STANDARD QWERTY KEYBOARD

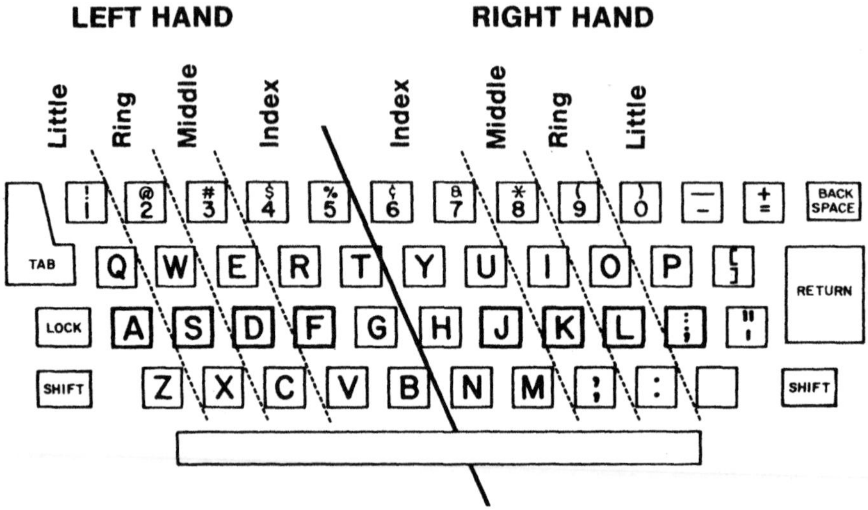

Cognitive Aspects of Skilled Typewriting

Edited by
William E. Cooper

Springer-Verlag
New York Heidelberg Berlin

William E. Cooper
Harvard University
William James Hall
33 Kirkland Street
Cambridge, Massachusetts 02138, U.S.A.

Current address:
Department of Psychology
University of Iowa
Iowa City, Iowa 52242, U.S.A.

Library of Congress Cataloging in Publication Data
Main entry under title:
Cognitive aspects of skilled typewriting.
Bibliography: p.
Includes index.
1. Typewriting—Psychological aspects. 2. Cognition.
I. Cooper, William E.
Z49.C63 1982 652.3 82-19237

With 48 Figures

Softcover reprint of the hardcover 1st edition 1983

Typeset by Publishers Service, Bozeman, Montana.

9 8 7 6 5 4 3 2 1

ISBN-13: 978-1-4612-5472-0 e-ISBN-13: 978-1-4612-5470-6
DOI:10.1007/978-1-4612-5470-6

Preface

This volume marks the 75th anniversary of the publication of William Book's 1908 *The Psychology of Skill,* in which typewriting received its first large-scale treatment from a psychological standpoint. As Book realized early on, this form of human behavior is particularly well suited to testing psychological theories of complex motor skill and its acquisition, presenting as it does a task that richly engages cognitive and motor components of programming, yet involves a form of response output that can be readily quantified. Now that typewriting is practiced so widely in workday circumstances, studying this activity offers the additional prospect of practical applicability.

Until recently, relatively few studies had been conducted on the psychology of typewriting. One might speculate that this dearth of interest stemmed in part from the fact that researchers themselves rarely undertook the activity, delegating it instead to the secretarial pool. Psychological research on piano playing has produced a literature more sizable than the one on typewriting, yet the latter activity has probably been practiced for many more total human hours in this century. But contemporary developments in word processing technology have moved the typewriter into the researcher's office, and in recent years interest in accompanying psychological issues has grown.

This book was conceived when the need arose for a source book of current research set against the backdrop of earlier efforts. By 1981, an international cast of psychologists were developing fruitful research programs, although relatively few published reports had emerged. Some prospective contributors shared my concern that the venture might be premature, but this worry was offset by those who expressed the belief that the time was now ripe for a basic volume on whose contents future studies could build. If psychological research on typewriting continues to develop in proportion to the increasing utility of this behavior in the workplace, there is reason to believe that these beginnings will give rise to a highly elaborated theory of this important skill with attendant applications in many circumstances.

As editor, I am especially grateful to the other authors for their dedication, enthusiasm, and promptness, all undeterred by a variety of environmental hazards during the course of this project. Thanks also go to Kristina Damon and Audrey Ham, who assisted in preparing aspects of the final draft, including many last minute details. Support was provided by a fellowship from the John Simon Guggenheim Memorial Foundation.

Spring 1983 William E. Cooper

Contents

Contributors

John M. Carroll, IBM Thomas J. Watson Research Center, Yorktown Heights, New York 10598 U.S.A.

William E. Cooper, Harvard University, William James Hall, Cambridge, Massachusetts 02138, U.S.A. Current address: Department of Psychology, University of Iowa, Iowa City, Iowa 52242, U.S.A.

Kristina Damon, Harvard University, William James Hall, Cambridge, Massachusetts 02138, U.S.A.

Susan F. Ehrlich, Advanced System Laboratory, Wang Laboratories, Lowell, Massachusetts 01851, U.S.A.

Donald R. Gentner, Department of Psychology, University of California at San Diego, La Jolla, California 92093, U.S.A.

Jonathan T. Grudin, MRC Applied Psychology Unit, CB2 2EF, Cambridge, England

Serge Larochelle, Institute for Perception Research, 5600 MB Eindhoven, The Netherlands

Gordon D. Logan, Department of Psychology, Erindale College, University of Toronto, Mississauga, Ontario L5L 1C6, Canada

John Long, Ergonomics Unit, University College London, London WC1H OAP, England

Robert L. Mack, IBM Thomas J. Watson Research Center, Yorktown Heights, New York, 10598, U.S.A.

Kevin G. Munhall, Department of Psychology, McGill University, Montreal, Quebec H3A 1B1, Canada

Ian Nimmo-Smith, MRC Applied Psychology Unit, Cambridge, England

Donald A. Norman, Department of Psychology, University of California at San Diego, La Jolla, California 92093, U.S.A.

David J. Ostry, Department of Psychology, McGill University, Montreal, Quebec H3A 1B1, Canada

David E. Rumelhart, Department of Psychology, University of California at San Diego, La Jolla, California 92093, U.S.A.

Andy Whitefield, Ergonomic Unit, University College London, London WCLH OAP, England

Hisao Yamada, Department of Information Science, Faculty of Science, University of Tokyo, Bunkyo-ku, Tokyo, 113, Japan

Chapter 1

Introduction

William E. Cooper

> Like a musical instrument, the typewriter is passive, and until played upon by the human hand it is useless.
>
> —William Allen Gilbert (1930, p. 89)

Since the act of typewriting involves such a close relationship between machine and human operator, the history and design features of the machine itself will be considered here as a prerequisite to a discussion of psychological issues. Like many complex inventions of the Industrial Revolution, the typewriter was developed over a lengthy period by numerous individuals working in diverse geographical areas. Its early history and contemporary development represent a truly international effort, combining the talents of man-machine engineering and business acumen.

Early History of the Typewriter

The recorded history of the machine begins on January 7, 1714, when Queen Anne granted to Henry Mill a British patent for

> an artificial Machine or Method for the Impressing or Transcribing of Letters Singly or Progressively one after another, as in Writing, whereby all Writing whatever may be Engrossed in Paper or Parchment so Neat and Exact as not to be distinguished from Print.

Unfortunately, the design of Mill's invention is not known, since no drawings of the machine have survived. Subsequent recordings of French and Italian inventions were similarly lacking in detailed description.

In 1829, William Austin Burt of Detroit received the first U.S. patent for a typewriter-like machine. Burt's only model, shown in Figure 1.1, operated much like a modern toy typewriter, but was destroyed by fire

Fig. 1.1. Burt's (1829) typographer (Herkimer, 1923).

only 7 years after the granting of the patent. By the mid-1800s, a variety of typewriter-like machines had been developed, incorporating some of the rudimentary features that characterize the modern machine. But most were large and inefficient, requiring more time to operate than was needed to write by hand. On the other hand, the benefits of clarity, uniformity, and potential use of the typewriter by handicapped individuals were recognized and spurred further efforts toward improvement.

The first practical model was constructed by Christopher Latham Sholes and two colleagues in Milwaukee. Sholes had read a *Scientific American* reprinting of a London article about an invention by John Pratt that incorporated the principle of the type wheel. Initially working with Carlos Glidden, who had been interested in developing farm equipment, and Samuel W. Soule, who like himself was a printer, Sholes developed a number of experimental models during the 1860s and 1870s, patenting the first efficient model on July 14, 1868. In 1873, following numerous improvements, Sholes contracted to have the typewriter manufactured with the gunsmith firm of E. Remington and Sons of Ilion, New York. The machine (see Figure 1.2) first appeared on the market the next year. Although the product incorporated a number of

Fig. 1.2. Sholes-Glidden typewriter, manufactured in 1973 (Herkimer, 1923).

features that are still standard today, it was not highly successful during the first few years. E. Remington and Sons went bankrupt in 1886, 12 years after the typewriter was first marketed. The assets were purchased by its sales agency, and the newly formed Remington Typewriter Company began to show strong sales the same year.

Professional authors were among the first to adopt the machine. The first typewritten book manuscript was Mark Twain's *Tom Sawyer*, prepared on a Remington. The widespread acceptance of the machine in the United States was aided by the rapid expansion of business and industry, which required more efficient and uniform modes of communication. The federal government showed an early interest, with typewriters introduced into the Department of Agriculture about 1878 by its Secretary, General Le Duc. Protocol prevented the adoption of typewriting in the Department of State and other federal departments for many years, but by 1900 the government was ordering about 10,000 machines each year. Early widespread use was spurred by the availability of carbon paper for the making of multiple copies of legal documents.

In Great Britain acceptance of the machine came more slowly. According to the Chicago Record (1898), a typewritten memo was not submitted to the House of Commons until 1898, and this memo was rejected by the Speaker of the House as a violation of the rule that all petitions must be written or lithographed. The Speaker chided the petitioner for infringing on the dignity of the House.

A number of mechanical developments quickly followed the first marketed typewriter model, including the use of a shift key for producing capital and lowercase letters, first marketed by Remington in 1878. The appearance of type that was immediately visible to the operator was introduced in 1883. A substantial improvement in efficiency was brought about by the use of an electric motor drive. A rudimentary electrical printing wheel (a machine that evolved into the modern ticker tape printer) was produced by Thomas Edison in 1872. James Smathers produced the first modern electric typewriter by 1920, building on numerous developments made during the intervening years.

The incorporating of electricity lent a versatility to the machine that paved the way for contemporary developments, including special-purpose inventions like the accounting machine, various composing machines, and the integration of the typewriter with the computer. This last achievement has exerted a profound impact on our civilization, permitting the development of business communications systems that are at once vast and highly efficient. It also necessitates an amendment to the statement by Gilbert presented at the onset of this chapter, so as to include the computer along with the hand as direct means of executing keystrokes.

As the typewriter developed, so too did the status of its human operators, leading to widespread social change. At first, the machine was operated primarily by male clerks. When female typists demonstrated an aptitude for the task, they gained an entering wedge into the world of business, without which, some surmise, they might not have attained their present degree of emancipation from the traditionally male-dominated form of Western society (see Figure 1.3; Yamada, 1980).

Typewriting from text copy has customarily been considered a clerical task, but many professionals at all levels have recently become enamored of typewriting in conjunction with computer usage and, in particular, with computerized text editing, in which material that has been typed into computer storage can be revised electronically. The advent of computerized text editing has also fueled the widespread

Fig. 1.3. Sholes as women's emancipator (Herkimer, 1923).

practice of *generative* or *composition typing* (as distinct from *copy* or *transcription typing*), in which the typist types his or her own ideas directly, as formerly practiced primarily by professional authors.

Methods of Typewriting and Keyboard Arrangements

The efficiency of typewriting depends jointly on the mechanical properties of the machine and on the method by which the typist strikes the keys. When the first typewriters were introduced, typists employed a hunt-and-peck method, using a single finger of each hand. The use of all fingers was first advocated by Mrs. L.V. Longley of Cincinnati in 1882. At that time, many typists did not believe that the all-finger method would permit speeds any higher than a modified version of the hunt-and-peck method in which two fingers of each hand were utilized.

The modern method of touch typing, in which the typist employs all fingers and refrains from looking at the keyboard, was first developed by Frank E. McGurrin of Salt Lake City. Touch typing was slow to gain acceptance, even though McGurrin demonstrated superior performance in a well-publicized typewriting contest in 1888 while competing against a highly proficient typist who employed only four fingers and looked at the keyboard. By 1900, most typewriting schools had adopted the all-finger method, with about half incorporating blind keying. Eventually, the combined advantages of increased speed and reduced fatigue earned touch typing its modern place as the standard method.

A mechanical factor closely related to the method of keying involves the precise arrangement of the keys themselves. The arrangement originally adopted by Sholes is almost identical to the modern standard, or "qwerty", system. A major rationale for Sholes's arrangement was the minimizing of key jamming, a serious problem in the early machine because keys returned to their resting places rather slowly, relying solely on the force of gravity. Sholes conducted experiments on the typing of various letter sequences in English and arranged the keyboard so that the individual keys utilized in the most common two-letter (digraph) sequences were located on opposite sides of the typebar basket. Unfortunately, this arrangement has persisted long after its original mechanical rationale disappeared, serving as an impediment to high-speed typing.

In the decades since the appearance of the Sholes arrangement, numerous suggestions have been proposed for alternative keyboard arrangements designed to facilitate higher speeds and greater accuracy. However, none of these alternative arrangements has succeeded in replacing the qwerty keyboard as the standard. The only serious contender that has been widely tested is the Dvorak simplified keyboard, developed by August Dvorak and colleagues at the University of Washington in the early 1930s (e.g., Dvorak, Merrick, Dealey, & Ford, 1936). The Dvorak arrangement, shown in Figure 1.4, featured a number of advantages over the qwerty system, including a larger home-row vocabulary (3,000 vs. 100 common words), greater utilization of right-hand keying, more balanced utilization of all fingers of each hand, greater utilization of alternative hand sequences (see Chapter 4), and minimization of awkward fingering sequences. Large-scale testing of the Dvorak and qwerty systems revealed that the Dvorak keyboard could be learned in about one-third the time needed to master the qwerty, and offered additional advantages of greater accuracy (approximately half as many errors), higher speeds (by about 15-20%), and reduced fatigue (for a review, see Yamada, 1980).

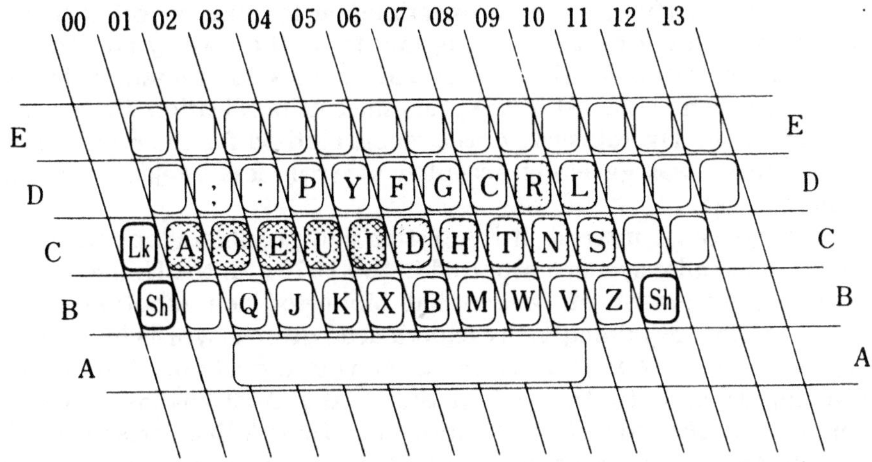

Fig. 1.4. Dvorak's (1936) keyboard. (Figure reprinted with permission from "A Historical Study of Typewriters and Typing Methods: From the Position of Planning Japanese Parallels" by H. Yamada, *Journal of Information Processing*, 1980, *2*, 175-202.)

Nevertheless, the Dvorak system has not replaced the qwerty arrangement as the standard, largely because the manufacturing of the qwerty and widespread training on it were entrenched by the time the advantages of the Dvorak system became apparent. Even so, the Dvorak system might have gained greater acceptance had it not been coupled with poor public relations and drastic changes in U.S. economic conditions. The Dvorak system was introduced during the Great Depression in the early 1930s, and Dvorak infelicitously publicized the system as advantageous on the grounds that its adoption would substantially reduce the number of both typewriters and typists required in business. Such publicity was largely unfavorable at a time when typewriter salesmen were in desperate need of new sales (often buying and destroying used typewriters so that new machines would be more in demand) and when typists themselves faced mass unemployment. In the early 1940s, the Dvorak system was gaining some ground, and Dvorak decided to link his system with the Remington noiseless typewriter, hoping that the combination of the two developments would outweigh the inertial advantages enjoyed by the qwerty. This maneuver also proved misguided, however, when it became evident that most typists preferred receiving auditory feedback in the form of the crisp clack associated with the standard typewriter. When World War II ensued, the U.S. government ordered 850,000 new typewriters, adopting the qwerty arrangement. At this time, most manufacturing facilities ordinarily employed for producing new typewriters were diverted to the manufacture of small arms, further impeding any momentum built up by the Dvorak system. The final blow to the modern campaign for the adopting of the Dvorak system came in 1956, when an experimental test was reported by the government comparing the training merits of the qwerty and Dvorak arrangements. Although the results and conclusions presented in this report have been criticized in the years since its publication, the report's rejection of the Dvorak system as a viable method for the retraining of qwerty typists was generally accepted as a wholesale rejection of the alternative system.

A resurgence of interest in the testing and possible adoption of the Dvorak and similar systems occurred in the 1970s. In the United States, the state government of Oregon has pioneered the adoption of the Dvorak system, retraining many experienced qwerty typists in a variety of agencies and encouraging Dvorak training in the schools. Committees on standards in both the United States and Australia have drafted recommendations for the adoption of Dvorak-like arrangements, although the future acceptance of these recommendations remains questionable. As Yamada (1980) observes, human beings are abundantly resistant to any change in the method by which a motor reflex skill is acquired. Individuals are not readily convinced of the potential advantages of retraining, nor do they envision retraining as a relatively easy task. In addition, businesses are reluctant to adopt any method of retraining that is costly and disruptive of routine activity.

Well aware of these factors, some designers of keyboard arrangements for languages with other character systems have advocated a thorough testing of alternative keyboard arrangements *before* manufacturing concerns can promote the adoption of an inferior arrangement that could not be easily displaced. Indeed, Yamada (1980) prepared his historical survey of Western typewriting from this standpoint, aiming to inform his Japanese audience about the shortcomings of Western typewriting so that these drawbacks might be avoided as the Japanese develop their own system (see also Chapter 13).

The Psychology of Typewriting

In sketching the history of the typewriter and methods of typewriting, I have hinted at the impact of various psychological considerations that have influenced the design of the machine and its mode of operation. In order to examine these and related psychological issues more fully, it is appropriate to review the major stages of human information flow that characterize typing during the planning and execution of this activity. A general model of information flow for typewriting from copy is presented in Figure 1.5.

Text Perception

At the first stage, the typist must perceive letters from the copy. Previous research on the study of typists' eye movements has been aimed at determining the extent to which typists read ahead as they type, and

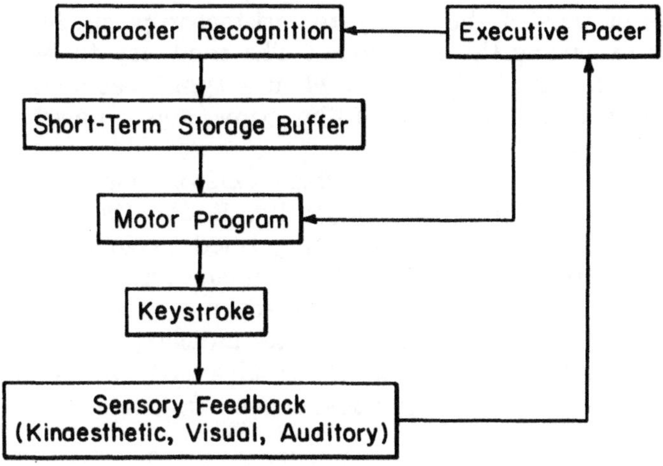

Fig. 1.5. Information-flow model of major stages in transcription typewriting.

the results indicate that skilled typists typically look about four to eight letters in advance (Butsch, 1932; Fuller, 1943). Compared with normal reading, typists exhibit more than three times the number of eye fixations and regressions. The locations and large number of the fixations and regressions that accompany typewriting indicate that this activity does not proceed by scanning the copy word by word. Rather, the eye typically looks a few letters ahead of the hand, with this span often (though by no means always—Shaffer, 1976) unrelated to the locations of word boundaries.

According to one representative study (Fuller, 1943), the mean eye-hand span in the typewriting of 100 advanced typewriting students was found to be .32 word, compared with about 1.1 words for the mean eye-voice span in reading. Pauses between saccadic eye movements were considerably longer in typewriting, averaging about .47 sec compared with .30 sec for normal reading. Overall, the rate of reading was thus about 5.7 times slower during typewriting. A similar pattern of results was obtained in an earlier study by Butsch (1932), who aptly summarized as follows:

> It is seen that the eye is not simply reading when it is obtaining copy for typewriting; and films obtained for reading for the same subjects reveal the fact that not only are the fixations more numerous but they are of longer duration. Apparently during typewriting the eye does not read at all at its maximum pace or even at the rate which is determined by the requirements of comprehension, but instead *reads only rapidly enough to supply the copy to the hand as it is needed* [my emphasis]. (p. 113)

Butsch also observed that the eye stays about 1 sec ahead of the hand, largely irrespective of the typewriting rate. Thus, fast typing is accompanied by greater eye-hand span, in accord with intuition. But even champion speed typists do not extend the eye-hand span beyond eight or so letters. Apparently, an overly enlarged eye-hand span leads to a deterioration of the ability to satisfactorily schedule motor programs for executing the keystrokes. The tendency to overextend the eye-hand span commonly occurs when a typist becomes absorbed in comprehending the meaning of the copy, and typewriting teachers generally discourage this practice.

The studies of eye movements place a major constraint on the scope of planning for copy typing. Originally, Book (1908) suggested that advanced typewriting skill was distinguished by increasingly enlarged reading spans. It was believed that the novice typist scanned individual words while the more skilled typist scanned word groups and even phrase units. The eye movement studies indicate instead that the eye-hand span is relatively short even for advanced typists, with the eye feeding copy to the hand as fast as it is needed.

Storage Buffer

Since typists do read ahead a few letters, a short-term storage buffer must be postulated to hold the information about subsequent letters that have been perceived but are yet to be typed (e.g., Thomas & Jones, 1970: Shaffer, 1976). The upcoming letters must be placed into this buffer in a queued sequence so that they are typed in the correct order. Since extending the eye-hand span beyond four to eight letters produces a deterioration in performance, we may assume that the short-term buffer has a limited capacity and/or a limitation on content retrieval. Similarly, pauses in typing appear to reflect occasions in which the buffer has been temporarily depleted (Shaffer, 1976). Champion typists exhibit an ability to minimize such occurrences, continually feeding new input into the buffer as they execute keystrokes.

Motor Program

Once the typist has perceived a few letters and placed these into the response buffer, the first letter is ready to be executed, a process that involves a number of motor commands to muscles of the fingers and hand. Motion picture studies of fluent typing indicate that the response commands for each letter are not strictly serial, insofar as the fingers may be in motion toward as many as three successive keystrokes simultaneously (see Chapter 5). Even before such evidence was available, Shaffer (1976) observed that the brief interkeystroke intervals of highly proficient typists made a strictly serial movement of the fingers unlikely in their case. Since the keys must be struck serially, the temporal orchestration of the muscle commands for different fingers in motion toward their targets at the same time represents a very complex type of motor programming.

Executive Pacer

At a global level of temporal control, there might exist an executive pacing mechanism, adjustable in order to achieve a given speed-accuracy trade-off in differing typing circumstances (Shaffer, 1976). When the source text was linguistically degraded, for example, one highly skilled typist exhibited longer interkeystroke latencies but was able to keep a fluent rhythm without large increases in latency variance (Shaffer, 1973, 1976, 1978). Shaffer suggested that the pacing device includes a metronomic beat that can trigger each keystroke with a random delay, although the detailed workings of the pacing device have not been examined. It is suspected that the pacing device would also be called upon to play an important regulatory role when physical characteristics of the source text are degraded, as when a typist must deal with handwritten source material.

In an effort to examine the nature of the executive pacer in normal circumstances, Shaffer (1978) conducted an experiment with the same highly skilled typist just mentioned, who averaged more than 100 words per minute (wpm) and participated in many of Shaffer's previous experiments. In this experiment, Shaffer included as source material three types of text, consisting of normal prose, sequences of words whose successive letters were typed with alternate hands, and sequences of words chosen from word lists in which the same sequence of three letters began various words (e.g., *fir, fire, firm, firmament*). The alternating-hand texts were included in an attempt to minimize the influence of contextual digraph dependencies on interkeystroke intervals when successive letters are typed with the same hand (see also Chapter 4). In actuality, typing the alternating-hand texts did reduce the variability of the interkeystroke intervals by about 30%, even though the typist was unaware of any difference in the text or in her response pattern. The data from the alternating-hand texts, then, seem to have provided a nearly optimal measure of the contribution of the pacing device, independent of other factors that normally influence interkeystroke timing. The embedding texts, in which the same sequence of three letters began different words, were included in order to test whether any systematic variation in the response distributions could be attributed to local contextual factors as opposed to executive pacing.

Autocorrelations were calculated for latency sequences in each text condition in order to examine whether a pacing control does exist and whether such a mechanism could be best described in terms of one of the following three types of process—metronome, feedback, or random walk. The results suggested that a higher order pacing device is in operation, as evidenced most clearly by the zero or negative autocorrelations for alternating-hand sequences, although the data did not offer a clear selection among the various types of pacer. The metronome and feedback types of process provided plausible representations of the pacer, whereas the random walk process failed to predict the negative and zero autocorrelations.

In addition to disclosing the influence of executive pacing, the data from the sequences of words that contained the same three-letter sequences provided evidence that both preceding and following local context can influence interkeystroke intervals within an invariant sequence. Although these effects of context are relatively small in comparison to global pacing, their presence complicates the overall time-keeping process considerably, and as Shaffer observes, there exist many options for representing how the general pacer and local context influences might be linked to the response commands (cf. Chapter 3, this volume).

Further Consideration of Storage Buffer and Motor Programs

The data from the invariant letter sequences also suggest, in accordance with earlier eye movement studies, that the typist did not always place all letters of a given word into a buffer before typing the first letter of the word. Latencies for the first letter of a three-letter invariant sequence were not systematically longer at the beginnings of relatively long words (e.g., *firmament* vs. *fir*).

This finding for latencies to begin typing words in the context of fluent typing contrasts with the results of a study by Sternberg, Monsell, Wright, and Knoll (1978) in which the latency to initiate typing a short string of letters increased linearly with the number of letters in the string, asymptoting at about five letters. A key difference between the study by Shaffer and the one by Sternberg et al. involves the contrast between continuous and single-trial typing. In the latter study, typists were first presented with the string array for an interval of 1 sec, followed by a 2.4-sec delay interval. Upon the presentation of a tone signal, the typist then began typing the letter string, with the objective of completing the string as soon as possible. Thus, in the Sternberg et al. study, the task was designed so that the typist was required to store the entire letter string in a short-term buffer before initiating the first keystroke, unlike the continuous typing experiment by Shaffer.

The contrast in the design features of these two studies illustrates a general issue that is worth keeping in mind throughout the discussion of typewriting research. This issue, which pervades many branches of experimentation, involves the extent to which a highly complex type of perceptual-motor skill like typewriting can be successfully studied in terms of component subsystems that can be more readily tested in a rigorous laboratory setting. In the study by Sternberg et al. the task was intentionally designed so that perceptual processes in reading text would not influence the results. The aim was to study detailed aspects of motor programming in isolation. Other studies of simple reaction time (e.g., Gatewood, 1920; Hoke, 1922; Hayes, 1978; Hayes & Halpin, 1978; Hayes, Wilson, & Schafer, 1977) have similarly studied typists' response latency to begin typing a single keystroke in response to a "go" signal and have provided baseline data on the inherent response latency differences among the individual fingers. For example, a study by Hayes and Halpin (1978) revealed that individual reaction times of the fingers were slowest to fastest for the fingers L4, L3, L1, L2, R1, R2, R3 and R4, where L4 designates the little finger of the left hand and where R4 represents the little finger of the right hand. The mean reaction time for L4 was about 30 msec slower than for R4. Although the results of this study provide useful information of the fundamental reaction times for the individual fingers in executing keystrokes, the study involves an extremely artificial task, with the typist executing a single keystroke on each trial. The task utilized by Sternberg et al. adds an important dimension of complexity to the reaction time task by requiring subjects to type more than a single keystroke on most trials. In order to study motor programming independently from the perceptual effects of reading text and from the possible influences of prior context, Sternberg et al. maintained a discrete trial task, with the subject typing a single brief letter string on each trial. In order to engage the influences of perceiving text and prior context, Shaffer and others have adopted a task of still greater complexity in which the typist is presented a continuous text. In some conditions, where the influence of higher order linguistic variables is not of interest, the continuous text is composed of short, wordlike letter strings. At the most complex level, grammatical prose is utilized, engaging all levels of processing that normally accompany fluent typing.

While many researchers agree that the long-term objective of experimentation with typewriting is an understanding of the processes that mediate fluent typing as it is customarily performed, there is far less agreement on the appropriateness of different experimental tasks that involve marked trade-offs between the rigorous isolation of a prospective subsystem and the natural engagement of fluent typing. As in any field of experimentation, the isolationists must demonstrate that the processes which can be isolated effectively are in fact actual subcomponents of normal typing, and that the study of such subcomponents in isolation leads to a significant advance in our ability to understand this complex form of behavior. For the naturalists, the burden of proof entails demonstrating that at the current stage of knowledge it is possible to extract further information about the processes that mediate typewriting by studying a highly complicated testing situation in which all of these processes are typically in simultaneous operation.

On the basis of the research conducted within these two traditions so far, it is not possible to determine whether one or the other method of study has enjoyed greater success, and it is not possible to foresee the relative merits of their contributions in the future. In all likelihood, both sources of information will prove valuable in constructing a detailed model of the processes that mediate fluent typing, although the distinction between the two appears useful in differentiating the more immediate aims of the various studies to be reviewed and presented in this volume. Regardless of where a given study lies on the isolationist-naturalist continuum, the challenge is to implement a design that allows one to probe fundamental aspects of this skill without simultaneously trivializing the task.

Feedback Systems

After the typist executes a keystroke, a monitoring system comes into play in order to detect possible errors. According to Shaffer and Hardwick (1969), skilled typists detect about half of their errors immediately; others have observed somewhat higher detection rates (Long, 1976a; Rabbitt, 1978). In many cases, an error appears to be detected even before its execution is terminated, as evidenced by the fact that typists often depress incorrectly selected keys more lightly than normal (Rabbitt, 1978). Thus, the monitoring system must be extraordinarily quick, relying on kinesthetic feedback for the most part as motor commands to the muscles are initiated. Shaffer (1973) suggests that the quickness of the error-detection system implies that the response codes are copied rather than moved from the buffer to the output, such that the original code remains in the buffer so that it can be compared with kinesthetic feedback. Despite its quickness, the monitoring system may sometimes operate over spans of at least two letters, as when transposition errors accompany high-speed performance (see Chapter 6). Such errors are often output as a rapid sequence but are then followed by a short pause.

Visual Feedback

In addition to kinesthetic feedback, the typist also receives visual and auditory feedback. Two forms of visual feedback are available, one provided by looking at the copy being typed, the other provided by the keyboard. The information provided by looking at the keyboard is primarily useful as a means of guidance rather than as feedback (Long, 1976a), since glancing at the keyboard serves primarily to help the typist maintain the fingers on the home row or to find an unfamiliar key before the relevant keystroke is initiated. In contrast, looking at the typed copy served as a means for checking errors and of examining format.

Visual consultation of both keyboard and copy play a vital role in the earliest stages of learning to type, but their role in skilled touch typing has been debated. In training schools, the typist is taught to keep eyes on the source text and to avoid looking at copy or keyboard; and in a study by Diehl and Seibel (1962), skilled typists showed comparable speed and accuracy whether or not they could see the copy, effectively masked in one condition by the use of cardboard. In another study (West, 1967), skilled typists were permitted to look at neither the copy nor the keyboard, with both masked by the placement of a cardboard shield connected to each typist's neck and waist. Typists' speed was approximately equal with and without the visual feedback in this case, but subjects committed about 60% more errors when visual feedback was unavailable. These findings, considered alongside those of Diehl and Seibel, suggest that skilled touch typists normally consult the keyboard in order to maintain their fingers on the home row and that without such feedback, substantially more errors in keying are committed. In discussing these studies, Klemmer (1971) suggested that the feedback checking of home-row position is manifest at all levels of skill, whereas checking the copy for errors is more prevalent in unskilled performance.

Unfortunately, no measurements of the typists' eye movements were recorded in these studies. However, Long (1976b) observed the number of times one skilled typist consulted the source, copy, and keyboard under a variety of typing conditions, providing some information about the extent of visual guidance and feedback. The typist, who normally typed between 70 and 80 wpm, consulted both the copy and keyboard occasionally (.4 consultation of the copy and .3 consultation of the keyboard per 100 keystrokes under normal conditions). When the same typist was required to type a completely errorless copy of a legal document, speed declined by about 60%, and both forms of visual consultation increased (4.21 consultations of the copy and 1.45 consultations of the keyboard per 100 keystrokes), implicating the function of maintaining accuracy. When the typist was given alphanumeric source material, consultation of both copy and keyboard also increased in comparison with normal typing, with the most substantial increase occurring for keyboard consultations, helpful in locating some of the numeric keys. The findings from these and other typing conditions of Long's study suggest that even skilled touch typists consult both copy and text occasionally in a variety of typical circumstances. Looking at the keyboard helps to maintain the fingers on the home row and to observe the locations of unfamiliar keys, both serving as guidance for avoiding errors. While Long's findings for this single typist are in general accord with intuition, there may also exist broad individual differences in the degree to which the copy and keyboard are consulted by skilled typists, and it would be useful to determine whether any such differences are related to individual differences in speed and accuracy among a group of skilled typists. It might also be revealing to consider the amount of time that has elapsed since the skilled typists received formal training. As mentioned earlier, formal training courses typically discourage visual consultation of copy and keyboard, and such discouragement appears helpful in trying to establish the method of touch typing. Yet, as the skilled typist becomes more accustomed to a posttraining working environment in which the daily requirements of accuracy often outweigh those of speed, the typist may begin to disregard the training instructions and practice visual consultation more frequently.

In additional experiments, Long (1976b) individually masked either the copy or the keyboard to determine the role of consulting each in regulating speed and in committing and correcting errors. When the keyboard alone was masked, both speed and accuracy declined. In this condition, an abnormally large number of keying errors involved the substitution of horizontally adjacent keys, suggesting the loss of a home-key starting state for the fingers. Errors were also associated with keys having unfamiliar locations. Taken together, these results provided further support for the notion that keyboard consultation under normal viewing conditions serves to help the typist maintain home-row position of the fingers and to help him or her locate unfamiliar keys. Long's experiments also showed that masking of the copy alone produced a decrement in the percentage of errors corrected by the typist. When corrections were not required, however, masking the copy did not affect performance. This result was consistent with the earlier findings of Diehl and Seibel, who also showed no effect of copy masking when subjects were not required to correct their errors. Since the study by West did include conditions of error correction, as well as both keyboard and copy masking, it is now more readily understandable why the influence of masking on performance was observed by West but not by Diehl and Seibel. More errors were committed under masking in West's study because masking of the keyboard impeded the maintenance of home-row finger locations and the locating of unfamiliar keys. Masking of the copy alone in the study of Diehl and Seibel would presumably have resulted in a decrement in the *correction* of errors, similar to Long's study, if subjects had been required to correct their mistakes (for further discussion, see Rabbitt, 1978).

Kinesthetic Feedback

Although it appears that visual guidance and feedback play a role in skilled as well as in unskilled typing, the primary source of sensory feedback in skilled typing is surely kinesthetic, including information about the position and movement of fingers as provided by muscles and joints. To a considerable extent, the development of skilled touch typing can be viewed in terms of an increasing reliance on this type of feedback and a reduced reliance on visual feedback. This view conforms to the general principle proposed by Paul Fitts (1951), who stated that the transfer from vision to kinesthesis as the primary source of feedback characterizes the development of perceptual-motor skills. In the case of typewriting, however, the decline in overall reliance on visual feedback is also accompanied by a change in the main function of this form of information. As Long (1976b) observes, as the typist makes the transition from visual to kinesthetic feedback for executing keystrokes, the visual modality is freed to take on the role as a backup system for locating unfamiliar keys and for checking the copy for possible errors.

Rabbitt (1978) tested skilled typists' ability to detect errors when visual feedback from both copy and keyboard was eliminated. By removing the typewriter ribbon from the machine, it was possible to remove copy feedback from the typist, while retaining a copy of the output for the experimenter by inserting a piece of carbon paper and another sheet of typing paper underneath the visible sheet. The results indicated that typists can monitor for error effectively via kinesthetic feedback.

Auditory Feedback

In addition to the visual and kinesthetic forms of feedback, auditory feedback is normally provided by the sound of the printing device striking the platen of the typewriter. In normal circumstances, this feedback is immediate, highly damped, and regular. As observed in the discussion of the machine's history, the Remington company was unsuccessful in marketing a "noiseless" typewriter that produced a dull thud sound, and it appears that typists prefer the crisp clacking sound provided by standard machines. But does such feedback help in the performance of typing? To the best of my knowledge, a systematic study has not yet been published on this issue.

Although the role of auditory feedback is probably minimal in ordinary circumstances, such feedback may be quite influential when it is delayed or irregular, as with certain teletype machines that include a buffer store for data entry. The buffer is incorporated in such machines so that data can be entered more rapidly than is otherwise possible with this type of transmission system. However, the introduction of a buffer store poses the potential disadvantage of impeding a typist's regular rhythm by providing delayed and irregular auditory as well as visual copy feedback. For tasks that involve more reliance on auditory control (e.g., speaking, singing, piano playing), a delay in auditory feedback considerably hinders rhythmic performance (e.g., Smith, Mysziewski, Mergen, & Koehler, 1963), but the influence of such a delay on typewriting is not immediately apparent. To investigate this possibility, Long (1975, 1976a) conducted experiments in which skilled typists' performance was assessed under normal and delayed auditory and visual feedback conditions. In the experiments, the delaying of feedback simulated the typical effect of a teletype buffer store by linking a standard teletype machine to a computer that had been programmed to impose variable delays. The results for a group of 16 typists showed a significant reduction in the speed for typing prose text in each of three delay conditions, with slightly greater reduction in speed at the longer delay intervals. An analysis of keying errors also revealed significantly more errors in the delay conditions. When corrected and uncorrected errors were analyzed separately, it was found that subjects committed significantly more uncorrected errors in the delay conditions but committed about the same number of corrected errors as in normal typing. This set of results suggested that the normal function of visual feedback in checking for errors was disrupted to some extent under the delay conditions.

Examination of the interkeystroke intervals also indicated that the delay in auditory feedback played a role in the impaired performance during the delayed conditions. In particular, interkeystroke intervals that were too brief to be accompanied by a visual consultation of the copy were generally slower in the delayed conditions. Subjects also reported that the delay in auditory feedback was disruptive, and that they adopted various strategies for trying to ignore the feedback.

In a related experiment, Long (1976a) examined the effects of delayed feedback on unskilled performance for keying digits. As in the previous study, the delay conditions were accompanied by a decrement in speed. An additional experiment was designed to test whether this effect would be reduced or eliminated as subjects became more familiar with the delay conditions. Three sessions of 2 hours each were administered over a week's period. Again, the delay conditions produced a decline in speed, and the decline was not eliminated over the testing period, although one might suppose that still greater familiarity with a given delay condition might circumvent this decline.

In these experiments, the unskilled typists implicated the delay in auditory feedback as the principal source of the decrement in their performance. A third experiment indicated that the effect was maintained even when the interkeystroke intervals were very fast, facilitated by the use of a task in which unskilled subjects simply typed sequences of 0's and 1's with alternate hands.

In considering the influence of delayed feedback on typing performance, Long (1976a) first presented two extreme types of open-loop and closed-loop feedback systems, shown here in Figure 1.6. According to an open-loop system, no effect of feedback delay is predicted, since keying is assumed to proceed without regard for the forms of visual and auditory feedback. Clearly, the results of Long's experiments rule out this extreme hypothesis. According to a strict closed-loop model, an individual keypress is not initiated until feedback about the previous one is received. In its simplest form, this model dictates that any delay in feedback should be directly reflected in a delay by the same amount in the interkeystroke intervals. The results

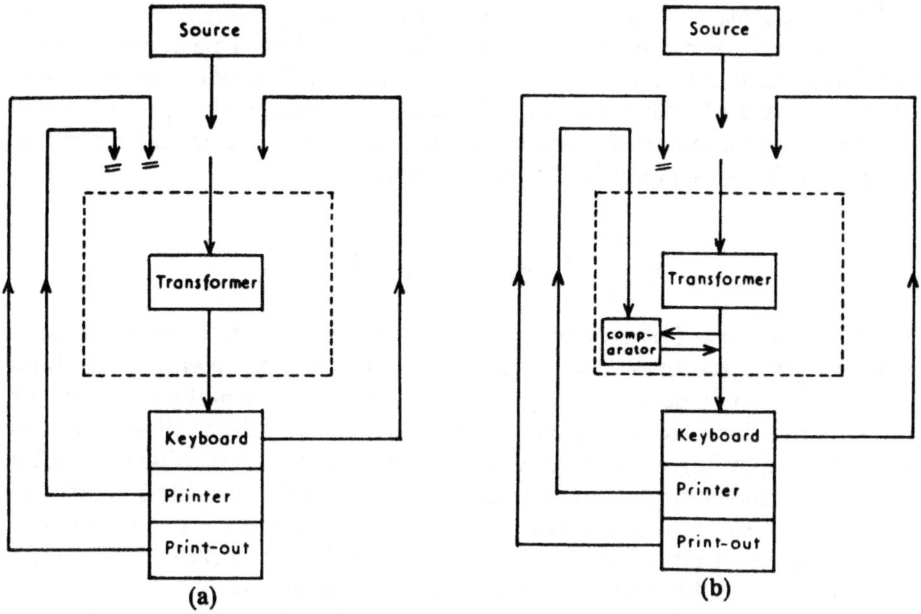

Fig. 1.6. Block diagrams showing the models of unskilled keying: (a) an open-loop version; (b) a closed-loop version. The broken lines delimit the processing system. (Figure and caption reprinted with permission from "Effects of Delayed Irregular Feedback on Unskilled and Skilled Keying Performance" by J. Long, *Ergonomics*, 1976, *19*, 183-202.)

of Long's experiments show an increase in the interkeystroke intervals with increases in feedback delay, but the amount of the increase in the interkeystroke intervals is not as great as the delay times. Thus, Long proposes a modified system, following a suggestion of Licklider (1960), in which an open-loop mode is adopted under normal feedback conditions but is switched to a closed-loop system under delayed feedback, at least initially. When related experiments on delayed feedback were conducted with skilled typists and text material, Long found that the decrement in performance under the delayed conditions was eliminated after about 2,000 keystrokes, or about 8 minutes. It appears, then, that skilled typists can adapt to the delay in auditory feedback, whereas unskilled typists substitute other forms of feedback, including kinesthetic feedback and visual guidance by looking at the keyboard.

Summary of Model Stages

At the most general level, typing from copy involves at least the following stages: perceiving text, storing perceived letters in a short-term storage buffer, executing a keystroke, and monitoring for errors via sensory feedback systems. At any given moment during typing, all of these processes are typically in operation *simultaneously* (see Long,

1976b; Rabbitt, 1978), and an executive pacing system might exert some control over the processes in order to achieve a particular speed-accuracy trade off under varying conditions. Although a great many characteristics of this general model remain to be specified, it will serve us here as a framework for introducing some of the major psychological issues that have been studied with typewriting.

Learning to Type

Unlike the act of speaking, touch typewriting is a form of motor behavior that requires extensive periods of training. Nearly all adults can speak their native language fluently, yet only a small percentage of such people learn to touch type. The considerable difficulties encountered by beginning typists provided impetus for the establishment of a variety of instructional classes to meet the need for skilled typists in business. These same circumstances prompted an interest in the psychological factors that underlie the learning of this complex motor skill (e.g., Book, 1908). Some psychological research has been devoted to the general objective of determining optimal training methods for the qwerty system. As mentioned in an earlier section, studies have also examined learning to type as a function of different keyboard arrangements, demonstrating a general superiority of the Dvorak simplified keyboard among students who are first learning to type. Finally, studies of learning have focused on attributes of the human operator, attempting to determine whether differences in learning are attributable to differences in sex, age, and previous experience of the typist.

As a general principle of learning, Woodworth (1938) claimed that learning is accomplished more quickly when the amount of training time is distributed over short sessions as opposed to longer ones. The advantage of distributed versus massed trial learning was considered to operate in a variety of learning circumstances with both human and animal subjects and was believed to include the task of skilled typewriting. More recently, a carefully controlled experiment by Baddeley and Longman (1978) has provided support for Woodworth's claim. In this study British postmen were trained as beginning typists in keying alphanumeric codes, with the subjects placed into four training groups, given either 1 or 2 hours of training per session and given either one or two sessions per day. The group that received a single 1-hour session per day showed more efficient learning (as measured in terms of correct keystrokes per minute after 60 or 80 total practice hours) than the groups given two 1-hour sessions per day or one or two 2-hour sessions per day. Interestingly, however, the subjects in the group receiving one session of 1 hour per day later reported less enthusiasm for this schedule than subjects receiving two 2-hour sessions per day. Thus, the greater learning efficiency observed for the group receiving the most distributed sessions is probably not attributable to a greater degree of motivation. As Baddeley and Longman point out, the disparity between efficient learning and subjects' satisfaction with the training schedule would need to be considered, along with various other factors such as the similarity of other tasks being learned by the subjects during the same general time period, when planning and evaluating large-scale training operations. Additionally, any broad conclusions about the differential effectiveness of distributed as opposed to massed trial learning for this task would need to await a companion study focusing on whether differences in instructor effectiveness accompany the different types of training schedules. The problem here, of course, is that instructor effectiveness per se can only be assessed indirectly by subjective measures, as in the case of measuring subjects' satisfaction with the scheduling. In any case, it does seem that Woodworth's original claim about the overall advantage of distributed over massed trial learning does apply to the initial learning of typing, at least within the restricted domain examined here.

Incidental Learning

Since the copy typist perceives the source material as input to typewriting, the question arises, To what extent does the typist comprehend the source material while typing? In contemporary secretarial schools, training emphasizes the inhibition of reading for meaning while typing, on the assumption that such reading will hinder high-speed performance. Some support for this assumption is derived from the introspections of champion speed typists, who report that they seldom recall the meaning from the source material incidentally. In addition, one can ask whether intentional reading of the source material for comprehension while typing actually impedes performance.

In one study, Marton and Sandqvist (1972) tested 64 Swedish secretaries who had taken a 1-year secretarial course. Half of the secretaries had received 5 hours of typing instruction per week, while the other half had received only 2 hours per week. In the test the secretaries from each training group received instructions to "think of what you are typing" in addition to the standard instruction to "type as well and as fast as you can." Following the typing, a retention test containing questions on comprehension of both global and detailed aspects of the text was administered.

The results showed that the instructions to think of what they typed produced significantly greater retention of the source material for both training groups. Thus, there appears to be some advantage of intentional over incidental learning of the source material, in accord with the general advantage often accorded intentional learning (e.g., Karen, 1956; cf. Saltzman & Atkinson, 1954). The intentional group also committed slightly more errors and typed at a slightly slower rate than the incidental group, although these effects of performance were not statistically significant. It remains to be determined whether intentional reading of text material produces a significant decline in speed and accuracy over a more lengthy text. It would also be interesting to find out whether, over a prolonged period, secretaries who performed at the same level after their training period remained matched in performance after half had become accustomed to reading for meaning while they typed. Reading for meaning might be more customary for secretaries in office jobs that routinely require draft copy typing in which some on-line editing is desired when typing the source material, as in letter correspondence originally given by dictation. Ironically, one of the most frequently heard complaints of professional personnel who employ secretaries is that the secretaries do not think of what they are typing, yet the inhibition of reading for meaning is considered a virtue during the formal training period for most secretaries.

A longer-term study of intentional versus incidental learning of material was conducted by Dawley and Dawley (1974); it was particularly noteworthy for the testing of comprehension of textbook material that required learning of complex material over a prolonged period rather than the simple recall of factual details. In this study, beginning typists copied 20 passages on economic concepts, each requiring 5 minutes to type, over a 5-week period. As in the Marton and Sandqvist study, one group of subjects was instructed to concentrate on the meaning of the source material as they typed, while the other group was given no special instructions regarding comprehension. After the typing period was completed, the subjects were tested for their understanding of the economic concepts presented in the source material, and it was found that the intentional learning group achieved significantly greater understanding. As in the Marton and Sandqvist study, no significant differences in speed or accuracy were found for the intentional versus incidental learning groups, and in this case there was even a trend for the speed of the intentional group to be superior to that of the incidental. Thus, it appears that intentional reading for meaning while copy typing can be practiced with significant gains in understanding without any clear decrement in typing proficiency, at least for beginning typists (the subjects here achieved speeds averaging about 35 wpm). Dawley and Dawley suggest that contrary to the assumption of most secretarial schools, reading for meaning may even help beginning typists achieve greater speed gains, although the data do not provide any strong evidence on this point.

Extensional Learning in Normal and Disabled Children

Aside from incidental learning of source material, a more general type of "extensional" learning has been studied, in which the typewriter appears to provide motivation to enhance the development of language-related skills. The development of typing skill in young children has been associated with improved learning over a prolonged period in spelling, vocabulary, and written composition. There also exists some evidence for related improvements in reading, although the evidence on this skill is less conclusive (e.g., Wood and Freeman, 1932). Generally speaking, it seems that the improvements in language skills attributable to the use of the typewriter in grade schools can be explained in terms of the children's greater familiarity with and enjoyment of printed English. Those children who type spend relatively more of their time writing and reading printed material, affording greater opportunity to improve spelling, reading, and writing. In addition, the use of the typewriter by these children leads to the production of written compositions that are far more legible than handwritten ones, and it is suspected that teachers are more likely to spend time giving constructive editorial feedback on typewritten manuscripts.

Normal Children

A large-scale study of this general topic was conducted in the 1930s with grade school children who had been trained to type and who utilized the typewriter in their daily lessons (Wood & Freeman, 1932). Four leading typewriter manufacturers—Remington Rand, Royal, Smith-Corona, and Underwood—lent more than 2,100 portable typewriters, placed in eight public school systems and five private schools. Within each of the public school systems, certain schools received typewriters and others served as control groups. The typewriters were utilized with children in kindergarten through grade 6, spanning the ages from 5 to 12. It was estimated that the children in the earlier grades spent an average of 50-80 minutes per week at their typewriters, while children in high grades averaged about 90-130 minutes per week. The children were trained and tested over a 2-year period, with both experimental and control groups tested at the end of each year on a variety of language skills. The results indicated that children who had used typewriters made more significant gains than the control children in spelling, vocabulary, and written composition. It was found that the children who typed wrote more material that the control children and enjoyed using their typewriters. At the same time, the handwriting of the children who also typed showed no evidence of deterioration. While the quantitative aspects of this study are difficult to interpret because of certain possible confounding factors, such as teacher caliber and expectations, the overall results suggested that the use of typewriters in grade schools promotes a good deal of extensional learning for language skills, and the subjective opinions of the teachers also supported this conclusion. More recent studies have lent further support for the link between the use of typewriters and improved language learning in early schooling (for a review, see Cothran & Mason, 1978).

Disabled Children

In addition to its use in normal childhood education, the typewriter offers special learning advantages for children with motor disabilities that inhibit the normal development of handwriting. Studies have been conducted to examine the effectiveness of the typewriter as an educational tool with children exhibiting abnormalities ranging from mild learning disability (with a motoric component) to cerebral palsy, in which motor coordination is minimal. In one study, Campbell (1973) tested the influence of typewriting on learning disabled children's development of reading skill. A group of 50 children, aged 7-10, were selected for the study on the basis of the following characteristics: their inability to learn to read satisfactorily, a developmental lag in psychomotor functioning (as tested by the Bender Visual Motor Gestalt Test), IQ scores of 80 and above, and an absence of diagnosed mental retardation, cerebral palsy, or emotional disturbance. Half of the children used a hunt-and-peck method of typewriting to do their classroom assignments, while the remaining half used handwriting in accomplishing the same tasks. An effort was made in the Campbell study to keep other variables of instruction method and content as closely matched as possible for the two groups so that any differences between the groups' performance could be attributed directly to the use of the typewriter. After a treatment period of about 3 months, the children who had typed their assignments showed a significantly greater gain in reading vocabulary than the control group, although both groups showed comparable gains in reading comprehension. The difference between the vocabulary and comprehension results was accounted for in terms of the greater emphasis on vocabulary learning at this early stage of development and possibly of the greater influence of the use of the typewriter in aiding the aspects of word recognition most closely tied to visual cues. However, the interpretation of the reading comprehension gains is made difficult by the fact that, unlike their vocabulary scores, the two test groups' pretreatment comprehension scores were not closely matched. In any event, the improvement in vocabulary learning does suggest that the typewriter aids learning disabled children who exhibit a developmental lag in motor performance. Whereas the reading development of such children appears ordinarily to be constrained by their lagging development in handwriting, the typewriter enables the children to surmount this motor disadvantage and establish a better reading vocabulary. It is not yet certain, however, whether the gains documented in the Campbell study represent a specific influence of the typewriter or a more general and indirect influence of the machine on improving pupils' attention and motivation to learn. Teachers typically report perceived improvements in the latter characteristics when typewriters are utilized in a study of this kind, and it would have been useful to include another measure of language or related ability for which gains were not predicted as a result of typewriter use. That comprehension gains did not differ substantially for the two groups in the Campbell study lends credibility to the notion that the vocabulary gains are specifically attributable to the use of the typewriter as a cognitive aid, although, as mentioned before, the pretreatment comprehension scores were not well matched for the two groups.

As in the case of studies with normal children, the demonstration of gains in reading and related skills with the use of the typewriter has not been accompanied by detailed studies that attempt to establish *why* the typewriter exerts this influence. In particular, it would be interesting to know how much of the gains are attributable to specific cognitive and language factors directly associated with the skills being taught. At the same time, it is encouraging that the typewriter does seem to promote gains in children's extensional learning, for whatever reasons.

In addition to learning disabled children, the use of the typewriter has been studied with educable mentally retarded children. Unlike the case of learning disabled children with motor lags, however, the rationale for applying typewriters with the mentally retarded is not readily apparent. In the former case, as with severely impaired cerebral palsied children, the typewriter clearly represents a tool for circumventing the degree of fine motor control necessary to produce handwriting, leading to improved language skills. With the mentally retarded, however, the impairment in language skills seems more related to general cognitive deficits, although some impairment in gross motor coordination may also be a factor in their impaired handwriting. Nonetheless, some studies have been conducted to determine the utility of the typewriter in teaching mental retardates. In the most systematic study on this topic to date, Gladis (1973) tested 56 such children, aged 8-15, whose IQs ranged from 55 to 84. The subjects were randomly assigned to experimental and control groups, matched for chronological and mental age, IQ, and educational achievement. The treatment included a 28-week period during which pupils in the experimental group were taught a modified version of touch typing and otherwise participated in language instruction similar to that of the control group. During the language program, the experimental groups typed their exercises while the control subjects wrote or printed them by hand.

The results generally showed greater gains in the experimental group, but not large enough to be statistically significant. Unfortunately, many of the particular design features of this study were not comparable to those of the study of learning disabilities conducted by Campbell, so it is not possible to draw any conclusions about whether the typewriter might be more useful for learning disabled children than for educable mental retardates. As Gladis observes, however, the small gains observed in language skills by the experimental group, coupled with the fact that this group learned a useful typewriting skill without any loss to other skills, suggests that the typewriter can be used to advantage with the mentally retarded (see also Karnes, Clarizio, & Zehrbach, Note 1). As in other studies, parents and teachers observed that the use of the typewriter seemed to improve the motivation of the pupils, although no follow-up studies were conducted to determine whether this influence on motivation was long lasting or confined to the first year of typewriting.

The use of the typewriter with cerebral palsied children who exhibit a considerable impairment in fine motor control represents one of the most clear-cut cases of the advantages of the typewriter in aiding disabled children to develop language skills. Cerebral palsied children are generally unable to learn printing or handwriting, but with training can often learn to type. Although systematic studies of such children's typing have not been conducted for the most part, it does appear from the results of one case study that operant conditioning techniques can be used to improve the development of typing (Yeatts & Brantley, 1976).

The typewriter has also been employed in the teaching of language skills to hearing-impaired children. Ziff (1974) describes one program in which touch typing was taught to such children for use in rewriting compositions after editorial feedback had been provided by the teacher on a first handwritten draft. Quantitative measures were not included in this study, but Ziff reports that the students exhibited improvements in their understanding of grammatical rules as well as in their enthusiasm for writing and ability to work independently. In this case, however, it is difficult to assess the possible influence of teacher enthusiasm on the pupils' performance, and a more controlled study of typewriting in hearing-impaired children remains to be conducted.

From the work with childhood disabilities, it seems apparent that the typewriter is primarily useful as a tool for circumventing the degree of fine motor control needed for handwriting, which is often impaired to a considerable extent in cerebral palsied children and in learning disabled children who also exhibit a motoric deficit. The use of the typewriter with these children seems to enhance their ability to learn language skills, including reading, although specific gains cannot be readily tied to specific aspects of typewriting. For other disabled groups, including the educable mentally retarded and hearing impaired, the typewriter may serve more as a motivational and attentional aid, much akin to that observed with normal children, and indirectly may thus enhance the children's learning of language skills. For the most part, however, the need persists for more tightly controlled studies on this topic in order to establish the general and specific advantages of typewriting for extensional learning in these childhood groups.

Retention of Skilled Typing

While a fair amount of previous research has been devoted to psychological factors involving initial learning with typing, relatively little attention has been paid to the retention and degeneration of this skill over prolonged time periods after formal training has been completed. A typical secretarial student might receive typing instruction over a 1- or 2-year period, then continue skilled typing in business for many years, even decades. The particular requirements of a typist's employer can vary substantially in terms of speed-accuracy trade off for draft material, the kinds of material typed, whether or not on-line editing is encouraged, and other factors. In addition, the typist in business might be asked to utilize different typewriting machines for specialized purposes in daily work or might have a familiar machine replaced by a new one, often involving computerized word processing capabilities. Even though far more labor hours are spent in skilled typing after the period of formal training has been completed, virtually no research has been systematically directed at the questions of retention and degeneration of skill over prolonged periods of time or as a function of changes in office requirements such as those just mentioned.

In the study of Baddeley and Longman (1978) reviewed earlier from the standpoint of distributed versus massed practice, retention of typing skill was assessed after periods of 1, 3, or 9 months after training had been completed. Only subjects who had not utilized the typewriter in the intervening period were examined for retention, and the results showed an approximately 30% reduction in speed, with greatest loss among the group who had received massed practice in the form of two 2-hour sessions per day during the training period. Thus, the results provided a further measure of support for the disadvantages associated with massed practice in the initial learning of this skill.

But studies have yet to be directed at the issue of long-term retention for typists who continue to utilize their skill after formal training. In particular, it would be interesting to determine how a typist's speed and accuracy might change over prolonged time periods, and the extent to which such changes are attributable to the kinds of material routinely typed, office requirements for errorless copy, and other factors, including psychological, social, and environmental. Intuition suggests that skilled typists often decline somewhat in speed after formal training if office conditions place a premium on errorless copy. Accompanying this loss in speed may be a greater reliance on visual guidance and feedback monitoring systems of the type discussed in an earlier section.

Domain of Planning

One of the cardinal issues in typing from copy involves the extent to which typists read material in advance of a given keystroke, storing this additional information in the short-term storage buffer in a queued sequence for eventual output. But the general notion of planning domains also extends to the execution of keystrokes themselves, since it appears that the fingers are typically in motion toward more than a single keystroke simultaneously.

In order to examine typists' planning domains at a general level, Shulansky and Herrmann (1977) tested both touch typists and non-touch typists in copying sentences that were either fully grammatical and meaningful, grammatical but semantically anomalous, or ungrammatical and semantically anomalous. In earlier studies (Miller & Isard, 1963; Marks & Miller, 1964), it had been observed that subjects are better able to recognize words in noise and learn sentences to the extent that they are grammatical and meaningful. The results, shown in Figure 1.7, indicate that the touch typists exhibited faster response latencies to begin typing than the non-touch typists. Furthermore, the touch typists commenced typing with about the same latency regardless of the type of sentence string being presented, whereas the non-touch typists exhibited longer latencies as the degree of grammaticality and/or meaningfulness declined. In addition, the touch typists showed no difference in their overall rate of typing for the various types of sentence strings, whereas the non-touch typists exhibited a substantial reduction in rate with successive degradations in linguistic form. Taken together, these results suggest that touch typists can effectively plan their typing without the need to consider syntactic or semantic constraints on word order. Further support for this conclusion comes from the fact that

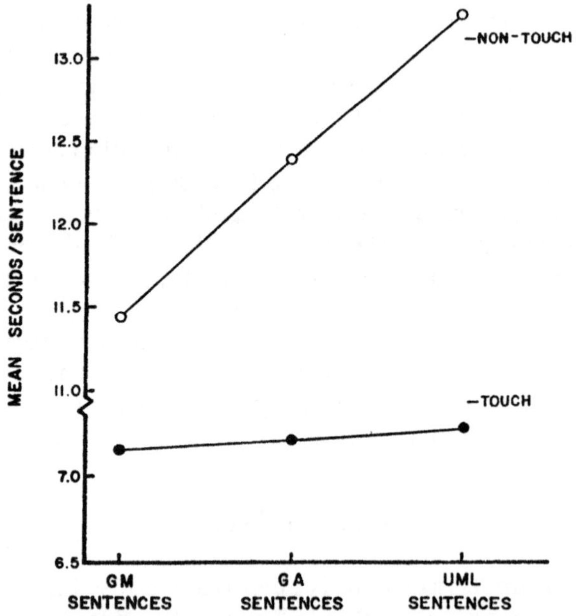

Fig. 1.7. Block diagram showing mean typing latency for touch typists and non-touch typists as a function of lexical complexity of sentences. (Figure and caption reprinted with permission from "The Influence of Linguistic Structure on Typing" by John D. Shulansky and Douglas J. Herrmann, *Language and Speech*, 1977, *20*, 83.)

highly skilled touch typists are often unaware of the content of what they are typing and can type prose and random word texts with the same approximate speed and accuracy (Shaffer & Hardwick, 1968). Performance for such typists does deteriorate, however, when the copy consists of zero-order random letter texts, in which all letters are equiprobable in their appearance (Shaffer & Hardwick, 1968). Thus, the typist does utilize some degree of local linguistic context to aid in the planning of subsequent keystrokes, and the available evidence suggests that for the most part skilled typists plan their responses in accordance with digraph characteristics (e.g., Rumelhart & Norman, Note 2; Evey, Note 3). However, other results suggest that digraph characteristics are not the exclusive determinants of typing speed, even among skilled touch typists. For example, Shaffer and Hardwick (1969) found that longer words are accompanied by longer interkeystroke latencies than shorter ones.

The emphasis on digraph characteristics has raised the issue of the extent to which syllabic structure influences typing speed. Shaffer and Hardwick (1969) showed that typists were faster at typing sequences of nonwords when these words obeyed the syllabic contraints of English than when they did not. In addition, Ostry and Munhall (Note 4) found that interkeystroke latencies were slower at the first syllabic break within a multisyllabic word. However, a similar effect was also obtained near the middle of a monosyllabic word, raising the possibility that the earlier effect might be attributable not to syllabic structure per se, but rather to an effect of the number of keystrokes already executed within the word. This issue could be resolved in an experiment in which syllabic divisions and the number of letters per syllable were varied independently in multisyllabic words, but such an experiment has not yet been conducted. In any event, the magnitude of the interkeystroke latency effects that might be attributable to syllabic structure or to the number of letters already typed in a word is relatively small in comparison with the effects of interkeystroke latencies that are attributable to the frequency of occurrence of given digraphs in the language or to such digraph factors as whether the successive letters are typed with the same hand (e. g., Rumelhart & Norman, Note 2; Evey, Note 3).

A large-scale study of syllabic structure and related factors that might influence interkeystroke latencies was conducted by Cooper, Ehrlich, Paccia, Weiss, and Damon (Note 5). Experiments were conducted with groups of 10-20 touch typists in order to examine whether interkeystroke latencies were influenced by the following factors: (a) major clause boundaries, (b) phrase boundaries, (c) syllable boundaries, (d) "silent" letters (e.g., the *b* in *plumber*), and (e) mismatches between common orthographic and phonological representations. The results failed to show significant results for any of these possible influences, although a strong trend was observed for interkeystroke latencies to be slower in the environment of silent letters. In all of the experiments, an effort was made to use digraph environments matched as closely as the English language would permit in order to test the influence of the independent variable in isolation, and in most cases it was possible to compare minimal or near-minimal pairs. Thus, for example, the same words were compared with or without the presence of an intervening clause or phrase boundary to test issues (a) and (b), while similar words containing the same key digraph were utilized in the study of the remaining issues (e.g., words like *reach* vs. *react* for the study of syllabic boundary effects). Since the test materials were controlled to this extent, and since a relatively large number of touch typists were tested in these experiments, the inability to reject the null hypothesis regarding the influence of these various linguistic factors certainly suggests that, to the extent that these factors might influence interkeystroke latencies at all, their influence is quite small. In addition, the data from these experiments revealed a good deal of intersubject variability in the interkeystroke latency differences for key comparisons, suggesting that subgroups of subjects may adopt somewhat different planning domains in pacing their typing rate in these circumstances. Detailed analysis of these individual differences revealed a trend for the more proficient typists to show syllabic and phonological influences on their interkeystroke latency profiles (cf. Chapter 4).

In particular, faster typists tended to be more influenced by any mismatches between common orthographic and phonological representations or by the presence of silent letters, suggesting that such typists normally exhibit some degree of visual-to-phonological recoding as they perceive the input and prepare to store it in a short-term buffer. This recoding stage was not included in the information-flow model presented in Figure 1.3 because its existence remains questionable, paralleling the controversy over phonological recoding in normal reading (e.g., Foss & Hakes, 1978), and there remains a need for more work on this topic.

Another source of evidence about domains of planning involves the response latency profiles for individual words typed at various places in a text. In reviewing such profiles, Shaffer (1973) observes that it is unlikely that most words are organized in terms of unique response procedures, suggested originally by Bryan and Harter (1899), Craik (1948), and Lashley (1951). For one thing, initial letters of words typically exhibit a shorter response latency than medial or final letters, contrary to the expectation that extra time would be needed to call up a word-level response profile at this juncture. This case against the word-level response unit is not airtight, however, since the unit response could be called during the execution of the ending of the preceding word (see also Terzuolo & Viviani, 1980). Second, although individual words often exhibit characteristic response profiles when typed at various locations in a text, the most salient aspect of such profiles involves the slowed typing of one or more letters rather than a characteristic fast response for most of the letters, as would be expected if fast typing were dependent on word-length response units.

Still another source of evidence that bears on the typists' planning scope involves an analysis of transposition errors, in which two letters are typed in incorrect order in the output (e.g., Shaffer, 1976; Chapter 6, this volume). Such errors are among the most common kinds of typing errors, and it is noteworthy that most such errors do not exceed syllable boundaries. That is, the two transposed letters typically belong to the same syllable, suggesting that the typists' indexing of proper letter location is processed largely on a syllable-by-syllable or even more restricted basis (Shaffer, 1976, p. 384).

Different Input Modes

In addition to typing from copy, typists may receive input in the form of spoken language, as in typing from dictation, or in the form of their own generative ideas. Typing from dictation requires the typist to make special adjustments for the rate of input. Ordinarily, the typist can operate a foot pedal or other device to start and stop the dictation at will, but the rate of speech input cannot be controlled by the typist, which renders this form of typing more difficult than copy typing. Unfortunately, systematic studies have yet to be conducted to compare these two forms of typing in terms of the kinds of stages described in the information-flow model presented earlier. In addition to the lack of control over input rate, typists who receive dictation input must perform the added operations associated with transforming the spoken input into an orthographic representation suitable for the initiating of keystroke commands, and it would be interesting to find out whether such typists encounter particular difficulties with words whose phonological and orthographic representations do not closely match (e.g., words containing silent letters). In addition, it would be interesting to determine the extent to which skilled typists from dictation can anticipate the speaker's pause patterns and utilize these as one means of catching up with the input in circumstances in which the short-term storage buffer is temporarily overloaded.

Even more intriguing from a psychological standpoint is generative or composition typing, in which a typist formulates ideas and translates these directly for typing without intervening spoken or written productions of the material. This form of typing is becoming increasingly widespread with the advent of computerized word processing equipment, encouraging professionals at all levels of business, government, medicine, and education to try their own hand at typing first-draft material "from their heads." In many cases, moreover, these people proceed to edit their rough drafts, thus eliminating the need for extensive retyping of various drafts. As with typing from dictation, very little is known about the psychological factors that mediate the learning and retention of this important skill.

In one study, Tannenbaum, Williams, and Wood (1967) investigated hesitation phenomena associated with generative speaking and typing of messages in response to viewing cards from the Thematic Apperception Test (TAT), displaying relatively unstructured situations. An analysis of the hesitations revealed that typing was characterized by fewer pauses having longer duration than during speech, with some pauses accompanying typing longer than 10 sec. A hesitation in typing tended to be followed by a lengthy uninterrupted sequence, sometimes including entire sentences. Two major differences between the modes of typing and speaking appear to be accountable for the differences in the kinds of hesitation that typically accompany the two forms of production. In particular, lengthy pauses of durations exceeding a few seconds are tolerated in typing but not in speaking because (a) the typist has a readily accessible printed record of the preceding material, whereas the speaker does not; and (b) the recipient of the typewritten message can read the message at a rate that does not place an overload on the recipient's short-term memory for preceding material. In effect, lengthy pauses are not permissible in speaking because both speaker and listener run the risk of losing track of what has just preceded the pause, and these problems are circumvented with typewriting because of the presence of a printed copy. Thus, from a psychological standpoint, we would expect that some of the mental operations that mediate generative typing differ in important aspects of temporal control from those that mediate generative speaking.

In further analyzing their data, Tannenbaum et al. (1967) found that the content of the typewritten messages tended to exhibit more grammatical structures involving subordination and a greater elaboration of noun phrases than in spoken messages. The authors suggest that this difference between typing and speaking may be attributable to the fact that formal grammatical training in the schools deals primarily with written rather than oral expression. On the other hand, as Tannenbaum et al. observe, the greater elaboration of grammatical structures in typing might be attributable to the lengthier pauses associated with typing, during which the typist can plan more complex syntactic frames.

Aside from this study and a somewhat related one by Tannenbaum, Wood, and Williams (1968) involving the generative typing of right- and left-branching sentences with or without visual feedback, studies of generative typing have largely been devoted to examining how this activity compares with other forms of language production as a means of effective on-line communication. In a series of studies, Alphonse Chapanis and his colleagues have investigated the effectiveness of the communication modes of speech, typewriting, handwriting, or unrestricted communication in group problem solving. The problems to be solved involve various real-world situations, ranging from how to wire a digital logic panel to argumentative topics like budget negotiations that typify much teleconferencing. The aim of the research has been to determine which mode or modes of communication are most effective in solving problems among small groups of individual participants. The general results of this work suggest that most types of problems are solved faster by groups when speaking is included in the communication setting (for details, see Chapanis, 1971, 1973, 1975, 1976; Chapanis, Ochsman, Parrish, & Weeks, 1972; Chapanis & Overbey, 1974; Chapanis, Parrish, Ochsman, & Weeks, 1977; Chapanis & Williams, 1976).

For the most part, the psychological factors that mediate generative typing remain undetermined. Skilled generative typists who utilize touch typing can often achieve relatively high speeds, yet this skill seems to be acquired with considerable difficulty and only after touch typing from copy has become facile. The degree to which the generative typist must concentrate on the formulation of ideas and their translation into a linguistic code clearly demands that the bulk of conscious attention not be devoted to the activity of typing itself. But we know nothing about the details of how the formulation of ideas and their initial translation are orchestrated on-line as the typist is simultaneously engaged in each of the other stages of typewriting outlined earlier in this chapter. Certainly much idea formation occurs during the long pauses that typify generative typing, but the translation of these ideas into particular sentences and phrases also seems to require a good deal of on-line decision making during execution.

In a recent study, Gould (1982) examined the general time course of generative typing and editing of routine letters with computer-based line-oriented text editors. The results, which showed that experienced users of text editors spent approximately two-thirds of their time pausing to plan the material, were similar to results found earlier for writing, dictation, and speaking (Gould, 1978). Judges rated the letters composed with the text editors as being of comparable quality to handwritten ones by the same author, although the text-edited letters took 50% more time to prepare than those that were handwritten, typed by a secretary, revised, and then retyped. With newer full-screen text editors, however, it is expected that the time consumed in preparing a text-edited letter would not be much longer than that spent preparing a handwritten one. Interestingly, authors made far more revisions in the text-edited letters than in the handwritten ones, as might be expected on the basis of the ease with which revisions can be made in the former context. However, that the quality of the two types of letters was judged to be about equal suggests that the first drafts of text-edited letters tended to be inferior to those of the handwritten counterparts, raising the suspicion that first-draft carelessness may be a characteristic of many text-edited materials.

The act of revising text with computerized text editing is itself a topic of psychological concern (see Chapters 11 and 12). With many text editors, the operator is faced with a number of command sequence options for making complex revisions, and studies have been conducted to determine how operators acquire the skill of efficient editing (Card, Moran, & Newell, 1980, 1982). In one study, Card et al. examined how an operator learns to rearrange clauses in a three-clause sentence, the task requiring the subject to change the sentence *The sun shines when it rains; our weather is funny* to *Our weather is funny; when it rains the sun shines*. Because the text editor permits the operator to move, copy, and delete elements in various sequences, it is possible to perform this task in a number of different ways. In this case, the operator displayed an improvement in editing performance over 1,100 trials, although as the authors note, it is difficult to assess the generality of this type of learning because the task involved manipulating only a single sentence on all trials. Card et al. view the text editing as a form of general problem solving and have proposed a detailed model of how the human operator reaches solutions to different types of editing requirements.

Different Output Modes

All of the psychological studies reviewed to this point dealt with the standard qwerty keyboard. However, there exist a number of studies that have examined typing with keyboards that involve either slight modifications of the qwerty system, typically including an exchange in the location of two or more letters (e.g., Stutsman, 1959; Gordon, Henry, & Massengill, 1975; Massengill, Gordon, & Henry, 1975), completely different arrangements of the keystrokes (e.g., Dvorak, Merrick, Dealey, & Ford, 1936), and most recently, keyboard arrangements for languages that do not utilize the Roman alphabet, such as Japanese (Yamada, 1980 and Chapter 13 in this volume) and Hebrew (Gopher & Eilam 1979). The work conducted on "non-qwerty" systems for the Roman alphabet has been largely devoted to the issue of performance changes during and after periods of retraining on a modified system, with little or no detailed examination of psychological factors. Hence, the work on non-qwerty systems for the Roman alphabet will not concern us here. However, recent research on non-qwerty systems for languages that rely on different alphabets has raised some important psychological considerations, to be presented in subsequent chapters. For example, in the case of Japanese, a considerable problem arises in constructing an efficient keyboard arrangement that includes a reasonable subset of the immense number of Japanese characters that are required for effective communication. According to Yamada (1980), a character set of a few thousand is required in this situation. Because it is desirable to have a relatively small number of keys on a keyboard, languages like Japanese prompt a consideration of alternative methods of keying, including chord keying of various keys simultaneously, multistroke keying of successive keys to produce a particular character, and multishift keying, with each key representing a number of characters that can be uniquely produced in combination with a particular shift key. Similar considerations arise for the Hebrew language (Gopher and Eilam, 1979), and some work has been directed at developing a form of chord keying that takes advantage of the ideographic similarity between Hebrew characters and chord keying patterns.

Conclusion

We have presented a general model of information flow for the mental processes that mediate typewriting, and have discussed some of the relevant issues and previous research that has been conducted on the psychological aspects of learning to type, incidental and extensional learning while typing, retention of typing skill, domains of planning in typing, and special problems associated with different input and output modes. The subsequent chapters deal with psychological aspects of on-line skilled typing activity in a manner that should allow us to specify a working model of this highly complex behavior in more depth.

Acknowledgment

In preparing the first section of this chapter, I found particularly helpful Hisao Yamada's 1980 article "A Historical Study of Typewriters and Typing Methods: From the Position of Planning Japanese Parallels." Thanks go to Richard Land for comments on an earlier draft.

Reference Notes

1. Karnes, M. G., Clarizio, H. F., & Zehrbach, R. R. *The effects of typing instruction on the personality and achievement of educable mentally handicapped children.* Unpublished manuscript, 1963. Champaign, Ill.: Community Unit 4 Schools, Department of Special Services.
2. Rumelhart, D. E., & Norman, D. A. *Simulating a skilled typist: A study for skilled cognitive-motor performance* (Tech. Rep. 102). La Jolla, Calif.: University of California at San Diego, Calif., Center for Human Information Processing, May 1982.
3. Evey, R. J. *How typists type.* Paper presented at the International Computer Conference, Hong Kong, October 1980.
4. Ostry, D. J., & Munhall, K. G. *Syllabic influences on the timing of typing.* Unpublished manuscript, McGill University, 1982.
5. Cooper, W. E., Ehrlich, S. F., Paccia, J., Weiss, E., & Damon, K. Unpublished data, Harvard University, 1981.

References

Baddeley, A. D., & Longman, D. J. A. The influence of length and frequency of training session on the rate of learning to type. *Ergonomics*, 1978, *21*, 627-635.

Book, W. F. *The psychology of skill: With special reference to its acquisition in typewriting.* University of Montana Publications in Psychology, 1908 Bulletin No. 53, Psychological Series No. 1.

Bryan, W. L. & Harter, N. Studies on the telegraphic language. *Psychological Review*, 1899, *6*, 345-375.

Butsch, R. L. C. Eye movements and the eye-hand span in typewriting. *Journal of Educational Psychology*, 1932, *23*, 104-121.

Campbell, D. D. Typewriting contrasted with handwriting: A circumvention study of learning disabled children. *Journal of Special Education*, 1973, 7, 155-168.

Card, S. K., Moran, T. P., & Newell, A. The keystroke-level model for user performance time with interactive systems. *Communications of the ACM*, 1980, *23*, 396-410.

Card, S. K., Moran, T. P., & Newell, A. *The psychology of human-computer interaction.* Hillsdale, N.J.: Erlbaum, 1982, in press.

Chapanis, A. Prelude to 2001: Explorations in human communication. *American Psychologist*, 1971, *26*, 949-961.

Chapanis, A. The communication of factual information through various channels. *Information Storage and Retrieval*, 1973, *9*, 215-231.

Chapanis, A. Interactive human communication. *Scientific American*, 1975, *232*(3), 36-42.

Chapanis, A. Interactive communication: Some findings from laboratory experiments. *Conference Record of the 1976 National Telecommunications Conference*, 1976, *2*, 17.1-1-17.1-9.

Chapanis, A., Ochsman, R. B., Parrish, R. N., & Weeks, G. D. Studies in interactive communication: I. The effect of four communication modes on the behavior of teams during cooperative problem-solving. *Human Factors*, 1972, *14*, 487-509.

Chapanis, A., & Overbey, C. M Studies in interactive communication: III. Effects of similar and dissimilar communication channels and two interchange options on team problem solving. *Perceptual and Motor Skills*, 1974, *38*, 343-374.

Chapanis, A., Parrish, R. N., Ochsman, R. B., & Weeks, G. D. Studies in interactive communication: II. The effects of four communication modes on the linguistic performance of teams during cooperative problem solving. *Human Factors* 1977, *19*, 101-126.

Chapanis, A., & Williams, E. Human considerations in interactive telecommunication. In E. I. Salkovitz (Ed.), *Science, technology, and the modern navy.* Arlington, Va.: Office of Naval Research, 1976.

Cothran, A., & Mason, G. E. The typewriter: Time-tested tool for teaching reading and writing. *The Elementary School Journal*, 1978, *78*, 171-173.

Craik, K. J. W. Man as an element in a control system. *British Journal of Psychology*, 1948, 38, 142-148.

Dawley, L. T., & Dawley H. H. Incidental and intentional learning of economic information in beginning typewriting. *Perceptual and Motor Skills*, 1974, *38*, 337-338.

Diehl, M. J., & Seibel, R. The relative importance of visual and auditory feedback in speed typewriting. *Journal of Applied Psychology*, 1962, *5*, 365-369.

Dvorak, A., Merrick, N. L., Dealey, W. L., & Ford, G. C. *Typewriting Behavior.* New York: American Book Company, 1936.

Fitts, P. M. Engineering psychology and equipment design. In S. S. Stevens (Ed.), *Handbook of experimental psychology*. New York: Wiley, 1951.

Foss, D. J. & Hakes, D. T. *Psycholinguistics: An introduction to the psychology of language*. Englewood Cliffs, N. J.: Prentice-Hall, 1978.

Fuller, D. C. *Reading factors in typewriting*. Unpublished Ed.D dissertation, Graduate School of Education, Harvard University, 1943.

Gatewood, E. L. Individual differences in finger reactions. *Psychological Monographs*, 1920, *28*(126, Whole No. 4).

Gilbert, W. A. *The orthographic keyboard*. Spokane, Wash.: Shaw and Borden, 1930.

Gladis, P. The influence of typewriting on selected language arts skills and motor development of the aducable mentally handicapped. *American Journal of Mental Deficiency*, 1973, *77*, 451-454.

Gopher, D. and Eilam, Z. Development of the letter-shape keyboard: A new approach to the design of data entry devices. *Proceedings of the Human Factors Society*, 23rd Annual Meeting, Boston, Massachusetts 1979, 41-44.

Gordon, M. E., Henry, H. G., & Massengill, D. P. Studies in typewriter keyboard modification: I. Effect of amount of change, finger load, and copy content on accuracy and speed. *Journal of Applied Psychology*, 1975, *60*, 220-226.

Gould, J. D. An experimental study of writing, dictating, and speaking. In J. Requin (Ed.), *Attention and Performance VII*. Hillsdale, N. J.: Lawrence Erlbaum Associates, 1978.

Gould, J. D. *Writing and speaking letters and messages* (RC-7528). *IBM Research Report*, 1979, *20*, 495-505.

Gould, J. D. Composing letters with computer-based text editors. *Human Factors*, 1982, in press.

Hayes, V. Relationship between typewriting rate and response to individual characters on the typewriter keyboard. *Perceptual and Motor Skills*, 1978, *46*, 1339-1343.

Hayes, V., & Halpin, G. Reaction time of the fingers with responses measured on a typewriter keyboard. *Perceptual and Motor Skills*, 1978, *47*, 863-867.

Hayes, V., Wilson, G. D., & Schafer, R. L. Typewriting rate as a function of reaction time. *Perceptual and Motor Skills*, 1977, *45*, 1179-1184.

Herkimer County Historical Society. *The story of the typewriter, 1873-1923*. Herkimer, New York, 1923.

Hoke, R. E. The improvement of speed and accuracy in typewriting. In E. F. Buchner (Ed.), *The John Hopkins University studies in education*. Baltimore, Md.: John Hopkins University Press, 1922.

Karen, R. L. Recognition as a function of meaningfulness and intention to learn. *American Journal of Psychology*, 1956, *79*, 650-652.

Klemmer, E. T. Keyboard entry. *Applied Ergonomics*, 1971, *2*, 2-6.

Lashley, K. S. The problem of serial order in behavior. In L. A. Jeffress (Ed.), *Cerebral mechanisms in behavior*. New York: Wiley, 1951.

Licklider, J. C. R. Quasi-linear operator models in the study of manual tracking. In R. D. Luce (Ed.), *Developments in mathematical psychology*. Glencoe, Ill.: The Free Press, 1960.

Long, J. B. Effects of randomly delayed visual and auditory feedback on keying performance. *Ergonomics*, 1975, *18*, 337-347.

Long, J. B. Effects of delayed irregular feedback on unskilled and skilled keying performance. *Ergonomics*, 1976, *19*, 183-202. (a)

Long, J. B. Visual feedback and skilled keying: Differential effects of masking the print copy and the keyboard. *Ergonomics*. 1976, *19*, 93-110. (b)

Marks, L. E., & Miller, G. A. The role of semantic and syntactic constraints in the memorization of English sentences. *Journal of Verbal Learning and Verbal Behavior*, 1964, *3*, 1.

Marton, F. I., & Sandqvist, G. Learning while typing. *Quarterly Journal of Experimental Psychology*, 1972, *24*, 287-290.

Massengill, D. P., Gordon, M. E., & Henry, H. G. Studies in typewriter keyboard modification: II. Relationships between individual differences in performance on standard and modified typewriters. *Journal of Applied Psychology*, 1975, *60*, 227-230.

Miller, G. A., & Isard, S. Some perceptual consequences of linguistic rules. *Journal of Verbal Learning and Verbal Behavior*, 1963, *2*, 217.

Rabbitt, P. Detection of errors by skilled typists. *Ergonomics*, 1978, *21*, 945-958.

Saltzman, I. J., & Atkinson, R. L. Comparison of incidental and intentional learning. *American Journal of Psychology*, 1954, *67*, 521-524.

Shaffer, L. H. Latency mechanisms in transcription. In S. Kornblum (Ed.), *Attention and performance* (Vol. 4). New York: Academic Press, 1973.

Shaffer, L. H. Intention and performance. *Psychological Review*, 1976, *83*, 375-393.

Shaffer, L. H. Timing in the motor programming of typing. *Quarterly Journal of Experimental Psychology*, 1978, *30*, 333-345.

Shaffer, L. H., & Hardwick, J. Typing performance as a function of text. *Quarterly Journal of Experimental Psycholgoy*, 1968, *20*, 360-369.

Shaffer, L. H., & Hardwick, J. Reading and typing. *Quarterly Journal of Experimental Psychology*, 1969, *21*, 381-383.

Shulansky, J. D., & Hermann, D. J. The influence of linguistic structure on typing. *Language and Speech*, 1977, *20*, 80-85.

Smith, K. U., Mysziewski, M., Mergen, M., & Koehler, J. Computer systems control of delayed auditory feedback. *Perceptual and Motor Skills*, 1963, *17*, 343-354.

Sternberg, S., Monsell, S., Knoll, R. L., & Wright, C. E. The latency and duration of rapid movement sequences: Comparisons of speech and learning. In G. E. Stelmach (Ed.), *Information processing in motor control and learning*. New York: Academic Press, 1978.

Stutsman, G. Reverse the "A" and "J" keys? *Journal of Business Education*, 1959, *6*, 249-250.

Tannenbaum, P. H., Williams, F., & Wood, B. S. Hesitation phenomena and related encoding characteristics in speech and typewriting. *Language and Speech*, 1967, *10*(3), 203-215.

Tannenbaum, P. H., Wood, B. S., & Williams, F. Effects of feedback availability upon generation of left- and right-branching sentence structures. *Language and Speech*, 1968, *11*, 12-19.

Terzuolo, C., & Viviani, P. Determinants and characteristics of motor patterns used for typing. *Neuroscience*, 1980, *5*, 1085-1103.

The Chicago Record, The typewriter barred out. April 16, 1898.

Thomas, E. A. C., & Jones, R. G. A. A model for subjective grouping in typewriting. *Quarterly Journal of Experimental Psychology*, 1970, *22*, 353-367.

West, L. J. Vision and kinaesthesis in the acquisition of typewriting skill. *Journal of Applied Psychology*, 1967, *51*, 161-166.

Wood, B. D., & Freeman, F. N. *An experimental study of the educational influences of the typewriter in the elementary classroom*. New York: Macmillan, 1932.

Woodworth, R. S. *Experimental psychology*. London: Methuen, 1938.

Yamada, H. A historical study of typewriters and typing methods: From the position of planning Japanese parallels. *Journal of Information Processing*, 1980, *2*, 175-202.

Yeatts, L. M., & Brantley, J. C. Improving a cerebral palsied child's typing with operant techniques. *Perceptual and Motor Skills*, 1976, *42*, 197-198.

Ziff, L. Utilization of visually-oriented media to motivate and develop language facility in hearing impaired children. *The Volta Review*, 1974, *76*, 178-181.

Chapter 2

A Glossary of Terms Including a Classification of Typing Errors

Donald R. Gentner, Jonathan T. Grudin, Serge Larochelle, Donald A. Norman, and David E. Rumelhart

A common terminology is essential when working in any area, and the study of typing is no exception. To aid ourselves and others, we have compiled a glossary of basic definitions useful in the description of the phenomena of typing. The glossary, which also contains a categorization of errors, has proved useful in several ways. Not only does it keep our terms consistent, but it has provided a framework for the description and classification of a number of typing errors. We hope this glossary will be of independent use, perhaps leading to standardization of the typing terms used throughout the typing literature.

Basic Terms

Keystroke, Latency, Interstroke and Interkeystroke Interval

The act of depressing the key on the typewriter keyboard is called the *keystroke*. With computer keyboards, this is synonymous with the making of the electrical contact, and the keystroke is assumed (defined) to have zero duration. With mechanical typewriters, there may be considerable duration to the keystroke. The *time* of the keystroke is taken to be the time at which the action is functionally completed, either when the type bar strikes the paper or when the electrical contact on the key is completed.

The term *latency* refers to the time elapsing between the receipt of sensory information and the first keystroke in response. The times between successive keystrokes are *interstroke* or *interkeystroke* intervals. In general, the term latency is not used in referring to continuous typing, but is reserved for discrete trial paradigms in which a single word or phrase is typed following a signal.

Digraph and Trigraph

Digraph denotes any sequence of two consecutive characters (letters, numerals, punctuation, space, etc.). The term *trigraph* denotes any sequence of three consecutive characters. Although the terms *digram* and *digraph* are used synonymously in the literature, we prefer digraph.

Terminology for Letter Sequences

Figure 2.1 shows the Sholes keyboard and the standard (American) mapping of fingers to keys. We classify letter sequences according to the fingers and hands involved. The following four cases are the ones we have found most useful.

2F Sequences in which the letters are all typed by the same hand, but with two different fingers. Thus, *ta* is a 2F digraph.

1F Sequences in which the letters are typed with the same finger (and therefore, with the same hand). Thus, *ceded* is a 1F sequence.[1]

2H Sequences that occur across hands. Thus, *the* is a 2H trigraph.

1H Sequences typed by one hand. This is used when the number of fingers used (1F, 2F,. . .) is not important. Thus, *beverages* is a 1H sequence.

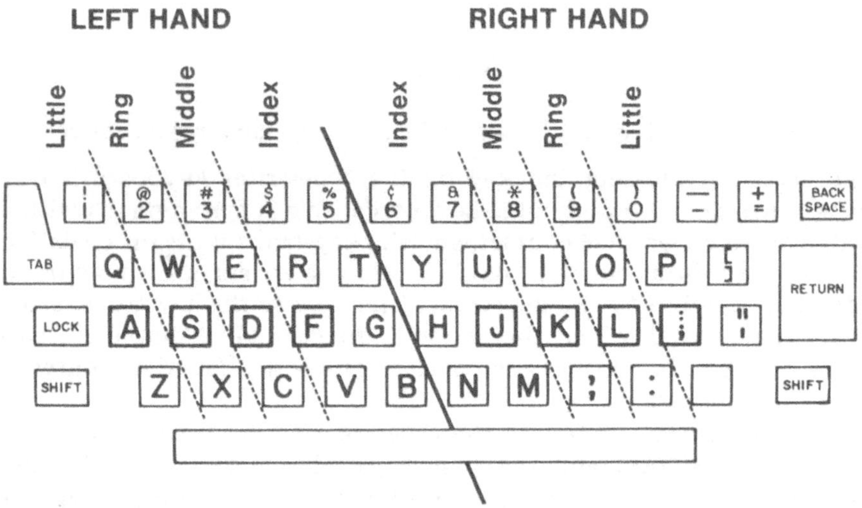

Fig. 2.1. The standard American (Sholes or "qwerty") keyboard and the mapping of fingers to keys.

[1] Some of our data (see Chapter 5) indicate the usefulness of distinguishing the special case of a 1F sequence in which the same letter is repeated from that in which the same finger types different letters. In these cases, the term 1F *doubles* can be used for the subset of 1F sequences involving the same key, and 1F *non-doubles* can then refer to the nondoubled single-finger sequences.

Specification of Hand, Finger, and Position: The [H,F,P] Triple

We specify the mapping between fingers and keys by the triple [H,F,P] where:

H specifies the hand (left or right);
F specifies the finger (little, ring, middle, index, or thumb);
P specifies the position, characterized in a coordinate space relative to the home position of the finger, where "up" and "down" correspond to motion along a column, and "inward" and "outward" refer to motion along rows, inward being toward the center of the keyboard.

Terminology for Errors

Error Categories Based on the Triple Notation

The [H,F,P] notation (and its application to errors) is useful in distinguishing among some classes of errors. Thus, consider the classes of errors that result from different combinations of errors in the specification of H, F, and P. Let "Ix" refer to erroneous specification of component I, so that [H,Fx,P] refers to erroneous specification of the finger:

[H,F,P] In this case, because the correct hand, finger, and position are specified, the correct letter is typed. Nonetheless, four classes of errors fit into this category: insertion, in which the letter typed does not properly belong in the text; transposition, in which the letter is typed properly, but has changed position with the next consecutive letter in the text; migration, in which the letter moves to an erroneous position in the text; and interchange, in which the letter changes position with another, nonconsecutive, letter in the text.

[H,F,Px] In this case the error is typed with the correct hand and finger, and only the finger position is erroneous.

[H,Fx,P] in this case the error is typed with the correct hand, and the finger moves to the correct position, but the wrong finger moves.

[Hx,F,P] This is a homologous error, for if only the choice of hand is in error, the letter typed is in the mirror-image position relative to the correct one on the keyboard.

Misstrokes

We define a misstroke to occur when the error can be traced to inaccurate motion of the finger, as when one finger strikes two keys simultaneously, or contacts another key in passing with sufficient force to activate it. In all other errors the hand-finger motion appears appropriate for the specification. Misstrokes can best be identified by stop-motion analysis of photographs or video pictures of the hand motions.

Errors of Transposition, Interchange, and Migration

One major set of errors occurs when the correct letters are typed, but not in the proper sequence. When consecutive text letters are switched, we call it a *transposition.* When two letters that are not consecutive are switched, we call it an *interchange across I letters*, and when one letter moves from its proper position to some other position *M* letters away, we call it a *migration across M letters.* (Note that although an interchange across zero letters and a migration across one letter are identical to a transposition, there are useful theoretical reasons for reserving the term transposition for these cases.)

Transposition errors. A transposition error occurs when two consecutive letters in a word are interchanged, as when *the* is typed as *teh.* Transpositions can also occur with the space or punctuation that precedes or follows the word, as when *a job* is typed as *aj ob.* Transpositions are classified according to the fingers and hands that are involved. Thus, if *kind* were typed as *iknd*, this would be a 1F transposition. If *this* were typed as *tihs*, a 2F transposition would be involved. When *the* is typed as *teh*, a 2H transposition is involved.

Interchange across I letters. In an interchange across *I* letters, two nonconsecutive letters get interchanged, with *I* letters intervening ($I > O$). The same subclassifications used for transposition errors apply to interchanges. Thus, if *major* is typed as *jamor*, this is classed as a 1F interchange across one letter.

Migration across M Letters. In a migration across *M* letters, one letter moves ("migrates") to a new position, with *M* letters intervening between its correct position and its end position ($M > 1$). If the word *that* is typed as *atht*, this would be categorized as a migration across two letters.

Omissions

An omission error occurs when a letter in a word is left out, as when *omit* is typed *omt.*

Insertions

Insertion errors occur when an extra letter is inserted into a text, as when *and* is typed *asnd.* Some insertions can be classed as misstrokes (when stop-motion analysis indicates that a faulty finger motion was involved).

Substitutions

A substitution error occurs when the wrong letter is typed in place of the correct letter. There are several classifications of substitution errors:

Column: When the key for the substituted letter is in the same column as the key for the correct letter and is adjacent to the correct key. Column substitutions are always typed with the correct finger and hand: [H,F,Px].

Row: When the key for the substituted letter is in the same row as the key for the correct letter and is adjacent to the correct key. There are two cases of row errors. In one case, the hand and finger are correctly specified, but the position is not, [H,F,Px]. In the other case, the hand and position are correctly specified, but the finger is not, [H,Fx,P].

Homologous: When the key for the substituted letter occupies the mirror-image position on the keyboard with respect to the key for the correct letter, and is therefore typed with the same finger, in the same row, but with the wrong hand, [Hx,F,P].

Nonspecified: When the substitution does not fit one of the foregoing classifications.

Doubling Error

In a doubling error, a word containing a repeated letter is typed so that the wrong letter is doubled; for example, *book* is typed *bokk.*

Alternation Error

An alternation error occurs when a letter alternates with another, but the wrong alternation sequence is produced, as when *these* is typed as *thses.*

Acknowledgments

The research reported here was conducted under Contract N00014-79-C-0323, NR 667-437 with the Personnel and Training Research Programs of the Office of Naval Research, and was sponsored by the Office of Naval Research and the Air Force Office of Scientific Research. Requests for reprints should be sent to Donald A. Norman, Institute for Cognitive Science C-015; University of California at San Diego; La Jolla, California 92093.

Chapter 3

Studies of Typing from the LNR Research Group

Donald A. Norman and David E. Rumelhart

Studies of Typing: An Overview

The study of typing comprises a fascinating mixture of elements from motor skills, typewriter mechanics, anatomy, and cognitive control structures. Our research group initially started to study typing because it seemed an ideal example of highly skilled performance, with readily available experimental subjects and, with the advent of computer-controlled keyboards, a possibility of collecting large amounts of response time data. We expected the topic to be interesting, but were unprepared for the complexity of the phenomenon. Typing brings together many different functions, some of them heretofore ignored in cognitive psychology, yet that are of critical importance in understanding human performance. In particular, some of the problems of typing force us to confront issues of the control structures involved in highly skilled parallel-output performance, as well as questions relating to the representation of skilled motor acts within the human memory and motor control systems, all of which apply to a much more general range of concerns than typing.

In this section we review the work of our research group at San Diego (the LNR Research Group). This group is large, and the work described here represents only a few of the different aspects of typing that we have studied. In general, we have used a variety of approaches to examine typing, including the study of continuous (transcription) typing and of discontinuous (discrete trials) typing, the examination of typists of several skill levels, the analyses of errors and of the interkeystroke time distributions, and examination of hand motions through video and film analysis. Several of our studies are presented in detail elsewhere in this volume—see Chapters 2 (to which we all contributed), 4, 5, and 6. Here we review the approach and the different areas that we have studied and present an overview of our typing simulation model.

Interkeystroke Interval Distributions and Errors

The first thing we did when we started our analyses of typing was to look at the phenomena. As a result, we started to collect interkeystroke intervals for a variety of typists. Much of the early work was done in the laboratory by simply timing the keypresses on the computer terminals that we used in the laboratory and in our offices. Examination of the resulting response time distributions provided some interesting hints of future issues: The distributions showed clear effects of the keyboard layout, and the times for keys typed with the same finger or same hand were clearly different from those for keys typed with different fingers or hands. For a while, we examined almost every conceivable aspect of the distributions, and it appeared that almost daily someone would provide yet another set of distributions reflecting specific letter or finger patterns.

At the same time that we were collecting and analyzing distributions, we were looking at the general patterns of typing. We are heavy users of a computer mail system, and this caused us to rely heavily on typed messages for many of our interactions, meeting announcements, and general discussion of issues. Because this form of communication is informal, typists do not always bother to correct their errors, and the error patterns that showed up were quite interesting. Once we realized the importance of looking at typing errors, we requested that people save their errors and forward them to us. Soon we bombarded one another with memos as we discovered more and more interesting errors. The important point was that they were regular—that we could begin to see that they exerted powerful constraints on the set of possible mechanisms. The analysis of the errors led us to some important conclusions about the representational issues that underlie the control of typing movements and that helped dictate the form of our typing simulation model. Most important, the doubling error convinced us that the representation could not contain individual "tokens" of each of the letters to be typed, but rather could have only "type" elements. This means that there cannot be any repeated letters in the representation of a string of elements to be typed. This poses an interesting limitation on the representation and, in our opinion, causes the development of a special unit to handle doubles and alternations. Moreover, the existence of doubling and alternation errors indicates that the binding between the unit and its arguments is only weakly specified, leading to occasional errors. We return to these issues later.

Hand and Finger Motions: Film and Video Analysis

In addition to the study of distributions and errors, we also decided to look at the hand and finger motions in typing. Gentner, Grudin, and Conway therefore arranged to take a high-speed motion picture of a skilled typist. The picture was filmed at 100 frames/sec and we took considerable care in the filming to use a text that would provide interesting patterns and a camera angle that would yield useful information. The camera was mounted directly over the keyboard, focused downward. A front-surface mirror was placed just above the keys so that the single camera frame recorded two views of the fingers, allowing the three-dimensional trajectory of the fingers to be determined. We have since learned that a video camera gives adequate temporal resolution (60 frames/sec, or 17 msec: We use a video camera that has a special high-speed shutter to avoid blur caused by movement). Video analysis has the advantage of allowing immediate playback and, with the use of a video disk, easy stop-frame analysis of the motion. We still use a camera position over the keyboard, with a front-surface mirror to give a second perspective on the movement (although we have modified slightly the configuration first used in the film). The report of the film analysis is given in Gentner, Grudin, and Conway (Note 1) and Gentner (Note 2).

The movie was a revelation to us, showing that much more was involved than the reaction time distributions could show. Moreover, it emphasized the overlapping nature of the processing. Viewing the film created an immediate impression of a fluid set of motions, of fingers moving in many directions at once. The movement of the fingers over the keyboard reminded us of sea grass weaving in the waves, gracefully bending this way and that, all in motion at the same time. If we ever believed that skilled typing was a serial process, performed one letter at a time, one viewing of the movie dispelled that belief.

Our analyses of films and videotapes of skilled transcription typists showed that although individual typists exhibited consistent patterns of finger movement and timing, there are large differences between typists that can be independent of overall typing rate. This is discussed in more detail in Chapter 5.

The Size of the Response Unit

One major issue in the study of typing has been the size of the response unit that governs the generation of the finger movements. In Shaffer's (1973) study of the units of typing for one skilled typist, reviewed in Chapter 1, he had his subject type normal prose, random words, random letters, and foreign words. He found almost no difference between typing prose and random words (the mean interkeystroke interval was 107 msec for prose and 104 msec for random words). Random letters were typed much more slowly than normal text (192 msec), and German text was typed at an intermediate rate (149 msec; the typist did not know German). Shaffer also found that when look-ahead was limited, the typist needed to see at least eight letters ahead of where she was typing in order to maintain her normal typing rate. (The rule of thumb that has emerged from this and similar studies is that a typist looks ahead at an amount of text that requires about 1 sec to type; slower typists look ahead fewer letters, faster typists more.) Grudin and Larochelle (in Chapters 6 and 4, respectively) discuss further the problem of determining the unit size of typing. They conclude that the unit should be at least the digraph or syllable.

In studies performed by Grudin (1981, Note 3) that are not reported in this book, he discovered that in the typing of transposition errors—for example, typing *waht* instead of *what*—the interkeystroke intervals are largely as they would have been had there been no error. That is, the timing pattern seemed to be preserved—an indication that there is some coordinated control of timing for at least two-letter sequences. The explanation most consistent with the data is that skilled typists represent short sequences of letters as a single unit and generate a pattern of timing pulses for each sequence. Additional evidence from the distribution of letter sequences occurring in errors supports this view and suggests that words are parsed into single-letter and two-letter units for execution. Furthermore, Grudin argued that transposition errors were usually errors that occurred within a response unit. This interpretation is further developed in his studies of the errors made by typists of different skill levels, reported in Chapter 6.

Larochelle studied discontinuous typing, a situation pioneered by Sternberg, Monsell, Knoll, and Wright (1978) and Ostry (1980 and Chapter 9 in this book) in which subjects are presented with a single word or word-size letter string and then, upon presentation of a signal, asked to type it. Two different times are important here: the *latency*, or time from the signal to the first keypress; and the *interkeypress interval*, the time between successive keypresses. Larochelle found that the changing from words to nonwords affected the performance of novice typists, but not that of skilled typists, as long as the nonwords preserved the same digraph frequency as the words. In general, he concluded that the orthographic representation of the letter sequences was still active during the execution of the typing response, and that the transformation of letters into keypresses is a continuing process that overlaps the execution of prior keypresses to a variable degree, depending on the skill of the subjects and the quality of the material. Novice typists seem to rely on the word structure of the material more than do skilled typists.

Terzuolo and Viviani (1979, 1980) have argued that the unit is the word, and that word-specific timing patterns are stored with each word. Gentner (1982), however, shows that their results can be explained by the effects of the contexts for digraphs, and that it is unlikely that the full word is the appropriate size of the unit in typing.

Maybe there is no unit. In fact, there probably is no "unit" of typing control. It is probably no more meaningful to talk about the correct unit size in the case of typing than it is in the case of reading. In analyses of reading, the interactive models of reading assume that all the various levels of structure contribute to the process: letters, digraphs, syllables, words, phrases, sentences, and so on. It would be misguided to search for a unit. This is a consequence of any "interactive" type of model. In typing, a similar situation exists. What has been shown is simply that there are digram frequency effects. All this means is that there are some "top-down" effects larger than a single keystroke. We conclude that it is not fruitful to seek out the magical value for the size of the response unit. It will surely turn out that responses are determined by a conspiracy of different pressures.

A Simulation Model of Typing

Our initial analyses of typing, coupled with the understanding of motor processes that was developed through interaction with the skills subsection of LNR[1] led us to experiment with possible formal models for the control of movement. The control of the hands is an interesting problem, obviously guided by the cognitive processes of generating words in composition typing and by the reading process in transcription typing. Excellent typists watch the text they are copying from (in transcription typing), not the keyboard (cf. Long, 1976); yet their hands, which often requiring fairly substantial movements to cover the keyboard (especially when typing on the number row or when pressing the return key), are guided accurately and rapidly over the keys. The timing presents some interesting problems, especially when one hand has a great deal to type before the other one, thereby allowing the free hand ample time to get to its key. Thus, in our film, we observed the typing of the word *vacuum*, in which the first three letters are struck with the left hand and the rest with the right. While the left hand types *vac*, the right hand has plenty of time to get ready for the *u*. Indeed, for the film that we analyzed, the hand got to the *u* key while the left hand was getting to the *a* key. How did the right hand then know when to do its typing? Did it hover over the key until it got a signal from the left hand that the left-hand sequence was completed? This seemed unlikely because the times involved were too short; with very skilled typists, when the two letters being studied are on different hands, the interstroke intervals can be very short, with times occasionally as low as 25 msec and often around 60 msec. The lower figure is less than the neural transmission time for a signal to go from one hand through the spinal cord to the brain and back to the finger muscles. Timing by means of feedback did not seem sensible. But how then? Was the timing done by

[1] Particiants in the skills group, in addition to the two of us, were Amy Geoffry, Donald Gentner, Jonathan Grudin, Geoffry Hinton, Michael Jordan, Serge Larochelle, Wynne Lee, Paul Rosenbloom, and Craig Will.

prediction? What if you suddenly slowed up a finger as it was typing—would this cause the next finger to go out of time? (The answer here is mixed. Grudin's analyses indicate that some transposition errors occur precisely because one finger is slowed up and the other types at its normal time. However, Terzuolo and Viviani, 1980, put weights on some fingers and found that although the weights slowed up those fingers, the typists easily compensated.)

We decided to see if we could derive typing performance without a central timing mechanism. In part, we were captivated by the films that showed the hand configuring itself in preparation for the future keys. Consider how the hand distorts to pick up a piece of paper together with a pencil and a coffee cup. Each of the picking-up motions is different than it would be in isolation as the hand adapts itself to the mutual constraints of the simultaneous tasks. So too with typing: The hand seems to adopt an optimization for the joint problem of getting to all the keys as quickly as possible, weighted so as to get to the keys in the proper order.

Our solution was based on the relaxation computational methods popular in computer vision. The hands were given the job of simultaneously configuring themselves to get to all the keys, a requirement in which one goal often conflicts with another. In the simulation, the hands move a tiny distance toward each of the goals, in all required directions, with the goals weighted according to temporal order, and with the constraints of possible hand and finger movements being obeyed. Repeated iterations of the small increments eventually lead to a compromise solution in which the hand-finger combination moves as far as possible toward all the targets, but guaranteeing arrival at the next target. From there, we still had to solve timing problems and other questions, but this relaxation iteration formed the basis for our exploration of the typing process. One other major consideration that guided us was our analyses of errors; we wanted a model that both captured the appropriate response timing and made the same classes of errors that our real typists exhibited. The resulting simulation model proved to be quite accurate, and it has formed a useful basis for the evaluation of our other work on typing.

Applying the Simulation Model: An Analysis of Keyboards

It seems obvious that the traditional typewriter keyboard—the "qwerty" or Sholes keyboard—presents many difficulties for nonexpert typists. The arrangement of the letters on the keyboard seems arbitrary and difficult to learn (see the discussion in Chapter 1). There appears to be no system to the layout, and beginners often ask why the keys cannot be laid out in alphabetical order. Indeed, a number of typewriter-like devices, including children's electronic toys (e.g., Texas Instruments' Speak and Spell), hand-held language translators, note-taking devices, and one of the most popular stockbroker's quotation terminals, do have their keys arranged in alphabetical order.

Although an alphabetical arrangement might be best for novices, different considerations are relevant for expert typists. Here the objective is to lay out the keys so as to maximize typing rate. Chapter 1 discusses one major redesign of the keyboard, known as the Dvorak keyboard. This is a keyboard arrangement based on human factors (time and motion study) principles that emphasizes an efficient layout of the keys to minimize hand and finger motion (Dvorak, 1943; Dvorak, Merrick, Dealey, & Ford, 1936). Proponents of the Dvorak keyboard have frequently demonstrated advantages in learning time and typing speed, but to little avail against the established dominance of the Sholes arrangement. We decided to examine just how big a difference keyboard layout makes for novice and expert typists.

Different layouts of keyboards produce considerably different loadings of the two hands, as well as different percentages of keypresses required off the home row. Detailed studies of the timing characteristics of typing have shown that between-hand letter digraphs are typed faster than within hand, and between-finger digraphs faster than within finger (Kinkead, 1975; Rumelhart & Norman, 1982; Gentner, Note 2). These and other factors indicate that for optimal typing speed, keyboards should be designed so that:

A. The loads on the right and left hands are equalized;
B. The load on the home (middle) row is maximized;
C. The frequency of alternating hand sequences is maximized and the frequency of same-finger typing is minimized.

The Dvorak keyboard does a good job on these variables, especially A and B; 67% of the typing is done on the home row and the left-right hand balance is 47-53%. Although the Sholes (qwerty) keyboard fails at conditions A and B (most typing is done on the top row and the balance between the two hands is 57% and 43%), the policy to put successively typed keys as far apart as possible favors factor C, thus leading to relatively rapid typing.

In our studies (Norman & Fisher, in press), we examined novices typing on several different arrangements of alphabetically organized keyboards, the Sholes keyboard, and a randomly organized keyboard (to control against prior knowledge of Sholes). There were essentially no differences among the alphabetic and random keyboards. Novices typed slightly faster on the Sholes keyboard, probably reflecting prior experience with it. We studied expert typists by using our simulation model. Here, we looked at the Sholes and Dvorak layouts, as well as several alphabetically arranged keyboards. The simulation showed that the alphabetically organized keyboards were between 2% and 9% *slower* than the Sholes keyboard, and the the Dvorak keyboard was only about 5% faster than Sholes. These figures correspond well to other experimental studies that compared the Dvorak and Sholes keyboards and to the computations of Card, Moran, and Newell (in press) for comparing these keyboards. These correspondences buttress our faith in the veracity of the typing model, and thereby also in its results for alphabetic keyboards.

Thus, the Sholes keyboard actually seems to be a sensible design, superior to all of the alphabetic arrangements that we have studied, and only 5-10% slower than the Dvorak keyboard, the one that was based on time and motion studies.

For the expert typist, the layout of keys makes surprisingly little difference. There seems no reason to choose Sholes, Dvorak, or alphabetically organized keyboards over one another on the basis of typing speed. It *is* possible to make a bad keyboard layout, however, and two of the arrangements that we studied can be ruled out. One of the slowest keyboards is the configuration of keys that people think of when considering alphabetic arrangements.

Some Basic Phenomena[2]

The Timing of Keystrokes

World champion typists can type at rates up to 200 words per minute (wpm). This involves a mean interval between key strokes of 60 msec, close to the neural transmission time between the spinal cord and the periphery (and obviously many keystroke intervals will be considerably less than the mean). There cannot be much feedback between strokes being performed so rapidly. Even relatively ordinary typists can routinely generate keystrokes at rates almost as rapid as this. For example, of the 1,656 time *th* was typed by one of our subjects, 414 times the interval was less than 63 msec. The *th* interkeystroke interval was less than 75 msec half of the time.

Speed, however, is the simplest of the phenomena that need to be accounted for. Overall, the timing phenomena that provide strong constraints on the structure of a possible model of typing include that:

(a) People can type very quickly;
(b) Cross-hand interkeystroke intervals (2H patterns) are shorter than those within hands (1F and 2F);
(c) Within-hand interkeystroke intervals appear to be determined by the patterns of fingers that are involved (i.e., doubles, 1F, and 2F) and by the reach from one key to the next;
(d) The time for a particular interkeystroke interval can depend on the context in which it occurs.

[2] This section is adapted from Rumelhart and Norman (1982).

Pattern of Errors

Errors are of special importance, for some of them give strong clues to the underlying mechanisms. Thus the existence of transposition, doubling, and alternation errors has played a major role in determining the structure of the model.

Transposition Errors

One of the most common and most interesting categories of errors is transposition, the reversal of two adjacent letters. The large majority of these errors occur across hands. Shaffer (1976) reports that of his subject's transposition errors, about 90% were cross-hand transpositions. We find the number to vary, being only 75% for one of our skilled typists. Examples of transpositions from our data include

because → *becuase*,
which → *whihc*.

Of the within-hand errors that we have examined, half involved adjacent keys (such as *e* and *r* and *o* and *p*), as in

supremely → *supermely*.

One interesting example was reported by Shaffer (1976):

went down → *wne todnw*.

The four keystrokes on the right hand (the *n*, space, *o*, and *n*) have all been displaced with respect to the five left-hand keystrokes.

Doubling Errors

When a word contains a doubled letter, the wrong letter is sometimes doubled. Thus, *look* can become *lokk*. This error was pointed out by Lashley (1951) and by Shaffer (1976) as being diagnostic as to the nature of motor control. Although our corpus of transcription typing includes only one example of a doubling error of this sort:

school → *scholl*,

we have collected many doubling errors from our samples of composition typing (while using the laboratory computer). For example:

gibbs → *giibs*,
Screen → *Scrren*.

Alternation Reversal Errors

These are akin to the doubling error, but with an alternating sequence. Thus in the word *these* the *ese* is an alternation. Samples observed during composition typing include

these → *thses,*
there → *threr,*
were → *wrer.*

Other Errors

In addition to the errors of transposition, doubling, and alternation, a number of other forms of errors occur. A large proportion of these errors are described and defined in Chapters 2 and 6, so there is no need to repeat them here. We believe that some of these errors come from factors outside the control of hand movements, either in the cognitive factors determining the choice of response schemas or in "slips" of performance, as discussed by Norman (1981).

The General Organization of Typing

Finally, there are two other observations that we have used as strong constraints: the overlapping of hand movements and the unit of organization of the strings to be typed.

Skilled Typists Move Their Hands Toward the Keys in Parallel

We have already mentioned the filming of hand movements that we have conducted by means of high-speed motion pictures and stop-frame video analysis. The results of these studies show the fingers of the hand in almost constant motion, with fingers starting to move toward their destination before the several preceding characters have been typed. A serial model of typing in which each finger in turn makes its stroke is incorrect. Rather, there seems to be a coordinated structure that allows the control of several fingers simultaneously.

A Cooperative Algorithm Simulation Model of Typing

In this section (which is taken from Rumelhart & Norman, 1981, 1982) we describe the operation of a working computer program that models a skilled typist. The program development was guided by the considerations of typing performance that we have just discussed. This section tells of the actual implementation. The completed model simulates a skilled human typist. The model output is both a set of keypress intervals and a graphic display of the hands moving across the keyboard.

Control of the fingers poses a number of complexities, and the cognitive specification of the actions to be performed must be compatible with existing knowledge of both mental structures and the phenomena of typing, especially the factors discussed in the previous sections. Our analyses of these components lead us toward a model that has the following properties:

(a) Control of action sequences by means of schemas;
(b) Selection of appropriate motor schemas through a combination of activation value and triggering condition;
(c) The representation of letter typing by means of a *pure type theory* (i.e., one with no type-token distinction);
(d) The need for distributed (local) rather than concentrated (central) control of movement.

We start with the assumption that motor control of a learned movement is represented by means of a motor schema, an organized unit of knowledge, differing from the form of knowledge widely studied in the literature on memory, language, and thought only in that it has as its output the control of body movements. This is not a new concept. Actually, the term *schema* was originally introduced into psychology for use in skilled motor control by Head (1926) and is still used for that purpose (cf. Schmidt, 1976).

We propose that one of the functions of schemas is to act as motor programs. The term *motor program* is to be understood by analogy with the term *computer program*. We believe there has been some confusion in the literature on skills in this regard, with critics of the notion of motor programming acting as if a program were a fixed action sequence, specified in complete detail before the actual movements. According to our view, motor programs are flexible, interactive control structures, capable of calling upon subprograms, passing parameters to be bound to program variables, and making local decisions as a result of current conditions (which might include information from feedback channels, perception, or other sources of knowledge). A motor program is not a fixed action pattern of movements. It is a set of specifications or control statements that govern the actions that are to be performed, with considerable flexibility in the specification of the actions. A program specifies the rules that are to be followed in the action, not the actual motions.

Issues Not Covered by This Simulation Model

Typing is a rich, complex skill, and although we examine and model a number of the characteristics of skilled typing, there is also much that we do not cover. We look only at skilled typing, and cover neither the mechanisms used by inexperienced typists nor the mechanisms involved in learning. We assume that all the necessary control and knowledge structures are already established. We do not examine how a skilled typist might vary typing rate in order to manipulate the speed-accuracy trade-off (although there are several parameters of our model that can readily be identified as potential candidates for this manipulation). We do not look at the mechanisms involved in perception or the encoding of the strings to be typed, nor in monitoring the accuracy of the typing. We do not simulate the deterioration of typing rate that occurs as the text is modified from normal prose to nonlanguage or random letters. Finally, we study only lowercase alphabetic characters and a limited number of other keys, ignoring most nonalphabetic keys.[3] Our work is readily extended to these other keys, however, so we do not consider this of fundamental importance. Nevertheless, there are insufficient data available for these other keys, and in many cases the keyboard locations are not standardized, so that typists are not as expert with them (or, as is often the case with number keys, may prefer to adopt a different mode of typing for them). Despite these omissions, there still has been considerable work for us to do.

The ATS Formalism

The basic framework that we follow is called an activation-triggered schema (ATS) system. The model consists of a set of schemas, each with activation values. A schema has an activation value that reflects the total amount of excitation that it has received. The normal resting value for a schema is zero. It can increase when the schema is "activated" or decrease when the schema is "inhibited." Schemas interact with one another, and the activation value reflects this interaction as well as the effects of decay and other sources of activation and inhibition. When appropriate conditions have been satisfied, a schema may be "triggered," at which time its procedures become operative and control whatever operations they specify.

Different schemas are often interconnected. Moreover, one schema may call upon other schemas to perform specific tasks, much as a computer program calls upon subroutines or coroutines. When one schema calls upon another, the initiating schema is called the *parent schema* and the called schema is the *child schema.* Each schema can serve in any or all of three ways: as a program in control of operations, as a parent schema that initiates the operation of other schemas, or as a child schema invoked by a parent.

A particular schema might be invoked by a parent schema, set into motion some operations, and then itself serve as a parent to its child schemas. Usually, but not necessarily, when a child schema has completed its operations, control returns to the parent schema. Thus, the schema for typing the word *the* might be initiated by the triggering of the parent schema for *the*, which then controls the activation and trig-

[3] In all of the analyses of typing data discussed in this section, we look only at lowercase alphabetic characters, spaces, and limited punctuation (period, comma, and semicolon). Other nonalphabetic characters, punctuation, numerals, and the use of the return and shift keys are not examined.

gering of the child schemas for the letters *t*, *h*, and *e*, which in turn activate the child schemas that control the actual finger, hand, and arm movements.

The Simulation Model

Figure 3.1 illustrates the basic structure of the model. The model incorporates the ATS system plus specific control mechanisms for the activations and selection of particular hand and finger movements. The input of the model is a string of characters that constitute the text to by typed. The output is a sequence of finger movements, either displayed on a visual computer-controlled display as the movement of the hands and fingers over a typewriter keyboard, or as a series of coordinate locations for the relevant body parts.

Figure 3.2 illustrates the basic assumptions of the activation process be using the word *very* as an example. First, the schema for the word is activated by the perceptual system and parser. This, in turn, activates each of the child schemas for keypresses. Each keypress schema specifies the target position, with position encoded in terms of a keyboard-centered coordinate system. These target positions are sent to the response system, which then must configure the palm and finger positions properly. Each keypress schema inhibits the schemas that follow it. This means that proper temporal ordering of the keypress schemas is given by the ordering of the activation values. In addition, the activation values are noisy, which leads to occasional errors.

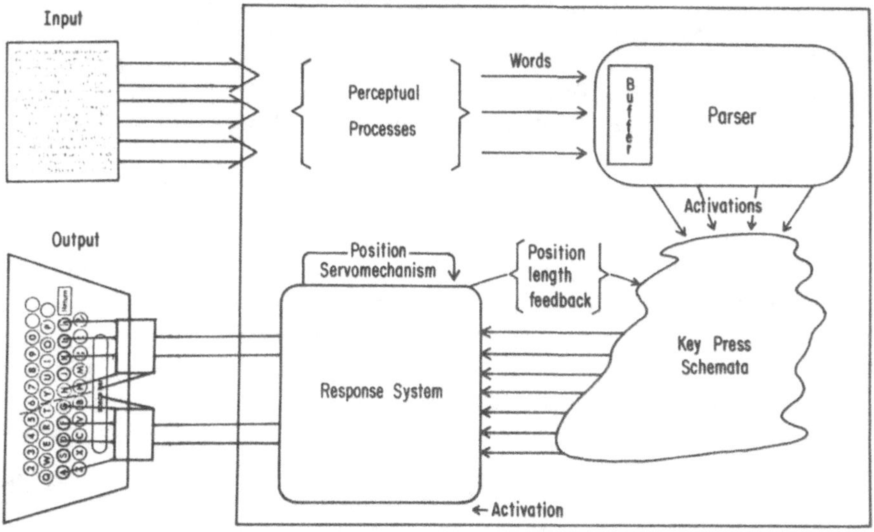

Fig. 3.1. The information processing structure used by the simulation model of typing.

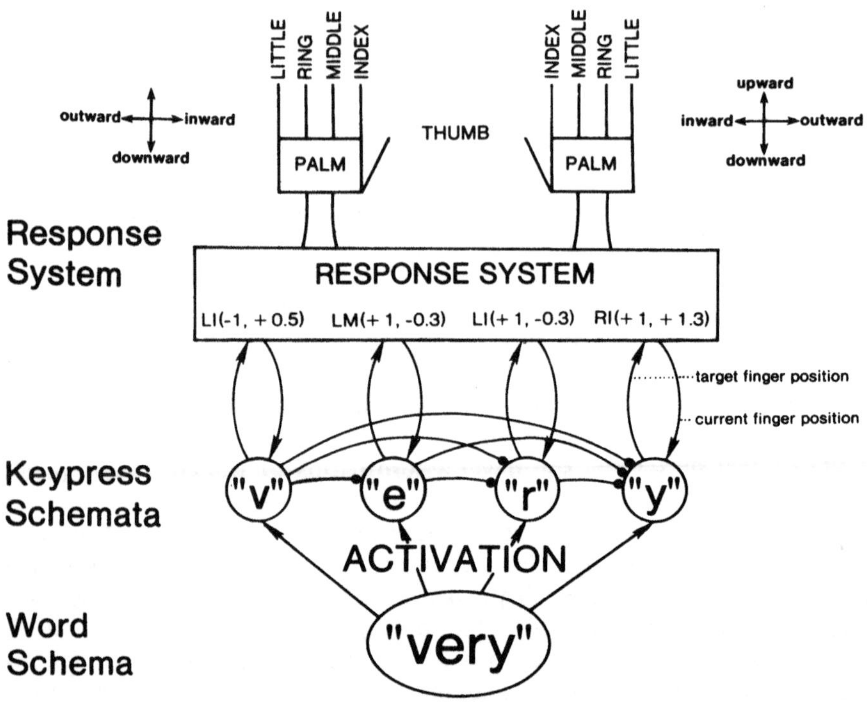

Fig. 3.2. The interaction of activations when the word *very* is to be typed. Inhibition is shown by the lines with solid circles at their termination.

The response system feeds back to the keypress system information about the current location of the fingers. Whenever the current finger position is within some criterion distance of its target position, and the relevant schema is the one most highly activated, then the triggering conditions are satisfied and the actual keystroke is launched.

Repeated Letters Imply That There Are No Token Schemas

The existence of doubling and alternation errors poses special problems. Consider the word *book*. According to the arguments we have just presented, the word would be represented by schemas for each of the letters *b o o k*. It is easy to see how such a representation could lead to transposition errors (such as *boko*) but not to doubling errors. It would be easy to make up a schema for a doubled letter (so that the word would be represented by the schemas *b DOUBLE-o k*), but this would not lead to the doubling errors either.

The doubling error turns out to have two major implications. First, it implies that there are special schemas that signal the existence of doubled letters, and that occasionally these schemas get applied to the wrong letters. In computational terms, this means that the binding between the arguments of the special schemas for doubling is occasionally made improperly. Second, the need for a special schema to mark doubled letters implies a difficulty in having the regular letter schema signal the double. Why is not the word *book* represented by the schemas *b o o k*? The reason would seem to be that this would require two instances (tokens) of the schema for *o*; the existence of the doubling error implies that such repeated tokens of a schema are not possible.

Thus, the existence of doubling errors forces us to a pure type model, in which each letter can have only a single keypress schema; the keypress schemas exist only as types, with no token schemas. There must be a special schema that signals the presence of a doubled letter. Moreover, there must be a weak binding between the special schema and the arguments upon which it operates. In the model, the arguments are not bound to the schemas, but are established via activation values. The most highly activated keystroke schema is triggered when it is within a criterion distance of its target. After triggering (and the resulting launch of the keystroke), this keypress schema can become bound to a doubling schema if one exists that has a higher activation value than its own. Because activation values are noisy, occasionally this leads to errors in the linking of keypress schemas to a doubling schema.

The existence of alternation errors leads to the same conclusion: There must be a special schema that signals the presence of alternating letters, with a weak binding between the schema and its arguments, and the mechanism proposed for alternations is similar to that for doubling.

Here is an example of the typing of a word with a doubled letter. The word *book* is represented by the activation of four schemas: *b*, *DOUBLE*, *o*, and *k*. Each schema inhibits all that follow it, in the regular fashion. The operation now is much as we illustrated before, except that after a keystroke schema has been triggered, it checks for the existence of a double schema whose activation value exceeds its own value. The *b* will initially be the schema most highly activated, and when the finger gets within a criterion distance from the key, the *b* keystroke will be launched. Now the *DOUBLE* schema will have the highest activation level. However, the *DOUBLE* schema does not command any motor responses, and it allows control to be passed to the schema with the next highest activation value. The next schema is the one for *o*. It proceeds normally. As the keystroke is launched, the *o* schema notes that there is a *DOUBLE* schema whose activation value is greater than its own. Whenever this condition occurs, the keypress schema deactivates the *DOUBLE* schema and, after the keystroke, does not deactivate itself. As a result, at the completion of the keystroke, the schema is again triggered, launching itself a second time. At the launching of this second keystroke the doubling schema is no longer present, so that typing of the rest of the word can continue. Noise in the activation levels occasionally causes this mechamism to go awry, so that the *DOUBLE* schema gets associated with the wrong keypress schema, causing the wrong character to be doubled.

This mechanism for doubling errors is, then, the same as the mechanism for transposition errors, except that here one of the two schemas that get transposed is the one representing *DOUBLE*. By this model, therefore, in a word like *book*, the underlying schema representation is *b D o k* (where *D* stands for *DOUBLE*), and so if any pair of schemas could transpose, we would expect the following typing sequences to be possible:

Transposed schemas	*Resulting schemas*	*Typed string*
None	*b D o k*	*b o o k*
b - D	*D b o k*	*b b o k*
D - o	*b o D k*	*b o k k*
o - k	*d D k o*	*b k k o*

Because the doubled letter results from explicit application of the *DOUBLE* schema, we would never expect to see an error of the form *boko*, where one of the pairs of the doubled letters transposes with another. This is simply not possible in our model. In principle, this provides us with a strong test of the model; in practice, however, the frequency of doubled letters is so low as to make critical tests unlikely without some artificial means for increasing the frequency of doubles or a massive study of large quantities of text.

We suspect that errors of alternation are caused by an underlying representation and mechanism similar to that proposed for doubles. Thus, a word such as *where* would be represented as *w h A e r* (where *A* stands for the schema for *ALTERNATION* of the two letters that follow). By the same transposition argument as used with doubles, this mechanism should lead to the following sequences with the word *where:*

Transposed schemas	*Resulting schemas*	*Typed string*
None	*w h A e r*	*w h e r e*
w - h	*h w A e r*	*h w e r e*
h - A	*w A h e r*	*w h e h r*
A - e	*w h e A r*	*Undefined*
e - r	*w h A r e*	*w h r e r*

Because there is only a single representation of the letter being alternated, we should not expect the alternating letter to be split, so an error of the form *wehre* is not possible with our model.

When we added this alternation mechanism to a version of the model, it led to difficulties. These were primarily with the typing of spaces. Let the symbol "-" stand for *space*. Words such as *-a-* that had but one letter were spelled *a-a* rather than *-a-*. It is possible that the problem here lies with the parsing mechanism, not with the alternation schemas. It is probably wrong to treat a word such as *a* or *I* as an alternation of *space letter space* (i.e., as the schemas *A space letter*); rather, each word should either be followed or preceded by a space (so that only a single space is ever tied in with a word). Because we did not attempt to model the perceptual and parsing process, we did not pursue this possible explanation. In similar fashion, in our list of possible alternation errors for the word *where*, transposition of the *A* and *e* schemas for *where* (yielding the schema sequence *w h e A r*) is undefined, because the alternation schema *A* requires two arguments. In our simulation model, the space following the word was picked up as the second argument, leading to the typing of the string *wher-r*. In our data we never observed errors of this form, where spaces were part of an alternation sequence.

The assumption that there are no token nodes causes special problems for any word that contains repeated instances of the same letter that is not part of a double or an alternation (e.g., the *e* and *p* of *perception*). As a result, if a word contains a repeated instance of a letter, at the first instance of the letter (say, the *e* in *perception*) the keypress schema for *e* becomes activated and therefore cannot be used to encode the repeated instance of the *e* until it has completed its duties (i.e., until *pe* has been typed). Parsing of the word into keystroke schemas is blocked at the repeated letter until the keystroke for the previous instance has been completed. Thus the parser sets up the keypress schemas for *p*, *e*, *r*, *c*. When the *p* and *e* have been typed, the parser is then free to set up the rest of the word: *e*, *p*, *t*, *i*, *o*, *n*. A similar blocking occurs in the case of repeated doubles, as in *bookkeeping*. Because there is only one node for *DOUBLE*, the parser can at first set up only *b*, *DOUBLE*, *o*, and then, when the doubled *o* has been typed, can add *DOUBLE*, *k*, and finally, when the doubled *k* has been typed, *DOUBLE*, *e*, *p*, *i*, *n*, *g*.

Movement

In the model, each active schema pushes its relevant hand and finger toward its desired key at the same time, and the final overall configuration is determined by the competition among these forces. Each schema pushes with a force proportional to its activation level. As a result, the forces are weighted so as to cause the letter schema that is next in line to be typed to approach its key most quickly. The actual location of each finger is determined by the sum of the extensions of the finger and the hand. To type a particular typewriter key, it is only necessary that the end position be correct. The end-point configuration is reached through an iterative relaxation process that involves only local computation. Because of the unequal weighting of activations, the process will eventually cause the most highly activated schema to move its finger-palm configuration to within a criterion distance from its target key, satisfying the trigger conditions and launching the keystroke. A more complete description of the model operation can be found in Rumelhart and Norman (1982).

Appraisal

In order to evaluate the model, we gave it a text of slightly over 2,000 words to type. The pattern of keystrokes and the times were collected from the simulation and analyzed in exactly the same fashion as we had followed for the data from our human subject. Overall, the fit of the model to the many phenomena of typing is good. Detailed analyses of the model performance indicate that the simulation results do show about the right pattern of interstroke intervals. Moreover, the correlation of model times with actual typing times for the 66 most common bigrams from our data with the data of six subjects yields an overall correlation between the model and the averaged data of about .86. The fit is not bad; however, the model clearly does not account for all that is happening. (Data for five of these subjects were collected by Donald Gentner. A more complete appraisal of the model is given in Rumelhart & Norman, 1982.)

The model does produce errors in typing, the most important ones being transposition errors, doubling errors, and misstrokes. The proportion of errors in the model is determined by the amount of noise in the activation levels. In our subjects' data we observed transpositions at about a rate of 1 for every 1,800 keystrokes. We adjusted the noise level to yield errors at a rate of about 1 for every 30 keystrokes. Despite the large difference in rate, the basic pattern of errors is similar. For example, a large majority (76%) of the transpositions in the simulation occur across hands. This is about the same as our subject and comparable to values reported for others. At the level of noise employed in the simulation, 17 doubling errors were generated.

Conclusion

We have constructed a working computer simulation of a model that captures the appropriate spirit of the phenomena observed with human typists, although it does not yet offer a complete account of the typing process. Despite the lack of an internal clock or metronome for timing, the model provides a resonably good account of the timing patterns observed among skilled typists, including the prediction of negative correlations among successive keystrokes, a characteristic of metronome models (see Chapter 1). In similar fashion, there are no specific context dependencies built into the model, yet the time that it takes to strike keys depends upon the context in which they occur. We have no specific stored timing patterns for specific words, yet the model predicts that words have characteristic time profiles. We have no specific mechanism for transposition errors, yet our model generates the correct types of transposition errors. Moreover, the coordinative structure assumed within the model yields a qualitative emulation of the pattern of overlapping movements shown in a high-speed film of a typist.

A number of conclusions can be drawn from our studies. First, the existence of doubling errors strongly implies the existence of a pure type representation of the keyboard schemas, with their arguments only loosely bound. Second, the nature of the skill requires simultaneous parallel control of the fingers and hands, and this requires some form of negotiation process to turn the potentially competitive movements into cooperative ones. The degrees of freedom problem can be turned into a degrees of freedom virtue. Third, the model must incorporate the entire environment within which the typist operates, from the reading of the text to the cognitive and motor control systems to the shapes and mechanical characteristics of the hands, finger, and keyboard. Indeed, some of the limitations of the current model may really result from limitations of how well we dealt with the environment surrounding the control processes. Perhaps the central conclusion to be drawn from our analysis of typing deals with the nature of skilled motor coordination. We propose that the motor control system carries out its computations relatively locally and in parallel. We presume that such a conclusion will be proven for all skills involving high-speed performance.

We consider that the typing simulation provides a useful first-order approximation to the final model of typing. This model demonstrates that many of the phenomena of typing can be reasonably well described by a structure that allows for parallel movements of the fingers, with no central timing mechanism. In normal operation, the timing is completely determined by how long it takes for each finger to reach its target position and for the inhibition from preceding fingers to be released. Thus, the timing is determined primarily by the physical constraints on finger and hand motions and by the mechanical layout of the keyboard.

Although the model works quite well, there is need for a revision, to a large extent because of the work reported in the chapters by the other members of the research group—Gentner, Grudin, and Larochelle. Among other things, a model of typing will have to account for the overlapping of preparation and execution, for the different effects of orthographic variables on the performance of skilled and novice typists, and for the spelling and timing patterns of errors. The result implies considerable structure in the internal units that guide the typing, with top-down effects taking place over groups of at least more than one or two letter units, but smaller than most words. A central timing mechanism does not seem to be necessary, but consideration of the role of the perceptual and working memory processes is probably necessary to account for the timing patterns.

Our computer simulation of typing does not satisfy all of these requirements, and the model is inadequate in some of its features and assumptions. However, it serves as a useful first approximation for the understanding of skilled typing. In the earlier section of the LNR approach we concluded that it was not fruitful to search for the magical value for the size of the response unit. It will surely turn out that responses are determined by a conspiracy of different pressures. Some of the pressures will be those well described by the model. Others will depend on other aspects of experience and the context. There are two points to be made here. Many things that one might have thought were the products of central control could have been generated by local interactions (as in the typing model). Some things that are observed, such as frequency effects, probably are the result of top-down processing forces. Presumably, were we to design our experiments carefully we could find other more subtle top-down effects. Some of the observations of the LNR group on error correction might suggest that there are syntactic and semantic effects, but we would not want to conclude that the sentence was the response unit. Nevertheless, it should not shock us to find that such things did have an effect (albeit subtle). Perhaps the suprising thing is not so much that there are traces of top-down effects, but how difficult it is to find and document them. The difficulty probably reveal more such effects in the future.

Acknowledgments

We thank Eileen Conway and Mark Wallen for their continued assistance in all phases of this research. All the members of the LNR research group played valuable roles in this research, but Donald Gentner, Jonathan Grudin, and Serge Larochelle were particularly important members of the LNR typing group. Craig Will contributed to our early studies of typing. Julie Norman worked with us in the early phases of the research and served as the typist for the initial film. Sondra Buffett joined later and helped in the completion of the manuscripts.

The research reported here was conducted under Contract N00014-79-C-0323, NR 667-437 with the Personnel and Training Research Programs of the Office of Naval Research, and was sponsored by the Office of Naval Research and the Air Force Office of Scientific Research. Requests for reprints should be sent to Donald A. Norman, Institute for Cognitive Science, C-015, University of California at San Diego, La Jolla, California 92093.

Reference Notes

1. Gentner, D. R., Grudin, J., & Conway, E. *Finger movements in transcription typing* (Tech. Rep. 8001). La Jolla, Calif.: University of California at San Diego, Center for Human Information Processing, May 1980.
2. Gentner, D. R. *Skilled finger movements in typing* (Tech. Rep. 104). La Jolla, California: University of California at San Diego, Center for Human Information Processing, July 1981.
3. Grudin, J. T. *Central control of timing in skilled typing* (Tech. Rep. 8202). La Jolla, Calif.: University of California at San Diego, Center for Human Information Processing, 1982.

References

Beeching, W. A. *Century of the typewriter.* New York: St. Martin's Press, 1974.

Card, S., Moran, T., & Newell, A. *Applied information-processing psychology: The human-computer interface.* Hillsdale, N.J.: Erlbaum, in press.

Dvorak, A. There is a better typewriter keyboard. *National Business Education Quarterly,* 1943, *11,* 58-66.

Dvorak, A., Merrick, N. L., Dealey, W. L., & Ford, G.C. *Typewriting behavior.* New York: American Book Company, 1936.

Gentner, D. R. Evidence against a central control model of timing in typing. *Journal of Experimental Psychology: Human Perception and Performance,* 1982, in press.

Grudin, J. T. *The organization of serial order in typing.* Unpublished doctoral dissertation, Universtiy of California at San Diego, 1981.

Head, H. *Aphasia and kindred disorders of speech* (Vol. 1) New York and London: Cambridge University Press, 1926.

Kinkead, R. Typing speed, keying rates, and optimal keyboard layouts. *Proceedings of Human Factors Society,* 1975, 159-161.

Lashley, K. S. The problem of serial order in behavior. In L. A. Jeffress (Ed.), *Cerebral mechanisms in behavior.* New York: Wiley, 1951.

Long, J. Visual feedback and skilled keying: Differential effects of masking the printed copy and the keyboard. *Ergonomics,* 1976, *19,* 93-110.

Norman, D. A., & Fisher, D. Why alphabetic keyboards are not easy to use: Keyboard layout doesn't much matter. *Human Factors,* in press.

Ostry, D. J. Execution-time movement control. In G. E. Stelmach & J. Requin (Eds.), *Tutorials in motor behavior.* Amsterdam: North-Holland, 1980.

Rumelhart, D. E., & Norman, D. A. An activation-trigger-schema model for the simulation of skilled typing. *Proceedings of the Berkeley Conference of the Cognitive Science Society.* Berkeley, Calif. 1981.

Rumelhart, D. E., & Norman, D. A. Simulating a skilled typist: A study of skilled cognitive-motor performance. *Cognitive Science,* 1982, *6,* 1-36.

Schmidt, R. A. The schema as a solution to some persistent problems in motor learning theory. In G. E. Stelmach (Ed.), *Motor control: Issues and trends.* New York: Academic Press, 1976.

Shaffer, L. H. Latency mechanisms in transcription. In S. Kornblum (Ed.), *Attention and performance IV.* New York: Academic Press, 1973.

Shaffer, L. H. Intention and performance. *Psychological Review,* 1976, *83,* 375-393.

Sternberg, S., Monsell, S., Knoll, R. L., & Wright, C. E. The latency and duration of rapid movement sequences: Comparisons of speech and typewriting. In G. E. Stelmach (Ed.), *Information processing in motor control and learning.* New York: Academic Press, 1978.

Terzuolo, C. A., & Viviani, P. The central representation of learned motor patterns. In R. E. Talbott & D. R. Humphrey (Eds.), *Posture and movement.* New York: Raven Press, 1979.

Terzuolo, C. A., & Viviani, P. Determinants and characteristics of motor patterns used for typing. *Neuroscience,* 1980, *5,* 1085-1103.

Chapter 4

A Comparison of Skilled and Novice Performance in Discontinuous Typing

Serge Larochelle

Much of the fascination of skilled activities has to do with the speed achieved in expert performance. By comparison, the slow and stumbling performance of novices seems rather bland and uninteresting. This may explain why most previous research devoted to transcription typing has been focused on the performance of skilled subjects. As a result, we have a much poorer characterization of the properties of novice typing. The problem is that without such a characterization, it is difficult to determine how expert speeds are achieved. The major motivation for the following studies was to step out of this vicious circle. In these studies the temporal properties of skilled and novice typing are compared and an attempt is made to specify some of the differences in processing that distinguish skilled from novice performance.

The studies are based on the discontinuous typing paradigm, used previously by Ostry (1980) and by Sternberg, Monsell, Knoll, and Wright (1978). In the discontinuous typing task, the subjects are presented with isolated words or word-size letter strings, which they are asked to type, on cue, as fast and accurately as possible. The variable of primary interest is the average time interval between the successive keystrokes. However, there is another temporal variable involved in discontinuous typing experiments, namely, the time between the signal to respond and the first keystroke (hereafter referred to as the latency period).

By its very nature, the discontinuous typing task deals with the transformation of lexical-orthographic information into an action sequence. The potential influence of syntactic and semantic factors on typing performance is eliminated altogether. However, the evidence accumulated so far indicates that the syntactic and the semantic structure of the material contributes very little to skilled performance in continuous transcription typing, as noted in Chapter 1. For instance, Shaffer and Hardwick (1968) failed to find any speed or accuracy difference between prose passages and passages made of a random distribution of the same words. By contrast, they found a deterioration in performance when the material was made of nonsense letter strings.

Similarly, in the discontinuous typing task, Sternberg, Knoll, and Wright (1978) found a difference in average interstroke interval between words and nonsense strings. However, they did not find the frequency of the digraphs composing the nonsense strings to have any effect on skilled performance. This lack of effect is somewhat at odds with results obtained in continuous typing experiments. For instance, in the previously cited experiment by Shaffer and Hardwick, a gradual deterioration in skilled performance was observed as the quality of the typing material was degraded from words to syllable strings to first- and zero-order letter strings.

Because of the neglect of novice performance alluded to earlier, we still do not know the role of syntactic and semantic structure in novice typing. We do know, however, that novice performance, like skilled performance, suffers from manipulations that destroy the word structure of the typing material. The problem one faces in evaluating the results is that the manipulations involved were rarely the same across skill groups, or that these manipulations were too radical to provide a good insight into the nature of the processes at work (Shaffer & Hardwick, 1970). By contrast, the stimulus strings used in the first experiment reported here are rigorously controlled, with very graded variations in their frequency composition. The experimental conditions are also the same across skill groups.

In order to get a more detailed view of the processes by which strings of letters are transformed into sequences of keystrokes, the motor composition of the sequences is also varied. It has been repeatedly shown (with skilled subjects again) that sequences of keystrokes that involve fingers of different hands (2H) are executed faster than sequences that involve different fingers of the same hand (1H). The first experiment deals with 1H and 2H sequences of different lexical-orthographic composition. The second experiment focuses on single-hand sequences, the analyses bearing on the results obtained with keystroke transitions that involve the repeated use of one finger (1F) and those that involve two different fingers (2F).

Experiment 1

Method

Subjects. Twelve right-handed subjects participated in the experiment. Four of them were skilled typists. These subjects were by no means experts. Their typing speed ranged from 65 to 73 words per minute (wpm), with an average of 70 wpm (171 msec/keystroke). Similarly, the eight novice subjects were not true beginners. They were college students who had learned the touch-typing method in high school. They had not reached a very high skill level then, nor had they practiced much since then. Their average typing speed was 21 wpm (571 msec/keystroke), with a range going from 15 to 26 wpm.

Stimuli. As mentioned previously, one set of stimuli consisted of letter strings that could be typed with the fingers of one hand (1H strings). The letter strings in the other set required a strict alternation between the fingers of each hand in executing the successive keystrokes (2H strings). The same letter could appear more than once within a given stimulus string but not in consecutive positions. About half of the 1H strings were typed by the right hand and the other half by the left hand. Similarly, among the 2H strings, about half of the strings started with a right-hand key, the other half starting with a left-hand key. In order to equate as much as possible the amount of work done by the left and the right hand, the letters *a*, *z*, *x*, and *c* were excluded from the composition of the strings because on the standard Sholes keyboard there are no letters in the corresponding positions under the right hand.

The stimulus strings were of three different categories with respect to their orthographic composition. First, there were words three to six letters long. Second, for each string length, a set of "pseudowords" was constructed by recombining the letters found in the set of words of that length while trying to preserve as many of the same digraphs as possible. No attempt was made to maintain the trigraph composition of the pseudowords equivalent to that of the words. As a result, the average digraph frequency of the pseudowords was very similar to that of the words, but there was a large difference in average trigraph frequency between these two categories of stimuli. Examples of the pseudowords used in the experiment are *ber*, *bret*, *stred*, and *bertse* for the 1H category (left-hand strings), and *voe*, *buth*, *rohtu*, and *shrdne* for the 2H category (left-starting strings).

Finally, a set of nonwords was constructed that preserved neither the digraph nor the trigraph composition of the words. The nonwords were made by recombining the letters found in the words of the same length, motor composition (1H vs. 2H), and starting hand (left vs. right). Except for the restrictions inherent in the experiment, this recombination process was random. As a result, the nonwords had a much lower average digraph and trigraph frequency than the other two types of stimuli. Examples of the nonwords used in the experiment are *bsd*, *tsge*, *dsrte*, and *efedet* for the 1H category (left-hand strings), and *fuv*, *tken*, *gubht*, and *bysndi* for the 2H category (left-starting strings).

In general, there were 16 different stimuli for each combination of the length, orthographic composition, motor composition, and starting-hand factors. Some of the length 6 conditions were underrepresented because not enough words could be found that satisfied all the requirements of the experiment. The method used to generate the nonsense strings guaranteed that the same imbalance would be present among the pseudowords and the nonwords as well. Strings of length 2 were also used in the experiment. These strings consisted of digraphs of varying frequency. Since the pseudoword-nonword distinction, as it was defined previously, does not apply to strings of length 2, the results obtained with these strings will not be considered here.

Design. Each subject was tested under all the stimulus conditions involved in the experiment. For most conditions, there were 12 test trials on which the subject had to type the string presented, and 4 catch trials on which no response was required from the subject. The conditions in which fewer than 16 different strings were available allowed for fewer catch trials, so that over all stimulus conditions, 23% of the trials were catch trials. The allocation of the strings to catch and test trials varied across subjects, and the number of times each string was used as a test stimulus and as a catch stimulus was proportionally the same for both skill groups.

The experiment required four sessions per subject, each session being held on a separate day and lasting approximately 45 minutes. The sessions involved three blocks of trials each: one block for the words, one for the pseudowords, and one for the nonwords. The order of the blocks varied over sessions and over subjects, in a balanced way across skill groups. The motor composition of the strings, the starting hand, and the string length varied randomly within each block.

The first session was considered a practice session, each block containing 40 trials. The stimuli used for practice were different from those used on experimental trials, but they were constructed following the same principles. In addition, the typing speed of the subject was estimated at the beginning of the first session from a sample of about 1,000 keystrokes of normal continuous transcription typing. For the last three sessions each block contained about 115 trials, the first 12 being considered practice. The trials on which the subject made an error were repeated at the end of the block in which the error had occurred.

Procedure. The experiment was performed on a Hazeltine 1500 terminal. Each trial was announced by the terminal's sounding a beep. Two hundred msec after the beep, a letter string was displayed for 1 sec in the center of the screen. Following the disappearance of the string, there was a period of 1.7 sec without any event before the subject heard a short burst of white noise. This first burst of white noise was followed 700 msec later by a second burst of white noise, which was followed another 700 msec later by a tone. Catch trials were signaled to the subject by a low tone (150 Hz), whereas a high tone (500 Hz) notified the subject to type the stimulus string "as fast and accurately as possible." The characters typed by the subject on test trials were recorded but they were not displayed on the terminal screen. A new trial was initiated 3 sec after the completion of the subject's last keystroke, or after the low tone when no response was required.

Results of the Skilled Group

The subject's means were submitted to two separate analyses of variance: one bearing on the latency data and the other on the average interstroke intervals. The trials with a latency longer than 3 sec and those in which one or more interstroke intervals were longer then 2 sec were eliminated prior to analysis. Note that the same cutoff points were used for all the experiments reported here. They resulted in the loss of .2% of the data collected with skilled subjects in the present experiment.

Orthographic composition. With respect to the orthographic effects, the results are exactly opposite to those obtained by Sternberg, Knoll, and Wright (1978) with typists of comparable ability. As is shown in Figure 4.1, the performance obtained with the words and the pseudowords was almost identical, at least up to length 5. By contrast, the curves obtained with nonwords diverge from the others much earlier.

At the statistical level, the overall orthographic effect on the interstroke intervals was found to be significant, $F(2,6) = 12.6$, $p < .01$.

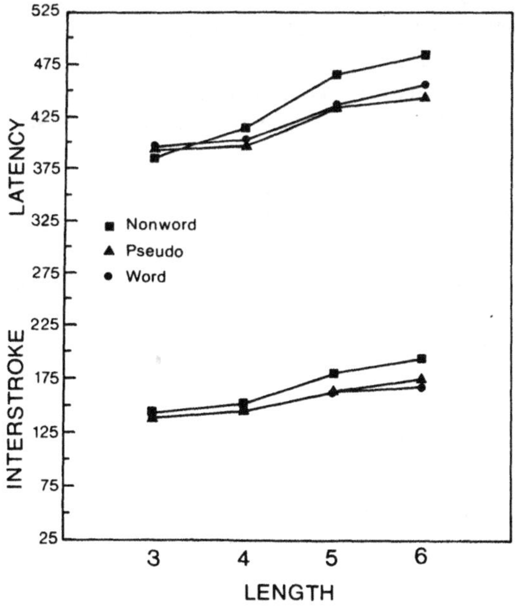

Fig. 4.1. Latencies and average interstroke intervals for the words, pseudowords, and nonwords composed of three to six letters. Results of skilled typists in Experiment 1.

Further interstroke interval comparisons showed a nonsignificant difference between the words and the pseudowords ($F < 1$), but a significant difference between the nonwords and the other two stimulus categories, $F(1,6) = 24.6, p < .01$. The overall length effect was significant, $F(3,9) = 37.8, p < .001$; and so was the length × orthographic composition interaction, $F(6,18) = 2.91, p < .05$.

Despite the general similarity between the latency results and the interstroke intervals, none of the above-mentioned effects or interactions reached the .05 level of statistical significance in the analysis performed on the latency data. It must be remembered that each trial in the experiment contributes many interstroke intervals, but only one latency observation. This probably accounts for the difference in power between the two analyses.

Finally, it is worth mentioning that the error rates paralleled the temporal data, with a nonsignificant 1% difference between the words and the pseudowords ($F < 1$) and a significant 4% difference between these two categories and the nonwords, $F(1,6) = 6.92, p < .05$. While the difference between the words and the pseudowords remained smaller than 2% at all string lengths, there was a tendency for the difference between the nonwords and the other two categories to increase with the length of the strings. As a result, the overall length × orthographic composition interaction was significant, $F(6,18) = 3.51, p < .05$.

Motor composition. On average, the typing of 2H sequences took 39 msec longer to initiate than did the 1H sequences, $F(1,3) = 4.41, p < .25$. However, the average interstroke intervals were 59 msec shorter for the 2H sequences, $F(1,3) = 280, p < .001$. These differences were fairly constant across the various orthographic categories. The F ratio for the interaction was smaller than 1 in the interstroke data, and it was 1.22 ($p < .50$) in the latency data.

As shown in Figure 4.2, the average interstroke intervals obtained with 1H and 2H sequences increased by about the same amount with increasing string length. A trend analysis performed on the interstroke intervals showed the linear component to be significant for both the 1H and the 2H sequences, with slopes of 5.9 and 7.2 msec/keystroke, respectively. However, both curves have significant, or marginally significant, residual components. Of the variance associated with the length × motor composition interaction, 75% was attributable to these higher order components. The interaction itself was not quite significant, $F(3,9) = 3.17, p < .10$. In the latency data, the slopes of the 1H and 2H sequences were estimated at 11.4 and 14.1 msec/keystroke, respectively. The F ratio for the length × motor composition interaction was of 2.16, $p < .25$.

The error rates, presented at the bottom of Figure 4.2, exhibit a monotonic increase with string length, $F(3,9) = 11.9, p < .01$, and a

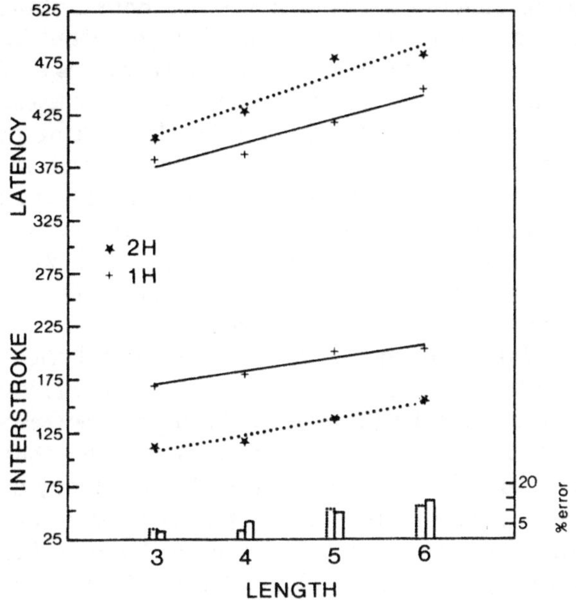

Fig. 4.2. Latencies and average interstroke intervals for the 1H and 2H sequences of three to six keystrokes, along with the best fitting linear trend. The bar histograms represent the error rates for the same conditions. Results of skilled typists in Experiment 1.

nonsignificant overall advantage in favor of the 2H sequences, $F(1,3) = 4.52$, $p < .25$. As in the interstroke data, there was a marginally significant interaction between the length and the motor composition of the sequences, $F(3,9) = 3.36$, $p < .10$, but no higher order interaction with the orthographic composition of the strings, $F < 1$. In short, there was no evidence of speed-accuracy trade-off in the performance of the skilled subjects.

Discussion

With respect to the motor composition effects, the results just reported are in agreement with those obtained by Sternberg, Monsell, Knoll, and Wright. Sternberg et al. also found the advantage in interstroke interval favoring the 2H sequence to be independent of the length of the sequences. However, the length effects they obtained with strings of two to five letters were strictly linear.

Following the logic of stage additivity (Sternberg, 1969), Sternberg et al. proposed a two-stage model to account for these results. According to their model, a motor representation of the stimulus string is established prior to the start of the typing response. This representation consists of a set of motor routines, each routine specifying the motor commands needed to execute a keystroke, or perhaps a short sequence of keystrokes. The motor routines are stored in an output buffer until the "go" signal is given. The typing of the stimulus string is achieved through the repeated operation of the following two processes. One process consists in searching the output buffer for the routine needed for the upcoming keystroke(s). The time required by the search stage is assumed to depend on the number of routines in the buffer, which is in turn a function of the length of the stimulus string. The nature of the motor transition between two successive keystrokes (1H vs. 2H) is assumed to affect the next stage of processing, which consists in "unpacking" the routine and executing the motor commands.

This model does not easily account for the lexical-orthographic effects obtained later by Sternberg, Knoll, and Wright. Since the motor routines, which are the basic units in the model, correspond to single keystrokes or short sequences of keystrokes, it seems that performance should be more sensitive to variations in the frequency composition of the letter strings than to differences in their lexical nature. Sternberg et al. found the opposite. Their results showed a lexical category effect but no digraph frequency effect. However, the two factors could easily have been confounded in Sternberg et al.'s experiment. They report no effort to maintain the digraph frequency of the words and nonsense strings equivalent. The results obtained here indicate that words and nonsense strings yield identical performance when such a control is enforced.

If the words and the pseudowords used in this experiment had a similar average digraph frequency, the words had an increasingly large frequency advantage at the trigraph and higher order *n*-graph levels. That these differences were not reflected in performance suggests that these higher levels of structure contribute very little to skilled typing, and that digraphs may be the largest units from which the motor component is derived.

With such constraint on unit size, Sternberg et al.'s model can easily accommodate the current results. The presence of an interaction between the length and the orthographic composition of the strings suggests that these two variables influence the same level of processing, namely, the search stage. In the model, the search is assumed to operate on a buffer containing the motor routines. If each routine specifies two keystrokes, the same number of routines will be needed to represent the words and the pseudowords used in the experiment, since these two stimulus categories had the same digraph composition. By contrast, the nonwords used in the experiment were made of much lower frequency digraphs, some of which never actually occur in English. For illegal digraphs, there cannot be any predefined motor routine in long-term memory, and the probability that such engrams exist for infrequent digraphs is also low. Consequently, the nonwords would have to be decomposed into smaller units, with some routines corresponding to single keystrokes. The greater number of routines in the buffer would be responsible for the longer search times obtained with nonwords.

This revised model is somewhat unsatisfactory in that it still leaves too many aspects of the typing process ill defined. However, it does provide a very economical account of skilled performance with which to contrast the properties of novice typing.

Results of the Novice Group

Forty-one trials (.7% of the data) were eliminated prior to analysis because their latency was longer than 3 sec or because some of the interstroke intervals exceeded 2 sec.

Orthographic composition. The lexical-orthographic composition of the strings had a significant effect on both the latency period, $F(2,14) = 6.41, p < .05$, and the average interstroke intervals, $F(2,14) = 7.64, p < .01$. The interaction between the length and the orthographic composition of the strings was also significant in both the latency data, $F(6,42) = 5.33, p < .001$, and the interstroke data, $F(6,42) = 4.21, p < .01$. As is shown in Figure 4.3, the nonwords produced much greater length effects than the words. Remember that a similar but weaker trend was

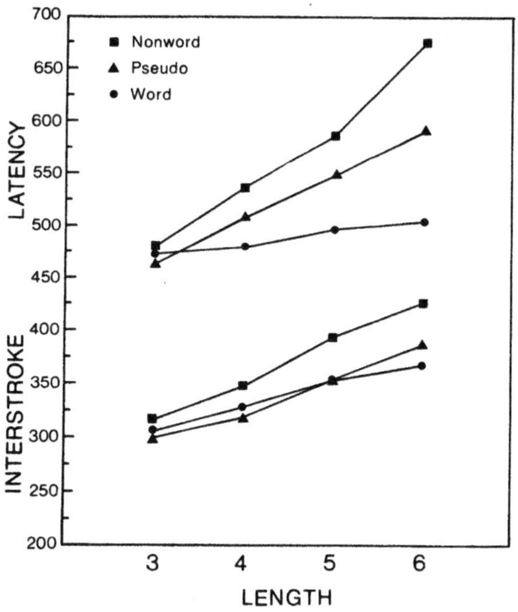

Fig. 4.3. Latencies and average interstroke intervals for the words, pseudowords, and nonwords composed of three to six letters. Results of novice typists in Experiment 1.

present in the results of the skilled typists. What is particular to novice performance is that the pseudowords also pronounced greater length effects than the words. This is especially evident in the latency data, $F(3,42) = 3.61, p < .05$, but the simple interaction was also significant in the interstroke data, $F(3,42) = 2.98, p < .05$. The overall difference between the words and the pseudowords was not significant in either the interstroke ($F < 1$) or the latency data ($F(1,14) = 3.19, p < .10$).

By contrast with the temporal data, the error rates showed a significant difference between the words (6.0% error) and pseudowords (9.7% error), $F(1,14) = 6.82, p < .05$. This result suggests that the fast typing rate obtained with the pseudowords was achieved at the cost of some accuracy. The nonwords produced significantly more errors (13.4%) than the other two stimulus categories, $F(1,14) = 18.9, p < .001$. As a result the overall lexical-orthographic effect was significant. The error rates showed the same patterns of interactions described previously for the temporal data.

Motor composition. Figure 4-4 shows the length effects on the sequences of different motor composition. In the latency data, the 1H sequences had a significant advantage ($F(1,7) = 8.15, p < .05$) over the 2H sequences. The advantage appeared at all string lengths. The slopes estimated

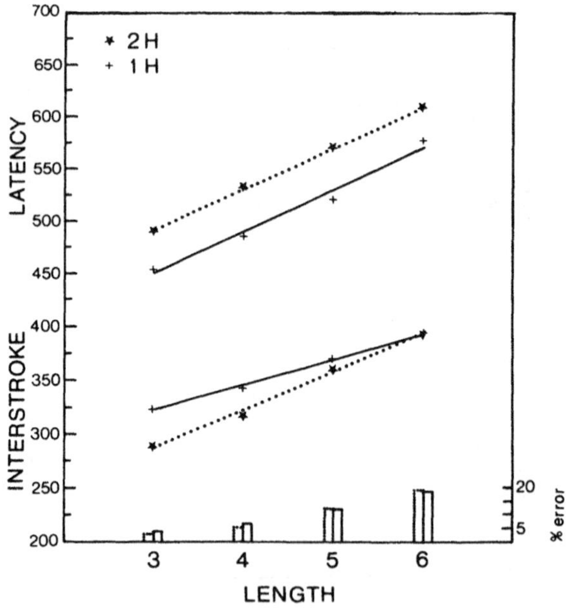

Fig. 4.4 Latencies and average interstroke intervals for the 1H and 2H sequences of three to six keystrokes, along with the best fitting linear trend. The bar histograms represent the error rates for the same conditions. Results of novice typists in Experiment 1.

for the 1H and 2H sequences were of 20.2 and 19.7 msec/keystroke, respectively. The F ratio for the length $\times$ motor composition interaction was less than 1. By contrast, there was a clear interaction in the interstroke results, $F(3,21) = 3.46, p < .05$. Of the variance associated with this interaction, 96% was attributable to the difference in slope between the 1H sequences (11.6 msec/keystroke) and the 2H sequences (17.9 msec/keystroke).

Neither the latency nor the interstroke results showed any interaction between the orthographic and motor composition (both $F < 1$). The three-way interaction, also involving the length of the strings, yielded an F ratio of .43 in the latency data. In the interstroke data, there was a tendency for the 1H and 2H functions to converge at a faster rate when nonwords were used as stimuli. The difference in slope between 1H and the 2H nonwords was 9 msec, the difference for the words being 4 msec. Despite this tendency, the overall three-way interaction was not significant: $F(6,42) = 1.46, p < .25$.

There was no difference in error rate between the 1H and the 2H sequences, nor was there any interaction between the length and the motor composition of the sequences (both $F < 1$). However, the three-way interaction, also involving the orthographic composition of the strings, was significant, $F(6,42) = 4.63, p < .01$.

Discussion

Neither Sternberg et al.'s original model nor the revised version discussed previously can easily be extended to account for the results of the novice subjects. The independence of the search and execution stages was the cornerstone of the model proposed to explain skilled performance. The presence of a length $\times$ motor composition interaction in the interstroke results obtained with the novices suggests, on the contrary, that a single stage of processing may be involved. So, when they are interpreted following the logic of stage additivity, the results of the novice and skilled subjects lead us to view the skill acquisition process as one through which the various operations involved in typing become increasingly separate in time and resources.

I wish to propose the totally different if not opposite view that the processes involved in typing can overlap in time, and that the amount of temporal overlap between the organization and the execution stages increases with the skill level of the subjects. However, before developing this view, I will consider an alternative explanation for the results. This explanation consists of attributing the differences between skilled and novice performance to a difference in the scope of the motor program that is established prior to the onset of the typing response.

Sternberg et al.'s model is a complete preprogramming model in the sense that the access to the motor engrams corresponding to the letters or digraphs composing a string is assumed to have occurred prior to the onset of the typing response. If indeed skilled typists can preprogram sequences of up to six keystrokes, novice subjects may not be able to do so. The necessity to do some on-line programming while typing the sequence could be at the origin of the length × motor composition interaction found in the interstroke data of the novice subjects. One need only assume that sequences of keystrokes that require hand alternations are more complex to program than 1H sequences, an assumption that is consistent with the longer latencies usually observed with 2H sequences. Because of their inability to fully preprogram the sequences, novice typists would have to maintain the orthographic representation of the string active during the execution of the typing sequence. This would explain why variations in the lexical-orthographic coherence of the strings had a greater impact on novice than skilled performance.

There are several difficulties with the notion that it is the extent of preprogramming that distinguishes skilled from novice performance. First, one would expect the length and the motor composition of the strings to have overadditive effects on the latency period in case of complete preprogramming. This prediction follows from the fact that the number of hand changes that must be preprogrammed increased with the length of the strings combined with the assumption made earlier that interkeystroke transitions that involve a hand change require more programming time than transitions that involve fingers of one hand. There was indeed a small difference in slope between the 1H and the 2H sequences in the latency data of the skilled subjects, but the interaction was far from significant.

The preceding argument is not in itself sufficient to warrant our rejecting the scope of programming explanation. It is possible that the latency period does not reflect the entire programming time. Some amount of programming could have occurred prior to the "go" signal, thereby preventing a length × motor composition interaction from showing up in the latency results of the skilled subjects. Furthermore, as Sanders (1980) has argued, it is quite difficult to interpret the absence of an interaction when the factors involved do not produce strong main effects. Remember that the motor composition of the strings did not produce a significant effect on the latencies of the skilled typists. The following argument is less vulnerable.

Serial position effects like those shown in Figures 4.5 and 4.6 are a typical finding in discontinuous typing experiments. Ostry (1980) has argued that the rise in the interstroke intervals toward the middle of a typing sequence reflects the time needed to program the latter part of the sequence. By contrast, the keystrokes occurring in last position presumably benefit from the fact that there are no further keystrokes to program, whereas those occurring in second position benefit from having been programmed during the latency period. So, if the converg-

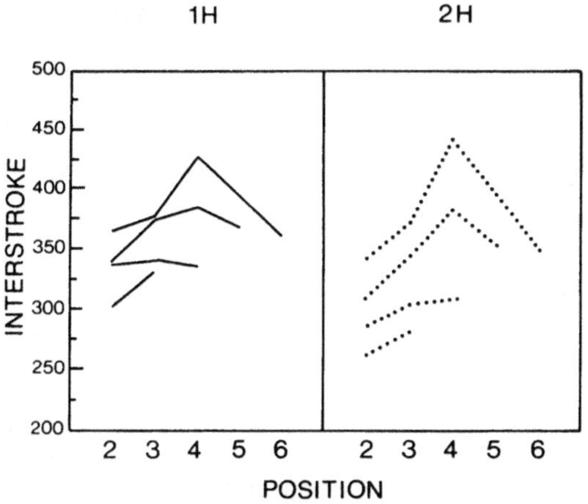

Fig. 4.5. Interstroke intervals for each position in 1H and 2H sequences of three to six keystrokes. Results of novice typists in Experiment 1.

ence of the 1H and the 2H sequences, which characterized the average interstroke intervals obtained with novice subjects, was due to the increasing need for on-line programming with longer strings, then this convergence should be much more pronounced at the peak of the serial position curves than in the second and last positions.

The serial position effects presented in Figure 4.5 are those obtained with novice subjects. A comparison of the left and right panels at position 2 shows a clear tendency for the differences between the 1H and the 2H sequences to decrease as the length of the strings increases. Furthermore, this tendency is about as strong as the one found at the peak of the serial position curves and in last position. Since the number of interstroke intervals varies with the length of the strings, it is difficult to directly test for the presence or absence of an interaction among the length, the motor composition of the sequences, and the keystroke position. However, none of the two-way interactions involving the motor composition of the sequences and the keystroke position was statistically significant (all $p > .10$) in any of the analyses performed on the strings of each length. The main position effect was significant ($p < .05$) for all strings except those of length 4 ($F < 1$).

Finally, if the skilled subjects were planning further ahead than the novice subjects, then the peaks of the serial position curves should have occurred in later positions, with no peaks in the case of complete preprogramming. The serial position curves obtained with the skilled typists are presented in Figure 4.6. Except for the four-letter strings ($F < 1$), all the curves show significant position effects. Furthermore, the 1H curves peak in the same position as the curves obtained with novice subjects. There is a tendency for the 2H curves to peak later than the 1H curves. However, this tendency was not strong enough to produce a sig-

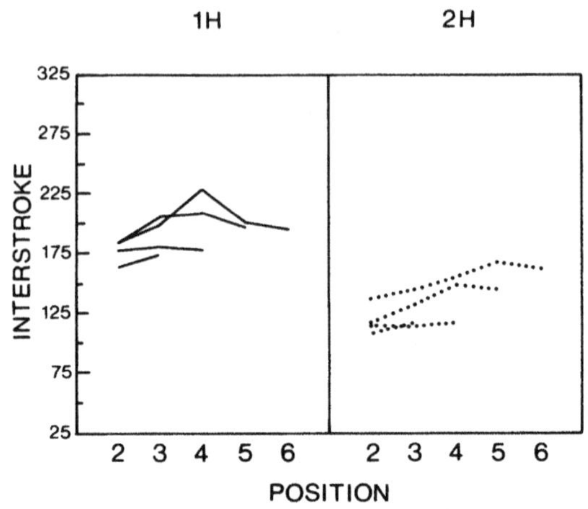

Fig. 4.6. Interstroke intervals for each position in 1H and 2H sequences of three to six keystrokes. Results of skilled typists in Experiment 1.

nificant motor composition × position interaction, even in the case of six-letter strings: $F(4,12) = 2.60, p < .10$.

In sum, the difference between the two skill groups is not in the presence versus absence of serial position effects, nor even in the shape of the serial position curves. The difference is in the distance separating the curves obtained with various sequence lengths, and in their steepness. So, I wish to propose that what distinguishes skilled from novice typing is the rate at which the various letters in a string are transformed into keystrokes instead of the number of letters that can be preprogrammed.

According to this view, the organization of the typing response starts in a search of the orthographic representation of the strings. The search is not viewed as a linear scan operating on the content of some buffer, but rather as an activation process of the type that is usually assumed to operate on a verbal representation. The minimal purpose of the search is to find which letter to type next. The search may also serve to determine the location of the keys associated with the letters and to choose the appropriate effectors: hand and finger. Finally, it is also possible that some motor engrams corresponding to sequences of letters are also found. This possibility will be discussed in more detail later.

The length effects, the orthographic effects, and the serial position effects are all thought to originate at this very high level of processing. Indeed it is presumably easier to remember the identity and especially the order of the letters when the strings form words than when they do not. Additional letters also increase the burden on memory, especially when the strings have little orthographic coherence. Finally, the position of the letters in the strings is also thought to affect their activation level. The model developed by Ratcliff (1978) shows how an activation-based memory access mechanism can produce serial position effects along with linear length effects.

After the spatiotemporal trajectory needed to reach the keys has been specified, the movements are executed. So the execution of a given keystroke must await the completion of the higher levels of processing. With increasing skill, however, it may become possible to search for the location of a key and to specify the spatiotemporal trajectory needed while executing a previous keystroke. In such a case, the interstroke intervals will reflect the temporal properties of the latter, execution stage, but they will not be influenced so much by the factors affecting the higher levels of processing. Within this framework, the smaller length, orthographic, and serial position effects obtained with skilled typists suggest that the preparation for future keystrokes was almost completed during the execution of previous ones.

Not only can there be overlap between the organization and the execution of the typing response, but there can also be temporal overlap within the execution level itself. In conditions where the higher level processes are faster than the actual execution times, the movements involved in typing a letter can be initiated prior to the completion of the previous keystroke. This overlap in movement does not result in a pure gain of time, however. The presence of overlap in movement will generate mechanical constraints on the fingers involved, except in the very rare occasions when the fingers are moving in the same direction. Such constraints will tend to be stronger in 1H than in 2H sequences. Indeed, the amount of work done by the fingers in typing 2H sequences is reduced by half compared to the amount of work done by the same fingers in typing 1H sequences. It is this difference in mechanical constraints that presumably accounts for the difference in the average interstroke intervals obtained with 1H and 2H sequences.

The amount of time gained in typing 2H sequences also depends on the speed of the higher level processes. With longer preparatory times, there will be less overlap in movements and consequently less difference in mechanical constraints between 1H and 2H sequences. Such an account is consistent with the length × motor composition interaction that was present in the interstroke data obtained with novice subjects. This account also leads us to expect interactions involving the orthographic composition of the strings. Remember that the three-way interaction among the length, the orthographic composition and the motor composition of the sequences failed to be significant, even with novice typists as subjects. However, such an interaction was present in the error data of the novice subjects. The practice obtained by repeating the trials on which errors had occurred may have prevented the interaction from being fully manifest in the interstroke results. The next experiment shows that an interaction among the interstroke intervals can be produced by degrading further the orthographic coherence of the nonsense strings and by putting more emphasis on the accuracy of the typing response.

The latency results did not exhibit the same length × motor composition interaction that characterizes the interstroke intervals obtained with novice subjects. So, how can the view of typing that was proposed to account for the interstroke results also account for the latency data? There is one seemingly trivial difference between the latency period and the following interstroke intervals that is of critical importance in understanding the difference in results—the latency period is not bounded by two keystrokes. Since the latency period extends from the "go" signal to the first keystroke, it can include whatever time is needed to reach and strike the first key. It can also include whatever organization time is needed at the start of the typing response. As was argued before, the interstroke intervals may not reflect much of the organization time needed for a keystroke if the planning is done during the execution of previous keystrokes. In cases where there is overlap in the movements leading to two successive keystrokes, the interstroke interval will even be shorter than the actual time needed for the execution of the second keystroke. In short, the interstroke intervals reflect a variable amount of organization and execution time, depending on the nature of the stimulus and on the skill level of the subjects. By contrast, the organization and execution of the first keystroke cannot overlap with the execution of previous keystrokes because there is no such previous keystroke. This may explain why the factors that are thought to affect the organization and execution times produced additive effects on the latencies. This may also explain why the latency results of the skilled and novice subjects were more similar than their interstroke results.

There is one final aspect of the results that needs to be considered, namely, the tendency for the 2H sequences to produce longer latencies than 1H sequences. This is a puzzling result considering that the difference in interstroke interval was in the opposite direction. The reason for this reversal is perhaps related to the freedom of movement involved in typing 1H and 2H sequences. I have argued earlier that the movements were less constrained in the case of 2H sequences, thereby allowing for shorter execution times than in the case of 1H sequences. The greater freedom of movement that characterizes 2H sequences could possibly have the opposite effect on the time needed to plan the movements. Keystroke transitions that involve a hand change may require more organization time because there is a greater number of possible spatiotemporal trajectories to consider than in the case of the more constrained 1H transitions. Alternatively, the organization of 2H transitions may be more complex because of the necessity to coordinate a greater number of dynamic links. The important point is that the interstroke intervals would not reflect such a difference in organization time if the planning of successive keystrokes (or interkeystroke transitions) occurred during the execution of previous ones. Since there is no keystroke before the first one, the latency period could reflect the difference in organization time between 1H and 2H sequences, provided that the planning done during the latency period extends up to the second keystroke.

The preceding argument concerning the reversal of the latency and the interstroke results remains quite speculative, but it follows naturally from a view of typing that allows the organization and execution of successive keystrokes to overlap. By contrast, a model like the one proposed by Sternberg et al., in which there is a strict seriality of processing all through the typing sequence, is hardly compatible with the finding that 2H sequences produce longer latencies but shorter interstroke intervals than 1H sequences.

Experiment 2

In explaining the results of the previous experiment, I have argued that the movements leading to successive keystrokes can overlap in time. However, the results themselves did not provide any evidence of the presence of overlap in movement. In this experiment, I analyze the conditions that give rise to movement overlap in skilled and novice typing.

Method

The method adopted is based on an extreme form of response-response incompatibility, namely, the fact that the same effector cannot move in two different directions at the same time. For instance, in typing the digraph *tr* with the standard method, the left index finger, which is responsible for typing both keys, cannot move toward the *r* before the *t* is typed. By contrast, in typing the digraph *dr*, two different fingers are used, so it is physically possible for the index finger to move toward the *r* key while the middle finger is still reaching for the *d* key. By comparing the interstroke intervals obtained in situations where the overlap is possible with those in situations where overlap is impossible, one can determine if overlap in movement contributes to the typing speed.

Subjects. The subjects participating in this experiment were different from those used in the previous experiment. All 10 subjects were right handed. The average typing speed of the five subjects in the skilled group was 60 wpm, compared with 23 wpm for the novice group.

Stimuli. The stimuli were letter strings composed of three to five letters. One half of the stimulus strings were typed by the fingers of one hand, the other half involved both hands.

The 1H strings were constructed in such a way that in each string, two of the letters were typed by one finger, none of the other fingers being used for more than one keystroke. In half of these strings, the repeated finger typed two successive letters. In this condition, called the 1F condition, it is the second keystroke executed by the repeated finger that is of critical interest because the interstroke interval precludes overlap in finger movement. The position where the finger repetition occurred varied across strings: In three-letter strings, the first two letters were typed by the same finger, so the critical keystroke was always in position 2. With strings of length 4, the critical keystroke was in either position 2 or position 3; with strings of length 5, it occurred in positions 2, 3, or 4. There was an equal number of strings for each of these positions, so that in the ensemble there was an increasing number of strings of lengths 3, 4, and 5.

The other half of the 1H strings were such that the two keystrokes produced by the same finger were separated by one intervening keystroke. This condition will be labeled the 2F condition because the finger responsible for the critical intervening keystroke was different from the finger used in typing the preceding key. Therefore the interstroke interval could reflect some overlap in movement. Different strings were constructed so that over all strings the critical keystroke occurred equally often in every possible position between the first and the last keystroke.

By contrast with the 2H strings used in the previous experiment, the ones used here involved only one hand alternation (two hand changes); hence all the keys but one were typed by the same hand. Half of the 2H strings were equivalent to the 2F strings just described except that the critical intervening keystroke was produced by a finger of the alternate hand. This finger was not homologous to any of the other fingers involved in typing the string. Since the critical keystroke was the only one executed by the alternate hand, this condition allowed for overlap in both hand and finger movement.

The same was true of the other set of 2H strings. However, the keystrokes immediately surrounding the critical one were executed by different fingers. The finger used in typing the critical keystroke was homologous to the one preceding or following it, depending on the string. This set of strings was introduced in the experiment mostly to balance the number of 1H and 2H strings. The results obtained with this set of stimuli will not be reviewed here, so that the 2H label will be used only to refer to the other set of two-hands strings.

Unfortunately, I could not find enough words that satisfied the constraints just described concerning the motor composition of the stimuli, so all the stimuli were nonsense strings. Half of them were composed of relatively high-frequency digraphs. These stimulus strings will be referred to for mnemonic purposes as *pseudowords*. The set of pseudowords was evenly split over both hands, half of the strings starting with a left-hand key and the other half starting with a right-hand key. No letter was allowed to appear more than once within a given string, and the letters *c*, *x*, and *z* were eliminated altogether from the composition of the stimuli (as had been done for the previous experiment). Since there are only two vowels under the left hand, however, it was impossible to eliminate the letter *a* and still obtain high-frequency strings. Instead, the letter *q* was eliminated from the construction of the pseudowords. With only one letter assigned to each little finger, the only fingers that could be used more than once within a given string were the index, the middle, and the ring. Over all strings, these fingers were used about equally often to type the critical keystroke. Examples of four-letter pseudowords used in the experiment are *swad*, *fegs*, and *doef* for the 1F, 2F, and 2H conditions, respectively. In these examples, the critical keystroke occupies the second position.

In order to obtain a set of stimuli with less orthographic coherence than the pseudowords, but with a similar motor composition, each of the pseudowords was subjected to a mirror-image transformation. This transformation, which was also used by Ostry (1980), consists of replacing each letter in a string by the letter located in the equivalent position on the other half of the keyboard. Since there is no letter in the same position as *a* on the right half of the Sholes keyboard, the letter *a* was replaced by the letter *p*. The letter *p* was replaced by the letter *q*. The strings so produced had a much lower average digraph and trigraph frequency than the pseudowords from which they were derived. They will be referred to as *nonwords*. Here are the nonwords corresponding to the pseudowords mentioned previously: *lopk*, *jihl*, and *kwij*.

Design and procedure. The pseudowords and the nonwords were presented in separate blocks throughout the experiment. The other factors involved in the composition of the stimuli varied randomly within each block. These factors were the length and the motor composition of the sequences, the position of the critical keystroke in the sequences, and the starting hand. There were 10 pseudowords and 10 nonwords for every possible combination of these factors. Of these 10 strings, 8 were used on test trials and 2 were used for catch trials, the subsets varying over the different subjects in a given skill group. Over all the subjects in a group, every string was presented four times as a test stimulus and one time as a catch stimulus. The stimuli used for practice were different from those used on experimental trials, but they were constructed according to the same general principles.

The experiment required five sessions per subject, the sessions lasting less than 1 hour each and being held on separate days. As usual, the first session was for practice. It consisted of two blocks of 50 trials each: one block for the pseudowords and the other for nonwords. There were 135 trials in each block of the following sessions, the first 15 trials in each block being considered practice. The order of trials within each block varied from subject to subject within a given skill group, and the order of the blocks varied both across subjects and across sessions. The same orders were used with both skill groups.

The procedure differed from the one used in the previous experiment on the following points. First, the subjects were asked to leave their fingers either on or slightly above the home-row keys, depending on which position felt more natural, until the signal to respond was given. The purpose of this request was to ensure some control over the position of the hands and fingers at the beginning of each trial, and to prevent the subjects from moving their fingers toward the keys to be struck prior to the signal. In order to motivate compliance with this request, the procedure followed on catch trials was modified. Rather than simply ignoring the letter string that had been presented and not responding, the subjects were asked to depress the fingers of both hands simultaneously on the home-row keys upon hearing the low tone. As in the previous experiment, test trials were signaled by a high tone. However, more emphasis was put on the accuracy of the typing response than in the previous experiment. The subjects were asked to "type the letter strings as fast as possible while keeping errors to a minimum." They were also explicitly told that their error rate should not exceed 10%.

Results of the Skilled Group

As usual, trials with extra long latencies and/or interstroke intervals were rejected prior to analysis. This resulted in a loss of less than 1% of the data collected with the skilled subjects. By contrast with the previous experiment, only one interstroke interval was extracted from the remaining sequences: the interval preceding the critical keystroke. These intervals were averaged over all the positions occupied by the critical keystroke in the sequences of various lengths, and then submitted to two separate analyses of variance. One analysis was limited to the conditions involving fingers of the same hand, namely, the 1F and the 2F conditions. The other analysis was devoted to the conditions involving different fingers within (2F) and across hands (2H). The results of all three conditions are presented in Figure 4.7. It is the contrast between the 1F and the 2F results that is of primary interest here. The 2F and 2H conditions are analogous to those involved in the previous experiment, so only the discrepancies in results or other important findings will be reviewed.

The same-hand conditions. As is shown in the left panel of Figure 4.7, the typing of pseudowords did benefit from a finger change. There was an average difference of 41 msec in the interstroke intervals between the 1F and the 2F conditions, a difference that corresponds to a nontrivial gain in typing speed of 10 wpm. The right panel of Figure 4.7 shows that the mirror-image transformation of the stimuli greatly reduced the advantage of the 2F transitions. The overall difference between the 1F and 2F conditions (motor composition effect) was significant, $F(1,4) = 8.38, p < .05$. However, the breakdown of the motor $\times$ orthographic composition interaction ($F(1,4) = 9.31$, $p < .05$) showed the difference to be significant only for the pseudowords.

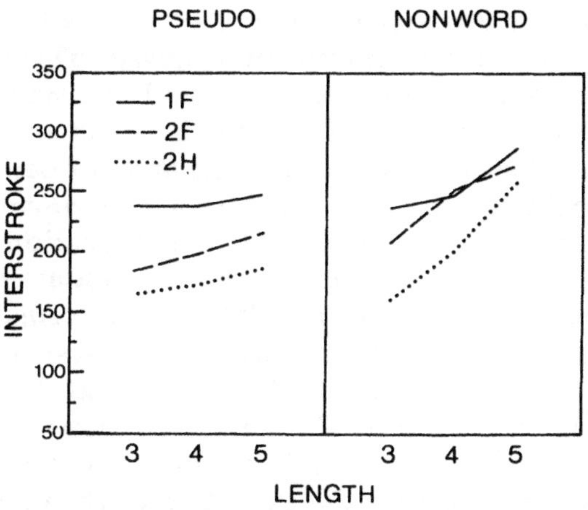

Fig. 4.7. Interstroke intervals preceding the critical keystroke for 1F, 2F, and 2H transitions embedded in sequences of three to five keystrokes. Results of skilled typists in Experiment 2.

The length effects obtained in the 1F and the 2F conditions were not sufficiently different to produce a significant length × motor composition interaction, $F(2,8) = 2.30$, $p < .25$. The three-way interaction involving the orthographic composition of the strings as well yielded an F ratio of 1.02, thereby indicating that the increase in length effects produced by the mirror-image transformation of the stimuli was of similar magnitude for the 1F and 2F conditions.

The different-fingers conditions. The results of the 2H condition show that, beyond the time gained from a finger change, there is additional time saved by a hand change. Indeed, the difference between the 2H and the 2F conditions was significant, $F(1,4) = 14.7, p < .05$. However, by contrast with the time gained from a finger change, the time gained from a hand change was not reduced by the mirror-image transformation of the stimuli. The motor × orthographic composition interaction was far from significant, $F(1,4) = 1.46, p < .50$. The three-way interaction also involving the length of the sequences was marginally significant, $F(2,8) = 3.25, p < .10$. This interaction reflects a tendency for the difference between the 2H and the 2F sequences to be greater among the nonwords, except at length 5. Such a tendency was absent from the results of the skilled subjects in Experiment 1, and it constitutes the only divergence between the two sets of results.

Discussion

The results obtained with same-hand transitions provide a clear indication that overlap in finger movement contributes to skilled performance, and that the amount of overlap in movement is related to the orthographic composition of the typing material. The question raised by these results is, How is overlap in movement achieved? This question is closely related to the issue of the units that underlie typing performance.

The presence of overlap in movement is not incompatible with the notion that single keystrokes are the basic units of performance. I have argued earlier that a search of the orthographic representation of a string was necessary, even if it serves only to find the location of the key associated with each letter and to choose the appropriate effector. As was shown by Rumelhart and Norman (1982), this information is sufficient to initiate the movements leading to any single keystroke. In the framework discussed here, the initiation of a given keystroke would therefore coincide with the completion of the search process. Overlap in movement would occur when the search required for the initiation of one keystroke takes less time than the execution of the previous keystroke.

If the view just summarized allows overlap in movement, it does not allow performance to exhibit overlap in movement along with strong length effects. Indeed, the presence of overlap in movement is an indication that it is the physical execution of the keystrokes that limits performance, as measured in terms of interstroke intervals. So factors that are assumed to influence higher level processes, like the length of the strings, should have minimal impact on performance when there is overlap in movement.

The results do not unambiguously support this view. The mirror-image transformation of the same-hand strings did produce an increase in length effect, and this increase was accompanied by a reduction of the amount of time saved by a finger change. However, the 2F condition showed a significant length effect, even among the pseudowords where there was a large advantage favoring the 2F transitions over the 1F transitions. Of course, it is possible that the length effect obtained with pseudowords originated in a few trials where there was no overlap in movement. The results obtained in the 2H condition provide stronger evidence for the separability of the length effects from the effects due to effector availability. Indeed, the mirror-image transformation of the 2H strings produced the usual increase in length effect but no reduction in the amount of time saved from a hand change.

That there was no general relationship between the size of the length effects and the amount of time gained from effector availability suggests that there may be some predefined response procedures that directly specify the coordination of the movements involved in a sequence of keystrokes. In this case, the presence of overlap in movement would not depend so much on the completion of some high-level search process, but rather on the content of the motor engrams corresponding to various digraphs or trigraphs. The search for these response procedures could proceed synchronously or asynchronously with the execution of previous ones, thereby allowing for sizable length effects in conjunction with overlap in movement.

One question raised by this view concerns the nature of the motor engrams. It has been suggested (Gentner, Note 1; Terzuolo & Viviani, 1980) that the motor program specifies the intercompletion time of successive keystrokes rather than their initiation times or some other dimension of the movements involved. This suggestion is hardly consistent with the results reported here. The nonwords used in this experiment were made of very low-frequency digraphs and higher order *n*-graphs. Presumably the response procedures for such sequences do not provide very efficient interstroke timing. This would explain why there was little difference between the 2F and the 1F transition among the nonwords. The problem is that in typing the nonwords, the 2H transitions should have produced results similar to those obtained with the 2F transitions. That there was a difference in interstroke intervals between these two conditions suggests that dimensions other than the interstroke times are specified in the response procedures.

The results of a high-speed videographic analysis of continuous typing suggest that response procedures for high- versus low-frequency sequences may be basically different. Grudin and Larochelle (Note 2) have presented an example of one type of movement reorganization that was centered on the times at which the fingers retracted from the keys after the execution of a keystroke. Grudin and Larochelle have shown that in typing the high-frequency sequence *ion*, the retraction of the middle finger from the *i* is often delayed until after the execution of the *o*, thereby facilitating the reaching motion of the ring finger toward the *o* and reducing the interstroke interval. A similar organization may not be present in typing low-frequency sequences. The resulting increase in the mechanical constraints on movement would produce an increase in interstroke intervals. Note that since the frequency effects are mediated by the mechanical constraints operating on the fingers of the same hand, one would not expect the same effects on transitions that involve a hand change. This is exactly what the results of this experiment show.

If some predefined response procedures exist for certain sequences of keystrokes, they must have been acquired with extensive practice in typing. The preceding argument suggests that the differences between skilled and novice typists should be especially manifest in the case of 2F transitions.

Results of the Novice Group

Exactly 1% of the trials were excluded from the analyses because of extra long latency and/or interstroke intervals.

The same-hand conditions. As is shown in the left panel of Figure 4.8, there was little time gained from a finger change in typing the pseudowords. The simple motor composition effect was not significant ($F < 1$),

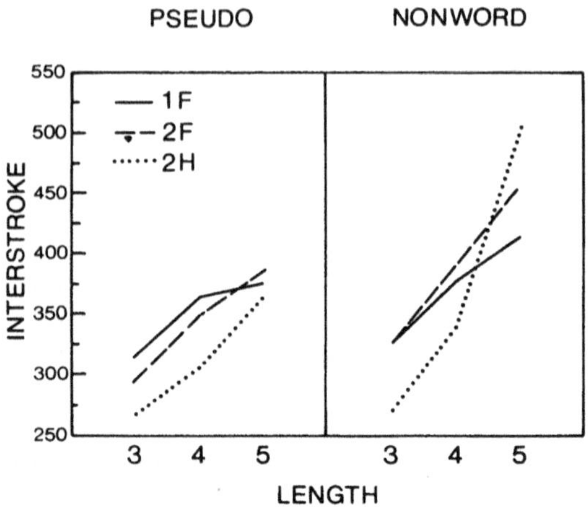

Fig. 4.8. Interstroke intervals preceding the critical keystroke for 1F, 2F, and 2H transitions embedded in sequences of three to five keystrokes. Results of novice typists in Experiment 2.

nor was the length × motor composition interaction, $F(2,8) = 1.36, p < .50$. Even the 20-msec difference between the 1F and the 2F transitions that was obtained with the pseudowords of length 3 was insignificant, $F(1,8) = 2.05, p < .25$. The mirror-image transformation of the pseudowords produced a reversal in the overall difference between the 1F and the 2F conditions, $F(1,4) = 4.79$, $p < .10$. Among the nonwords, the 1F transitions had a marginally significant advantage over the 2F transitions, $F(1,4) = 4.64$, $p < .10$, but the simple length × motor composition was still not significant, $F(2,8) = 2.30, p < .25$. It is only at length 5 that the difference between the 1F and the 2F nonwords was statistically significant, $F(1,8) = 9.01, p < .05$.

Further analyses revealed that some artifact in the composition of the stimuli may have contributed to the reversal of the 1F and 2F conditions across orthographic categories. The differences between the 1F and 2F transitions were limited to the left-hand strings. Among the left-hand pseudowords, the 2F strings (and the critical digraphs) had a large frequency advantage over the 1F strings (and critical digraphs). Among the left-hand nonwords, it is the 1F condition that had the frequency advantage over the 2F condition. Note that this type of bias was almost inevitable, given the disposition of the letters on the standard Sholes keyboard. A more complete discussion of the laterality effects that are induced by the configuration of the Sholes keyboard (when used with the standard method) can be found in Larochelle (1981).

The different-fingers conditions. If novice performance did not benefit much from a finger change, it did benefit from a hand change. In the typing of pseudowords, there was an average difference of 30 msec between the 2F and the 2H transitions, $F(1,4) = 19.1, p < .05$. This difference remained fairly constant at all string lengths, the F ratio for the simple interaction being smaller than 1. By contrast, there was a significant length × motor composition interaction among the nonwords, $F(2,8) = 13.49, p < .01$. This interaction is due to the reversal of the 2F and 2H conditions at length 5.

Discussion

Among the results of the novice subjects it is the performance observed with the five-letter nonwords that is perhaps the most intriguing. In this condition, the 2H transitions produced longer interstroke intervals than the 2F transitions. This result contrasts with the pattern of interstroke intervals obtained in all the other conditions (as well as with skilled typists), but it does correspond to the pattern of latencies usually observed. The times involved are also very close to those that characterize the latency period. For sequences in which the critical transition immediately followed the first keystroke, there was an overall difference in the novice subjects' latencies of 46 msec between the 2H and 2F conditions. I have suggested earlier that this latency difference originates in the organization of the motor response. That a difference similar to the one exhibited by the latencies was present among the interstroke intervals obtained with the five-letter nonwords suggests that the same processes are still active during the execution of the typing sequence.

It is worth mentioning that there was also a tendency, in this experiment, for the 2F condition to produce longer latencies than the 1F condition. For instance, with novice typists there was an overall difference in latency of 28 msec between the 2F and 1F conditions when the critical transition immediately followed the first keystroke. The differences in interstroke intervals were usually in the opposite direction. So there seems to be a general complementarity of the latency and the interstroke data with respect to the freedom of movement involved in typing 2H, 2F, and 1F transitions. If it is true that the latency period reflects more of the planning processes, then the results suggest that more organization time is needed when the constraints on movement are smaller.

General Discussion

The experiments reported here provide a view of the interactions between globally defined levels of processing and of some of the changes that take place with skill. The results can be synthesized in the following way: As the constraints on movement decrease from 1F to 2H transitions, the impact of the combined length and orthographic effects on the interstroke intervals increases. This type of underadditive interaction is an indication, but not a definite proof, of the presence of temporal overlap among the stages of processing involved (see Taylor, 1976; also

McClelland, 1979). Since it is difficult to see how the length and orthographic effects could originate at the motor level, I have argued that these factors influence higher levels of processing involved in the preparation of the typing response. The suggestion that the organization and execution of successive keystrokes can overlap is not new. The same notion is present in the type of model proposed earlier by Shaffer (1976).

When viewed in this perspective, the results do guide our speculations about the acquisition of the typing skill. In order to type with the touch-typing method, one must first learn the position of the keys and the fingers that are associated with each key. This phase corresponds to what Rumelhart and Norman (1978) labeled the *accretion stage*. Until this knowledge is well established, typists would rely very heavily on the visual guidance and monitoring of the movements. At this stage, the preparation and the execution of successive keystrokes would proceed in a largely serial fashion, and the interstroke intervals could be even longer than the time needed to reach and depress the keys. As the basic knowledge gets established and the need for the monitoring of movements decreases, some resources can be allocated to the anticipation of future keystrokes. There is probably a long *tuning phase* during which the amount of overlap between the preparation and the execution of successive keystrokes gradually increases, until there can finally be overlap in the movements leading to successive keystrokes. At this stage, the interstroke intervals become gradually shorter than the actual movement times. The presence of overlap in movement raises some difficulties not previously encountered concerning the distribution of the work over the various dynamic links in the arms and hands. For instance, it may be efficient to move the hand as a whole in reaching for keys located on the same row, but when the keys are on different rows, it may become more efficient for the fingers to move separately. This type of problem could give rise to some reorganization of the movements involved in typing. The consequence of such reorganization, called *restructuring* by Rumelhart and Norman, would be the existence of specific response procedures for specific sequences of keystrokes.

Two final comments are in order. First, although I have distinguished three phases in the skill acquisition process, I do not view these phases as distinct time periods. Rather, I think of them as being tied to the frequency with which letters and sequences of letters are encountered. So, it would be possible for a relatively unskilled typist to have already elaborated a response procedure for the very frequent sequence *the* while still having difficulty in reaching for the letter *q*. In sum, I would not expect a longitudinal study of typing to show plateaus in global measures of performance.

The second comment concerns the scope of the response procedures. The results of the first experiment suggest that if such predefined procedures contribute to skilled performance, they do not generally span more than two keystrokes. Remember that the skilled subjects of Experiment 1 produced identical performance with words and pseudowords, despite the differences in trigraph and higher order *n*-graph frequency between these two stimulus categories. Such a result is hardly consistent with the theories of skilled typing that are based on the assumption that there are predefined response procedures corresponding to specific words (Leonard & Newman, 1964; Terzuolo & Viviani, 1980). It is true that the evidence supporting these theories does not come from global performance measures of the sort discussed here. What Terzuolo and Viviani found is that despite variations in typing speed, the ratio of each interstroke interval to the total time needed to type a word remained fairly constant from one occasion to the next. It is not clear, however, if the phenomenon holds for many words, or if frequent words exhibit more regularity than infrequent ones (as they should). The view developed here is also consistent with some regularity in typing, the sources of regularity being the frequency composition of the strings, the nature of the motor transitions involved, and the amount of movement overlap (which also restricts effector availability).

Acknowledgments

The research reported here was conducted at the University of California at San Diego, under Contract N00014-79-C-0323, NR 157-437 with the Personnel and Training Research Programs of the Office of Naval Research. The preparation of this report was done at the Institute for Perception Research while the author was the recipient of a research fellowship from the University of Technology, Eindhoven, The Netherlands.

Reference Notes

1. Gentner, D. R. *Skilled finger movements in typing* (Tech. Rep. 104). La Jolla, Calif.: University of California at San Diego, Center for Human Information Processing, July 1981.
2. Grudin, J., & Larochelle, S. *Digraph frequency effects in skilled typing* (Tech. Rep. 110). La Jolla, Calif.: University of California at San Diego, Center for Human Information Processing, February 1982.

References

Larochelle, S. *Temporal aspects of typing*. Unpublished doctoral dissertation, University of California at San Diego, 1981.

Leonard, J. A., & Newman, R. C. Formation of higher habits. *Nature*, 1964, *203*, 550-551.

McClelland, J. L. On the time relations of mental processes: An examination of systems of processes in cascade. *Psychological Review*, 1979, *86*, 287-330.

Ostry, D. J. Execution-time movement control. In G. E. Stelmach & J. Requin (Eds.), *Tutorials in motor behavior*. Amsterdam: North-Holland, 1980.

Ratcliff, R. A theory of memory retrieval. *Psychological Review*, 1978, *85*, 59-108.

Rumelhart, D. E., & Norman, D. A. Accretion, tuning and restructuring: Three modes of learning. In J. W. Cotton & R. Klatzky (Eds.), *Semantic factors in cognition*. Hillsdale, N.J.: Erlbaum, 1978.

Rumelhart, D. E., & Norman, D. A. Simulating a skilled typist: A study of skilled cognitive-motor performance. *Cognitive Science*, 1982, *6*, 1-36.

Sanders, A. F. Stage analysis of reaction processes. In G. E. Stelmach & J. Requin (Eds.), *Tutorials in motor behavior*. Amsterdam: North-Holland, 1980.

Shaffer, L. H. Intention and performance. *Psychological Review*, 1976, *83*, 375-393.

Shaffer, L. H., & Hardwick, J. Typing performance as a function of text. *Quarterly Journal of Experimental Psychology*, 1968, *20*, 360-369.

Shaffer, L. H., & Hardwick, J. The basis of transcription skill. *Journal of Experimental Psychology*, 1970, *84*, 424-440.

Sternberg, S. Memory-scanning: Mental processes revealed by reaction-time experiments. *American Scientist*, 1969, *57*, 421-457.

Sternberg, S., Knoll, R. L., & Wright, C. E. Experiments on temporal aspects of keyboard entry. In J. P. Duncanson (Ed.), *Getting it together: Research and applications in human factors*. Santa Monica: Human Factors Society, 1978.

Sternberg, S., Monsell, S., Knoll, R. L., & Wright, C. E. The latency and duration of rapid movement sequences: Comparisons of speech and typewriting. In G. E. Stelmach (Ed.), *Information processing in motor control and motor learning*. New York: Academic Press, 1978.

Taylor, D. A. Stage analysis of reaction time. *Psychological Bulletin*, 1976, *83*, 161-191.

Terzuolo, C. A., & Viviani, P. Determinants and characteristics of motor patterns used for typing. *Neuroscience*, 1980, *5*, 1085-1103.

Chapter 5

Keystroke Timing in Transcription Typing

Donald R. Gentner

Over the past few years, in collaboration with Jonathan Grudin, David Rumelhart, Donald Norman, and Serge Larochelle, I have been studying transcription typing in the laboratory. Typically, typists would be asked to transcribe normal English prose from typewritten copy. This corpus of naturalistic data, now totaling over half a million keystrokes, has been a rich vein of information on the development and performance of a highly practiced skilled action.

Method

Typists

Most of this chapter is based on data collected from six professional typists (Typists 1-6) who were normally employed as university secretaries. I refer to this group as the *expert typists*. Their typing speeds on the experimental text (assuming five keystrokes per word and with no adjustment for errors) ranged from 61 to 90 words per minute (wpm). A second group of four typists (Typists 7-10), the *super typists*, were recruited from local businesses in order to study the upper end of typing skill. The super typists' speeds ranged from 85 to 112 wpm on the experimental text. A third group of eight typists (Typists 21-28), the *student typists*, were students in a beginning typing class from a local high school. The student typists were studied once a week in the 3rd through 8th weeks of their typing class. The students did not type all the letters of the alphabet until the 4th week, so data from the 3rd week were not included in these analyses. Their typing speeds on the experimental texts ranged from 13 wpm for one student in the 4th week to 41 wpm for another student in the 8th week. The data from the student typists were collected by Jonathan Grudin and kindly furnished by him.

Texts

The text typed by the expert and super typists was adapted from a *Reader's Digest* article on diets; it will be referred to as the *diet text*. The diet text was approximately 12,000 characters long and was presented as double-spaced typewritten copy. After a 10-minute warm-up with another text, the typists were asked to transcribe the diet text at their normal rapid rate, without correcting errors. The student typists were given several different texts to transcribe. The texts for the 4th and 5th weeks consisted of a number of unrelated prose paragraphs. The remaining texts for the student typists were prose passages adapted from *Reader's Digest* articles.

Apparatus

The typists worked at a high-quality electronic keyboard (Microswitch model 51SD12-4 with "tactile feel"). The keyboard layout was identical to that of the normal IBM Selectric typewriter (see Figure 2.1). Keypresses and the corresponding times (with a resolution of 1 msec) were recorded by a microcomputer. The typed characters were displayed on a cathode-ray tube (CRT) in front of the typist. While the typists were transcribing the diet text, their finger movements were recorded on videotape by means of a Sony RSC 1050 Rotary Shutter camera. A mirror mounted at the top of the keyboard at a 45-degree angle allowed simultaneous recording of two views of the typist's fingers (normal and parallel to the plane of the keyboard). The video fields, recorded every 16.7 msec, were serially numbered with an electronic video counter, and selected portions of the videotape were later analyzed, field by field, with a Sony SVM 1010 Video Motion Analyzer. Finger and hand coordinates were digitized from a video monitor by superimposing a joystick-controlled cursor on the video image. (Resolution with the cursor was .5 mm, with a reproducibility of about 1 mm.) These coordinates were used to calculate the successive positions of the fingers and hands in three-dimensional space. Finger position was measured at the fingertip. Some analyses were based on the relative finger and hand movements. The hand position was measured at the skin above the point where the right index finger joins the palm (the metacarpophalangeal joint). The position of the fingertip was then determined relative to that point on the hand.

Development of Typing Skill

A typical office typist, typing at 60-80 wpm, is averaging five to seven keystrokes per second. How does a typist develop these rapid, accurate movements?

The Range of Typists

Figure 5.1 illustrates the progression of interstroke interval distributions for a student typist at 4 and 8 weeks, for an expert typist, and for a super typist. The most obvious change is a major increase in typing speed from 13 to 112 wpm and a corresponding decrease in the median interstroke interval from 852 to 96 msec. In fact, when the distributions in Figure 5.1 are normalized by dividing the interstroke intervals by each typist's median interstroke interval, the four distributions are remarkably similar. But this similarity in the overall distributions masks major developmental differences. The interstroke intervals can be usefully grouped according to the class of digraph associated with them. Sequences of two keys typed by a single finger are called one-finger (1F) digraphs (the typewriter keyboard is shown in Figure 2.1); the 1F digraphs can be further subdivided into one-finger doubles, such as *dd*, and one-finger nondoubles, such as *de*. Sequences typed by two fingers on the same hand, such as *se*, are called two-finger (2F) digraphs. Sequences typed by different hands, such as *pe*, are called two-hand (2H) digraphs. When the distributions were separated into the four classes, a significant qualitative difference became apparent. The relative times to type the four classes were different for beginning and skilled typists. The slowest students typed 1F doubles much more rapidly than 1F nondoubles, 2F digraphs, or 2H digraphs. The fastest typists showed

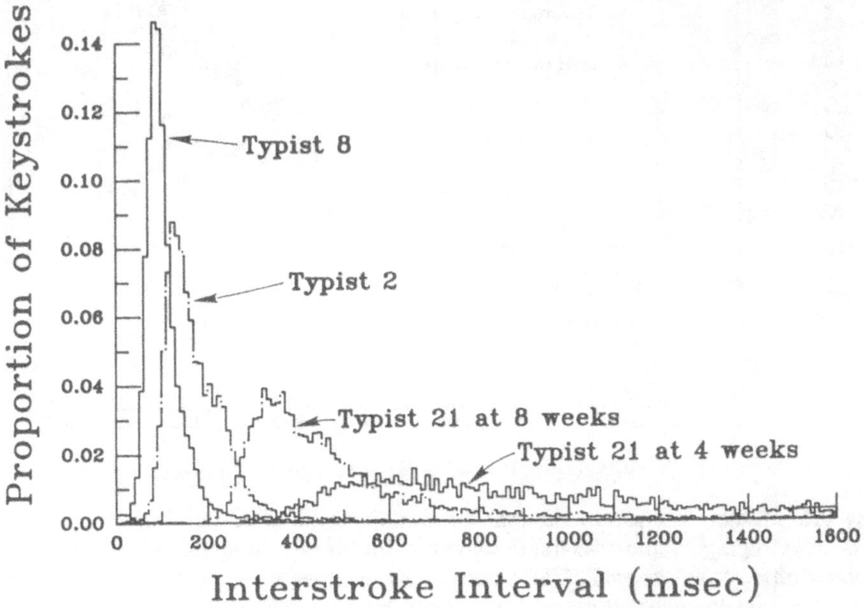

Fig. 5.1. Distribution of all interstroke intervals for Typist 21 after 4 weeks (13 wpm) and 8 weeks (25 wpm) of typing class, Typist 2 (66 wpm), and Typist 8 (112 wpm).

quite a different pattern: 1F digraphs, both double and nondouble, were typed more slowly than 2F and 2H digraphs. Figure 5.2 displays the median interstroke interval of the four digraph classes for all typists studied. Figure 5.2 also shows a subtler progression for the 2F and 2H digraphs. In general, 2H digraphs were slower than 2F, but they tend to be similar for the slowest (below 25 wpm) and fastest (above 80 wpm) typists. For the middle range of typists, the median interstroke interval for 2F digraphs is about 30% slower than for 2H digraphs.

Learning to Type

The patterns seen when contrasting student, expert, and super typists also hold when the progress of individual students is followed over several weeks. Newell and Rosenbloom (1981) found that for a wide variety of tasks, a plot of the time to perform the task versus the number of trials produced a straight line in log-log coordinates. The slope of this line (with the sign changed) is the learning rate. Therefore, I calcu-

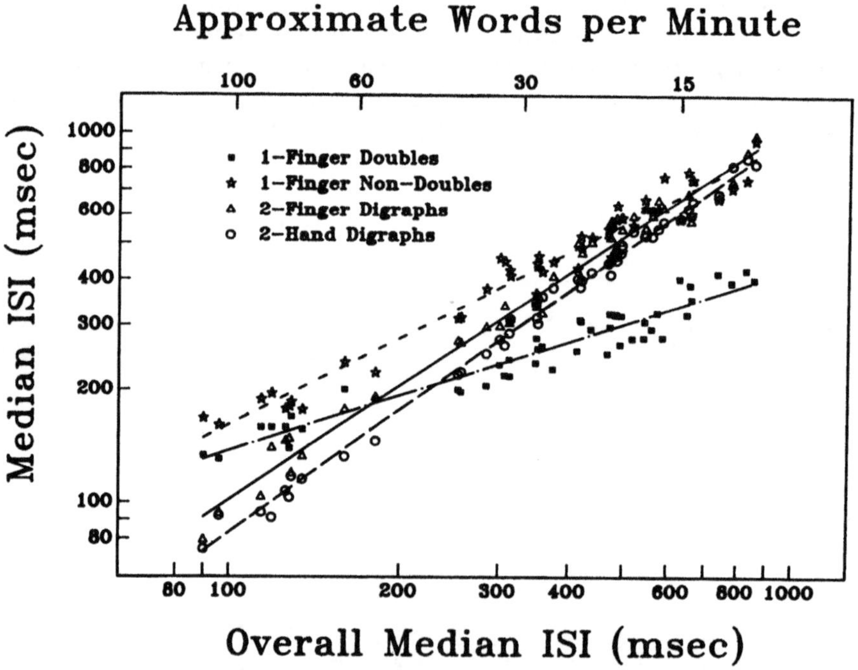

Fig. 5.2. Median interstroke interval for one-finger doubles, one-finger nondoubles, two-finger digraphs, and two-hand digraphs plotted as a function of typists' overall median interstroke interval. The fastest typist (112 wpm) is on the left, the slowest (13 wpm) on the right. Data at the left are from 10 skilled typists; data at center and right are from 37 sessions with eight student typists in the 4th-8th weeks of a beginning typing class. Note that one-finger doubles are among the slowest for skilled typists but fastest for students.

lated learning rates by plotting the median interstroke interval against the number of weeks in the typing course. Although this is not quite legitimate, because the number of repetitions of a given digraph class varies from week to week, the procedure gives at least a reasonable estimate of the learning rate for these data. Typist 21 was the slowest typist initially and showed the greatest learning rate. Figure 5.3 shows the improvement of Typist 21 on the different digraph classes over the period of the study. Typist 21's learning rates for 2F and 2H digraphs were more than twice that for 1F digraphs. Six of the eight students had a higher learning rate for 2F and 2H digraphs than for 1F digraphs. Table 5.1 gives the learning rates of all students for the three digraph classes. On average, compared with the 1F digraphs, the learning rate was 83% higher for 2F digraphs and 54% higher for 2H digraphs.

Table 5.2 shows related data, the median interstroke intervals on Week 4 and Week 8. On Week 4, 1F digraphs were fastest, 2H digraphs were intermediate, and 2F digraphs were slowest. (The only exception to this pattern was Typist 25, who had some previous typing experience and typed at 31 wpm on Week 4. None of the other students got above 27 wpm by Week 8, so it is not surprising that Typist 25 exhibited the pattern of a more experienced typist.) Because of the higher learning rate for 2F and 2H digraphs by Week 8, the median interstroke intervals for the different digraph classes were much closer than on Week 4.

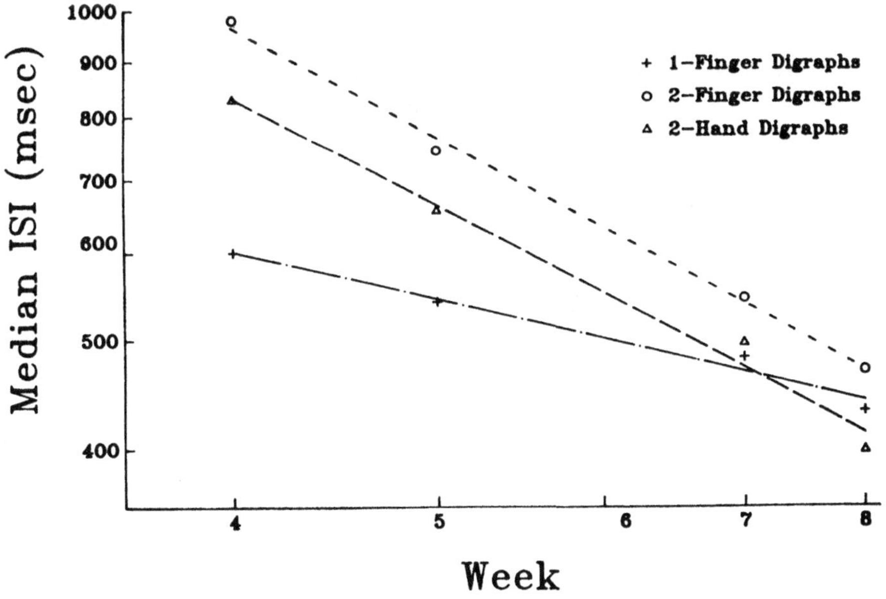

Fig. 5.3. Learning curves for Typist 21 in the 4th-8th weeks of a beginning typing class. The learning rate for two-finger and two-hand digraphs was about twice the learning rate for one-finger digraphs.

Table 5.1. Learning Rate

	Digraph Class		
Typist	1F	2F	2H
21	.45	1.04	1.01
22	.28	.80	.35
23	.36	.64	.62
24	.56	.52	.68
25	.38	.32	.28
26	-.02	.33	.21
27	.35	.57	.58
28	.45	.92	.60
Mean	.35	.64	.54

Note. The learning rate is the slope when the median interstroke interval (in msec) is plotted against the time in the typing class (in weeks) in log-log coordinates.

The same developmental pattern is apparent when the individual digraphs are examined, although these data are more variable because of the smaller number of observations. Figure 5.4 shows some typical examples from Typist 21 for the digraphs *ed* (1F), *in* (2F), and *ha* (2H).

Variability in Skilled Typing

The keystrokes of skilled typists are remarkably rapid, typically five to eight keystrokes per second. Nonetheless, there is considerable variation in the interstroke intervals. The distribution of interstroke intervals for a typical typist (Typist 4 in this study) had a median of 135 msec and a half-width (the difference between the 1st and 3rd quartiles) of 58 msec. This section examines the variability of interstroke intervals in skilled transcription typing.

Table 5.2. Median Interstroke Interval (in msec)

	Week 4 Digraph Class			Week 8 Digraph Class		
Typist	1F	2F	2H	1F	2F	2H
21	600	979	828	432	470	398
22	345	575	412	296	312	313
23	593	885	857	480	581	586
25	369	338	265	426	518	448
26	440	657	549	291	271	220
27	440	489	463	474	482	450
28	426	593	523	356	337	315
Mean	459	645	557	394	424	390

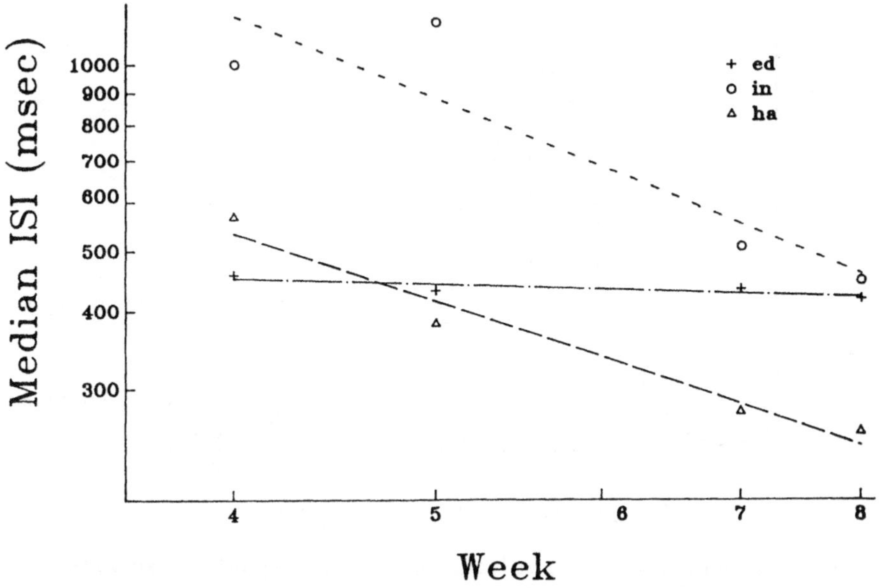

Fig. 5.4. Individual digraph learning curves for Typist 21 in the 4th-8th weeks of a beginning typing class. Student typist made rapid progress on *in* (a 2F digraph) and *ha* (a 2H digraph), but median interstroke interval for *ed* (a 1F digraph) changes very little.

Effects of the Surrounding Character Context

The interstroke intervals in typing have almost always been categorized in terms of the digraphs being typed. Some authors have subdivided the digraphs on the basis of the class of finger movements required to type the digraph (Coover, 1923; Kinkead, 1975; Terzuolo & Viviani, 1980; Gentner, Note 1), but the digraph has remained the unit of description. One study that considered a more extensive context than the digraph was reported by Shaffer (1978). Shaffer found that the interstroke interval for a given digraph was affected by context both preceding and following the digraph. I conducted a systematic study of how interstroke intervals are affected by the surrounding character context.

Because interstroke interval distributions are highly skewed, I have followed Shaffer (1973) in characterizing them by medians and quartiles. The spread of an interval distribution was measured in terms of the half-width: the difference between the 3rd and 1st quartile (the 75th and 25th percentile). I also repeated these analyses using the standard deviation rather than the half-width as a measure of the spread of the distribution, but that did not change any of the results reported here.

Figure 5.5 shows the distribution of all interstroke intervals for a typical typist. The half-width of the overall distribution is 63 msec. On analysis it became clear, however, that this distribution was a composite

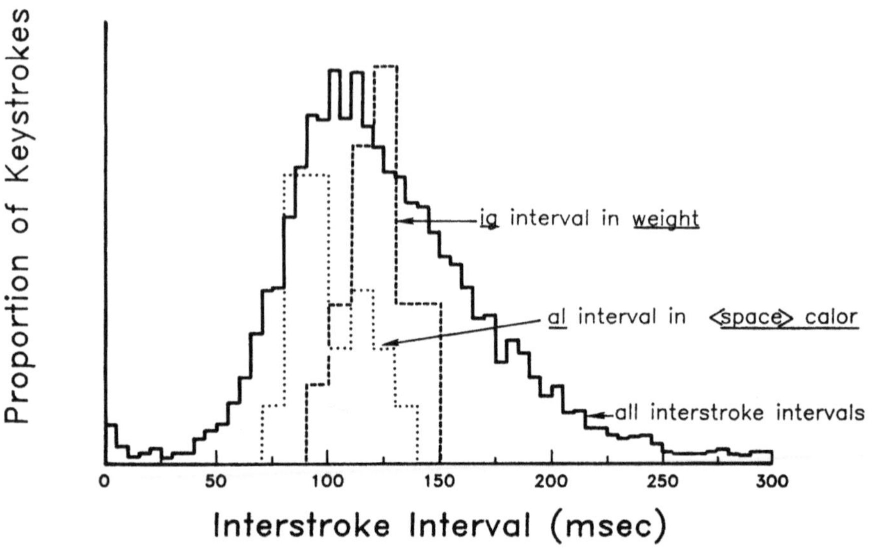

Fig. 5.5. Distribution of all interstroke intervals for Typist 3 (half-width = 63 msec). Also shown is the distribution of intervals for the digraph *al* in the sequence ⟨*space*⟩*calor* (half-width = 30 msec), and the distribution of intervals for the digraph *ig* in the sequence *weight* (half-width = 17 msec). Median half-width for all such interval distributions with six characters of context fixed is 18 msec, indicating that the distribution of all interstroke intervals is composed of many narrower distributions with varying medians.

of many narrower distributions. When the context of the interstroke interval was highly constrained by fixing the six-character string containing the interval (the three characters before and after the interval), the interval distributions had a median half-width of 18 msec. Two such narrower distributions are also shown in Figure 5.5, which illustrates the extremes of context effects, going from no context at all (the distribution of all intervals) to the highly controlled context provided by a string of six characters. Here, I explore the effects of context by determining the half-width of interval distributions as context characters are sequentially added to the left and right of the interval. In a later section, I show that these context effects are independent of the word unit. It is not the case that controlling the context is effective merely because it helps specify the word in which the digraph occurs.

The effects of specifying context are shown in Table 5.3. The row labeled "All" gives the half-width of the distribution of all interstroke intervals (the mean half-width across all typists is 56.7 msec). The median half-width of interval distributions for the individual characters, shown in row C, is the median half-width of the distributions of interstroke intervals ending with *a*, *b*, *c*, and so on. The median half-width for individual characters (55.2 msec) is essentially the same as for all characters combined, indicating that specifying the character being typed

Table 5.3. Median Half-Widths of Interval Distributions (in msec)

Fixed String[a]	N^b	Typist 1	2	3	4	5	6	Mean
All	1	56	73	63	51	57	40	56.7
C	26	57	76	59	50	52	37	55.2
cC	206	35	39	34	30	24	28	31.7
ccC	238	27	33	27	23	21	23	25.7
cccC	94	26	29	26	21	22	22	24.3
Cc	210	44	58	47	41	43	34	44.5
Ccc	237	34	40	42	35	38	29	36.3
ccCc	94	23	25	23	19	17	19	21.0
ccCcc	58	24	25	19	19	16	18	20.2
cccCc	59	23	25	21	19	17	19	20.7
cccCcc	20	25	22	18	20	16	21	20.3

Note. Based on all six-character strings composed of lowercase letters, period, comma, and space occurring 10 or more times in the diet text.

[a] The "All" row is for the distribution of all characters combined. The labels for the other rows specify the fixed string, with "C" indicating the character that terminates the interval and "c" indicating additional context characters. For example, the label "ccC" refers to a series of 238 distributions, including the distribution of *an* intervals in the string *tan*.

[b] *N* is the number of distributions analyzed for each typist.

has little effect on the variability of interstroke intervals. In contrast, specifying one additional character to the left of the character being typed ("cC") reduces the half-width by almost half to 31.7 msec. This is the strongest context effect observed and is the basis for the common practice of describing interstroke intervals in terms of the corresponding digraphs. Table 5.3 also shows that the effect of context extends farther than one character to the left of the character being typed. Specifying a second character to the left ("ccC") further decreases the half-width of the distributions to 25.7 msec. Specifying a third character to the left ("cccC") has little effect. Somewhat surprisingly, context to the right of the character being typed also affects the intervals. It appears from the data in Table 5.3 that specifying one character ("Cc") or two characters ("Ccc") to the right also reduces the half-width of the interval distributions.

The data in Table 5.3 are confounded, however. Because the data are based on normal English text, the distribution of letters in words is not balanced and, for example, specifying right context also puts constraints on the left context. To separate these factors, consider the case when the character being typed and two characters to the left are specified ("ccC"). A total of three characters are specified, and the mean half-width is 25.7 msec. A fourth character can be added to the context by specifying either a third character to the left ("cccC") or one character to the right of the typed character ("ccCc"). Adding a character on the left to the context decreases the half-width by 1.4 msec, but adding a character on the right decreases the half-width by 4.7 msec. This effect holds for every individual typist, and indicates that adding context to the right does more than merely constrain left context. A similar argument shows that the second character of right context has little effect (cf. row ccCc with row cccCc vs. row ccCcc). In summary then, the interstroke interval for typing a given character is influenced by the neighboring two characters to the left and one character to the right.

Effect of Digraph Class

It is well established that the interstroke intervals differ for the different digraph classes (Coover, 1923; Terzuolo & Viviani, 1980). This analysis is concerned with variability of the interstroke intervals within and among typists.

Considering first the question of within-typist variability, I found 2F digraphs as a class to be generally more variable than 1F or 2H digraphs. These data are shown in the first part of Table 5.4. The mean half-width for 2F digraphs is 56 msec, compared with 39 msec for 1F and 2H digraphs. Examples of these distributions for two typists are shown in Figures 5.6 and 5.7.

A different picture emerges, however, if we examine the individual digraph distributions (e.g., the distribution of *er* or *do* interstroke intervals). The median half-widths of the individual digraph distributions are presented in the middle part of Table 5.4. The individual 2F and 2H digraphs were similar in variability, but they were about twice as varia-

Table 5.4. Median Half-Width of Distribution (in msec)

Digraph Class	Typist						Mean
	1	2	3	4	5	6	
	All Interstroke Intervals of a Given Class						
1F	32	40	47	34	47	33	38.8
2F	67	79	57	57	41	37	56.3
2H	41	47	39	36	36	34	38.7
	Individual Digraph Specified						
1F	21	21	20	16	20	19	19.5
2F	37	47	36	31	24	30	34.2
2H	38	41	36	35	33	30	35.5
	Digraph Plus Two Surrounding Characters Specified						
1F	15	21	12	17	15	19	16.5
2F	21	28	17	17	15	18	19.3
2H	28	25	27	19	19	19	22.8

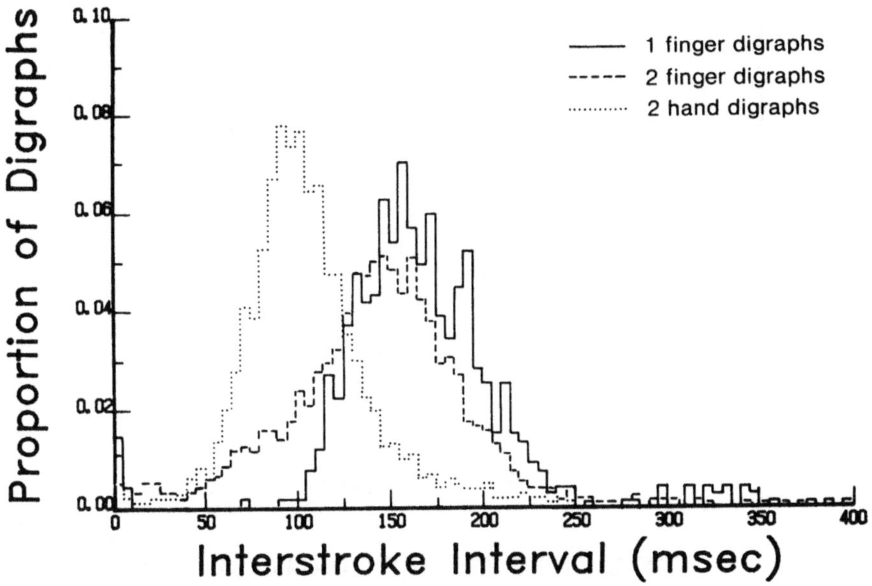

Fig. 5.6. Distribution of interstroke intervals for all lowercase letter-letter digraphs for Typist 3. Interstroke intervals for one-finger digraphs (median = 164 msec) were generally longer than for two-hand digraphs (median = 103). Distribution for two-finger digraphs (median = 147) was most similar to that for one-finger digraphs. Interstroke intervals of less than 5 msec were all errors, when an adjacent key was struck at approximately the same time as the correct key.

ble as the 1F digraphs, even though 1F digraphs had a longer interstroke interval. The lower variability of 1F digraphs undoubtedly occurs because the position of the relevant finger is fixed before and after the interval. For example, consider the 1F digraph *ce* and the 2H digraph *ne*. When typing *ce* the left middle finger strikes the *c* key at the start of the interval and the *e* key at the end, but when typing *ne* the position of the left middle finger is undetermined at the start of the interval. The difference in this case is striking: Averaged over the typists, the *ce* distribution has a median of 204 msec and a half-width of 20 msec, but the *ne* distribution had a median of 120 msec and a half-width of 41 msec.

If 2F and 2H digraphs were more variable because the finger position was not fixed at the beginning of the interval, controlling the surrounding characters should reduce their variability. The last part of Table 5.4 shows that this was true. On average, controlling the four-character context surrounding the interstroke interval reduced the half-widths for 1F distributions by 15%, but reduced the half-widths for 2F and 2H distributions by 44% and 36%, respectively. With the context thus controlled, the differences between the three digraph classes were reduced, but 1F digraphs were still generally least variable and 2H digraphs were generally most variable.

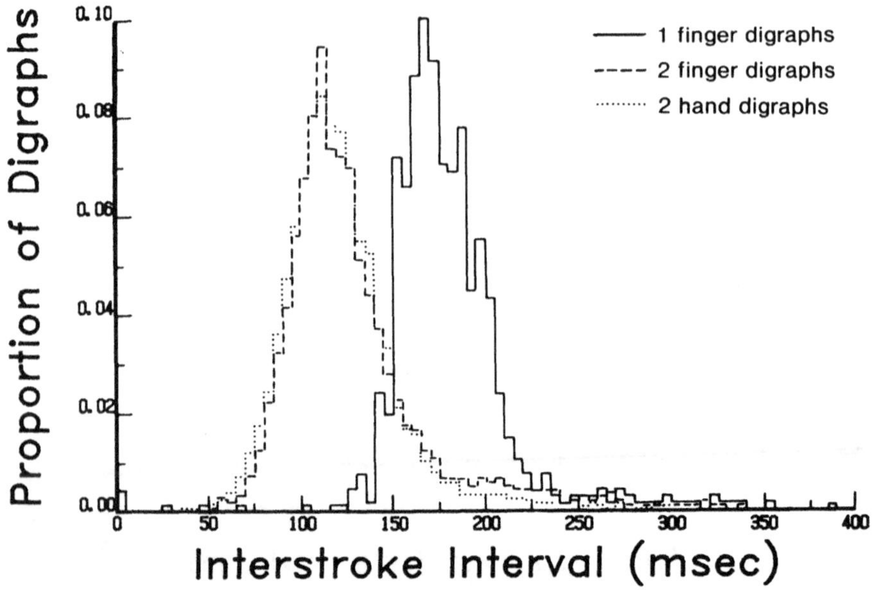

Fig. 5.7. Distribution of interstroke intervals for all lowercase letter-letter digraphs for Typist 6. Interstroke intervals for one-finger digraphs (median = 176 msec) were generally longer than for two-hand digraphs (median = 117). In contrast to Typist 3, however, the interval distribution for two-finger digraphs (median = 119) was almost identical to that for two-hand digraphs. The distributions for the other four typists were intermediate between these extremes.

Variability Among Typists

Table 5.5 gives the median intervals of 1F, 2F, and 2H digraphs for the six typists. For every typist, 1F digraphs were typed slowest, 2F digraphs were intermediate, and 2H digraphs were typed fastest. The 2H digraphs were presumably fastest because typists were able to overlap movements on separate hands. Overlapped movements are obviously not possible for 1F digraphs, since the same finger is used to type both letters. Overlapping movements for a 2F digraph would require independent finger movements on one hand, and I show later that typists vary greatly in the independence of their finger movements.

As shown by the standard deviations in Table 5.5, intervals for 2F digraphs were most variable among typists. This pattern is even more pronounced when the surrounding character context is controlled. I calculated the standard deviation across the six expert typists for all digraphs appearing 10 times or more in the same four-character context. For example, I calculated the standard deviation across typists of the median interstroke intervals for *ve* in the string *ever*. The median standard deviations were 24.0 msec for 1F digraphs, 39.8 msec for 2F digraphs, and 22.8 msec for 2H digraphs. That is, 2F digraphs are about twice as variable across typists as 1F or 2H hand digraphs.

Table 5.5. Letter-Letter Digraphs

Typist	Median Interstroke Interval (in msec)				
	Overall	1F	2F	2H	Savings[a] (%)
1	114	180	103	94	90
2	160	225	176	132	52
3	128	164	147	103	28
4	135	167	132	115	67
5	181	209	190	145	30
6	129	176	119	117	97
7	81	157	79	75	95
8	96	149	93	92	98
9	117	183	139	91	48
10	129	168	145	107	38
Mean	127	178	132	107	64
SD	28.7	23.3	35.1	20.9	

[a] $\text{Savings} = \dfrac{\text{1F interval} - \text{2F interval}}{\text{1F interval} - \text{2H interval}}.$

Table 5.5 also shows that the six typists vary when the interval for 2F digraphs is compared to the intervals for 1F and 2H digraphs. If the difference between 1F and 2H intervals is taken to represent 100% of the savings resulting from the possibility of overlapping movements, the percentage of savings seen in the 2F interval ranges from 28% for Typist 3 to 98% for Typist 8. Note that Typist 3 and Typist 6, who are near the extremes in the amount of savings for 2F digraphs (28% and 97%), had similar overall typing rates (76 wpm for Typist 3 and 82 wpm for Typist 6).

The differences in median interstroke interval for the digraph classes are reflected in the distributions of interstroke intervals shown in Figures 5.6 and 5.7. For Typist 3, the 2F digraphs were most similar to the 1F digraphs. Typist 6 shows a completely different pattern; the 2F digraphs were almost identical to 2H digraphs. Figure 5.8 presents a more detailed comparison of the 77 highest frequency digraphs in the diet text for Typists 3 and 6. Typist 3 was faster on 1F and 2H digraphs and Typist 6 was faster on 2F digraphs.

Variability in Finger and Hand Movement

All six expert typists were faster when typing 2H digraphs than when typing 1F digraphs. Because there is no possibility of overlapping the successive keystrokes in 1F digraphs and because typists have been observed to overlap keystrokes with 2H digraphs (Olsen & Murray, 1976; Gentner, Grudin, & Conway, Note 3), the shorter interval of

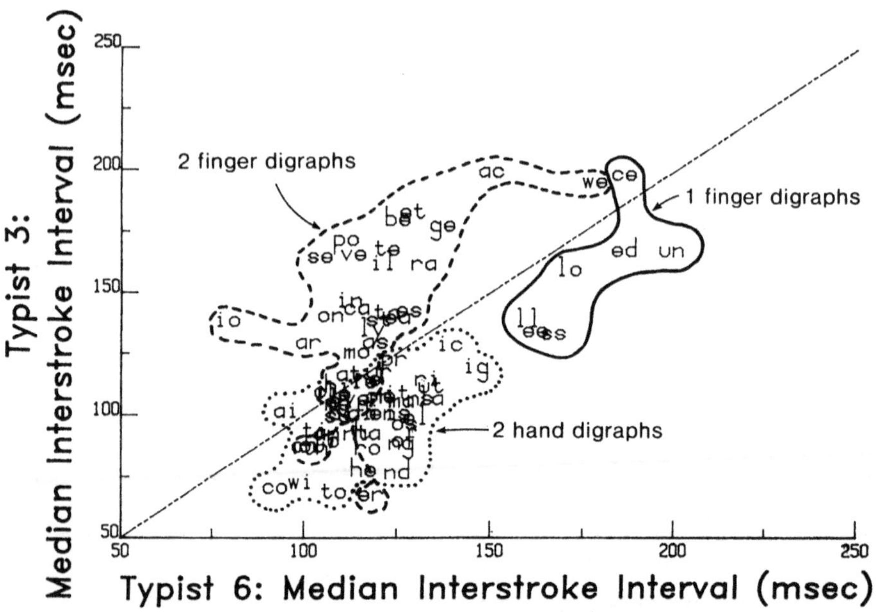

Fig. 5.8. Comparison of median intervals of the 77 highest frequency digraphs for Typists 3 and 6. Digraphs plotted below the diagonal line were typed faster by Typist 3; those above the diagonal were typed faster by Typist 6. Although Typist 3 was faster with one-finger and two-hand digraphs, Typist 6 was faster with two-finger digraphs. Their overall typing rates were similar.

2H digraphs has been attributed to overlapped movements. This perspective suggests that the variation in the relative interval of 2F digraphs could be caused by a variation in different typists' ability to overlap movements within a hand.

To examine this issue, I determined the typists' finger and hand movements from the videotape recordings. I analyzed the finger and hand trajectories during the typing of a letter sequence that appeared a number of times in the diet text. The string *thing* occurred eight times in various words in the diet text. The actual words were *things* (twice), *anything* (twice), *nothing* (twice), *thing*, and *everything*. Figure 5.9 shows the trajectories of the right index finger while typing *hin* in the string *thing*. (The right index finger types *h* and *n*; the right middle finger types the *i*. See Figure 2.1 for the keyboard layout.) The finger trajectories of Typists 2, 4, and 6 appear similar: direct, regular, smooth movements of the index finger from the *h* key to the *n* key. This can be seen quantitatively in Table 5.6. The means and standard deviations of the path length were smallest for Typists 2, 4, and 6. By contrast, Typists 1 and 3 had longer and more variable finger trajectories. Typist 5 had the longest finger trajectories of all (almost three times those of Typist 6), although they were fairly regular relative to their length.

There was a general correlation between the length of the finger trajectory and the time between striking *h* and *n*. Comparing typists, I

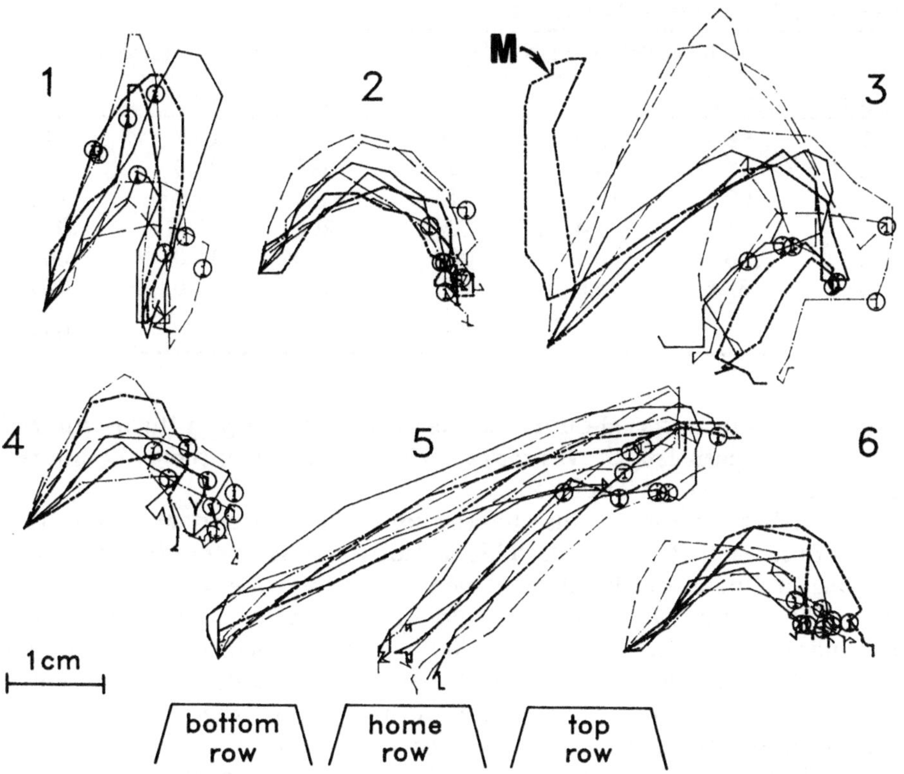

Fig. 5.9. Trajectories of the right index finger while typing the sequence *hin* in the string *thing* for Typists 1-6. The projection of trajectory on the *y-z* plane is shown, as if the finger were viewed from the right end of the keyboard. The letters *h* (right end of the trajectory) and *n* (left end of the trajectory) are typed by the right index finger. The circled *i* indicates the time when the *i* key was struck by the right middle finger. The trajectories have been adjusted to superimpose their end points when the *n* was struck. Approximate location of typewriter keys relative to the finger trajectory for Typist 5 is indicated at the bottom of the figure. Eight finger trajectories are shown for each typist except Typist 3, who made an error in one of the words. Another trajectory of Typist 3 (labeled "M") contains an apparent misstroke and was not included in the analysis.

found the correlation between the mean path length and the mean *hn* interval to be +.75 (nonsignificant), and the correlation increased to +.95 when Typist 2 was excluded. When the keystrokes were compared separately for each typist, path length and interval were significantly correlated for Typists 1, 3, and 4 (mean $r = +.85$), but the correlations were insignificant, although still reasonably high, for Typists 2, 5, and 6 (mean $r = +.55$).

A final observation of note is that for a given typist, the time between striking the *h* and *n* is more regular than the length of the finger trajectory. If the ratio of the standard deviation to the mean is taken as a measure of relative variability, the mean variability in path length (.141)

Table 5.6. Variability in Typing *hin*

	Finger Path Length (in mm)			Interstroke Interval (in msec)		
Typist	Mean	*SD*	*SD*/Mean	Mean	*SD*	*SD*/Mean
1	56.4	12.9	.229	231	10.7	.046
2	41.3	3.7	.090	298	31.9	.107
3	90.8	19.5	.215	279	47.9	.172
4	41.5	4.4	.106	201	10.2	.051
5	108.8	8.7	.080	349	17.9	.051
6	38.5	4.9	.127	213	20.0	.094
Ave.			.141			.087

for the six typists was about twice the mean variability in the *hn* interval (.087). The path length was more variable than the interstroke interval for all typists except Typist 2.

An earlier section of this chapter contrasted 2F and 2H digraphs in terms of interstroke intervals. This section extends the contrast to observations of finger and hand movements. Consider the sequences *hin* and *hen*. The within-hand sequence, *hin*, is composed of 2F digraphs, and the alternating-hand sequence, *hen*, is composed of 2H digraphs. Although typists are generally faster at typing alternating-hand sequences than within-hand sequences, I showed earlier that there are large individual differences in the extent to which 2H digraphs can be typed faster than 2F digraphs. I found similar differences when comparing the sequences *hin* and *hen*. The times taken to type *hin* and *hen* are compared in Table 5.7.

Typists 2, 4, and 6, who displayed the short, regular finger trajectories, actually typed the sequence *hin* an average of 12% faster than the sequence *hen*. This shows that within-hand sequences are not necessarily slower than alternating-hand sequences. One reason for these fast performances may be that *hin* is a high-frequency trigram, in the top 4% of trigrams listed by Underwood and Schulz (1960). High-frequency

Table 5.7. Median Interstroke Intervals (in msec)

	Typist					
Interval	1	2	3	4	5	6
hin in *thing*	231	289	261	197	346	223
hen	191	329	196	255	294	241
hin/hen	1.25	.89	1.38	.81	1.19	.93
All *hi*	82	125	113	105	155	109
All *in*	78	144	148	102	190	112
hi in *thing*	160	131	114	100	145	107
in in *thing*	76	160	146	102	202	108

digraphs such as *er* and *hi* were usually among the most rapidly typed digraphs even though they are typed by one hand.

In contrast with the performance of Typists 2, 4, and 6, Typists 1, 3, and 5 were about 27% slower when typing *hin* compared with *hen*. In all three cases, interference between movements to type the *i* and *n* appeared to be responsible for the slower performance when typing *hin*. Figure 5.9 shows that typists 3 and 5 moved their right index finger toward the top row of the keyboard while typing the *i* with their right middle finger. After striking the *h* key, Typists 3 and 5 typically moved their index fingers 10 and 30 mm, respectively, in the direction of the top row. This forces a much longer movement to type the *n*. In contrast, the average movement toward the top row by Typists 2, 4, and 6 was less than 1 mm. Thus, it appears that Typists 3 and 5 are slower because the movement of the right middle finger interferes with, and delays, the movement of the right index finger.

The case of Typist 1 was more puzzling at first. Typist 1 usually typed 2F digraphs almost as fast as 2H digraphs (see Table 5.5), yet she typed *hin* 25% slower than *hen*. The clue came from the analyses in Table 5.7. Note that the interstroke intervals observed for *hin* were essentially identical to the normal *hi* and *in* interstroke intervals in every case except one: For Typist 1 the median *hi* interval was 82 msec, but it was 160 msec in the sequence *hin*. When I checked all of the timing data for Typist 1, I found that the mean *hi* interval was 165 msec when *hi* was followed by *n* or *m*, but 72 msec when followed by any other letter. The two distributions do not overlap at all. No other typist showed this large difference, although the difference of the means for Typist 2 (137 vs. 117 msec) was statistically significant. An analysis of the hand movements of Typist 1 suggests that typing the *n* interfered with typing the *i*. After striking the *h* key, the other typists usually kept the hand fixed or moved it toward the upper row while striking the *i* key. On average, Typists 2-6 moved the hand 3 mm toward the upper row before striking the *i*. Typist 1, however, actually moved the hand toward the lower row of the keyboard an average of 6 mm before striking the *i* key. Presumably this made the *i* a longer and more difficult keystroke. For each typist, movement of the hand toward the top was correlated (nonsignificantly) with a short *hi* interstroke interval. This correlation was greatest (.61) for Typist 1. The difference in hand motion is reflected in the finger trajectories shown in Figure 5.9. The index fingers of Typists 2-6 were above the middle or upper row of the keyboard when the *i* is struck, but the index finger of Typist 1 was halfway to the *n* key before the *i* is struck. Another related observation is that for Typist 1, and none of the other typists, the time between the *h* and *n* keystrokes was more regular (SD = 10.7 msec) than either the *hi* interval (SD = 35.5 msec) or the *in* interval (SD = 27.4 msec). It is as if the sequence *hn* had been programmed, with the *i* keystroke allowed to fall somewhere in between.

The quantitative measures of finger movement just reported describe the movement of the fingertip relative to the keyboard. This movement can be decomposed into a movement of the hand relative to the keyboard and a movement of the fingertip relative to the hand.

Table 5.8 lists the amount of hand movement and the amount of finger movement relative to the hand for each typist during the sequence *hin*. The table also lists the ratio of relative finger to hand movement, calculated for each movement individually, and the ratio of *hin/hen* time intervals. The range extends from Typist 3, who had about equal amounts of finger and hand movements, to Typist 4, whose finger movements were more than twice the size of her hand movements. Comparing across typists, I found the amount of hand movement to be significantly correlated ($r = +.89$) with the *hin/hen* interval. Typists with less hand movement typed *hin* relatively faster.

Models of Keystroke Timing

No Evidence for a Word Level

Terzuolo and Viviani (1980) showed that in a number of cases the interstroke interval for a given digraph differed significantly depending on the word in which it was embedded. For example, they report that for one typist, the *an* interstroke interval (the time between the *a* and *n* keystrokes) was 147 msec in the word *thank*, but 94 msec in the word *ran*. They cite these differences as evidence for a word-specific stored timing pattern. An alternative explanation, however, is that the interstroke interval could be modulated at the time of execution by the surrounding character context, without requiring any stored timing pattern. In the word *thank*, for instance, it could be that the right index finger types the *n* more slowly than usual because it was recently occupied with typing the *h*. There would be no comparable delay in the word *ran* because the *r* and *a* are typed by the left hand, giving the right index finger plenty of time to position itself over the *n* key.

Table 5.8. Median Path Lengths (in mm)

	Typist					
	1	2	3	4	5	6
Right hand	32.9	25.4	54.2	17.1	49.5	20.5
Right index finger (relative to hand)	44.6	35.2	65.5	38.4	98.4	37.6
Median finger/hand ratio	1.21	1.38	1.14	2.28	1.92	1.86
hin/hen interval ratio	1.25	.89	1.38	.81	1.19	.93

An earlier section described in detail the effects of surrounding character context on the interstroke interval. It could be argued that the interstroke interval for a given digraph is specific to the word, and in specifying the context we are merely limiting the set of words in which the digraph occurs. There are three major lines of evidence against this argument: First, the effects of context cross word boundaries; second, intervals in the same context, but in different words, do not differ; third, context effects can be produced without word-specific timing patterns.

1. *The effects of context cross word boundaries.* To determine whether context effects apply only within words or could also be found between two words, I compared cases in which the left context was within the word with cases where it crossed a word boundary. As indicated in Table 5.9, the half-widths of distributions for intervals preceding lowercase letters narrowed as the left context was further specified (cf. row C with row cC and row _ C). The character context was clearly more effective than the ⟨*space*⟩ context, reducing the half-width to a mean of 30.8 msec, compared to 42.7 msec for the ⟨*space*⟩ context. The important point for this analysis, however, is that specifying a second character of left context further reduced the half-width of the distributions by similar amounts whether the intervening character was a lowercase letter or a space. When it was within-word context ("ccC"), the second character of context reduced the half-width by 6.5 msec on average, and when it was across-word context ("c_ C"), the second character of context reduced the half-width by 7.4 msec. Context effects crossed word boundaries for all six typists.

Table 5.9. Context Effects Within and Across Words: Median Half-Widths of Interval Distributions (in msec)

Fixed String[a]	N^b	Typist 1	2	3	4	5	6	Mean
C	23	57	74	56	50	51	37	55.2
cC	161	35	37	32	28	24	29	30.8
ccC	104	27	30	25	21	21	22	24.3
_C	20	45	50	53	50	32	26	42.7
c_C	36	33	41	50	37	28	23	35.3

Note. Based on all strings composed of six lowercase letters occurring 10 or more times in the diet text. Some of the half-widths in this table are slightly different from the corresponding half-widths in Table 5.1 because "C" and "c" in Table 5.1 include lowercase letters, period, comma, and space, but "C" and "c" in this table are restricted to lowercase letters.

[a] The labels specify the fixed string with "C" indicating the letter terminating the interval, "c" indicating additional context letters, and "_" indicating a *space* character. For example, the label "c_C" refers to a series of 36 distributions including the distribution of ⟨*space*⟩*t* intervals in the string *e*⟨*space*⟩*t*.

[b] *N* is the number of distributions analyzed for each typist.

In accord with this result, Shaffer (1978) found that the initial interval in a word could be affected by the previous word. For example, the mean ⟨*space*⟩*s* interval was 91 msec in the phrase *win supply* but 121 msec in the phrase *ratio supply*. He found significant effects of the previous word in 12 of the 39 cases examined. Shaffer's results indicate not only that context effects can cross word boundaries, but that the pattern of intervals found in a given word is dependent on the previous word—additional evidence against a word-specific timing pattern.

2. *Intervals in the same context, but in different words, do not differ.* I examined all words in the diet text that shared a string of four or more letters to see if there would be any effect of the word being typed, once two letters of left context and one letter of right context were specified. For example, I compared the *er* interval in the words *permanent* and *supermarket.* Since the text was not specifically chosen for this test, the number of possible comparisons was small. Nonetheless, out of 77 pairs of intervals compared in the same context but in different words, none of the means were significantly different at the 5% level. Although a null result is never very convincing, this finding supports the view that it is the surrounding character context, rather than the word, that determines the interstroke interval.
3. *Context effects can be produced without word-specific timing patterns.* Examination of the typewriter keyboard (Figure 2.1) suggests how these wider context effects can be accounted for without having to postulate word-specific timing patterns. Consider the *it* interval in the sequences *bit* and *wit*. The typing of the *t* by the index finger on the top row could be delayed in the sequence *bit*, relative to the sequence *wit*, because the index finger is pulled away from the top row to type the *b* on the bottom row (the *w* is typed by the ring finger on the top row). Five of the six typists had a longer median *it* interval in the sequence *bit* (mean over typists = 130 msec) than in the sequence *wit* (mean = 112 msec). The means were significantly different by a t test ($P < .05$).

   It is less obvious how context to the right of the digraph could affect intervals. To see how this might come about, consider the sequences *tin* and *tio*. The *i* and *o* are typed by the right hand on the top row, but the *n* is typed by the right hand on the bottom row. If the attempts to type neighboring letters overlap somewhat in time, we could expect the *ti* interval to be longer in the sequence *tin*; a tendency to move to the bottom row to type the *n* would conflict with the movement to the top row to type the *i*. This conflict would not exist when typing the sequence *tio*. All six typists had a longer median *ti* interval in the sequence *tin* (mean over typists = 126 msec) than in the sequence *tio* (mean = 100 msec). The means were significantly different by a t test ($P < .01$).

These data from typists are supported by results from the simulation model of typing developed by Norman and Rumelhart (Chapter 3). Their simulation model has no word-specific timing patterns. Instead, keystroke timing is determined by the layout of the keyboard and the physical constraints of the hands and fingers, which may be attempting to type several letters at once. Norman and Rumelhart report effects of right context very similar to those obtained by Shaffer. I did several experiments with their computer simulation model, having it type the diet text as well as specially controlled texts. I found context effects from characters two to the left and one to the right similar to those shown by typists. For instance, the mean *it* interval produced by the simulation model in the sequence *bit* was 1.6 times as long as in the sequence *wit*. The mean *ti* interval in the sequence *tin* was 1.3 times as long as in the sequence *tio*. In both cases the means were significantly different by a t test.

Parallel Versus Serial Models of Keystroke Timing

The presence or absence of a unit larger than the individual keystroke has been a recurrent issue in studies of keystroke timing. That is, is the time for a given keystroke specified in parallel with a larger sequence of keystrokes, or is it specified serially, relative only to the previous keystroke? At the extreme of parallel models, the unit could be the entire sequence to be typed, and all times would be specified relative to the beginning of typing. Wing and Kristofferson (1973; Wing, 1980) developed a metronomic model of finger tapping on this basis, with the times of each response in the sequence related to an internal timekeeper. Shaffer (1978) argued for a metronomic model of timing based on data from one fast typist. In a series of papers, Terzuolo and Viviani (1979, 1980; Viviani & Terzuolo, 1980) proposed a parallel model of typing with the word as the basic unit.

In the simple parallel model, the times of successive keystrokes are independent. The time for the nth keystroke is given by

$$t_n = T_n + e_n. \tag{1}$$

The interstroke interval for the nth keystroke is

$$i_n = t_n - t_{n-1} = T_n - T_{n-1} + e_n - e_{n-1} \tag{2}$$

where t_n is the observed time of the nth keystroke, T_n is the planned time of the nth keystroke, e_n is a random error term for the nth keystroke, and i_n is the observed interstroke interval for the nth letter of the unit.

Note that, in Equation 2, the error term e_{n-1} enters into i_n with a negative sign, but would enter into i_{n-1} with a positive sign. This relation leads to a negative correlation between successive interstroke intervals for parallel models of timing. (For further discussion of the negative correlations in parallel timing models, see Wing, 1980, and Gentner, Note 2.)

In the corresponding serial model,

$$t_n = t_{n-1} + I_n + e_n \tag{3}$$

and

$$i_n = I_n + e_n \tag{4}$$

where I_n is the planned interstroke interval of the nth keystroke. In this simple serial model, successive interstroke intervals are independent and uncorrelated.

It would be easy to distinguish between these simple parallel and serial models on the basis of the correlation between successive keystrokes. Other factors, however, complicate the analysis. For example, fluctuations in the overall typing rate over time will make the correlations more positive for both models.

I calculated the correlation between successive interstroke intervals for all expert and super typists while transcribing the diet text. These data are shown in Table 5.10. The correlations were all positive, ranging from .05 to .34, with a mean of .16. The large variations in interstroke interval caused by differences in the digraph and surrounding context contribute a lot of noise to these correlations, however, so I also calculated the correlations for successive intervals in repeated typings of several common letter strings. I examined both within-hand sequences (*ever*, *ion⟨space⟩*, *⟨space⟩you*) and alternating-hand sequences (*⟨space⟩and⟨space⟩*, *⟨space⟩for⟨space⟩*, *ight⟨space⟩*, *⟨space⟩the⟨space⟩*, *⟨space⟩with*. These data are from an earlier, similar study in which Typists 1-5 transcribed six magazine articles. The results are shown in Table 5.11. Overall, the correlations were mostly positive, with within-hand sequences exhibiting more positive correlations than alternating-hand sequences, but this pattern does not hold for every typist.

Table 5.10. Correlation Between Successive Interstroke Intervals for Entire Text

Typist	Correlation	Typist	Correlation
1	.171	6	.341
2	.318	7	.124
3	.134	8	.052
4	.154	9	.217
5	.088	10	.036
Mean			.164

Note. Interstroke intervals greater than 800 msec (1.2%) were excluded.

The more negative correlations observed with alternating-hand sequences need not be an indication of parallel timing control. For example, if timing across hands is more variable than timing within a hand, then in alternating sequences, such as *the*, the *th* and *he* intervals will be negatively correlated. This is the case for some of the typists. For Typists 1 and 3, the *te* intervals in the word *the* were actually less variable than the *th* or *he* intervals, leading to large negative correlations of -.5 to -.7 for the *th* versus *he* intervals. For these two typists, the time between striking *t* and *e* in *the* was almost identical to a normal *te* interval—for instance, in the word *tell*. In contrast, for the other eight expert and super typists, the *te* interval in *the* was much longer than a normal *te* interval. This again suggests that when Typists 1 and 3 type the word *the*, the left hand types the sequence *te* with timing relatively independent of the typing of the *h* by the right hand.

Discussion

The layout of the typewriter keyboard and the physical constraints of the hands appear to be the most important determinants of keystroke timing in skilled typing. When two successive keys are typed by the same finger (1F digraphs), there is no possibility of overlapping the two movements in time, and these digraphs have the slowest interstroke intervals. If the two successive keys are typed by different fingers on the same hand (2F digraphs) or different hands (2H digraphs), the second movement can overlap the first movement in time or at least be unaffected by the first movement. Skilled typists typically type 2F and 2H digraphs with interstroke intervals three-quarters to one-half the length of those required for 1F digraphs.

The pattern is just the opposite for beginning typists. The interstroke intervals for 2F and 2H digraphs are much slower than for 1F digraphs. A likely possibility is that the limiting factor for student typists is the time to plan and coordinate movements, and that these processes take

Table 5.11. Correlations Between Successive Interstroke Intervals for Repeated Letter Strings

Typist	Within-Hand Sequence	Alternating-Hand Sequence
1	-.16	-.01
2	.38	.45
3	.23	-.19
4	.12	.14
5	.40	.03
Mean	.19	.08

longer when two fingers are involved. As student typists get more practice, they move toward the physical limits that dominate the performance of skilled typists.

Although skilled typists share many characteristics, they also exhibit surprisingly large differences, both within and across typists, that have not been eliminated by thousands of hours of practice. Considered as classes, the interstroke intervals of 2F digraphs were the most variable for a given typist. When the digraph and the surrounding context were controlled, however, all digraph classes were much less variable. Averaged over typists, the median half-widths of the interstroke interval distributions were 16.5, 19.3, and 22.8 msec for 1F, 2F, and 2H, respectively. These differences suggest that timing is most accurately programmed when the action involves one finger, intermediate when it involves two fingers on one hand, and least accurate when it involves two hands. An alternate explanation is that 2H digraphs are more variable because factors such as the relative elbow position are not being controlled, but they are of necessity controlled for 2F and 1F digraphs that involve only one hand. According to this second explanation, it is the execution of the action, rather than the programming of it, that is responsible for the observed differences in variability.

The interstroke intervals for 2F digraphs were the most variable between typists. For some typists they were like the rapid 2H digraphs; for other typists they were like the slow 1F digraphs; for the remaining typists, 2F digraphs were intermediate in speed. These differences were not always related to overall typing speed. Typists 3 and 6 were near the extremes for the speed of 2F digraphs relative to 2H digraphs, but had similar overall typing rates. Analysis of finger and hand movements on videotape recordings showed that the differences in relative speed for 2F digraphs were correlated with the independence of within-hand finger movements. Three typists who moved their fingers independently were able to type a within-hand sequence (*hin*) as rapidly as an alternating-hand sequence (*hen*). The other three typists coupled their within-hand finger movements. When typing a 2F digraph, the movement to strike the first key often interfered with the movement of another finger to strike the second key. In general, the typists who show independent within-hand finger movements have higher overall typing speeds, but there are clearly exceptions to this rule.

In the cases studied, the time period of a movement was generally more regular than the path length of the movement. This suggests that it is the time parameters of the movement, rather than the spatial parameters, that are specified by the motor program. Kelso, Southard, and Goodman (1979) came to a similar conclusion with a very different task. They had subjects move two hands toward different targets and found that although the speed and distance of the movements varied widely, the time patterns of the two movements were in synchrony.

There is no evidence from keystroke timing of the importance of word-level or higher level units. The sequence of letters being typed, as it establishes the interaction between keyboard layout and the physical constraints of the hand, is the primary determinant of keystroke timing for skilled typists. Serial models of timing provide a better fit to the data than parallel models, but that appears to be primarily a reflection of the semiserial nature of the finger movements. Thus, within-hand sequences, where the physical constraints are more likely to enforce sequential movements, generally fit a serial model of timing better than alternating-hand sequences.

Transcription typing was originally appealing because of its simple, highly repetitive nature. On closer examination, it is a complex process with performance strongly dependent on task context, and with large individual differences between skilled typists. Perhaps we were a little misled by viewing typing at the level of the keystroke, with its discrete outcome (the typed letter) and an exact, if somewhat arbitrary, time. The keystroke is a narrow window into a skill involving reading, mental processing, planning, coordination, and execution of continuous movements.

Acknowledgments

The other people of the LNR Research Group made important contributions to the research reported in this chapter. In addition to the authors of other chapters, Eileen Conway assisted with many of the experimental studies and data analysis.

The research reported here was conducted under Contract N00014-79-C-0323, NR 667-437 with the Personnel and Training Research Programs of the Office of Naval Research, and was sponsored by the Office of Naval Research and the Air Force Office of Scientific Research.

Requests for reprints should be sent to Donald R. Gentner, Center for Human Information Processing, C-009; University of California at San Diego, La Jolla, California 92093.

Reference Notes

1. Gentner, D. R. *Skilled finger movements in typing* (Tech. Rep. 104). La Jolla, Calif.: University of California at San Diego, Center for Human Information Processing, July 1981.
2. Gentner, D. R. *Evidence against a central control model of timing in typing* (Tech. Rep. 8108). La Jolla, Calif.: University of California at San Diego, Center for Human Information Processing, 1981.
3. Gentner, D. R., Grudin, J., & Conway, E. *Finger movements in transcription typing* (Tech. Rep. 8001). La Jolla, Calif.: University of California at San Diego, Center for Human Information Processing, May 1980.

References

Coover, J. E. A method of teaching typewriting based upon a psychological analysis of expert typing. *National Education Association*, 1923, *61*, 561-567.

Kelso, J. A., Southard, D. L., & Goodman, D. On the coordination of two-handed movements. *Journal of Experimental Psychology: Human Perception and Performance*, 1979, *5*, 229-238.

Kinkead, R. Typing speed, keying rates, and optimal keyboard layouts. *Proceedings of Human Factors Society*, 1975, 159-161.

Newell, A., & Rosenbloom, P. S. Mechanisms of skill acquisition and the law of practice. In J. R. Anderson (Ed.), *Cognitive skills and their acquisition*. Hillsdale, N.J.: Erlbaum, 1981.

Olsen, R. A., & Murray, R. A., III. Finger motion in typing of texts of varying complexity. *Proceedings, 6th Congress of the International Ergonomics Association*, 1976, 446-450.

Shaffer, L. H. Latency mechanisms in transcription. In S. Kornblum (Ed.), *Attention and performance* (Vol. 4). New York: Academic Press, 1973.

Shaffer, L. H. Timing in the motor programming of typing. *Quarterly Journal of Experimental Psychology*, 1978, *30*, 333-345.

Terzuolo, C. A., & Viviani, P. The central representation of learned motor patterns. In R. E. Talbott & D. R. Humphrey (Eds.), *Posture and movement*. New York: Raven Press, 1979.

Terzuolo, C. A., & Viviani, P. Determinants and characteristics of motor patterns used for typing. *Neuroscience*, 1980, *5*, 1085-1103.

Underwood, B. J., & Schulz, R. W. *Meaningfulness and verbal learning*. Chicago: Lippincott, 1960.

Viviani, P., & Terzuolo, C. Space-time invariance in learned motor skills. In G. E. Stelmach and J. Requin (Eds.), *Tutorials in motor behavior*. Amsterdam: North-Holland, 1980.

Wing, A. M. The long and short of timing in response sequences. In G. E. Stelmach & J. Requin (Eds.), *Tutorials in motor behavior*. Amsterdam: North-Holland, 1980.

Wing, A. M., & Kristofferson, A. B. Response delays and the timing of discrete motor responses. *Perception & Psychophysics*, 1973, *14*, 5-12.

Chapter 6

Error Patterns in Novice and Skilled Transcription Typing

Jonathan T. Grudin

Errors have long been viewed as an important source of insight into the organization underlying performance. In this study, the general patterns of errors made by novice and expert typists suggest how skill in this complex motor task is organized and developed.

Early accounts of typing errors were largely descriptive (e.g., Lessenberry, 1928; Dvorak, Merrick, Dealey, & Ford, 1936). Lashley's (1951) suggestion that they are a potentially valuable source for inferring the processes in skilled performance was picked up in the 1960s and thereafter by MacNeilage (1964), Shaffer and Hardwick (1968, 1969), Long (1976), and Rabbitt (1978). Sophisticated process models for typing have been proposed (e.g., Shaffer, 1978; Sternberg, Monsell, Knoll, & Wright, 1978; Terzuolo & Viviani, 1980; Rumelhart & Norman, 1982). The increased availability of computer and video systems, which are particularly suited for analysis of typewriting, makes it possible to correct and extend previous accounts. This study goes beyond initial descriptive categorizations to suggest functional classifications that support the divisions of Chapter 2 and to support constraints on a model of typing explored elsewhere (Grudin, 1981).

Lessenberry (1928) compiled letter confusion matrices in which 60,000 typing errors are categorized according to the letter intended and the latter actually struck. I have extended the analyses of Lessenberry's data and compiled two additional confusion matrices to allow a more detailed comparison of novice and expert performance.

One of my tables was constructed from all substitution errors found in a large corpus of text transcribed by expert typists. The second consisted of all substitution errors from a practice exercise by about 70 beginning high school typists. These confusion matrices constitute the Appendix to this chapter.

The Lessenberry Confusion Matrix

Important contextual information is lost when only the key intended and the key actually struck are considered. As Dvorak et al. (1936) mentioned, the context usually supplies information necessary for determining the cause of a given error. Nevertheless, some patterns emerge from Lessenberry's large corpus.

The correct character was replaced by a character immediately adjacent and in the same row in 43% of the errors. (These are referred to as row errors.) Substitutions of a neighboring letter from the same column (column errors) accounted for 15%.

Most common after neighboring letters is the substitution of the homologous (mirror-image) letter, typed by the same finger in the same position but the wrong hand. This error is typically the second or third most frequent substitution. It accounts for 10% of the errors overall, even though several letters have no corresponding homologous letter. (The Lessenberry data were restricted to letters, with no information on substitutions involving punctuation.)

Note that the keyboard is not quite symmetric. Because of mechanical constraints on early typewriter design, the vertical columns are actually on a diagonal. This complicates the determination of homology for keys in the bottom row. It also permits us to contrast purely spatial symmetries with "movement symmetries."

For example, relative to the positioning of the hands at the keyboard, the letters *m* and *c* are in homologous positions, but the *m* is typed by the index finger and the *c* is typed by the middle finger. There were relatively few substitutions of *m* for *c* or *c* for *m*.

At What Level Do Homologous Errors Occur?

The confusion that leads to a homologous intrusion could conceivably occur at any of a number of levels: (a) in the selection of the motor program (the set of commands to muscle groups); (b) in the specification of the hand, finger, and finger position that determine the key to be typed; (c) within a more abstract representation of the keyboard (e.g., a spatial representation). These are clarified below.

A confusion of motor programs would result from a possible association between symmetric movements. The special relationship between symmetric motions is manifest in the relative difficulty of making different motions with the hands—it is more difficult to pat your head and rub your stomach simultaneously than to pat or rub both.

A confusion at the "movement component" level could occur if keys are at some point specified in terms of hand, finger, and finger position, and if one of these components, in this case hand, is specified incorrectly. This differs from a confusion at the motor program level in that, for example, it could lead to the specification of three components not typically associated, such as "right middle finger down and inward." Because the middle finger does not normally make such a movement, presumably no motor program has been formed for that particular movement, so such a confusion could not occur at the motor program level.

A confusion at the abstract representational level can be pictured by specifying keys with Cartesian coordinates on a grid that has one axis down the middle of the keyboard. A homology would occur if the sign of the x coordinate were reversed.

I argue that (a) is responsible for some, although not all, of the errors, and that (b) probably accounts for most. Although (c) could be made to account for some, there is no evidence that requires positing such a level of abstraction.

First, consider (a). If learned motor programs for letters are likely to be confused when they result in mirror-image or homologous movements, the failure to get *m-c* homologies is explained—there are no learned mirror-image programs for these letters. A down-and-inward movement exists for the middle finger of the left hand and results in typing *c*, but there is no learned down-and-inward pattern for the right middle finger. So no confusion occurs. This also explains the *v-n* homology, but it runs into trouble with the relatively numerous *v-m* confusions. The motor programs for these should be quite different, one being inward and the other outward. There is a similar problem in explaining the *b-n* confusions, which outnumber even the *v-n* substitutions.

Explanation (b), a confusion of movement components, can explain the *v-m* and *b-n* confusions if we assume finger position specifications like "down" for *m* and *v*, and "down and inward" for *n* and *b*. This also explains the absence of *m-c* substitutions (different finger assignments). But it does not predict *n-v* homologies, which are even more common than those of *m-v*. Since *n-v* are motorically homologous, (b) and (a) together cover all of the errors.

The failure to find an *m-c* homology would eliminate (c), the confusion at the level of an abstract mental representation, if the typist's representation of the keyboard were an undistorted version of the actual keyboard. But imagine a representation in which the rows have been aligned, as in Figure 6.1. This alignment is a natural one, in that the keys in each column are typed by the same finger. In fact, when I gave skilled typists a set of loose keys and asked them to arrange them as on a keyboard, they invariably produced this pattern. Given this distortion, (c) is effectively indistinguishable from (b). (Below I show that it is also necessary to increase vertical separations relative to horizontal separations and to place a larger separation between the center alphabetic keys than between other keys to make the abstract representation useful. None of these modifications is really implausible, but such a representation is not needed to account for any data.)

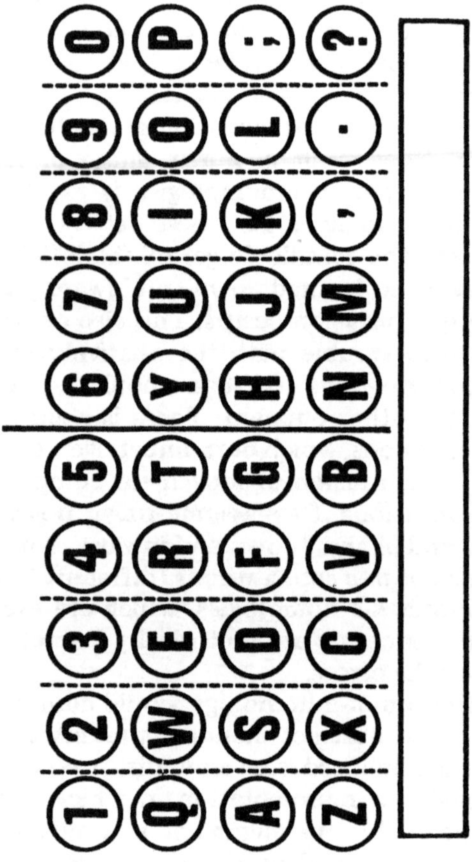

Fig. 6.1. A symmetric alignment of the keyboard.

Letter Frequency Effects

Consider the symmetry of homologous errors. Is a typist more likely to replace a left-hand letter with its right-hand homologue than to replace a right-hand letter with its left-hand homologue? Is a person more likely to replace a lower frequency letter with its higher frequency homologue than a higher frequency letter with its lower frequency counterpart? I found no effect of hand, but a strong effect of frequency. For example, *d* has a higher frequency than its homologue *k*. The letter *d* was struck for *k* 484 times, whereas *k* was struck for *d* only 287 times. However, the absolute frequency of error is not the best test. For example, although *o* is more frequent than *w*, *o* was substituted for *w* only 104 times while *w* was struck for *o* 122 times. This is misleading, because the typists had fewer opportunities to err on *w*, since *w* was encountered less often. We need to control for letter frequency; that is, to examine the *proportion* of the occurrences of a letter that leads to a substitution. To allow such controlled comparisons, I constructed a normalized confusion matrix for each raw data matrix (see Appendix). After normalization for letter frequency, it is always the case that higher frequency letters are more likely to replace lower frequency letters in homologous substitutions.

Summary of Lessenberry Data Analyses

The most common error is the striking of a key immediately adjacent, either horizontally or vertically, to the intended key. Also highly frequent is the striking of the homologous or mirror-image key. The best explanation for most of the homologous errors is that the representation of a keystroke includes a specification of the hand to be used, and that an error in this specification leads to the homologous intrusion. Finally, a higher frequency letter is more likely to be typed for a given lower frequency homologous letter than vice versa.

Although the size of the corpus makes Lessenberry's data useful, we know little of the circumstances in which it was gathered. Russon and Wanous (1973, p. 205) describe the typists as "students." For this reason, I constructed confusion matrices from the errors of novice and expert typists to corroborate and extend the forgoing analyses.

Novice and Expert Confusion Matrices

Method

Six professional typists transcribed magazine articles totaling approximately 60,000 characters. In some sessions, typing was done on a computer keyboard with which the typists were familiar; in the others, on a Microswitch keyboard designed to look and feel identical to an IBM Selectric typewriter keyboard. The text was presented as double-spaced typed copy on individual sheets of paper. After a 10-minute warm-up with another text, the typists were given an article and asked to transcribe it. They were told not to worry about errors and to type for speed. Keypresses and the corresponding times were recorded by a microcomputer.

In addition, novice typists were recruited from the beginning typing classes at a local high school. Eight students spent 1 hour each week transcribing text on the Microswitch keyboard, using the procedure just described. In addition, class papers were collected 6 weeks into the class, when the students had been acquainted with all letters of the keyboard for 2 weeks, and a three-paragraph exercise was scored for errors.

Some sessions of novice and expert typing were videotaped with a rotary shutter camera aimed down at the keyboard from above. Two views of the fingers were obtained by placing a mirror behind the keyboard at a 45-degree angle. By forming its image in less than 2 msec, the rotary shutter yields an image quite free of blur. The video fields were serially numbered with an electronic video counter and analyzed by using a Sony video motion analyzer.

I undertook separate analyses of novice and expert data. Table 6.1 gives the typing speeds, error rates, and a categorization by purely descriptive error type for each skilled typist and for the novices as a group. (The typing speed for students is a good approximation; all rates are based on a five-character word and make no adjustment for errors.)

Substitution, insertion, and omission errors all refer to single-letter errors in otherwise correctly typed words. Many of the miscellaneous ("other") novice errors are, in fact, words in which two substitutions appear to have been made. Thus, substitution errors completely dominate the errors of students. These are substantially reduced in experts, where they are the second most common error. Insertion errors, the most frequent for experts, are not necessarily the most interesting: The overwhelming majority of a randomly selected subset examined on videotape

Table 6.1. Typing Speeds and Error Rates

Typist	Speed (wpm)	Error Rate (%)	Error Type (% of all errors)				
			Ins.	Omi.	Sub.	Tra.	Oth.
1	90.4	1.1	28	21	27	10	13
2	65.6	0.5	17	11	69	3	0
3	76.1	1.9	75	5	6	4	10
4	74.9	1.0	47	15	4	4	29
5	61.3	0.4	53	19	9	11	9
6	81.9	0.8	35	12	21	11	20
Novices	20	3.2	9	4	75	4	11

Note. Error types listed are Ins., insertion; Omi., omission; Sub., substitution; Tra., transposition, Oth., other.

are misstrokes, two keys struck by one finger. For this reason, only substitution errors were used to generate confusion matrices. These included some 3,300 and 500 substitutions for novices and experts, respectively.

Results

Immediately adjacent keys of the same row accounted for 59% of the novice substitutions and 31% for the experts (compared with 43% for Lessenberry). Errors of the same finger in the same column were 8% of novice substitutions, 16% of experts, and 15% in Lessenberry's data. The proportion of substitutions that fit the description of homologous error were 4% for the experts and 16% for the novices. Lessenberry's data showed 10% of this type. Possibly Lessenberry examined intermediate typists or, more likely, a range of skill levels.

Homologous Substitutions

Chance level for producing homologous errors by random substitution of letters is about 3%. However, substitution errors are not random. Seventy-eight percent of skilled typist substitutions and 72% of novice typist substitutions are within hand. If we restrict the analysis to 2H errors, homologies account for 17% of expert and 62% of novice errors (chance being 7%). Thus, there may be homologous substitution by skilled typists, although infrequently compared with novices. (See also Chapter 10 for further evidence of homologous errors in typing.)

Lessenberry's data were for letters only, leaving open the question whether novices homologously confuse letters and punctuation—the *a* and the semicolon, for example, or the *c* and comma. In my corpus there is no example of such an error. Punctuation is struck for adjacent letters—the semicolon for the *l*, the comma for the *m*—but never for the homologous key. Possible reasons for this are discussed in the next section.

Homologous errors by novices can be found in sequence or with an intervening key typed correctly, as in *learn* → *siarn* and *think* → *thend.*

Twenty-three homologous errors by eight novices were examined on videotape. In 18 cases only one finger moved. Twice, fingers moved toward the homologous keys simultaneously. In three cases, the correct finger moved to the correct key, withdrew, and then the error was made. This indicates that the error is often, but not always, made early, more likely in the specification of the components of action than at the level of the motor program.

Frequency Effects in Homologous Errors

As we have seen, Lessenberry's data show a frequency effect. For each homologous letter pair, the higher frequency letter is more likely to intrude in place of its mirror-image than vice versa. My study of novices confirmed the effect. Nine of the 10 pairs showed the pattern. The set of substitution errors by skilled typists contained only 19 homologous mistakes and did not show the same pattern, with 10 intrusions by higher frequency keys and nine by lower frequency keys.

Some of the homologous errors in their context indicate that multicharacter response units may be represented during performance. In particular, homologous errors rarely create low-frequency digraphs. For example, the letter *k* appeared in three words in the novice typing exercise: *stroking*, *think*, and *know*. Students mistyped it as *d* 46 times. In the first two words, the substitution of a *d* produces no unusual letter combinations. These accounted for 45 of the 46 homologous errors. Only once did a typist type *dnow*, which includes the unusual digraph *dn*. Similarly, the word *sequences* was typed on different occasions with homologous errors in the second, third, fifth, and sixth positions, but not in the fourth, which would have produced the illegal digraph *qr*. In fact, substituting *q* for *p*, which would usually form an illegal digraph, is proportionally the rarest homologous error in both Lessenberry's corpus and my own.

The effect of letter frequency—that in the more common novice errors, higher frequency letters are more likely to intrude—may explain the failure to find homologous errors involving punctuation keys. Both punctuation keys and the letters in positions homologous to them are low in frequency (with one exception). Low-frequency keys, by definition, seldom occur, so there is little chance for substitution. The exception, *a*, is homologous to the semicolon, which has extremely low frequency. Thus, semicolon is unlikely to replace *a*, and there are few opportunities for *a* to replace semicolon. Of course, other factors may be at work. For example, most homologies involving punctuation would create low- or zero-frequency digraphs, which, as we have seen, rarely occur in substitution errors.

Adjacent-Letter Substitutions

Most substitution errors in both unskilled and skilled typing occur when an immediate neighbor of the target key is struck in its place. Every researcher investigating typing errors has noted the prevalence of these errors, particularly for horizontally adjacent keys. It is reasonable to suppose that these represent aiming or trajectory errors. On videotapes of skilled and novice typists, I located instances of substitution by a horizontally adjacent letter. I restricted the set to those in which the two keys would normally be typed by different fingers (e.g., *small* → *smsll*, *each* → *wach*, *golf* → *gold*). In each case the intended and typed keys are adjacent on the keyboard but are struck by different fingers.

In these substitutions the question is, Which finger strikes the key? For 22 of the 25 skilled typist errors and 42 of the 44 novice errors examined on videotape, the key was struck by the finger that usually strikes it. The errors could not be attributed to errant finger trajectories.

Thus, typists are more accurate in the execution of keystrokes than might have been supposed, but occasionally err in their specification of finger. This is the more interesting explanation, since it indicates that the finger to be used is explicitly represented during execution.

Column substitutions are a moderate source of error, accounting for 8% of novice and 16% of expert errors. Analysis of the videotapes to determine whether a finger strikes a key squarely or not is more difficult than determining which finger strikes a key, but in most cases it is clear. Of the 14 examples examined, in 8 cases there was a clean motion to the wrong key; 3 were misstrokes, landing between the keys; and the remaining 3 were difficult to judge. Thus it is likely that most vertical errors are also specification errors.

Immediate neighbors are much more likely to be substituted than distant letters in the same row or column. The data in Table 6.2 support this observation. Each number represents the median number of substitution errors within the pairs in the specified category. For example, the top row indicates that for row substitution errors involving one finger (1F) and a distance between the correct and struck letter of one (i.e., they are immediately adjacent), Lessenberry's (normalized) data show the median number of substitutions to be 1,521. This would be such pairs as *r–t*.

The next three rows of the table indicate that the likelihood of substitution falls off quickly with distance across the keyboard. These rows show pairs typed by two fingers of the same hand (2F) with separations of

Table 6.2. Substitution Errors: Median Number for Pairs in Each Category

Error type	H/F	Distance	Lessenberry	Novice	Expert
Row substitution errors	1F	1	1521	145	10
	2F	1	974	60	9
	2F	2	149	4	0
	2F	3	60	1	1
	2H	1	562	21	3
	2H	2	81	6	1
	2H	3	122	3	1
Column substitution errors	1F	1	623	18	5
	1F	2	152	1	0
Diagonal substitution errors	1F	1	232	13	2
	2F	1	163	1	0
	2H	1	91	1	0

one, two, and three letters. Examples of these would be *a–s*, *a–d*, and *a–f*, respectively. The column errors show a similar effect of proximity.

Across-hand (2H) and diagonally adjacent pairs are included for comparison. For example, a 2H error of distance 1 is a substitution by an immediately adjacent key typed by the other hand, such as a *t* for a *y*. For 2H substitution errors of distances 1 and 3, the numbers are high because several pairs are homologous. Diagonal errors are notably fewer than either row or column adjacent errors, even in 1F diagonal confusions such as *f–t*, where hand and finger are constant. Perhaps diagonality is not a position equivalent to the vertical or horizontal. Alternatively, the paucity of errors could arise from the lack of diagonal movements of the other fingers, and a consequent reduced probability of a confusion in this specification.

Given the relatively few 2H errors, physical proximity alone is not adequate to explain the predominance of substitutions of immediately adjacent neighbors. Neighboring fingers share musculature, and postural compensations for finger movements may be similar for neighboring fingers. As was argued earlier from the pattern of homologous errors, the confusion probably occurs at the level of the movement components of hand, finger, and finger position, or at the lower level of the motor program itself.

Frequency Effects in Adjacent Errors

As with homologous errors, there are large frequency effects in adjacent errors in Lessenberry's data. Once again, after normalizing for frequency in the language, a typist is more likely to substitute a higher frequency letter for a neighboring low-frequency letter than vice versa. This asymmetry held for every pair of row adjacent keys and 15 of 16 pairs of column adjacent keys.

We are now in a position to use the disproportionate likelihood of immediately adjacent letter intrusions to explain why MacNeilage (1964) found a preference for substituting home-row keys. Home-row keys have two adjacent vertical neighbors, whereas keys on the upper and lower rows have only one. Thus, there is no intrinsic preference for the home row. The perference is for higher frequency letters. (Other data of MacNeilage can be explained by this frequency effect as well.)

The frequency effect was confirmed in my novice study, with 31 row or column adjacent pairs favoring the higher frequency letter and 7 pairs favoring the lower frequency letter: chi-square(1) = 22.04, $p < .01$. Because the skilled typists made proportionally fewer row and column errors, as well as fewer errors overall, their data are noisier, with many empty cells. Of those pairs with one or more substitutions in each direction, 18 favor the higher frequency letter (after normalization) and only 6 favor the lower frequency letter, a significant difference: chi-square(1) = 5.04, $p < .025$.

We can eliminate the possibility that the frequency effects result from the typist's more careful scrutiny of relatively unfamiliar low-frequency keys during performance. Such scrutiny could lead to early detection of potential errors in which low-frequency letters are about to be typed. However, the relatively high proportion of substitutions within pairs such as *z–x* and *j–k* suggests that low-frequency letters do not get particularly careful inspection before they are typed. Thus it is more likely that intrusion by the higher frequency letter brings about the substitution error.

Permutation Errors

Novices and experts show different patterns of letter transpositions. Experts average around 80% across-hand transpositions, and almost always exchange two successive letters from the text. Only twice in the corpus did a letter migrate across more than one position (*deliberately* → *deliberatyel*, *outweigh* → *ouweight*), and only once did letter components appear to switch (*simple* → *simo;e*). Although a world champion typist (Owen, 1919) reported that she eventually began to transpose words rather than letters, our typists did this only twice. More common were "interchanges," the switching of two separated letters, such as *big* → *gib*, *figuring* → *firuging*, and the more complicated examples *denomination* → *demonimation* and *and more* → *amd nore*. As the examples indicate, these were almost all within-finger errors.

Novices are almost as likely to make within-hand as across-hand transpositions (40% vs. 60%). They are more likely than experts to transpose homologous letters (25% vs. 12% of 2H transpositions). Novices, more than the experts, move a key past two intervening keys (e.g., *sequences* → *sequeences*, *lower* → *leowr*). Every novice permutation falls into one of three categories: transpositions, interchanges, and migrations across two positions. (These constitute fewer than half of the theoretically possible permutations.)

The data suggest that migrations and most transpositions involve one mechanism and interchanges a different mechanism. Most transpositions involve nonhomologous 2H letter sequences. In contrast, interchanges (e.g., *major* → *jamor*, *also* → *aosl*) by experts and novices are generally 1F: The two keys involved (but not the intervening key) are typed by the same finger. Hand and finger, two of the three principal components determining a keystroke, are shared. Most of the remaining interchanges are 2F and involve row adjacent keys, and again two components—hand and position—are shared. Finally, of the few 2H interchanges, most involve homologous keys, sharing finger and position.

For 96 of 163 transpositions by experts, the result of the error is to place a lower frequency letter in front of a higher frequency letter. The effect is significant chi-square(1) = 5.52, $p < .02$. Five typists are in accord, with Typist 4 running strongly counter to the others: 18 of her 25 errors move a higher-frequency letter into the first position.

In a videotape study of 66 transposition errors, I found that for both novices and experts, the finger that made the first motion toward the key was usually the finger that first struck a key. Thus, the reversal may typically occur early in execution.

Learning. To determine the effects of practice, I examined a sample of novice typing taken 1 month later. In this extra month, the novices had 67% more experience with typing and up to three times the experience with the last keys introduced in the last class.

As expected, performance was generally closer to but not equal to expert performance. There are fewer errors overall. Of all transpositions, 28% are within hand. Homologous reversals account for 29% of 2H transpositions, which is still more than skilled typists. The misplacement of a letter by more than one position is rarer than before, bringing the students in line with expert performance in this regard. Interchanges still occur, and as before usually involve keys sharing two of the three movement components of hand, finger, and finger position.

Other Errors

Norman (1981) uses the term *activation error* to describe an error in which a similar but more common or more recent performance is substituted for the behavior one had intended. A number of errors made by skilled typists seem to be of this sort. In the error *Even experts* → *Even Experts* the (space)-*e* sequence in *experts* may have reactivated the (space)-(shift)-*e* sequence. Another example is the mistyping of "chew everything carefully, never gulp" into "chew everything carefully, nevery gulp."

Substitution errors not yet accounted for include a large number of vowel-for-vowel substitutions (even after normalizing for their high frequency of occurrence), and confusions of the letters *c, g, s, t, w*. Both may represent an activation of a multiletter response unit, perhaps one recently active, by the presence of component letters. In the case of the five consonants, the units could be digraphs ending with the letter *h*. Thus, most substitutions of the five consonants (except *s* with *w*, those being adjacent keys) are in such cases as *Ruth* → *Ruch, Rugh; three* → *chree; show* → *whow; check* → *sheck.*

Misstrokes, which are not a major source of substitution errors, are more evident in instances where an extra letter is inserted into the text—a finger strikes two keys simultaneously. Well over half the insertion errors by experts are potentially such errors, and most examined on videotape are two keys struck by the same finger. In other cases, the finger adjacent to the key being struck moves along with it and hits a key, causing an insertion. These two mechanisms account for all the examined insertions by Typist 3, who alone accounts for over half of all insertion errors by skilled typists. One skilled typist (Typist 5), whose retraction from striking the space bar normally causes her right middle finger to skim close to the *k*, actually strikes it occasionally—but only when the letter about to be typed is a *p*: The motion toward the *p* on top of the retraction from the space bar causes the middle finger to hit the key. Her only insertions of the letter *k* thus come before words beginning with *p*.

Most insertion errors of the misstroke description occur when an index finger is reaching inward or diagonally for one of the six center keys. Many insertions that do not appear to be misstrokes consist of typing a letter that appears elsewhere in the word, usually later—for example, *fiber* → *bfiber*, *crash* → *cracsh*. However, this is true for only two of the six typists. These two typists are shown elsewhere (Gentner, Note 1) to have particularly independent finger movements, leading to more overlapping finger motion. There are several possible explanations. With a number of fingers approaching keys simultaneously, anticipatory keystrokes might be more likely. Also, these errors could be transpositions, interchanges, or migrations that were subsequently corrected. (Examples are *notion* → *ntotion*, *ravenous* → *vravenous*.)

Errors of omission by skilled typists follow the general serial position pattern described by MacNeilage (1964) for errors of this type: They are rare in the first-letter position and most common in the next few positions. Videotape analysis indicates that for approximately half there is no motion toward the omitted key. When there is motion toward the key, it varies in its degree of completion: At times the finger seems to contact the key, while at other times the finger simply moves over the key but never strikes at it. We note in Gentner, Grudin, and Conway (Note 2) that there are often two clearly delineated parts to a keystroke: the motion toward the key and a rapid downstroke. On still other occasions, the finger positions itself over the key and makes a very weak thrust in the direction of the key, coming nowhere near it. I see no pattern to these different responses.

Omitted letters are likely to appear, typed correctly, in the word preceding or following the word being typed, or elsewhere in that word itself. (For example, three typists omitted the third *i* in *artificial*.) This was true for over 60% of all omissions. In the video study the letter is significantly more likely to precede the omission; in another study the letter is almost equally likely to follow the omission. Omissions of one of a double-letter pair occurred only 17 times, but this is 20% over chance based on the percentage of doubles in the text.

The low incidence of omissions in the first-letter position in a word suggests that that letter is particularly strongly activated, and for that reason possibly subject to less noise. Therefore, I looked particularly carefully at the 31 omissions that did occur in the first position. In 42% of them the omitted letter was also one of the three preceding letters, usually the immediately preceding letter, as when *the entire* was typed *the ntire* or *keep putting* was typed *keep utting*.

In many of the remaining omissions, the finger previously used was the finger that should have typed the omitted letter. For example, three words dropped an initial *p* or *l* when that letter was immediately preceded by a carriage return, which uses the same finger. This suggests that the "deactivation" of a letter for motor program following a keystroke has, in these cases, interfered with the typing of a subsequent key.

There were a small number of doubling errors, in which the wrong letter is doubled (e.g., *well* → *weel*), and just one error fitting the description of an alternation error (*where* → *whrer*), by Typist 3. Of the 124 alternating sequences in the text, *ere* is among those typed most quickly by Typist 3, despite being within hand.

Lashley (1951), Shaffer and Hardwick (1968), and Rumelhart and Norman (1982) argue that doubling and alternation errors indicate the use of special markers for such sequences—when the marker is applied to the wrong letter, an error occurs. The omission errors suggest why such special measures may be necessary—without them, the deactivation process following a keystroke would interfere with the quick retyping of the same key.

The Development of Skilled Typing

In this section, I summarize the results of the investigations of typing errors and discuss the implications as they bear on three developmental changes in error patterns: (a) the disappearance of homologous errors with the acquisition of skill; (b) the reduction in the proportion of adjacent substitution errors; (c) the marked increase in the percentage of across-hand transpositions.

The major categories of substitution error are row, column, and homologous errors. In most cases, the error is due to a deliberate stroke by the finger appropriate for the key actually struck, with no motion toward the correct key. Thus, these errors are best explained as occurring prior to the active involvement of the motor program, when the keystroke is specified in terms of hand, finger, and finger position. For touch typists, this mapping of finger to key is particularly orderly. In those errors where two fingers are in motion simultaneously, the confusion may have occurred later, possibly among motor programs.

Although novices make more errors than experts, their errors are orderly. The majority are substitution errors, of which 75% are substitutions of immediately adjacent keys. Fifty-one percent of the remainder are homologous errors. Experts make proportionally fewer substitution errors, and fewer of them are adjacent keys. Skilled typists make very few homologous errors.

Evidence for multicharacter response units in skilled typing, digraph units in particular, is presented elsewhere (Grudin, 1981). These units may help optimize postural and positional adjustments across a series of movements. As digraphs are relied on more heavily, substitutions based primarily on errors in hand, finger, and finger position specification may decline, since they often produce sequences of low or zero frequency; and movement components governing hand, wrist, and arm could come into play with the development of digraph response units. The greatest violation of such global preparations is a keystroke by the wrong hand, so homologous errors drop off quickly. Vertical movements require wrist and arm motion, so column errors would conflict with such preparation more than row errors. Among row errors, those of the same finger are most compatible, those of adjacent fingers reasonably compatible, but those of distant fingers might require different postural adjustments, and thus be less likely to occur. This parallels the distribution of these errors.

The pattern of substitution errors is marked by strong frequency effects. A higher frequency letter is more likely to substitute for a lower frequency neighbor or homologue than vice versa. This appears to result from an intrusion of the more common letter, which in an activation model could yield to either a recency or frequency explanation. A long-lasting residual activation could follow the typing of a key; keys active more recently or more often would have more residual activation. Alternatively, the activations for higher frequency elements could have higher resting levels or lower thresholds for initiating action.

Residual effects of deactivation are indicated by the pattern of omission errors. A letter is more likely to be omitted if the same letter was recently active (and thus recently deactivated). This suggests that deactivation may be a source of variability in typing: When a letter is insufficiently deactivated, a substitution error may follow, whereas when a letter is too strongly deactivated, the same letter appearing soon afterward may fail to be typed.

In addition, omissions are strongly influenced by serial position within the word being typed, with initial letters least likely to be omitted and medial letters most likely. This matches other determinations of the relative strengths of letters, and suggests an initial profile of letter activation.

For novices and experts, all errors in which the correct letters are permuted result from either the misplacement of a single letter or the switching of two letters. The great majority of these are either transpositions or interchanges, with the former more frequent. Interchanged letters almost always share components, most often being two letters typed by the same hand and finger, while transpositions are typically typed by different hands. A possible reason is that transposed letters are part of a multicharacter response unit, whereas interchanged letters belong to different response units.

Elsewhere I argue from the timing of transposition errors the presence of centrally issued "trigger" pulses for the two letters involved (Grudin, 1981). Thus, within a unit, subordinate letters may be transposed because keystroke times have little flexibility. If one finger is out of position, another finger might come in early. Transpositions are likely to be 2H for several reasons: In such a sequence, a movement or mispositioning of one hand can influence one finger while not affecting the other; the second letter has more freedom to reach its key early if it is on a different hand; interstroke intervals are shorter for 2H sequences, and the activation levels guiding the keystrokes may accordingly be more equal. If interchanges, by contrast, involve two response units, they are free of these timing constraints, and are more likely to be affected by response similarities of the letters involved.

The different patterns of transposition errors in the typing of novices and experts may be due to the greater reliance of skilled typists on multicharacter response units. Novices transpose two letters typed by the same hand twice as often as experts. This is consistent with the argument that the prevalence of 2H transpositions in skilled typing is due to constraints on timing within multicharacter sequences (Grudin, 1981). Some novice transpositions may be interchanges involving single-character response units, interchanges with no intervening letter. Just as interchanges involve keys sharing components, 69% of 1H novice transpositions are horizontally or vertically adjacent letters, and 25% of the 2H cases are reversals of homologous keys. Thus, 41% of novice (and only 16% of expert) transpositions share two of the hand, finger, and finger position specifications.

The remaining novice 2H transpositions may, in fact, represent multicharacter sequences already being learned. Over half of them are in function words—*the*, *that*, *than*, *for*, *to*, and *and*. The average length of a word containing a 2H transposition is under four letters, while the length of a word containing a 1H transposition averages over six letters. A similar effect holds for our experts. Words containing 2H transpositions average 6.1 letters while words with 1H transpositions average 7.8 letters. This significant difference results from the absence of short words containing 1H transpositions: there are 21 across-hand and no 1H errors in words of two and three letters (there are many 1H function words, such as *are*, *as*, *at*, *be*, *in*, *on*, and *was*). Short words may be executed as units, less susceptible to the errors based on shared components (which includes most 1H errors) that I associate with errors across response units. This analysis also suggests that longer words are not executed as units.

Are these multicharacter response units "syllables"? Shaffer (1975) reported that most transpositions occur within a syllable. This was true for 91% of our transpositions of letters. However, 87% of all letter-letter transitions are within syllable in the text. The difference is not significant, so transpositions provide no evidence for syllable representation in typing.

There is further evidence that novices have begun abstracting patterns. The special treatment of double letters, inferred by Lashley (1951), Shaffer and Hardwick (1968), and Rumelhart and Norman

(1982) from the existence of errors such as *ill* → *iil*, is indicated by such novice errors as *speed* → *spped*, *spiid*, and *letter* → *leteer*, *lettee*, *lettrr*. But novices also produce errors such as *speed* → *spede* and *letter* → *lerter*, which suggest that they do not always handle double letters as units.

When novices move a letter past two intervening letters, as in *that* → *atht*, the skipped letters are usually digraphs with high frequency or high transitional probability—*th*, *or*, *at*, *qu*. This raises the question why I found no transpositions of multicharacter sequences in skilled typing. Two-letter insertions, omissions, and even substitutions occur (though much less frequently than single-letter errors), but not multicharacter transpositions. Possibly typists strongly inhibit the activation of distant multicharacter units. Most likely, typists detect potentially multicharacter errors and stop typing after only one or two incorrect keystrokes. Typists do detect most errors during execution, virtually always within one or two letters of the error (Long, 1976; Rabbitt, 1978). If detected following one keystroke, a partly executed digraph transposition would appear as an anticipatory insertion. If detected following two keystrokes, it might appear as a two-letter omission.

Summary

Studies of the errors made during transcription by novice and skilled typists allow the correction and extension of previous analyses of typing errors, with implications for representation at various levels of the motor system during performance. Videotape records suggest that a keystroke is explicitly represented in terms of the hand, finger, and finger position that uniquely specifies it, and that a common source of error is the incorrect assignment of one of these three components. Further analyses provide support for previous indications that multicharacter response units, notably digraphs, are represented during execution, and that certain errors occur within, and other errors across, such units. The formation of such multicharacter units could explain differences in the patterns of novice and expert errors. Finally, the special problems arising from "deactivation" of representations in order to avoid perseveration may explain other errors, as well as mechanisms developed to avoid them.

Acknowledgments

I thank Craig Will and Don Gentner for their assistance and many discussions, Don Norman for his advice and contributions, and the LNR Research Group for its encouragement and support of this work. I also thank the typists who contributed to these studies, including students in typing classes conducted by James Henderson at La Jolla High School. Mark Wallen developed software; Patty Haden assisted with data analysis, and Eileen Conway with manuscript preparation.

The research reported here was conducted under Contract N00014-79-C-0323, NR 667-437 with the Personnel and Training Research Programs of the Office of Naval Research, and was sponsored by the Office of Naval Research and the Air Force Office of Scientific Research.

Reference Notes

1. Gentner, D. R. *Skilled finger movements in typing* (Tech. Rep. 104) La Jolla, Calif.: University of California at San Diego, Center for Human Information Processing, July 1981.
2. Gentner, D. R., Grudin, J. T., & Conway, E. *Finger movements in transcription typing* (Tech. Rep. 8001). La Jolla, Calif.: University of California at San Diego, Center for Human Information Processing, May 1980.

References

Dvorak, A., Merrick, N. L., Dealey, W. L., & Ford, G. C. *Typewriting behavior.* New York: American Book Company, 1936.

Grudin, J. T. *The organization of serial order in typing.* Unpublished doctoral dissertation, University of California at San Diego, 1981.

Lashley, K. S. The problem of serial order in behavior. In L. A. Jeffress (Ed.), *Cerebral mechanisms in behavior.* New York: Wiley, 1951.

Lessenberry, D. D. *Analysis of errors.* Syracuse, N.Y.: L. C. Smith and Corona Typewriters, School Department, 1928. (Reprinted in A. Dvorak, N. Merrick, W. Dealey, & G. Ford, *Typewriting behavior.* New York: American Book Company, 1936.)

Long, J. Visual feedback and skilled keying: Differential effects of masking the printed copy and the keyboard. *Ergonomics*, 1976, *19*, 93-110.

MacNeilage, P. F. Typing errors as clues to serial ordering mechanisms in language behaviour. *Language and Speech*, 1964, 7, 144-159.

Norman, D. A. Categorization of action slips. *Psychological Review*, 1981, *88*, 1-15.

Owen, Margaret B. *The secret of typewriting speed.* Chicago: Forbes, 1919.

Rabbitt, P. Detection of errors by skilled typists. *Ergonomics*, 1978, *21*, 945-958.

Rumelhart, D. E., & Norman, D. A. Simulating a skilled typist: A study of skilled cognitive-motor performance. *Cognitive Science*, 1982, *6*, 1-36.

Russon, A. R., & Wanous, S. J. *Philosophy and psychology of teaching typewriting* (2nd ed.). Cincinnati: South-Western Publishing, 1973.

Shaffer, L. H. Control processes in typing. *Quarterly Journal of Experimental Psychology*, 1975, *27*, 419-432.

Shaffer, L. H. Timing in the motor programming of typing. *Quarterly Journal of Experimental Psychology*, 1978, *30*, 333-345.

Shaffer, L. H., & Hardwick, J. Typing performance as a function of text. *Quarterly Journal of Experimental Psychology*, 1968, *20*, 360-369.

Shaffer, L. H., & Hardwick, J. Errors and error detection in typing. *Quarterly Journal of Experimental Psychology*, 1969, *21*, 209-213.

Sternberg, S., Monsell, S., Knoll, R. L., & Wright, C. E. The latency and duration of rapid movement sequences: Comparisons of speech and typewriting. In G. E. Stelmach (Ed.), *Information processing in motor control and learning.* New York: Academic Press, 1978.

Terzuolo, C. A., & Viviani, P. Determinants and characteristics of motor patterns used for typing. *Neuroscience*, 1980, *5*, 1085-1103.

Appendix

NOVICE ERRORS

(read: column item 'a' was struck for row item 'c' 1 time, etc.)

#	a	b	c	d	e	f	g	h	i	j	k	l	m	n	o	p	q	r	s	t	u	v	w	x	y	z
a	-	0	1	0	35	0	1	5	0	0	0	0	0	4	29	1	1	1	72	2	2	0	0	1	0	2
b	0	-	0	1	0	0	0	0	0	0	0	0	1	19	0	0	0	0	0	1	0	22	0	0	0	0
c	0	1	0	3	3	0	0	0	0	0	0	0	0	3	0	0	0	0	3	0	0	7	0	0	0	0
d	1	1	16	-	18	4	3	0	0	0	46	9	0	2	0	0	0	1	70	1	0	0	0	0	1	0
e	26	0	0	36	-	0	0	3	53	0	1	1	0	1	19	1	1	131	6	9	3	0	54	0	4	1
f	0	1	1	11	0	-	11	2	0	2	1	0	0	0	0	0	0	7	0	3	0	4	1	0	0	0
g	0	3	0	0	0	10	-	21	0	0	1	0	0	0	0	0	0	0	0	1	0	1	0	0	0	0
h	0	0	0	0	0	4	1	-	0	16	1	0	0	4	4	0	0	1	3	1	0	0	1	0	9	0
i	1	0	0	0	138	0	0	0	-	0	2	1	0	1	84	0	0	2	3	0	36	0	1	0	1	0
j	0	0	0	0	0	8	0	14	0	-	5	0	9	1	1	1	0	1	2	3	4	0	0	0	0	0
k	0	0	0	105	0	0	1	8	1	2	-	22	0	0	1	0	0	0	2	0	1	0	0	0	0	0
l	4	0	0	9	0	0	0	6	0	1	20	-	0	0	7	0	0	1	7	6	2	0	0	0	0	0
m	0	2	0	0	0	0	0	0	0	0	0	0	-	140	0	0	0	0	1	0	0	0	1	0	0	0
n	0	2	0	2	1	0	1	6	0	2	0	0	111	-	1	2	0	4	5	1	0	2	4	0	3	4
o	14	0	0	0	44	0	0	3	55	0	0	21	0	3	-	38	0	2	1	6	9	0	4	0	4	0
p	5	0	0	0	3	0	0	0	0	0	0	0	0	0	65	-	4	3	0	0	0	0	1	0	3	0
q	2	0	0	0	2	0	0	0	0	0	0	0	0	0	0	2	-	0	1	1	0	0	5	0	1	0
r	1	0	0	0	88	5	0	0	0	0	0	0	0	5	1	2	1	-	12	73	12	0	3	0	3	0
s	71	0	9	112	25	1	0	0	0	0	6	10	0	7	3	0	0	9	-	4	1	0	28	8	0	1
t	1	0	0	5	22	26	2	2	1	0	0	1	0	14	7	8	0	198	2	-	2	0	1	0	62	0
u	1	0	1	0	2	0	0	0	4	3	0	0	0	0	6	1	0	19	0	4	-	0	1	0	131	0
v	1	39	7	0	1	0	0	0	0	0	0	0	2	3	0	0	0	2	0	0	0	-	0	0	0	0
w	2	0	0	2	68	0	0	0	0	0	0	0	0	1	10	0	9	0	33	5	0	0	-	0	3	0
x	0	0	13	0	0	0	0	0	0	0	0	0	0	0	0	0	0	0	4	0	0	0	2	-	0	10
y	1	0	0	0	1	1	0	5	0	0	0	2	0	0	0	1	0	5	0	28	47	0	0	0	-	0
z	2	0	0	0	0	0	0	0	1	0	0	0	0	0	0	0	1	0	0	0	0	0	0	2	0	-
,	0	0	0	1	0	0	0	0	0	0	1	0	6	0	0	0	0	0	0	0	0	0	0	0	0	0
.	0	0	0	0	1	0	0	0	0	0	0	0	0	0	0	0	0	0	0	0	0	0	0	0	0	0
;	0	0	0	0	0	0	0	0	0	0	0	5	0	0	1	5	0	1	0	0	0	0	0	0	0	0
4	0	0	0	0	0	0	0	0	0	0	0	0	0	0	0	0	0	1	0	0	0	0	0	0	0	0
5	0	0	0	0	0	0	0	0	0	0	0	0	0	0	0	0	0	1	0	1	0	0	0	0	0	0
7	0	0	0	0	0	0	0	0	0	0	0	0	0	0	0	0	0	0	0	0	1	0	0	0	0	0
8	0	0	0	0	0	0	0	0	1	0	0	0	0	0	0	0	0	0	0	0	0	0	0	0	0	0
9	0	0	0	0	0	0	0	0	1	0	0	0	0	0	0	0	0	0	0	0	0	0	0	0	0	0
0	0	0	0	0	0	0	0	0	0	0	0	0	0	0	0	1	0	0	0	0	0	0	0	0	0	0
-	1	0	0	0	1	0	0	0	0	0	0	0	2	3	0	0	0	0	0	0	0	0	0	0	0	0
1/2	0	0	0	0	0	0	0	0	0	0	0	0	0	0	0	8	0	0	0	0	0	0	0	0	0	0

NOVICE ERRORS, NORMALIZED FOR LETTER FREQUENCY

(reflects probability of substitution)

#	a	b	c	d	e	f	g	h	i	j	k	l	m	n	o	p	q	r	s	t	u	v	w	x	y	z
a	-	0	2	0	8	0	5	3	0	0	0	0	0	2	8	1	10	0	29	1	2	0	0	10	0	20
b	0	-	0	1	0	0	0	0	0	0	0	0	2	11	0	0	0	0	0	0	0	110	0	0	0	0
c	0	5	0	2	1	0	0	0	0	0	0	0	0	2	0	0	0	0	1	0	0	35	0	0	0	0
d	0	6	32	-	4	7	15	0	0	0	153	9	0	1	0	0	0	0	28	0	0	0	0	0	1	0
e	9	0	0	24	-	0	0	2	66	0	3	1	0	1	5	1	10	47	2	3	2	0	54	0	2	10
f	0	5	2	7	0	-	55	1	0	20	3	0	0	0	0	0	0	2	0	1	0	20	1	0	0	0
g	0	15	0	0	0	17	-	13	0	0	3	0	0	0	0	0	0	0	0	0	0	5	0	0	0	0
h	0	0	0	0	0	7	5	-	0	160	3	0	0	2	1	0	0	0	1	0	0	0	1	0	6	0
i	0	0	0	0	32	0	0	0	-	0	7	1	0	1	24	0	0	1	1	0	30	0	1	0	1	0
j	0	0	0	0	0	13	0	9	0	-	17	0	15	1	0	1	0	0	1	1	3	0	0	0	0	0
k	0	0	0	70	0	0	5	5	1	20	-	22	0	0	0	0	0	0	1	0	1	0	0	0	0	0
l	1	0	0	6	0	0	0	4	0	10	67	-	0	0	2	0	0	0	3	2	2	0	0	0	0	0
m	0	10	0	0	0	0	0	0	0	0	0	0	-	82	0	0	0	0	0	0	0	0	1	0	0	0
n	0	10	0	1	0	0	5	4	0	20	0	0	185	-	0	2	0	1	2	0	0	10	4	0	2	40
o	5	0	0	0	10	0	0	2	69	0	0	21	0	2	-	35	0	1	0	2	8	0	4	0	2	0
p	2	0	0	0	1	0	0	0	0	0	0	0	0	0	19	-	40	1	0	0	0	0	1	0	2	0
q	1	0	0	0	0	0	0	0	0	0	0	0	0	0	0	2	-	0	0	0	0	0	5	0	1	0
r	0	0	0	0	20	8	0	0	0	0	0	0	0	3	0	2	10	-	5	21	10	0	3	0	2	0
s	24	0	18	75	6	2	0	0	0	0	20	10	0	4	1	0	0	3	-	1	1	0	28	80	0	10
t	0	0	0	5	3	43	10	1	1	0	0	1	0	8	2	7	0	71	1	-	2	0	1	0	39	0
u	0	0	2	0	0	0	0	0	5	30	0	0	0	0	2	1	0	7	0	1	-	0	1	0	82	0
v	0	195	14	0	0	0	0	0	0	0	0	0	3	2	0	0	0	1	0	0	0	-	0	0	0	0
w	1	0	0	2	11	0	0	0	0	0	0	0	0	1	3	0	90	0	13	1	0	0	-	0	2	0
x	0	0	26	0	0	0	0	0	0	0	0	0	0	0	0	0	0	0	2	0	0	0	2	-	0	100
y	0	0	0	0	0	2	0	3	0	0	0	2	0	0	0	1	0	2	0	8	39	0	0	0	-	0
z	1	0	0	0	0	0	0	0	1	0	0	0	0	0	0	0	10	0	0	0	0	0	0	20	0	-
,	0	0	0	1	0	0	0	0	0	0	3	0	10	0	0	0	0	0	0	0	0	0	0	0	0	0
.	0	0	0	0	0	0	0	0	0	0	0	0	0	0	0	0	0	0	0	0	0	0	0	0	0	0
;	0	0	0	0	0	0	0	0	0	0	0	5	0	0	0	5	0	0	0	0	0	0	0	0	0	0
7	0	0	0	0	0	0	0	0	0	0	0	0	0	0	0	0	0	0	0	0	1	0	0	0	0	0
8	0	0	0	0	0	0	0	0	1	0	0	0	0	0	0	0	0	0	0	0	0	0	0	0	0	0
9	0	0	0	0	0	0	0	0	1	0	0	0	0	0	0	0	0	0	0	0	0	0	0	0	0	0
0	0	0	0	0	0	0	0	0	0	0	0	0	0	0	0	1	0	0	0	0	0	0	0	0	0	0
-	0	0	0	0	0	0	0	0	0	0	0	0	3	2	0	0	0	0	0	0	0	0	0	0	0	0
1/2	0	0	0	0	0	0	0	0	0	0	0	0	0	0	0	7	0	0	0	0	0	0	0	0	0	0

SKILLED TYPIST ERRORS

(read: column item 'a' was struck for row item 'e' 9 times, etc.)

*	a	b	c	d	e	f	g	h	i	j	k	l	m	n	o	p	q	r	s	t	u	v	w	x	y	z	,	.	;	sp
a	-	0	0	0	9	1	0	1	1	0	0	1	0	0	1	0	1	3	4	3	1	0	1	0	0	0	0	0	0	0
b	1	-	0	0	0	1	0	3	0	0	0	0	1	1	1	1	0	0	0	2	0	5	0	0	0	1	0	0	0	0
c	1	1	-	6	2	0	1	0	0	0	0	0	0	0	1	0	0	0	4	7	0	3	0	3	0	0	0	0	0	0
d	0	0	2	-	11	9	2	0	0	0	3	1	1	1	0	0	0	0	4	2	0	0	0	0	0	0	0	0	0	0
e	7	1	1	2	-	0	3	0	2	0	2	2	0	0	0	0	0	3	3	4	1	3	6	0	1	0	0	0	0	1
f	0	1	0	3	0	-	5	0	1	1	0	0	1	1	0	0	0	7	0	0	0	0	0	0	0	0	0	0	0	0
g	0	4	1	0	0	7	-	1	1	0	0	0	0	0	0	0	1	0	1	3	0	0	0	0	0	0	0	0	0	0
h	1	0	0	0	0	0	2	-	0	0	0	0	0	0	0	0	0	0	0	0	0	0	1	0	1	0	0	0	0	0
i	3	0	0	0	3	0	0	0	-	0	0	0	0	0	9	0	0	1	0	2	6	0	0	0	0	0	0	0	0	0
j	0	0	0	0	0	1	0	1	0	-	0	0	2	0	0	0	0	0	0	0	1	0	0	0	0	0	0	0	0	0
k	0	0	0	2	2	0	0	0	0	0	-	2	2	1	0	0	0	0	0	0	0	0	0	0	0	0	0	0	0	0
l	1	0	1	0	2	0	0	0	1	0	0	-	0	0	0	0	0	0	0	0	0	0	0	0	2	0	0	0	0	1
m	2	1	0	0	1	0	1	0	0	0	0	0	-	6	0	0	0	0	0	0	0	0	1	0	0	0	1	0	0	0
n	3	1	0	0	1	0	0	0	1	0	0	1	7	-	0	0	0	3	0	1	0	0	0	0	0	0	0	0	0	0
o	6	0	1	0	0	1	0	0	9	0	0	2	0	1	-	2	0	1	0	1	2	0	0	0	1	0	0	0	0	0
p	0	0	0	0	2	0	0	0	0	0	0	0	0	0	3	-	0	2	0	0	0	0	0	0	0	0	0	0	0	0
q	1	0	0	0	0	0	0	0	0	0	0	0	0	0	0	0	-	0	0	0	0	0	0	0	0	0	0	0	0	0
r	4	1	0	0	6	1	0	0	0	0	0	0	1	0	1	0	0	-	1	6	1	1	0	0	0	0	0	0	0	0
s	14	0	9	4	4	0	0	1	1	0	0	0	0	2	1	1	0	2	-	3	0	0	1	1	0	0	0	0	0	0
t	1	4	1	1	5	4	4	0	2	0	2	1	0	2	3	0	0	4	3	-	1	0	3	0	1	0	0	0	0	0
u	0	0	1	0	0	0	0	0	4	0	0	0	0	1	5	2	0	0	0	1	-	0	0	0	0	0	0	0	0	0
v	1	3	2	0	0	4	1	0	1	0	0	0	0	1	0	0	0	0	0	0	0	-	0	0	0	0	0	0	0	0
w	0	0	0	0	4	0	0	0	0	0	0	0	0	0	0	0	2	0	6	4	0	0	-	0	0	0	0	0	0	0
x	0	0	1	0	0	0	0	0	0	0	0	0	0	0	0	0	0	0	8	0	0	0	0	-	0	1	0	0	0	0
y	0	0	0	0	1	0	0	2	0	0	0	0	0	0	0	0	0	0	1	1	5	0	0	0	-	0	0	0	0	0
z	2	0	0	0	0	0	0	0	0	0	0	0	0	0	0	0	0	0	1	0	0	0	0	1	0	-	0	0	0	0
,	0	0	0	0	0	0	0	0	0	0	0	0	0	0	0	0	0	0	1	0	0	0	0	0	0	0	-	12	0	0
.	0	0	0	0	0	0	0	0	0	0	0	3	0	0	0	0	0	0	0	0	0	0	0	0	0	0	8	-	0	0
;	0	0	0	0	0	0	0	0	0	0	0	1	0	0	0	0	0	0	0	0	0	0	0	0	0	0	0	0	-	0
sp	0	0	6	0	4	0	0	0	0	0	0	1	1	5	0	0	0	0	1	0	0	1	0	0	0	0	1	0	0	-
/	0	0	0	0	0	0	0	0	0	0	0	0	0	0	0	0	0	0	0	0	0	0	0	0	0	0	0	6	0	0
3	0	0	0	0	1	0	0	0	0	0	0	0	0	0	0	0	0	0	0	0	0	0	0	0	0	0	0	0	0	0
5	0	0	0	0	1	0	0	0	0	0	0	0	0	0	0	0	0	1	0	0	0	0	0	0	0	0	0	0	0	0
6	0	0	0	0	0	0	0	0	0	0	0	0	0	0	0	0	0	0	0	1	0	0	0	0	0	0	0	0	0	0
8	0	0	0	0	0	0	0	0	1	0	0	0	0	0	0	0	0	0	0	0	1	0	0	0	0	0	0	0	0	0
9	0	0	0	0	0	0	0	0	0	0	0	0	0	0	3	0	0	0	0	0	0	0	0	0	0	0	0	0	0	0
0	0	0	0	0	0	0	0	0	0	0	0	0	0	0	0	1	0	0	0	0	0	0	0	0	0	0	0	0	0	0

SKILLED TYPIST ERRORS, NORMALIZED FOR LETTER FREQUENCY

(reflects probability of substitution)

*	a	b	c	d	e	f	g	h	i	j	k	l	m	n	o	p	q	r	s	t	u	v	w	x	y	z	,	.	;	sp
a	-	0	0	0	3	1	0	1	1	0	0	1	0	0	0	0	44	2	2	1	1	0	2	0	0	0	0	0	0	0
b	0	-	0	0	0	1	0	2	0	0	0	0	2	1	0	2	0	0	0	1	0	17	0	0	0	53	0	0	0	0
c	0	2	-	6	1	0	2	0	0	0	0	0	0	0	0	0	0	0	2	3	0	10	0	37	0	0	0	0	0	0
d	0	0	2	-	3	13	4	0	0	0	14	1	2	1	0	0	0	0	2	1	0	0	0	0	0	0	0	0	0	0
e	3	2	1	2	-	0	5	0	1	0	9	2	0	0	0	0	0	2	2	2	1	10	14	0	2	0	0	0	0	0
f	0	2	0	3	0	-	9	0	1	37	0	0	2	1	0	0	0	4	0	0	0	0	0	0	0	0	0	0	0	0
g	0	10	1	0	0	10	-	1	1	0	0	0	0	0	0	0	44	0	1	1	0	0	0	0	0	0	0	0	0	0
h	0	0	0	0	0	0	4	-	0	0	0	0	0	0	0	0	0	0	0	0	0	0	2	0	2	0	0	0	0	0
i	1	0	0	0	1	0	0	0	-	0	0	0	0	0	4	0	0	1	0	1	7	0	0	0	0	0	0	0	0	0
j	0	0	0	0	0	1	0	1	0	-	0	0	3	0	0	0	0	0	0	0	1	0	0	0	0	0	0	0	0	0
k	0	0	0	2	1	0	0	0	0	0	-	2	3	1	0	0	0	0	0	0	0	0	0	0	0	0	0	0	0	0
l	0	0	1	0	1	0	0	0	1	0	0	-	0	0	0	0	0	0	0	0	0	0	0	0	4	0	0	0	0	0
m	1	2	0	0	0	0	2	0	0	0	0	0	-	3	0	0	0	0	0	0	0	0	0	12	0	0	2	0	0	0
n	1	2	0	0	0	0	0	0	1	0	0	1	11	-	0	0	0	2	0	0	0	0	0	0	0	0	0	0	0	0
o	3	0	1	0	0	1	0	0	5	0	0	2	0	1	-	4	0	1	0	0	2	0	0	0	2	0	0	0	0	0
p	0	0	0	0	1	0	0	0	0	0	0	0	0	0	1	-	0	1	0	0	0	0	0	0	0	0	0	0	0	0
q	0	0	0	0	0	0	0	0	0	0	0	0	0	0	0	0	-	0	0	0	0	0	0	0	0	0	0	0	0	0
r	2	2	0	0	2	1	0	0	0	0	0	0	2	0	0	0	0	-	1	2	1	3	0	0	0	0	0	0	0	0
s	6	0	10	4	1	0	0	1	1	0	0	0	0	1	0	2	0	1	-	1	0	0	2	12	0	0	0	0	0	0
t	0	10	1	1	1	6	7	0	1	0	9	1	0	1	1	0	0	2	2	-	1	0	7	0	2	0	0	0	0	0
u	0	0	1	0	0	0	0	0	2	0	0	0	0	1	2	4	0	0	0	0	-	0	0	0	0	0	0	0	0	0
v	0	7	2	0	0	6	2	0	1	0	0	0	0	1	0	0	0	0	0	0	0	-	0	0	0	0	0	0	0	0
w	0	0	0	0	1	0	0	0	0	0	0	0	0	0	0	0	89	0	3	2	0	0	-	0	0	0	0	0	0	0
x	0	0	1	0	0	0	0	0	0	0	0	0	0	0	0	0	0	0	4	0	0	0	0	-	0	53	0	0	0	0
y	0	0	0	0	0	0	0	2	0	0	0	0	0	0	0	0	0	0	1	0	6	0	0	0	-	0	0	0	0	0
z	1	0	0	0	0	0	0	0	0	0	0	0	0	0	0	0	0	0	1	0	0	0	0	12	0	-	0	0	0	0
,	0	0	0	0	0	0	0	0	0	0	0	0	0	0	0	0	0	0	1	0	0	0	0	0	0	0	-	35	0	0
.	0	0	0	0	0	0	0	0	0	0	0	3	0	0	0	0	0	0	0	0	0	0	0	0	0	0	20	-	0	0
;	0	0	0	0	0	0	0	0	0	0	0	1	0	0	0	0	0	0	0	0	0	0	0	0	0	0	0	0	-	0
sp	0	0	7	0	1	0	0	0	0	0	0	1	2	3	0	0	0	0	1	0	0	3	0	0	0	0	2	0	0	-
/	0	0	0	0	0	0	0	0	0	0	0	0	0	0	0	0	0	0	0	0	0	0	0	0	0	0	0	18	0	0
5	0	0	0	0	0	0	0	0	0	0	0	0	0	0	0	0	0	1	0	0	0	0	0	0	0	0	0	0	0	0
8	0	0	0	0	0	0	0	0	1	0	0	0	0	0	0	0	0	0	0	0	1	0	0	0	0	0	0	0	0	0
9	0	0	0	0	0	0	0	0	0	0	0	0	0	0	1	0	0	0	0	0	0	0	0	0	0	0	0	0	0	0
0	0	0	0	0	0	0	0	0	0	0	0	0	0	0	0	2	0	0	0	0	0	0	0	0	0	0	0	0	0	0

LESSENBERRY ERROR MATRIX

(read: column item 'a' was struck for row item 'b' 69 times, etc.)

*	a	b	c	d	e	f	g	h	i	j	k	l	m	n	o	p	q	r	s	t	u	v	w	x	y	z
a	-	69	106	71	560	102	24	139	148	26	15	136	58	61	126	60	89	104	1012	116	46	96	100	33	46	139
b	36	-	37	43	33	44	163	42	12	8	3	25	57	262	43	13	1	7	28	40	21	773	7	6	15	9
c	59	43	-	486	98	67	22	19	36	7	27	14	20	84	25	1	7	30	174	28	14	466	22	133	8	9
d	65	43	436	-	755	394	117	23	73	27	484	58	7	80	27	6	2	72	862	119	22	21	30	22	11	1
e	494	28	149	651	-	72	76	114	1019	20	25	141	66	75	174	27	5	813	276	273	95	44	638	17	77	7
f	43	80	92	524	72	-	586	56	66	176	24	38	6	27	56	47	3	419	71	153	12	159	12	1	8	1
g	35	241	34	166	75	541	-	461	24	54	41	17	9	59	8	5	8	37	30	267	18	51	9	3	8	3
h	40	44	43	22	42	47	389	-	100	207	111	21	19	275	46	15	6	26	36	117	44	11	9	4	99	1
i	159	10	17	73	907	28	25	84	-	30	211	81	50	90	915	21	13	59	78	150	560	54	20	2	27	1
j	11	6	10	11	21	140	62	489	46	-	217	49	242	188	28	7	1	6	4	40	128	5	1	2	10	2
k	17	10	34	287	29	11	16	66	172	101	-	521	37	44	56	10	2	17	23	16	7	2	2	4	3	0
l	119	44	16	59	116	54	24	42	106	54	413	-	62	97	567	92	7	40	150	77	29	3	8	7	14	3
m	52	16	11	8	41	6	15	13	27	60	56	21	-	1577	77	24	5	17	25	14	36	39	6	3	2	2
n	93	135	33	44	87	19	68	151	90	28	17	50	1249	-	68	10	6	27	74	67	25	63	8	6	22	3
o	210	18	23	30	134	82	20	68	1290	26	52	671	54	63	-	346	36	154	78	112	154	22	104	8	22	3
p	33	11	9	6	56	11	10	14	28	3	6	46	15	24	405	-	36	23	14	43	19	6	13	3	15	1
q	232	6	5	3	21	11	12	7	9	3	0	4	10	3	10	22	-	6	16	66	20	17	109	3	6	6
r	111	15	40	139	1043	334	36	24	92	5	7	27	14	70	140	33	8	-	186	1488	398	58	67	19	28	7
s	954	23	260	1061	300	106	23	16	69	6	24	162	27	91	68	12	8	156	-	150	57	59	410	157	15	19
t	97	38	24	105	212	185	254	129	157	26	20	65	15	58	79	23	55	1407	168	-	58	7	55	45	327	5
u	33	59	10	28	64	17	15	49	519	124	23	40	13	35	123	21	40	217	81	99	-	22	25	52	419	12
v	45	1001	430	39	71	137	38	28	35	1	2	10	34	101	17	2	18	44	24	11	40	-	11	11	20	1
w	89	9	10	76	927	26	6	19	15	3	1	17	16	22	122	30	96	136	382	95	18	26	-	10	12	26
x	33	12	292	35	24	1	3	11	8	5	1	2	9	8	11	5	5	21	225	23	23	10	12	-	16	191
y	44	10	5	18	57	11	26	109	33	13	3	12	18	31	12	11	5	32	138	508	502	90	43	13	-	8
z	288	7	6	7	6	2	3	2	10	1	3	3	1	5	4	4	6	13	34	6	2	9	30	108	6	-

LESSENBERRY ERROR MATRIX, NORMALIZED FOR LETTER FREQUENCY

(reflects probability of substitution)

*	a	b	c	d	e	f	g	h	i	j	k	l	m	n	o	p	q	r	s	t	u	v	w	x	y	z
a	-	115	95	44	110	106	30	63	51	433	58	83	56	21	40	83	2747	46	402	30	43	245	119	458	61	5110
b	11	-	33	27	6	46	204	19	4	133	12	15	55	91	14	18	31	3	11	10	19	1972	8	83	20	331
c	19	72	-	304	19	70	28	9	13	117	104	9	19	29	8	1	206	13	69	7	13	1189	26	1847	11	331
d	21	72	389	-	149	410	146	10	25	450	1862	35	7	28	9	8	62	32	342	31	20	54	36	306	14	37
e	156	47	133	407	-	75	95	52	354	333	96	86	63	26	56	38	154	357	110	71	88	112	760	236	101	257
f	14	133	82	328	14	-	733	25	23	2933	92	23	6	9	18	65	93	184	28	40	11	406	14	14	11	37
g	11	402	30	104	15	560	-	210	8	900	158	10	9	20	3	7	247	16	12	70	17	130	11	42	11	110
h	13	73	38	14	8	49	486	-	35	3450	427	13	18	95	15	21	185	11	14	30	41	28	11	56	130	37
i	50	17	15	46	179	29	31	38	-	500	812	49	48	31	293	29	401	26	31	42	519	138	24	28	36	37
j	3	10	9	7	4	146	78	222	16	-	835	30	233	65	9	10	31	3	2	10	119	13	1	28	13	74
k	5	3	30	179	6	11	20	30	46	1683	-	318	36	15	18	14	62	7	9	4	6	5	2	56	4	0
l	38	73	14	37	23	56	30	19	37	900	1588	-	60	34	182	128	216	18	60	20	27	8	10	97	18	110
m	16	27	10	5	8	6	19	6	9	1000	215	13	-	548	25	33	154	7	10	4	33	99	7	42	3	74
n	29	225	29	28	17	20	85	69	31	467	65	30	1201	-	22	14	185	12	29	17	23	161	10	83	29	110
o	66	30	21	19	26	85	25	31	448	433	200	409	52	22	-	481	1111	68	31	29	143	56	124	111	29	110
p	10	18	8	4	11	11	13	6	10	50	23	28	14	8	130	-	1111	10	6	11	18	15	15	42	20	37
q	73	10	4	2	4	11	15	3	3	50	0	2	10	1	3	31	-	3	6	17	19	43	130	42	8	221
r	35	25	36	87	205	348	45	11	32	83	27	16	13	24	45	46	247	-	74	388	369	148	80	264	37	257
s	302	38	232	663	59	110	29	7	24	100	92	99	26	32	22	17	247	68	-	39	53	151	488	2181	20	699
t	31	63	21	66	42	193	318	59	55	433	77	40	14	20	25	32	1698	617	67	-	54	18	65	625	430	184
u	10	98	9	18	13	18	19	22	180	2067	88	24	13	12	39	29	1235	95	32	26	-	56	30	722	551	441
v	14	1668	384	24	14	143	48	13	12	17	8	6	33	35	5	3	556	19	10	3	37	-	13	153	26	37
w	28	15	9	48	182	27	8	9	5	50	4	10	15	8	39	42	2963	60	152	25	17	66	-	139	16	956
x	10	20	261	22	5	1	4	5	3	83	4	1	9	3	4	7	154	9	89	6	21	26	14	-	21	7022
y	14	17	4	11	11	11	33	50	11	217	12	7	17	11	4	15	154	14	55	132	465	230	51	181	-	294
z	91	12	6	4	1	2	4	1	3	17	12	2	1	2	1	6	185	6	13	2	2	23	36	1500	8	-

Chapter 7

Skilled Typing: A Characterization Based on the Distribution of Times Between Responses

John Long, Ian Nimmo-Smith, and Andy Whitefield

Introduction

In 1946, Stella Pajunas, now Mrs. Garnard, typed 216 words in 1 minute using an IBM typewriter (McWhirter, 1981). In 1981, one of us (JL) typed 24 words in 1 minute, also using an IBM machine. The two examples serve to delimit the dimension of skilled typing. At one end, the champion typist succeeds in typing an average of 18 keystrokes per second, giving a mean interresponse time of 55 msec (interresponse time is the time between two successive keystrokes; words are considered to consist of five characters, including a space). At the other end of the dimension, the hunt-and-peck typist manages to type only an average of 2 keystrokes per second, giving a mean interresponse time of 500 msec. The champion is almost 10 times as fast as the beginner. Although speed is one of the most noticeable differences between these two levels of skill, other differences are as easily observed.

A champion typist such as Mrs. Garnard reads the text to be typed and presses the keys at the same time. Preview of at least two words is necessary for fast typists to attain normal speeds (Shaffer, 1976). A hunt-and-peck typist such as JL, however, first looks at the text to be typed, then looks at the keyboard in order to see which keys are to be pressed. For the former, once the hands are referenced with respect to the keyboard, keypressing is guided by memory for key location. For the latter, the keys are located by means of a visual search. Looking at the keyboard implies that the position in the text being copied needs to be relocated visually before further material can be read. The champion

---

Note: The ordering of authors is alphabetic. Psychological enquiries should be addressed to the first author; statistical enquiries to the second. This research was supported in part by a grant to the first author from the Central Research Fund of the University of London.

typist has a fixed assignment of fingers to keys, using either the straight (by column) or the standard fingering method (Crooks, 1964). There is also a full assignment of fingers to keys, including the use of thumb(s) to operate the space bar. JL, on the other hand, has only a partial assignment of fingers to keys—two fingers (index and middle) on the right hand plus thumb for the space bar and only one (index) on the left hand. Further, the assignment of fingers to keys is not fixed. In general, JL's typing gives the impression of discontinuity. Keypressing alternates with reading of the text. During keypressing, searching for keys alternates with striking the keys. The discontinuity can be seen in the frequent changes in the direction of gaze from the text to the keyboard and back again. It can be heard in terms of the long pauses between the printer's successive striking of the platen. In particular, however, the sequential nature of the output from the typewriter—a string of typed characters in the appropriate order—seems to reflect the essentially sequential nature of the movements of hands and fingers. Little overlap between movements seems to occur, with the exception perhaps of movements between hands. In contrast, and in general, the performance of a champion typist gives the impression of continuity. Keypressing and reading proceed together, and pauses between keystrokes or groups of keystrokes are rare. In particular, moreover, the sequential nature of the output from the typewriter seems at variance with the continuous flurry of activity exhibited by the fingers and hands. It seems almost impossible that a correctly ordered string of single events should result from so many simultaneous movements. It is precisely the anticipatory nature of the simultaneous movements, however, that permits the champion typist to achieve such high speeds. Successive keystrokes tend to overlap (Olsen & Murray, 1976). Movements toward keys may be initiated out of the order in which the letters are eventually typed (Gentner, Grudin, & Conway, Note 1). The flurry of simultaneous activity characterizes very high-speed typing and is a necessary precondition for it to occur.

Although the champion typist and the hunt-and-peck typist may be conveniently taken to delimit the dimension of skilled typing, both will be considered to fall outside normal skilled typing and hence will be excluded from the characterization presented here. The champion typist is excluded because only about 1% of typists exceed 100 words per minute (wpm), which is less than half the speed attained by Mrs. Garnard. In the absence of detailed data, it would be premature to assume that the characterization of normal skilled typing should be taken to include typing performance at the championship level. The hunt-and-peck typist is excluded because skilled typing presupposes touch typing, that is, typing that does not generally depend on sight of the board for key location. Only about 1% of touch typists perform slower than 36 wpm, which is half as fast again as JL. Thus, the present characterization is concerned only with touch typing that falls somewhere between the performance of the champion and the hunt-and-peck typist. Speed estimates for these touch typists, defined as the middle 99%, indicate a mean range from 36 to 94 wpm or 120 to 330 msec per response (Droege & Hill, 1961).

It might be doubted that such a large range of performances (in spite of excluding the extremes) can be usefully characterized, particularly in terms of the single parameter of interresponse time. Individual differences in the performance of perceptual-motor skills are legion (Fleishman, 1975). They are nowhere more apparent than in typing (West, 1969; Long, 1975). However, these large and obvious differences in speed belie marked similarities between the performance of skilled and unskilled typists in terms of the distribution of an individual's interresponse times for the typing of a piece of text. Examination by eye of the 16 interresponse time distributions from the experiment by Long (1975) showed 15 to have a single peak; 16 to be right skewed; 14 to have a positively accelerating leading edge; and 14 to have a negatively accelerating trailing edge. Typing performance over a reasonably wide range seems to be characterized not only by large differences in speed, but also by similarities in terms of the shape of the interresponse time distributions. The aim of this chapter is to report our attempts to characterize skilled typing by capturing numerically the differences and similarities between interresponse time distributions, and to relate the characterization to models of typing.

The chapter is divided into seven parts. In this part we delimit the notion of skilled typing. In the second part, we describe the different numerical techniques that we have applied to the data reported in Long (1975), in an attempt to characterize individual differences in typing performance. Two of the techniques failed to provide an adequate—that is, orderly—characterization (mixture methods and parametric distribution methods). They are nevertheless documented for the sake of completeness. Two techniques, however, provided a successful characterization. One used conventional summary statistics of the interresponse time distributions—skewness and kurtosis—and the relations between them. The other involved selecting percentiles to represent the interresponse time distributions and deriving a two-dimensional manifold from them. In this part we also introduce the notion of fluency in order to interpret the characterizations, which are essentially descriptions of the data, in terms of the typing activity itself.

In the third part of the chapter, we describe how the two successful techniques were next applied to characterizing the acquisition of typing skill by a beginning typist undergoing training. In the fourth part, the scope of the techniques was extended by applying them to characterizing the effects on performance of changes in the typing task—the presence or absence of sight of the keyboard (Long, 1976a). In the fifth part, the techniques were successfully applied to characterizing the voluntary changes of speed brought about by changes in instruction. In the sixth part of the chapter, we report an experiment designed to bring fluency under experimental control by varying the need for consulting the keyboard and the copy. This was achieved by varying the difficulty of the source material to be typed.

The final part of the chapter presents an overall discussion and our conclusions. We first present the characterizations of skilled typing derived from the data. Next we interpret the characterizations in terms of fluency. We then go on to relate fluency to more general notions of skill that have been proposed in the psychological literature. Fluency is further related to information processing models of typing, which are evaluated relative to the characterizations we have proposed. We suggest the need to distinguish a primary system, which generates responses, from a secondary system, which subserves the referencing of the hands to the keyboard and the execution of visually guided movements. Finally, we indicate how the techniques we describe might usefully be developed in both an applied and a theoretical context.

Characterizing Individual Differences

Method

As indicated earlier, the initial aim was to characterize the differences and similarities between individuals in typing skill. The data were taken from a previously published study designed to evaluate the effects of randomly delayed visual and auditory feedback on typing (Long, 1975). Only data from the control condition involving no delay were used (termed originally condition *Normal 1*). The subjects were 16 female members of the Medical Research Council Applied Psychology Unit's panel. All were touch typists actively engaged to varying degrees in transcription typing. Their ages ranged from the early twenties to early fifties.

The material typed was standard English prose extracted from non-technical books. The texts were chosen from those published in the Pitman magazine *Memo* as speed and accuracy tests for typists. The data reported here for each typist consisted of a single text, different for each subject and each 2,000 characters long.

The experimental procedure required the subjects to type as fast as possible while making approximately 1% errors. They were instructed to correct errors by immediate double spacing and retyping from the incorrect word or symbol. In all, 1.85% errors were made, of which 1.07 were corrected. The texts were typed on a Honeywell solid-state keyboard. Interresponse times were recorded by a Modular One computer. Further details are available in the original publication.

The interresponse time distributions for each subject are shown in Figure 7.1. The distributions are plotted as both frequency polygons and cumulative frequency curves.

Techniques

The distribution of interresponse times occupies an intermediate position as a record of the events of a session of typewriting. It has shed the information concerning the order of the keystrokes and the identities of the keys that were struck. Further, it contains no information about activities related to the source text, for example, inspection of the keyboard or of the printout. It has, however, an a priori claim to the

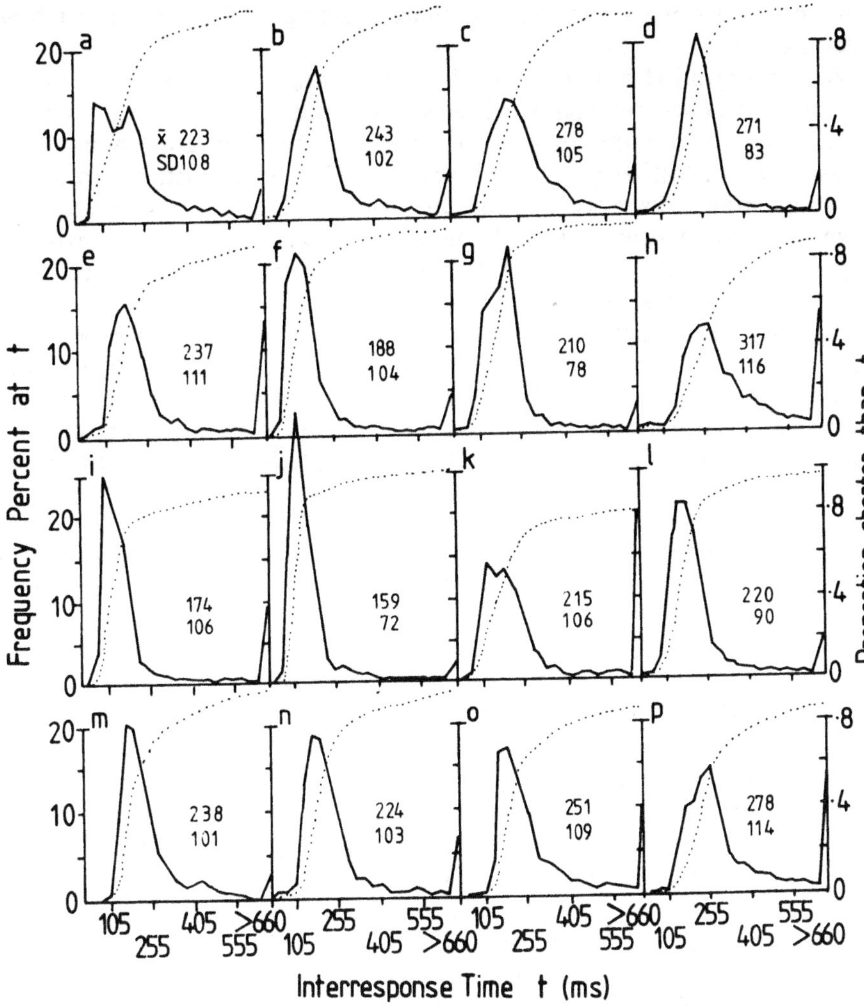

Fig. 7.1. Interresponse time distributions characterizing individual differences, shown as frequency polygons and as cumulative frequency curves.

embodiment of more than can be derived from a single statistic, such as the mean interresponse time. It is a deliberately selected constraint of the analyses described in this chapter that they are based on no finer detail of data than the interresponse time distribution. We recognize that this distribution is not a homogeneous entity, that it is in fact a mixture of various component distributions that we expect to be more homogeneous. However, besides its explicit representation of the amount of time that was spent among shorter and longer interresponse times, there are potentially other aspects of the data that the interresponse time distribution captures. Coupled with the notion that there are some questions for which the interresponse time distribution represents the appropriate level of detail for adequate answers, it is sensible to see how far one can proceed in characterizing skill by using just these distributions.

We have applied and evaluated a wide range of techniques for the analysis and characterization of these distributions. We think that it is of interest to document our experiences: Not all approaches were equally useful, but they are methods that will occur naturally to people thinking about distributions of interresponse times. Moreover, our experiences with these methods have given us some clues as to whether they may be of use later if applied to more homogeneous components of the interresponse time distribution.

The techniques fall into a number of distinguishable classes, although there are some overlaps between them: (1) mixture methods, (2) parametric distribution methods, (3) summary statistics, and (4) empirical nonparametric methods. As a reference text for readers unfamiliar with distributions and the associated terminology, see Kendall and Stuart (1969).

Mixture methods. It is a truism that the interresponse time distribution is a mixture of more homogeneous components. A mixture model is one that specifies in some terms what components and how they are combined. For instance, it is appealing to think of a multimodal distribution as being a mixture of the appropriate number of unimodal distributions. Multimodality is not a usual feature in the distributions of Figure 7.1. However, an initial approach was made that attempted to separate the slower tail of the interresponse time distribution from its faster central portion. Two distributions constitute the minimum number contained in any mixture. Further, it was hypothesized that the tail of the distribution might result from discontinuities in typing performance. Permutt (Note 2) started out from the observation that the tail of the distribution is decreasing exponentially: $f(t) = K \exp(-\beta t)$ for large t, where $f(t)$ is the density function of the distribution. This observation was based on the empirical log-survivor plots of the pooled distributions of Long (1975): The linearity of the tails of this transformation of the distribution is a necessary and sufficient condition for the distribution to have an exponential tail. Permutt postulated a density function of the form

$$f(t) = (1-p)\,g(t) \qquad \text{for} \quad t < t_0 ,$$

$$f(t) = (1-p)\,g(t) + p\beta e^{-\beta t} \quad \text{for} \quad t > t_0 .$$

Here $g(t)$ is the unknown density of the fast distribution, whose tail is assumed to decay faster than exponentially; t_0 is the unknown time at which the exponential tail component starts; p is the unknown proportion of the exponential tail in the mixture; and β is the parameter that defines the rate of decrease of the exponential tail.

The data of the distributions of Figure 7.1 are counted in 22 bins of width 30 msec, together with a 23rd bin for interresponse times greater than 660 msec. The supposition was that interresponse times greater than 420 msec (bin 15 onward) came from the slow exponential distribution. The probability that an interresponse time from this exponential distribution falls in the interval between t_1 and t_2 is equal to

$$\exp(-\beta t_1)\left\{1 - \exp[-\beta(t_2 - t_1)]\right\};$$

for the kth bin, $t_1 = 30(k-1)$ and $t_1 - t_2 = 30$ (bin width), or infinity when $k=23$. So the logarithm of the likelihood of the data in the tail of the distribution, from the 15th bin onward, is given by the expression

$$\sum_{k=15}^{22} n_k[-(30)(k-1)\beta + \log(1-e^{-30\beta})] - n_{23}(30)(22)\beta,$$

where n_k is the number of interresponse times in the kth bin. Setting the derivative with respect to β of this expression equal to zero yields the following formula for the maximum likelihood estimator of the parameter β.

$$\hat{\beta} = \left(\frac{1}{30}\right) \log \left(\frac{\sum_{k=15}^{23} (k-1)n_k}{\sum_{k=15}^{22} (k-2)n_k + 22n_{23}} \right)$$

The estimate $\hat{\beta}$ was not sensitive to variation of starting point between bins from the 13th to the 17th. The fast distribution was unmixed from the raw interresponse time distribution by means of subtraction. This required the estimation of p and of t_0. By the nature of the relation between these two parameters and the absolute thickness (as opposed to rate of decrease) of the exponential tail, their estimates are necessarily strongly negatively correlated, and there is also an appreciable range of mutual indeterminacy. This is a common feature of problems concerning mixtures (Everitt & Hand, 1981). It was not possible to assume that $t_0 = 0$, since this would produce negative estimates of $g(t)$. The indications of the data are that any exponential tail must begin after a delay of between 60 and 200 msec. The resulting density functions $g(t)$ are bell shaped, right skewed, and leptokurtic (standardized fourth moment greater than that of a normal distribution); their means and standard deviations were very similar, in contrast to those of the complete interresponse time distributions. In addition, although there was no simple relationship among p, β, and the mean of the complete distribution, there was an indication that longer mean interresponse times were associated with either larger p (thicker tails) or lower β (slower decreasing tails). As a characterization of the complete interresponse time distributions, this must be judged as only a partial success.

Parametric distribution methods. The approach here is to assume that the interresponse time distributions come from a low-dimensional family of distributions, characterized by the values of the appropriate set of parameters. Here *low* is usually taken to mean four or less.

The lognormal family, for instance, has two parameters: It is the distribution of a measure X such that $\log(X)$ is normally distributed and the mean and variance of $\log(X)$ are the parameters of the lognormal distribution. This family can be extended to the linear lognormal family of linear transforms of X, $X+b$. (There is no extra generality to be gained from introducing a scale parameter, since this is equivalent to selecting an appropriate new mean and standard deviation for $\log(X)$.) The usefulness of this extended three-dimensional lognormal family is assessed by its ability to represent a large number of distributions that occur in practice. Similarly, the normal distribution gives a two-dimensional family, parametrized by mean and standard deviation, and the linear gamma family has three dimensions, including an offset together with the scale and degrees of freedom parameters.

It has been conventional for statisticians to say that two distributions have the same *shape* if one is a linear transform of the other, or equivalently, if they each have the same standardized form. Standardization means transformation by subtracting the mean and dividing by the standard deviation. For a measure with any particular distribution, this gives a linearly transformed measure that has mean 0 and standard deviation 1 and otherwise has the same shape of distribution. Thus, for each family of distributions that contains any linear transform of each of its members, there is a family of underlying shapes that has two less dimensions. There is a one-dimensional family of lognormal shapes, a one-dimensional family of gamma shapes, and a unique normal shape.

There are two two-dimensional systems of shapes, those of K. Pearson and those of Johnson (Elderton & Johnson, 1969; Pearson & Hartley, 1972, pp. 75-87 and Figure 7), that have been sufficiently explored to make the fitting of data a practicable proposition. Beyond this numerical advantage, the justification for using these rather than any other system of distribution forms is largely arbitrary. The Pearson system does contain several of the standard statistical distributions as special cases (e.g., normal, Student's t, chi-square or gamma, and beta). Similarly, the Johnson system contains the one-dimensional lognormal family as a boundary between two distinct classes of shape.

The conventional application of these systems of curves is to smooth, graduate, or approximate an empirical distribution, such as an interresponse time distribution. For this one needs to find the member of the family that lies closest to the data. This is done by estimating two parameters β_1 and β_2 from the data; the definition of these parameters and how they are estimated are discussed in the next subsection. For our present purposes we can think of them as coordinates that describe the position of the distribution in what we call the (β_1, β_2) plane.

The Pearson system consists of three broad types (I, IV, and VI) corresponding to regions of the (β_1, β_2) plane, with certain transitional types in between. In the (β_1, β_2) plane the lines delimiting the domains of the principal types are straight, or nearly straight. As regards the present set of data, 12 of the interresponse time distributions (a, b, e, f, i, j, k, l, m, n, o, p) in Figure 7.1 are of the Pearson Type I (reversed J-shaped beta); two of the exceptions (c and h) are of Type I (bell shaped), and the other two (d and g) are of Type IV (bell shaped). This is a partial confirmation of some communality of shape, but otherwise is too coarse a characterization to be of use.

The Johnson system has two subsystems (S_B and S_U) separated in the (β_1, β_2) plane by the lognormal line. The distinction between these two classes of distribution is that the members of S_B take a range of values that are bounded, but those of S_U can, like the normal distribution, take any positive or negative values. The lognormal distributions have a lower bound, but no upper bound, to their values. All 16 distributions have (β_1, β_2) values that belong to the S_B system.

Comparison between empirical distributions and the members of the Pearson or Johnson family that match β_1 and β_2 gives rise to some disquiet. The Pearson Type I (J) curve is zero up to some time t_0, then jumps to an infinite density, which then declines monotonically out into the tail. The data tend to show a distinct slope leading up to the mode, rather than a vertical cliff. The fitted Johnson S_B curves, on the other hand, are indeed tangent to the axis at the start; however, they tend to rise to their mode more sharply, and to give a higher value to the modal density, than the data do. Both of these types of curve terminate at some upper cutoff, t_1. Additionally, there are technical problems concerning the limits for (β_1, β_2) values for which ancillary tables of values are at present available (Johnson, Note 3).

The conclusion, then, is that conventional "universal families" such as those of Pearson or of Johnson will not produce a fine enough degree of characterization, and indeed appear to miss potentially characteristic features of the interresponse time distributions. Also, it is not clear how one would use the approximating curve as a characterization, even though such a curve (if giving an adequate fit to the data) does have a valuable practical and predictive role to play.

Summary statistics. Here, the idea is not to capture the whole distribution in the form of a mathematical equation, but to express some set of features of the interresponse time distribution in numerical form. The features examined correspond to conventional statistics: measures of central tendency such as mean (m_1), mode, and median; measures of spread or scale such as standard deviation (s) and interquartile range; skewness ($\sqrt{b_1}$); and kurtosis (b_2). The method of calculating the latter two statistics is briefly described: They are defined as standardized third and fourth moment ratios of a distribution, and are estimated by the method of moments, that is, by treating the moments calculated from a sample of data as if they are the exact values for the distribution that is sampled. The first four central moments, m_1, m_2', m_3', m_4', are calculated. We use the convention that Greek and Latin symbols correspond respectively to theoretical values from a complete distribution and empirical values based on a sample of data:

$$m_1 = \frac{\Sigma\, x_k}{n}, \qquad \mu_1 = E(x),$$

$$m_2' = \frac{\Sigma\,(x_k - m_1)^2}{n}, \qquad \mu_2' = E[(x-\mu_1)^2],$$

$$m_3' = \frac{\Sigma\,(x_k - m_1)^3}{n}, \qquad \mu_3' = E[(x-\mu_1)^3],$$

$$m_4' = \frac{\Sigma\,(x_k - m_1)^4}{n}, \qquad \mu_4' = E[(x-\mu_1)^4].$$

The parameters β_1 and β_2 are given by standardizing μ_3' and μ_4' with respect to $\sigma = \sqrt{\mu_2'}$, the standard deviation of the distribution. The resulting quantities are called the standardized third and fourth moment ratios, and are given, for the complete and sample distributions, by the formulas

$$\sqrt{\beta_1} = \frac{\mu_3'}{\sigma^3}, \qquad \sqrt{b_1} = \frac{m_3'}{s^3},$$

$$\beta_2 = \frac{\mu_4'}{\sigma^4}, \qquad b_2 = \frac{m_4'}{s^4},$$

where σ and s denote the standard deviation of the theoretical and empirical distributions, respectively. Note that the quantities $\sqrt{\beta_1}$ and

$\sqrt{b_1}$ are given in square root form: The reason for this is given below. For binned data, as here, we conventionally assign the value at the center of the bin to all the observations in the bin. Continuity corrections are ignored: Empirically it makes little difference whether one uses the corrections or not. All these quantities were calculated for the truncated interresponse time distributions, that is, omitting observations greater than 660 msec, which happened to be the cutoff value in the experiment and was expected to cover most of the distribution.

The correlations among mean, mode, and median were high, and it was decided to keep the mean interresponse time as the principal numerical index of speed. The correlations among m_1, b_1, and b_2 are all significant: Higher speed goes with higher skewness and higher kurtosis. The correlation between b_1 and b_2 ($r = .94$) is higher than that between m_1 and either b_1 ($r = -.90$) or b_2 ($r = -.83$); the correlation between s and b_1 is $-.53$ and between s and b_2 is $-.77$, both of which are higher than that between m_1 and s ($r = .42$), but lower than those between m_1 and b_1 and b_2 given above. Since b_1 and b_2 are, by definition, mathematically independent of location (mean m_1) and scale (s), this means that there are systematic variations in the relative shapes of the interresponse time distributions across the 16 individual typists. In Figure 7.2 the b_1 and b_2 statistics for these 16 distributions are plotted against each other. The two lines in the figure are for the gamma and lognormal families of distributions, which meet at the point (0,3) belonging to the normal distribution. The gamma line is a straight line; the lognormal line is not very curved. If they were plotted in terms of the coordinates $(\sqrt{b_1}, b_2)$, these lines, and those of other families of distributions, would appear rather curved. There are a number of important aspects of this plot: (1) The distributions fall on or near a straight line in the (b_1, b_2) plane given approximately by the equation $b_2 = 1.25 b_1 + 2.0$; (2) position on this line is not perfectly correlated with speed ($r = .67$, untruncated mean with position of projection on this line), and position expresses differing degrees of the combined presence of a combination of peak *and* tail; (3) the distributions fall in a region of the (b_1, b_2) plane not generally inhabited by statistical life (cf. the 15 empirical distributions of Pearson & Please, 1975), both in terms of the direction of the line on which our interresponse time distributions lie and because of the high values of b_1 and b_2 we have encountered.

It is useful to make here two points concerning the interpretation of the relative position of distributions in the (b_1, b_2) plane. First, since (b_1, b_2) are *standardized* measures, two distributions that differ only by an added constant or by a constant scale change, or by a combination of the two, will (ignoring sampling variability) correspond to the same point in the (b_1, b_2) plane. So differences (e.g., in speed) brought about by changes of this type will not produce a change in position in the (b_1, b_2) plane. Second, always remembering that b_1 and b_2 are relative measures of shape, we must be careful in interpreting their joint mean-

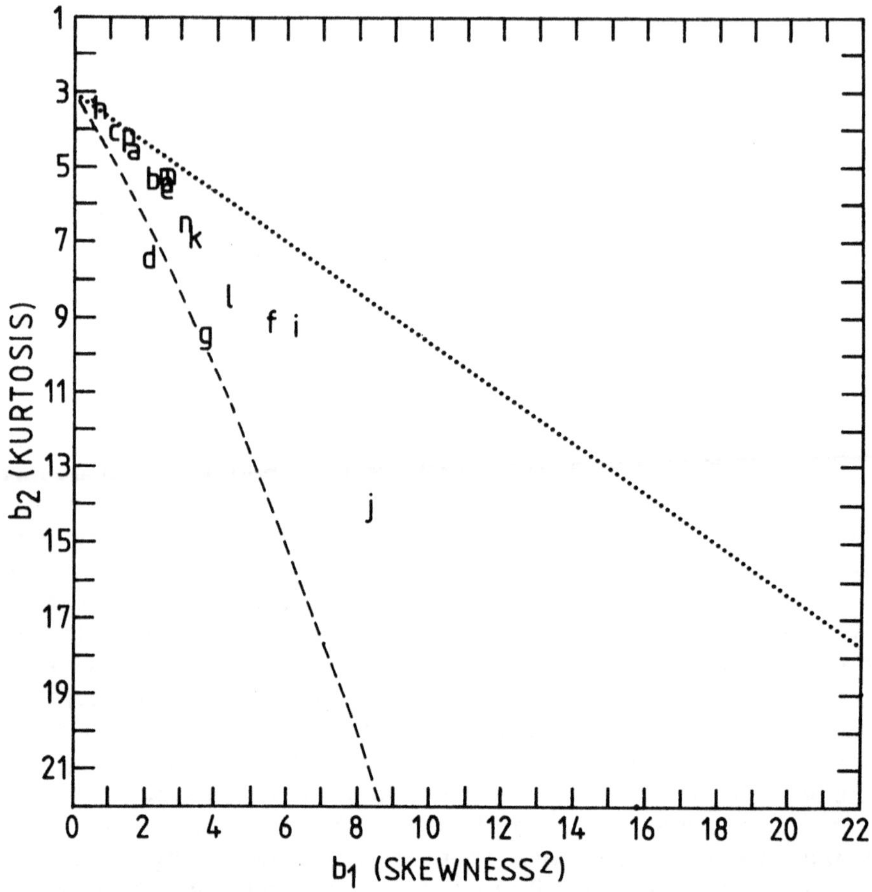

Fig. 7.2. Graph of b_1 (skewness^2) against b_2 (kurtosis) of the interresponse time distributions characterizing individual differences, together with the lognormal line (dashed) and gamma line (dotted).

ing. Finucan (1964) has described kurtosis (b_2) as an indicator of "a prominent peak" *and* "a prominent tail" with concomitant "lack of shoulders" in the distribution.

So we judge that the application of summary statistics has been a successful method. That the 16 distributions fall near a line in the (b_1, b_2) plane is highly suggestive. There is no a priori reason why this should be the case. Distribution shapes exist for all positions within the feasible region of the (b_1, b_2) plane. Instead, it appears that there is a joint relationship between the relative sizes of the peak and the tail of the interresponse time distributions, such that the more prominent the relative peak, the more prominent the relative tail. Moreover, it appears that this combined prominence is correlated with absolute speed (i.e., mean interresponse time). Two distributions (*d* and *g*) perhaps fall a little below the line associated with the other 14 distributions.

Empirical nonparametric methods. The gamma family and the lognormal family (and other less familiar families) have a one-dimensional variety of shapes that occupy lines in the (b_1, b_2) plane that are straight, or nearly straight. This suggests a family affinity among the interresponse time distributions, manifested by this lawlike relationship between b_1 and b_2. But prompted by our lack of success in applying existing families, we have developed a new approach to the characterization of the interresponse time distribution. It attempts to take the intercorrelations of mean, standard deviation, b_1, and b_2 into account, as well as to look for expressions of this and other relationships in the *cumulative* distribution functions of the data.

In effect it says: There is a family resemblance among these distributions; by measuring various aspects of the distributions, and applying an appropriate statistical method, discover the ways in which the distributions differ most from each other. By implication, ways in which they do not differ embody the family resemblance; moreover, this method will enable one to describe how a new interresponse time distribution relates to these 16 distributions, by saying where in the family it falls.

This program was put into operation in the following manner. The 16 distributions were compared in terms of their cumulative frequency functions (these are plotted with the frequency polygons in Figure 7.1). This was done by computing for each distribution seven percentiles: the 5th, 10th, 30th, 50th, 60th, 70th, and 80th. The selection of these values is arbitrary within the constraints that (1) the head, peak, and tail of the distribution should be measured; (2) no further detail of the tail beyond the 80th percentile could be obtained from *all* 16 distributions in common, since Subject k had 20% of her interresponse times greater than 660 msec; and (3) no further detail of the shape of the peak of the distribution could be obtained from *all* 16 because Subject i had 32% of her interresponse times within the range of 120-150 msec. Linear interpolation was used to estimate these seven percentiles for the 16 distributions. Figure 7.3 shows the "profiles" produced in this way for six of the distributions: It is not possible to plot all 16 in the same figure without a great loss of clarity. Various features are striking. Most of the profiles do not intersect one another. The flatter ones at the bottom are for the faster typists (e.g., Subject j), with smaller gaps between percentiles. The steeper ones at the top are for the slower typists (e.g., Subject h), with larger gaps between percentiles. Contrasting profiles intersect in an informative way.

If distribution A is identical to distribution B *except* that B is delayed by a constant, then A and B will produce profiles that are parallel, displaced vertically by this constant amount; the distributions for Subjects d and g are nearly of this form. This suggests that their displacement from each other in Figure 7.2, parallel to the "family line," may be due in part to truncation, since the b_1 and b_2 measures were calculated for the truncated distributions. The fact that they are *both* displaced is no

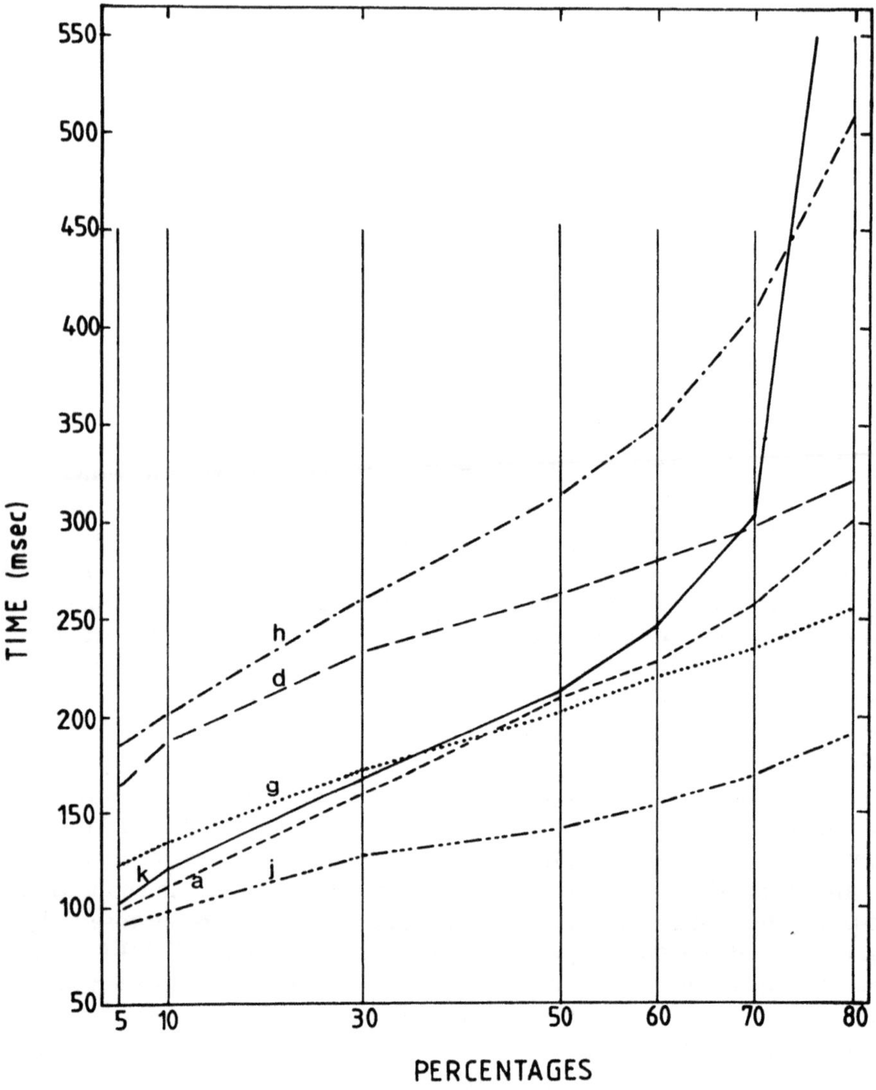

Fig. 7.3. Interresponse times at seven percentiles of six of the distributions characterizing individual differences.

doubt a reflection of the degree to which they share a resemblance that contrasts to some extent with the other distributions. On the other hand, look at Subjects a and k: they are virtually identical up to their 50th percentile at approximately 210 msec, but by the 80th percentile they are approximately 360 msec apart—truncation in the b_1, b_2 calculations has placed them close together in Figure 7.2. If distribution C differs from distribution D only by a scale change, so that each percentile of C is a constant multiple of the corresponding percentile of D (and if we assume that this constant is greater than 1), then the profile of C is the same shape as that of D except that the linear segments have a slope that differs by this same constant factor. Typists d and a are very approximately related in this way, for their higher percentiles, with a scale change of about 1.6.

In order to express the dimensions along which the profiles of Figure 7.3 differ, the method of principal component analysis was applied to the 16 sets of seven profile measures. The first two components were (arbitrarily) selected as an alternative two-dimensional representation of the space in which such interresponse times lie. These two components accounted for 99.2% of the total variance (83.8% and 15.4% individually). The method of calculating these components for any interresponse time distribution, relative to the present set of 16 distributions, is given below.

Figure 7.4 shows how the 16 distributions lie in relation to one another in the space of the first two principal components. This figure corresponds to the perpendicular projection of the 16 profiles on the empirically defined plane, through the mean profile of the 16, with axes given by these two principal components. The scaling of these axes has been standardized so that the standard deviations of both the first and second principal component scores for the 16 distributions are equal to 1; these scores are uncorrelated, by definition of the method of principal component analysis.

Table 7.1 gives the mean profile and the two sets of weights and the scaling factors needed to project any empirical profile into this profile-analysis plane: From each percentile, subtract the corresponding mean percentile of the 16 distributions and multiply by the appropriate weight from the first set of weights; add these seven products and then divide by the scaling factor of the first principal component. This yields the first profile-analysis coordinate. The second coordinate is produced in the same way by using the second set of weights and their scaling factor. This method allows one to locate any interresponse time distribution in a plane that represents the two maximal orthogonal contrasts that exist between the 16 profiles. In subsequent sections, we will see how distributions of other data look in relation to this reference set.

Table 7.1 indicates that the first component has all its weight positive, increasing with percentile. This reflects variously the fact that all the percentiles tend to be positively correlated, and that there is greater variation among the higher percentiles than among the lower ones. As such this component is also highly correlated with speed and represents a generalized weighted average interresponse time. The second component, by contrast, has all the first six weights positive and approximately equal, and has a larger negative weight for the 80th percentile. Thus, a distribution will score low on its second profile-analysis component if the mean of its first six percentiles is lower than average and/or its 80th percentile is higher than average; conversely for a high

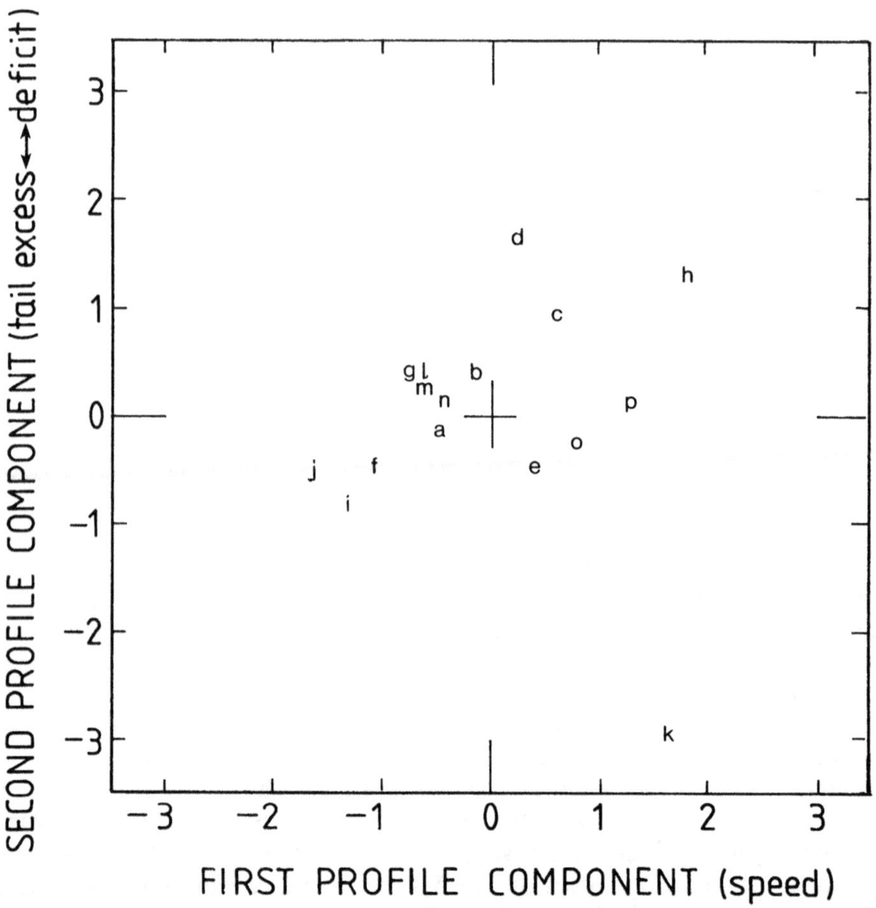

Fig. 7.4. Graph of the first two (standardized) principal components of the interresponse time distributions characterizing individual differences.

Table 7.1. Mean Profile, Weights, and Scaling Factors for Profile Analysis

	Percentile							Scaling factor
	5th	10th	30th	50th	60th	70th	80th	
Average profile (in msec)	126.7	140.4	180.8	217.9	239.7	273.0	353.9	—
First-component weights	.128	.148	.205	.253	.296	.400	.779	144.48
Second-component weights	.286	.317	.363	.355	.350	.284	−.597	61.95

Note. Presented are the average profile at seven percentiles of the 16 interresponse time distributions characterizing individual differences, together with the weight vectors derived for the first two principal components in the profile space of the 16 individual distributions and the scaling factors to normalize the components of their projections into the profile-analysis plane of these two principal components.

score on this component, a distribution must have the first six percentiles higher than average and/or its 80th percentile lower than average.

Thus the second component expresses a contrast between the central portion and the tail of the distribution. Low second component means "excess tail" for a given rate of faster responses, and high second component means "deficit of tail" for a given rate of faster responses. The fact that the distribution for Subject k is particularly indicated as having an excess of tail may mean that Subject k's presence in the sample has to some extent emphasized this form of the second profile-analysis component.

Summary

Mixture methods and parametric methods both failed to produce an adequate characterization of the interresponse time distributions. Two methods succeeded, however, thus confirming the initial impression of visual similarity among the distributions. Summary statistics suggested that similarities are characterized by a dimension relating the peak of the distribution (as expressed by kurtosis) to the tail (as expressed by skewness). The fastest typist, j, compared to the slowest typist, h, has a more peaked distribution and a tail that, although smaller in absolute terms, is more pronounced. The differences among individuals in terms of performance are characterized by locations along the dimension. Profile analysis, on the other hand, suggested that the similarities between distributions can be captured by two components. The first component was associated generally with speed, for example, Typist j fast and Typist h slow; the second component was associated with a relative deficit or excess in the tail of the distribution, for example, Typist d exhibiting a deficit and Typist k an excess. The two methods suggest a different emphasis. Summary statistics emphasize the linear relations within the space defined by the two parameters. Profile analysis emphasizes the dispersion of the data within the space defined by the two components. Together, however, they emphasize the relations among the speed of typing, the peak of interresponse time distribution, and the tail.

Given the restricted nature of the data, it is not possible to relate the detailed aspects of the characterizations directly to the typing activity itself. It is possible, however, to hypothesize generally concerning those relations. We might assume, for example, that the peak of the distribution contains, in the main, fluent responses, and the tail, again in the main, nonfluent ones. Fluent responses are finger movements that are made normally, unassociated with any discontinuity or interruption, and at a speed related to level of typing skill. Nonfluent responses are finger movements that are not made normally, for a number of different reasons. These may be unrelated to the activity of typing—for example, distraction from the immediate environment. They may also be occasioned by external processes required in the exercise of the skill, for example, fixating the keyboard to locate an unfamiliar key, or checking the typed copy for errors (Long, 1976a). They may also result from internal processes that have been executed with only partial success—for example, an initial failure to remember the location of a normally familiar key.

In all cases an unusually long interresponse time results. This notion of fluency captures in a more restricted form the extremes of continuity and discontinuity exemplified respectively, by the champion touch typist and the hunt-and-peck typist referred to earlier. Fluency increases with skill (as indexed here by the speed of performance) and can be used to interpret the characterizations of the interresponse time distributions at the level of the typing activity itself. Increased fluency seems to involve three aspects, as exemplified by the differences between the highly skilled Typist j and the less skilled Typist h. First, as skill increases, interresponse time decreases for both fluent and nonfluent responses. Second, increased skill is associated with a reduction in the number of nonfluent responses. Third, for the highly skilled typist, there is less absolute difference between fluent fast and fluent slow interresponse times. The distribution becomes more peaked; the fluent responses are more similar in terms of speed. This suggests that skill consists in generally speeding up all responses, whether fluent or not; in speeding up particularly already fluent responses (although not apparently all by the same amount); and in reducing the absolute number of nonfluent responses.

In terms of the typing activity itself, these changes in skill can be variously interpreted. It would appear that finger movements are generally becoming faster, whether or not they are associated with discontinuities in performance (as reflected in long interresponse times). Whatever the causes of discontinuity, recovery is quicker. Finger movements unassociated with discontinuities of performance, however, do not become faster by the same amount. Perhaps some movements, such as repeated responses or interhand responses, are initially fast, thus leaving less scope for increases in speed. Alternatively, at higher levels of skill, physical constraints such as finger strength may be a more important limitation on performance, and this limitation will have differential effects on movements. Lastly, discontinuities in performance decrease with increased skill, whether they are occasioned by the need to reference the hand to the keyboard, or by the need to type unfamiliar characters with the aid of vision, or by some other need. It is as if the skill involves a (differential) increase in the efficiency with which finger movements attain their targets, plus an improvement in the coordination and control that both makes touch typing possible and offsets discontinuities in performance. Individual differences in typing appear to consist of the differential contribution of these two aspects of finger movement and control.

Characterizing Skill Acquisition

Method

It is tempting to think of the difference in the speed of performance between individual typists as illustrated by the interresponse time distributions of Figure 7.1 only in terms of the acquisition of typing skill. Following this line of thought, summary statistics (Figure 7.2) and profile analysis (Figure 7.4) both offer a characterization of individual differences in which Subject j would be considered to have acquired the highest level of typing skill and Subject h the lowest level. By implication, were Typist h to become as skilled as Typist j, she might be expected to pass successively through the locations in the (b_1, b_2) plane and the profile plane occupied by the other subjects (excluding the less typical locations occupied by Subjects d and g in Figure 7.2 and by Subject k in Figure 7.4). However, the temptation to equate performance and level of skill must be rejected. An increase in skill will improve performance, but the improvement represents a relatively permanent change (Walker, 1967). An increase in motivation will also improve performance, but the improvement will be transient (Fitts & Posner, 1967). Hence, some of Subject j's superiority over Subject h may have been due to motivational factors. Further, task factors may also have affected performance—for example, the general conditions under which the experiment was run, including the particular electronic keyboard used (which may have been more familiar to some subjects than to others). It may be that acquisition, motivation, and task factors affect performance similarly in terms of the two characterizations offered. Alternatively, the three types of factor may affect performance differently, and the characterizations themselves may be some product of the differences. The data presented so far do not permit the two possibilities to be distinguished.

It was thus decided to apply the two techniques that had been successfully used to characterize the differences between individuals at the same point in time to the acquisition of skill by the same typist at different points in time. In this way, it was hoped to minimize motivational and task factors. Such factors cannot be entirely eliminated, but they were expected to be subsidiary to the overall pattern of skill change. Further, rather than test a few typists over a small number of sessions, it was decided to test a single typist over a large number of sessions. This was to maximize the changes in the interresponse time distributions, thereby affording the techniques more scope.

The subject (MG) was 18 years old when first tested and had recently enrolled in a secretarial and commercial course at a technical college. Over a period of 9 months, MG was tested 20 times at approximately fornightly intervals. She had about 25 hours of typing practice prior to her first test and 250 hours over the period of testing, including the experimental sessions. MG was a member of the MRC Applied Psychology Unit panel and was paid for her participation.

The material typed consisted of the same texts used in the experiment reported earlier. The apparatus was also the same, in terms of both the keyboard and the recording of responses. The only difference concerned the time beyond which keystrokes were not classified individually—650 msec in the previous experiment, 1,400 msec here. The data, however, have been truncated at 670 msec to bring them into line with the earlier set.

Each session began with a practice period. MG then typed three texts with a rest between each. The texts were 2,000 characters long. She was instructed to type as fast as possible while not making more than 1% errors. The mean percentage of errors per session ranged from .10 to 1.10, with a mean of .71. There was no trend in the error scores over the period of testing. The sessions lasted about 2 hours initially but decreased somewhat as the speed of typing increased. The interresponse time distributions are shown in Figure 7.5. For reasons of space, only the data from the second text typed at each session have been shown. The analysis and conclusions, however, hold for all the texts typed.

Characterization

Examination by eye of the 20 distributions shows them to be remarkably similar, particularly from the fourth session onward. Seventeen distributions have a single peak, sessions 1-3 providing the (very marginal) exceptions. All 20 distributions are right skewed and have a positively accelerating leading edge and a negatively accelerating trailing edge. All interresponse times become faster, the truncated means decreasing over the sessions from 477 msec to 286 msec. At the same time, the peak of the distribution becomes more pronounced and the tail in absolute terms contains fewer interresponse times.

Summary statistics. The b_1 and b_2 statistics for the 20 distributions are plotted against each other in Figure 7.6. By inspection, they all fall on or near the same line in the (b_1, b_2) plane. The position on this line is not perfectly correlated with speed or session, but in general, as speed increases over sessions, the position of the distributions moves down the line, kurtosis and skewness increasing together.

Profile analysis. For the 20 distributions, the values of the first and second components were calculated, normalized with respect to the data of the 16 typists reported earlier. The two components are shown plotted against each other in Figure 7.7. In terms of the first component, as might be expected, the data points generally move from right to left, indicating increasing speed with increased practice. In terms of

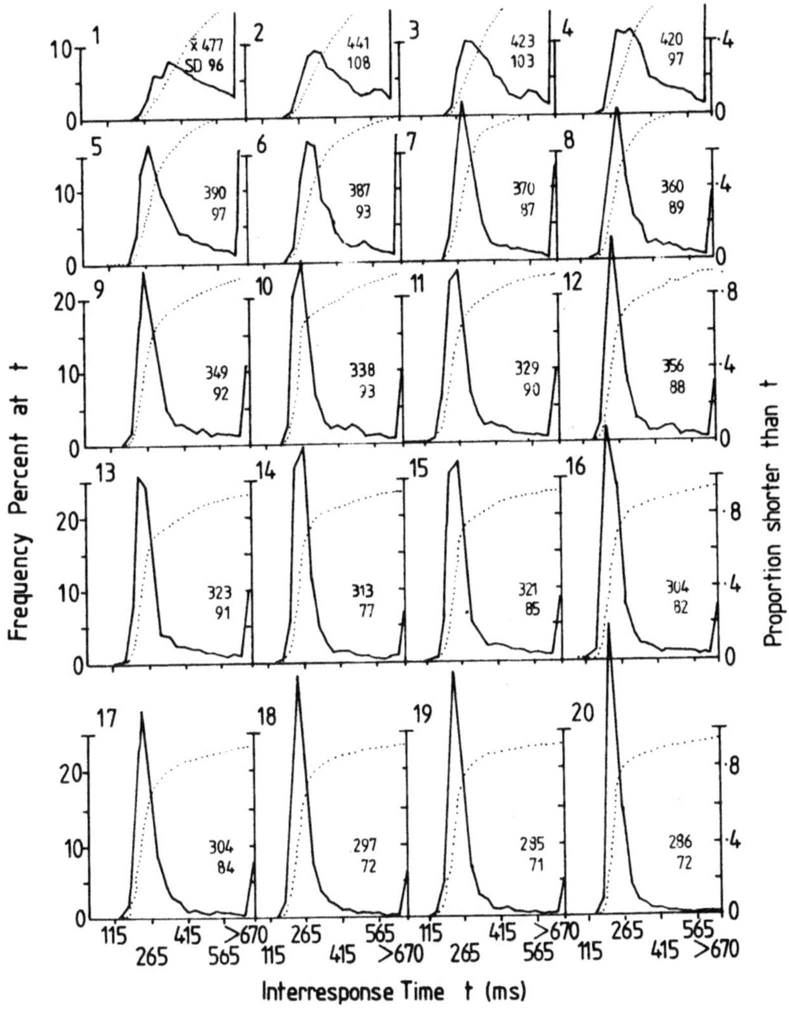

Fig. 7.5. Interresponse time distributions characterizing skill acquisition, shown as frequency polygons and as cumulative frequency curves.

the second component, there appears to be an approximately linear reduction in the deficit associated with the tail of the distribution over the first 10 sessions, with little systematic change thereafter.

Summary

The two methods that successfully characterized the individual differences among typists were also successful in characterizing the improved performance associated with a single typist learning to type. MG's distributions, particularly over the later sessions, contained very pronounced peaks and appeared similar to those of Typists i and j. In terms

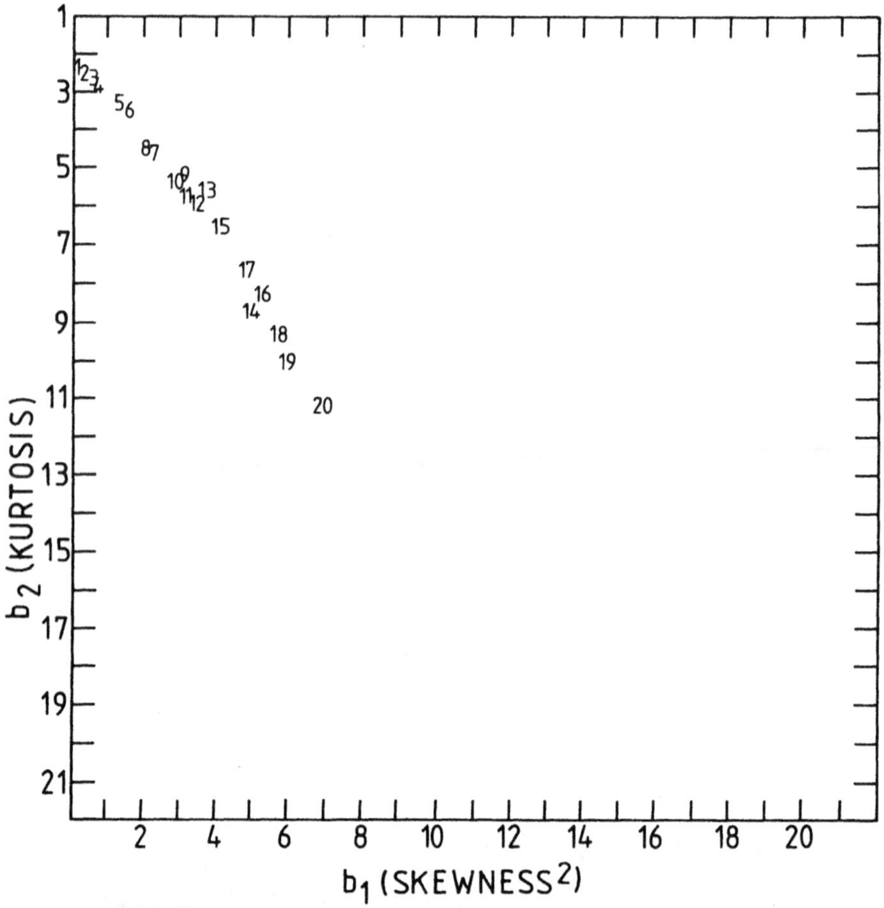

Fig. 7.6. Graph of b_1 (skewness^2) against b_2 (kurtosis) of the interresponse time distributions characterizing skill acquisition.

of summary statistics, MG's line in the (b_1, b_2) plane was essentially the same as that projected for the 16 typists. By session 5, MG occupied a location almost identical to that of Typist h (the slowest typist), although Subject h was the faster of the two (a mean interresponse time of 317 vs. 390 msec). By session 20, MG occupied a location midway between Typists i and j (although still very much slower, with a mean interresponse time of 286 msec vs. 174 and 159, respectively), having passed through or near the positions occupied by the remaining typists (with the exception of Typists d and g). In terms of profile analysis, it took MG 10 sessions to approximate the slowest typist's (Typist h) position on the first component. By session 20, MG occupied a position midway between Typists b and d, still somewhat slower than the average of the group. Overall, MG's final distributions were most like those of Typist d, showing by the second component a relative deficit in the tail of the distribution.

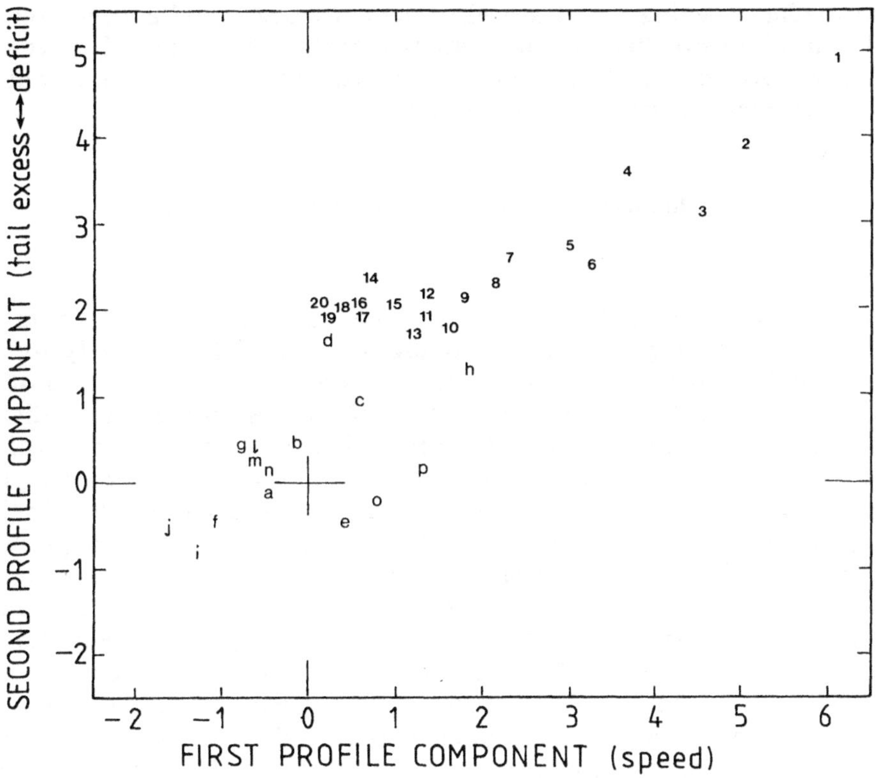

Fig. 7.7. Graph of the first two principal components of the interresponse time distributions characterizing skill acquisition in the profile-analysis plane of the initial 16 subjects, together with those of 15 of the subjects from Fig. 7.4.

In comparison with the 16 typists, MG's acquisition of the skill of typing was far from complete. Nevertheless, both methods of characterization indicate that during the course of acquisition, MG passed through locations in the respective planes occupied by other typists. Since progression in the (b_1, b_2) plane with respect to speed was similar for both the 16 typists and for the learning data of MG, it is reasonable to accept the characterization of individual differences presented earlier in terms of the acquisition of typing skill. The same supposition can be made on the basis of profile analysis, provided that no assumption is made as to the generality of MG's progression through the space represented by the two components, since they are orthogonal. Thus, applying the methods to the acquisition data of MG both increases their scope of successful application and provides converging evidence that they are essentially characterizing the skill of performance rather than any other aspects. The interpretation of the characterization of skill offered earlier in terms of fluency can therefore be retained. In line with the individual differences data, it appears that as a typist becomes more skilled, there is a general speeding up of all responses, both fluent and nonfluent; a particular speeding up of already fluent responses; and a reduction in the absolute number of nonfluent responses. The increased speed of finger movements and the context of control and coordination in which they are effected are developed together.

Characterizing the Effect of a Task Variable

Method

As indicated earlier, typing performance may change as a function of differences among individuals, among levels of skill, among types of task, and among levels of motivation. Summary statistics and profile analysis successfully characterized the differences both among individual typists and among levels of typing skill attained by the same typist. It was decided to extend further the scope of the techniques by applying them to characterizing the effects on performance of changes in the typing task. Skill is not only a matter of fast performance; it presupposes an ability to be flexible and to type successfully over a broad range of conditions. It was therefore considered appropriate to characterize skilled performance as a function of changing task conditions.

The data were taken from an experiment reported earlier by Long (1976a), in which 12 subjects typed with and without sight of the keyboard. In the latter condition, the keyboard and the typist's hands were concealed by means of a shaped aluminum mask. The experiment was concerned with the role of visual feedback in skilled typing. Although it is often assumed that skilled typists never consult the keyboard during typing, a pilot study showed that consulting the keyboard during transcription constituted part of normal typing activity and that the frequency of consultation was a function of specific task demands (e.g., creating own vs. machine right-hand margin; typing alphanumeric vs. alphabetic only material). Masking the keyboard produced more errors —particularly substitution errors—due most likely to a combination of "drift," that is, in referencing of the hand to the keyboard, such that keys adjacent to the correct ones were struck, and of an inability to locate some keys—especially control keys such as the carriage return and line feed—without the aid of vision. Masking the keyboard also caused typists to slow down, which is the performance change to be characterized.

The data presented here are taken from Experiment 2, in which (unlike the previous experiments) there was no requirement to correct errors. The two conditions were termed *normal* (the control condition) and *keyboard masked*. The material and the apparatus were the same as for the two data sets reported earlier. The cutoff for the individually classified interresponse times was 1000 msec. They are truncated here at 650 msec to bring them into line with the data already presented.

Further details are to be found in Long (1976a). The interresponse time distributions are shown in Figure 7.8.

Examination of the 24 distributions shows them to be very similar, both to one another and to the distributions of the 16 typists and of MG (Figures 7.1 and 7.5, respectively). The similarity holds for both the control condition and the experimental condition: 21 of the distributions have a single peak (2—A and D—have bimodal peaks in the control condition, and 1—D— has a bimodal peak in the experimental condition); all the distributions are right skewed; 22 have a positively accelerating leading edge (exceptions are D and F, both in the control condition); and all have a negatively accelerating trailing edge. It should be noted that although all typists were slower with the keyboard masked on the basis of the complete data (mean interresponse time 335 vs. 260 msec), only 7 were slower on the basis of the truncated distributions (239 vs. 231 msec). In terms of the latter data, some typists (B and E)

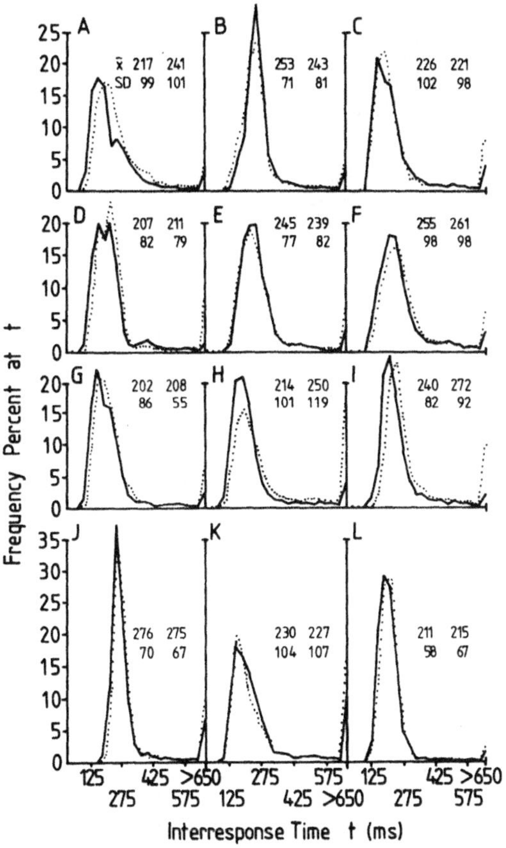

Fig. 7.8. Interresponse time distributions characterizing the effect of a task variable, shown as frequency polygons and as cumulative frequency curves (solid line, with sight of the keyboard; dotted line, without sight of the keyboard).

actually keyed marginally faster with the keyboard masked, some (J and K) changed their speed hardly at all, and some (A, H, and I) slowed down quite considerably.

Summary statistics. The b_1 and b_2 statistics for the 24 distributions are plotted against one another in Figure 7.9. By inspection, they all fall on or near the same line in the (b_1, b_2) plane, although there may be more spread in the data than for the equivalent plots for the 16 typists and MG. If the best fitting line from the latter two sets of data is superimposed on Figure 7.9, the points of a number of typists fall below

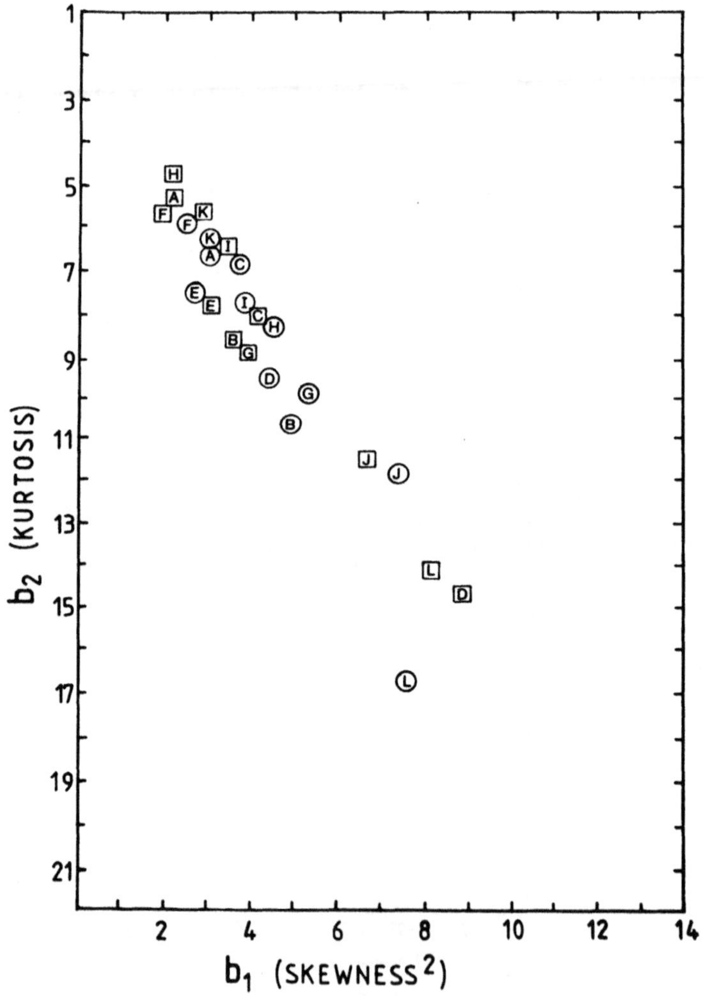

Fig. 7.9. Graph of b_1 (skewness^2) against b_2 (kurtosis) of the interresponse time distributions characterizing the effect of a task variable. Circles denote typists able to see keyboard, squares those with masked keyboards.

the line for both the control and the experimental conditions (e.g., B, D, and G). As regards the effect of the experimental manipulation, some typists' data points remain stationary in the space (e.g., E and F). This is not surprising, since they also show little change in truncated mean interresponse time. Of the remainder, all except L move up or down the line when the keyboard is masked, although some (J and K) move but little. Most move up the line (A, B, G, H, I, J, and K), as would be expected from the fact that masking the keyboard slowed performance and from the direction of movement exhibited both by the slower of the 16 typists and by the earlier sessions of MG. Of the typists whose data points move up the line, A, H, and I all slow down by a nontrivial amount and clearly move up the line in the (b_1, b_2) plane. Both remaining typists (C and D) move in the opposite direction, that is, down the (b_1, b_2) line, although their change in mean interresponse time is marginal (5 and 4 msec, respectively).

Profile analysis. The first and second profile components for the 24 distributions were calculated and are plotted in Figure 7.10, normalized with respect to the data of the 16 typists. In terms of the first component, typists' locations in the space generally move to the right when the keyboard is masked (A, D, E, F, G, H, I, and K), although some (B, C, J, and L) change very little. In terms of the second component, typists are split evenly in the direction of movement occasioned by the masking of the keyboard. Four typists (A, D, G, and I) move upward, exhibiting an increase in the relative deficit associated with the tail of their distribution; four (C, F, J, and L) remain stationary; and four (B, E, H, and K) move downward, exhibiting an increase in the excess of their distributions' tail. Even if the magnitude of the decrease in performance under keyboard masked conditions is taken into account, there is still considerable variety in the direction of the movement associated with the second component. For example, of the six typists showing the largest decrease, three (D, G, and I) move upward and three (E, H, and K) move downward. Of the six showing the smallest decrease, one (A) moves upward, one (B) moves downward, and four (C, F, J, and L) remain stationary.

Summary

Just as for the individual differences and for the acquisition of skill, both statistical methods together successfully characterized performance under conditions designed to evaluate a task variable—in this case the sight of the keyboard. Masking the keyboard slowed down performance considerably, although the major decrement seems to be reflected in the tail of the distribution beyond the point where the interresponse times were truncated, as if already nonfluent responses were made even less fluent. Because much of the decrement in performance was not

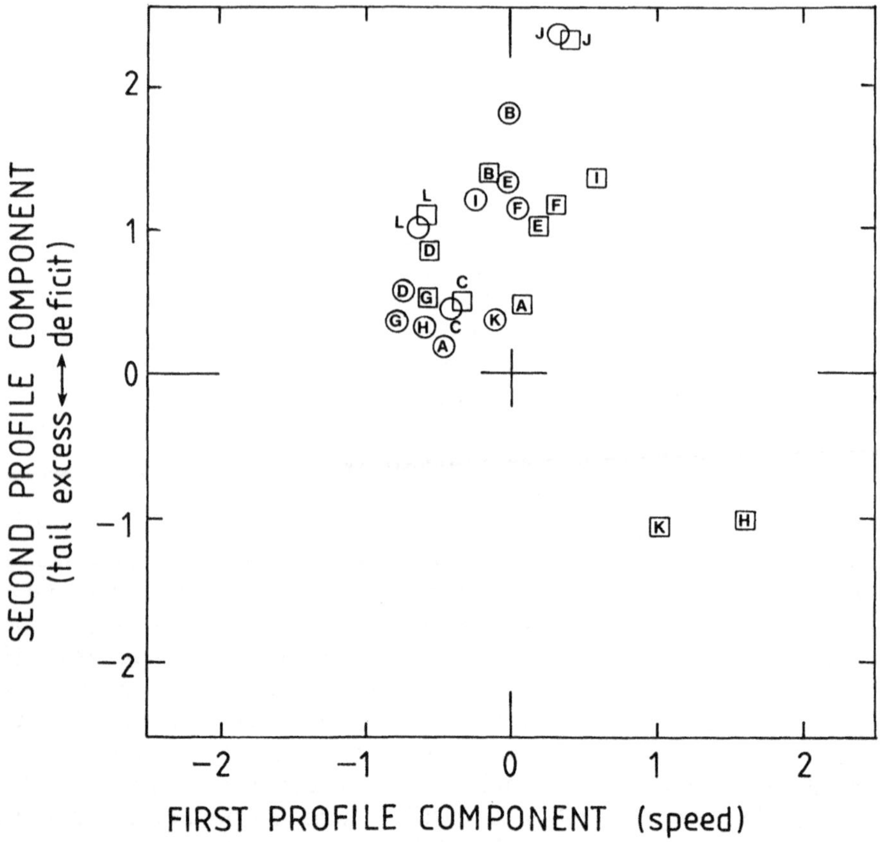

Fig. 7.10. Graph of the first two principal components of the interresponse time distributions characterizing the effect of the task variable in the profile-analysis plane of the initial 16 subjects. Circles denote typists able to see the keyboard, squares those with masked keyboards.

reflected in the truncated response times, effectively limiting any movement in the (b_1, b_2) plane, and because the direction of movement along the line was not obviously consistent over typists, it is unclear how well summary statistics characterized the *change* in performance effected by the task variable. It may be, however, that consistency of directional change over typists is a misguided assumption with respect to performance decrements under changed task conditions. The different task conditions may lead typists to the recruitment of different strategies to effect an intentional slowing down of performance. Alternatively, typists may react more passively to task changes, recovering as best they can from the extra difficulties imposed on them—locating an already unfamiliar key, for example, without sight of the keyboard. In either case, summary statistics may be successfully characterizing some very important aspects of performance change.

This line of thinking is encouraged by the directional inconsistency over typists, demonstrated by the second component of profile analysis, although the meaning of the inconsistency is not the same for both methods. That the analysis is not based on truncated data further supports the view. At the very least, one must seriously entertain the possibility that directional inconsistency over subjects, in the case of both summary statistics and profile analysis, indicates differential effects of changes in task variables or different strategies for effecting changes in speed. In terms of fluency, for example, slowing down might involve the reverse changes exhibited by the difference between fast and slow typists from the group of 16 and by the initial and final sessions of MG. All interresponse times may be slowed (although not necessarily by the same amount), with an increase in nonfluent responses and an increase in the absolute difference between fluent fast responses and fluent slow ones, which would occasion a movement *up* the line in the (b_1, b_2) plane. Alternatively, fluent fast responses may be slowed with no change in fluent slow responses or in the number of nonfluent responses, which would occasion a movement *down* the line in the (b_1, b_2) plane. Appropriate variations in the overall interresponse times, the number of fluent and nonfluent responses, and the relative similarity of fluent fast and fluent slow responses would analogously produce movements in opposite directions along the second component of profile analysis.

Characterizing the Effect of a Motivational Variable

Method

Motivation has been shown to affect performance. Typically performance is improved by the provision of appropriate feedback either during performance or following performance in the form of knowledge of results (Annett, 1969). The effect is assumed to derive in part from the establishment by the subject of an appropriate standard for performance, based on the information provided by the feedback (Fitts & Posner, 1967). The standard expected for performance can also be varied by instructions to the subject. Even if subjects trade speed for errors (Pew, 1969), instructions can be considered to affect a subject's motivation in terms of an intention to attain a certain standard with respect to the major parameters of skilled performance—speed and accuracy. The following experiment was therefore set up to evaluate how well summary statistics and profile analysis were able to characterize changes in performance resulting from instructions intended to manipulate the typist's motivation. Voluntary changes in speed were also intended to be contrasted with the previous data sets presented. Changes in performance due to skill acquisition are not voluntary in this sense. Changes due to task variables may be voluntary—that is, under the typist's direct control. Changes brought about by instructions are voluntary, since the change is under the typist's control. Hence, the changes in performance may differ from those considered earlier. The experiment had a further aim, which is detailed in the next section.

The subjects were six female touch typists, aged between early twenties and middle forties. Their level of typing activity varied, with only one being a full-time typist. The materials were three texts adapted from a typing course from Scheidegger (1969). The nature and purpose of the changes will be made clear in the next section. Only two of the three texts concern us here (the third will be discussed in the next section). The first 2,500 characters typed by the typist were recorded.

Subjects typed at a Lynwood DAD-2 visual-display unit (VDU) keyboard, and interresponse times were recorded by a CED LSI-2 processor. The material to be typed and the typists' output both appeared on VDU screens. The typists were not required to format their output or to correct errors. The first text was typed at normal speed. For the second text, the typists were instructed to increase their speed, although specific instructions about the amount of increase were not given. They were told that a small increase in errors would be acceptable (mean errors increased from 1.56% to 2.97%). They were given a 300-character practice text before the second text, so that both experimenter and subject could be satisfied that an increase had taken place. In order to obtain an accurate estimate of "normal" typing speed, experimental conditions were not counterbalanced for order. Warm-up and learning effects may therefore be confounded with voluntary changes of speed. However, previous research indicates few within-session changes due to these factors (Long, 1976a).

Figure 7.11 shows the interresponse time distributions for each typist in each condition, together with the means and standard deviations (calculated on times truncated at 660 msec). The means for all typists are faster in the increased speed condition, showing that typists can voluntarily increase their speed if desired (the mean interresponse time, averaged across subjects, moved from 187 to 165 msec). It can also be seen that the distributions in the fast condition generally have a peak that is higher and occurs sooner.

Characterization

Examination by eye of the 12 distributions shows them to be similar both to all the earlier data sets and among themselves. Eleven distributions have a single peak (the exception is Typist 3 in the fast condition); all distributions are right skewed; 11 have a positively accelerating leading edge (Typist 6 in the normal condition is the exception); and all distributions have a negatively accelerating trailing edge.

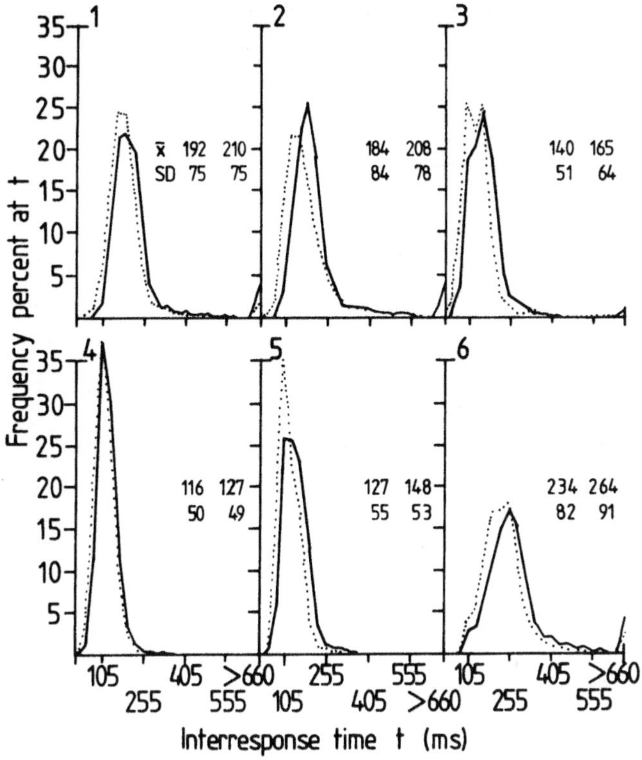

Fig. 7.11. Interresponse time distributions characterizing the effect of a voluntary change in speed, shown as frequency polygons and cumulative frequency curves (solid line, normal speed; dotted line, fast speed).

Summary statistics. The b_1 and b_2 statistics for the 12 distributions are plotted against each other in Figure 7.12. By inspection, they all fall on or near the same line in the (b_1, b_2) plane. The extreme values from the earlier data sets can be projected onto the same line (*h* and *j* from the 16 typists; sessions 1 and 20 from MG; Typists H and D from the task variable data). Hence, the characterization is successful. However, the directional inconsistency noted in the task variable data set is also apparent here. Typists 1, 4, 5, and 6 move down the line as their speed increases, consistent with the movement from slow to fast typists in the group of 16 and from the earlier to later sessions of MG. Typists 2 and 3, however, move up the line. The directional inconsistency results neither from marginal changes in the (b_1, b_2) plane nor from marginal changes in speed, since Typists 2 and 3 speeded up their performance by somewhat more than the average.

Profile analysis. The normalized first and second components for the 12 distributions were calculated and are shown plotted against each other in Figure 7.13. In terms of the first component, and in line with

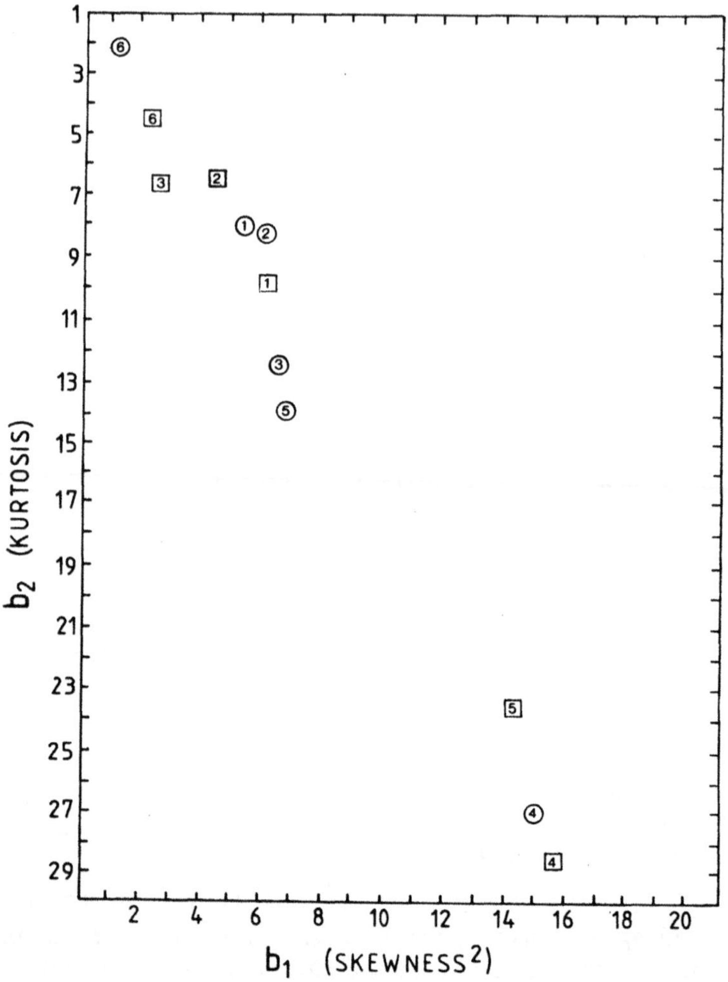

Fig. 7.12. Graph of b_1 (skewness^2) against b_2 (kurtosis) of the interresponse time distributions characterizing the effect of a voluntary change in speed. Circles denote normal speed, squares fast speed.

all the data presented so far, faster typing is reflected in a move to the left by the data points of all six typists. In terms of the second component, all typists show a downward movement in the faster condition, indicating a relative excess in the tails of the distributions. Directional consistency of movement, therefore, holds on both components and for all subjects. Further, all the data points fall on or near the same line in the component space. Unlike summary statistics, this suggests that subjects act similarly under conditions requiring an increase in the speed of performance.

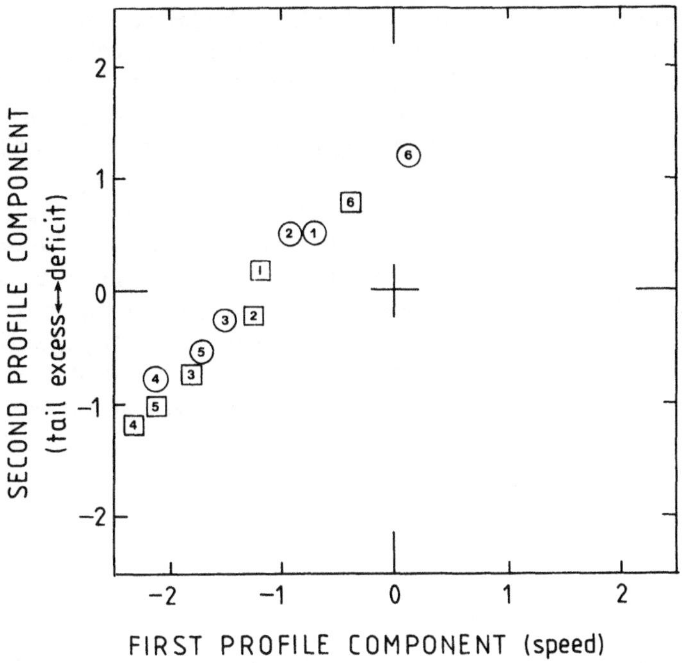

Fig. 7.13. Graph of the first two principal components of the interresponse time distributions characterizing the effect of a voluntary change in speed in the profile-analysis plane of the initial 16 subjects. Circles denote normal speed, squares fast speed.

Summary

Both methods again successfully characterized typing performance, as with earlier data. They also characterized successfully the differences in performance for the same typists during the same session, differences occasioned by instructions to increase the speed of typing. The methods, however, suggest different interpretations of the changes in speed. Summary statistics indicate directional inconsistency of movements in the (b_1, b_2) plane over typists, suggesting, as does the task variable data, that typists may recruit different strategies to effect changes in speed or may more passively react differentially to the consequences of typing faster. As an example of strategies, typists might speed up only slow fluent responses or only fast fluent responses, while leaving the number of nonfluent responses unchanged. The former strategy would produce a movement down the (b_1, b_2) line; the latter a movement up the line. As an example of passive reactions, typists might speed up fluent responses by a constant and either change some nonfluent responses into fluent ones, by reducing the frequency of checking the keyboard or the copy, or accept that some excessively fast fluent responses may be changed into nonfluent ones. Again, the former reaction would produce a movement down the (b_1, b_2) line, the latter a movement up the line. On the other hand, profile analysis suggests directional consistency with changes of speed and along the same line in the component space. The reason for the difference between the two methods is unclear at this time. It may be related to the truncation of the data, but this seems unlikely, since as indicated earlier, truncation usually produces consistency of directional movement in the (b_1, b_2) plane. Alternatively, summary statistics may be more sensitive to changes in the peak of the distribution, whereas profile analysis may be more sensitive to changes in the tail. If this were so, the method suggesting directional consistency would vary with the particular nature of the changes that occurred. In the present case, the changes would be associated with differences in the peaks of the distributions of Typists 2 and 3 rather than in the tails.

Bringing Fluency Under Experimental Control

Method

The fluency of skilled typing has been a continuing theme of this chapter. It has served to interpret the characterization derived from the distributional data. As such, it constitutes a major characteristic of the skill. For the purposes of interpretation, we have proposed that fluent responses be generally associated with the peak of the interresponse time distribution and nonfluent responses with the tail. However, none of the experiments reported here, so far, have attempted to manipulate fluency explicitly in terms of the relationship of the peak of the distribution to the tail. If the notion of fluency is to be developed further, it is necessary to bring it under experimental control. This was the aim of the next experiment.

Bringing fluency under experimental control is not straightforward, because it is difficult to define operationally. It is tempting to define fluent responses as those appearing in the peak of the distribution. However, some nonfluent responses may also appear in the peak. For example, a marginally deviant finger movement may slow down a fast transition between letters, making it nonfluent, but not enough to move it from the peak of the distribution to the tail, only from the early part of the peak to the later part. A more promising approach is to define nonfluent responses as those appearing in the tail. If they are slow enough to appear in the tail, it is implausible that they have been executed normally. Nonfluent responses, however, have more than one origin. For example, some may be due to distraction, others to a partial failure of memory. A single experimental manipulation would be unlikely to affect both. However, previous research suggests that one important origin of nonfluent responses is the need to consult the keyboard and the copy (Long, 1976a). The copy may be consulted to confirm a suspected error, or more generally to control the quality of the typed output. The keyboard may be consulted to re-reference the hands, or to locate by sight unfamiliar or less familiar keys. Such consultations appear to be a routine part even of skilled typing activity.

It was decided, therefore, to manipulate fluency, in terms of the nonfluent responses (defined operationally as those appearing in the tail of the distribution), by varying the need for consulting the keyboard and the copy. This was done by varying the difficulty of the source material, where difficulty was defined by the relative contribution of alphabetic characters versus numeric and punctuation characters to the material to be typed. It was also necessary to measure interresponse times occurring during fixation of the source material (termed *source-on* responses) separately from interresponse times occurring during fixations other than of the source material (termed *source-off* responses). Certainly, some fluent responses would be expected to occur during consultation of the keyboard (e.g., the typing of the familiar characters making up a word between the unfamiliar quotation marks surrounding them), and some nonfluent responses would be expected during consultation of the material to be typed (e.g., momentary losses of the location in the text). However, the increase in nonfluent responses resulting from the increase in the nonalphabetic characters would be expected to occur outside consultation of the source text. The manipulation, therefore, would be expected to reduce the number of source-on responses, while increasing the number of source-off responses appearing in the tail of the distribution—independently of any effect it might have on the peak or the relation of the peak to the tail.

This experiment was run at the same session as the previous one, and both therefore share the same subjects and equipment. Based on Scheidegger (1969), three texts were constructed, each of which existed in two versions—easy and difficult. The easy versions consisted solely of alphabetic characters, commas, and periods. The difficult versions included in addition a great deal more punctuation (e.g., hyphens, parentheses, semicolons, colons, single and double quotation marks) and some numeric characters. The three easy texts contained an average of 57 characters that were not lowercase letters or spaces, whereas the three difficult versions contained an average of 324 such characters. Each text was approximately 2,700 characters long, but only the first 2,500 characters typed were recorded. (Only easy versions of the texts were used in the previous experiment.)

In order for us to determine consultations, the subjects wore a headband attached to which was an ultrasonic (40 kHz) transmitter. Receivers were placed at the VDUs presenting the source material and the output copy, and these signals were input to the computer. Subjects each typed three texts. The two that concern us here are one easy and one difficult text (the third was an easy text typed at a faster speed and was discussed in the previous section). Mean errors for the easy text were 1.56% (range .36 to 2.68), and for the difficult text they were 1.95% (range .64 to 3.12).

Data

Figure 7.14 shows the frequency distributions of interresponse times for each subject in each condition, along with the means and standard deviations (calculated on data truncated at 660 msec). All subjects typed more slowly on the difficult texts, with the mean interresponse time, averaged over subjects, increasing from 187 to 216 msec. Examination of the distributions shows that in each case the difficult text produces a smaller peak and a thicker tail. In order to establish that the tail does in fact contain more interresponse times, the percentile corre-

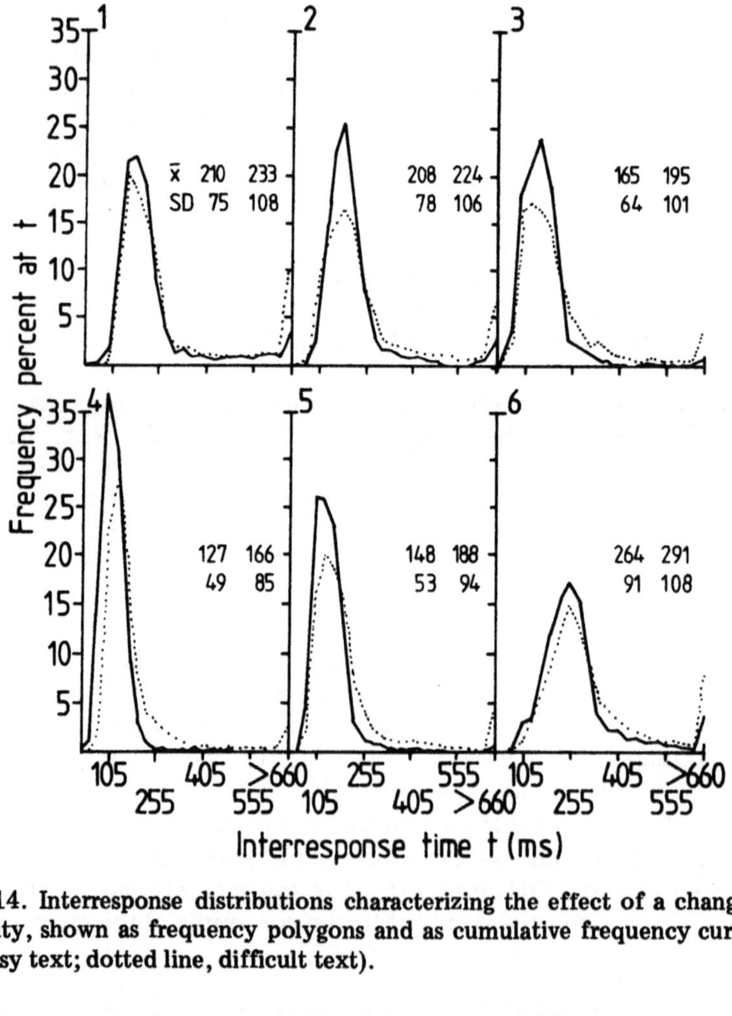

Fig. 7.14. Interresponse distributions characterizing the effect of a change in text difficulty, shown as frequency polygons and as cumulative frequency curves (solid line, easy text; dotted line, difficult text).

sponding to the time of the mean plus 1 standard deviation was established for each distribution. In all cases the percentiles for the difficult text distributions were lower than those for the easy texts, signifying the greater amount in the tail (mean percentile: easy, 89; difficult, 83). This was also true when the percentile for the mean plus 1.5 standard deviations was established (mean: easy 92; difficult, 86), and was true in four out of six cases for the mean plus .5 of a standard deviation (mean: easy, 79; difficult, 77). The manipulation has therefore increased the absolute size of the tail, that is nonfluent responses, as defined here.

Given an increase in nonfluent responses, we can now consider their origin. Figure 7.15 shows for easy and difficult texts the interresponse times occurring during fixation of the text to be typed (source on—except for the first interresponse time following a consultation elsewhere —which would be expected to be long, since the subjects have to find their place in the text again) and during fixation elsewhere (source off). The numbers of interresponse times have been summed over typists because individual subjects made very few responses during source off. The figure shows that the reduction in the peak and the increase in the tail for difficult texts illustrated by Figure 7.14 is associated with source-off distributions and not source-on ones. The tails of the source-on distributions are almost identical for easy and difficult texts. Thus, increasing the amount of nonalphabetic material to be typed increased the number of nonfluent responses as defined as those appearing in the

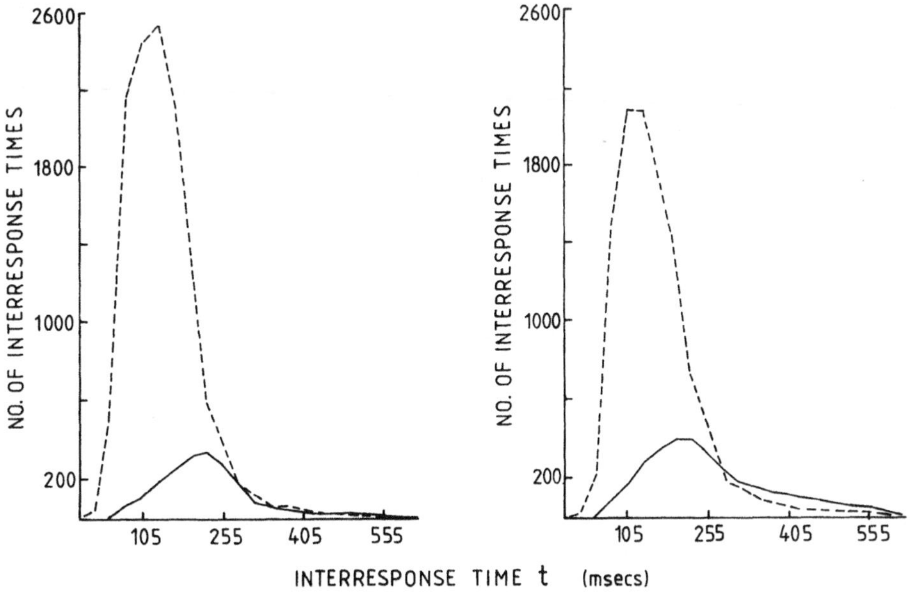

Fig. 7.15. Frequency distributions of source-on and source-off interresponse time characterizing the effect of a change in text difficulty, summed over six subjects (solid line, source off; broken line, source on; left, easy text; right, difficult text).

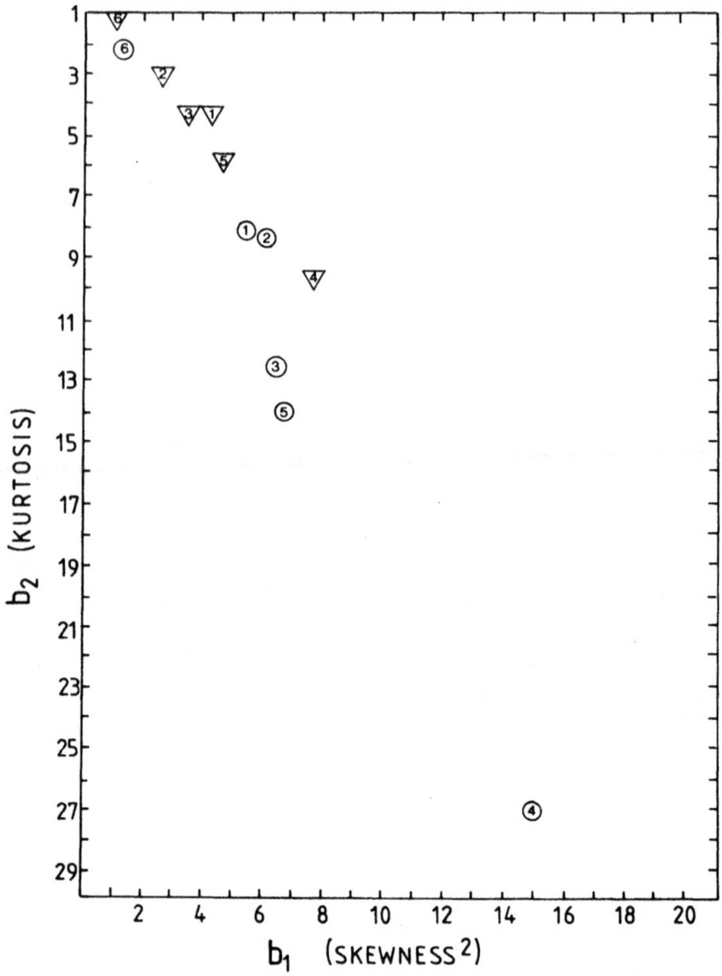

Fig. 7.16. Graph of b_1 (skewness^2) against b_2 (kurtosis) of the interresponse time distributions characterizing the effect of a change in text difficulty. Circles denote the easy text, inverted triangles the difficult text.

tail—responses that occurred while the typists looked either at the keyboard, the copy, or elsewhere.

Characterization

Further examination of the 12 distributions shows them to be similar to earlier data sets and to themselves. All distributions have a single peak; all are right skewed; 11 distributions have a positively accelerating leading edge (the exception is Typist 2 on the difficult text); and all distributions have a negatively accelerating trailing edge.

Summary statistics. The b_1 and b_2 statistics for the 12 distributions are plotted against each other in Figure 7.16. By inspection they all fall on or near the same line projected from the earlier data sets. In addition, there is a tendency for data points for the difficult texts to move downward, reflecting increased skewness values, as might be expected given the fatter tails. All six points associated with the difficult texts lie above a line drawn through the two highest easy distribution points, for Typists 2 and 6 (in the previous section all six fast distribution points fell below the same line). In terms of the direction of movement, all typists move up the line when typing the difficult text. None of the changes in speed and none of the movements along the (b_1, b_2) line (with the exception perhaps of Typist 6) were marginal.

Profile analysis. The normalized first and second components for the 12 distributions are plotted in Figure 7.17. In terms of the first component and in line with all data presented so far, slower typing of the difficult texts is reflected in a move to the right of the data points of all six typists. In terms of the second component, there is a downward movement associated with difficult texts for four typists (1, 2, 3, and 6), reflecting an excess in the tails of the distributions; and an upward movement for the remaining two typists (4 and 5), reflecting a deficit.

Summary

An increase in the difficulty of the text to be typed succeeded in increasing the number of interresponse times in the tail of the distribution, and in particular in the tail of the distribution associated with nonfixations of the source material. In terms of our operational definition, nonfluent responses were increased, thus bringing them under experimental control. The finding that their increase was associated with nonsource fixations can be interpreted as indicating that their origin was consultation of the keyboard to guide punctuation and numeric keypresses requiring vision for their execution.

Both methods successfully characterized typing performance as well as the differences in performance resulting from the two levels of text difficulty. In contrast to the previous data set, which characterized voluntary changes of speed, summary statistics here indicates directional consistency of movements in the (b_1, b_2) plane, whereas profile analysis indicates inconsistency. Since the variable of text difficulty affected the tail of the distribution, this might be taken to support the notion presented earlier that summary statistics may be more sensitive to changes in the peak of the distribution, while profile analysis may be more sensitive to changes in the tail.

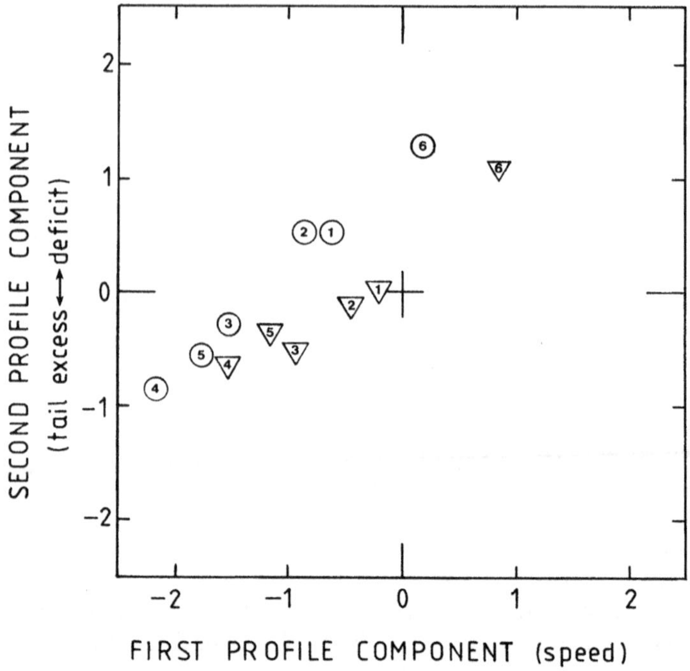

Fig. 7.17. Graph of the first two principal components of the interresponse time distributions characterizing the effect of a change in text difficulty in the profile-analysis plane of the initial 16 subjects. Circles denote the easy text, inverted triangles the difficult text.

Overall Discussion and Conclusion

Summary

In this final section, we shall begin by summarizing the visual evidence of similarity between interresponse time distributions. Next, we describe the characterization of skilled typing offered by summary statistics and profile analysis at the data level. We then propose an interpretation of the characterization mediated by the notion of fluency. Fluency is then related both to wider notions of skill and to process models of typing. A distinction is proposed between a primary system, responsible for producing fluent responses, and a secondary system, responsible for nonfluent responses. Finally, possible applications of the techniques to human factors research are reviewed, together with possible developments of the techniques themselves.

Characterizing Skilled Typing

The similarity between interresponse time distributions observed in the initial set of data was confirmed in subsequent sets. If performance under normal typing conditions is considered alone (and excluding the data of MG), there are 34 sets in all. Of these, 31 distributions have a single peak; 34 are right skewed; 29 have a positively accelerating leading edge; and 32 have a negatively accelerating trailing edge. It is also possible to observe by eye that, in general, distributions with sharper peaks accompany faster performance. The difference is most easily observed at the extremes of performance, for example, between very fast and very slow typists and between early and late stages of skill acquisition. This relationship and the configuration of features, therefore, appears to be general to our sample and would be expected to characterize the population of touch typists at large.

The characterization of the distributional data was accomplished by two methods. Summary statistics suggested a characterization based on the relationship between the peak of the distribution and the tail. Faster performance was accompanied by a more pronounced peak and a (relatively) more pronounced tail. The relationship was expressed as a line in the (b_1, b_2) plane, faster performance showing itself generally as an increase in kurtosis and skewness and hence a movement down the line. The stability of the relationship and its orderly change with changes in the speed of performance can be inferred from the fact that the *same* line can be projected onto all the data sets reported. It is remarkable that differences induced by such different factors as individual differences, learning, task change, and motivation should be characterized so similarly. It suggests that the characterization is fundamental with respect to the nature of the skill of typing. The second method, profile analysis, suggested a characterization based on a general speed component associated with the early part of the distribution, including the peak, and a second component associated with a relative deficit or excess in the tail of the distribution. Although the two components are orthogonal, some of the data (especially those reflecting voluntary changes in speed—see Figure 7.13) suggest that faster performance may be associated with orderly changes in direction on both components. Both methods, however, indicate that all typists do not effect all performance changes similarly. Directional inconsistency over subjects was exhibited by both summary statistics and profile analysis, although not on identical data sets. The fact that directional inconsistency was shown by profile analysis for performance changes affecting the tails of the distributions (see Figure 7.17) and by summary statistics for performance apparently affecting the peaks of the distributions (see Figure 7.12) suggests that profile analysis may be more sensitive to changes in the tail of the distribution and summary statistics more sensitive to changes in the peak. This in turn suggests that the methods are not alternatives and that both may be required for a complete characterization of some data sets. Nonlinear transformation of the distributions might produce more consistent movements over subjects in the (b_1, b_2) and profile-analysis planes. There is no a priori reason, however, to assume this to be the case for the present data. It is a possibility that might usefully be explored.

Interpretation of the Characterization in Terms of Fluency

Summary statistics and profile analysis both characterize skill only at the level of the data, expressed here in interresponse times. To interpret the characterization in terms of skill at the level of the typing activity itself, we have had recourse to the intermediary notion of fluency. We have distinguished fluent and nonfluent responses by associating them, respectively, with the peak and the tail of the distribution, both basic features of the data characterization. Increased skill, as interpreted in terms of fluency, appears to involve three aspects: first, there is an overall reduction in interresponse time for both fluent and nonfluent responses; second, there is a decrease in the number of nonfluent responses; and third, there is less absolute difference between fluent fast and fluent slow interresponse times. These aspects are apparent whether the differences in skill are exhibited by different typists or by the same typist during the course of skill acquisition. When the typing task is made more difficult, either by masking the keyboard or by increasing the number of nonalphabetic characters, it is as if performance becomes less skilled. Typing not only becomes slower, which would be expected, but the number of nonfluent responses increases and the fluent fast and fluent slow interresponse times become more dissimilar. Likewise, when typists are asked to speed up performance, it is as if performance becomes more skilled. We speak hypothetically here advisedly, since the directional inconsistency over subjects either in terms of summary statistics or in terms of profile analysis strongly suggests that typists do not all effect performance changes similarly. The differences may be considered in terms of the active recruitment of strategies or in the more passive recovery from the effects of task change. Successful strategies, even if they slowed performance, would have to be interpreted in some sense as an extension of skill. More passive reactions for coping might then be interpreted as exhibiting in some sense a decrease in skill, since they would include more nonfluent responses. Further research, however, is obviously required before any firm conclusions can be drawn concerning the relationship between speed change and individual strategies. In summary, then, skilled performance can be characterized as a mixture of fluent and nonfluent responses whose relationship varies systematically with changes in the level of skill.

Fluency and Skill

This characterization of skill can be directly related to others that have been proposed in the psychological literature. For example, Fitts and Posner (1967) suggested three phases in the acquisition of skill. The first or cognitive phase involves the selection of an initial repertoire of subroutines from the available ones that have been developed previously, as the first step in the development of an executive program for running the skill. In typing, this would include reading the text, remembering the spelling of words, and pressing the keys. The second or associative phase involves the construction of new subroutines more appropriate for carrying out the skill. In typing, this would include learning to locate the keys without the aid of vision and to press the keys simultaneously with reading the text. The third or autonomous phase involves the automatization of the component processes of the skill. In typing, this would include the individual finger movements.

Since touch typing is by definition a skill, it is tempting to associate it with Fitts and Posner's third or autonomous phase of acquisition, particularly since even MG, who was less experienced than many typists tested, had practiced for 250 hours over the period of the experiment. However, the characterization of skilled typing proposed here emphasizes the presence of both fluent and nonfluent responses as well as their relationship. To preserve the distinction between the two types of response within the autonomous category, we propose first to distinguish within the category between "automatic" and "controlled" responses (following Shiffrin, Dumais, & Schneider, 1981), and second to identify fluent responses with automatic and nonfluent responses with controlled. Essentially automatic processes do not use general processing capacity and cannot be inhibited (see also Chapter 8). In typing, this might be a common sequence of keystrokes. Controlled processes, in contrast, do use general resources. In typing, this might be a finger movement to an unfamiliar target key executed with the aid of vision. In these terms, then, skilled typing involves both automatic and controlled responses (this is analogous to Shiffrin et al.'s claim that automatism and controlled processing are theoretical states and that performance in almost all tasks will be carried out with a contribution from both types of process). Following the extension of the characterization of skill offered here, we might expect increased skill to involve the general speeding of both automatic and controlled responses; the reduction of controlled responses in favor of automatic ones; and increased similarity in the times taken by fast automatic and slow automatic responses. The instantiation of this claim over processes (predominantly perceptual or motor) and over skills should prove informative with respect to the nature of skill itself. It should be noted in passing that it is not possible to identify nonfluent responses uniquely with controlled processes, because failed automatic processes are also likely to result in nonfluent responses.

Alternatively, the distinction between fluent and nonfluent responses with the autonomous category might be preserved by identifying fluent responses with open-loop control and nonfluent responses with closed-loop control (Adams, 1968, 1971). Open-loop control presupposes some central program for the control of finger movements, executed without reference to feedback or in this case without reference to exteroceptive feedback such as vision (see Summers, 1981, for a discussion of the different levels at which feedback may operate). Closed-loop control presupposes that (exteroceptive) feedback is built into the procedure for executing the movement—for example, in typing, the use of vision to locate an unfamiliar key. If open-loop and closed-loop theories of movement control are eschewed in favor of schema theories (Pew, 1974; Schmidt, 1975, 1976), the distinction between fluent and nonfluent responses can be preserved by assuming that fluent responses derive directly from the schema instance, whereas nonfluent responses require the use of additional information such as vision to translate the schema instance into a temporal string of motor commands. Programming notions, however, may be rejected altogether (Kelso, 1981). Order and regulation of movement may be conceived as local by-products of a system's dynamic properties, rather than as centrally generated in the manner of schema theories. Within this perspective, typing movements (of the hand or of the fingers) might be interpreted as essentially oscillatory in nature, modulated by the need to attain different spatial targets. In this view, fluent responses might be identified with basic oscillatory processes, and in particular with those producing timing invariance over movements executed at different speeds (Viviani & Terzuolo, 1980), while nonfluent responses might be identified with those involving only a single cycle. In summary, then, the characterization of skill presented here in terms of fluency can be related to a wide range of more general notions of skilled performance, provided that the distinction between fluent and nonfluent is preserved and that it is accepted that skilled performance consists of a combination of each. It should be noted that fluency as used here is superordinate to rhythm, whether in the form of temporal patterning, regularity, or stress.

Fluency and Models of Typing

As well as interpreting the characterization proposed here in terms of more general notions of skill, it is also possible to interpret it with respect to particular models of the typing process (Shaffer, 1976; Sternberg, Monsell, Knoll, & Wright, 1978; Viviani & Terzuolo, 1980; Rumelhart & Norman, Note 4). It is tempting, for example, to interpret changes in speed, whether resulting from changes in skill, in task conditions, or in instructions, directly in terms of the models. A direct interpretation, however, is not consistent either with the data or with the characterization. For example, Shaffer (1976) proposed a two-stage model with each stage involving buffer storage and a translation process (with bulk transfer between buffers). The first buffer contains strings representing words; the second contains strings representing response specifications. Output from the second stage is serial, in time with an internal clock or metronome. Speeding up could be accomplished by increasing the metronome rate. This, however, would produce a constant decrease over all interresponse times, an outcome not consistent with our data, which exhibit systematic changes in the (b_1, b_2) plane (as opposed to stationarity). Elsewhere, Sternberg et al. (1978) have proposed that typing responses follow a self-terminating search through a nonshrinking output buffer. Speeding up could be accomplished by increasing the speed at which the buffer is searched. This would produce a proportional reduction in interresponse times, which again is inconsistent with our data. Viviani and Terzuolo's model (1980) is based on such relative speed changes, and constant ratios between the timing of successive motor commands are assumed to be represented in the central template, which controls typing output in terms of the words or letter sequences. Again, our data are not consistent with such a model, which implies stationarity in the (b_1, b_2) plane with changes of speed. Last, Rumelhart and Norman (Note 4; also Chapter 3, this volume) have proposed a distributed model of typing that has no central processor nor any central representation of the timing pattern between letters. A response is triggered when a letter representation reaches a sufficiently high level of activation, each letter inhibiting those that follow it. Interresponse times are thus a by-product of movement organization and not a controlling feature. It is not obvious how this model could be changed. One could just select a different time unit base, which would be equivalent to a relative change. Since the time units are already arbitrary, however, this is hardly a principled change. It may be that alterations of some parameters of the model, such as the level of inhibition, would produce speed changes, but it is difficult to see how these could be other than relative. As such, they would not produce the data reported here, particularly in terms of summary statistics.

We accept, of course, that the models may be optionally incomplete with respect to nonfluent responses, their aim being to account only for fluent responses. The inconsistency of the models with the data, however, raises the interesting question what modifications might be necessary to produce consistency. It might be argued, for example, that since the models are normative, the predictions all assume normal processing. A judicious mixture of failed and successful processes might then be consistent with one or other of the models *and* consistent with our data. The argument can most easily be sustained with respect to voluntary changes in speed, because the external context, including the task, remains the same, which minimizes the number of confounding factors. The argument's strength will depend on how the models are extended to handle failed or at least initially unsuccessful processes.

Leaving aside the optional incompleteness and the normative assumptions of the models, however, there are two compelling reasons why it is not possible to identify the changes of speed in our data directly with the models. First, the models describe asymptotic performance and not how performance comes to be asymptotic, for example, in terms of skill acquisition in the manner of MG (for a more extended discussion of this point see Rabbitt, 1981). Second, the models do not include the support system necessary to subserve touch typing and hence do not reflect the operation of the system. To be more explicit, touch typing is more efficient than vision-aided typing, because reading and typing occur concurrently and because search time for the target key is eliminated along with slower visually guided movements. However, touch typing has overheads in the form of the support system necessary to ensure that key pressing is accurate. For example, for the correct key to be pressed, the hands have to be appropriately referenced to the keyboard. The typist learns only relative movements within the spatial context of the keyboard. The context, therefore, has to be both established and checked. This setting-up and control system is in addition to the system generating the responses. In the case of the non-touch typist, the visual specification of the key to be pressed avoids the need for an additional context and hence for such a system.

In order for our data to be directly related to the models, then, they need to be extended in a principled way to cover changes brought about by learning. For some models, changing the speed at which processes crucial to sequencing occur might be appropriate (e.g., the rate or regularity at which an internal metronome is able to operate—Shaffer, 1976; or the rate at which an output buffer is scanned—Sternberg et al., 1978). Changing the group size of the elements being processed together might be appropriate for others, since it might be assumed that between-group interresponse times would normally be slower than within-group ones (Viviani & Terzuolo, 1980; Rumelhart & Norman, Note 4). The models also need a support system to subserve touch typing. If the system generating the responses is assumed to constitute the primary system (e.g., any of the models cited earlier), a secondary system can be assumed; (1) to set the context for touch typing by referencing the hand to the keyboard; (2) to monitor the adequacy of referencing (either by sight—of the hands and keyboard or of the typed copy—or by kinesthetic feedback relating the adequacy of the finger location to the key during depression); and (3) to reinstate appropriate referencing conditions if they fall below some criterion of adequacy. Since the three functions of the proposed secondary system are also those required to execute less familiar movements that can only be made with the aid of sight, the system would be able both to subserve the primary system and to act as a backup system in the event that the specifications of the movement by the primary system were inadequate. On the basis of these proposals, the models can now be related directly to our findings. Fluent responses result directly from the processes assumed to operate in the primary system. They constitute in the main the peak of the interresponse time distribution. If an initially unsuccessful process is nevertheless completed successfully within the primary system, the response will be nonfluent and will appear in the tail of the distribution (unless recovery was particularly fast). If a response is inadequately specified by the primary system, control is passed to the secondary system, which executes the movement on the basis of additional information, usually visual. Again, a nonfluent response results, which appears in the distribution's tail.

As typing skill is acquired, fluent responses become faster, either by speeding up the primary system processes or by increasing the group size of the elements being processed. At the same time, secondary system responses may also be assumed to speed up, perhaps because the amount of additional information is reduced, thus decreasing the interresponse times associated with nonfluent responses. In short, there is a general speeding up of all responses. Further, the specification of more movements becomes complete, so that control passes less often to the secondary system, which reduces the number of nonfluent responses. It is unclear why fluent fast and fluent slow responses become more similar, particularly for those models assuming only the speeding of a single parameter (metronome or buffer-search speed). Plausibly, however, for models that assume that increases in skill are in part due to increases in the group size of elements processed together as an output unit, the original elements may be less advantaged in speed than the additional elements.

Let us now consider changes in speed not related to the acquisition of skill. If the keyboard is masked, typists may slow down primary system processes; they may be slower at implementing secondary system processes because, in the absence of vision, both hand referencing and unfamiliar character location are likely to require tactile guidance. Since the main effect of masking was on the tail of the distribution, the most likely explanation is in terms of slower nonfluent responses originating in the secondary system. If the number of nonalphabetic characters in a text is increased, this may be expected to increase the number of times control is passed to the secondary system, thus increasing the nonfluent responses in the distribution's tail.

Concerning directional inconsistency over subjects, particularly in the (b_1, b_2) plane for speed changes associated with instructions or text difficulty, individual strategies would be expected to recruit the primary and secondary systems differentially. For example, in order to type faster, typists might actively increase the group size of the elements to be typed; assuming that between-group interresponse times are normally slower than within-group ones, this would reduce the interresponse times of the fluent slow responses relative to the fluent fast responses, without having more frequent recourse to the secondary system. Alternatively, typists may speed up primary system processing excessively, such that more frequent use has to be made of the secondary system to re-reference the hands. With more difficult text, typists may slow down primary system processing or maintain the same speed as for normal text, while in both cases passing control more frequently to the secondary system for the typing of characters inadequately specified for touch typing.

In summary, it is possible to extend current process models of typing in a way that allows them to be directly related to the characterization of skilled typing proposed here. The relationship, however, raises a number of questions. These include, for example, how speed changes are effected by the models; how upper limits on speeding up processes are determined and controlled; and what control, if any, typists have over nonfluent responses. The techniques proposed here for characterizing interresponse time distributions should provide a useful tool for conducting the further research necessary to answer such questions.

Application and Development of the Techniques

We have been mostly concerned here with techniques underlying the characterization of skilled typing and the interpretation of the characterization in terms of skill and of typing models. Both aspects are likely to find a wide practical application. Data input via keyboards, particularly to computer systems, is the object of a considerable amount of human factors applied research (see West, 1969, and Seibel, 1972; also Baddeley & Longman, 1978; Fletcher, Note 5; Glencross, Note 6). Further, computer control of experiments has led to the measurement of individual interresponse times rather than simply the mean time per character keyed (Kinkead, 1975; Long, 1975, 1976a, 1976b; Neal, 1977; Pollard & Cooper, 1979). However, unless techniques are developed that adequately characterize changes in performance reflected by interresponse time distributions, and unless interpretations are also developed to extend the characterization beyond the level of the data, there is a risk that the additional information provided by distributions will go unused (e.g., Allen, 1981). Further practical applications can be expected to derive from the orderliness of performance changes, particularly as expressed in movements along the dimension in the (b_1, b_2) plane. The dimension could be used for the purposes of extrapolation, for example, to adjust for the learning effects that may occur over a long-term typing experiment. The dimension could also be used to relate the performance of different groups of keyboard users—for example, an experimental population that differed systematically from the target user population. The characterizations, in conjunction with the distributional information itself, can also be used to calculate system parameters not easily inferred from mean interresponse times—for example, the required buffer size of a terminal linked to a line whose transmission rate is slower than fluent fast interresponse times (Long, 1975). Lastly, with the increasing interest in word processors, text editing, and document preparation prompted by the development of new technology, there is considerable scope for the techniques to be used to separate keying processes from planning and compositional processes (Card, Moran, & Newell, 1980; Allen, 1981; Gould, 1981). We would expect, then, to see the scope of the application of the techniques considerably extended.

Finally, we would like to consider briefly how the techniques themselves might be further extended and developed. The method of profile analysis used here was based on a small population (16 distributions only) with a limited degree of resolution (because of binning and truncation). The method would increase in validity if the profile-analysis plane were based on a larger number of distributions, and if some attention were given to the question what constitutes an adequate set of percentiles to define the profile. The use of the summary statistics, b_1 and b_2, and their relationships with profile analysis, will also be clearer when the limitations due to truncation are removed (although some truncation will always be necessary for the very longest interresponse times). We expect that the techniques associated with unmixing mixtures of distributions and with parametric curve fitting will be of considerable value at the stage when different subdistributions have been identified and their interrelationships are being explored. In relation to mixtures of distributions, we expect that the profile-analysis technique will have a more direct extension than is possible with summary statistics. The relationship between the values of b_1 and b_2 for the whole distribution and for its constituent subdistributions is not simple. In profile analysis, however, by virtue of its linear origins, there will be a simple linear relationship between the profile components of the constituents and of the whole.

Reference Notes

1. Gentner, D. R., Grudin, J., & Conway, E. *Finger movements in transcription typing* (Tech. Rep. NR 157-437). Personnel and Training Research Programs, Office of Naval Research, Arlington, Va., 1980.
2. Permutt, T. J. *Applied field project report for diploma in mathematical statistics.* Unpublished essay, Cambridge University Statistical Laboratory, 1975.
3. Johnson, N. L. (1970). *Tables to facilitate fitting S_B curves* (Mimeo Series No. 557). University of North Carolina, Institute of Statistics.
4. Rumelhart, D., & Norman, D. *Simulating a skilled typist: A study of skilled cognitive-motor performance* (Tech. Rep. 102). La Jolla, Calif.: University of California at San Diego, Center for Human Information Processing, May 1981.
5. Fletcher, J. H. *An interim report on aptitude tests for postal coding desk operators and coding desk keyboards.* Dollis Hill, London: Post Office Research Department, 1974.
6. Glencross, D. J. *The Flinders typing project.* South Australia: Flinders University Report, 1976.

References

Adams, J. A. Response feedback and learning. *Psychological Bulletin*, 1968, *70*, 486-504.

Adams, J. A. A closed-loop theory of motor learning. *Journal of Motor Behavior*, 1971, *3*, 111-150.

Allen, R. A. Composition and editing of text. *Ergonomics*, 1981, *24*, 611-622.

Annett, J. *Feedback and human behaviour*. Harmondsworth: Penguin, 1969.

Baddeley, A. D., & Longman, D. J. A. The influences of length and frequency of training sessions on the rate of learning to type. *Ergonomics*, 1978, *21*, 627-635.

Card, S. K., Moran, T. P., & Newell, A. Computer text editing: An information processing analysis of a routine cognitive skill. *Cognitive Psychology*, 1980, *12*, 32-74.

Crooks, M. *Touch typing for teachers*. London: Pitman, 1964.

Droege, R. C., & Hill, B. M. Comparison of performance on manual and electric typewriters. *Journal of Applied Psychology*, 1961, *45*, 268-270.

Elderton, W. P., & Johnson, N. L. *Systems of frequency curves*. New York and London: Cambridge University Press, 1969.

Everitt, B. B., & Hand, D. J. *Finite mixture distributions*. London: Chapman and Hall, 1981.

Finucan, H. M. A note on kurtosis. *Journal of the Royal Statistical Society (Series B)*, 1964, *26*, 111-112.

Fitts, P. M., & Posner, M. I. *Human performance*. Belmont, Calif.: Brooks/Cole, 1967.

Fleishman, E. A. Toward a taxonomy of human performance. *American Psychologist*, 1975, *30*, 1127-1149.

Gould, J. D. Composing letters with computer-based text editors. *Human Factors*, 1981, *23*, 593-606.

Kelso, J. A. S. Contrasting perspectives on order and regulation in movement. In J. B. Long & A. D. Baddeley (Eds.), *Attention and performance* (Vol. 9). Hillsdale, N.J.: Erlbaum, 1981.

Kendall, M. G., & Stuart, A. *The advanced theory of statistics* (3rd ed., Vol. 1). London: Charles Griffin, 1969.

Kinkead, R. Typing speed, keying rates, and optimal keyboard conjoints. *Proceedings, 19th Annual Human Factors Society Meeting*, 1975.

Long, J. B. Effects of randomly delayed visual and auditory feedback on keying performance. *Ergonomics*, 1975, *18*, 337-347.

Long, J. B. Visual feedback and skilled keying: Differential effects of masking the printed copy and the keyboard. *Ergonomics*, 1976, *19*, 93-110. (a)

Long, J. B. Effects of delayed irregular feedback on unskilled and skilled keying performance. *Ergonomics*, 1976, *19*, 183-202. (b)

McWhirter, N. (Ed.) *Guinness book of records*. Enfield, London: Guinness Superlatives, 1981.

Neal, A. S. Time intervals between keystrokes, records, and fields in data entry with skilled operators. *Human Factors*, 1977, *19*, 163-170.

Olsen, R. A., & Murray, R. A. Finger motion analysis in typing of texts of varying complexity. *Proceedings of the 6th Congress of the International Ergonomics Association*, 1976, 446-450.

Pearson, E. S., & Hartley, H. O. *Biometrika tables for statisticians* (Vol. 2). New York and London: Cambridge University Press, 1972.

Pearson, E. S., & Please, N. W. Relation between the shape of population distributions and the robustness of four simple test statistics. *Biometrika*, 1975, *62*, 223-241.

Pew, R. The speed-accuracy operating characteristic. *Acta Psychologica*, 1969, *30*, 16-26.

Pew, R. W. Human perceptual-motor performance. In B. H. Kantowitz (Ed.), *Human information processing: Tutorials in performance and cognition*. Hillsdale, N.J.: Erlbaum, 1974.

Pollard, D., & Cooper, M. B. The effect of feedback on keying performance. *Applied Ergonomics*, 1979, *10*, 194-200.

Rabbitt, P. Cognitive psychology needs models for change in performance with old age. In J. B. Long and A. D. Baddeley (Eds.), *Attention and performance* (Vol. 9). Hillsdale, N.J.: Erlbaum, 1981.

Scheidegger, W. *Learn with Scheidegger* (8th ed., Booklet 3). London: Scheidegger, 1969.

Schmidt, R. A. A schema theory of discrete motor skill learning. *Psychological Review*, 1975, *82*, 225-260.

Schmidt, R. A. The schema as a solution to some persistent problems in motor learning theory. In G. E. Stelmach (Ed.), *Motor control: Issues and Trends*. New York: Academic Press, 1976.

Seibel, R. Data entry devices and procedures. In H. P. Van Cott and R. G. Kincade (Eds.), *Human engineering guide to equipment design*. Washington, D.C.: American Institutes for Research, 1972.

Shaffer, L. H. Control processes in typing. *Quarterly Journal of Experimental Psychology*, 1975, *27*, 419-432.

Shaffer, L. H. Intention and performance. *Psychological Review*, 1976, *83*, 375-393.

Shiffrin, R. M., Dumais, S. T., & Schneider, W. Characteristics of automatism. In J. B. Long and A. D. Baddeley (Eds.), *Attention and performance* (Vol. 9). Hillsdale, N.J.: Erlbaum, 1981.

Sternberg, S., Monsell, S., Knoll, R. L., & Wright, C. E. The latency and duration of rapid movement sequences: Comparisons of speech and typewriting. In G. E. Stelmach (Ed.), *Information processing in motor control and learning*. London: Academic Press, 1978.

Summers, J. J. Motor programs. In D. Holding (Ed.), *Human skills*. Chichester: Wiley, 1981.

Viviani, P., & Terzuolo, C. Space-time invariance in learned motor skills. In G. E. Stelmach and J. Requin (Eds.), *Tutorials in motor behavior*. Amsterdam: North-Holland, 1980.

Walker, E. L. *Conditioning and instrumental learning*. Belmont, Calif.: Brooks/Cole, 1967.

West, L. J. *Acquisition of typewriting skills*. New York: Pitman, 1969.

Chapter 8

Time, Information, and the Various Spans in Typewriting

Gordon D. Logan

Introduction

Skilled typewriting is a complex activity that requires the coordination of several independent, concurrent processors. At any moment in time, different processors are concerned with different parts of the text being typed. Processors "earlier" in the information flow (i.e., closer to the receptors) are generally ahead of the "later" processors (i.e., processors closer to the effectors), focusing on parts of the text that the later processors are not yet ready to deal with. The difference in focus may be measured in units of information (i.e., keystrokes) or in units of time, and is called the *span*. Since there are several processors working together in typing, there should be several spans. How should we study them? One approach would be to identify the processors and then deduce the spans between them. This would require more detailed knowledge about the nature of typing than we have at present (but see Rumelhart & Norman, 1982; Shaffer, 1976). A second approach would be to discover the spans empirically, by examining the existing studies of spans in typewriting and then trying to distinguish spans in terms of their properties. The second approach was adopted in this chapter.

Altogether, there are seven different methods for studying typewriting spans in the literature, and they converge on three different spans that may be distinguished by their length (in characters), their duration, and the linguistic units they are sensitive to. A summary of methods, results, and theories is presented in Table 8.1.

The best known span in typing is the *eye-hand span*: In a variety of circumstances, the eyes are typically six to eight characters ahead of the fingers. With a special procedure, this span can be stretched to 40-odd characters; then it is influenced by different variables, and becomes the *copying span*. The third span, the *stopping span*,

Table 8.1. Theory, Methods, and Data in Studies of Span in Typewriting

Span theory	Technique	Span data	Duration (sec)	Unit
Stopping span	Stop signal	1-3		
	Change	3	.2-.5	Letter
	Error detection	0-1		
Eye-hand span	Eye movements	4-8		
	Preview	6-8	1	Word
	Text structure	5-7		
Copying span	Alternate looking and typing	40	10	Phrase

Note. Span data are the number of characters in the span; duration is the time required to type the number of characters in the span; and unit is the highest level of linguistic structure that affects the span.

reflects what typists are committed to typing (i.e., what they cannot avoid typing), and is usually shorter than three characters.

The plan of this chapter is to introduce the different spans, revealing their empirical characteristics, and then to search for theoretical interpretations for them. We shall consider two interpretations in particular: The first describes the spans in units of information (i.e., characters or words) and identifies them with contents of different buffer memories that mediate communication between processors. From this perspective, spans may be artifacts of differences in the units used by different processes. One unit in one process may translate into several units in another process, and a buffer memory may be necessary to hold the several units until the second process can deal with them. The second interpretation describes the spans in units of time, and identifies them with the processes themselves. From this perspective, spans may be artifacts of reaction time, reflecting how far one process must be ahead of another in order to be able to provide it with a steady supply of data. The two interpretations are not mutually exclusive, but instead provide complementary perspectives on the meaning of the various spans.

Span Data

Eye-Hand Spans

Eye movements. Of the three methods used to study the eye-hand span, the eye movement method is the most direct. Eye movements and keystrokes are recorded simultaneously, and at each point in time the character fixated is compared with the character struck. The eye-hand span is simply the number of characters or words that elapse between them.

The only published study using this method is that of Butsch (1932). He studied 19 typists, including a world champion who typed 100 words per minute (wpm). The other 18 typist ranged in (rated) speed from 40 wpm to 75 wpm. On a test that involved typing connected text, the average eye-hand span for the group was 4.82 characters, ranging from 3.24 to 7.60 in individual subjects. Butsch provided distributions of the eye-hand span, which I collapsed across subjects and level of skill to form a single distribution (plotted in Figure 8.1). It is based on 689 observations. Plotted with it to provide contrast is a stopping span distribution from a study by Logan (1982) in which subjects were told to stop typing when they heard a tone and the text disappeared (see the section on the stopping span below. The stopping span is the number of characters typed after the tone; the distribution in the figure is based on 1,200 observations.

In Butsch's data, eye-hand span correlated significantly with typing speed, $r(17) = .679$, $F(1, 17) = 14.55$, $p < .01$ (my calculations from Butsch's Table 1), indicating that the more skilled typists tended to have longer spans. As a possible account for this relation, Butsch (1932) noted that "the eye keeps at an average distance ahead of the hand such that the time interval between seeing a letter and writing it is approximately one second, no matter what the speed of writing" (p. 114). His Table 4 indicates that over the range of typing skill from 40 to 100 wpm, the observed eye-hand span is closely approximated by the number of characters typed in 1 sec, that is,

$$\text{eye-hand span} = \text{letters/sec} \times 1 \text{ sec.}$$

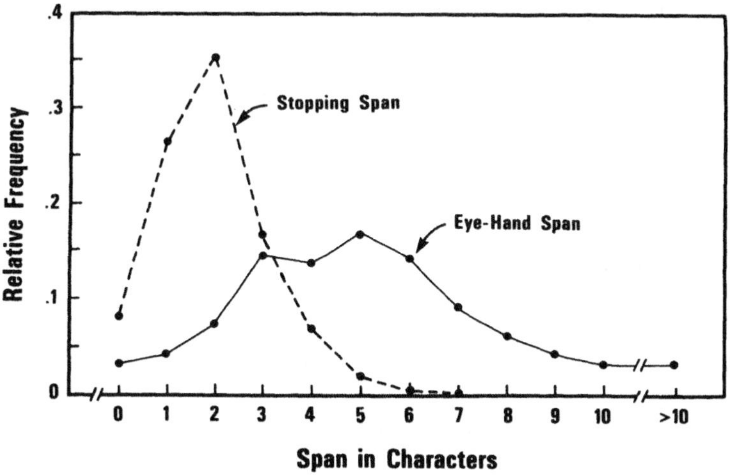

Fig. 8.1 Frequency distributions for the eye-hand span and the stopping span. The eye-hand span data are from a study by Butsch (1932, Table 3) in which eye movements and keystrokes were recorded simultaneously; the stopping span data are from Logan (1982, Experiment 3).

We shall return to this observation later in discussing interpretations of the different spans, focusing on the meaning of the 1-sec interval. For now, note that Butsch was the first to consider span in units of time instead of in units of information (Characters or words).

In separate tests with a world champion, Butsch examined eye-hand span as a function of text structure, and found no difference between spans when typing connected text (6.50 characters) and when typing sequences of disconnected words (6.59 characters). This suggests that the eye-hand span is not affected by structural relations between words, a conclusion that is consistent with studies that manipulate text structure described below.

Preview method. The second method for studying the eye-hand span involves manipulating the amount of the text that typists can view. Special display systems are constructed that show a specified number of characters to the left (postview) and to the right (preview) of the character being typed. Generally, typing speed increases as the amount of preview increases, reaching asymptote between six and eight characters (Hershman & Hillix, 1965; Shaffer, 1973), The amount of preview at which typing speed reaches asymptote is taken as a measure of the eye-hand span. Clearly, this method measures the eye-hand span less directly than the eye movement method does; nevertheless, the agreement between methods is encouraging.

Typical data from a single 100-wpm typist studied by Shaffer (1973, Table 3) are presented in Figure 8.2. Note the clear asymptote at eight characters preview, and note that the bulk of the benefit from preview accrues from increasing preview from one character to three. Note also that with 40 characters preview random words were typed as fast as prose.

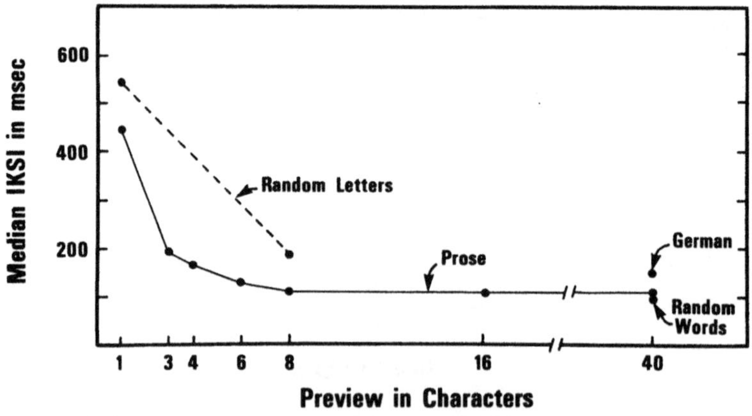

Fig. 8.2. Median interkeystroke interval (typing speed) as a function of preview of the text to be typed (from a study by Shaffer, 1973, Table 3). Note that random letters benefit from preview about as much as prose does.

A special advantage of the preview method is that it allows a direct test of the importance of the eye-hand span for speed and fluency in normal typing: If the eye-hand span is important in normal typing, skilled typists should not manifest their characteristic speed and fluency unless the amount of preview equals or exceeds their eye-hand span. In both studies, it was very clear that skilled typists could not attain high speeds without preview, which indicates that the ability to look ahead is an essential ingredient of typing skill.

The preview method also suggests that the eye-hand span may be related to typing skill. Skilled typists reach asymptotic speed with six to eight characters preview (Hershman & Hillix, 1965; Shaffer, 1973), whereas unskilled typists reach asymptote with shorter previews. The evidence here is from a study by Shaffer and Hardwick (1970) in which nontypists were practiced for 13 sessions on a reduced keyboard (12 characters and a space). At the end of practice, subjects typed about 25 wpm and reached asymptotic speed with three characters preview. Like the eye-movement study, this suggests that skilled typists manifest longer eye-hand spans than unskilled typists. However, some aspects of Shaffer and Hardwick's data mitigate this conclusion somewhat: Their unskilled subjects benefited from increasing preview the first time it was manipulated (after they had three sessions of experience on the task, during which they typed with unrestricted preview). When preview was first manipulated, typing speed reached asymptote (about 17 wpm) with three characters preview, just as it did at the end of practice (see Shaffer & Hardwick, 1970, Figure 2). Nevertheless, subjects benefited more from preview as they gained more skill, even if the point at which they reached asymptote did not change.

The three preview studies in the literature all manipulated the structure of the text as a way to converge on the conclusions drawn from the analysis of the preview effect. Generally, the preview at which typing speed reaches asymptote increases with increases in the structure of the text to be typed, from random letter strings through orders of approximation to English words to random word texts (Hershman & Hillix, 1965; Shaffer & Hardwick, 1970). However, the effects of structure are small in contrast with the effects of preview. For example, Shaffer and Hardwick (1970) found an interaction between preview and structure (random letter vs. syllable vs. word texts) such that typing speed reached asymptote at longer previews with more structured texts. However, the interaction was weak in contrast with the main effect of preview; increasing preview form zero to five characters reduced the interval between successive keystrokes (interkeystroke interval) by about 200 msec in random letter texts and about 250 msec in word texts (see their Figure 1). Further, Shaffer (1973) found the opposite interaction in the single 100-wpm typists he studied: Increasing preview from one to eight characters reduced interkeystroke interval by about 353 msec in random letter texts and about 333 msec in prose texts.

Thus, the conclusion that typists can take advantage of preview only if there is sufficient structure in the text receives no support (cf. Hershman & Hillix, 1965; Shaffer, 1973; Shaffer & Hardwick, 1970).

Text Structure. The third way to study the eye-hand span is to manipulate the structure of the text to be typed. There are several reasons why typists might be expected to type structured texts faster than unstructured texts (e.g., economy of coding, redundancy of coding, practice with common sequences of keystrokes). In order to benefit from structure, however, the elements linked by the structure must be "available" to the typist at the same time; that is, they must fall within the eye-hand span. Different structures relate elements at different distances in the text to be typed, and the eye-hand span can be estimated from the longest "span" of structural relations that results in an increase in typing speed (i.e., the structural relations at which typing speed reaches asymptote).

The data are very clear: Fendrick (1937) and Shaffer and Hardwick (1968) found that typing speed increased from random letter strings to random word texts, but showed no further increase from random word texts to connected discourse (also see Shaffer, 1973, and Figure 8.2), suggesting an eye-hand span about one word long. Given that words are typically five to seven characters long, this agrees nicely with estimates from eye movement and preview methods.

How does eye-hand span, as measured by manipulating text structure, vary with typing skill? Fendrick (1937) had subjects at six different levels of typing ability (11, 17, 30, 38, 48, and 104 wpm) type eight texts that differed in structure. His major data were the number of keystrokes typed in 5 minutes. I have converted these to estimates of average interkeystroke interval, and plotted them in Figure 8.3. Clearly, each group was faster on random word texts than on random letter texts, but was no faster on connected discourse than on random word texts. Thus, it would appear that eye-hand span is not related to typing skill; all groups benefited from structure. However, all groups did not benefit equally. In absolute terms, the slower groups benefited more than the faster groups (i.e., the slowest group gained 437 msec per keystroke by going from random letters to connected text, whereas the fastest group gained 140 msec per keystroke). In relative terms, the faster groups benefited more than the slower groups (e.g., the slowest group reduced their average interkeystroke interval by 33% upon going from random letters to connected text, whereas the fastest group reduced theirs by 56%). The findings in relative terms resemble the finding of Shaffer and Hardwick (1970) that the preview at which typing speed reached asymptote did not change as subjects became more skilled, but the amount by which their speed improved when given asymptotic preview did increase with skill. Possibly the preview method and the text structure method are not sufficiently sensitive to detect the change in the eye-hand span with skill.

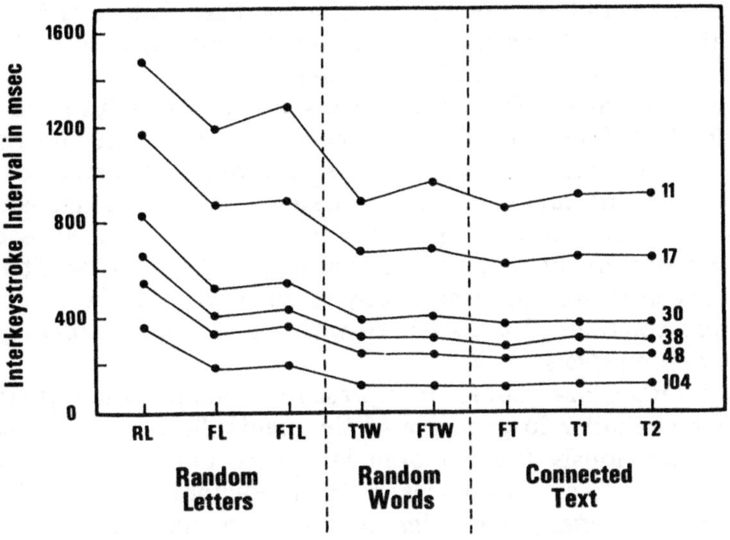

Fig. 8.3. Interkeystroke interval as a function of the text being typed (from Fendrick, 1937, Table 2). Numbers on curves identify groups of typists by mean typing speed in words per minute. Connected text: FT, text made from the 500 most frequent words in English; T1 and T2, different samples of connected discourse. Random words: FTW, text made by scrambling the words in the frequent-word text, FT; T1W, text made by scrambling the words in T1. Random letters: FTL, text made by scrambling the letters from FT; Rl, a random ordering of rare letters (PWFGVKJXQZ); a random ordering of frequent letters (ETAOSINRHL).

Summary. The three procedures agree in estimating an eye-hand span of six to eight characters or 1-1.5 words. The span increases with typing skill, and appears to be necessary to produce the speed and fluency associated with skilled typing. The eye-hand span increases with structure within words, but is not affected by structure between words. This suggests that the word is the unit of organization in the eye-hand span, but there is no direct evidence to support this conjecture.

The Copying Span

In all three procedures for studying the eye-hand span, subjects read and typed concurrently. If subjects are not allowed to read and type at the same time, a different span emerges; the number of characters typed between successive glances at the text to be copied reflects the *copying span*. There is only one study of the copying span in the literature, but the spans observed there are so different from the eye-hand span that it seems both necessary and prudent to distinguish them.

Rothkopf (1980) had five typists copy 17 texts by alternating between typing and reading, and found an average span of 40 characters between successive glances at the text. The 17 texts differed in difficulty as measured by the Flesch Reading Ease Index, and Rothkopf found that the eight easier texts produced longer spans (46 characters) than the eight harder texts (34 characters).

In order to assess the relation between text structure and copying span, Rothkopf calculated Cloze scores for each text and compared them with the copying span. Cloze scores were calculated by deleting every sixth word, and having 120 college students try to guess the missing words. Texts containing words that were guessed correctly by a higher proportion of subjects received higher Cloze scores. The correlation between Cloze scores and copying span was significant, indicating that more constrained texts (those with higher Cloze scores) produced longer copying spans.

Rothkopf's Cloze procedure represents a manipulation of text structure that is similar in principle to the manipulations of text structure discussed previously (i.e., random letters vs. random words vs. text). Cloze scores reflect differences in the predictability of words in text, and so would reflect the difference between random word texts and connected discourse in the previous studies (i.e., random words would receive lower Cloze scores than connected text). Thus, it is possible to compare the copying span and the eye-hand span in their response to a common manipulation (i.e., sensitivity to linguistic structures larger than the word). This comparison suggests that they are different: The copying span increases as words become more predictable, but the eye-hand span does not.

Since only five typists were studied, the relation between span and skill could not be assessed reliably. However, there were significant correlations across texts between typing rate and copying span, indicating that texts that were typed faster produced longer copying spans. It was clear that the variation in typing rate was due to variation in the difficulty of the texts; the correlation between reading rate and typing rate was significant. Possibly the correlation between span and typing speed would remain if typing speed varied between subjects as a result of differences in skill.

The units of the copying span appear to be clauses or phrases. It is certain that the units are not smaller than single words; Rothkopf reported that subjects rarely ended their spans in midword (see Rothkopf, 1980, p. 569). At the other end, copying spans were clearly smaller than the sentence; for all but one text there were more characters in the average sentence than in the average copying span. This leaves units larger than words and smaller than sentences, such as clauses or phrases.

Rothkopf found that typists were most likely to end their spans at punctuation points (i.e., at phrase, clause, and sentence boundaries). Discounting spans that ended at punctuation points, he observed that spans ended after content words with greater than chance frequency (i.e., at content-function or content-content boundaries) and ended after function words with less than chance frequency (i.e., at function-content or function-function boundaries). Since phrases often begin with function words and end with content words, this suggests the phrase as the unit of the copying span.

The time taken by the copying span is about 10 times as long as the time taken by the eye-hand span. The average 40-character span took 9.16 sec to type at a typing rate of 229 msec per character, and about 3.32 sec to read at a reading rate of 83 msec per character. The total time taken by the copying span is thus 12.48 sec, which is considerably longer than the 1-sec duration of the eye-hand span.

The Stopping Span

A third kind of span can be assessed with procedures that require subjects to interrupt their typing in response to some arbitrary event, such as an error, a tone, or a change in the display. The number of keystrokes that occur between the critical event and the termination of typing is called the *stopping span.* It has been measured in three ways: by asking subjects to stop typing when they detect an error; by asking subjects to stop typing when they detect an arbitrary signal from the experimenter; and by asking subjects to stop typing old text and begin typing new text when the display changes.

Error-Detection Method. As mentioned in Chapter 1, Long (1976) and Rabbitt (1978) had subjects report the errors they made while typing continuous text. Long's subjects stopped and tried to correct the error, whereas Rabbitt's subjects stopped and typed an asterisk. Both found that typists stopped most often immediately after an error, and rarely typed more than two characters before reporting the error. To be exact, in Long's data (extracted from his Figure 5), 69% of the detected errors were reported with zero characters intervening, 13% with one character intervening, and 8% with two characters intervening. In Rabbitt's Experiment 1, the figures are 95%, 3%, and 1% for zero, one, and two intervening characters, respectively, and for his Experiment 2, 89%, 10% and 2% for zero, one, and two intervening characters, respectively.

These spans are substantially shorter than the eye-hand span and the copying span, which suggests that they warrant separate attention. Upon finding such short spans, both Long and Rabbitt argued that typists must monitor the accuracy of each individual keystroke. This suggests the single letter as the unit of the stopping span.

It is instructive to consider the error-detection span in terms of the time it represents. Subjects seem to detect an error and abort the planned sequence of keystrokes within one interkeystroke interval of its occurrence. This represents 100-150 msec for skilled typists, a very short time indeed. However, this analysis rests on the assumption that keystrokes are executed serially, so that the next one cannot begin until the current one is finished. Recent high-speed films of a skilled typist call this assumption into question: Gentner, Grudin, and Conway (Note 1) found an average of 261 msec elapsing between the onset and termination of the movement for a single keystroke, compared to an average interkeystroke interval of 124 msec. Moreover, the movement for the next keystroke began before the movement for the current one finished on 96% of the occasions on which keystrokes alternated between hands.

Clearly, keystrokes are not executed serially. They often begin more than one interkeystroke interval before they are registered on the keyboard. This is important, because there is evidence that typists may detect their errors before they register on the keyboard: Shaffer (1975) found that error latencies were often longer than the average interkeystroke interval, suggesting that subjects detected their errors before they occurred and tried to inhibit them. Rabbitt (1978) found that errors were often struck with less force than correct responses, suggesting that they were detected before their occurrence and "pulled."

Putting this together with the evidence that keystrokes may be executed in parallel suggests that typists may be able to detect their errors more than one interkeystroke interval before they occur. In principle, errors may be detected any time between the initiation of the erroneous movement and the (expected) termination of the keystroke following the error (i.e., movement time for the error plus one interkeystroke interval). In the typist filmed by Gentner et al. (Note 1), an error-detection span of zero characters represents a maximum interval of 385 msec (i.e., 261 msec of movement time plus 124 msec of interkeystroke interval). This renders less impressive the speed of error detection. Nevertheless, it represents a substantially shorter period of time than the eye-hand span or the copying span.

Three aspects of the error-detection procedure suggest that the spans discussed here may not represent the "true" stopping span. First, Rabbitt's figures are based on single errors only; errors involving more than one character were excluded from analysis. Single errors constituted 56% of the total error corpus in Experiment 1 and 36% in Experiment 2. By definition, errors involving more than one character must represent spans longer than zero characters (i.e., if a subject typed *rae* ch* for *reach*, the span from the first error to the report, *, would be one, and the span from the second to the report would be zero). Rabbitt excluded these errors because of the inherent ambiguity in classifying them, and as a result, he may have inadvertently underestimated the stopping span. It is not clear from Long's report whether he included or excluded errors involving more than one character.

Second, subjects in Rabbitt's and Long's studies detected only 70% of their errors. It is not clear what would have happened if the rate of error detection were higher.

Finally, it is important to note that errors are significant events to a skilled typist, and special strategies may have been developed to cope with them. Possibly, typists can anticipate when an error is likely to occur, and adopt a special mode of control to prevent them. Thus, the control that typists manifest when errors occur may not represent the control processes used more typically.

Stop signal method. One way to alleviate many of the problems with the error-detection method is to ask subjects to stop typing when they detect some arbitrary event controlled by the experimenter (e.g., a tone or a change in the display). The onset of the stop signal can be specified exactly, and it can be presented independent of the subject's typing. Thus, it is easier to interpret, and may reflect a more typical stopping span.

The only studies using this method were reported by Logan (1982). He conducted four experiments that differed in the type of text and the type of stop signal they employed. Three experiments used discrete trials on which single words were presented. In two of them, the stop signal was a tone presented on 20% of the trials. In these cases, subjects typed an average of 1.6 and 1.4 characters before stopping. In the third study, the stop signal was a change in the display; the single word changed into a new word on 25% of the trials. There the average span was 2.8 characters. The difference in span could be due to the difference in the probability of occurrence of the stop signal, since this is an important variable in stop signal studies (Logan, 1981), or it could be due to the difference in the type of stop signal. Reaction time is often faster to an auditory stimulus than to a visual one, and in the typing studies, the difference would be exaggerated by any tendency to look at the keyboard while typing (since subjects must look at the display to detect the change in the display, but need not look anywhere in particular to detect the tone). I suspect that the difference in the stop signals is the important variable.

The fourth study used sentences, and the stop signal was a tone and a change in the display (the display extinguished at the onset of the tone). In that study, the average span was 2.2 characters. The span was longer than the 1.4- and 1.6-character spans from the single-word tone signal studies, either because of the sentence context or because of differences in the probability of occurrence of the stop signal. (In the sentence study, the stop signal occurred with 33% of the sentences, or equivalently, with 7% of the words.) The distribution of the number of characters typed after the stop signal in the sentence study is presented in Figure 8.1. It is based on 1,200 observations. Presented with it is the distribution of the eye-hand span from Butsch (1932). Although there is some overlap between distributions, they are clearly different.

A major purpose of Logan's experiments was to determine whether the units of the stopping span were single letters or single words. This was assessed from the way the stopping span was affected by word length and by *stop signal delay* (i.e., the delay between the onset of the word and the onset of the stop signal, or the delay between the onset of typing and the onset of the stop signal). If subjects typed whole words before stopping, span should be strongly affected by stop signal delay and word length, since for a given word length, more letters remain to be typed the shorter the delay; and for a given delay, more letters remain to be typed the longer the word. On the other hand, if subjects could stop after individual letters or clusters of two or three, the span should not be affected by delay or word length. In all four experiments, the span was unaffected by stop signal delay and by word length, ruling out the former alternative and supporting the latter. The mean spans from the study in which the display changed are presented in Figure 8.4.

In this study, subjects performed one of three tasks when the display changed (a new word replaced the old one). In the stop task, they stopped typing the first word; in the change task, they stopped typing the first word and began typing the new word as quickly as possible;

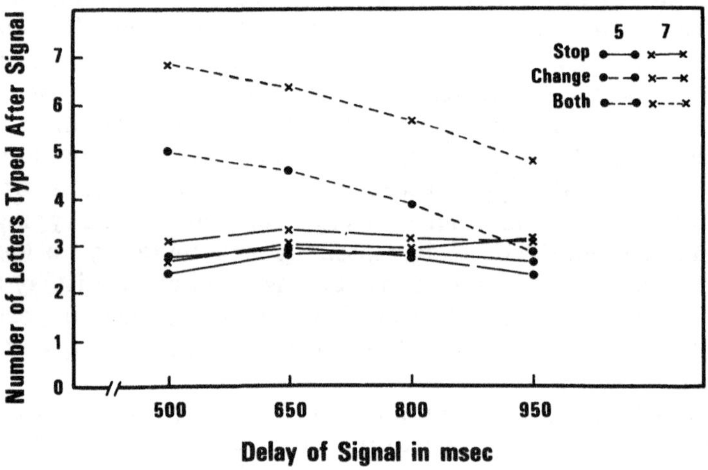

Fig. 8.4. Mean number of letters typed after signal (change in display from one word to another) as a function of signal delay. Two word lengths (five and seven characters) and three task conditions (stop: stop typing when the word changes; change: stop typing the first word and type the second and soon as possible; and both: finish typing the first word and type the second as soon as possible) are shown (from Logan, 1982, Table 7). Note that word length and signal delay had substantial effects in the both condition (since at a given delay, more letters remain to be typed in the longer words, and since for a given word length, more letters remain to be typed the shorter the delay) but neither length nor delay affected the stop or change task. Typists can interrupt their typing in midword. Mean spans were about the same in the stop task and in the change task.

and in the type both task, they completed the first word and typed the second as quickly as possible. Thus, the spans from the type both task represent quantitative predictions of the spans from the stop task on the hypothesis that subjects must type out whole words before stopping. The data in the figure clearly disconfirm the hypothesis: Spans in the stop task were not affected by delay or word length, and were substantially smaller than the spans in the type both task. Subjects rarely completed whole words before stopping.

The only exception occurred in the sentence study, when subjects typed the word *the*. The average span around *the* was 2.7 characters, significantly longer than the 2.0-character span at comparable places in the sentence. Analysis of span distributions suggested that the mean increased because subjects often completed the word and the following space before stopping (see Logan, 1982, Figure 3). This is interesting because it suggests that familiar words or letter sequences may be typed ballistically; typists may not be able to stop them without completing them.

The general finding that subjects can easily stop typing in midword is consistent with the conclusion from error-detection studies that the single letter is the unit of the stopping span. This suggests that the stopping span is influenced by a much lower level of linguistic structure than is the eye-hand span or the copying span, which indicates once again that they are different.

Another difference between the stopping span and the eye-hand span is that the stopping span is independent of typing skill. Altogether, Logan tested 19 subjects in the three experiments that used a tone as a stop signal and shared the same test of typing speed (some subjects served in more than one experiment). Their typing speeds ranged from 47 to 87 wpm, and their mean spans ranged from 1.2 to 3.0 characters; however, there was no correlation between speed and span: $r(17) = .197$, $F(1, 17) < 1$. This contrasts with the positive relation between speed and span in the eye-hand span (Butsch, 1932), again suggesting that the stopping span and the eye-hand span are different beasts.

The stopping spans represent an interval of about 250-500 msec. The single-word studies with auditory stop signals produced spans of 1.6 and 1.4 characters, which took 281 and 245 msec to type, respectively. The sentence study, which also used auditory stop signals, produced spans of 2.2 characters, which took 304 msec to type. The single-word study with a display change as the stop signal produced 2.8-character spans, which took 478 msec to type. These intervals are about the same as the time taken by the error-detection spans, and are considerably shorter than the 1-sec interval for the eye-hand span and the 10-sec interval for the copying span.

Changing the display. When the display changes, replacing old text with new, it is possible to ask subjects to stop typing the old text and begin typing the new as soon as possible. This provides another estimate of the stopping span under conditions that differ from the stop signal task in interesting ways. The only study using this method was reported by Logan (1982), together with the stop signal studies discussed earlier.

Spans obtained with the change task reflect subjects' ability to stop a response sequence in order to reprogram the motor system. These spans can be compared with spans obtained in the stop task in order to determine whether the requirement to reprogram the motor system affects the ability to stop. The mean spans from Logan's stop and change tasks are presented in Figure 8.4. Clearly, there was no difference in the spans produced by the different tasks: Subjects typed 2.8 characters after the display change in the stop task, versus 3.0 in the change task.

In the change task, the latency from the onset of the new word to the typing of the first character of the new word is an interesting datum, particularly when it is contrasted with the latency from the onset of the new word to the first character of the new word in the type both condition (in the type both condition, subjects complete the old word and then type the new one when the display changes). The comparison allows us to determine whether the internal components of the typing response stop when the external components (overt movements) stop. Possibly the external components can stop in midword, but the internal components cannot; instead, they must finish dealing with the word before a new one can be programmed. If this were true, initial latencies to the second word should be no different in the change task and the type both task. On the other hand, if subjects are able to interrupt the internal components and the external components in midword, initial latencies to the new word should be substantially faster in the change condition than in the type both condition. The data clearly support the latter alternative: In the change condition, the mean initial latency to the new word was 892 msec, whereas in the type both condition, the mean initial latency was 1158 msec.

According to the arguments presented earlier about the effects of word length and signal delay, the data in Figure 8.4 indicate that the unit of the change span is smaller than the word. Further, the change span was not related to typing speed: $r(9) = -.327$, $F(1, 9) = 1.07$. The 3.0-character span from the change task took 498 msec to type, compared to the 478 msec required to type the 2.8-character span in the stop task (the same subjects performed the two tasks). Thus, the change span and the stop span appear to be very similar.

The initial latency to the new word in the change task may represent a "reprogramming span," which may have different properties than the change span. It is substantially longer than the change span (892 msec vs. 498 msec) and is related to typing speed: Faster typists manifested shorter initial latencies to the new word: $r(9) = .610$, $F(1, 9) = 5.32$, $p < .05$. The meaning of this interval will be discussed later in the context of the duration of the eye-hand span.

Summary. The stop signal and display change methods suggest a stopping span of 1.5-3 characters, and the error-detection method suggests a span of 0-1 character. The difference between the methods disappears when span is considered in units of time instead of in units of information; in all three methods, the spans represent an interval of 250-500 msec. The unit of the stopping span is smaller than the word, and appears to be the single letter. Finally, the stopping span is not related to typing skill, as measured by typing speed. Thus, it is markedly different from the eye-hand span and the copying span.

Theoretical Issues

There is clear evidence for three separate spans in typewriting, distinguished by their length and the kinds of structure they are sensitive to. What does it all mean? This section is concerned with how they may be distinguished theoretically, and how they function together in the course of "normal" typing. First we consider general interpretations of spans in units of information and in units of time. Keeping the advantages of each perspective in mind, we then consider how the three spans might fit into a set of processes that might underly typing, and whether it seems more appropriate to interpret each span in terms of the time or the information it represents.

Span as Information or Span as Time?

An "ancient" truism in modern cognitive psychology is that information is processed over time. This implies a sort of reciprocity between information and time such that it is often as appropriate to think of a process in terms of the time it takes as in terms of the information it transmits. This appears to be true of spans in typewriting. The possible reciprocity suggests different perspectives on the spans, which reveal different properties.

Span in units of information. The different processes underlying typewriting must communicate in some way to produce output. The communication may be mediated by *buffer memories* that accept output from "earlier" processes and make it available to "later" processes. In this context, spans may represent the contents of the different buffers between processes (i.e., the information they contain). The different processes need not parse the text into the same units. If one unit in an earlier process translates into several units in a later process, the buffer memory between the processes must hold the several units until the later process is ready to deal with them. From this perspective, spans may be artifacts of differences in unit size; spans will occur as an inevitable consequence of translation whenever one unit in an earlier process yields more than one unit in a later process.

Why should typists adopt units of different sizes for different processes? Clearly, adult readers can organize their reading in many ways, and it would be possible to read text letter by letter, so each process could deal with the same unit (letters). The advantages of larger units are redundancy and economy of coding: Several lower level units can be packed into one higher-order unit, and this unit can be passed in less time with a lower probability of error than could the several lower order units that it comprises (imagine repeating a five-letter word three times vs. saying each of its letters once). Coding in higher order units also allows the typist to correct errors in higher order structures. For example, misspelled words could be recognized correctly, and upon recognition, the correct spelling could be retrieved. Grammatical errors or semantic slips could be detected and corrected. (Note that this discussion assumes the task of copy typing; an author composing at a typewriter probably generates the text to be typed by thinking in higher order units.)

Apart from their alleged necessity, buffer memories or spans may ease communication and simplify coordination between processes. Buffer memories absorb time-of-arrival differences between different inputs. If a later process that "reads" its input from the buffer does so one unit at a time, taking the next unit in the buffer as soon as it is finished with the current one, it does not matter whether there are several units queued in the buffer or whether the succeeding units have yet to enter the buffer, as long as there is another unit for the later process to read when it finishes with the current one. This allows considerable flexibility in timing communication between processes; the earlier process can put the next unit into the buffer immediately after it finishes putting the current one there, or it could wait until the buffer is empty (i.e., until the later process has emptied the buffer). This may represent a substantial period of time. For example, if five units were queued in the buffer, it would not have to be filled again until the later process had cycled five times. By contrast, if there were no buffer, the two processes would have to be closely synchronized, the earlier passing the next unit to the later whenever the later is finished with the current one. This would require communication once in each cycle of the later process, which is a much shorter period of time than would be available were there a buffer. Thus, there are advantages to a full buffer that may induce typists to look a little farther ahead than one unit.

Span in units of time. The three spans differ in the amount of time they represent as well as the amount of information. How can we interpret spans in units of time? Spans may reflect an adaptation to temporal constraints on communication between the component processes underlying typing. Each component may require a substantial amount of time to process a single unit, which we call the *cycle time* of the process, and span may be an artifact of cycle time: In order to have finished with a unit at some particular point in time (i.e., when a later process is ready to accept it), a process must begin dealing with it one cycle time earlier than it is needed. If the process begins less than one cycle time earlier than the unit is needed, the later process will be forced to wait, slowing the rate of typing and reducing its regularity. From this perspective, spans play an important role in maximizing speed and regularity; spans represent how far ahead a process must be in order to prevent gaps in typing (i.e., one cycle time).

To be more precise, how far one process must be ahead of another in time depends on three factors: the cycle time of the earlier process (CTe), the cycle time of the later process (CTl), and the number of later process units produced per cycle of the earlier process (N). The product $N \times$ CTl represents the time taken by the later process to deal with the output of one cycle of the earlier process. The relation between this time and the cycle time of the earlier process has important implications for typing performance. Consider the following three cases:

$$N \times \text{CTl} > \text{CTe}; \tag{1}$$

$$N \times \text{CTl} = \text{CTe}; \tag{2}$$

$$N \times \text{CTl} < \text{CTe}. \tag{3}$$

In Case 1, the later process takes more time to deal with earlier process output than the earlier process takes to produce it. Consequently, the earlier process is not rushed for time, compelled to function at its maximum rate. This is a desirable state of affairs, since there is plenty of time to absorb perturbations in the timing of the earlier process. The earlier process may have the option of beginning the next unit before the later process is finished with the current one, thus increasing the amount of information in the buffer. In turn, this would increase the magnitude of the inequality in processing times, further relaxing the temporal constraints on the earlier process.

In Case 2, the later process deals with earlier process outputs as quickly as the earlier process can produce them. This represents a limiting case of Case 1; typing can remain smooth and fast as long as the earlier process functions at its maximum rate, and as long as there are no severe perturbations in timing. Otherwise, gaps would appear in the typing.

In Case 3, the later process deals with earlier process outputs faster than the earlier process can produce them. Gaps will appear in typing unless the earlier process can reduce its effective cycle time by processing its own units in parallel. Parallel processing is possible at some levels of processing in typing; the high-speed films of Gentner et al. (Note 1) show unequivocally that the movements of the different fingers occur in parallel. It is possible that at higher levels of processing only one unit can be dealt with at a time, so Case 3 may sometimes produce gaps (i.e., it may not be possible to compose two thoughts at once, hence the long gaps in typing as I compose this chapter).

This analysis has interesting implications for the development of skill in typing: As typists acquire skill, their typing becomes faster and more regular. Presumably at least part of this change occurs because some of the component processes become faster. Can we say which ones? The present analysis suggests that it is more important that an earlier process gain speed than a later process. Case 3 represents slow, irregular typing, characteristic of an unskilled typist, and Case 1 represents fast, smooth typing, characteristic of a skilled typist. The transition from Case 3 to Case 1 mimics the acquisition of skill. This transition can occur in two ways: by slowing down the later process (increasing CTl $\times$ N) or by speeding up the earlier process (reducing CTe). Since practice generally speeds processing, the second possibility is more likely if we wish to interpret the transition from Case 3 to Case 1 as the acquisition of skill.

A second possibility is that skill develops partly as a result of increased ability to process units at the same level in parallel. This could reduce the effective cycle time of early or late processes, moving from Case 3 to Case 1 or vice versa (respectively). However, its most important effect would be to maintain a full buffer, producing a transition from Case 3 to Case 1 by increasing the effective N.

The two alternatives can be distinguished empirically. The first predicts that skilled typists should differ from unskilled typists in the speed of their early processes more so than in the speed of their late processes. One way to test this would be to measure the speed of finger movements of skilled and unskilled touch typists. The difference in finger speed should not account for much of the difference in typing speed if the first alternative is correct. Further, any evidence that skilled and unskilled typists differ more in the speed of their later processes than of their earlier processes would damage the first alternative.

Such evidence would be consistent with the second alternative, since the second alternative suggests that skill depends on parallel processing and may be independent of the speed with which a single unit can be processed. It need not predict that later processes would be relatively faster in skilled typists than in unskilled typists. It does predict more parallel processing in skilled typists than in unskilled typists, however.

Later, we test these predictions in the eye-hand span, trying to account for Butsch's (1932) correlation between speed and span on the one hand, and Logan's (1982) correlation between speed and the latency to the first letter of the second word in the change task on the other (which represents the cycle time of the earlier process in the eye-hand span).

Spans and the Components of Typing

So far, our discussion of the processes underlying typing has been very general, distinguishing only between early and late processes. Now it is time to consider specific processes and to relate them to specific spans. The discussion will remain fairly general, since we have grounds only for distinguishing processes connected by a buffer memory or span, and there are only three spans to consider. The set of processes and memories (spans) we will consider are presented in an information-flow diagram in Figure 8.5.

People type for a purpose, and the purpose dictates which processes will be required. In general, we distinguish between *transcription* typing, in which typists copy text presented to them to type, and *composition* typing, in which the typist generates the text to be typed. They involve different routes through the memories and processes depicted in Figure 8.5. All of the studies discussed in this chapter have involved transcription typing.

Transcription typing. Transcription typing involves a flow of information through a perceptual system, through a translation process, to the execution of physical keystrokes (see Figure 8.5). The perceptual system will vary with task requirements; subjects can type from written copy of from dictation. Either perceptual system is probably a collection of several systems interacting in a complex manner to produce input for the translation process. For example, Butsch (1932) found evidence of regressive eye movements in his typists, suggesting a close link between the eye movement system and the visual-cognitive system to maximize the gain of information (i.e., a typist may make regressive eye movement to confirm an interpretation of the text). However, the complex interaction is probably hidden by the eye-hand span, which would absorb time of arrival differences in information coming from the perceptual system (i.e., most often, Case 1 applies to transcription typing).

It is clear that transcription will entail the eye-hand span and the stopping span; what is not clear is the extent to which the copying span is also entailed. Recall the extreme procedure Rothkopf (1980) had to employ to produce the copying span (forced alternation between reading the text to be typed and typing it). The fact that the written text to be copied is continuously available to the visual system minimizes the necessity of relying on memory to retain it; the written text serves as an external memory. The copying span may be more important in typing from dictation, since speech is transitory and the words to be typed would be harder to recover than they would in the case of vision.

Composition typing. In composition typing, typists generate their own text. Thus, the perceptual system is replaced by a "construction" pro-

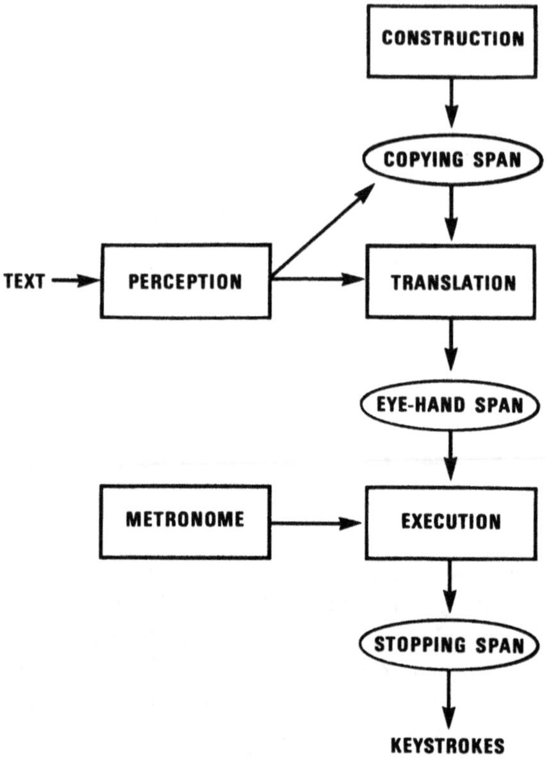

Fig. 8.5. Possible processes and buffer memories underlying typewriting. Transcription typing and composition involve different sets of processes: Transcription requires perception of the text to be copied, translation of the text into a motor program, and execution of the motor program. Transcription typing requires a buffer between translation and execution, reflecting the eye-hand span, and a buffer between execution and the external world, reflecting the stopping span. It may or may not involve a buffer between perception and translation, reflecting the copying span. Composition involves construction of ideas, propositions, and sentences, translation of these structures into motor programs, and execution of the motor program. Composition requires buffers between translation and execution and between execution and the external world, as does transcription. The buffer between construction and translation, which is optional in transcription typing, is necessary in composition. The metronome is a timing process that generates rhythmic pulses that pace the execution of keystrokes in both transcription and composition.

cess (see Figure 8.5) that generates ideas and turns them into sentences, clauses, or phrases. The construction process is certainly a complex system involving many interacting processes. The construction process is very slow relative to translation and execution, so the later processes must often wait until the next idea comes along. Thus, most often, Case 3 applies to composition typing. Anyone who has ever composed at a typewriter knows that gaps often occur in the typing itself, and the gaps can be very long. The duration and spacing of the gaps may reveal important properties of the construction process (e.g., Tannenbaum, Williams, & Wood, 1967).

In composition typing, the copying span probably represents a working memory, holding words representing sentence fragments in a queue. These are translated word by word into motor programs, which are held in the buffer that represents eye-hand span in transcription typing. Then the keystrokes are executed. Since little is known about composition typing (little is known about composition itself), these remarks are highly speculative.

The Three Spans Revisited

The copying span. Is it more appropriate to think of the copying span in terms of the information it contains or in terms of the time interval it represents? It seems to me (and to Rothkopf, 1980) that the copying span represents the conventional short-term memory or the more modern working memory (e.g., Hitch, 1980). That is probably its role in composition typing. Thus, the copying span reflects information more than time. If five-letter words are assumed (as is conventional in typing), the 40-character copying span represents about eight words, well within the span of short-term memory, since the words are connected grammatically and semantically. Consistent with this is the earlier suggestion that the units of the copying span are clauses or phrases; the words in the span may chunk into a single structural unit.

Alternatively, the copying span may reflect an extended eye-hand span; in exceptional circumstances, typists may be able to hold up to 40 keystrokes in queue for execution. This seems unlikely, given conventional views about the capacity of short-term storage. Moreover, specific theories argue for a relatively short eye-hand span. In Rumelhart and Norman's model (1982) only unique keystrokes are queued for execution; the queue is considered full the first time a letter is repeated. This is necessary in order to distinguish between doubled letters (e.g., the *e*'s in *street*) and repeated letters (e.g., the *e*'s in *delete*). Otherwise, their model would have trouble simulating the ordering of keystrokes.

The eye-hand span. The eye-hand span mediates between translation and execution in composition and transcription tasks (see Figure 8.5). Is the eye-hand better conceived of in units of information or in units of time? The answer is probably both.

There is abundant evidence that the eye-hand span reflects structure up to the word level, but no higher (see above). In the present context, this suggests that the translation process works with words and the execution process works with letters. Since most words contain more than one letter, a word-length span is forced on the system. Thus, it seems necessary to think of the eye-hand span in units of information.

It is also appropriate, however, to think of the eye-hand span in units of time. Recall Butsch's (1932) claim that the eye-hand span represents the number of characters that can be typed in 1 sec. The discussion above about spans in units of time suggests that the 1-sec interval might represent the cycle time of the translation process, or alternatively, the cycle time of the whole set of processes prior to execution.

Is there any reason to believe that the earlier processes might require 1 sec to cycle? The earlier processes encode a word from the written text and translate it into a motor program that specifies a series of keystrokes. Rough estimates of the cycle time of these processes can be obtained from measures of interkeystroke interval when subjects have no preview of the text (e.g., Shaffer, 1973), from the latency to the first keystroke of a word in discrete trials typing tasks (e.g., Logan, 1982; Ostry, 1980; Sternberg, Monsell, Knoll, & Wright, 1978), and from the latency to the first keystroke of the second word in Logan's (1982) word change procedure. Let us consider each in turn.

With no preview, typists cannot see the next letter to be typed until the current keystroke is registered. The interval between the registration of the current keystroke and the registration of the next one includes the time to encode the next letter, translate it into a motor program, and execute it. The cycle time of the preexecution processes can thus be estimated from such interkeystroke intervals. The intervals in the literature turn out to be a little too fast: Shaffer (1973) found a 450- to 500-msec interval in one highly skilled typist (see Figure 8.2), and Shaffer and Hardwick (1970) found intervals of 700-750 msec in relatively unskilled typists trained on a reduced keyboard.

Initial latencies in discrete trials typing tasks may also reflect the cycle time of preexecution processes. In the discrete trials procedure, a single word is presented and the subject is told to type it as quickly as possible. If subjects are allowed to encode the word at leisure and then type it in response to a "go" signal, initial latencies are on the order of 300 msec (Ostry, 1980; Sternberg et al. 1978), far too fast for a 1-sec cycle time. The go signal procedure leaves many of the interesting preexecution processes outside the latent period (i.e., the word is encoded before the go signal). If subjects are required to type a word as soon as it appears, without waiting for a go signal, the latency of the first keystroke is on the order of 700 msec (Logan, 1982; Ostry, 1980). This interval includes the interesting preexecution processes, but again is too fast for the 1-sec cycle time we are looking for.

Apart from suggesting intervals that are too fast, the no-preview task and the discrete trials task differ from continuous transcription typing in one respect that may be important. In transcription typing, typists normally encode one word while they are typing another. This feature is missing in the no-preview task and the discrete trials task, and it is possible that the estimates of cycle time they suggest would be increased substantially, moving them closer to the desired 1-sec interval, if subjects were typing while they were encoding. The word change procedure of Logan (1982) takes one step toward removing this discrepancy. Two of the tasks typists had to perform when the word changed involved encoding the new word while typing the old. These were the change task, in which subjects were told to stop typing the first word and begin typing the second, and the type both task, in which subjects were told to complete the first word and then type the second. The latencies to the first letter of the second word in these two tasks include the interesting preexecution processes, and so may provide a more appropriate measure of on-line cycle time.

The latency from the change task represents a minimal cycle time, since subjects were allowed to abort the old word and begin typing the new word as soon as they possibly could. The mean latency to the second word was 892 msec, relatively close to the 1-sec interval we want. The latency to the first letter of the second word in the type both task may represent a more typical cycle time. Subjects may finish encoding the second word before they finish typing the first. This would allow some temporal slack in encoding and translating the second word (i.e., Case 1, such as might occur in normal typing). Here, the mean initial latency was 1158 msec, slightly longer than the desired 1-sec interval, but clearly in the neighborhood.

This analysis suggests a reformulation of the equation representing Butsch's hypothesis. Butsch's equation,

$$\text{eye-hand span} = (\text{letters/sec}) \times 1 \text{ sec},$$

becomes

$$\text{eye-hand span} = (\text{letters/sec}) \times \text{CTtranslation},$$

where letters/sec is the reciprocal of the cycle time of the execution process and CTtranslation is the cycle time of the preexecution processes. In Logan's (1982) change task, the mean interkeystroke interval was 165 msec and the mean latency to the second word was 892 msec, yielding a predicted eye-hand span of 5.41 letters. In his type both task, the mean interkeystroke interval was 174 msec and the mean latency to the second word was 1,158 msec, yielding a predicted eye-hand span of 6.66 letters. These values are well within the normal range of the eye-hand span (see Figure 8.1).

The foregoing arguments and the logic developed in the section on interpreting spans in units of time suggest an interesting interpretation of Butsch's (1932) finding that the eye-hand span increased with typing skill. In the earlier section, we considered two ways in which typing skill may develop—by increasing the speed of component processes or by increasing dependence on parallel processing. The increase in span with skill supports the latter alternative. To see why, consider how the cycle times of translation and execution would have to change in order for span to increase with skill: According to the equation above, which expresses eye-hand span in terms of the cycle times of translation and execution, eye-hand span could only increase by increasing the speed of the execution process relative to the speed of translation (i.e., by increasing letters/sec). The correlation between speed and span suggests that this must be true. This follows because the increase in span with skill means that more characters are typed in the same time (i.e., the cycle time of translation). (Note that there is evidence that the speed of the preexecution processes may increase as well; this is what is suggested by Logan's 1982 finding that latency to the second word in the change task correlates with typing skill. In order for span to increase with skill, the execution process must gain speed at a faster rate than the translation process does.)

Increasing the speed of execution relative to translation would create a problem: According to the analysis of Cases 1, 2, and 3, it would produce gaps in typing (i.e., a transition from Case 1 to Case 3). However, gaps in typing tend to occur less frequently as a typist acquires skill (Shaffer & Hardwick, 1970), so something must be done to prevent them. The only way to eliminate gaps in typing is to have the translation process deal with its units in parallel, so the buffer between translation and execution always contains letters to be executed. Thus, typing skill must depend on the ability to process in parallel as well as on an increase in speed.

The stopping span. In Figure 8.5 the stopping span represents a final buffer between execution and the keystokes themselves. Is this buffer necessary? The answer to this question bears on the answer to another, which expresses the theme of this section: Is it appropriate to think of the stopping span in units of information or is it better to think of it in units of time? Let us consider why execution may need a buffer.

An execution buffer may be important in timing keystrokes and typing rhythmically. Typing may be paced by an internal metronome, as Shaffer (1978) has suggested. This is not to say that a central timing mechanism is responsible for all temporal patterning in the interkeystroke interval data; Rumelhart and Norman (1982) argue convincingly that the physical constraints imposed by the hands and the keyboard are responsible for most of the patterning. However, constraints in the hands and the keyboard do not determine the rate at which keystrokes are executed; this requires some central oscillator or metronome. I believe that the metronome provides timing pulses that act as temporal targets against which the motor system attempts to synchronize keystrokes. The timing pulse combines with the constraints of the keyboard and hands to produce the observed temporal patterning in the interkeystroke intervals. The keyboard and the hands may determine the variance of interkeystroke intervals, but the metronome determines the mean.

From this perspective, the next keystroke to be typed may wait in an execution buffer until its timing pulse comes along, and the stopping span reflects the contents of this buffer. Possibly the contents of the buffer must be exhausted before typing can stop (thus the short stopping spans).

It seems more appropriate to think of the stopping span in terms of the time it represents. The different tasks produced a variety of estimates ranging between 200 and 500 msec. This likely represents the time required to detect a signal and stop the execution process. Since simple reaction time to the kinds of stop signals employed in these studies is on the order of 200-300 msec, these short spans indicate that the execution process can be stopped very quickly indeed.

It is interesting to compare stopping times with starting times: Ostry (1980) and Sternberg et al. (1978) used a version of the discrete trials procedure in which subjects were allowed to encode the letter string to be typed but were not allowed to type it until a go signal occurred. Latency to the first keystroke after the go signal was on the order of 300-400 msec, well within the range of times representing the stopping span.

The go signal task is very similar to the stop signal task. In both cases, the preexecution processes have produced a string of characters ready to be executed. The go signal task reflects how quickly the execution process can begin dealing with them; the stop signal task reflects how quickly the execution process can stop dealing with them. It is interesting that it takes about the same amount of time to stop and start the execution process. It is as if there were a switch for turning the process on and off, like a go bit in a computer clock.

The quickness of the stopping times suggests that typists have relatively close temporal control over their typing, able to stop or change what they are doing within a keystroke or two of thinking of it. One way typists could manifest such close control would be to engage a feedback loop that monitors the occurrence of individual keystrokes, releasing the next one in sequence when it receives some signal indicating that the current keystroke is under way (e.g., Long, 1976). This would require close attention to the motor system in skilled typing in order to produce keystrokes every 100-150 msec. This would be consistent with a "late selection" theory of attention in which all stimuli are processed completely, in parallel, without interference, and capacity limitations only come into play in selecting responses (e.g., Duncan, 1980; Norman, 1968). From this perspective, attention is focused on the response end of typing, so subjects can stop very quickly by interrupting the feedback loop. A late selection theory would have trouble accounting for the evidence that the perceptual processes are highly interactive (e.g., the regressive eye movements observed by Butsch, 1932). Presumably interactions between perceptual processes would require attentional control as much as interactions between motor processes. Perhaps perceptual and motor components could be time shared, with attention switching back and forth between them. However, this would require attention shifts every 100-150 msec in skilled typists, which is very fast.

An alternative veiw suggests that the components of typing are controlled by constraining the communication between them (e.g., Logan, 1982). From this view, typing can be stopped by severing the lines of communication between components so that they no longer have information to process. For example, if typing were paced by timing pulses from a metronome, typing could be stopped within one keystroke by preventing the next timing pulse from reaching the execution process. This would be consistent with a hierarchical theory of attention, in which attention has no specific locus in the chain of processes between stimulus and response, but rather controls and coordinates them by establishing the chain and adjusting its parameters to maximize performance (e.g., Broadbent, 1977). However interesting this may be, there are no data to distinguish this alternative from the late selection view, so we need not speculate further.

Concluding Remarks

The literature suggests there are at least three spans underlying typewriting performance—the copying span, the eye-hand span, and the stopping span. The spans differ in the types of linguistic structures they are sensitive to and in the amount of information and time they represent. They seem to play an important role in typewriting, allowing the typist to maintain high speed and a steady rhythm.

Are there other spans in typewriting? Possibly. From the theoretical stance adopted here, spans represent buffers or channels of communication between the component processes of typing. We have distinguished only five processes; obviously a finer grained analysis would reveal more. For each process identified, there should be spans linking it to the processes it communicates with. The difficult part is to find experimental manipulations that will allow us to observe these spans. However, there seems to be no limit to the ingenuity of experimental psychologists, so we can expect new discoveries in the future. (We could also benefit from further study of the spans described here; many of my conclusions are based on analogies across experiments and procedures, and it would be better to have them tested directly in one experiment.)

The contrast between time and information has been very interesting to me, since it highlights the features of typing that reflect the continuous operation of the different components. I have been accustomed to thinking of latencies in a discrete stages framework in which only one stage is working at once. It is very clear that typing cannot be described adequately by discrete stage theory, and it has been instructuve to consider what aspects of timing are informative in a continuous stage or cascade model (cf. McClelland, 1979): Continuous performance is dominated by the cycle time of the slowest process, which often masks the contribution of the other processes.

The typing task itself is different from the tasks typically used to study human cognition in interesting ways that may suggest different kinds of experiments in other domains. Typing is a continuous task, and typists typically have unlimited preview of the text to be typed. This allows them to plan ahead, and to make anticipatory and compensatory adjustments. By contrast, most studies in cognitive psychology use discrete trials in which there is only one (motor) response per trial. Care is taken to randomize the sequence of trials so the subject cannot benefit from knowledge of the past sequence of stimuli, and the next stimulus is not presented until the subject responds to the current one, so the subject cannot choose to process stimuli in parallel or to adjust his or her processing to accommodate the transition between the current trial and the next one.

Many of the tasks we perform in everyday life are more like typing than the discrete trials tasks typically studied in the laboratory. Thus, the skills that emerge in continuous tasks (planning and compensation) are probably important in everyday cognition, and it is unfortunate that most of our research "controls" them out of the picture. Typing thus provides a healthier perspective, since it depends on these emergent abilities. However, typing is only one task, and it highlights motor limitations on performance, so it would not be appropriate to base a whole theory of cognition on typewriting. It would be interesting to study other continuous tasks, and draw together the conclusions that survive shifts in paradigms. Then we would have the beginnings of a valid psychology of everyday cognition.

Reference Note

1. Gentner, D. R., Grudin, J., & Conway, E. *Finger movements in transcription typing* (Tach. Rep. 8001) La Jolla, Calif.: University of California at San Diego, May 1980.

References

Broadbent, D. Levels, hierarchies, and the locus of control. *Quarterly Journal of Experimental Psychology*, 1977, *29*, 181-201.

Butsch, R. L. C. Eye movements and the eye-hand span in typewriting. *Journal of Educational Psychology*, 1932, *23*, 104-121.

Duncan, J. The locus of interference in the perception of simultaneous stimuli. *Psychological Review*, 1980, *87*, 272-300.

Fendrick, P. Hierarchical skills in typewriting. *Journal of Educational Psychology*, 1937, *28*, 609-620.

Hershman, R. L., & Hillix, W. A. Data processing in typing. *Human Factors*, 1965, 7, 483-492.

Hitch, G. J. Developing the concept of working memory. In G. Claxton (Ed.), *Cognitive psychology: New directions.* London: Routledge & Kegan Paul, 1980.

Logan, D. G. Attention, automaticity, and the ability to stop a speeded choice response. In J. Long & A. D. Baddeley (Eds.), *Attention and performance* (Vol. 9) Hillsdale, M. J.: Erlbaum, 1981.

Logan, G. D. On the ability to inhibit complex movements: A stop-signal study of typewriting. *Journal of Experimental Psychology: Human Perception and Performance*, 1982, *8*, 778-792.

Long, J. Visual feedback and skilled keying: Differential effects of masking the printed copy and the keyboard. *Ergonomics*, 1976, *19*, 93-110.

McClelland, J. On the time relations of mental processes: An examination of systems of processes in cascade. *Psychological Review*, 1979, *86*, 287-330.

Norman, D. A. Toward a theory of memory and attention. *Psychological Review*, 1968, *75*, 522-536.

Ostry, D. J. Execution-time movement control. In G. E. Stelmach & J. Requin (Eds.), *Tutorials in motor behavior.* Amsterdam: North-Holland, 1980.

Rabbitt, P. M. A. Detection of errors by skilled typists. *Ergonomics*, 1978, *21*, 945-958.

Rothkopf, E. Z. Copying span as a measure of the information burden or written language. *Journal of Verbal Learning and Verbal Behavior*, 1980, *19*, 562-572.

Rumelhart, D. E., & Norman, D. A. Simulating a skilled typist: A study of skilled cognitive-motor performance. *Cognitive Science*, 1982, *6*, 1-36.

Shaffer, L. H. Latency mechanisms in transcription. In S. Kornblum (ed.), *Attention and performance* (Vol. 4) New York: Academic Press, 1973.

Shaffer, L. H. Control processes in typing. *Quarterly Journal of Experimental Psychology*, 1975, *27*, 419-432.

Shaffer, L. H. Intention and performance, *Psychological Review*, 1976, *83*, 375-393.

Shaffer, L. H. Timing in the motor programming of typing. *Quarterly Journal of Experimental Psychology*, 1978, *30*, 333-345.

Shaffer, L. H., & Harkwick, J. Typing performance as a function of text. *Quarterly Journal of Experimental Psychology*, 1968, *20*, 360-369.

Shaffer, L. H., & Hardwick, J. The basis of transcription skill. *Journal of Experimental Psychology*, 1970, *84*, 424-440.

Sternberg, S., Monsell, S., Knoll, R. L., & Wright, C. E. The latency and duration of rapid movement sequences: Comparisons of speech and typewriting. In G. E. Stelmach (Ed.), *Information processing in motor control and learning.* New York: Academic Press, 1978.

Tannenbaum, P. H., Williams F., & Wood, B. S. Hesitation phenomena and related encoding characteristics in speech and typewriting. *Language and Speech*, 1967, *19*, 203-215.

Chapter 9
Determinants of Interkey Times in Typing

David J. Ostry

Typewriting, musical instrument playing, spoken language, and dance involve sophisticated motor skills and associated symbol schemes. Researchers in cognition have been interested in these abilities because they enable the study of relations between the structure of motor behavior and the organization of the associated formal system. Typewriting, in particular, is of interest because of the remarkable rate and complexity of finger and hand movements involved and because its performance is readily quantifiable. However, if typewriting is to be used to study either cognitive or motor organization, the factors contributing to its temporal structure must be identified.

In this chapter I present the findings of several studies that examine variables that influence the pattern of interkey times in typing. In addition to providing evidence on the constituents of control in typing, the studies provide a basis for the examination of proposals by Ostry (1980) and Sternberg, Monsell, Knoll, and Wright (1978) that certain aspects of typing control are inherently tied to the execution of the sequence. The suggestions arise from observations that patterns of initial latency and interkey time are not changed by the introduction of a delay between stimulus presentation and a response signal. The inability to take advantage of a preparation interval seems to indicate that the programming of typing movements is intimately linked to their execution.

Hand Movements

A common experience for both the novice and the expert is that it is easier to type words such as *for*, in which successive characters involve the fingers of opposite hands, than words such as *was* or *wed*, in which successive characters involve the repeated use of the fingers of a single hand and sometimes the repetition of the same finger. The phenomenon raises the question how much of the timing of typing is due to motor coordination between the fingers of the two hands as opposed to the lexical and orthographic structure of the material being copied.

The issue is relevant in the context of recent claims by Terzuolo and Viviani (1980) that the timing of typing reflects an underlying "engram" for the word as a whole. Terzuolo and Viviani found that on repeated typing of a single word, the duration of intervals from one keystroke to the next was scaled in proportion to changes in speed. The scaling of interval durations resulted in a characteristic interkey time profile for the word as a whole. This was interpreted as evidence for a central program for a word.

The interkey time patterns in typing are known to differ substantially between words (Harding, 1933; Shaffer, 1978: Terzuolo & Viviani, 1980). Part of the difference may be due to the particular hand movements involved, independent of the words that are actually typed. For example, on the repetition of isolated letter pairs, performance is more rapid when successive characters involve fingers of opposite hands than when two fingers of the same hand are used (Coover, 1923; Dvorak, Merrick, Dealey, & Ford, 1936). Similarly, with sentences, alternating between hands for successive characters is more rapid than repeating the use of a single hand (Lahy, 1924).

The first study was undertaken to examine the effects of hand movement on typing, independent of differences between words. In describing the study, the term *hand alternation* will be used when successive letters are typed with fingers of opposite hands; *hand repetition* will be used when two fingers of a single hand are used for successive letters. Because it was desirable to examine all possible combinations of hand alternation and repetition movements at a given word length, the study was restricted to five-letter words. For example, the same sequence of hand movements was represented by each of *right*, *blame*, *chair*, and *laugh*. A different sequence was represented by *grape*, *lunch*, *scale*, and *brake*. In total, there are 16 different patterns of hand alternation and repetition possible for five-letter words. Fifteen different monosyllabic words were tested for each of the 16 different movement sequences, with order of presentation randomized.

Subjects in the study were 15 students whose speeds on prose ranged from 37 to 89 words per minute (wpm). (The wide range of speeds enabled tests of performance change with differences in skill.) The words were presented in uppercase on a video screen, at a rate of one word every 5 sec. A brief audio signal was synchronized with the onset of each word. An IBM Selectric was used for testing; the interkey times were recorded with 1-msec accuracy by means of a PDP-11/20 computer. Subjects were instructed to start typing when the stimulus was presented and to type rapidly while maintaining as low an error rate as possible. (The effects of different instructions to subjects are reported later in the section on single-word strategies.) The data are based on words that were typed without error. Error rates in the study ranged from .02 to .11 with an average of .053.

Initial latencies and interkey times were examined separately. Initial latencies were greater than interkey times and also varied with the movement composition of the word. Initial latencies were longer when the first movement within the word (letter 1 to 2) involved alternation as opposed to repetition of hands, $F(1, 15) = 32.39$, $p < .01$, $SE = 2.41$ msec. Latencies preceding a hand alternation averaged 756 msec, while latencies preceding a repetition averaged 739 msec. In contrast, the total number of repetitions or alternations in a word did not affect initial latency in any systematic manner.

Interkey time patterns, excluding initial latencies, are shown in Figure 9.1 for the 16 different movement patterns that were tested. Each of the panels shows interkey times averaged over typists and over the 15 different words used for a particular movement sequence. In general, hand alternation movements were more rapid than hand repetitions, but the extent of the difference seemed to depend on the particular sequence of hand repetitions and alternations involved.

The data on movements within a word were also partitioned in order to examine differences in interkey time between hand alternations and repetitions, without regard to the actual movement sequence. Analysis of variance across typists found alternations reliably faster than repetitions, $F(1, 14) = 265.49$, $p < .01$, $SE = 1.38$ msec. In this study, the mean interkey time for hand alternation was 147 msec and that for repetition was 192 msec, a difference of 45 msec. The analysis was repeated for each of the 15 subjects individually. In all cases interkey times for hand alternations were reliably less than for hand repetitions.

A further analysis examined differences in interkey times for hand alternation and repetition movements as a function of typing speed. As shown in Figure 9.2, timing differences between hand repetition and hand alternation movements were relatively constant over differences in speed.

The constant difference between interkey times for hand alternation and repetition cannot be accounted for strictly in terms of a biomechanical constraint on the repeated use of one hand. This interpretation would require the assumption that slow typists were performing as near to their biomechanical limit for hand repetition as fast typists. Alternatively, the constancy of the delay brought about by the repeated use of a single hand may be associated with the motor organization of movements whose constituents are repeated or overlap. Delays brought about by movement repetition have been reported for both handwriting (Wing, Lewis, & Baddeley, 1979) and speech (Sternberg et al., 1978). The repetition of letters in handwriting causes a slowing relative to sequences in which different letters are produced. The slowing depends on the over-

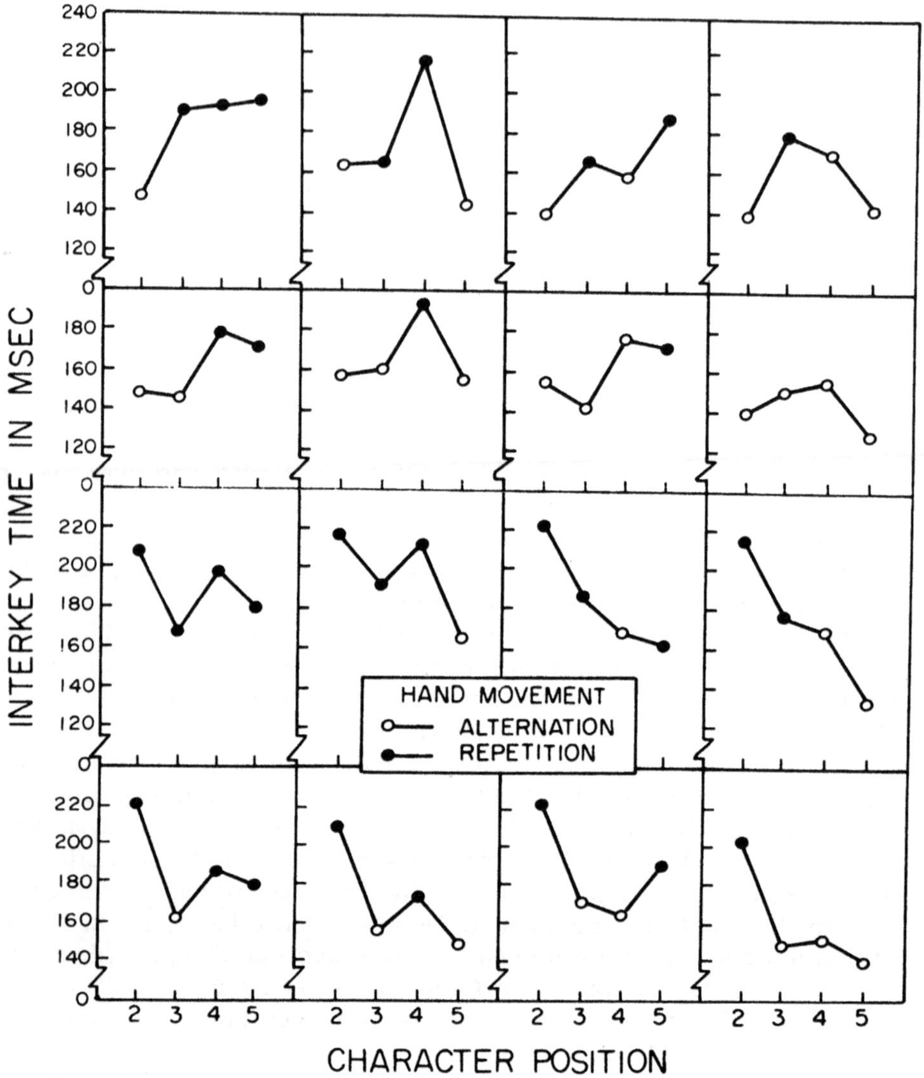

Fig. 9.1. Average interkey times for all sequences of hand alternation and repetition in five-letter words. Times shown at any character position represent average interkey time between character *n* - 1 and character *n*.

lap of movements rather than the actual repetition of the letters; the production of handwritten sequences involving both upper- and lowercase forms of a letter does not produce a comparable slowing of performance. Similarly, when subjects are instructed to say a particular word repeatedly, the production rate is slower than when subjects repeat a sequence of different words.

In contrast to the greater interkey times observed for hand repetition movements, initial latencies were greater prior to initial hand alternation. The finding is consistent with reports by Larochelle (Chapter 4) and

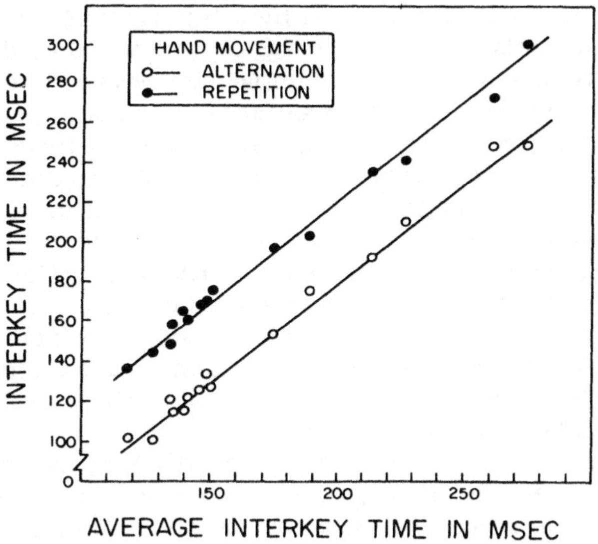

Fig 9.2. Average interkey times for each subject for hand alternation and hand repetition in five-letter words. Times for alternation and repetition are shown for each subject as a function of average typing speed.

Sternberg et al. (1978) as well as with demonstrations of movement timing within words. Both Ostry (1977) and Shaffer (1978) have observed that there is a slowing of movement in the interval preceding a hand alternation. Thus, although alternation of hands seems to improve interkey times in typing, the time occupied prior to response initiation may indicate that bimanual activity actually involves greater underlying complexity than unimanual control.

In summary, the pattern of hand alternation and repetition movements produces substantial differences in the timing of typing. Attempts to assess lexical or orthographic components of typing must account for differences due to movements alone. The delay in interkey times brought about by the repeated use of a single hand suggests that organization at the level of the movements themselves must extend at least to character pairs. Differences in initial latency dependent on the movement from letter 1 to letter 2 likewise implicate a motor organization that extends at least to adjacent movements.

Word Length

Interkey time functions in typing characteristically display a nonmonotonic inverted U-shaped pattern over successive characters. The pattern has been reported for sets of both words (Ostry, 1980; Shaffer & Hardwick, 1970) and nonwords (Ostry, 1980; Sternberg et al., 1978) and is obtained both when subjects start typing immediately on presentation of the stimulus and when performance is delayed for 1 sec. In single words the pattern is masked by substantial differences in timing due to movements between the hands (see the preceding section).

Several writers have interpreted initial latencies and interkey times as indicators of the underlying organization of typing (e.g., Shaffer & Hardwick, 1970; Sternberg et al., 1978). Initial latency and average interkey time have been shown to increase with sequence length when the stimuli are words or letter strings of five letters or less. Except for short sequences, however, the influences of length have not been explored systematically. To the extent that organization in typing is applied to the sequence as a whole, it should be evident over differences in sequence length. The results of several studies in which words of various lengths are typed either alone or in sentences are reported below. The stimuli have been balanced to eliminate differences due to hand alternation and repetition movements.

One set of studies was conducted with words from five to eight letters in length. At each word length, 80 words were selected, such that between any two successive characters the total number of hand alternations and repetitions was approximately equal. For example, approximately half of the 80 words at length 5 required hand alternation from letter 1 to letter 2. Likewise, half (40) required alternation from letter 2 to letter 3, and so on for all character positions and word lengths. All but 5 of the 320 words tested were bisyllabic.

The actual frequencies of hand alternation at word length 5 were 35 alternations between letters 1 and 2; 45 alternations between letters 2 and 3; 38 between letters 3 and 4; and 44 between letters 4 and 5. Corresponding letter pairs at length 6 had hand alternation frequencies of 35, 37, 41, 40, and 41, respectively. Alternation frequencies at length 7 were 43, 36, 40, 42, and 32, and at length B the frequencies were 44, 37, 39, 42, 46, 42, and 30. Proportions of high-frequency words (AA and A, respectively, in Thorndike & Lorge, 1944) were likewise similar at the four word lengths. The proportions of AA-frequency words were .21, .20, .20, and .15 for word lengths 5 to 8, respectively. Proportions of A-frequency words were .21, .25, .21, and .23. The aim of these procedures was to ensure that the patterns of performance described below would not be accounted for by either by the linguistic frequency of the test words or the sequence of hand movements involved in their typing.

In an initial study with these stimuli, the words were presented in uppercase on a video screen at a rate of one word every 5 sec. The order of presentation was randomized with respect to word length. A brief audio signal was synchronized with the onset of each stimulus. Fifteen different subjects, whose speeds on prose were 30 to 82 wpm, were tested. Subjects were screened prior to the experiment for standard finger-key assignments, including spacing with the right-hand thumb. An IBM Selectric was used for testing, and as in the first study, interkey times were measured with 1-msec accuracy by a PDP-11/20 computer.

Subjects were instructed to type rapidly while maintaining as low an error rate as possible. Each subject provided mean interkey times for correctly typed words at each character position and all word lengths. Error rates ranged from .02 to .13, with an average of .07.

The data were partitioned with respect to initial latency and interkey time. Initial latencies were evaluated as a function of word length in characters. Initial latencies were longer than interkey times as a result of the single-word format but they were not otherwise affected by differences in word length, $F(3, 42) < 1$, $SE = 4.51$ msec. Average latencies were 836, 834, 833, and 839 msec for word lengths 5 to 8, respectively. Initial latency also varied with differences in skill, where shorter initial latencies were associated with greater average typing speeds, $r(13) = .64$, $p < .01$.

Interkey times were likewise assessed with respect to word length. The obtained patterns, averaged over typists, with initial latencies excluded, are summarized in Figure 9.3 (the times shown at any character position represent the average interkey time between character $n - 1$ and character n). The initial latency was followed by a relatively short interval from character 1 to character 2. Interkey time increased in the interval from character 2 to character 3 and, with the exception of word length 5, again from character 3 to character 4. Interkey time then decreased toward the end of the word, with performance tending toward an asymptote at word lengths 7 and 8. The maximum interkey time at midword and the times toward the end of the word both increased with word length.

Except at word length 5, the pattern of short interkey times at the beginning and the end of a word and slower performance in the middle

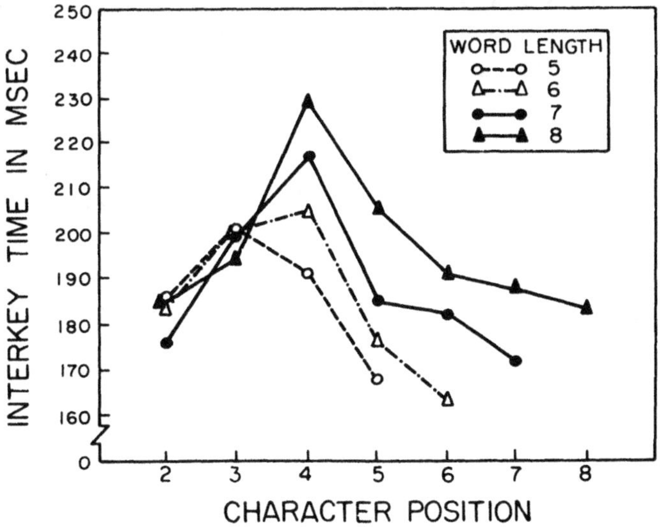

Fig 9.3. Average interkey times over successive character positions for five- to eight-letter words.

was obtained for all typists and word lengths. For five-character words, 6 of the 15 typists produced functions in which interkey time monotonically decreased from the first to the last interval in the word.

Differences in the set of interkey times at each word length were tested by analysis of variance. These analyses were reliable in all cases, indicating that performance varies over word length: $F(3, 42) = 10.99$, $p < .01$, $SE = 4.16$ msec; $F(4, 56) = 20.03$, $p < .01$, $SE = 3.89$ msec; $F(5, 70) = 13.52$, $p < .01$, $SE = 4.58$ msec; $F(6, 84) = 12.12$, $p < .01$, $SE = 4.68$ msec, respectively. Differences between interkey times for character 1 to character 2 and times for the longest interval at midword were tested by using Scheffé contrasts. At all word lengths, the character 1 to character 2 interkey times were found to be reliably less than the interkey times at midword: $F(3, 42) = 13.68$, $p < .01$; $F(4,56) = 28.04$, $p < .01$; $F(5, 70) = 80.07$, $p < .01$; $F(6, 84) = 88.49$, $p < .01$, respectively. Differences between the interkey time preceding the final character and the longest time at midword were also tested. Differences were again reliable in all cases, indicating a significant increase in speed toward the end of a word: $F(3, 42) = 62.83$, $p < .01$; $F(4, 56) = 116.96$, $p < .01$; $F(5, 70) = 98.21$, $p < .01$; $F(6, 84) = 99.79$, $p < .01$, respectively.

Tests for differences among the four functions were also carried out, in order to assess the reliability of the observed divergence among the functions beyond the third character position in the word. The analysis of variance compared performance at all word lengths up to character position 5 (the part common to all test items). The patterns were found to differ at the four word lengths, $F(9, 126) = 13.66$, $p < .01$, $SE = 2.94$ msec. Tests for simple main effects showed no differences among the curves at character positions 2 and 3—$F(3, 168) = 2.31$ and $F(3, 168) = 1.02$, respectively—and reliable differences at both character position 4, $F(3, 168) = 29.35$, $p < .01$; and 5, $F(3, 168) = 27.97$, $p < .01$.

The contribution of typing skill to this pattern was assessed by examining, for each subject, the difference between the maximum interkey time at midword and the shortest time at word end. Estimates averaged over the four word lengths ranged from approximately 20 msec for rapid typists to about 75 msec for slow typists. The average difference between the times at midword and those at word end decreases with increases in typing speed, $r(13) = .61$, $p < .01$. As typists become more skilled, there is a less pronounced slowing at midword.

The finding that the extent of the midword slowing varies with the skill of the typist is consistent with the suggestion that sequence level aspects of typing organization take place while the response is actually in progress. In this context, the midword slowing can be viewed as a loading effect due both to the efficiency of organization and to sequence length.

Delayed Response

Because of the possibility that the interkey time patterns just reported resulted from an insufficient opportunity to complete the perceptual processing of the stimulus or the organization of its response, the single-word procedure was repeated with varying delays introduced between the presentation of an item and an audio signal to respond. Greater delays should enable the completion of perceptual processing, and to the extent that the observed interkey time pattern results from the immediate response condition, an advantage to the delayed condition should be seen in the timing of the subsequent motor sequence.

The stimuli were the same items tested above (80 items at each of word lengths 5-8). They were presented one at a time in uppercase and were followed, after a delay of 0, 50, 100, 200, 400, or 800 msec, by a brief audio signal to respond. The trials were blocked on response delay, with the order of test items differently randomized for each block.

Ten subjects, none of whom participated in the first studies, were tested. Their speeds on prose ranged from 35 to 80 wpm. A Cybernex electronic keyboard and PDP-11/20 were used for the test. The subjects were instructed to prepare their response when an item appeared on the screen and to begin typing as soon as possible after the audio signal. The results are based on correctly typed items. Error rates ranged from .01 to .09, with an average of .048. Similar error rates were observed at all six delays.

The data indicated that the benefits of greater preparation time extended only to the first character in a word (Figure 9.4), and that, at least for longer words, the nonmonotonic interkey time pattern was obtained after an 800-msec delay. Thus, the interkey time pattern reported in the preceding section does not seem to have resulted from the immediate response condition.

The initial latency decreased from an average of 615 msec at a response delay of 0 msec to a value of 310 msec at the 800-msec delay, but the benefit of greater preparation time did not appear to extend beyond the first character in the word. A monotonically decreasing interkey time pattern was observed at word lengths 5 and 6; the nonmonotonic pattern of Figure 9.3 was obtained at word lengths 7 and 8. However, with the exception of the initial latency, none of the actual output patterns was altered, even at delays of 800 msec.

Initial latencies were independent of word length at all response delays. The initial latencies decreased from values of 619, 610, 609, and 617 msec at delay 0 msec to values of 305, 305, 313, and 311 msec at the 800-msec delay. At all delays the initial latencies varied in a nonsystematic manner as a function of word length.

The analysis of variance tested differences in performance as a function of response delay for each word length separately. With initial

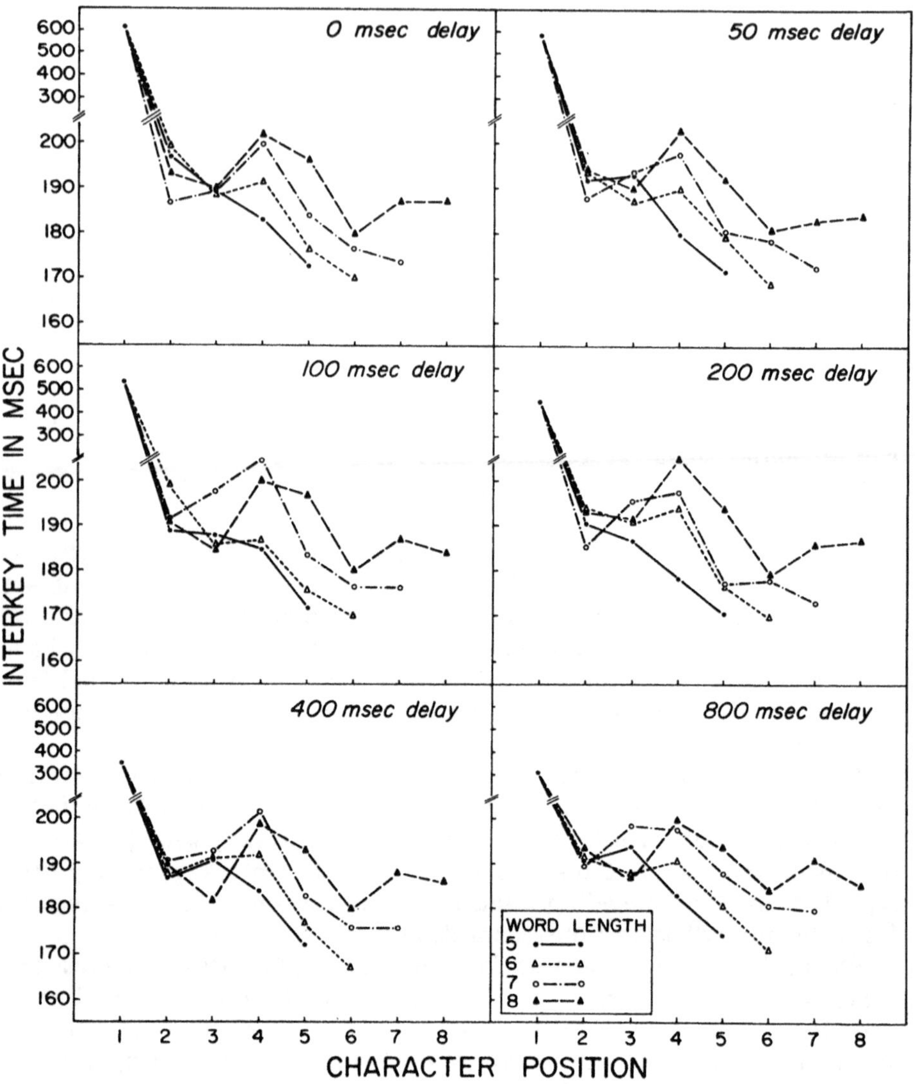

Fig. 9.4. Average interkey times over successive character positions in five- to eight-letter words as a function of response delay.

latencies included in the analysis, interactions between interkey times and response delay were obtained at each of word lengths 5-8: $F(20, 180) = 256.31$, $p < .01$, $SE = 3.52$ msec; $F(25, 225) = 240.74$, $p < .01$, $SE = 3.25$ msec; $F(30, 270) = 229.21$, $p < .01$, $SE = 3.04$ msec; $F(35, 315) = 218.68$, $p < .01$, $SE = 2.97$ msec, respectively. The interactions were all due to a decrease in the initial latency as a function of increased response delay. The patterns of interkey time were not otherwise affected by the delay manipulation, and in fact, at any specified word length and character position, there was little variation in the values obtained at the different response delays. The interkey times were within 6 msec of one another for over 80% of the data points at any character position, and in all cases the range of interkey times was no greater than 10 msec.

The slowing that was observed at midword in the previous study was not obtained at word length 5 or 6. This may be a result of the introduction of an electronic keyboard. However, differences in the interkey time pattern are more likely a reflection of the subjects themselves; patterns such as this were observed for 40% of the subjects tested at word length 5 in the single-word study of the preceding section. The nonmonotonic interkey time patterns of Figure 9.3 were obtained for word lengths 7 and 8, where Tukey contrasts verified a reliable slowing between character position 2 and the point of slowest performance, at two of six and five of six response delays, at word lengths 7 and 8, respectively. This increase in interkey times was also tested with planned contrasts, which showed reliable midword slowing at all response delays for both seven- and eight-letter words.

The finding that the nonmonotonic interkey time pattern reported above cannot be eliminated by extending the period before response initiation is consistent with the notion that aspects of motor organization at the level of the sequence or perhaps the word take place while the movement is in progress.

Typing Sentences

In a final study with this stimulus set, words were embedded in sentences and presented to subjects one sentence at a time. While there is little evidence that typing organization extends to the phrase or the sentence, the subject may adopt different strategies for single words than for continuous typing. Shaffer and Hardwick (1970), for example, have demonstrated that when visual preview is restricted, performance is not degraded until fewer than eight characters are available. Similarly, Butsch (1932) showed that even with extremely rapid typists the eyes rarely lead the hands by more than two words. Further, Fendrick (1937) and West (1969) have shown that performance is only slightly more rapid for prose than for the same words randomly ordered and that the advantage to prose is unrelated to skill.

Fifteen subjects (speeds on prose from 32 to 94 wpm right-hand thumb for spacing) copied sentences one at a time. A brief audio signal synchronized with the presentation of each sentence served as a starting tone. The sentences were from 7 to 10 words in length, and the words were no more than eight letters each. The sentences were constructed to include all of the words used earlier (these will be referred to as test words) and as many others as necessary for meaning and continuity.

The sentences were presented to subjects on double-spaced 22- by 28-cm pages. The subjects read all sentences before the experiment began. An IBM Selectric was used for testing. For each sentence, all interkey times, including times to move to and from the space bar, were recorded. For purposes of analyses, the first and last words in each sentence were excluded to eliminate overall start-up and ending effects. All words with errors were likewise removed.

Initial latencies for test words were evaluated as a function of word length and, as in the single-word condition of the preceding section, they were not found to differ, $F(3, 42) = 1.92$, $SE = 3.52$ msec. The obtained values were 220, 228, 227 and 231 msec for word lengths 5-8, respectively. The initial latencies were considerably shorter than those observed when single words were tested, but they were similar to values obtained at the points of slowest performance in the middle of the word (longest interkey times at midword for word lengths 5-8 were 222, 212, 227, and 229 msec, respectively).

The interkey times for test words were partitioned with respect to word length (Figure 9.5). The obtained patterns were similar to those reported above. The initial latency was followed by a short interkey time preceding character 2, and a maximum interkey time between characters 2 and 3 for word lengths 5 and 6 and between characters 3 and 4 at word lengths 7 and 8. Unlike the single-word condition, there was little evidence that interkey times reached an asymptote at the ends of longer words. As in the previous studies, however, interkey times beyond midword were greater at longer word lengths. Each word was terminated by striking the space bar. The interval from the final character to the space averaged 186 msec, and its duration was uninfluenced by word length. Similar patterns were observed for all typists.

Differences in interkey times at each word length were tested by analysis of variance and were found to be reliable in all cases, which indicates that performance varied over word length: $F(5, 70) = 9.30$, $p < .01$, $SE = 5.40$ msec; $F(6, 84) = 12.72$, $p < .01$, $SE = 4.75$ msec; $F(7, 98) = 10.84$, $p < .01$, $SE = 5.52$ msec; $F(8, 112) = 9.97$, $p < .01$, $SE = 5.24$ msec, for word lengths 5-8, respectively. Scheffé contrasts confirmed that interkey times from character 1 to character 2 were reliably less than values at the point of slowest performance in the middle of the word: $F(5, 70) = 30.79$, $p < .01$; $F(6,84) = 17.93$, $p < .05$; $F(7, 98) = 60.45$, $p < .01$; $F(8, 112) = 57.13$, $p < .01$, again for word lengths 5-8; and that differences between the final interkey time in the word (excluding the space) and the point of slowest performance at midword were likewise reliable: $F(5, 70) = 42.75$, $p < .01$; $F(6, 84) = 28.33$, $p < .01$; $F(7, 98) = 45.71$, $p < .01$; $F(8, 112) = 21.46$, $p < .01$, respectively.

The movement between the final character and the space generally produced short interkey times. Further tests of the spacing sequence

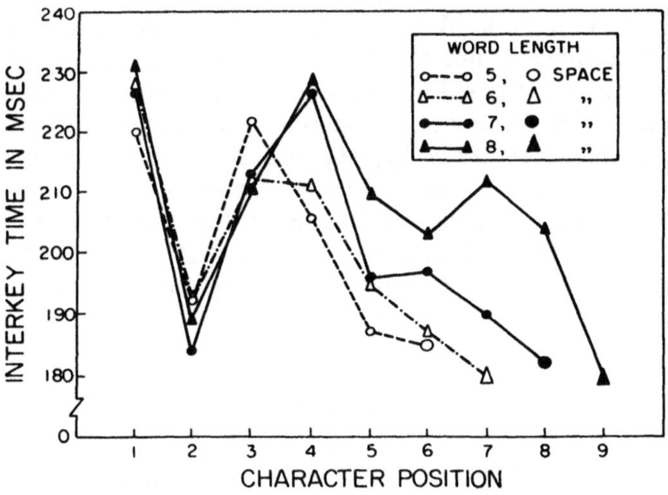

Fig. 9.5. Words in sentences. Mean interkey times over successive character positions as a function of word length.

studied its relations to hand alternation and repetition (all typists used the right-hand thumb for the space bar; thus a word ending in a *d* required a hand alternation, whereas one ending in a *k* required a repetition). The analysis of variance found reliable time differences between spacing movements involving hand alternation and those involving hand repetition, $F(1, 14) = 13.28, p < .01, SE = 3.31$ msec. Alternating hands to move to the space bar was faster than using the same hand for both the last character of a word and the space. Average times were 177 msec for hand alternation and 194 msec for repetition. The duration of the spacing movement was not related to word length, $F(3, 42) < 1.00$, $SE = 2.39$ msec; the average time for spacing was 186 msec at all word lengths tested.

Because of its advantage in speed, the space stroke was presumed to reflect characteristics of skilled performance. A test was conducted to examine the time difference in spacing movements as a function of typing speed for hand alternation as opposed to hand repetition. The analysis suggested that the time difference between repetition and alternation in spacing may increase as typists increase in speed, $r(13) = .43, p \cong .05$. Alternations in spacing were about 10 msec faster than repetitions for slower typists, whereas for faster typists the difference increased to approximately 30 msec.

There is a parallel between the difference in interkey times observed in spacing and the time difference between hand alternation and repetition movements within words (see the section on hand movements at the beginning of the chapter). In both, with increases in speed, there are proportionately larger deviations from uniformity in successive interkey times. In effect, for both spacing movements and movements within words, improvements in skill seem to result in relatively greater departures from temporal uniformity (see Harding, 1933, for a related demonstration of departure from temporal uniformity with increases in typing skill). The finding is not at odds with the reported decrease in midword slowing for faster typists (see the section on word length), since the data presented earlier in the word-length section are based on performance averaged over differences in hand alternation and repetition. Thus, although performance is generally streamlined with increases in skill, the timing of the individual typing movements becomes less periodic relative to their average speed.

Longer Words

A final assessment of the effects of word length involved the examination of typing performance for longer words, from 8 to 11 letters. The stimuli were four sets of 60 words each, all two to four syllables in length. Hand movement pattern and digraph frequency were balanced at each word length separately (see below). The proportion of high-frequency words was low in all conditions, with 3 of 60 words at word length 8, 4 of 60 at length 9, 3 at length 10, and 0 at length 11 having frequencies of occurrence of 100 per million or greater (Thorndike & Lorge, 1944).

As in the foregoing studies, the set of 60 words at each word length was balanced for the total number of hand alternations and repetitions between any two successive characters. The balancing never departed by more than 10% from equal numbers of alternation and repetition movements at a given word length and character position, with stimulus sets at word lengths 8, 9, and 10 being perfectly balanced. The proportion of high-frequency digraphs (frequencies greater then 750 per 20,000 words; Mayzner & Tresselt, 1965) was likewise similar at all character positions and word lengths. The overall proportion of high-frequency digraphs was .17 with obtained proportions within .05 of this value at all character positions at each word length.

The stimuli were presented one at a time in uppercase with order of presentation randomized. As earlier, an audio signal was synchronized with the onset of each stimulus and served as a starting tone. An IBM 2741 terminal was used for testing. Sixteen subjects whose speeds on prose ranged from 39 to 84 wpm participated in the study. Subjects were instructed to begin typing when a word appeared on the screen, to type rapidly, and to maintain as low an error rate as possible. Both initial latency and interkey times were measured. Error rates ranged from .005 to .07, averaging .04.

The interkey times were examined at each word length separately (there were no systematic differences due to initial latency; values of

635, 652, 625, and 632 msec were obtained for word lengths 8-11, respectively). Interkey times followed a pattern similar to that obtained at shorter word lengths (Figure 9.6). After a relatively short interval preceding character 2, performance slowed, reaching a maximum interkey time at character position 4 at word lengths 8, 9, and 11 and at position 5 for word length 10. Interkey times then progressively decreased until the final interval in the word, where an increase of about 10 msec was observed.

Differences in interkey times at each word length were tested with analysis of variance. These analyses were reliable in all cases, indicating an overall difference in speed across the word: $F(6, 84) = 9.41, p < .01$, $SE = 3.88$ msec; $F(7, 98) = 11.91, p < .01$, $SE = 4.41$ msec; $F(8, 112) = 14.54, p < .01$, $SE = 4.34$ msec; $F(9, 126) = 12.05, p < .01$, $SE = 4.83$ msec, respectively. Differences between interkey times at character position 2 and the maximum values observed at midword were reliable by planned comparisons. The slowing that is seen in the final interval was not reliable by Tukey tests at any word length.

Similar patterns of interkey times have been observed in the studies described here. In these studies, word length in characters has been varied from 5 to 11 letters. In general, interkey times display a nonmonotonic inverted U-shaped pattern over successive letter positions. More specifically, interkey times are relatively short at the beginning of a word, progressively increase to reach a maximum at about position 4, and then decrease monotonically over the remainder of the word. The magnitude of the maximum interkey time may increase with word length; however, its location in the word is relatively constant. Interkey

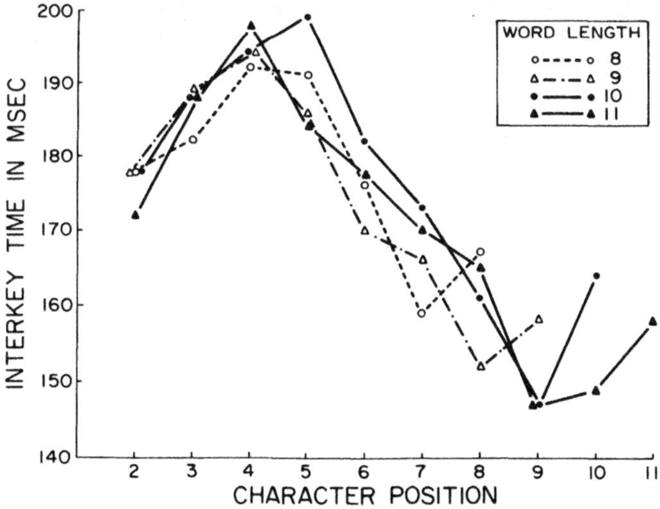

Fig. 9.6. Average interkey times over successive character positions for words from 8 to 11 letters in length.

times at a given character position are similar for different word lengths prior to the slowest point at midword. Beyond midword, interkey times are greater for longer words (exceptions are discussed in the last section of this chapter). Initial latencies are not found to vary as a function of word length in the range from 5 to 11 letters.

An organization extending to the sequence as a whole may be indicated by the finding that beyond the maximum interkey time near position 4, times at any character position are greater for longer words. The pattern observed here cannot be attributed to hand movement, digraph or word frequency, or differences in typing skill. It does not result from the presentation of the stimuli one word at a time, incomplete perceptual processing, or an inadequate period for motor organization prior to movement. Possible influences on interkey times that were not controlled in these studies are syllabification, the use of words as stimuli, and the implicit strategies the subject might adopt in typing.

Syllabification does seem to account somewhat for the form of the interkey time function in typing. Ostry and Munhall (Note 1) tested subjects with mono-, bi-, and trisyllabic words that were otherwise balanced for differences in word length, hand movement, and digraph and word frequency. They obtained patterns similar to those reported here for both bi- and trisyllabic stimuli. With monosyllabic words a somewhat different nonmonotonic pattern was obtained. Specifically, an initial decrease in interkey times was followed by a slowing of performance later in the word and a subsequent increase in speed for the final characters.

In contrast, the overall form of the interkey time function does not appear to depend on the use of words as stimuli. Larochelle (Chapter 4) has demonstrated that when words and nonwords are balanced for digraph frequency, the interkey time patterns and the extent of midword slowing at a given sequence length are similar in the two conditions.

The form of the interkey time function—a single slowing of performance early in the word followed by a monotonic increase in speed that continues to the final characters—raises the possibility that the nonmonotonic pattern is the reflection of a strategy used for typing. The following study examined this possibility.

Single-Word Strategies

The nonmonotonic pattern of interkey times may reflect a strategy, presumably implicit, that subjects adopt for typing. Alternatively, it may be a relatively rigid characteristic of the structure of typing, a "rise time" effect associated with rapid seriation. If the initial slowing in the interkey time function results from a start-up or rise time effect, it would be expected only at the beginning of the word and should not be modifiable by instructions to subjects.

A final study was conducted with the aim of explicitly manipulating the strategies subjects use in typing. The effects of three instructions on the typing of single words were examined. One instruction was to start typing as soon as possible after a word appeared on the video screen and to continue at a normal rate after starting. A second instruction was to be fully prepared before starting to type, and to finish as soon as possible once started. A third instruction was simply to type each word as it appeared on the screen. These instructions were combined either with the information that errors were unimportant or that errors were to be minimized. Subjects were tested in all six conditions with order of conditions balanced according to a Williams square (Cochran & Cox, 1957) in order to eliminate first-order carry-over effects.

The stimuli were 64 words at each of word lengths 4-7. The stimuli were selected in order to balance for differences in hand movement, and digraph and word frequency. All possible combinations of hand alternation and repetition were tested at each word length. At length 4 there are eight possible combinations of hand alternation and repetition; at length 5 there are 16 combinations; at length 6 there are 32 combinations; and at length 7 there are 64. The complete set of 64 words was obtained by using eight different words for each of the eight hand alternation-repetition combinations at length 4, four different words for each of the 16 combinations at length 5, and so on. The proportion of high-frequency words (frequencies greater than 100 per million; Kucera & Francis, 1967) was .25 at all word lengths. The proportion of high-frequency digraphs (frequencies greater than 750 per 20,000 words; Mayzner & Tresselt, 1965) was .15 ± .07 at all character positions and word lengths.

Eighteen subjects, whose speeds ranged from 27 to 74 wpm, participated. The stimuli were presented one at a time in uppercase on a video screen, with a brief audio signal simultaneous with the stimulus onset. The testing was carried out on an IBM 2741 terminal. Each subject was tested over a period of six sessions, with a different set of instructions at each session. Items that were typed incorrectly were re-presented at random later in the session.

Initial latencies and interkey times were examined separately. Initial latencies varied systematically with instructions to the subject. Latencies increased in conditions in which errors were to be minimized (753 vs. 730 msec). They were shortest when subjects were instructed to start typing as soon as possible (660 msec) and longest when subjects were to prepare fully before starting to type (825 msec). Initial latency did not vary systematically as a function of word length (736, 736, 736, and 756 msec for lengths 4-7, respectively).

Interkey times for each of the six conditions are shown in Figure 9.7. The three main instructions each resulted in different interkey time patterns. The instruction to begin typing as soon as possible produced an increase in interkey time at character position 2 that accompanied

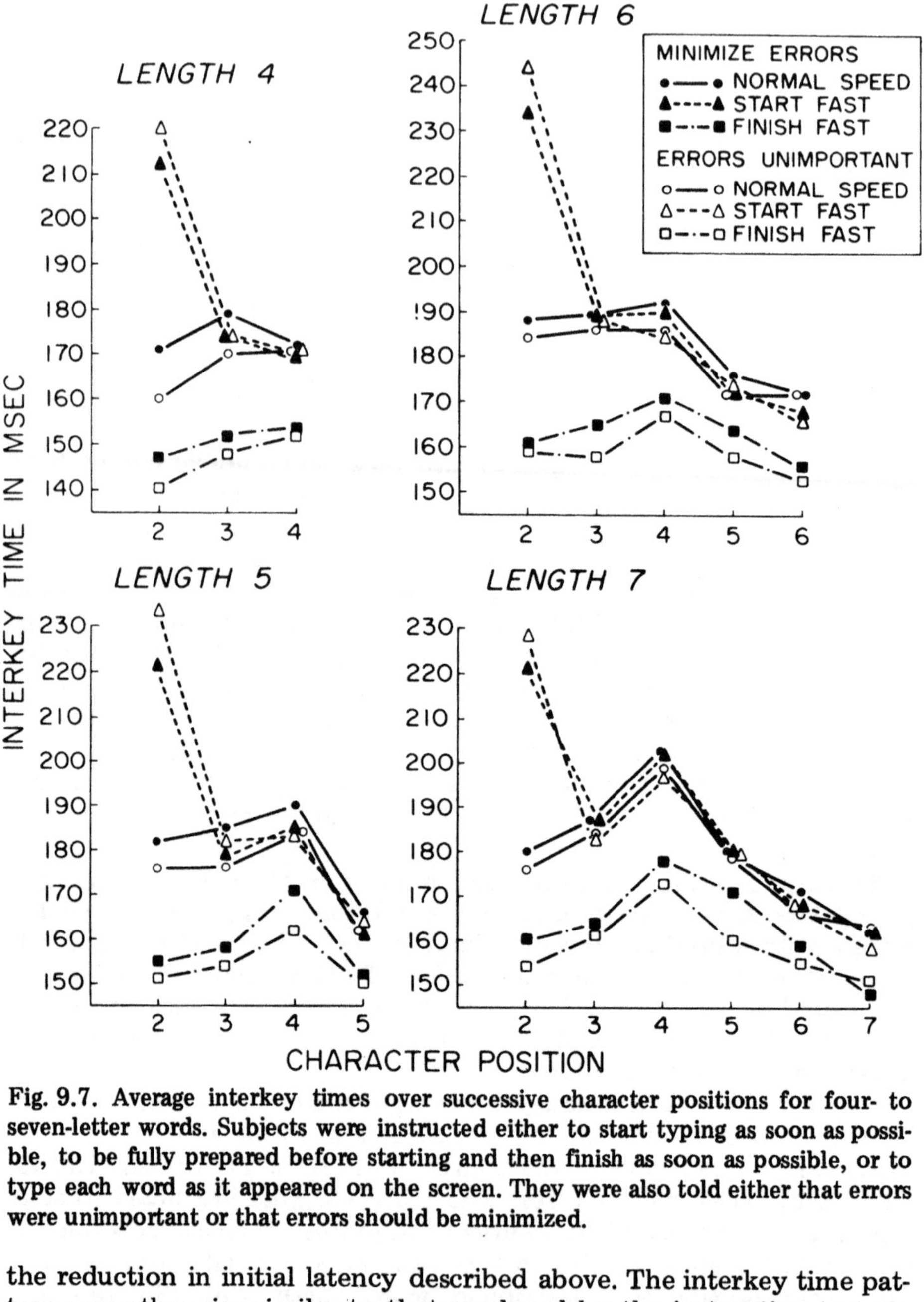

Fig. 9.7. Average interkey times over successive character positions for four- to seven-letter words. Subjects were instructed either to start typing as soon as possible, to be fully prepared before starting and then finish as soon as possible, or to type each word as it appeared on the screen. They were also told either that errors were unimportant or that errors should be minimized.

the reduction in initial latency described above. The interkey time pattern was otherwise similar to that produced by the instruction to type each word as it appeared on the screen. The instruction to start only when fully prepared and then finish as soon as possible produced a reduction in interkey times but no change in the form of the overall function.

The error rate manipulation did not affect interkey times to the same extent as the other instructions. It did, however, result in the anticipated changes in error rates. Error rates averaged .049 in conditions where errors were to be minimized and .086 in conditions where errors were unimportant. The average error rate was .047 for the normal speed condition, .066 in the condition where the typist was to start as rapidly as possible, and .090 in the condition where the typist was to finish as rapidly as possible.

The increase in interkey times over successive character positions at word length 4 has been reported previously for three- and four-letter words (Chapter 4, this volume; Ostry, 1980). A similar increase in interkey times, from character position 2 to approximately 4, is also observed at longer word lengths. It is possible that interkey time functions at all word lengths may be similar in this range.

The overall form of the interkey time pattern was not substantially affected by the different instructions. The instruction to start typing as soon as possible seemed to result in a one-character slowing after the first keypress and then a return to the nonmonotonic pattern that is otherwise observed. The instruction to finish as soon as possible shifted the entire curve as if a gain setting had been changed, but the overall form of the function did not appear to be altered. Therefore, the characteristic interkey pattern does not appear to be the result of a flexible strategy that subjects adopt for typing. The slowing that occurs over the first characters in the word may be a rise time or start-up effect accompanying the initiation of each movement sequence.

General Discussion

Determinants of interkey times in typing were examined in a series of studies in which movements, word length, and instructions to subjects were manipulated. Effects were obtained both for movements between letter pairs and for the sequence as a whole. The interkey time pattern in typing was relatively insensitive to attempts to manipulate strategies.

In a study of movement patterns, timing differences were assessed between letter pairs that involved the successive use of two fingers of one hand and movements in which letters were typed with two fingers of alternate hands. Three main findings were described. First, sets of words requiring different sequences of hand alternation and repetition resulted in different interkey time patterns. Second, the average time difference between hand alternation and hand repetition movements was constant, independent of differences in typing speed. Finally, interkey times were reliably less for hand alternation movements, but initial latencies were less preceding initial hand repetitions.

The first finding suggests that the sequence of movements between hands is a main contributor to the pattern of interkey times for a given word. The Terzuolo and Viviani (1980) observation that each word has a distinctive pattern is perhaps a reflection of this fact, rather than a reflection of a motor engram per se.

The constant difference between interkey times for hand alternation and repetition was interpreted as a property of motor organization associated with the repetition or overlap of successive movements. Repetition of letters in handwriting and words in speech produces similar delays (Wing et al., 1979; Sternberg et al., 1978). The difference between alternation and repetition movements is in part the result of a mechanical advantage in hand alternation. However, the constant difference, independent of typing speed, makes it unlikely that the effect can be accounted for strictly in biomechanical terms.

The longer interkey times for movements involving the repetition of a hand can be contrasted with their shorter initial latencies. The latency pattern suggests differences in the organizational complexity of bimanual and unimanual control. The differences in initial latency dependent on the movement from letter 1 to letter 2 along with delays in interkey times brought about by the repeated use of a single hand both suggest that organization at the level of the movements themselves extends at least to character pairs.

The study of movement patterns also led to the observation of proportionately greater departures from temporal uniformity with increases in typing speed, both within words and in spacing. (The constant difference between interkey times for alternation and repetition within words necessarily produces proportionately larger deviations from uniformity with increases in speed.) The observation is not consistent with the notion of exact periodicity in movement timing. Indeed, Shaffer (1982) has suggested recently that there is little evidence that the control of typing movements is based on a strictly periodic timing mechanism.

The pattern of interkey times was also examined as a function of word length. In general, performance could be described by a nonmonotonic inverted U-shaped function in which interkey times were short in the interval from letter 1 to letter 2, lengthened over the next several letters to reach a maximum at about character position 4, and then decreased over the remainder of the word. The first part of this function, approximately to character 4, was similar in form at most word lengths (including length 4). (Some exceptions are discussed below.) The second part of the function, from the position of maximum interkey time onward, involved a progressive increase in speed, with the average interkey time at a given character position being somewhat greater for longer words. The sets of stimuli used in these studies were balanced with respect to hand movement, digraph frequency, and word frequency. Thus, the observed pattern of interkey times cannot be attributed to these factors. The pattern did not depend on whether the words were typed in sentences or alone, or whether the typist was to start immediately on presentation of the stimulus or after a delay. Instructions aimed at changing the strategy the subject adopts for typing did not alter the overall form of the interkey function.

The slowing of performance that was observed over the first four letters in a word may be a rise time effect associated with the initiation of a sequence. If so, it seems to be sufficiently basic to rapid seriation that it is not modifiable by instructions to induce strategy shifts. It should be noted, however, that the slowing was not observed for every subject, particularly at shorter word lengths. A tempting possibility was that faster subjects produced the monotonically decreasing interkey time functions whereas slower subjects showed the nonmonotonic pattern present in the averaged displays. An examination of the data was not consistent with this suggestion. For example, in the manipulation reported earlier in the section on word length, 6 of 15 subjects tested produced monotonically decreasing interkey times over successive character positions at word length 5. The average interkey time for this group was 190 msec, while the average for subjects who produced the more common nonmonotonic pattern was 197 msec. The slowest typist in the study was one of the subjects whose pattern was monotonic.

The divergence of interkey time functions beyond the position of slowest performance suggests an effect on organization at the level of sequence length. However, there is little evidence that this should be interpreted as organization at the level of words. West (1969), for example, found only a modest advantage in speed in typing words rather than high-frequency letter pairs and likewise showed that the advantage to words was unrelated to skill. Lexicality per se does not seem to be entirely responsible for interkey time effects either, since functions similar to those reported above have been obtained for both words and nonwords (Chapter 4, this volume; Ostry, 1980; Shaffer & Hardwick, 1970).

Manipulations of word length also indicate that certain sequence level aspects of control in typing occur after the initiation of the response. Even if an extended period is provided for response preparation, an initial increase in interkey times is observed, followed by a decrease whose rate varies with both sequence length and skill. The dependence on length and skill suggests that output timing reflects both the overall load and the efficiency of organization of movement after response initiation. The insensitivity of the pattern of interkey times to response delays and strategies suggests that the function depends on properties of a relatively rigid system that is activated at the initiation of movement.

Acknowledgments

This research was supported by the Natural Sciences and Engineering Research Council of Canada and the FCAC program of the Quebec Department of Education. The author thanks K. G. Munhall for his comments and suggestions.

Reference Note

1. Ostry, D. J., & Munhall, K. G. *Syllabic influences on the timing of typing.* Unpublished manuscript, McGill University, 1981.

References

Butsch, R. Eye movements and the eye-hand span in typewriting. *Journal of Educational Psychology*, 1932, *23*, 104-121.

Cochran, W., & Cox, G. *Experimental designs.* New York: Wiley, 1957.

Coover, J. E. A method of teaching typewriting based on a psychological analysis of expert typing. *National Educational Association, Addresses and Proceedings*, 1923, *61*, 561-567.

Dvorak, A., Merrick, N., Dealey, W., & Ford, G. *Typewriting behavior.* New York: American Book Company, 1936.

Fendrick, P. Hierarchical skills in typewriting. *Journal of Educational Psychology*, 1937, *28*, 609-620.

Harding, D. Rhythmization and speed of work. *British Journal of Psychology*, 1933, *23*, 262-278.

Kucera, H., & Francis, C. M. *Computational analysis of present-day American English.* Providence, R.I.: Brown University Press, 1967.

Lahy, J. *Motion study in typewriting.* Boston: World Peace Foundation, 1924.

Mayzner, M., & Tresselt, M. Tables of single-letter and digram frequency counts for various word-length and letter position combinations. *Psychonomic Monograph Supplement*, 1965, *1*, 13-22.

Ostry, D. J. *Organization of typewriting performance.* Unpublished doctoral dissertation, University of Toronto, 1977.

Ostry, D. J. Execution-time movement control. In G. E. Stelmach & J. Requin (Eds.), *Tutorials in motor behavior.* Amsterdam: North-Holland, 1980.

Shaffer, L. H. Timing in the motor programming of typing. *Quarterly Journal of Experimental Psychology*, 1978, *30*, 333-345.

Shaffer, L. H. Rhythm and timing in skill. *Psychological Review*, 1982, *89*, 109-122.

Shaffer, L. H., & Hardwick, J. The basis of transcription skill. *Journal of Experimental Psychology*, 1970, *84*, 424-440.

Sternberg, S., Monsell, S., Knoll, R. L., & Wright, C. E. The latency and duration of speech and typewriting. In G. E. Stelmach (Ed.), *Information processing in motor control and learning.* New York: Academic Press, 1978.

Terzuolo, C., & Viviani, P. Determinants and characteristics of motor patterns used for typing. *Neuroscience*, 1980, *5*, 1085-1103.

Thorndike, E., & Lorge, I. *The teacher's word book of 30,000 words.* New York: Teacher's College, 1944.

West, L. J. *Acquisition of typewriting skills.* New York: Pitman, 1969.

Wing, A., Lewis, V., & Baddeley, A. The slowing of handwriting by letter repetition. *Journal of Human Movement Studies*, 1979, *5*, 182-188.

Chapter 10

Mirror-Image Movements in Typing

Kevin G. Munhall and David J. Ostry

The human arms and hands can function together in many ways, including movement in rapid succession, such as in drumming and typing; movement in unison, such as in clapping and two-handed catching; and complementary movement, as in such tasks as striking a match, knot tying, and complex manipulation. Even casual observation of these activities reveals both the coherence and the complexity of the limb interaction.

The study of bimanual coordination has revealed that the individual hands are not kinematically independent for certain movements. For example, it appears to be difficult for the hands to produce different and harmonically unrelated rhythms (Cohen, 1970; Klapp, 1979; Peters, 1977; but cf. Shaffer, 1981, for evidence that skilled pianists can produce different rhythms). Further, in simultaneous rapid movements the hands tend to have similar starting and ending times as well as similar velocity profiles even when the targets differ in size and the movements are of different extent (Kelso, Southard, & Goodman, 1979; but cf. Marteniuk & MacKenzie, 1980).

Rapid bimanual activities such as typewriting may also involve linkages or dependencies between the hands in spite of their speed and apparent flexibility. In fact, certain "natural" intermanual relationships may be sufficiently rigid that they endure in a skill in which they do not provide any evident coordinative advantage. Since dependencies between the limbs have been demonstrated most readily in symmetric intermanual activities, we have used successive symmetric movements to test for similar linkages in typing.

Coordination between the hands in typing was examined in terms of the timing of movements from one hand to the other in the course of typing a word. Spatial and anatomical correspondence of successive movements was varied. To this end a stimulus set was constructed that enabled the examination of three types of movements between hands:

(1) successive movements that involve the same fingers on each hand, with movements going to mirror-image positions on the keyboard (see the section on method for details); (2) successive movements that involve the same fingers on each hand, but that differ with respect to the spatial trajectories of the movements (e.g., index finger, left hand upper row to index finger, right hand, lower row); and (3) successive movements that involve different fingers on each hand (e.g., first finger, left hand to third finger, right hand). Bimanual coordination was examined in terms of differences in timing among the three conditions.

The study was supplemented by a reanalysis of typing substitution errors originally tabulated by Lessenberry (1928) and Davis (1935; both matrices are reprinted in Dvorak, Merrick, Dealey, & Ford, 1936). The analysis compared the frequencies of occurrence of errors involving the substitution of mirror-image positions, the substitution of letters typed by the same fingers of the two hands (but not mirror image), and substitution errors involving letters typed by different fingers of the two hands.

Method

Subjects

Sixteen McGill University students participated as subjects. Typing speeds for prose averaged 47.8 words per minute (wpm), with a range from 33 to 92 wpm. Subjects were screened prior to the experiment for a minimum typing speed of at least 30 wpm and standard finger-key assignments.

Stimuli

The stimuli were 96 seven-letter words that were classified on the basis of the type of movement between the hands and the position in the word at which the movement occurred. Three movements were examined: (1) movements between mirror-image positions (successive movements involving the same fingers of opposite hands and the same keyboard rows, e.g., from *g* to *h*); (2) movements involving the same fingers of opposite hands, but not between mirror-image locations (successive movements involving the same fingers but different keyboard rows, e.g., from *g* to *u*); and (3) movements involving different fingers of opposite hands (e.g., from *g* to *o*).

The layout of the typewriting keyboard is such that the designation *mirror image* requires clarification. For alphabetic characters, hand assignments on the keyboard are divided along an axis running at an oblique angle between letters *t* and *y*, *g* and *h*, and *b* and *n*. Each digit (excluding the thumbs) has a home-row key assignment and, with the exception of the index fingers, a single key assignment in each of the upper and lower rows. The index fingers each have two key assignments on each of the three rows. The mirror-image designation was based on corresponding finger and row assignments. For the index finger, the mirror-image assignment was based on both row and proximity of keys to the axis dividing the keyboard. Because of this layout, the mirror-image movements involved related but not always indentical mirror-image trajectories.

The three movement types were examined at all positions in seven-letter words, that is, from letter 1 to letter 2, from letter 2 to letter 3, and so on. A single value, corresponding to the interkey time (time from character $n - 1$ to character n) for the movement of interest, was obtained from each word typed. For example, for the movement from character 1 to character 2, three of the stimuli were *worship*, *sounded*, and *context*. In these examples, *w* and *o* are mirror-image movements, *s* and *o* are both typed by the index finger, and *c* and *o* are typed by different fingers of each hand. The data points here are the times between the responses for the first letter in the word and the letter *o*.

For each of the six letter pairs in seven-letter words there were four words of movement type 1 (mirror-image), four words of movement type 2 (same finger) and eight words of movement type 3 (different finger). (See Appendix for stimuli.)

Average log word frequencies per million for words containing movement types 1, 2, and 3 were respectively .82, .66, and .97, (Carroll, Davies, & Richman, 1971). Average log digraph frequencies per 20,000 words for the letter pairs tested were 2.24, 2.23, and 2.42 for movement types 1, 2, and 3, respectively (Mayzner & Tresselt, 1965). The percentage of movements from the left to the right hand for the letter pairs tested was 42% for each of the three movement categories.

Procedure

Subjects were given an opportunity to familiarize themselves with the keyboard (IBM 2741). Following this, each was given a 3-minute speed test that served as a screening for the minimum typing speed. The test was a prose passage that was copied from a typed sheet.

In the experiment, the subjects copied words that were presented one at a time on a Tektronix screen. They were instructed to begin typing as soon as they could following word presentation, and to maintain normal typing speed. An audio signal occurred simultaneously with the presentation of each item. Stimulus presentation was paced by the subject's pressing of the return button on the terminal after completing a word. When an error occurred the stimulus was re-presented at random later in the block. All subjects received a short warm-up on this procedure before the experiment.

Each of the 96 stimulus words was typed five times by each subject with order randomized. Subjects received short breaks after every 80 words. Interkey times were recorded by a PDP-11/34 computer for each word typed. The timing program was accurate within 1 msec. For each subject, median interkey times for each movement type and character pair were computed across the four (or eight) words and five repetitions of each. These were used as individual observations in the analyses of variance.

Results and Discussion

A movement type by position in the word analysis of variance was performed on the data. A significant main effect was obtained for movement type, $F(2, 30) = 18.32, p < .01, SE = 2.5$ msec, indicating that the timing of the movement of one hand was influenced by the preceding movement of the other hand. As can be seen in Figure 10.1, the effect was due to slower performance on mirror-image movements. A Scheffé

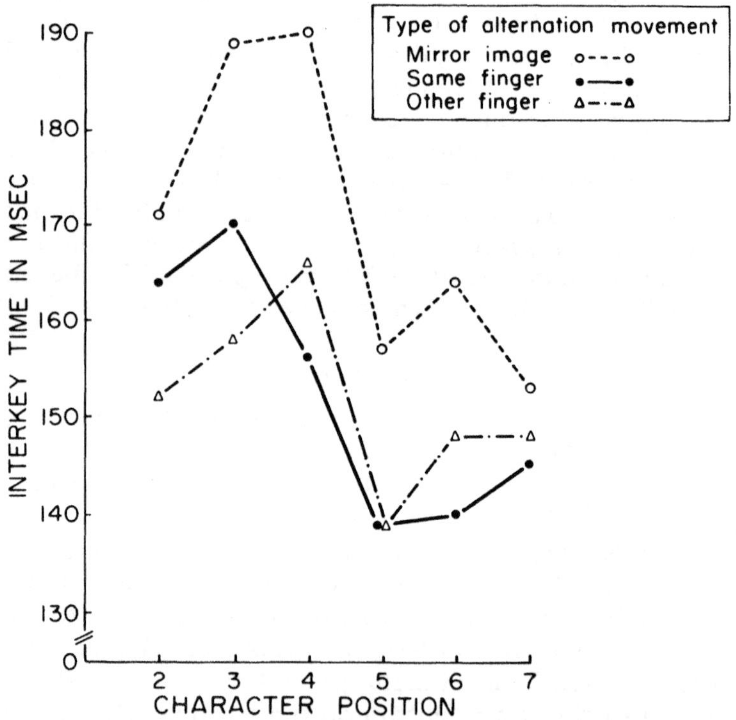

Fig. 10.1. Average interkey times for mirror-image, same finger, and other finger movements between the hands. Interkey time for position n is the time between character n - 1 and character n. Data points for each movement type were taken from different sets of words. Points are joined for visual presentation only.

test showed that the mirror-image movements were reliably slower than the mean of the other two movement types, $F(2, 30) = 37.20, p < .01$. The timing of performance also varied with the position of the movement in the word, $F(5, 75) = 5.19, p < .01$, $SE = 5.1$ msec, but did not interact with movement type, $F(10, 150) = 1.80$, $SE = 5.0$ msec.

The subjects were divided into two skill levels on the basis of their typing speed on the initial screening test. (Rank orderings of subjects on the basis of speed on the initial screening test and overall average interkey times in the experiment were identical.) The average interkey times for the stimuli tested here were 116 msec for the faster group and 201 msec for the slower group. A skill by movement type by position in the word analysis of variance was performed. It revealed significant effects for skill, $F(1, 14) = 23.81, p < .01$, $SE = 12.4$ msec; position, $F(5, 70) = 5.19, p < .01, SE = 5.1$ msec; and movement type, $F(2, 28) = 18.23, p < .01$, $SE = 2.5$ msec. None of the interactions were reliable. The average interkey times for the three conditions (mirror image, same finger, other finger) were respectively, 126.1, 108.8, and 111.8 for the faster group, and 215.5, 196.0, and 191.9 for the slower group.

In summary, the analyses indicated that movements between mirror-image locations on the keyboard were reliably slower than other movements. Further, this relationship did not seem to change with differences in skill or the position of the mirror-image movement in the word.

The organization of mirror-image movements in typing was further assessed by reanalyzing two confusion error matrices, one compiled by Lessenberry (1982), the other by Davis (1935; both are reprinted in Dvorak et al., 1936). (See Chapter 6 in this volume). Tables 10.1 and 10.2 present these matrices, which specify the frequency with which each letter in the alphabet was struck in place of each other letter. The Lessenberry matrix was based on more than 60,000 substitution errors on the conventional qwerty keyboard. The Davis matrix analyzed 3,300 errors on the Dvorak simplified keyboard. The keyboards are similar in the spatial layout of the rows and the keys but differ with respect to the assignment of letters to keyboard positions. (The keyboard layout and other details of the Dvorak keyboard can be found in Dvorak et al., 1936, and West, 1969; see also Chapter 1 in this volume.)

In the present analysis, only errors that involved confusions between the hands were considered. (Most errors in typing are substitutions involving adjacent keyboard positions; see MacNeilage, 1964. For both the conventional and the simplified keyboards, there are 330 possible substitution errors involving the use of fingers of the incorrect hand. These include 22 mirror-image substitution errors, 80 same finger substitutions, and 228 substitutions involving different fingers of the incorrect hand. (The mirror-image pairs for the conventional keyboard are *g* and *h*, *f* and *j*, *d* and *k*, *s* and *l*, *t* and *y*, *r* and *u*, *e* and *i*, *w* and *o*, *q* and *p*, *b* and *n*, and *v* and *m*. The mirror-image pairs for the Dvorak simplified keyboard are *i* and *d*, *u* and *h*, *e* and *t*, *o* and *n*, *a* and *s*, *y* and

Table 10.1. Substitution Error Frequencies for the Qwerty Keyboard

	A	B	C	D	E	F	G	H	I	J	K	L	M	N	O	P	Q	R	S	T	U	V	W	X	Y	Z
A was struck for		69	106	71	560	102	24	139	148	26	15	136	58	61	126	60	89	104	1012	116	46	96	100	33	46	139
B was struck for	36		37	43	33	44	163	42	12	8	3	25	57	262	43	13	1	7	28	40	21	773	7	6	15	9
C was struck for	59	43		486	98	67	22	19	36	7	27	14	20	84	25	1	7	30	174	28	14	466	22	133	8	9
D was struck for	65	43	436		755	394	117	23	73	27	484	58	7	80	27	6	2	72	862	119	22	21	30	22	11	1
E was struck for	494	28	149	651		72	76	114	1019	20	25	141	66	75	174	27	5	813	276	273	95	44	638	17	77	7
F was struck for	43	80	92	524	72		586	56	66	176	24	38	6	27	56	47	3	419	71	153	12	159	12	1	8	1
G was struck for	35	241	34	166	75	541		461	24	54	41	17	9	59	8	5	8	37	30	267	18	51	9	3	8	3
H was struck for	40	44	43	22	42	47	389		100	207	111	21	19	275	46	15	6	26	36	117	44	11	9	4	99	1
I was struck for	159	10	17	73	907	28	25	84		30	211	81	50	90	915	21	13	59	78	160	560	54	20	2	27	1
J was struck for	11	6	10	11	21	140	62	489	46		217	49	242	188	28	7	1	6	4	40	128	5	1	2	10	2
K was struck for	17	10	34	287	29	11	16	66	172	101		521	37	44	56	10	2	17	23	16	7	2	2	4	3	—
L was struck for	119	44	16	59	116	54	24	42	106	54	413		62	97	567	92	7	40	150	77	29	3	8	7	14	3
M was struck for	52	16	11	8	41	6	15	13	27	60	56	21		1277	77	24	5	17	25	14	36	39	6	3	2	2
N was struck for	93	135	33	44	87	19	68	151	90	28	17	50	1249		68	10	6	27	74	67	25	63	8	6	22	3
O was struck for	210	18	23	30	134	82	20	68	1290	26	52	671	54	63		346	36	154	78	112	154	22	104	8	22	3
P was struck for	33	11	9	6	56	11	10	14	28	3	6	46	15	24	405		36	23	14	43	19	6	13	3	15	1
Q was struck for	232	6	5	3	21	11	12	7	9	3	—	4	10	3	10	22		6	16	66	20	17	109	3	6	6
R was struck for	111	15	40	139	1043	334	36	24	92	5	7	27	14	70	140	33	8		186	1488	398	58	67	19	28	7
S was struck for	954	23	260	1061	300	106	23	16	69	6	24	162	27	91	68	12	8	156		150	57	59	410	157	15	19
T was struck for	97	38	24	105	212	185	254	129	157	26	20	65	15	58	79	23	55	1407	168		58	7	55	45	327	5
U was struck for	33	59	10	28	64	17	15	49	519	124	23	40	13	35	123	21	40	217	81	99		22	25	52	419	12
V was struck for	45	1001	430	39	71	137	38	28	35	1	2	10	34	101	17	2	18	44	24	11	40		11	11	20	1
W was struck for	89	9	10	76	927	26	6	19	15	3	1	17	16	22	122	30	96	136	382	95	18	26		10	12	26
X was struck for	33	12	292	35	24	1	3	11	8	5	1	2	9	8	11	5	5	21	225	23	23	10	12		16	191
Y was struck for	44	10	5	18	57	11	26	109	33	13	3	12	18	31	12	11	5	32	138	508	502	90	43	13		8
Z was struck for	288	7	6	7	6	2	3	2	10	1	3	3	1	5	4	4	6	13	34	6	2	9	30	108	6	

Note. This table of over 60,000 typing errors is from *Analysis of Errors* by D. D. Lessenberry, Syracuse, N.Y.: L. C. Smith and Corona Typewriters, 1928; reprinted in Dvorak *et al.*, 1936.

Table 10.2. Substitution Error Frequencies for the Dvorak Simplified Keyboard

	A	B	C	D	E	F	G	H	I	J	K	L	M	N	O	P	Q	R	S	T	U	V	W	X	Y	Z
A was struck for		4	—	3	32	—	1	9	26	—	—	3	3	4	217	1	—	5	12	5	2	2	1	—	1	—
B was struck for	3		1	18	2	1	—	—	—	—	3	—	23	4	2	1	—	—	—	—	1	—	1	—	1	—
C was struck for	1	—		1	5	—	12	1	2	—	—	1	—	1	—	—	—	18	2	34	—	—	1	—	—	—
D was struck for	2	19	—		1	8	3	22	18	—	—	1	—	1	1	—	—	1	3	5	1	—	—	1	2	—
E was struck for	18	1	3	3		1	—	10	27	—	—	3	—	2	153	—	1	6	5	23	26	2	1	—	3	—
F was struck for	—	—	—	9	2		26	—	3	—	—	1	—	—	1	—	—	1	—	—	—	1	—	—	19	—
G was struck for	—	—	11	1	—	61		6	—	—	—	—	1	2	—	17	—	—	—	—	2	—	—	—	4	—
H was struck for	3	4	1	50	10	5	—		1	—	1	—	26	6	2	1	—	—	3	47	12	—	—	1	—	—
I was struck for	12	—	—	18	25	1	1	5		—	1	3	—	11	12	1	—	8	7	9	35	—	—	1	3	—
J was struck for	1	—	1	—	2	—	—	—	—		6	—	—	—	—	1	1	1	1	—	1	—	—	1	—	—
K was struck for	—	4	—	—	—	—	—	—	2	1		—	—	1	—	—	—	—	—	—	1	1	—	13	—	—
L was struck for	—	1	1	2	7	3	—	1	2	—	—		—	2	—	13	—	24	41	2	1	—	—	—	—	—
M was struck for	1	50	—	1	—	—	1	17	1	—	2	—		2	1	1	—	—	2	3	1	7	21	—	—	—
N was struck for	—	—	3	6	1	—	1	6	10	—	—	2	7		17	—	—	57	40	50	1	16	2	—	—	—
O was struck for	134	2	1	4	167	5	1	1	14	1	—	5	3	12		1	—	13	17	6	15	—	4	—	5	—
P was struck for	—	3	—	1	2	3	17	—	1	—	—	1	—	—	3		—	14	—	1	13	—	—	—	34	—
Q was struck for	1	—	—	—	1	—	2	—	—	1	—	—	—	—	5	—		—	—	—	—	—	—	—	—	—
R was struck for	4	—	27	—	7	2	—	—	8	—	—	31	—	60	15	3	1		1	9	2	5	—	—	4	—
S was struck for	5	—	3	6	7	—	—	5	3	1	—	50	3	46	5	—	—	10		12	—	—	1	—	—	1
T was struck for	1	—	38	15	42	6	—	44	7	—	2	—	—	46	9	—	—	4	9		5	—	22	—	3	—
U was struck for	10	1	—	—	56	2	—	2	50	—	—	2	—	5	7	4	—	3	1	3		—	2	—	1	—
V was struck for	1	1	1	—	—	—	—	—	—	—	—	—	—	44	—	—	—	1	10	—	—		10	2	—	1
W was struck for	—	—	6	—	2	1	—	—	—	2	—	—	22	4	4	—	—	—	—	19	—	12		—	1	—
X was struck for	—	8	—	—	—	—	—	—	3	—	11	—	—	—	—	—	—	—	—	—	—	1	1		—	—
Y was struck for	2	—	—	—	3	19	4	—	9	—	—	—	2	—	1	37	—	2	—	3	1	—	—	—		—
Z was struck for	2	—	—	1	—	—	—	—	6	1	—	—	—	—	—	—	—	—	4	—	—	—	—	—	—	

Note. From D. W. Davis, *Journal of Business Education*, 1935; reprinted in Dvorak et al., 1936.

f, *p* and *g*, *x* and *b*, *k* and *m*, *w* and *j*, and *v* and *q*.) The total frequency of occurrence of each of these three between-hand error types was calculated separately for the two error matrices.

The analyses of confusion errors revealed patterns in the frequencies of between-hand substitution errors (Table 10.3) that were similar to the pattern observed in the timing data reported above. Substitution errors involving mirror-image locations on the keyboard occurred disproportionately often relative to other substitution errors with the opposite hand. The differences were highly reliable by chi-square tests. Whereas mirror-image pairs accounted for only 6.9% of the possible key pairings between hands, mirror-image substitutions accounted for 38.2% of all between-hand errors with the conventional keyboard and 35.1% of between-hand errors with the simplified keyboard. (The effect also seems to be present in the 623-item corpus analyzed by MacNeilage, 1964.)

The possibility that the observed proportion of mirror-image substitutions was related to the frequency with which mirror-image pairs are adjacent in English was tested by comparing error rates and digraph frequencies for all between-hand letter pairs. One might predict that letters that occur adjacent to each other frequently in English might be substituted for one another in typing at a higher rate than letters forming low-frequency digraphs. In this analysis the total frequency of occurrence of letter pairs (Mayzner & Tresselt, 1965) was calculated for each of the three movement types. As can be seen from Table 10.3, the digraphs associated with mirror-image locations on the keyboard account for only 5.6% and 7.1% of the total frequency of occurrence of between-hand digraphs on the conventional and simplified keyboards, respectively. This is far less than the 38.2% and 35.1% of between-hand errors resulting from mirror-image substitutions.

Mirror-image positions on the keyboard are associated with slower interkey times and are more likely to be substituted for one another than other keyboard positions involving the two hands. The similar substitution error patterns for the two completely different keyboard layouts indicates that linguistic or motor factors specific to the conventional typing keyboard do not lead to the differences observed for the mirror-image classification. Further, the fact that the timing of mirror-image movements does not interact with skill or with the characteristic interkey time pattern over the length of the word (Ostry, 1980, for words; Sternberg, Monsell, Knoll, & Wright, 1978, for letter strings) suggests that a general aspect of motor organization, and not simply a typing-specific one, may be involved.

Mirror-image movements involve the same fingers of opposite hands and similar movement trajectories. The tendency to confuse these locations may indicate that there is a bilateral activation of symmetric movements. The related observation that the interkey times of mirror-image

Table 10.3. Frequency of Between-hand Substitution Errors

	Qwerty Keyboard		
	Mirror Image	Same Finger	Other Finger
Observed frequency (Lessenberry, 1928)	6,379	2,685	7,615
Total observed between-hand errors (%)	38.2	16.1	45.7
Total number of possible between-hand errors	22	80	228
Total possible between-hand errors (expected distribution of between-hand errors %)	6.7	24.2	69.1
Total frequency of between-hand digraphs	2,051	9,160	25,095
Total frequency of between-hand digraphs (expected distribution of errors %)	5.6	25.2	69.1
	Dvorak Simplified Keyboard		
Observed frequency (Davis, 1935)	245	96	357
Total observed between-hand errors (%)	35.1	13.8	51.1
Total number of possible between-hand errors	22	80	228
Total possible between-hand errors (expected distribution of between-hand errors %)	6.7	24.2	69.1
Total frequency of between-hand digraphs	3,213	6,367	35,793
Total frequency of between-hand digraphs (expected distribution of errors %)	7.1	14.0	78.9

movements are longer than those of other movements of the two hands is perhaps a result of attempts to prevent errors when mirror-image positions have to be typed sequentially. Alternatively, the slowing of interkey times may result from movement overlap or sequence repetition. This alternative would account for the slowing of performance that is reported for the repetition of letters in handwriting (Wing, Lewis, & Baddeley, 1979) and words in speech (Sternberg et al., 1978).

Evidence from studies of simultaneous or rhythmic bimanual movement has indicated that there are limits on the independence of the individual hands and arms (Kelso et al., 1979; Klapp, 1981; Marteniuk & Mackenzie, 1980; Peters, 1977). In the present study, the demonstration of consistent relationships between the hands has been extended to a task involving rapid serial output. The findings underscore the fundamental nature of interlimb dependence even in the production of complex movements.

Appendix

Mirror image	Same finger	Other finger	
sliding	display	silence	auction
rubbish	fulfils	context	flicker
eidetic	soaring	fingers	curious
worship	sounded	torture	compare
bowling	postage	painted	forming
leisure	edition	distant	husband
island	hostage	welfare	neutral
trumpet	phrases	private	pistons
chiefly	nakedly	storage	fluster
courage	figures	release	someone
growing	insoles	request	enforce
falsely	closing	whistle	crystal
achieve	smokers	fathers	outcome
network	imposed	product	outside
disrupt	confuse	garment	mention
foreign	pencils	conduct	advised
culture	propose	authors	problem
pansies	blanket	exhaust	centaur
impulse	helpful	teaches	despise
shadowy	purpose	against	furnish
prairie	provoke	routine	receipt
flavour	without	remarks	tendons
kernels	embryos	persons	trouble
somehow	mistake	wrinkle	pursuit

Note: The interkey times reported above are the times between the underlined letter pairs.

Acknowledgments

This research was supported by the Natural Sciences and Engineering Research Council of Canada. The authors thank S. Lichtman for helping with data collection and Jonathan Grudin for helpful comments.

References

Carroll, J. B., Davies, P., & Richman, B. *The American Heritage word frequency book.* Boston: Houghton Mifflin, 1971.

Cohen, L. Interaction between limbs during bimanual voluntary activity. *Brain,* 1970, *93,* 259-272.

Dvorak, A., Merrick, N., Dealey, W., & Ford, G. *Typewriting behavior.* New York: American Book Company, 1936.

Kelso, J. A. S., Southard, D. L., & Goodman, D. On the coordination of two-handed movements. *Journal of Experimental Psychology: Human Perception and Performance,* 1979, *5,* 229-238.

Klapp, S. T. Doing two things at once: The role of temporal compatibility. *Memory and Cognition,* 1979, 7, 375-381.

Klapp, S. T. Temporal compatibility in dual motor tasks II: Simultaneous articulation and hand movements. *Memory and Cognition,* 1981, *9,* 398-401.

Lessenberry, D. D., *Analysis of errors.* Syracuse, N.Y.: L. C. Smith and Corona Typewriters, School Department, 1928. (Reprinted in A. Dvorak, N. Merrick, W. Dealey, & G. Ford, *Typewriting behavior.* New York: American Book Company, 1936.)

Mac Neilage, P. F. Typing errors as clues to serial ordering mechanisms in language behavior. *Language and Speech,* 1964, 7, 144-159.

Marteniuk, R. G., & MacKenzie, C. L. A preliminary theory of two-handed co-ordinated control. In G. E. Stelmach and J. Requin (Eds.), *Tutorials in motor behavior.* Amsterdam: North-Holland, 1980.

Mayzner, M., & Tresselt, M. Tables of single-letter and digram frequency counts for various word-length and letter position combinations. *Psychonomic Monograph Supplement,* 1965, *1,* 13-22.

Ostry, D. J. Execution-time movement control. In G. E. Stelmach and J. Requin (Eds.), *Tutorials in motor behavior.* Amsterdam: North-Holland, 1980.

Peters, M. Simultaneous performance of two motor activities: The factor of timing. *Neuropsychologia,* 1977, *15,* 461-465.

Shaffer, L. H. Performances of Chopin, Bach and Bartok: Studies in motor programming. *Cognitive Psychology,* 1981, *13,* 326-376.

Sternberg, S., Monsell, S., Knoll., & Wright, C. The latency and duration of speech and typewriting. In G. E. Stelmach (Ed.), *Information processing in motor control and learning.* New York: Academic Press, 1978.

West, L. J. *Acquisition of typewriting skills.* New York: Pitman, 1969.

Wing, A., Lewis, V., & Baddeley, A. The slowing of handwriting by letter repetition. *Journal of Human Movement Studies,* 1979, *5,* 182-188.

Chapter 11
Actively Learning To Use a Word Processor

John M. Carroll and Robert L. Mack

Introduction

In the early days of cognitive psychology, it was often necessary to rail against "stimulus-response" analyses of learning that went like this: Items in the world come around and get paired with responses (or dispositions to respond) in the organism (generally because the pairing leads to a good effect of some sort). This is a somewhat barren analysis of human learning, and cognitive psychology succeeded in doing away with it. The solution offered by cognitive psychology, then and now is to turn the question of learning into the question of memory. This was probably a good idea; after all, successful learning ought to lead to memory, and stimulus-response psychology had nothing to say about how even simple aspects of memory organization could be explained.

In turning the question around like this, however, cognitive psychology overlooked another striking problem with the stimulus-response analysis of learning: Learning—in that view—is a mechanically *passive* matter of pairing and then incrementing the strength of pairing. The active initiatives of the learner do not figure in at all. In turning the learning question into the memory question, cognitive psychology effectively finessed this problem: Memory structures, after all, *ought* to be stable, relatively static, and so on. Reducing the analysis of memory to a set (albeit an increasingly large set) of mechanisms was viewed as an entirely proper scientific approach to the matter. (But cf. Jenkins, 1974).

Both stimulus-response psychology and cognitive psychology—in their approaches to the problems of analyzing learning and memory, respectively—share a basic orientation: The processes involved are passive with respect to the initiative of the learner-memorizer. They in fact share one other basic orientation. Neither school of psychology focused much empirical concern on the analysis of full-scale problems of human behavior and experience. This is as true of the classic Sperling and Sternberg brand of memory research as it is of the classic Skinnerian studies of pigeon pecking. Although it may be true that in highly constrained situations, or in infrahuman species, active self-initiative is muted, this may not bear at all on the nature of real and complex human learning.

In this chapter we consider the full-scale task of learning to use a word processor. We argue, based on our empirical study of this task situation, that learning is fundamentally active, fundamentally driven by the initiatives of the learner—which are in turn based on extensive real-world knowledge and on reasoning processes that are systematic yet highly creative. The picture of learning we develop here can be embedded within the framework of current cognitive science (see Norman, 1981).

Method and Overview

The research we will discuss consists of studies of office personnel learning to use word processing equipment. In this chapter we are not concerned with issues relating to particular systems (see Mack, Lewis, & Carroll, Note 1). Our principal focus will be on a class of learning strategies that we have identified in the course of this work. We refer to these strategies as *learning by thinking.* (See Carroll & Mack, 1982, for a more extensive discussion of learning strategies.)

Our view is that these are natural—albeit complex—strategies for people to adopt when confronted by a learning task of nontrivial complexity. What is especially noteworthy in the present case is that the learners we have studied are almost entirely "innocent" with respect to computer technology. Because of this, these natural strategies entrain severe and wide-ranging learning problems. Analysis of these problems, in turn, suggests research directions for the analysis of real human learning within cognitive science and practical directions in which computer word processing systems, and the educational technologies that support their training and use, might evolve.

The Learners and Their Task

In this research project 10 office temporaries spent 4 half-days learning to use one of two possible word processing systems in our laboratory. Four were given a subset of the word processing operations for a general-purpose command-based system. The other six were asked to learn basic functions of a commercially available word processor that was menu based.

These people were highly experienced in routine office work, but quite naive with respect to computers in general and word processors in particular. We asked them to imagine a scenario in which a word processing system had recently been introduced into their office and they had been asked to be the first to learn it (in order to pass this knowledge on to colleagues). The point was that they were to learn to use the system by using the training materials that accompany it as their only resource. The manual we used was designed for use as the nucleus of a self-study training method, although such materials are rarely used in complete isolation from other methods, such as tutorial assistance (which is not surprising in light of our results; see below).

The materials we asked our learners to study covered basic letter entry and revision skills (including formatting, printing, document retrieval, and document merging), and in the case of the commercially available system, the use of command menus, the interpretation of messages, and the use of the on-line help facility.

Learners spent varying amounts of time with this task, but we stopped them in any case after about 12 hours in order to ask them to try a simple transfer task that involved typing in, revising, formatting, and then printing out a one-page letter. This transfer task was not part of the self-study manual; it served as a sort of benchmark achievement test. Finally, we asked learners about their prior work background, made specific queries that occurred to us during the course of the learning sessions, and elicited the participants' overall impressions of the system and the experience.

Our concern here is not to detail the results of the project; they can be found in Mack et al. (Note 1). Suffice it to say that a great many problems cropped up during the sessions and that even after the 12 hours or so of self-study learning not a single learner was able to complete the transfer task without some kind of serious difficulty. Indeed, the only subtask successfully completed was the initial creation of a document (i.e., just the initiation of input; *not* the successful typing in of a complete letter)!

Two very general points should be stressed about this project. First, the domain in which we studied learning is part of the real world of actual learning that real people must cope with: We studied real word processing systems and books targeted for them. We take this project to constitute an "ecologically valid" investigation of human learning. Second, the systems and the manuals that were our materials for this work are state of the art. Thus, our findings—especially those pertaining to learner problems—are not abstract effects of "materials," but rather have immediate and specific practical implications for the design of technology in the word processing domain (see Mack et al., Note 1).

Thinking Aloud

Our method involved prompting learners to think aloud as they worked through the training materials. They were to report questions that were raised in their minds, plans and strategies they felt they might be considering or following out, and inferences and knowledge that might have been brought to awareness by ongoing experiences. We remained with the learners in order to keep them talking and to intervene if at any time it appeared that a problem was so grave that a learner might leave the experiment if we did not help out. Our prompting remained nondirective, and indeed once learners got going we needed to prompt very infrequently. We had to actually intervene only rarely.

Throughout the learning sessions, video and sound recordings were made (in what we hoped was an unobtrusive manner). Our analysis consisted first of an enumeration of "critical incidents," which were cataloged and classified in various ways. This classification was constrained by the consensus of the three experimenters (the authors and Clayton Lewis). The chief goal of this was to form a picture of the typical experience of a learner, and it is this induced "prototype" learning experience to which we will refer in what follows (for details see Mack et al., Note 1). Our method of reporting will be to cite induced generalizations and to illustrate these by concrete examples transcribed from our audio recordings.

We are aware that the thinking aloud technique has been of great methodological interest recently, but this topic lies outside the scope of this chapter (see Ericsson & Simon, 1980; Nisbett & Wilson, 1977).

How People Learn

Perhaps the most apt description of the world of the new user of a word processing system is that often quoted phrase of William James, "a bloomin' buzzin' confusion." People in this situation see many things going on, but they do not know which of these occurrences are relevant to their immediate concerns. Indeed, they do not know if their current concerns are the appropriate concerns for them to have. The learner reads something in the manual, sees something on the display unit and must try to connect the two—to integrate, to interpret. It would not be surprising to find that people in such a situation experience conceptual—or even physical—paralysis, since they have so little basis on which to act.

Yet people do act. Indeed, perhaps the most pervasive tendency we have observed is that people simply strike out into the unknown. If the rich and diverse sources of available information cannot be interpreted, then some of them will be ignored. If something *can* be interpreted (no matter how specious the basis for this interpretation), then it will be interpreted. Ad hoc theories are hastily assembled out of these odds and ends of partially relevant and partially extraneous information, and these theories are used for further prediction. Whatever initial confusions get into such a process, it is easy to see that they are at the mercy of an at least partially negative feedback loop: Things quite often get worse before they get better.

Designers of word processors and training technology probably would have liked things to have been different. The easiest way to teach someone something is, after all, to tell them. However, what we see in the learning to use a word processor situation is that people are so busy trying things out, thinking things through, and trying to relate what they already know (or believe they know) to what is going on that they often do not notice the small voice of structured guidance crying out to them from behind the manual and the system interface.

What's wrong? We believe that the learning practices people adopt here are typical, and in many situations adaptive. The problem in this learning situation is that new learners of word processors are *innocent* in the extreme. Each feature of a word processing system may indeed have a sensible design rationale from the viewpoint of a systems' engineer, but this rationale is frequently far beyond the grasp of the new user. "Word processor," so far as we know, is not a natural concept. People who do not know about word processors have little, possibly nothing, to refer to in actively trying to learn to use them. Innocence turns reasonable learning strategies into learning problems.

Learning by Thinking

Learners actively—indeed relentlessly—try to make sense of their experience with the word processing system. Learning passively by rote assimilation of information is atypical, and perhaps impossible given the complexity of current computer interfaces. Rather, learners actively try to develop interpretations about why the computer works the way that it does.

These quests after meaning can be triggered by new and salient facts, or by discrepancies between what is expected and what happens. They can be motivated by the learner's attempts to solve problems and to address an ever-growing personal agenda of goals and queries, referred to as new opportunities arise. They can arise in attempts by learners simply to identify and integrate the elements of procedures relevant to accomplishing goals of current interest. In each case, learners' lack of knowledge about word processing operations makes it difficult for them to reason out coherent solutions that accurately represent the objective operation of the computer.

We will exemplify each of these aspects of active learning by examining three transcript excerpts from three of our learners. The first learner, as detailed in Table 11.1, is trying to sign on to the computer and to carry out a simple exercise in typing and deleting a string of characters in a menu field. The second learner (see Table 11.2) tries to correct a typing error during an exercise on a prerequisite cursor movement operation. Table 11.3 provides a glimpse of a third learner trying to discover how to delete an underscore and replace a lowercase *t* with its uppercase counterpart.

The next three subsections develop three aspects of the active strategy of learning by thinking: construction and verification of creative interpretations, analysis and integration of multiple pieces information, and self-initiated problem solving.

Constructing Interpretations

Learners do not assimilate their experiences in an unanalyzed form. They construct interpretations for these experiences based on what they believe they know or can reason out. Thus, when a command is invalid, people are inclined to say something like "The computer won't accept it when I'm on this menu"—thus going beyond the particular experience to an interpreted generalization of that experience. Unfortunately, this strategy is also invoked in circumstances where the relevant generalization about the system interface is obscure to the learner.

For example, more than one learner was troubled by an inconsistency in the functions that are used to move the cursor around the screen. One set is used to move the cursor within a menu display, whereas another is used to move it around a typing display. One learner reconciled herself to the distinction by reasoning that a cursor movement function that moved the cursor from one line of a document file to another would not work in a menu display because there could be more than one field on a line of a menu and she decided the function would not be able to move from one field to another within a line of a menu. The learner could have simply accepted the way things were accomplished. Instead, she tried to construct an interpretation for why things were done the way they were.

Another example is shown in Table 11.1, where a learner has pressed an invalid key that has locked the keyboard. After a series of frustrating attempts to discover what various functions do in this context, she correctly hypothesizes (end of Segment 5) that she has done something to lock the keyboard. This insight is still insufficient to allow her to discover the cause of her problem, or its remedy, and it is only in the context of other problem solving activities (discussed later) that the problem is finally solved.

We should not assume that interpretations like this one are obvious: The number of possible interpretations is much greater for new users than for experienced. The former have less relevant knowledge to use in constructing interpretations. Another learner was in a similar situation, unable in this case to move the cursor in a protected area of the screen. In contrast to the learner in Table 11.1, this person concluded that the reason the cursor would not move was that it was already in the correct

Table 11.1 Signing on the Word Processing System

(1) *Learner has been trying to type the letter string* abc *on display in order to observe cursor movement and to practice backspacing. She is typing this string on the "operator name" field for the sign-on task menu. As a result of a number of errors, which include prematurely trying to sign on with* abc *as the incorrect operator name, the learner decides to simply start over.*

L: So now let's see. Could I turn it off and start all over? That's what I would do. Will it hurt anything?

E: You're in control.

L: Let's see what happens. If I were all alone that's what I would do.

E: Yup! You're all alone!

Turns power off, and immediately back on. Previous display is replaced with a diagnostic pattern and then a new sign-on menu display.

(2) *Learner correctly types operator name* learner6 *in the sign-on menu field labeled "operator name."*

L: Uh the six [i.e., of learner6] was right next to it [i.e., no space] and it entered without typing anything. Do I have to make it, press "enter" to make it stay? No. Didn't say anything about that so we will forget about that.

Reference unclear, but she does not "enter" the filled-in sign-on menu. Instead, she continues with the next exercise, involving typing the letters abc *and backspacing. This is intended to be done on the sign-on menu to illustrate how one can correct mistakes made while filling in menu parameters.*

(3) Okay now we are off. [*Reads aloud.*] "If you have worked with this type "abc" and watch the cursor move."

Now she types abc *right after the operator name, which causes an error, signaled by: a beep, a message at top left, reset/help indicator light that comes on, and a locked keyboard, which can only be unlocked by pressing a reset key.*

L: Whoops!

E: What do you think happened then?

L: A bell rang. A buzzer or something.

(4) [*Reads instructions on sign-on menu display.*] "Enter to finish." Okay let's see what happens. [*Presses the enter key.*]

E: You pressed enter?

L: I pressed enter and nothing happened. [*The keyboard is locked. Learner reads more fragments of manual, stops at* "Ask your training adminstrator for help."] How do I get the menu? Request the menu again. All right. Press "request," "cancel."

Presses keys labeled request and cancel, and to no effect because of the locked keyboard. Reference to "the menu" is not clear but may reflect her current understanding that she has not signed on yet.

Okay. I didn't get the original menu to press anything.

Learner believes she needs a different menu, one that lists the tasks or commands available. It appears after one signs on.

Table 11.1 (*continued*)

Presses enter, which would have the effect of bringing up another display, but to no effect because of locked keyboard.
Now presses request key, which is not relevant to anything here.

E: You pressed request?

L: Request and enter. Trying to find that menu page because this page is not, I don't know how to get off this page. [*Not clear what she is referring to here, but clearly she believes that she must have a different display to work on.*]

All right. Come on. [*Reads more fragments of manual, referring to functions, which move the cursor from one menu field to another.*] Okay. Pressed that.

E: Variable Advance?

L: Right. "Watch the cursor. . . ." Nothing. [*Keyboard is still locked.*] Great!

E: Okay, what are you pressing there?

L: "Variable advance." [*then*] "Enter" to see if anything different might happen. Okay. Let's try it once more [*does so*]. Nothing!

(5) Still nothing. Okay. If I wanted to go back I would use the . . . ". . .look on the front." Where is the code key? Now I'm trying the variable advance key and the code key to see if anything happens. Nothing happens! For all the punching I'm doing nothing at all is happening.

E: Do you have any idea why that might be?

L: Ah I can't understand why it isn't entering, even entering the mistakes if I'm making mistakes. It's coming up with nothing. They did not tell me to get off this page.

[*New audio tape; some interaction may have been lost*]

Now I'm touching the backspace key and it is not erasing anything [*because keyboard remains locked*]. So I have made some kind of error that has locked everything in here.

E: Nothing seems to be working?

(6)

L: Right. Reset/help? [*presses reset key, which is remedy*].

E: Pressing reset?

L: I pressed reset/help to see what would happen there.

E: What do you think happened?

L: Nothing really. [*In fact, reset/help indicator light went off, signaling unlocking of keyboard.*]

E: Why did you press that?

L: I'm trying to get back to a beginning. To start over. All right. What would happen if I put it on "test"? [*Referring to a button on VDU that is labeled "test status." It is used to diagnose problems with display. It is totally irrelevant.*]

[*Turns test status "on" and a diagnostic pattern overlays screen*] Beautiful!

E: What happened?

L: I decided to put it on Test. Status is "test" rather than normal. Now let's see what happens if you backspace. [*Backspace works and she does so, deleting the incorrect string "learner6abc"*] Oh my gosh are you sure this isn't hurting everything? Oh hey hurrah! Good! Very good! Now we are in business.

Table 11.1 (*continued*)

Now if we backspace it takes it off. Okay. Fine. Now where did it tell me that I should have started at "Test"?

(7)

E: Can you summarize what you were just doing there?

L: Well I was looking at this 1-8 [*page*]. I was looking at this diagram and it says "The reset/help indicator is on." So then I figured out that these are indicators. I didn't know that before this. [*Summarizes what other indicator lights mean.*] Now I pressed the correct key and nothing happened, which is exactly what they tell you in the directions will happen. "When you are in a reset [*condition*] you cannot move the cursor or type anything." Now this was my problem before. But I wasn't up to page 1-9 so I didn't know that if the rest/help key, uh indicator is on the machine is going to do nothing. So you need to press . . .

E: Was that your problem before?

L: Yes.

E: Huh!

L: I didn't realize that it would not act as long as that was on, that I have to do something to get it back to acting again.

Okay. To be able to continue you need to press the reset key. So I press that. Now the . . . did they call it a code? An indicator. The indicator went off. The reset help indicator went off. So evidently we are back in business.

(8) Well um. Do you want . . . maybe I should go back and put it on normal and see if I could do the same thing?

E: Well you're in control.

L: [*Puts "test status" button on normal setting*] Now it's on normal. Let's do everything we did and see if it will work on this because we may still have been on the reset help button over there. I don't know.

We'll type the *abc* [*types abc in the operator name sign-on menu field*] and see what happens. Then we'll try to backspace [*does so, deleting the abc she has just typed*] Does that alright. We'll go backwards and do the things they told us to do.

[*Tries variable advance and return fucntions, which work.*] Which moves the cursor. Now they want us to move back. We'll code it in [*i.e., use the code key with variable advance to get variable return function*] and we're back.

Okay. I'm running back through the instructions and it is working with it set on normal. [*Reads fragments of manual—repeats exercise on making "invalid key" errors and pressing reset.*] Okay I could have done the exercise on normal.

E: Is that what you conclude?

L: That's what I concluded. Evidently when I heard the bell before and I didn't know that the reset/help indicator was on or didn't realize what was happening in that column. In other words I got into trouble before I got to [*page*] 1-8! So now we know why nothing was registering because I hadn't read on page 1-9 that I had to press the reset key.

Okay. Now I am going on to exercise two. We're going to find out how to sign on.

At this point begins following directions to sign on.

location for entering her password. That nothing appeared on the screen when she typed the password was unfortunately consistent with the fact that passwords are typically not displayed by computers.

The extreme complexity of current word processor interfaces provides many specious hints to the new user trying to diagnose a problem, resolve a question, or otherwise interpret the system's operation. Table 11.2 provides an example: In Segment 6 of this table, the learner has inadvertently inserted a blank line between two lines of text and wants to delete it. However, she does not think of her problem in this way, but rather as one of "bringing back" the bottom line to be immediately under the top one. This description suggested to her that a key labeled "required return" might be relevant: In fact, it is just another version of the (carriage) return function, and resulted in her inserting yet another blank line.

In another example, not shown in the tables, a learner tried to decide if a "file" command had stored a document file away. The command had not done so because it was entered in a text input mode where all typed strings are interpreted as text and not as commands. But she assumed that the file had been stored, and tried to confirm this interpretation. Not knowing what is really relevant, the learner found two features of the screen that were superficially similar to what one might hypothesize if the file command had been successful, and thus she concluded that the document had been stored. For example, at one point she noticed a status message "input mode 1 file," which indicates that she was in the text input mode. However, the word *file* matched her file command, and this was enough to suggest to her that her file (as in "store document") command had worked.

How can we characterize these reasoning processes? To a first approximation, these processes exemplify deductive and inductive reasoning. For example, Segment 5 in Table 11.1 involves generalizing from a number of examples of failures to make function keys work to the induction that something has caused the keyboard to lock. In Segment 8 the learner tries to find evidence for a hypothesis she has generated about the origin of her locked-keyboard problem. She correctly deduces that a procedure for unlocking the keyboard will allow her to carry out the steps of an earlier procedure, and verifies this deduction by repeating these steps.

In many other cases, the reasoning mechanism that learners engage diverges sharply from formal modes of logic like induction and deduction. In particular, hypotheses are often generated and/or verified on the strength of a *single fact* or *observation*—and this can happen despite other inconsistent but concurrently available data! Induction presupposes multiple and a priori similar facts, and deduction presupposes a logically complete connection between a set of premises and a predicted fact. Novices learning to use computers are typically not this systematic. They often rely on abduction and adduction.

Table 11.2 Correcting a Typing Mistake Prematurely

(1)
E: What are you thinking?
L: I'm trying to figure out what exercise is supposed to be for line advance. Supposed to be an exercise on errors, but am I supposed to be trying to make errors and then move back?
Types first three lines of file. At end of third line types comma instead of a period. Realizes her mistake after she has already carrier returned. Wants to know how to move the cursor back to make the correction.

(2) Oh, I see, so now . . .
E: What are you thinking?
L: I made a mistake up here, now if I want to go back I guess I would . . . [*Looks in the manual for information.*]
E: What are you looking at, page 3-4? [*Pause*] What is that telling you?
L: Well, I'm trying to figure out how I can go back to correct that mistake. Am I supposed to correct my mistake yet, or am I supposed to just not worry about the mistakes or . . . I'm going to try to go back.

(3) *Backspaces with the cursor at the beginning of current line in order to move cursor back to immediately preceding line. This is not allowed and incurs a beep error message.*
Oh! It didn't like that.

(4) *Presses line return, which moves the cursor to the beginning of the previous sentence with the comma that she wants to correct.*
E: Ok, what did you hit?
L: I pressed line return.
E: On page 3-4 again, what's that telling you?
L: I'm still trying to figure out . . . press and hold down line return until the cursor moves to the first line . . . that's a step but . . . [*Trying to adapt the manual instructions to her situation.*]

(5) *Hits the space bar, which puts a space at the beginning of the line. Then immediately backspaces, which deletes it.*
E: You hit a space then a backspace?
L: Yes. I'm just going to leave that mistake and press return.

(6) *The cursor is at the beginning of the third line, so when she presses return she inserts a blank line above it.*
Whoa!
E: OK, what are you thinking?
L: I didn't know it was going to do that. Wonder how I can bring it back.

(7) *Hits code*
E: What did you hit?
L: I pressed code . . .
E: What are you thinking?
L: I'm going to try to bring it back to where it was.
E: Bring what back?
L: Bring back the line, although I'm not really sure if it matters . . . space in between there [*points to blank line*]. I press return . . .

Table 11.2 (*continued*)

(8) [*Presses required return and inserts yet another empty line.*] Don't go any further . . . I'm having difficulty because I'm trying to bring it back up.
[*Pause in tape*]
Uses line advance to move cursor down to the line that needs to be "moved back up."
I'm trying to remember how to bring it back. I don't even know if it matters if it has a space in between. I can just continue typing.

Peirce (1958) defines the process of *abduction* as accepting a hypothesis when it, together with other assumptions the learner may already hold, allows the individual to deduce some fact or observation. The concept of abduction describes the type of reasoning mechanism that learners appear to engage when they generate hypotheses. The reasoner starts with some fact to be accounted for, and abduces a hypothesis that can account for it. Reliance on abduction, however, magnifies the "inductive risk": Learners construct ad hoc interpretations that may seriously misrepresent the situation they are actually in. (See Lewis and Mack, Note 2 for further discussion.)

In Table 11.1 (Segement 6), a learner with a locked keyboard believes that she has succeeded in unlocking the keyboard with a button labeled "test." She abduces the hypothesis that as a new user she should have been operating in this special test mode, and that *that* was the basis of her locked-keyboard problem. We saw another example earlier of a learner who locked the keyboard while trying to move the cursor in a protected area of the screen. She hypothesized that the cursor would not move because it was already in the right place to do what she wanted to do!

When a hypothesis is already held, learners frequently seek to verify it by *adducing* whatever evidence can be taken as relevant. Rarely do people systematically deduce and test the consequences of their hypotheses. Rather, they tend to reason only from confirming evidence and to overlook potentially disconforming evidence (see Nisbett & Ross, 1980, for similar observations). The learner who moved her cursor into a protected area and then tried to type her password adduced the failure of any characters to appear on the screen as evidence that she was proceeding correctly: Passwords are not displayed. But she simply ignored the fact that the cursor failed to move *at all* and that a "reset" error light came on. These facts were inconsistent with the hypothesis she was testing.

The mechanisms of abduction and adduction are important because they afford a way of generating and verifying new knowledge without requiring extensive prerequisite knowledge. In contrast, classical methods of reasoning—both deductive and inductive—impose this requirement. Deduction requires an extensive knowledge base of principles from which univocal predictions can be derived. Induction requires an extensive and systematic empirical data base—and in any case cannot guarantee the validity of its conclusions. Nevertheless, induction and deduction play a role in the learning mechanism—at least as a conservative check on the more radical, and reckless, processes of abduction and adduction. The roles of and interrelations between these several reasoning processes within the overall mechanism that learners employ remains to be detailed.

Integrating Information

The learner's ultimate goal is to discover procedures for accomplishing meaningful tasks. State-of-the-art training materials (which generally means step-by-step manuals) attempt to present such procedures as a matter for drill and practice. Learners are expected to read through a procedure specification and then to practice it within prescribed exercises until it is mastered. But this scenario is wrong in every way. Learners do not always read; they jump right into problem solving and exploration. They do not follow exercises very consistently, and when they do they are frequently derailed by the most trivial errors (we have found programmed exercises to be notoriously fragile—see Mack et al., Note1). Even when they do read about procedures, the meaning of actions and events referred to is not immediately apparent.

Identifying key elements of procedures and integrating them into a smooth operation often proceeds by successive approximation: Learners form some general schema or idea of what elements are relevant to a procedure, and then fill it out in the course of interacting with the computer. The process looks much more like slightly unsystematic scientific research than it does like drill and practice.

Table 11.3 shows two protocol excerpts from a learner who is trying to delete the underscoring for the three words *will not change*. The underscoring itself looks normal but it is marked by a special underscore character that is a block of reversed video highlighting superimposed on the space immediately following the word. To delete it, the user must position the cursor under the character in such a way that the message "word underscore" appears on an information line at the top of the display.

The learner's attempts to coordinate her initial understanding of this delete operation demonstrate the *revelatory nature* of trying things out: A sequence of actions and events is consolidated into a procedural concept. The learner has the correct general idea of positioning the cursor under a character and then using a delete function to delete it (evidenced in Segments 1 and 2), but does not incorporate the critical feedback from the information line at the top of the screen. The procedure has been incompletely instantiated. Even though the learner has read about these elements of the operation and, as the example shows, will read about it all again (e.g., Segment 5), its significance becomes

Table 11.3 Deleting a Word Underscore and Replacing a Letter

(1) *The learner is trying to delete the underscore from the second of three words, will not change. She is not locating the cursor in a way that identifies the special underscore character.*

L: What happened? The line [*underscore line*] didn't disappear, now what did I do? Was I over too many spaces? I could of been.

(2) Let me try again, I can replace the other one anyway. [*Presses character delete, deleting the c of the third word, change. Not clear why she did this.*]
What's happening?
Positions cursor immediately after the third word and "under" the underscore instruction so that character delete correctly deletes the underscore from the word.
It worked on that one, I don't understand. [*Learner did not enter underscore instruction at the correct location for the second word but did so for the third. Therefore the procedure worked for the latter, although the learner still does not realize how to know when the cursor has identified the underscore instruction, even for the third word.*]

(3) *Presses word delete and deletes the third and fourth words.*

E: What did you just press there?

L: I just pressed word delete.
Moves cursor to the next word and deletes it.
Oh, wait a minute that keeps moving all of them.
[*Looks in manual for information*] Checking out something here under [*the topic of*] word delete.

E: What is it that you're looking for?

L: I'm just trying to see . . .

(4) *Not is still underlined and every word in the line after not has been deleted.*
I got a little paranoid when I saw everything moving backward, I thought "wait a minute." Now, I realized I wanted to erase the whole thing anyway and retype it and then . . . Because I lost a space in there and I couldn't get rid of the line under *not*.

E: What were you looking for when you looked under word delete?

L: Yes, for some reason I was afraid I saw this moving over and I saw this moving over and I was afraid that I was going to erase . . . I don't know I'd . . . I'd forgotten that everything was going to move over anyway as you erase, as you delete. So, I didn't want to go on to the next, although actually I may have to erase that also. Ok, I'll see, I'll see if I can type this, retype this line . . .
Types in the rest of the sentence, after underscored not.
Oh, that's Ok, alright.

(5) *Moves the cursor back to the space before the underscored not.*

E: What are you looking for now?

L: Ok, I'm just looking to see what it says here again. [*I want to*] start again with the underscore . . . deleting the underscore . . . Yes, no I'm just going over what I did before.
Still trying to delete the line under not, places the cursor under the space after the t and deletes a space.
Oh, what did I do?

Table 11.3 (*continued*)

(6) [*Moves the cursor under the t in not, then moves the cursor to the space after the t*]. I see, Ok, I didn't realize that before. I didn't realize it [*the cursor*] has to pass through . . . the underscore. It has to pass through the underscore from what I understand.

E: How did you find that?

L: Um, under the, under the delete underscore instructions. [*Moves the cursor under the t, the word under message appears on the information line.*] I did that automatically before . . . It was supposed to be under the last letter of the underscore. [*Presses character delete and the underscore is deleted.*]

(7) *Learner moves on to another instruction for revising, this one involving replacing of a t with a T in the word the, which is the first word of a newly revised sentence.*

(8) *She deletes the t in the to produce the string he with the cursor positioned under the h. But before she tries to type the T she moves the cursor back to the space before the he: i.e., "___he". When she types T she actually inserts the T in front of the space to produce "T___he".*

E: What are you thinking?

L: Ok, um, when I deleted the *t* and typed the capital *T*, I created a space. Why is it doing this?

(9) *Looks in manual for help.*

E: Where are you reading now?

L: OK, I'm reading under character delete, I'm just . . . I'm trying to find out why when I retyped another character in place of the one I just deleted . . . um, I'm just wondering, there's another space after that now separating *T* and *h*.

(10) *Places the cursor in the space between T and h and inserts another T. Perhaps she is convincing herself that this really happened. Then she turns back to the manual section on deleting material.* It says they move together.

E: Was that a particular thing you just said?

L: Ok, it says, the instructions say that when you delete something the letters will move together to fill it in. Ok, now that . . . I don't understand why there's a space there as soon as I type the other one.

(11) [*Sometime later learner speculates*] When you delete you take out. Do you add when you put in?

apparent only through careful and detailed attempts (Segment 6) to integrate and practice the procedure.

One obstacle to integrating the elements of procedures, again, is the learner's innocence. For example, Table 11.3 also shows (beginning of Segment 8) that the learner has great difficulty understanding that the word processor is always in an insert mode. Hence, "replacing" is no longer a simple operation of overtyping (as it might be on a typewriter with a correcting ribbon). The learner tries to replace a *t* with a *T* in the word *the*. She deletes the *t* correctly, but then formulates her goal of replacing it with a *T* to be one of replacing the space at the front of the string *he* rather than of simple inserting the *T* at the beginning of the string.

Of course, the *T* is in effect inserted in the existing string, which now includes a space, producing the string *T he*. In Segment 11 she struggles to interpret this outcome by tying the "addition" of text to her earlier experience deleting it. As she puts it: "When you delete you take out. Do you add when you put in?" Her real problem however, is not recognizing that an important element of this procedure is the fact that the word processing system is always in an insert mode (i.e., characters, spaces, and even line breaks are inserted into the text line wherever the cursor happens to be).

These examples suggest that even the simplest operations present learners with serious challenges. They must translate expository descriptions of operations into actions. They must coordinate multiple sources of information (on the display unit, in the manual, and from memory); and it is evident that the significance of these various elements (i.e., what they accomplish, what prerequisites are needed, what relevant outcomes are etc.) only becomes clear to learners in the context of their interacting with the word processing system.

Setting Goals and Solving Problems

The interpretations that learners make are often in the service of broader goals, such as accomplishing tasks or solving problems that arise. Learners are hampered by their innocence of the appropriate problem space, or domain of possible actions and interpretations relevant to accomplishing goals and resolving problems. Accordingly, their strategies are often local and fragmentary: They have difficulty integrating information and formulating their concerns in ways that map congruently onto how the computer operates. One way learners cope with this situation is by constructing a personal agenda of goals and queries as they go along, and trying to resolve them in light of new experiences.

The learner in Table 11.2, for example, got into trouble trying to answer a long-standing question about how to correct a typing error. When she makes a typing error in the course of practicing cursor movement she is provided with an opportunity to try to resolve this question. The learner sets about doing so in a goal-directed manner, setting up subgoals of moving to the revision point and then finding functions appropriate for deleting the erroneous material. Yet her attempt to carry out these basic word processing operations founders for want of relevant knowledge.

For example, even though the exercise as a whole pertains to cursor movement, the learner tries to move the cursor by using the return key and space bar. Because the computer is also in insert mode, these keys (unlike their role on a typewriter) insert blank lines and spaces. These outcomes surprise the learner and she abandons her goal. The fragmentary character of her problem solving is revealed in part by the fact that she does not relate the goals of the exercise to her problem. That is, she does not explore the possibility of using these cursor movement keys to accomplish the subgoal of moving the cursor.

Table 11.1 also provides examples of the local and fragmentary character of the learner's problem solving. The learner sets many goals in the course of trying to type a letter string and learning how to delete it. For example, once the learner hypothesizes, toward the end of Segment 3, that she is not on the right "page" or menu to try what she wants, she attempts to find an alternative screen to work on. Her inability to do so results from entanglement with another problem that she has diagnosed (i.e., the keyboard is locked) but is not able to solve in time to accomplish her original subgoal. The learner ultimately solved her problem opportunistically. As Segments 7 and 8 show, the learner later encounters information that suggests an alternative interpretation of her earlier difficulty. Not only does she reconsider her erroneous interpretation, but as we saw earlier, she successfully adduces evidence for her new hypothesis by stepping back through the previous actions.

A major challenge to characterizing learners' reasoning and problem solving behavior in this task domain of word processing is the lack of a well-defined problem space. Although learners may understand the general task domain of office tasks, they do not know how this translates into the actions and concepts relevant to the specific problem domain for word processing. Their lack of knowledge makes it difficult to know what is relevant to achieving their goals, and what constraints to put on interpretations and goal-related actions.

We have focused here on the problems learners encounter when they are both innocent and active. But indeed this is the normal case: Active learning pervades our protocols. When learners tried to "go by the book" and play the passive role, they frequently—and very quickly—fell into some error or tangle of errors that compelled them to resort to more active strategies; and in those few cases in which a learner succeeded in *both* following the training materials passively and avoiding errors, they often turned to us and asked "What did we do?"

We would of course like to correct learner innocence: That, after all, is the whole object. But we may be able to do little to alter the learner's preference for active learning. In any case, the course of least resistance is clearly to try to design system interfaces that *facilitate* active learning by innocent learners, rather than to penalize people for their initiative: Computer interfaces are easy to change; human cognition may not be. To this end we now sketch the kind of system environment that we imagine might facilitate active learning.

Learning in an Exploratory Environment

If the picture of learning we have given here is anything close to correct, it suggests that an optimal learning environment for new users will differ from that provided by current systems. Indeed, the disparity between what exists currently and what would seem to constitute a reasonable learning environment is so great that we are able to capture only the grossest properties of what we imagine would be an optimal learning environment. By definition we will refer to this setting as an *exploratory environment;* our reason for choosing this term will become clearer presently.

Task Orientation

One property of an exploratory environment is that it provides learners with an appropriate orientation toward the task: Learners approach the task of learning to use a word processor with highly discrepant expectations about what it will be like and how difficult it will be. They—and their supervisors—may understand from popular misconception that word processors are easy to learn to use and that using them will result in immediate and substantial productivity increases. This might even be true if the means of instruction is personal tutoring. If the means of instruction is contemporary self-study, however, this outcome is far from the current reality—as our studies demonstrate. *Realistic expectations* about the difficulty of learning to use word processing equipment would at the very least discourage attributions of self-blame on the part of learners, and this in turn would make learning to use these systems more pleasant.

Another aspect of realistic task orientation involves *learner responsibility and control.* Manuals and system interfaces implicitly attempt to place the learner in a passive role; but as we have seen, learners take charge regardless. Nevertheless, the conflict between a manual-system ensemble that prescribes rote exercises on, say, cursor movement, and an active learner who decides in spite of this to explore techniques of error correction is problematic: The learner will "fail" in some sense no matter what the outcome. An exploratory environment establishes and reinforces a role of responsibility and control for the learner via the system interface and training materials. (Some of our current research work is addressed to providing such a learning environment and we return to it briefly in the final section of this chapter.)

Simplicity, Clarity, and Safety

A second property of an exploratory environment is *system simplicity:* Capacities of the system that to new users seem unrelated ought to be functionally independent—insofar as this is possible. Current systems contain many subtle interdependencies. In one of the systems we studied the command to print a document renders that document inaccessible for further editing until it is removed from the print queue by being either printed or deleted. The edit command still causes the document to be displayed, but no delete or insert operations work. Learners who inadvertently tried to edit such inaccessible documents were unable to make the correct attribution. They were convinced that something had gone wrong *within* the edit capability itself. In an exploratory environment, functions like printing and editing would be distinct: Straightforward attributions would be correct.

Simplicity connects directly to other properties of exploratory environments, in particular to *clarity* and *safety*. Systems are often unclear in the sense that they do not inform the user of the state they are currently in, what they are currently doing, or even what they have just done. In one system we studied, even the command to sign off occasioned no confirmation message at all: The system merely put up the sign-on menu (presumably for the next user). New users do not recognize that "hello" means "good-bye" in this system. They quite frequently signed on again and then asked us how they were ever going to get off of the system!

In the same system, the command to print a document elicited a confirmation message that was routed to a message reservoir. Here the message waited for the user to request it to be displayed. The trouble is that a user might not realize what has happened and/or might not know how to display a message. This could result in the message's being displayed at a time much later than that at which it was sent. Thus when one least expected it, one could learn that file such-and-such had been printed—which from the user's point of view is quite misleading. However, these problems of the availability and the timing of feedback can be headed off before they create misleading feedback situations: Why not have some feedback available and present it in a more timely fashion? (The relevant design trade-off in this case is that the presentation of feedback might interrupt succeeding operations and distract the user; but this rationale does not make printing any less inscrutable for the learner.)

A further, and far less trivial, feedback problem is that the content of messages is not typically problem oriented. Learners do not want to read messages like "parameter omitted or not valid"; they want to find out what they did wrong *in that case* with regard to their own current goals, and they would like to know what to try next to acheive those goals. This kind of situation can be troublesome for current help systems. We have often seen subjects examine a help screen that in fact contained the information they needed, but presented that information in a problem-neutral manner. Since the learners were construing their needs in a problem-oriented vocabulary, they simply failed to see the relevance of the help. An example is a learner who correctly employed on-line help to check the maximum permitted document name length. Instead of getting information focused on her specific need, she got a screenful of general information about naming documents. Overwhelmed by this display, she gave up.

Addressing this problem at all would require a task-analysis-driven approach to interface design that regards *learning* as a key user task. Addressing it comprehensively would require building some sort of "intelligence" into the system interface. Nevertheless, an exploratory environment is clear in the sense that it provides abundant, timely, and problem-oriented feedback to the learner.

Safety is the capacity of the system to protect the learner from demoralizing penalty. The issue arises because, as we have seen, the learning strategies that people adopt lead them into trouble with current word processors. If the strategy of learning by thinking is to operate effectively, the inferences, deductions, and abductions that people are prone to make must be correct. In some cases, this point can be codified simply: Operations that have apparent natural inverses (space and backspace, cursor up and cursor down) should indeed *be* inverses, each should undo the other's effects; and they should have predictably inverted names (Carroll, 1982a). In many other cases, designing systems that can be learned by being reasoned out is not nearly so straightforward. We simply do not understand human reasoning in these complex task environments well enough to derive appropriate design strategies from first principles.

Motivation

These properties straightforwardly suggest the hypothesis that learning, as we have described it here, is facilitated in an exploratory environment. In closing this section, however, we want to observe that this facilitation may not be merely "cognitive." Exploratory environments may enhance task-oriented motivation as well. Computer games manifest many of the properties of exploratory environments, and it has been argued that they increase task-oriented motivation (Malone, 1981, Note 3). The argument is murky, though, since the games differ from word processors in a great many irrelevant ways as well.

The game of Adventure may be an important case with respect to this point, both because it is so popular and because its maze-learning problem scenario is analogous in many ways to mastering the conceptual maze codified in a structure of interconnected menus in a word processor (Carroll, in 1982b). Indeed, the similarities between Adventure and word processing systems are abundant, which raises the question why the game is so attractive. Part of the answer might be that the types of properties we have clustered into the concept of an exploratory environment—properties like feedback, safety, and learner control—nurture a motivational orientation in game learners that is precluded for learners of current word processors.

Clearly these are empirical questions that can be addressed only by developing word processing systems that comprise exploratory environments and by studying how people manage to learn to use them. This is the direction of our current work.

Finale: Active Learning

At the outset of this chapter we broadly reviewed the recent treatment of learning in both stimulus-response psychology and (subsequently) cognitive psychology. Both share a picture of learning as passive with respect to the initiative of the learner. Both share a methodological orientation that focuses analysis on highly constrained laboratory situations. Our examination of a full-scale learning situation questions these premises. Learning to use a word processor provides a study of real complex human learning that is fundamentally active.

Where do we go from here? Our examinations of current word processing systems have led us to a conception of learning, and in particular of learning to use a word processor. In the two preceding sections we have summarized and projected in very general terms what we think we have learned. However, recognizing that current word processing systems might be improved from the learner's perspective by creating an exploratory environment is far short of understanding what learning would be like in such a situation. If the problems that learners experienced were less debilitating, we might be able to analyze learning at a finer grain and expose cognitive mechanisms that are simply lost in the confusion when people try to learn current systems. At the least, we could contrast learning in the two situations.

We are now attempting to codify our suggestions for training and system design into concrete experimental prototypes. A rude approximation involves merely altering the training materials that are provided for learners. The system they interact with is one we have studied previously, and one that has very little in common with exploratory environments. Nevertheless, by providing modular, problem-oriented training and training materials that make explicit the basic elements of procedures (e.g., what the goal is; what actions are required, including prerequisites; and what the outcomes are), we have been able to reduce training time without impairing learning performance (as measured by our transfer task).

These are preliminary results (our analysis is in progress) but they are encouraging. The next step for us is to exert direct control over the system interface itself. Only in this way can we seriously assess what learning may be like in an exploratory environment.

The nature of active learning remains for the most part an open question in current cognitive science. Since theory in this area is not very developed or abstract, the most promising strategy seems to be one of representatively examining a variety of accessible and realistic learning domains. Each domain must of course be probed as deeply as possible on its own terms, since we have no way of knowing beforehand which of the generalizations we identify will turn out to be domain independent and which will turn out to be properties that are specific to particular domains or sets of domains. The current study can be placed in this programmatic framework: Its chief results are its indications of what needs to be done next.

Acknowledgments

We are greatly indebted to Clayton Lewis, who was a full collaborator in this research and an originator of many of the ideas presented here. He was unable to participate in writing the chapter. We are also grateful to Karen Greer, who helped to transcribe from tape recordings the material presented in the tables. Some of the material in this chapter appears in a slightly different form in Carroll and Mack (in press).

Reference Notes

1. Mack, R., Lewis, C., & Carroll, J. M. *Learning to use word processors: Problems and prospects.* Unpublished manuscript, 1982.
2. Lewis, C., & Mack, R. *The role of abduction in learning to use a text-processing system.* Paper presented at the annual meeting of the American Educational Research Association, 1982.
3. Malone, T. W. *What makes things fun to learn? A study of intrinsically motivating computer games* (Xerox PARC Rep. CIS-7), 1980.

References

Carroll, J. M. Learning, using, and designing command paradigms. *Human Learning: Journal of Practical Research and Applications.* 1982a, *1*, 31-62.

Carroll, J. M. *The adventure of learning to use a small computing system: Travels in an exploratory environment. Computer,* 1982b, *15:11*, 49-58.

Carroll, J. M. & Mack, R. Learning to use a word processor: By doing, by thinking, and by knowing. In J. Thomas & M. Schneider (Eds.), *Human factors in computer systems.* Norwood, N.J.: Ablex, in press.

Ericsson, K., & Simon, H. Verbal reports as data. *Psychological Review*, 1980, *87*, 215-251.

Jenkins, J. J. Remember that old theory of memory? Well, forget it! *American Psychologist,* 1974, *29*, 785-795.

Malone, T. W. What makes computer games fun? *Byte,* 1981, 258-277.

Nisbett, R., & Wilson, T. Telling more than we can know: Verbal reports on mental processes. *Psychological Review*, 1977, *84*, 227-236.

Nisbett, R., & Ross, L. *Human inference: Strategies and shortcomings of social judgment.* Englewood Cliffs, N.J.: Prentice-Hall, 1980.
Norman, D. A. (Ed.) *Perspectives on cognitive science.* Norwood, N.J.: Ablex, 1981.
Peirce, C.S. The logic of drawing history from ancient documents. In A. Burks (Ed.), *Collected papers of Charles Sanders Peirce.* Cambridge, Mass.: Harvard University Press, 1958.

Chapter 12

Knowledge of Word Frequency as an Aid for Text Editing

Susan F. Ehrlich, Kristina Damon, and William E. Cooper

In this chapter we will consider how a writer's memory for his own writing may influence his ability to edit with a word processor. Word processing systems provide the ability to search for character strings automatically. This option allows the writer to locate segments of text quickly in order to make editing changes. In many systems, one of the most efficient ways to locate a particular segment is to search for a unique word that is used only in that segment. Writers' ability to take advantage of this option is dependent on their ability to recognize unique words in their own manuscripts. The research described here investigated the ability of four female subjects to locate such unusual words. Two procedures were used. First, each subject was shown a series of isolated words from her manuscript and was asked to estimate the number of times she had used each word. Second, each subject was asked to go through her manuscript and mark each word that she thought she had used only once. Both procedures allowed us to examine the writer's knowledge of single-occurrence words that would be useful for searching with a word processor. The first procedure also allowed us to examine the subject's ability to estimate frequency for words that were used more than once.

Before presenting the data, two theoretical perspectives will be discussed that concern the nature of the writer's memory representation. On the one hand, we might predict that a writer would perform with a high level of accuracy because she has a very accurate representation of the surface details of the sentences that have been produced. After all, the decisions about content, structure, and lexical form were originally made by her. On the other hand, we might assume that the writer's knowledge of self-generated prose is much like her knowledge of manuscripts that have been written by others (Bransford & Franks, 1971; Sachs, 1967). That is, the writer may maintain knowledge of the content of the manuscript but lose knowledge of the surface details of the sentences, such as whether a passive or active verb was used, or whether the word *make* or *produce* was used. An intermediary position is also possible. Subjects may maintain a conceptual representation as well as some knowledge of particular structural and lexical decisions. Memory for surface-level information might be more accurate when the writer spends an unusual amount of time finding the correct syntactic form or correct word to express an idea. There is little if any literature on memory for self-generated prose, but our personal observations suggest that memory for such text is largely conceptual.

Consider the following attempt by the first author of this chapter to reproduce the introductory paragraph from memory, immediately after writing the first few pages. An attempt was made to reproduce the paragraph verbatim, although the writer had not planned in advance to perform this exercise. The first draft was as follows:

> One of the greatest advantages of word processing systems is that they drastically reduce the time required to edit a manuscript. Retyping is kept to a minimum and "cutting and pasting" is carried out with a few strokes. Another great advantage of word processing systems is the fact that we are able to search for particular parts of the text efficiently so we can make additions or deletions or other types of corrections. A newcomer to a word processing system may at first be tempted to scan down the screen for the critical location in the text where the change is to be made even if that change might be made in a location that is a few pages farther into the text than the current location. However, the novice quickly learns that he can depend on more efficient means. In particular, he learns to search his memory for words that are unique to the critical location and he then searches for that critical word with one simple command.

Reproduction of first paragraph from memory:

> One of the greatest advantages of word processing systems is that they allow us to edit manuscripts very efficiently. Retyping is kept to a minimum and "cutting and pasting" is carried out with a short series of key presses. One of the other advantages of word processing systems is that they provide us with an efficient means for searching for particular locations so additions, deletions and other kinds of changes can be made. A newcomer to a word processing system may initially attempt to search for particular locations by scanning down the page even though the critical location may be far in advance of his current location. With experience, the novice learns that the most efficient means for getting to a critical location is to search memory (or a hard copy of the text that he may be working from) for some unique word and to search for that word with a simple command.

The parenthetical insert was a new thought that was inserted during the second writing. Except for this insert, very few *content* changes are evident when the two paragraphs are compared. In fact, all of the main ideas of the second paragraph appear in the same order as in the original. On the other hand, the surface realization of those ideas changed quite a bit. Syntactic structure changed considerably; with Version 1 stating "they drastically reduce the time required to edit a manuscript" and Version 2 having "they allow us to edit manuscripts very efficiently."

Although many of the words were maintained across the two versions (e.g., *word processor* and *retyping*), many others were changed. Notice the alternate realizations of the efficiency concept in the phrases given in the two versions. Even words at the beginning of sentences were changed, with "However, the novice quickly learns" becoming "With experience, the novice learns."

Observations such as these lead us to hypothesize that the writer's representation of self-generated text is primarily conceptual in nature. If this is true, then we would expect that writers' ability to find and use unique words (in order to search with a word processor) would also be dependent on conceptual knowledge. Conceptual confusions would be a hindrance during the editing process.

Case 1

The first case involved a graduate student in the department of religion at Harvard University and the 22-page introduction to her Ph.D. thesis. Her introduction was obtained 3 days after it was input into the word processor. During the next day, a frequency count of the words in her manuscript was performed and a subset of those words was selected for presentation. The following day, the subject was asked to read through her manuscript once without making any editing changes. The subject was told that this reading was in preparation for a test of memory for text. She was then asked to read through her manuscript again as it appeared on the screen of the word processor (the "vi" editor in the UNIX operating environment, implemented on a PDP11/44 computer). The subject inserted an asterisk in front of each word that she thought occurred only once in the manuscript. She was instructed to differentiate between capitalized and lowercase letters. This task took about one hour. The subject then took a half-hour break and returned for the second task, which involved estimating the frequency of occurrence of particular words. These words were displayed one at a time on a Radio Shack TRS-80 microcomputer, and the subject typed in her estimates. Response latencies to begin typing were also recorded. The subject gave estimates for 232 words, which were presented in a random order and segmented into four blocks. This procedure also took about an hour.

To provide some context for the data that will be reported, a distribution for the number of words with particular frequencies is given in Figure 12.1. Notice that the large majority of words occurred only once and that the number of words with higher frequencies dropped off very sharply, hitting a floor at about 10. Thus there were a large number of low-frequency candidates to choose from for the isolated word esti-

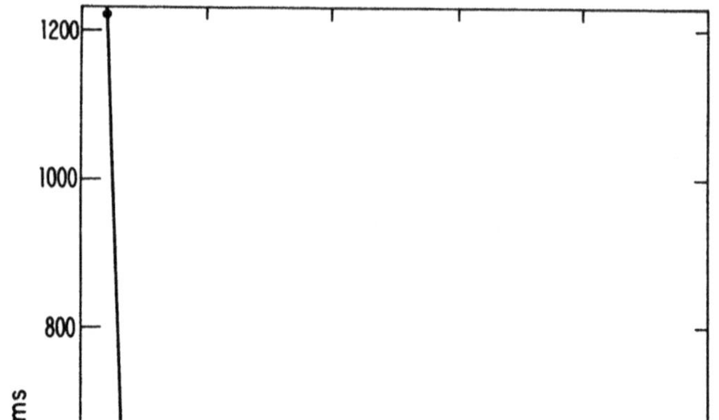

Fig. 12.1. Number of uses of words from the manuscript of Case 1.

mation task. Also, there were a large number of single-occurrence words for the subject to find when she marked the text with asterisks.

The data for the initial asterisk task are presented in Table 12.1. The words that were found by the subject and marked as unique were broken down into five categories: nouns, verbs, adjectives, adverbs, and function words. Function words included prepositions, conjunctions, determiners, quantifiers, and pronouns. The assignment of a word to a category was made on the basis of how the word was actually used in the text. There were two potential errors that the subject could have made. First, she could have *failed to find* some words that occurred only once. Second, she could have *incorrectly marked* words that were actually used more than once.

This subject was more likely to find unique nouns than any other category. The next most frequently marked category was adjectives, with verbs next. Only three single-occurrence adverbs and *no* function words were marked with asterisks. Of the two potential errors, failures

Table 12.1. Case 1: Subject Search for Single-Frequency Words

Part of speech	Total number of words marked	Incorrectly selected words	Total number in text	Percentage correctly selected
Noun	154	19	442	30
Verb	41	1	291	14
Adjective	65	6	154	38
Adverb	3	0	44	7
Function	0	—	50	0

to mark words far outweighed errors of marking a word that occurred more than once. Most of this second type of error occurred on capitalized nouns, and it is of interest that many of these cases involved a second use of a proper name in a footnote. Thus this subject tended to be conservative in judging whether particular words occurred only once. A count was made of the number of single-occurrence words in the manuscript for each category. This made it possible to obtain the percentage of the *available* words in each category that the subject *realized* were used only once. This subject seemed to be particularly good at picking out single-occurrence adjectives, marking 38% of the total number. She seemed to be next most sensitive to nouns (30%). The subject was surprisingly insensitive to verbs and adverbs, and she seemed to have no ability to recognize single-occurrence function words, even though there were 50 of them in the manuscript.

The subject's relative insensitivity to single-frequency verbs and function words is consistent with the idea that she had stored the content of the manuscript in a conceptual rather than surface format. Function words generally carry very few semantic features and are used in many different contexts. Such words would not often be specific enough to allow a profitable search of conceptual memory. Also, certain kinds of words with purely syntactic functions (e.g., relative pronouns, conjunctions) may be input into surface structure at the time of writing without having any conceptual basis per se (see Ehrlich, Note 1). If this is true, then the subject could not use a conceptual representation to verify the number of times such words were used. A similar analysis applies to the poor performance in recognizing unique verbs. Single-occurrence verbs may be distinguished from other verbs simply on the basis of tense and number. The tense and number of a verb are highly dependent on the syntactic context in which it is used, independent of the actual time of occurrence that the verb represents. If the tense and number of a verb are selected on the basis of the syntactic requirements of the sentence (see Ehrlich, Note 1) and syntactic decisions are not represented in the subject's memory for the text, then the subject would have no means for distinguishing the frequency of usage for different tenses of the same verb. We will provide further evidence supporting this conclusion.

The data for the isolated word estimation task are presented in Table 12.2. The 232 words that were used in the frequency estimation procedure included 15 single-occurrence, 15 double-occurrence, and 15 triple-occurrence words for each of the five word classes, whenever possible. In some cases, fewer than 15 of a particular type of word were used in the manuscript (see Table 12.2). Also included were 30 words whose frequency ranged from 15 to 20 occurrences and 10 words that never occurred in the manuscript. The subject was instructed to type the frequency estimates, and she was told that none of the words had been used more than 20 times. She was also told that there were a small number of words that did not occur in her manuscript, so that zero was an appropriate response. The zero-occurrence words and the 15- to 20-occurrence words were used to encourage the subject to use a wide range of estimates.

The first characteristic to notice in Table 12.2 is the high level of accuracy. This subject's estimates of frequency did indeed increase with the number of uses, even when single increments are considered. If this is a general skill, then we could conclude that searching for words that are unique or of low frequency in a manuscript would be a useful strategy for editing a manuscript. Notice that these frequency estimates complement the data in Table 12.1. The subject was less accurate at estimating frequency for those categories that she was less likely to mark as unique in the manuscript. The one exception was for adverbs. The subject was fairly accurate at estimating their frequency, although she failed to mark them uniquely in the manuscript. Both results can be interpreted in the same way. If the subject had a conceptual representation of the text that she produced, she would have good information about the number of times she used particular *concepts* but little infor-

Table 12.2. Case 1: Average Estimated Frequency of Occurrence

	Noun	Verb	Adjective	Adverb	Function	Average
Zero	*	*	*	*	*	1.00
N						(10)
Single	3.70	4.06	2.46	1.73	6.00	3.58
N	(15)	(15)	(15)	(15)	(15)	(75)
Double	3.36	5.13	3.33	3.80	6.73	4.57
N	(15)	(15)	(15)	(5)	(15)	(65)
Triple	4.46	4.64	3.37	—	7.38	5.09
N	(15)	(14)	(8)	(0)	(13)	(50)
15-20	*	*	*	*	*	14.36
N						(30)

Note: *N* denotes the number of words presented to the subjects in each category. Asterisks indicate cells for which no data were collected. Because the Zero category and the 15-20 category filler items were not selected on the basis of their part of speech, only average frequency ratings were obtained for these items.

mation about surface details of the manuscript, such as function words and verb tense.

The claims that have been made about the nature of the subject's memory representation have further implications that can be investigated with a more careful look at the available data. If the subject was indeed sensitive to the number of times a particular concept was used but not to tense and number, we would predict that verb frequency would be overestimated in cases where other tenses of verbs were employed. We might also expect overestimates in cases where the same *concept* was represented by a synonym. Table 12.3 presents the single-frequency verbs, nouns, adjectives, and adverbs whose frequency was overestimated. The subject's estimate is given next to each word, followed by (1) a list of words that had the same base morpheme and their frequency counts, and (2) a list of words that might be considered synonyms of the tested word and their frequency counts. Nine of the 12 verbs whose frequency was overestimated had counterparts with the same morphological base, usually a verb with a different tense. In some cases, verb synonyms seemed to account for the overestimates. Although the subject was more accurate in estimating frequency for words belonging to other categories, the occasional overestimates were often made in cases where synonyms were used in the manuscript.

The subject correctly judged the frequency of 22 single-frequency words. Only 6 of these had counterparts with the same morphological base in the manuscript. Those words with counterparts all happened to be adverbs. Notice that although this subject made accurate estimates for adverbs, many of those words represent some very general concepts that might apply to many of the relationships in the text: *easily*, *notably*, *greatly*, *essentially*, *directly*. Perhaps the forced judgments in the asterisk task did not reflect judgments based on access to these concepts in the conceptual memory representation of the text but instead reflected the subject's knowledge of general frequency of use for adverbs.

This idea receives some support from the final measure that was obtained from this subject, namely, the response latency to produce a frequency estimate. The correlations between the time to respond with an estimate and the size of the estimate are given below for each grammatical category. These correlations included data from the words that occurred once, twice, or three times in the manuscript. The high-frequency and zero-frequency filler items were not included.

Noun	Verb	Adjective	Adverb	Function
.31	.40	.20	−.01	.00

The correlation coefficients are interesting given the small frequency range. Note in particular how well reaction time correlated with the estimated frequency for verbs. On the other hand, times to produce estimates for function words and adverbs did not correlate at all with the estimates themselves. The response latencies may in general reflect

Table 12.3. Case 1: Potential Conceptual Confusions for Single-Frequency Words

Nouns	Subject estimate	Same root	Frequency in text	Synonym	Frequency in text
trees	2	tree	4	—	
comparison	9	comparing	1	other	9
		compared	1	contrasting	1
audience	7	—		readers	1
pains	8	painful	1	torment	4
				torments	5
edition	7	—		version	9
				versions	7
				translation	3
actions	3	reactions	1	deeds	9
origin	5	—		source	2
				sources	1
cloud	2	—			
purpose	5	—		reason	1
				theme	5
				idea	3
habitation	3	inhabited	1	place	4

Verbs	Subject estimate	Same root	Frequency in text	Synonym	Frequency in text
appeared	3	appearing	1	occur	1
		appear	1	occurs	1
		appearance	1	occurred	1
		appears	6		
externalized	2	—			
gives	17	given	3	providing	1
		give	6		
		Give	1		
walked	3	—		went	2
				Travelling	1
lived	2	Life	1	existence	1
shows	10	shown	2	reflected	1
		show	2	reveal	1
greets	2	greeted	2	welcomed	1
flourished	2	—		(see develop)	
leads	2	lead	1		
		led	3		

Verbs					
develop	8	developed	1	make	1
		development	1	formed	1
help	4	helper	1	provide	1
				providing	1
				provided	1
				support	1
disclose	3	disclosure	1	show	2
		disclosures	2	shows	1
				shown	2
				reveal	1
Adjectives					
little	3	—		few	1
				nothing	5
				least	1
greatest	3	greatly	1	most	6
		great	2		
		greatness	2		
		Great	1		
		greater	3		
fifteenth	3	fifty-	1	fourteen	1
		five	1	four	4
				fourth	1
				15	8

late	2	later	7		
critical	2	hypocritical	1	judgment	3
				Judgment	3
recurrent	8	recurs	3	repeatedly	1
				again	1
Adverbs					
undoubtedly	2	doubts	2	(of) course	4
directly	3	direction	1	right	1
		indirectly	2		
immediately	3			just	10
				after	6
				After	2
repeatedly	2	—		recurrent	1
spiritually	3	spirits	2	soul	16
		spirit	4	souls	14
				Soul	1
				Souls	2
greatly	3	greatness	2	much	2
		greater	3	very	3
		greatest	1		
		Great	1		
		great	2		

Table 12.3. (*continued*)

	Subject estimate	Same root	Frequency in text	Synonym	Frequency in text		Subject estimate	Same root	Frequency in text	Synonym	Frequency in text
righteous	7	righteousness	1	pure	1	intriguing	2	Intrigued	1	interesting	2
		right	1	sinners	4					interest	1
				Sinners	1						
				virtues	1	inevitably	2	—		(of) course	4
										necessary	1

the time used to search within the memory representation. If this is true, then the lack of correlation for adverbs and function words suggests that these words were not available in the memory representation of the text and that estimates were made on some other basis, perhaps with the use of knowledge of general word frequency in the language as a whole. This conclusion receives further support from the facts that the subject failed to find these two word classes in the asterisk task and that accuracy in estimating the frequency of function words was poor.

Taken together, the various sources of data reported suggest that this subject did indeed have quite detailed knowledge of the number of times she used low-frequency concepts. However, the application of such knowledge to the task of manuscript editing on a word processor would require that a number of factors be taken into account. In particular, surface information is sometimes required in order to single out words, and the data from this first case suggests that such information is not necessarily available in memory. Single-occurrence nouns and adjectives seem to be particularly useful, perhaps because such nouns are not likely to have synonyms and because adjectives are used sparingly and tend to be content rich.

Because of the idiosyncrasies of particular manuscripts, analysis of groups of subjects seems to be an inappropriate approach to the issues that have been discussed. It is our position that testing of generality at this stage would be more informative if done on a case-by-case basis. Data have been collected for three other subjects in our laboratory. For the third and fourth subjects, only the frequency estimate task was carried out.

Case 2

The second case involved a graduate student in the Department of Psychology and Social Relations at Harvard and her 20-page term paper. In relation to Case 1, this manuscript showed a comparably high level of organization and content density. The procedures used in the second case were essentially the same as those of the first case, with the exception that response latencies were not collected for the frequency estimation procedure. Table 12.4 presents the data collected from the asterisk task. This subject also tended to be conservative in marking unique words, although she did mark more multiple-occurrence words as single-occurrence words. The number of words selected in each category paralleled the first case, with nouns being marked most frequently and function words being marked least frequently. When the percentage marked correctly is considered, the subject again paralleled the first subject, except that she seemed to be far more sensitive to adverbs, marking 40% of the them. This subject also was more sensitive to single-frequency function words. The words in this cateogy that she correctly marked were *hence*, *Nowhere*, *himself*, *insofar*, *vs.*, and *Up*. Some of

Table 12.4. Case 2: Subject Search for Single-Frequency Words

Part of speech	Number of words marked	Incorrectly selected words	Total number in text	Percentage correctly selected
Noun	160	25	296	45
Verb	90	11	280	28
Adjective	124	13	174	64
Adverbs	31	5	61	40
Function	6	0	40	17

these words are used infrequently in the language as a whole. Two of the words were capitalized, serving as the initial words of sentences. The subject may have been able to judge that these words had a very low probability of being used more than once at the beginnings of sentences without searching for other potential instances in memory.

The frequency estimation data for Case 2 are presented in Table 12.5. This subject showed a very high level of accuracy, with her estimates increasing with the number of actual occurrences. Perhaps the most important distinction between this subject and the preceding one was that her average estimates for function words were very low. In fact, she *underestimated* 9 out of 13 triple-occurrence function words, judging that 5 of those words were *never used* in the manuscript. Although her function word estimates were very different from those of the first subject, the same general conclusion seems to be warranted. Her knowledge of frequency of usage was poor for this word type.

Table 12.6 presents the synonym and common morpheme information for this subject. Again the overestimates generally reflected instances where the same root morpheme was used in different contexts or where synonyms were used. Of the 28 single-frequency words that

Table 12.5. Case 2: Average Estimated Frequency of Occurrence

	Nouns	Verbs	Adjectives	Adverbs	Function	Average
Zero	*	*	*	*	*	1.53
N						(15)
Single	1.66	2.53	1.73	1.86	1.66	1.89
N	(15)	(15)	(15)	(15)	(15)	(75)
Double	3.20	3.73	2.53	3.33	2.66	3.09
N	(15)	(15)	(15)	(15)	(15)	(75)
Triple	3.53	3.26	3.00	3.50	2.08	3.08
N	(15)	(15)	(12)	(10)	(13)	(65)
15-20	*	*	*	*	*	9.38
N						(29)

Note: *N* denotes the number of words presented to the subjects in each category. Asterisks indicate cells for which no data were collected. Because the Zero category and the 15-20 category filler items were not selected on the basis of their part of speech, only average frequency ratings were obtained for these items.

were correctly estimated, 11 had counterparts with the same morphological base. Of these, 4 were adverbs. This subject judged that 4 single-occurrence words never appeared in her manuscript.

Case 3

The third case involved a 14-page research manuscript, submitted for publication by a graduate student in the department of psychology and social relations at Harvard. This manuscript appeared to be comparable to those considered in Cases 1 and 2 in terms of level of organization and content density, but it also adhered to a specific journal format. Frequency estimation data are presented in Table 12.7. The subject did not happen to use any triple-occurrence adverbs in the manuscript.

The same basic pattern of results was found. Estimates increased with the number of actual occurrences. Like the other subjects, she had particular trouble with verbs and function words. Overestimates seemed to be based on the confusions at the conceptual level, as illustrated in Table 12.8.

Case 4

The last case involved a 45-page short story written by an undergraduate at Harvard. This manuscript differed considerably in style from the other three cases, with much less integration of the content across different paragraphs and sections. Frequency estimation data appear in Table 12.9. This subject was extraordinarily accurate in estimating word frequency with the single exception of the function word category. The generally high level of accuracy is particularly noteworthy in light of the fact that the manuscript was two to three times as long as the other manuscripts that have been discussed. The potential conceptual confusions in Table 12.10 provide some insight into the level of accuracy of this subject. Of the 38 correctly estimated single-occurrence words, only 13 had counterparts with the same morphological base. Also, relatively few synonyms were used. Both characteristics seem to be a function of the type of manuscript. The story moved from one scene to the next, without a lot of rehashing of old relationships and implications, as is often the case in term papers and research reports.

Summary

Although the four cases presented show somewhat different profiles, together they present a surprisingly consistent picture. Each of the subjects was familiar with the content of her manuscript to the extent that she could estimate frequency of words to within a very narrow range.

Table 12.6. Case 2: Potential Conceptual Confusions for Single-Frequency Words

Nouns	Subject estimate	Same root	Frequency in text	Synonym	Frequency in text
rationale	2	—		reasons	1
				reasonable	2
limitations	4	limit	2	restricted	1
		limited	3	handicap	3
				problem	12
clouds	2	Clouds	1		
observations	3	unobservable	1		
		observable	1		
character	3	characterization	1	quality	1
		characterized	2		
argument	2	argue	1	discuss	1
				discussed	2
failure	2	fail	1	success	2
		Failure	1	successful	2
				successfully	1

Verbs	Subject estimate	Same root	Frequency in text	Synonym	Frequency in text
giving	2	given	7	—	
		give	8		
		gives	1		
		Given	1		
showed	10	show	2	taught	1
		shows	1	teaching	3
		shown	3	teachers	4
		showing	2		
applied	2	—			
assume	2	assumption	1	presumably	2
		assumed	1		
require	2	requiring	1	necessitate	1
				necessary	6
necessitate	3	necessary	6	causes	3
		necessarily	1		
compensate	3	Competence	1	—	

Verbs					
create	7	creatively	1	makes	2
		created	1	making	3
		creates	2	make	9
		creativity	18	Make	3
		creative	20		
		Creative	3		
		Creativity	1		
represent	3	representative	2	shows	1
				shown	3
				showing	2
				show	2
				showed	1
Adjectives					
clever	6	cleverest	1	intelligence	2
subtle	2	—		inobvious	1

certain	4	certainly	1	particularly	2
				some	14
careful	3	carefully	1	wary	1
Adverbs					
certainly	3	certain	1	particularly	2
possibly	3	possible	11	conceivable	1
		possibility	1		
		possibilities	2		
verbally	2	verbal	7	words	2
		Verbal	1	word	3
previously	5	previous	1	first	6
				before	3
constantly	2	—		always	3
physically	2	physical	1	—	
typically	2	nontypical	1	common	3

Table 12.7. Case 3: Average Estimated Frequency of Occurrence

	Nouns	Verbs	Adjectives	Adverbs	Function	Average
Zero	*	*	*	*	*	0
N						(10)
Single	2.06	4.46	1.60	2.80	5.00	3.18
N	(15)	(15)	(15)	(15)	(15)	(75)
Double	3.46	6.00	3.40	4.60	4.46	4.46
N	(15)	(15)	(8)	(4)	(15)	(57)
Triple	6.00	6.60	6.00	—	7.09	6.48
N	(15)	(15)	(30)	—	(11)	(44)
15-20	*	*	*	*	*	17.29
N						(17)

Note: *N* denotes the number of words presented to the subjects in each category. Asterisks indicate cells for which no data were collected. Because the Zero category and the 15-20 category filler items were not selected on the basis of their part of speech, only average frequency ratings were obtained for these items.

Those cases where frequency was overestimated very often seemed to reflect conceptually based confusions. Knowledge of frequency for function words was consistently poor, although one of the subjects tended to underestimate frequency for those words rather than overestimate it.

Although further research with different subjects and different types of manuscripts is clearly needed in order to establish the generality of the results, it is reasonable to conclude that (a) the knowledge of the conceptual structure of a manuscript can be a boon to a writer who may be attempting to locate information during text editing, and (b) use of this knowledge must be tempered by an understanding of its limitations, namely, that surface details are not readily available.

Efficient Search During Text Editing

Given the assumption of the largely conceptual nature of memory for self-generated text, how might a user of a word processing system become more efficient at locating particular portions of the text? Often the user will obtain a printout of the original manuscript and will mark the printout with editing changes. In order to implement these changes on the electronic copy, the writer can scan the printout for a unique word that is near the location of the desired change. Because a large proportion of words in a manuscript are used only once, the likelihood of finding a unique word on a page is very good. The user can then search for the unique word with the search procedure that is built into the word processing system. For cases where a unique word cannot be found, it would be possible to search for a word pair, capitalized word, or word with neighboring punctuation. A two-step search procedure might also be adopted, where the user would first command the word processor to locate the section containing the critical region. The user

Table 12.8. Case 3: Potential Confusions for Single-Frequency Words

	Subject estimate	Same root	Frequency in text	Synonym	Frequency in text
Nouns					
basis	6	based	1	—	
lessons	2	lesson	2	teaching	2
				teacher	24
				teachers	89
				teach	1
				Teacher	2
				Teachers	1
test	4	—		examines	1
				examine	2
				examined	3
				example	2
reliabilities	3	—		accurate	1
				accuracy	3
issue	2	—		question	5
				questions	7
characteristics	2	—		nature	1
authors	3	—		experimenter	6
discussion	2	discussing	1	—	
		discussed	1		
		Discussion	1		
significance	5	significantly	1	importance	1
		significant	4		
Verbs					
knew	5	knows	1	concluded	1
				Conclusion	1
discussing	2	discussed	1	argued	1
		discussion	1		
		Discussion	1		
compensated	5	compensate	2	—	
		compensation	2		
		compensating	4		
selected	4	—		chosen	3
voiced	3	—		expressed	3
				express	1
				expressing	6
discussed	5	(see above "discussing")			

Table 12.8. (*continued*)

	Subject estimate	Same root	Frequency in text	Synonym	Frequency in text
Verbs					
introduced	7	—		—	
lessened	3	*less*	3	diminish	1
		less	11		
concluded	3	Conclusion	1		
considering	3	Considering	2	think	7
				thought	5
averaging	7	average	2	usual	2
				Mean	1
supported	8	support	3	—	
breaking	2	—		—	
Adjectives					
enthusiastic	3	enthusiasm	3		
plausible	3	—		credit	1
				believed	1
				nonsuspicious	2
negative	2	—		None	1
				no	6
				not	2
close	2	closer	1		
stable	2	—		last	1
sure	3	insure	1	—	
		surer	1		
		unsure	2		
long	2	along	1	—	
		longer	5		
		length	8		
free	2	—		—	
Adverbs					
coolly	4	cool	1		
		coolness	1		
		cooly	1		
experimentally	2	Experimenter	1	test	1
		experimenter	2		
		experimenter	6		

		experimental	8		
		experiments	1		
significantly	3	significance	1	importance	1
		significant	4		
substantially	2	—			
previously	4	Previous	1	before	4
		previous	1	first	1
		prior	1		
exceptionally	5	exception	1	unusually	1
randomly	3	—			

slightly	4	—		somewhat	1
differently	5	differential	2		
		difference	4		
		differ	1		
		differences	1		
generally	2	generality	1	usual	2
hesitantly	2	hesitant	5		
		hesitated	1		
		hesitate	1		
unusually	2	usual	2	exceptionally	5

Table 12.9. Case 4: Average Estimated Frequency of Occurrence

	Nouns	Verbs	Adjectives	Adverbs	Function	Average
Zero	*	*	*	*	*	.60
N						(10)
Single	1.40	1.26	1.50	1.93	4.55	1.92
N	(15)	(15)	(15)	(15)	(9)	(69)
Double	2.30	1.80	2.06	2.33	3.20	2.28
N	(15)	(15)	(15)	(15)	(10)	(70)
Triple	2.50	2.86	2.80	3.28	4.50	3.12
N	(15)	(15)	(15)	(7)	(12)	(64)
15-20	*	*	*	*	*	4.97
N						(29)

Note: *N* denotes the number of words presented to the subjects in each category. Asterisks indicate cells for which no data were collected. Because the Zero category and the 15-20 category filler items were not selected on the basis of their part of speech, only average frequency ratings were obtained for these items.

Table 12.10. Case 4: Potential Confusions for Single-Frequency Words

	Subject estimate	Same root	Frequency in text	Synonym	Frequency in text
<u>Nouns</u>					
costs	4	cost	1	price	5
				prices	1
				valued	1
year	4	years	2		
lie	2	—		true	1
				story	3
				True	1
<u>Verbs</u>					
entrusted	2	—		giving	1
				given	2
				give	3
				gave	1
				Give	1
answer	2	answers	1	respond	1
		answered	1		
glanced	2	glancing	1	looks	1
		glance	1	looked	2
				looking	2
				look	7
				Look	5

Table 12.10. (*continued*)

	Subject estimate	Same root	Frequency in text	Synonym	Frequency in text
claimed	2	claim	1	said	15
				saying	1
				say	8
				argument	1
				arguing	1
Adjectives					
bizarre	2	—		unusually	1
				abnormal	1
				unnaturally	1
				unheard of	1
drab	2	—		bored	2
				poor	4
constant	2	—		always	7
widespread	2	wide	1	lot	3
				Several	1
major	3	—		most	3
				larger	3
				important	8
				Most	1
awful	3	awfully	1	bad	3
				disgusting	1
				disgust	1
Adverbs					
awkwardly	3	awkward	1	skill	1
				foolishly	1
foolishly	2	fool	2	awkwardly	1
relatively	2	relationship	1	fairly	1
				compare	1
cleanly	3	clean	2	sharp	1
		cleanest	1		
anxiously	2	—		worries	1
				worried	2

Table 12.10. (*continued*)

	Subject estimate	Same root	Frequency in text	Synonym	Frequency in text
admittedly	2	admitted	1	(of) course	4
simultaneously	3	—		same	1
				during	1
				times	2
				time	10
				Times	1
suddenly	5	Suddenly	1	abruptly	2
				quickly	3

can then scan the section for words that are unique within that *section* in order to hone in on the exact location. This two-step search method would be most efficient if the author could assign some unique label to each subsection of the original manuscript.

The strategy of identifying and searching for unique words may evolve naturally, but explicit instruction to do so, which takes into account the nature of the user's memory representation, would ensure increased efficiency for users with minimal word processing experience. This search strategy can be modified to conform to individual writing styles and individual differences in sensitivity to unique words.

Acknowledgments

This work was supported by NIH Grant NS-15059 and the Computer Based Laboratory at Harvard University.

Reference Note

1. Ehrlich, S. F. *Propositional networks as the basis of language production.* Manuscript submitted for publication, 1982.

References

Bransford, J. D., & Franks, J. J. The abstraction of linguistic ideas. *Cognitive Psychology*, 1971, *2*, 331-350.

Sachs, J. S. Recognition memory for syntactic and semantic aspects of connected discourse. *Perception & Psychophysics*, 1967, *2*, 437-442.

Chapter 13

Certain Problems Associated with the Design of Input Keyboards for Japanese Writing

Hisao Yamada

Introduction

Traditional Japanese typewriting is basically a hunt-and-peck method using approximately 3,000 base characters. Because of its cumbersome operation and slow speed, typewriting has not been as common in Japan as in the United States or Europe.

Recent developments in the field of electronics are rapidly relaxing various limitations on the mechanical aspects of typewriter design. For example, with regard to printing mechanisms, 24 × 24 wire-dot printers are now commercially available at a reasonable cost, and thermal transfer or ink-jet printers, among others, are expected to be economical and noiseless within a few years. All of these devices are plain paper printers. As for the pattern generation of Chinese characters (*kanzis*[1]), in a few years very large-scale integrated (VLSI) circuits will substantially reduce the cost of font pattern storage. Hence, a Japanese (character) typewriter similar in size to contemporary Western typewriters may soon be manufactured at a *cost* of only about $500, provided that a given manufacturer turns out 100,000 or more units a year. It is estimated by the U.S. federal government that there are two to four million professional typists in the United States today, and nearly two million typewriters are produced every year. If Japanese typewriters and word processors that can be used as easily as English ones are developed, and if Japanese society evolves into one in which typists enjoy the same socioeconomic benefits as their Western counterparts, then it is not unreasonable to expect the number of professional typists in Japan to exceed 1,500,000 and the annual output of typewriters and word processors for Japanese to reach several hundred thousand.

---

[1] A Chinese character is usually called a *kanji*. However, we shall use the government standard (*kunrei*) spelling of Japanese for this and other words, except proper names, throughout this chapter.

To attain this goal, the input method problem must be solved, because at present input, particularly its speed, is about the only difference between typewriters in the West and in Japan. Yet, since the mode of input for Japanese is seemingly so different from that for English, the implications of the advances in electronics for the input of Japanese characters took us almost by surprise. Various input methods have been proposed to meet the demand for a means of machine processing Japanese text; many have been designed and tested, and half a dozen are now commercially available. Since Japan lacks the hordes of professional typists common to the West, practically all of these input devices are designed to be used by untrained clerical personnel and professional people; hence they are not likely to be suitable, as regards speed and the psychological tension and fatigue associated with their prolonged use, for the well-trained typist of the future.

In spite of the increasing use of word processors, which are daily becoming easier to use even by untrained typists, we are convinced that well-trained professional typists in the Western sense will continue to have a place in society, and we have been pursuing the design of the typewriter/word processor that will be optimally productive yet least fatiguing when operated by well-trained typists.

This chapter is a summary of the Japanese problem, the approaches that are generally used, the approaches I advocate, and the philosophy behind the latter. From Japan, the question of input method seems to have been answered in the West, and we have the impression that we cannot look to the West for much help with this problem even though we still benefit from general research activities in the West, as this chapter shows in part. At the same time, problems in Japan are complicated by the more complex writing system involved. Naturally our efforts have been groping. After the fact, it seems that we must try to take advantage of the right cerebral hemisphere lateralization of typing functions in well-trained typists, although the issue is still far from settled. We feel that our investigation has raised more questions than it has solved, and many of the statements made in this chapter are tentative, as we shall note at the appropriate points. We also examine some current practices from our somewhat speculative viewpoint, in order to test the adequacy of our reasoning.

Since our thinking is still that of a minority, even in Japan, partly because the notion of touch typing is not well understood by the public in Japan, we have at times to give certain explanations that may be redundant to Western readers. On the other hand, certain explanations, such as that of the Japanese writing system, are essential for non-Japanese readers. Also, this chapter is not meant to resolve every problem by all-convincing demonstrations, nor even to elaborate on facts already established; rather, it is our modest wish to act as a direction finder, although we do not know for sure at the moment whether it will direct us to the right destination.

Japanese Writing System

By far the most common Japanese writing system is based on the mixed use of kanzis, hiraganas, katakanas, the Roman alphabet, Arabic numerals, and other alphabets and symbols.

Kanzis are Chinese characters, and most of the kanzis in use today were adopted from Chinese, although many new ones have been devised in Japan to meet our domestic needs. We cannot go into detail here about the way kanzis are constructed (Wieger, 1927). Originally they were mostly pictograms and ideograms, as can be seen in Figure 13.1, but these now constitute only 10% or less, and most kanzis are logograms constructed by combining semantic indicators (determinatives) and phonetic indicators, and often with phonetic transfers (Gelb, 1963, pp. 97-107). Furthermore, the shapes have undergone a succession of changes, as shown in Figure 13.2, and they no longer resemble pictures.

	Meaning						
Form	dog	river crossing (river + two feet)	town (crossroads + two feet)	fish	stop (one foot; two feet for "walk")	hand	water
Contemporary	犬	渉	街	魚	止	手	水
Ancient							

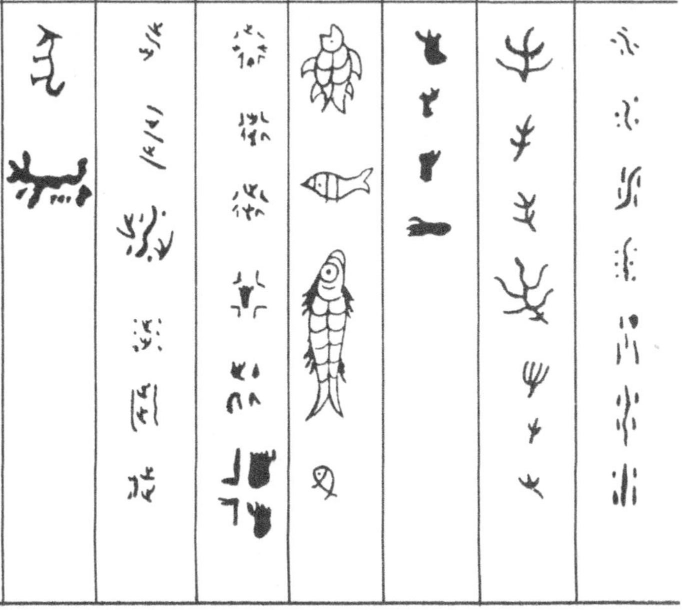

Fig. 13.1. Ancient pictographic form of kanzis.

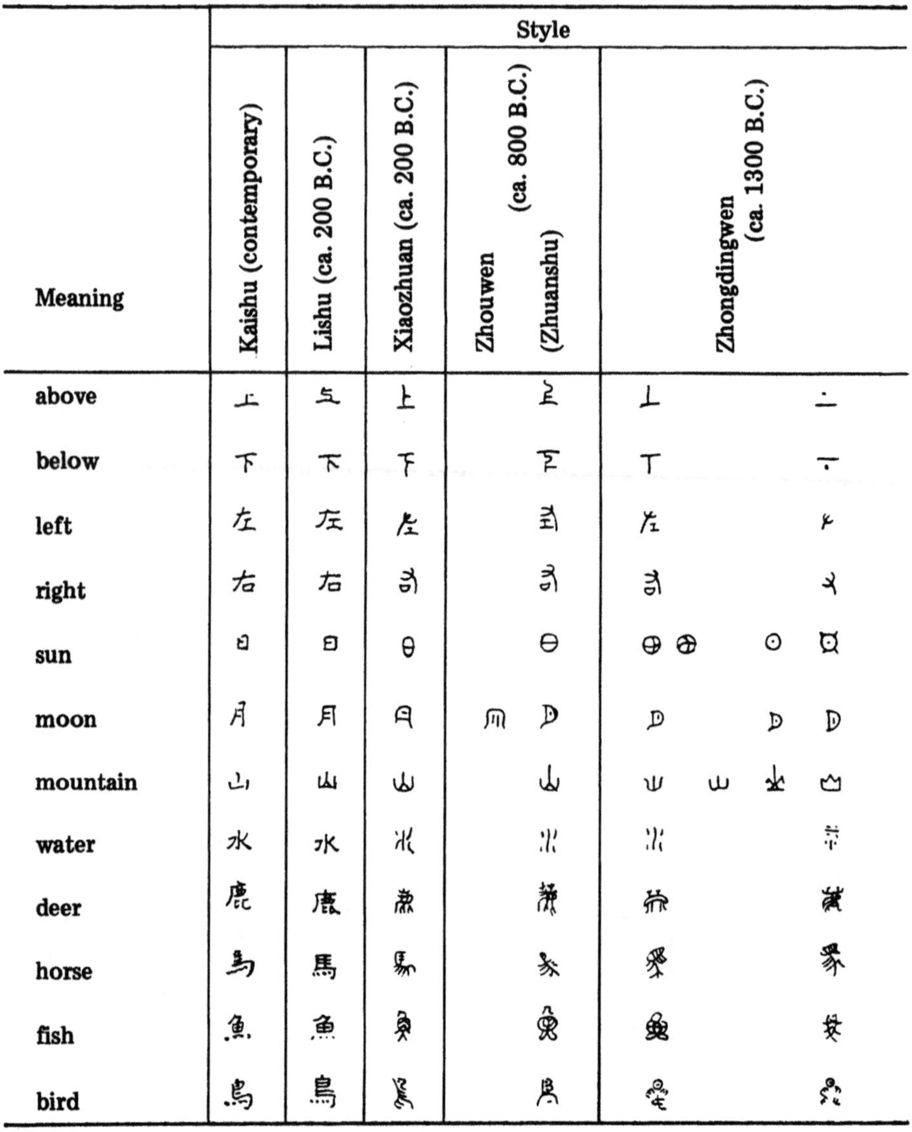

Fig. 13.2. Change of kanzi shapes in time.

The largest kanzi dictionary today lists more than 50,000 distinct kanzis, not including locally used regional characters nor older forms like the ones in Figures 13.1 and 13.2. No one knows how many there are when these are included; the number also depends on the way they are collected or catalogued.

For ordinary use, however, Table 13.1 is a *reasonable* measure of the number of different kanzis needed for various purposes. It should be noted from this table that a typist in the Western sense has to deal with

Table 13.1. Kanzi Sets Used for Various Purposes

Purpose	Number
Individual writing[a]	800
Elementary education	1,000
Daily usage set	2,000
(Zyôyô kanzi	1,945)[b]
Newspapers	2,500
(JIS C-62261 (1978) first level	2,965)
Small printer's set	3,500
Medium printer's set	6,000
(JIS C-6226 (1978) first and second levels	6,349)
Large printer's set	10,000
Desk-top dictionary	10,000
Largest dictionary	50,000

[a] Except literary authors.
[b] Parentheses indicate various Standard Sets.

only about 1,000 or so kanzis for daily office routine, although the contents of this set may shift gradually over the years as the nature of the activities in an office changes. Even within a given office, however, a basic kanzi set varies from individual to individual, and when the number of persons that a typist serves increases, the size of the necessary kanzi set also increases, up to perhaps 1,500 or so for an office of 10 people. The situation is entirely different in a printer's shop where manuscripts on many different topics must be dealt with.

Kana consists of two subsets of syllabaries, hiraganas and katakanas, each of which in turn is made up of about 80 letters, some of which are used only in special cases, such as old writings. Of each kana set about 25 may be decomposed into another kana and one of two diacritical marks, and they are represented as such on kana typewriters.

In Japanese there is no orthography in the Western sense, and a sentence may be "spelled out" entirely in hiraganas or in katakanas (or even in a mixture of the two). However, almost all normal writing is a mixture of kanzis, hiraganas, and katakanas (and others). Kanzis are used for nouns and for the root parts of verbs, adjectives, adverbs, and the like. Hiraganas are used to write inflections and other grammatical parts of sentences, and katakanas are used mainly for the transcription of foreign words. Kanzis and kanas have sufficiently different appearances that we need not use word segmentations (i.e., spaces). Hence, if we simulate kanzi-kana writing by using kanzis in an English sentence, it looks like Figure 13.3, where in part (b) the katakanas are simulated by italics.

Numerous studies have dealt with the cumulative percentage of text coverage in terms of the number of characters ordered by their fre-

(a) English

What's in a name? that which we call a rose,
By any other name would smell as sweet.

Act 2, Scene 2
Romeo and Juliet
by William Shakespear

(b) Kanzi-alphabet English

何'sina名前? thatwhich我呼a*rose*,
byany他名前 would 匂as甘.

第2幕, 第2場
*romeo*and*juliet*
by*william*•*shakespear*

(c) Kanzi-Kana Japanese

名前が何でしょう。 他の名前で呼ばれたって
やっぱりバラは甘く匂いますわ。

ウイリアム・シェイクスピア作
ロメオとジュリエット
第2場 第2幕

Fig. 13.3. English simulation of a kanzi-kana sentence.

quency of appearance; Figure 13.4 is a schematic summary of some such studies. In connection with this graph, we note first that the percentage of kanzis in ordinary texts is about 35% (25-45% range), and the rest is kanas, alphabet, numerals, and some symbols, which total about 120 in number. Figure 13.4 is based only on the 35% of the text that consists of kanzis; the remaining 120 characters are disregarded. Taking this factor into consideration, 1,600 characters suffice for 99% of newspaper texts (National Language Laboratory, 1976), 1,100 characters are sufficient for almost 100% of the technical journal of the Information Processing Society of Japan (Watanabe, Note 1), and 900 characters suffice for technical reports produced by a research group in a company (Sakashita, Abashi, Yamashina, & Kimura, 1981). Therefore, the task of a specific Japanese office typist (in the future) will not be as bad as it sounds from the total number of kanzis in dictionaries.

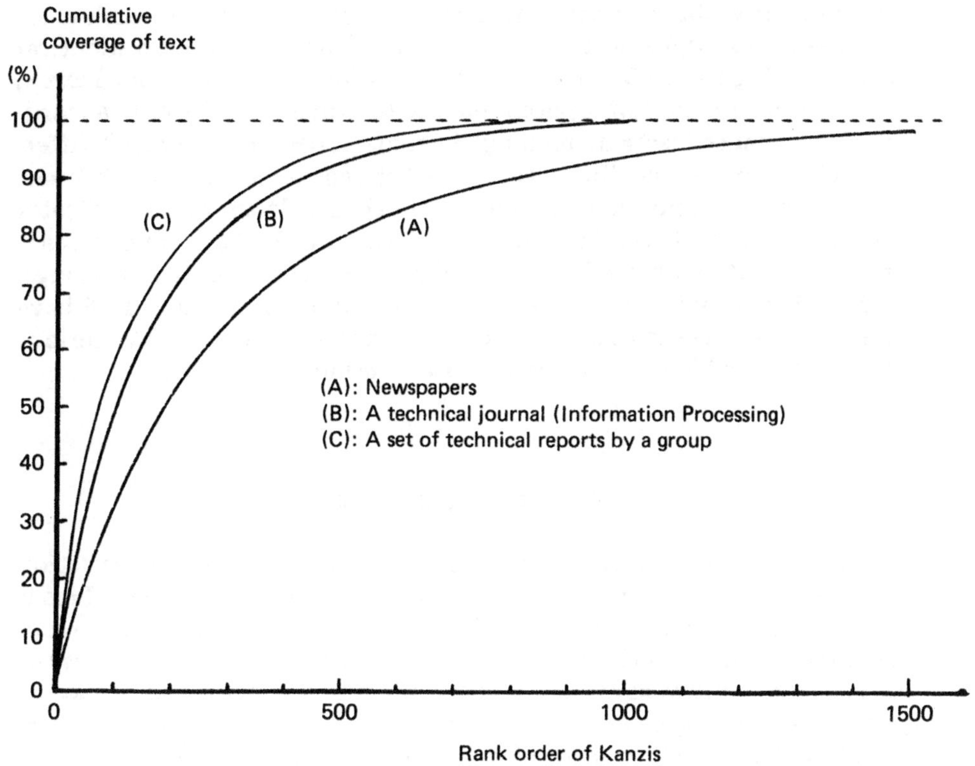

Fig. 13.4. Cumulative percentage coverage of various texts in terms of the number of different kanzis used.

Other basic information concerning kanzis that is essential in order to appreciate the difficulty of Japanese text handling is that (a) a single kanzi may be read in several different ways; and (b) many different kanzis having different meanings may have the same reading (i.e., the homophone problem). Although in China a kanzi almost always has a single reading, the same kanzi may be read in Japan in Wu sound (*Go-on*, of the 6th century), Tang sound (*Kan-on*, of the 8th century), Song sound (*Tô-on*, of the 10th century), and Qing sound (*Ka-on*, of the 17th century) as well as in the Chinese-style Japanese sound (*Niti-on*). Although all except the last originally derived from Chinese sounds and are called *on* sounds, they have undergone substantial phonetic changes in Japan that they cannot be recognized by Chinese speakers. In addition, each kanzi is read as a Japanese word by its meaning (*kun* sound), just as it would be read as an English word in the English simulation in Figure 13.3b. As a consequence, some characters have over 50 different readings, and one has an incredible 260 (Yamada, 1977, Note 2).

Among various readings of kanzis, the most frequent ones are the *on* sounds of Chinese origin. Unfortunately, the phonetic structure of Chinese, especially after it has been phonetically butchered by Japanese and rendered without tonal distinctions, is rather restricted; each character has a monosyllabic sound and many characters have an identical *on* sound. Figure 13.5 shows the distribution of 1,819 basic kanzis, over the sizes of the homophone classes to which they belong, according to their most frequent readings in texts. There are only 268 different readings in all, and the largest class happens to contain 58 different kanzis with the same reading sound. The shaded leftmost bar indicates that out of these 1,819 kanzis, only 57 (i.e., 3.1%) have unique readings. All the others have 1-57 other characters with identical readings. Of the 1,819 kanzis, 50% have 10 or more homophones and 15% have more than 30. The average size of such homophone sets has serious consequences, which will be seen in later sections.

Typewriting in Japan

It is generally accepted that a typist's speed under extended production conditions is half that person's speed under contest conditions. This is still about four times the speed of neat longhand copying done under daily production conditions, as we shall see in the next section. Because of this speed advantage as well as the legibility and esthetic appearance of typed documents, typewriters and typists have been an indispensable part of daily office activities in the United States for almost 100 years now.

Statistics of the U.S. Bureau of the Census (1976) and others (Rutzick & Swerdloff, 1962) show that the combined force of secretaries, stenographers, and typists in the United States increased steadily from .78% to 1.84% of the total population, or from 2.3% to 4.7% of the total labor force, from 1940 to 1970. These figures take into account the people who make their living by the daily use of their keyboard skill as the major part of their work, but do not include keypunchers for computer input. We have not checked more recent figures, but since good typists are in short supply today, it is safe to assume that the current percentages are not significantly lower. The number of typists in France is estimated to be about 800,000, or 1% of the population (Nora & Minc, 1978).

In contrast, although the Japanese Wabun typewriter was invented in 1913 and immediately put into production, it was not widely adopted in offices in Japan, not only because it is not significantly faster than longhand, but also because it is stressful and tiresome to use, as we shall see in a later section. Hence, even today most business documents are prepared in longhand, and when a fair amount of typing is needed, the work is often farmed out to privately owned printing shops. The mimeographic process was perfected by Sinzirô Horii in 1894 in Japan, and began to be used for the production of small quantities of office documents from hand-cut stencils. After Horii invented the mimeographic

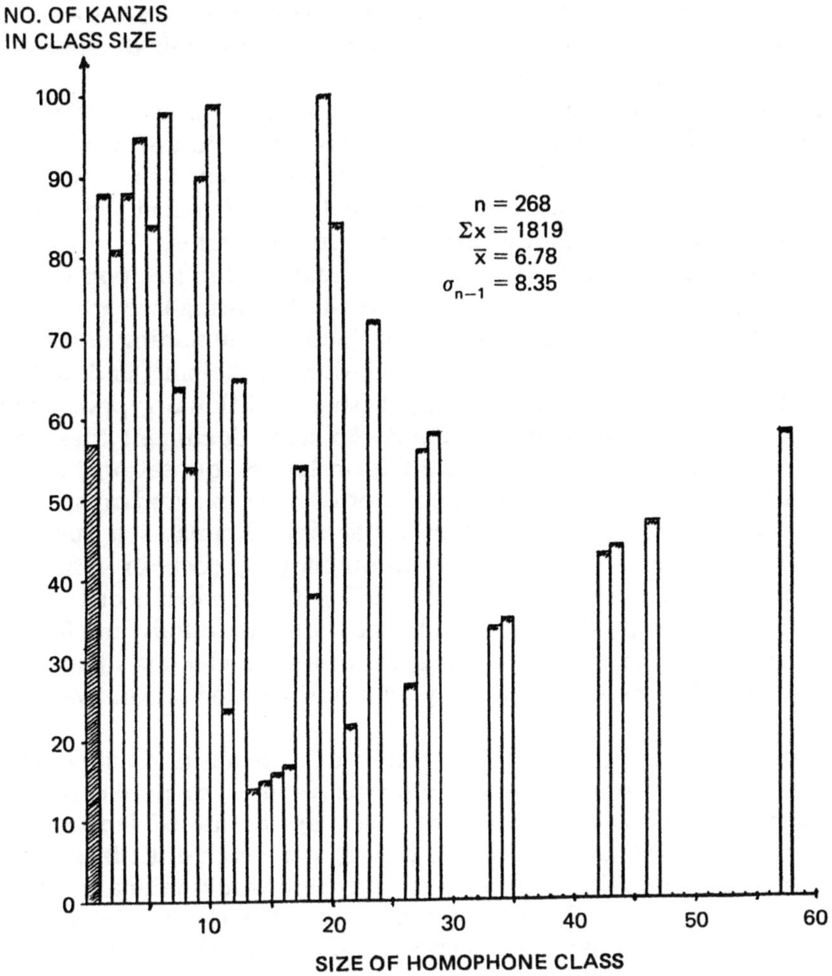

Fig. 13.5. Number of kanzis in homophone classes of various sizes.

rotary press in 1910, outside printers began to handle more and more of the processing of documents for office distribution, although most stencils were still cut by hand. Reliance on such outside printing services meant that minor revisions and corrections were more difficult to make and that the turnaround time for document preparation was relatively long. This system also fostered the undesirable practice of extensive author's revisions on galley proofs, and it is reported by printers that on occasion authors rewrite as much as one third of their galley proofs. Such practices have impeded the modernization of the printing industry in Japan.

During the post-World War II period of economic expansion in Japan, while labor costs were still low, companies began to hire more Wabun typists for the paper work for which a better appearance was desired, and the "document section" in office organization charts began to grow.

Since the oil crisis of 1973, this trend has slowed and has even been reversed as many institutions reduced the size of their document sections and turned again to outside services.

The first Japanese word processor for commercial use was put into service in 1978, no doubt as a result of the reputation of word processors in Western nations. Its success was prompt, since such equipment enhanced the trend toward office automation in Japan at the time, and there are now dozens of word processors on the market.

However, if we look closely at the reasons for the popularity of Japanese word processors, we find that the following two are the most important: (a) they have good editing facilities, including easy correction of typing errors, insertion and deletion, formatting, and table generation—functions that are not easy with a traditional typewriter; and (b) their memory function—the ability to store document files—makes possible the generation of standard form letters, quotations, invoices, contracts, and the like, by making minor changes in standard specimens prepared and stored earlier. This capability eliminates a substantial amount of paper work—and the accompanying cost—in offices. But more important is that the control of office paper work is once again in the office, where it should be, and that the turnaround time for document production is greatly reduced, the effect of which is already being felt by the light printing industry as a business reduction (Morikawa, 1982).

When it comes to the very raw input of substantial documents of a one-shot type, such as research proposals, reports, or publications, the input speed has not been much increased by the use of Japanese word processors. In Western offices, the typing of a rough draft from a handwritten manuscript that took 1 hour to prepare would take a good typist somewhere between 10 and 15 minutes. In contrast, the preparation of a neat copy takes a Japanese secretary 1-2 hours, whether by longhand copying or a Wabun typewriter. Hence, typing and retyping a document three times, depending on the author's revisions, is not a practical procedure, as regards both the time and cost involved and the psychological inhibition we feel about red-inking a prepared copy that took so much effort. Even today in Japan it is customary to submit handwritten manuscripts to publishers, a practice abandoned in the West well over 50 years ago.

As a consequence, typed copy is usually something special in Japan, and we normally have to contend with relatively poorly prepared documents, or even with the lack of proper documents of various kinds, when compared with Western society, even though our society is encumbered by a greater amount of red tape. We have reported elsewhere (Yamada, 1980) the details of the impact the typewriter has had on Western society, so we will not go into them here. One thing we can safely say is that the combination of the typewriter and typist functions in Western society as a transformer of quantity into quality, or as an intelligence amplifier.

Since career typists in the Western sense do not exist in Japan, the effectiveness of professional typists and secretaries is neither understood nor valued; hence, the majority of the word processors commercially available today have an input means that is designed to be used by anyone, including hunt-and-peck varieties on a 3,000-character board, or kana-to-kanzi conversion systems that are still very tedious to use because of the incessant decisions regarding homophones that must be made because the conversion algorithm involves difficult linguistic processing that, even after extensive developmental effort, is yet to be perfected.

One consequence is that we are very slow at phasing out the traditional business practice of keeping on staff too many overqualified college graduates to do mostly routine document preparation by longhand. This practice, inevitable in the past, has contributed to the lower productivity (at least 33% lower according to one estimate (Woronoff, 1981)) of white collar workers in Japan. In document preparation alone, the productivity figure is a mere one third of that in the West. The introduction of word processors would generally improve productivity in this area, just as it has in the West (e.g., Downing, 1980). Occasionally, however, the introduction of a word processor has lowered the productivity of key professional personnel, and the use of word processors is gradually being delegated to those who are more skilled. We suspect that a core of specialists in the use of word processors will emerge sooner or later, and they will ultimately become professional typists.

Some argue that the Japanese office is managed by group decisions, and that the introduction of a management system based on clearly defined and specialized job functions is alien to it (Takahashi, 1982). Although there is some truth in this contention, I also believe that this style of Japanese management is in part an outcome of the lack of competent secretaries able to produce documents quickly and accurately, as in the West, and that it is perhaps an intermediate state in the evolution of Japanese business practices. I shall return to this question later in my concluding remarks.

Various Typing Methods for Japanese Writing

Because of the complexity of the Japanese writing system, a variety of typing methods have been devised in the past, yet none is considered satisfactory for all purposes. Some major methods are summarized in Table 13.2.

Before the advent of electronics, there was no choice but to use a piece of type to print each character, and typing was effected by dis-

Table 13.2. A Classification of Japanese Typing Methods

Characterization				Category and Examples
				Sight (hunt and peck) typing
unilateral	full display	chord key	One-to-one	Pen touch Bar-code Wabun typewriter Alps Push Key
unilateral	full display	chord key / sequential key	Multishift	Kanzi teletypewriter Shaken Sabebe Yokokawa HP Wordix Brother Proword
				Blind (touch) typing
unilateral	coded input	chord key	Stenographic	NEC[a] Hitachi[a] Saeki[b] Wides 80[c]
unilateral	coded input	sequential key / standard keyboard	Uniform-length code	Yamura Shinkô Rainputto Ricoh TX620
unilateral	coded input	sequential key / standard keyboard	Uniform-length code with shifting	Daikei, Kantec Ricoh-Hitachi
unilateral	coded input	sequential key / standard keyboard	Variable-length code	IBM's Apollo[a]
				Pseudo-touch typing
interactive	kana-kanzi conversion	sequential key / standard keyboard		Hitachi's "additional designation"
interactive	kana-kanzi conversion	sequential key / standard keyboard	Contiguous	Various experimental
interactive	kana-kanzi conversion	sequential key / standard keyboard	Word group segmentation	Toshiba JW-10
interactive	kana-kanzi conversion	sequential key / standard keyboard	Kanzi designation	CanoWord 55[d]
interactive	kana-kanzi conversion	sequential key / standard keyboard	Homophone display-select	Oki Lettermate 80 Alps's "cylindrical table"
interactive	kana-kanzi conversion	chord key	Kanzi designation	Fujitsu Oasys 100

[a] Experimental.
[b] Proposal.
[c] Not operable by touch typing.
[d] Also alphabetical.

playing a full character set from which to choose, and by devising some means for the selection of a type piece for each character. This class is the full-display one-to-one keying method. The classic example is the Wabun (i.e., Japanese sentence) typewriter (an example is shown in Figure 13.6), which is based on the original invention of Kyôta Sugimoto in 1913. Using the mushroom-shaped handle seen in the middle, the operator moves the whole platen assembly (it weighs several kilograms)

Fig. 13.6. Wabun typewriter: Hayasi's Horse 55.

over the type matrix, which contains 2,500-3,500 metal characters, until the desired character is selected. Then the handle is pressed down, activating the mechanism that grasps and swings the type against the platen to print the character.

When using a one-to-one device, the typist has to pick one character at a time, according to the manuscript. This procedure requires that the typist look at the manuscript and then the keyboard in turn. In addition, since the error rate due to misselection and/or mistouching of the displayed characters (each is typically 4.5 × 4.5 to 6 × 6 mm square) is high, the typist also has to look at the page being typed rather often. Naturally the typing speed is low—about 25-35 characters a minute under normal production conditions. Operation of these devices also lacks rhythm, not only because of the low speed, but also because the hand motion associated with character selection is a random excursion over the large character display area.

For lack of alternatives, however, the Wabun typewriter has been in use almost exclusively since 1913 in Japanese offices as the sole means of document typing, although because of its slow speed and cumbersome operation, as well as the fatigue associated with its use (all of which contribute to its low cost effectiveness), it is used much less than typewriters in Western offices are.

In order to use such a typewriter as the input device for a computer, some early models printed certain bar-codes along with the characters so that they could be optically read in order to generate signals to be used as input. With the advent of modern electronics, Alps's Push Key input device actually provided about 3,500 push keys, each 6 mm square, for direct inputting. However, the most widely used device of this sort today is the touch-sensitive "pen touch" table, an example of which is shown in Figure 13.7.

At the height of electromechanical technology in the early 1950s, the Asahi Newspaper Company and Yamura Shinkô Company jointly developed the kanzi teletypewriter (kantele) system for the transmission of news items, and other newspaper companies quickly followed suit. Figure 13.8 shows an example of the kantele keyboard. It is essentially a chord keyboard in that there are 150-250 main keys having 12-16 characters engraved on each, with as many shift keys as the number of characters on a main key. The selection of a kanzi is effected by choosing two keys—the main key having the character on it, and the shift key, whose relative location among others corresponds to the relative location of the kanzi among those on the main key—and then depressing both simultaneously. The most frequently used characters are generally grouped at the lower right area of main keys, because the larger size of the main keys enables an experienced typist to select many high-frequency characters by touch without seeing their main keys or shift keys, thus increasing the typing speed to 40-60 characters/minute in production work. Although the multishift keyboard is still basic-

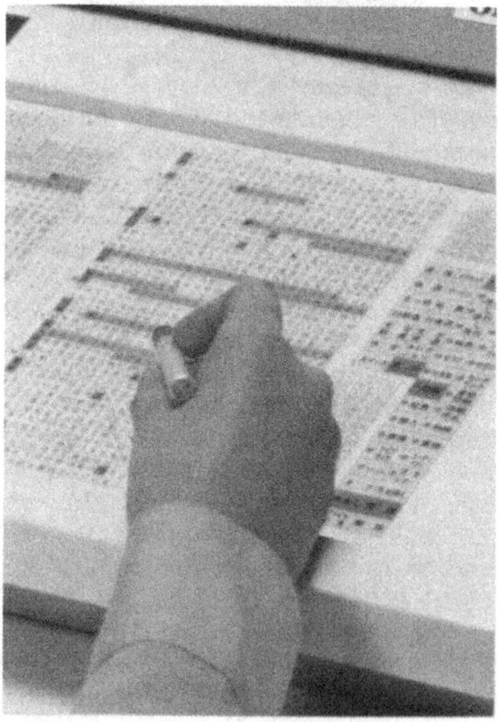

Fig. 13.7. Pen touch keyboard: Oki's Lettermate 80 word processor (about half the area is shown).

ally a sight keyboard, it is also partly a touch keyboard. Some word processors with this keyboard are now beginning to be marketed.

One-to-one and multishift machines are intended for the sight (or hunt-and-peck) typing system, which requires the use of eyesight on the keyboard. Within this limitation, efforts to optimize the physical shape of the keyboard as well as the character arrangement on it have been pursued in order to make its use more effective and less fatiguing. To name some examples, Akiba (1961) studied the typing performance of Wabun typists, using electromyography as well as oculography. Brown (1975) analyzed hand and arm motions on both an early pen touch keyboard and a multishift keyboard. Watanabe and Ohgishi (Note 3, pp. 31-42) measured the performance of typists on pen touch keyboards. In order to reduce the area to be covered by hand motions, Miyamoto, Futamura, Kanai, Ôshima, and Inose (Note 4) implemented some ingenious pen touch keyboard hardware by partitioning the kanzi set into several pages and displaying by command only a subset at a time in a smaller area. Ikeda, Hirohata, and Kiyono (1978) displayed on a cathode-ray tube (CRT) a table of those characters that have been chosen up to the current point of each session. The selection of a character can then be made from this table as well as from the master table. This procedure takes advantage of the fact that the kanzis used for a short, specific input task are usually quite limited in number as well as in category, to enable the user to work with a smaller table of 400-800 characters. However, the locations of kanzis on the display will be different from session to session, which is a disadvantage. Matsui (1982) has been studying the adequacy of photocomposing machines with the one-to-one type of input, mainly in the hands of physically handicapped people.

The next category in Table 13.2 is the touch typing (or blind typing, or blind touch typing) system; in principle, typists using it need not look at the keyboard when typing.

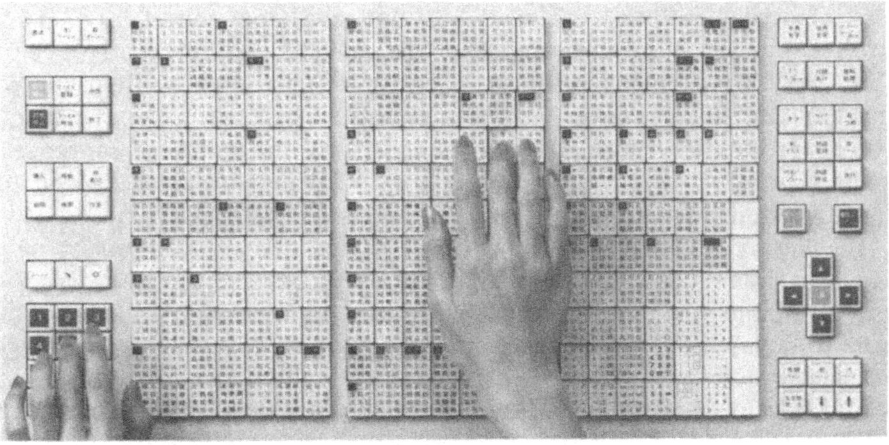

Fig. 13.8. Multishift keyboard: Yokogawa's Wordix word processor.

Among them, the stenographic variety is essentially a Japanese version of English (Miller, 1942; Palantype, 1963) or French (Pesch, 1955) stenotypewriters. In spite of extensive experimentation, it is not yet practical, and this system for Japanese is dormant at present. The reason for the difficulty is twofold: First, as with English, stenographic input is highly coded and requires computer decoding (Galli, 1962). That is not an easy task, not only on account of the variability of codes from person to person (as is the case with English) but also because of homophone problem discussed earlier. Second, the speed of stenotypy is achieved by the complex coding of words, phrases, and sometimes even sentences, not by the inherent speed of chord keying. It is known that Japanese stenotypy (developed by A. Kawakami and called *sokutaipu*) entails the simultaneous depression of about 6.3 keys on average by means of an average of about 4.7 fingers. The limiting average speed of keying is about 3 strokes/sec, and even the average of 2.5 strokes/sec is difficult to maintain.

From what we have learned from sokutaipu operators, we strongly suspect that there may be an essential difference between the one-at-a-time keying on an ordinary typewriter and the chord keying on a stenotypewriter with respect to the queueing in the brain of instructions for hand and finger motions. That is, if we plot the skill acquisition "surface" for typing with respect to two parameters, chord complexity and amount of practice, it should look schematically like Figure 13.9, and there should be a sharp drop in speed from $K = 1$ (one-at-a-time keying) to $K \geqslant 2$ (chord keying), as depicted. At any rate, we have not been able to find experimental data for a surface like the one in this figure, and the sharp drop between $K = 1$ and 2 is only our conjecture at this point.

Parenthetically, the upper limit known today for $K = 1$ is the 216 words per minute (i.e., 18 strokes/sec) sustained for 1 minute by Stella Pajunas (now Mrs. Garnand) on an IBM typewriter in an official test in 1946 (McWhirter & McWhirter, 1977, p. 448). Lenore Fenton (now Mrs. George MacClain) achieved 182 net words per minute (i.e., 15.2 strokes/sec) for 1 minute while she was being filmed in the presence of U.S. Navy Department officials in early 1940s (letter to Belmont W and Thelma Adams, May 15, 1978; see also "Reform in typewriting," 1945). Presumably both of these records were on practiced sentences, while the 11 strokes/sec used in Figure 13.9 is the average speed of contest winners for a 1-hour typing period with first-sight texts.

H. Tatuoka, who was also involved in the early development of a Japanese stenotypewriter, says that the adoption of chord keys was the only available option in those days of mechanical designs, and that if he were to develop a stenotypewriter anew today, he would take advantage of electronics to make sequential keys of hair-trigger sensitivity and would develop a suitable coding scheme for abbreviations as a means of achieving speed.

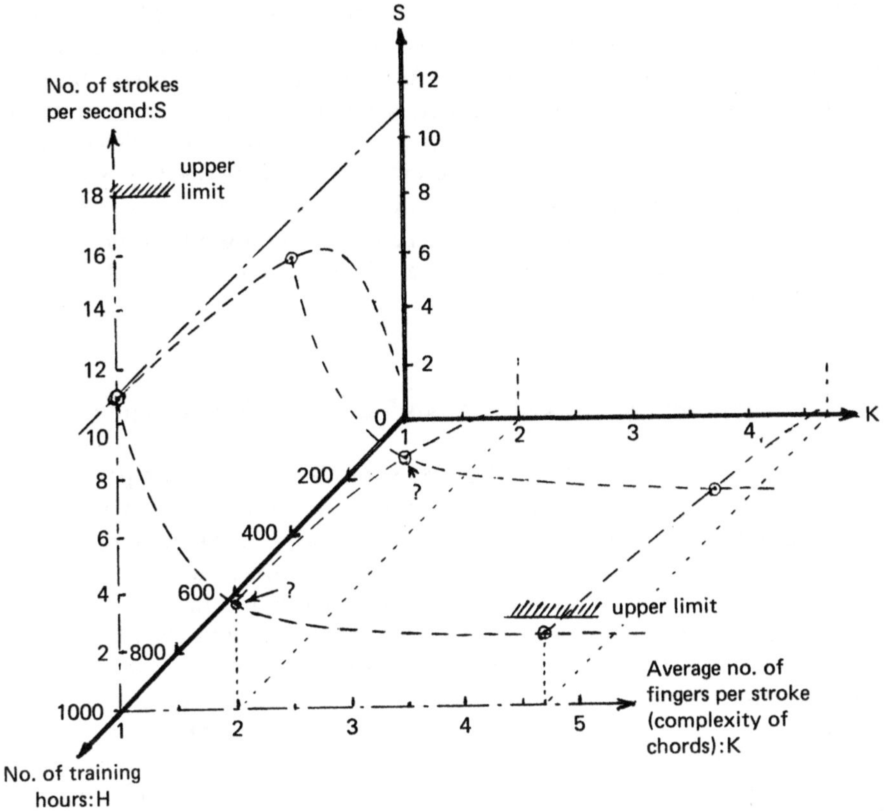

Fig. 13.9. Influence of chord complexity and practice time on typing speed.

Incidentally, we have used the average number of fingers from both hands as a measure of the complexity of chords, but the average number of keys simultaneously depressed may be used instead. For experimental purposes, chords may be designed with a uniform number of keys and/or fingers simultaneously involved.

Despite its speed advantages, stenotyping in its present form may be too difficult even for professional typists to learn. Hence, simpler chord keyboards, for example, with at most two simultaneous key depressions, are often suggested as a means of increasing speed without substantially increasing operational and learning difficulties. The Oasys family of kana-to-kanzi conversion word processors is one such example. Basic data such as those in Figure 13.9 are deemed essential in order to evaluate such proposals intelligently.

All the remaining systems in Table 13.2, including the pseudo-touch-typing systems, feature a keyboard that is physically almost identical to the standard English keyboard (except the Wides 80, Alps's cylindrical table, and Oasys 100, each of which uses its own design); and including these exceptions, all use multistroke codes for characters, although the details of codes vary considerably from one to another. The systems in the table are broken down into coded input systems and kana-to-kanzi conversion systems. The difference between the two is that the latter aspire to use purely phonetic input, whereas the former do not. All coded input systems, except Hitachi's with its "additional designation" code, employ unilateral inputting methods, whereas kana-to-kanzi conversion systems (and the Hitachi system just mentioned) are interactive.

Before we go into the details of these touch-typing and pseudo-touch-typing systems, we review the nature of touch typing and the ways it differs from sight typing.

Ergonomic Aspects of Various Tasks and Touch Typing

It is common knowledge in Western societies today that professional typists invariably type by the touch method. Hence, it may be considered superfluous to explain what touch typing is. However, it is precisely the lack of understanding of the nature of touch typing on the part of the majority of the Japanese that stands in the way of general recognition and acceptance of the value of professional typists in Japanese offices. Surprisingly, this ignorance may be seen even among those few who have been trained as touch typists. It was recently reported by H. Tatuoka, a typing consultant, that a touch typist on a "two-stroke" system for Japanese text confessed to him her sense of inferiority because her hands hardly move when she types (her system's optimized kanzi code minimizes hand and finger motions), whereas the hands and fingers of her counterparts on a kana-to-kanzi conversion system with a JIS (Japanese Industrial Standards) keyboard (which is known to be far from optimal from the standpoint of hand and finger motions) fly impressively all over the keyboard. Another example will be mentioned in a later section ("Evaluation of Codes Based on Hand and Finger Motions"). This ludicrous event becomes more understandable when we recall that it was 14 years after the first typewriter was commercially produced in the United States when Frank E. McGurrin demonstrated, in a much publicized contest with Louis Taub in 1888, that an accomplished sight typist is no match for a well-trained touch typist. Moreover, it took another 27 years before all typing schools in the United States adopted the touch-typing method (Yamada, 1980).

Because of the large size of the character set needed for Japanese text, by far the majority of the input work in Japan is still done by a sight method of one kind or another, as we mentioned in the preceding section. Hence, it appears useful to review here what is meant by touch typing.

The characteristics of touch typing from a written manuscript in English by an accomplished copy typist are as follows:

1. As a rule, the typist looks not at the keyboard but at the manuscript. Checking of typed text is minimal; it may be done at the end of each paragraph, or even less frequently.
2. The sequential motion of the fingers is mostly the result of the subconscious cortical reflex of the cerebrum in response to visual stimuli received from the manuscript.
3. The unit of typing motion is not an individual letter but a sequence of letters, such as a syllable, a word, or even a sequence of words (e.g., *trans-*, *-ment*, *that is*, *out of the*). An accomplished typist is thought to have acquired 2,000-3,000 such typing patterns (i.e., scheduling unit of continual typing, which are, however, interruptible) as units of finger motion.

Apparently there is some disagreement about multiple-word units for English typing. This may be the result of the use of the space bar. Since Japanese is an agglutinate language in which word boundaries are not so clearly definable, and since our coded Japanese typing system does not use a space bar or shift key, as we shall see, our typists are definitely developing pattern typing for a train of words. At any rate, a more precise definition of patterns is needed before this point can be discussed intelligently.

4. As a consequence, it takes about 400 hours of practice in order to develop the skill of this cortical reflex for so many patterns, and about 1,000 hours of experience in all are needed to be a truly smooth and relaxed copy typist.

This last point is based on the author's personal interviews with many good typists in the United States and some in Australia. It is interesting to note that 400 and 1,000 are also about the number of practice hours often said to be required in order for ordinary people to become skilled and excellent, respectively, in various sports that demand quick motor reflexes, such as tennis and fencing.

If we take the various manual tasks we perform and dichotomize them according to the use of eyesight and to the degree of consciousness involved, we can group one set under "sight (or hunt-and-peck) method" and the other under "touch (or blind) method." (The latter is also sometimes called the "blind touch method.") Table 13.3 gives some examples of each, along with the characteristics of each for factors related to typing.

One essential difference between the sight and touch systems of typing is that the former requires a sequence of conscious decisions in order to locate one character after another on the 3,000-character keyboard, whereas the latter is executed by cortical reflexes of the cerebrum. We shall consider this difference in detail later, in the sections on hemispheric lateralization and on the best method of copy typing.

Fatigue is greater when working with the Wabun typewriter than with the English typewriter for at least three reasons: (a) with the Wabun

Table 13.3. Characterization of Typing Methods

	Method	
	Sight (hunt and peck)	Touch (blind)
Examples	Consulting a dictionary	Piano playing
	Wabun typewriter	English typewriter
Characteristics of typing example		
Sight	Much used (looking at texts, locating characters, and constant verifications)	Enough to look at texts while typing
Speed	Low	High
Rhythm	Little	Much
Decision	Conscious	Reflex
Fatigue	Much	Little
Mental stress	Much (mental instability likely to occur)	Little
Occupational hazard	Likely to occur (neck-shoulder-arm syndrome; tenosynovitis)	Less at the initial stage special techniques required
Morale	Low	High

typewriter one arm, weighing several kilograms, has to be moved constantly over the keyboard, which is approximately 40 × 25 cm in area, whereas the English machine requires the fingers and hands to move but a few centimeters; (b) the extensive use of the eyes to locate entries on the 3,000-character board and to look from keyboard to manuscript contributes greatly to fatigue; and (c) the need for constant conscious decisions when choosing characters is extremely taxing. In fact, the last two aspects cause not only physical fatigue but also mental strain, as we shall see in the section "Some Two-Stroke Touch-Typing Systems " It is common knowledge in the Japanese light printing industry that Wabun typists are likely to quit a job without cause and drift to another with comparable working conditions; this behavior is taken to be a sign of mental instability due to the stress inherent in the work. It is also reported that the so-called neck-shoulder-arm syndrome (nonspecific complaints) and tenosynovitis (tendovaginitis) are observed among Wabun typists more often than among other office workers, although exact data are difficult to obtain because of their sensitivity in management-labor relations.

On the other hand, use of the Wabun typewriter requires no special training other than familiarizing oneself with the locations of characters on the keyboard and/or display, whereas 400 hours or more of prior training are usually required to become a professional English typist. This fact is often cited in support of the use of Wabun typewriters rather than other input means for Japanese text. However, the attainment of (even not-so-impressive) speed on the Wabun typewriter is effected by sheer brute force, so to speak, as in a 2-km dash, whereas speed on the English typewriter is attained by diligent practice, as in skating. The training necessary for touch typing is an initial investment that is well justified for a prospective professional typist. Not so much technique is needed to learn to use the Wabun typewriter, whereas (as we shall discuss later) the way a person acquires touch-typing skill would make a difference in the time needed to acquire it and even in the level of proficiency eventually attainable.

Lastly, I have observed that Wabun typists tend to have less professional pride than typists in the United States. This is understandable when we consider that Wabun typists are less trained, can be readily replaced by laymen, and play a less crucial role in the office than their U.S. counterparts. This fact is also witnessed, and perhaps even encouraged, by the way Wabun typewriters are advertised: Manufacturers often claim (although it is far from true) that a person can become a professional typist in one day with their product.

Touch Typing Viewed as a Choice Versus Reaction Time Paradigm

It is often said in Japan that it is easy to type in English because there are only 26 letters in the alphabet, and that the typing of Japanese text is an altogether different matter because it requires a means to deal with at least 2,000 different characters (e.g., Itokawa, 1981). Yet, as we stated in the preceding section, it takes somewhere between 400 and 1,000 hours of experience at the keyboard to become an accomplished English typist. This confirms that there is more to typing than the simple comparison above suggests.

The typing process can be viewed as a psychological experiment of choice versus reaction time paradigms, where the viewing of sentences of the manuscript is the stimulus set and the depression of appropriate keys is the response set. From the experiment of J. Merkel in 1885 it is known that the time required to depress a designated key increases linearly as the base-2 logarithm of the number of alternative stimulus-response combinations is varied from 0 to 3.32 (i.e., the number of combinations from 1 to 10). Posner (1966) summarized later studies and classified the stimulus-response combinations into three categories, according to the compatibilities between the stimulus (S) and the response (R), as follows where RH (right hemisphere) and LH (left hemisphere) refer to the right and the left cerebral hemisphere, and their implications will become clear later in "possible Hemispheric Lateralization of Cerebral Functions in Typing.":

(a) Incompatible S-R, involving a transformation between a symbolic code and a spatial code. Examples are
  i. from an arabic number to pressing the corresponding key (LH to RH); and
  ii. from a spatial array of lights to the spoken digit (RH to LH).

(b) Semicompatible S-R, involving a transformation from a spatial stimulus to the corresponding spatial response in different planes—for example, from light arrays in the vertical plane to key arrays in the horizontal plane (RH to RH′).

(c) Compatible S-R, involving either symbolic stimuli and response codes or spatial stimuli and response codes within the same plane. Examples are
  i. from arabic numerals to spoken digits (LH to LH);
  ii. from lights to directly pointing them (RH to RH); and
  iii. from key vibration to pressing that key (LH to LH, and RH to RH).

Figure 13.10 is a schematic adaptation of Posner's summary of the reaction time in various stimulus-response categories, in terms of the number of possible S-R choices. One example cited by Posner shows that after extensive practice, a subject's performance graph in a semicompatible S-R task coincided with that of the compatible category.

In terms of the foregoing classification, the typing tasks of a novice are clearly in the incompatible S-R combination category. Yet the per-

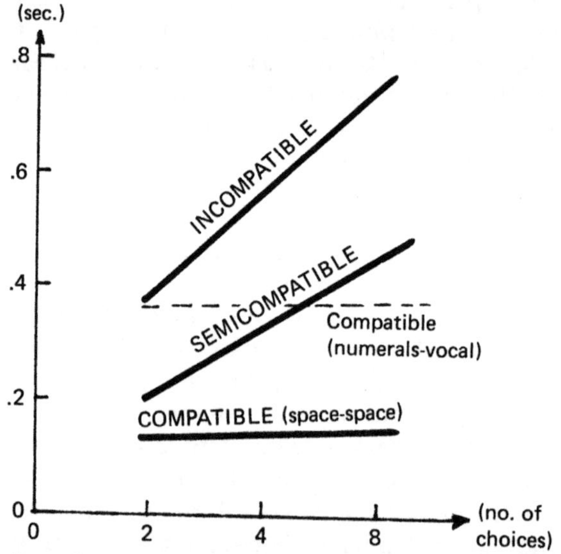

Fig. 13.10. Reaction time for various S-R categories (schematic adaptation from Posner, 1966).

formance of a very experienced typist approaches that of compatible space-space combinations, even when the number of choices exceeds 80 (see, e.g., Figure 6 in Yamada, 1980). This may be accounted for in two ways: (a) after extensive practice, performance on incompatible S-R tasks approaches that on compatible S-R tasks; and (b) the S-R tasks in typing are not treated as separate tasks. Instead, they are grouped into sets of more complex patterns made up of clusters of characters, as mentioned in the preceding section. Figure 13.10 shows that even if the reaction time for keying is brought down to the level of a compatible space-to-space task, it would be still on the order of .15 sec for only eight choices. On the other hand, the key-to-key time of champion typists averages less than .09 sec and there are some who, with more than 80 different keystrokes to choose from, would bring that rate down to less than .06 sec, as we stated earlier (in "Various Typing Methods for Japanese Writing"). This clearly indicates the overlapping of the execution of the sequential motions of fingers (see also Chapter 5 in this volume). These two factors explain why English typists have to spend hundreds of hours practicing before they attain professional status.

Recent years have seen the emergence of educational techniques, such as the Sight and Sound originally developed by the British Navy, intended to expedite and simplify the training of touch typists and claims are made to produce touch typists in 13 hours (or 17 hours for kana typing). While the pedagogic value of these plans in the early stage of training is undeniable, we must recognize that after 13 hours trainees will have mastered little beyond the depressing of the correct keys one at a time without looking at the keyboard, which is far short of forming some sort of symbol-space compatibility and pattern typing reflexes in the cerebral cortex. We will return to this question later in conjunction with cerebral functions.

Some Two-Stroke Touch-Typing Systems

In order to be able truly to touch-type in the way described earlier (in "Ergonomic Aspects of Various Tasks and Touch Typing"), it is necessary to limit the number of keys on the keyboard. For average people, it is very easy to touch-type on 30 keys, manageable on 40 keys, and virtually impossible on more than 50 keys. Therefore, unless otherwise noted, we shall henceforth assume the use of the International Standards Organization (ISO) standard keyboard, which has 48 printing keys.

The principle of touch typing for Japanese text is now described: Take a 48 $\times$ 48 matrix, and fill the 2,304 cells with the 2,304 most frequently used characters, for the moment in any arrangement. Then each character in the matrix is addressable by the row and column coordinates of the matrix, each of which is out of 48 possible choices.

Assign 48 keys to the 48 row coordinates and then 48 column coordinates, one to one. Each matrix entry can now be addressed by successively stroking the corresponding two keys, one after the other. (The physical selection and activation of an actual character is to be performed by hardware.)

Now, (a) if a typist can learn the 2,304 two-stroke codes by heart (actually by fingers), and (b) if after a suitable training period, she (or he) can type those codes in sequence according to the text as fast as her (or his) English counterpart can, then we will have touch typing for Japanese text. (We disregard for the moment characters other than the 2,304 basic ones.)

The most common reaction to this statement is that it is impossible to memorize such a code table, and that even if the code table could be memorized after much effort, it would not be possible to type Japanese text according to such a complex code correspondence. However, it has been shown that the acquisition of such a typing skill is no more difficult nor time consuming than that for proficient English typing. Before elaborating on this statement, we present a brief early history of such touch-typing efforts for Japanese text.

As far as I have been able to ascertain, the first person to practice two-stroke touch typing of Japanese text was Morimasa Natori of the Asahi Newspaper Company in Japan. Asahi, jointly with the Yamura Shinkô Company, developed the first multishift keyboard system (the kanzi teleprinter, or kantele for short) and installed it in 1957 for their news service activities. The kantele used (and still does) punched paper tape as its operational medium for the manuscript. Each character is represented by two columns of six-hole codes on the tape.

Natori was a Morse kana code telegraph operator for Asahi, and he used kana typewriters with a paper tape punch in transcribing messages received in Morse code. Since the specifications for the punched paper tape kantele system are the same as those for the kana typewriter (except that kana codes for the latter consist of a single column of six holes on the tape), Natori realized that each character on the kantele could be sent by two strokes on a kana typewriter, on which he had been touch typing for more than 20 years. Because of its size, a multishift kantele keyboard requires hunting and pecking. In order to eliminate the need to fixate the keyboard, he had a kana typewriter adapted for kantele use, memorized the equivalent two-stroke kana codes for kantele character codes, practiced touch typing by the two-stroke kana codes, attained a production typing speed of about 150 characters (i.e., 300 strokes) per minute, and started to use it for his daily functions in 1961.

His approach was later taken up by the Yamura Shinkô Company and was developed into the SC 4000 teletypewriter and others in 1971 and thereafter. About 180 such units are now in use, by the Bureau of Research and Documentation of the Cabinet, the Meiji Life Insurance

Company, Kumagai Printing Company, and others. A patent was applied for in 1968 (Ogawa, 1981). At the moment the vendor does not appear too eager to market the products, mainly because there are no standards for the two-stroke codes for kanzis. (cf. Ogawa, Hori, & Kokubun, 1972; Hori, 1973; Kurishima, 1976.)

Another pioneer of the two-stroke kanzi typing system is Akira Kawakami (Kawakami & Kawakami, 1972, 1974) of the Rainputto Company, who also developed the Japanese stenotypy system in the early 1940s. He commenced his work on the two-stroke kanzi coding in 1965 in order to help the stenotypists at the Japanese courts of justice, applied for a patent in 1970 (Kawakami, 1975), had the prototype paper tape puncher built in 1969, and made a public announcement in 1970 (Tatuoka, 1970). At present, Rainputto has systems built for themselves, leases the units, and trains operators for the renters, in addition to offering text inputting services. The number of systems produced so far is only about 100, mainly as a result of Rainputto's very conservative management policy and closely guarded technical know-how.

A third early system was that of Akihiko Itô of the Daikei Company, a data input service in Ôsaka. His patent application (Itô, 1974) was made in 1971, the system was put into service in 1974, and he now employs about 250 typists who input kanzi material, constituting about 15% of the total input business, on his systems. Daikei has its systems made to order for its own use only.

Besides these three "classical" systems, there are other newer production and experimental systems, as well as proposals; several of them will be discussed in later sections in conjunction with various technical approaches for two-stroke coding.

One way to evaluate the degree of difficulty in acquiring typing skill in the two-stroke kanzi codes is the learning curve. Figure 13.11 is a schematic presentation of learning curves for three systems in two-stroke touch typing of Japanese and for two in English. The curve for the qwerty (i.e., standard English) keyboard by U.S. high school students in a typing class is taken from Thurstone (1919), who used the data of 51 students out of 83 (i.e., 61.4%) in the class in order to eliminate data from students whose performance was erratic because of irregular attendance or sheer lack of interest. The asymptote for the Thurstone curve is computed to be 54 words per minute (wpm), or the equivalent of 135 kanzis per minute, stroke for stroke. Another reliable source of data, not plotted here, is the composite of studies made by Carmichael, by Kibby, and by Kochka, reported by Dvorak, Merrick, Dealey, and Ford (1936). Their data give about 180 strokes per minute (or the equivalent of 90 kanzis per minute) after 200 hours for the student who is 25% below the top in the class. This value is slightly lower than that of Thurstone.

Dvorak et al. also give data for the class *average* of some U.S. high school students on the rationalized DSK keyboard; these results far sur-

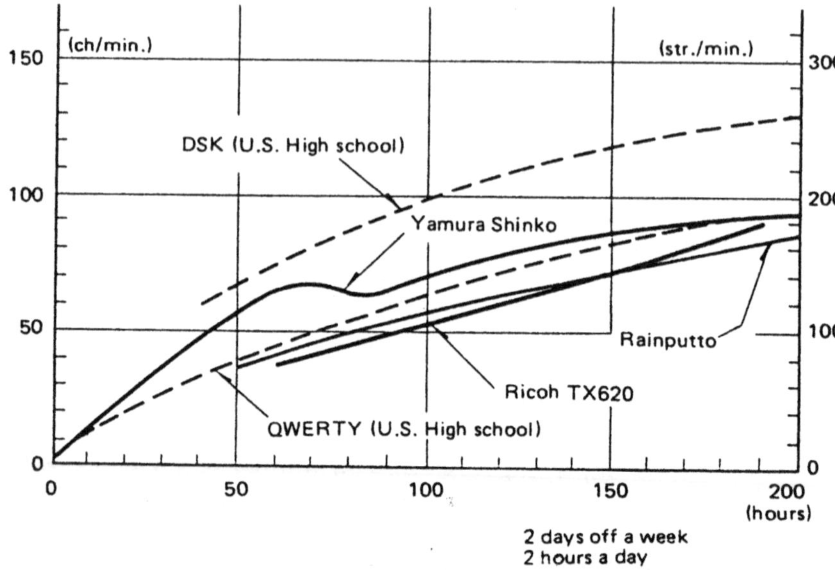

Fig. 13.11. Schematic comparison of learning curves:
3 2-stroke Kanzi Code Typing
2 English Typing (U.S. High School)

pass those on the qwerty, as seen in Figure 13.11. This shows that a good keyboard arrangement is a crucial factor in good typing (see, e.g., Yamada, 1980).

As regards Japanese touch typing, the learning curve on Yamura Shinkô's SC 4000 system (Ogawa et al., 1972) represents the data for two female college graduates. The dip at around 80 hours is due to the rapid increase of new kanzi codes to learn. Since then, Yamura Shinkô has trained more than 20 additional typists for its customers and their learning curve is said to be similar to this one.

The learning curve for Rainputto by Kawakami (Kawakami & Kawakami, 1972) is part of the 400-hour curve for 26 female high school graduates. Since then the company has trained a few hundred typists for their customers, and the dropout rate is said to be 2-3%. Another system for which the learning curve is available is the Ricoh TX620, an experimental system revealed in 1979 (Ricoh Company, 1979), which we shall discuss later (in "Some Examples Optimized for Hand and Finger Motions").

It is interesting to note in Figure 13.11 that the learning curves for all systems, English and Japanese (except for DSK English typing), go through a fairly narrow band, called a *window*, even though kanzi code typing appears to be much more difficult than English typing. At first we thought there was something sacred about the location of the window as an indicator of capacity for human skill acquisition, until we found out about DSK. Nevertheless, it is reassuring to find that the difficulty associated with Japanese touch typing is of more or less in the same magnitude as that of English.

Any remaining skepticism about the ease of typing Japanese text despite the seemingly complex procedure can be eliminated if we recall a study of English typing in abbreviated form. In order to reduce the number of keystrokes and increase typing speed, some experiments have been conducted in which high-frequency words were entered via their abbreviations. For example, Tirrell and Klemmer (Note 5) used 200 abbreviated words and found that after 25 hours of practice, typists had almost regained their previous keying rates, which resulted in a 15% increase in input speed. Schoonard and Boies (1975) used 130 encoded words (which constituted 24% of the total text used) and arrived at similar conclusions. The percentages of coded words here are less than, but close to, that of kanzis in Japanese texts.

Psychophysiological Evaluation of Touch Typing

To quantitatively evaluate the degree of fatigue arising from extended engagement in various types of tasks involving activity that is more mental than muscular, pupil dilation, voice stress, electroencephalography, critical flicker fusion (CFF) frequency (Simonson & Brozék, 1952), and other indicators can be measured, and subjective reports by typists can be elicited.

Figure 13.12 shows the CFF frequency data of a Ricoh research team (Kojima, Note 6) for multishift typing, two-stroke touch typing, and vocal transmission of a manuscript by telephone. Plots A-D show the percentage shift of CFF frequencies at 30, 60, and 90 minutes after the start of tasks, with respect to the CFF frequencies at the outset. Plot B shows the data for six subjects on the multishift (kantele) keyboard. The graph is the average of values for all subjects, and crossbars indicate the range of the values. Plot C shows the data for seven subjects on two-stroke touch typing, and Plot D for six subjects at the telephone, vocally transmitting a manuscript. The last is shown here because the task involved should be similar to the use of a voice-activated typewriter, if such be made practical at some future date. Note that the variability of frequency shift increases from Plot B to Plot D. A task is considered reasonable if the deviation stays within the range of 5% around the zero level, and not an acceptable routine if it exceeds the 10% range. Plot D suggests that the use of a voice-activated typewriter may not be as desirable a device for extended use as it is often depicted by futurologists.

As for the general tendencies of the plots, it is generally held that tasks with a curve resembling Figure 13.12C, with an indication of recovery after a small dip, are the most agreeable kind. Tasks with a continued downshift curve like that in Figure 13.12B are next most

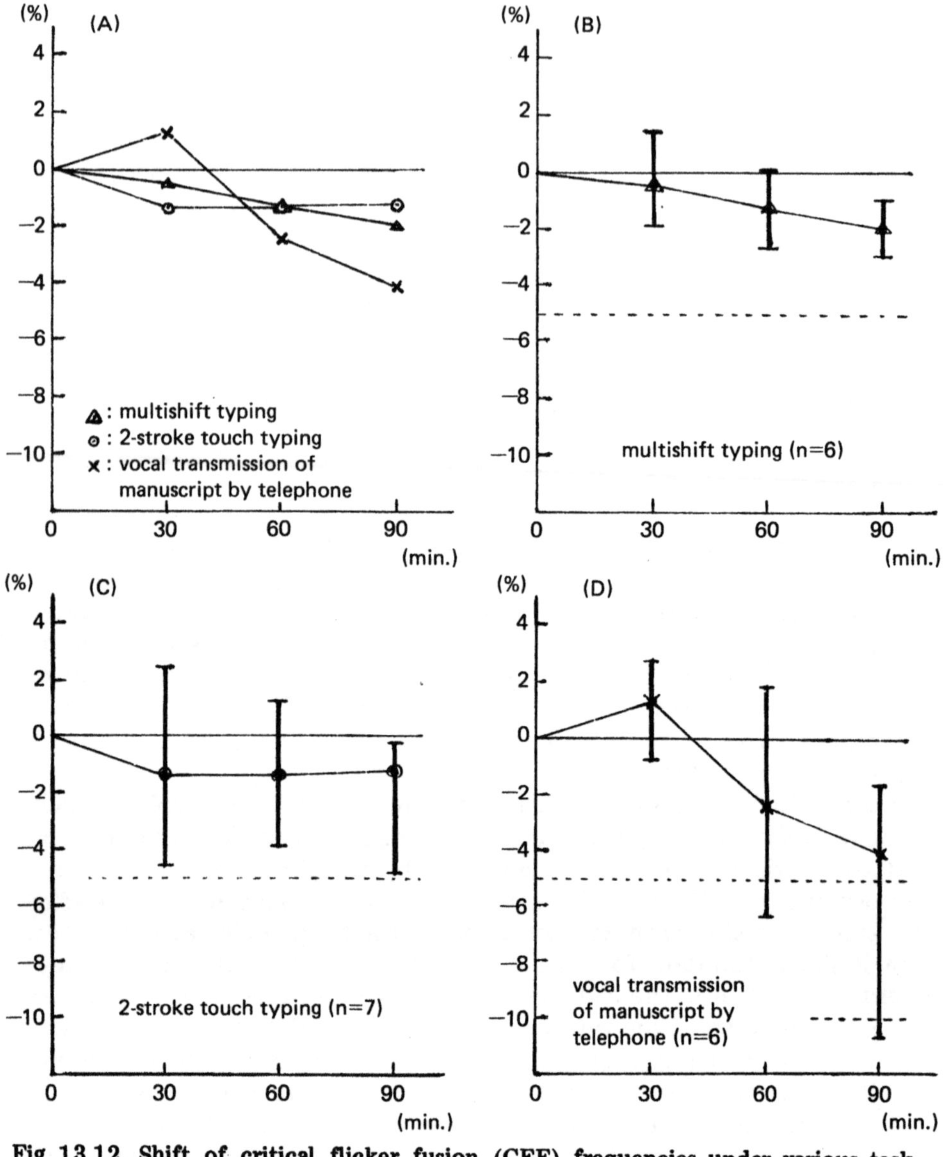

Fig. 13.12. Shift of critical flicker fusion (CFF) frequencies under various task conditions (adapted from Kozima, Note 6).

agreeable, and those with a curve having an initial rise and then a sharp decline, like Plot D, are considered taxing, stressful, and generally not desirable. Plot A is the superposition of the three curves in order to show their relationship more clearly.

From these measurements, it appears that two-stroke touch typing is perhaps a better choice than multishift typing as a method of typing for professional use. The variability in Plot C is larger than that in Plot B.

It should be borne in mind, however, that unlike the accomplished typists in Plot B, the test subjects of Plot C were still in training, which may have contributed to the result, whereas the subjects in Plot D required no special skills. Another possibility is that the training procedures the Plot C subjects were undergoing were suboptimal or badly regulated (see the section "Educational Aspects"), and this may have caused the wider range of shifts. We shall return to the question of training procedures later.

The reporting of various subjective symptoms of typists was also studied by the Ricoh team (Kojima, Note 6). The evaluation is based on a questionnaire developed by the Industrial Fatigue Research Committee of the Japan Society of Industrial Health (Yoshitake, 1970). Operators were asked to indicate their awareness of the symptoms listed in Table 13.4 in yes-no choices after 90-minute sessions of the specified tasks in the morning and again in the afternoon. The average values of the results are shown in Table 13.5.

These results also indicate that two-stroke touch typing is by far the best of the three systems. Since it is known that the measurements of these symptoms and of CFF frequencies generally do not correlate well, (Yoshitake, 1972)—that is, they give measures of fatigue in different dimensions—the well-correlated results of these two tests for touch typing with kanzi codes may be taken to reinforce one another as indicative of the desirability of Japanese touch typing with codes.

Coding of Kanzis Based on Linguistic and Graphic Structures

Although the character codes and the keyboard are inseparably related, there are certain handles with which we may begin our investigation. We can separate characters into kanzis and kanas for coding purposes, and we can choose a keyboard from among the kana keyboard, the qwerty keyboard, the combination (kana-qwerty) keyboard, and some unorthodox keyboards. The first three are more or less standard keyboards in Japan, while some examples of unorthodox ones are the Romazi (i.e., Latin alphabet) keyboards for Japanese, or a keyboard (such as Kawakami's) expressly designed for the present purpose. When we design kanzi codes, various factors should be taken into consideration, including the following:

(a) The linguistic or graphic structures of kanzis, to make the memorization of codes easier; this may be based on (i) the reading sounds of kanzis; (ii) the mnemonics for, or association with, the meaning of kanzis; or (iii) the description of the graphic structures of kanzis.
(b) The optimization of hand and finger motions, which includes such factors as (i) the distribution of usage over keyboard rows, (ii) the loading of hands and fingers, (iii) the extent of alternate use of

Table 13.4. List of Subjective Symptoms

Physical	Mental	Sensory
Heaviness of head	Difficulty thinking	Headache
Body fatigue	Weary to talk	Stiff neck
Leg fatigue	Nervousness	Back pain
Yawning	Inability to concentrate	Breathing difficulty
Muddled/hot head	Lack of enthusiasm	Dry mouth
Drowsiness	Inability to recall	Hoarse voice
Eyestrain	Increase in errors	Dizziness
Clumsiness	Anxiety	Eyelid spasm
Unsteadiness on feet	Loss of good posture	Tremor in limbs
Want to lie down	Loss of persistence	Sickness

hands, and (iv) the degree of awkward sequencing when successive one-hand keying occurs.

As for coding based on the linguistic and graphic structures of kanzis, it is known that, at least for the usage of kanzis in the Japanese language, the reading of a kanzi in general carries denser information than the varieties of constituent strokes of which it is composed (Mori & Hirahara, 1969). Therefore, a natural tendency in a layman, especially a salesman of a potential product, is to prefer a kanzi coding based on their sounds, because it seems "obvious" to the Japanese that the effort involved in learning codes would be minimized if most of the codes were based on transcriptions of the sounds of kanzis. Contrary to this belief, however, is some experimental evidence, and a preliminary explanation based on some experimental results in psychology, as we shall see in "Association Codes and Interference with Pattern Typing."

For the time being, assume that we use a kana typewriter, and that we assign distinct two-kana codes for distinct kanzis from the most frequently used kanzi down, based as much as possible on their sounds, until such assignments are no longer possible because of homophone problems. We have approximately 2,000 kanzis that are supposedly the most frequently used overall. When used, most of them are most often pronounced in their monosyllabic *on* (i.e., of Chinese origin) sounds; hence they should be assigned *on*-sound codes. The trouble is that there are relatively few different *on* sounds, and for each of them there are

Table 13.5. Reported Symptoms (%) Averaged over Items and Subjects

	Symptoms			
Tasks	Physical	Mental	Sensory	All
Multishift	25.5	17.0	19.5	20.7
Two-stroke	1.5	0.0	2.0	1.2
Voice transmission	13.0	12.0	12.5	12.5

many homophonic kanzis—an average of several, but 15% of them have more than 30, as we saw earlier in "Japanese Writing System."

As an example, Table 13.6 shows a two-stroke code assignment for kanzis having the sound "so-o," of which there are 33 out of 1,945 Zyôyô kanzis. In our classical spelling system, depending on the case, the *so* in "so-o" is spelled either *so* or *sa*, and *o* is spelled *o*, *ho*, *wo*, *u*, or *hu*. Not all possible combinations are actually used, but in categories A(1) and A(2) of Table 13.6, all are used as codes, including "␣" (space). Category A(3) is the class of *kun*-sound codes. Category B is in combination with the sounds of a component, either (1) *on* sound or (2) *kun* sound. Category C shows some examples of codes made up of the sounds of component parts, and category D shows codes made up of the sound of a common phrase using kanzis. Finally, category E is an example of the use of foreign words for kanzis as kanzi codes. (The codes shown in Table 13.6 are for purposes of illustration; although

Table 13.6. Two-Stroke Codes for "So-o" Class

A. Sound of Whole Character

(1) *On* Spelling		(2) Classical *On* Spelling		(3) *Kun* Spelling	
1. 走	so-␣	7. 荘	sa-␣	13. 倉	ku-ra
2. 総	so-o	8. 曹	sa-o	14. 霜	si-mo
3. 奏	so-ho	9. 遭	sa-ho	15. 草	ku-sa
4. 僧	so-wo	10. 槽	sa-wo	16. 桑	ku-wa
5. 送	so-u	11. 争	sa-u	17. 窓	ma-do
6. 層	so-hu	12. 葬	sa-hu		

B. With Sound of Component

(2) *On* Sound			(2) *Kun* Sound		
18. 装	so-i	(衣 = i)	23. 巣	so-su	
19. 想	so-si	(心 = sin)	24. 喪	so-mo	
20. 藻	so-so	(草 = soo)	25. 燥	so-hi	(火 = hi)
21. 騒	so-ma	(馬 = ma)	26. 操	so-te	(手 = te)
22. 壮	so-do	(土 = do)	(3) Others		
			27. 創	so-ri	(リ = ri)

C. From Component Structures

28. 双	nu-nu	(又 = nu)
29. 相	ki-me	(木 = ki, 目 = me)

D. From Common Phrases

30. 掃	so-zi	(掃除 = so-zi)
31. 捜	so-sa	(捜査 = soo-sa)
32. 挿	so-nu	(挿入 = soo-nyuu)

E. From Foreign Words

33. 早	a-ri	(early)

based on the principles of some existing coding systems, they are fictitious.) If we examine these assigned codes in terms of the foregoing classifications, category A codes are based purely on reading, but category B employs reading of components as well as mnemonic devices in order to facilitate differentiation of characters having the same sound. Categories D and E are much more associative in that in category D the reading of words using the target kanzis as a part is used, and in E a foreign kanzi "reading" in the sense of Figure 13.3b is used. Category C exemplifies codes that are based on structural decomposition and the reading of resulting components. Category B may be viewed as standing between A and C.

We note that if the procedure given here is carried out for all kanzis, then we are bound to encounter a conflict within the class of kanzis having the same sound or even with kanzis in other classes having different sounds. When that happens we are forced to use codes of remotely related sounds or even codes that are neutral (i.e., unrelated).

At any rate, a coding scheme incorporating such a memory crutch appears desirable, especially for occasional users of the system. Therefore, when we designed our first system, we used such associative codes (Tanaka & Yamada, Note 7). After some experience with our system, however, we found that the seemingly more difficult neutral codes present fewer problems to the constant user of the system, whereas codes with associative devices, especially those based on sound information, often conduce to errors of replacement by characters with similar sounding codes. This finding was corroborated by the typists in an experiment conducted earlier at the IBM Human Factors Center in San Jose, California. Since these results run counter to laymen's intuition, we had to look for an explanation in the framework of a psychological theory of learning, which we will discuss in the next section.

At any rate, the propensity to use kanzi codes with phonetic association is strong because of its seeming naturalness. In spite of its good human engineering in Dvorak's sense, Kawakami's Rainputto system uses highly mnemonic coding. This and other associative codes are discussed further in a later section ("Association Codes and Interference with Pattern Typing").

Another direction to take in devising a kanzi code is to base it on the graphic structure of kanzis. The Chinese writing system has different problems from Japanese in that (1) it requires at least 3,500 and normally 6,000 kanzis, even in the simplified writing adopted in mainland China; (2) the homophone problem for kanzis is as great as in Japanese; (3) Chinese is an isolating language, and words are mostly of one or two simple syllables; hence there are very few distinct morphemic handles that the identification of parts of speech and subsequent syntactic analysis can utilize; and (4) there is vast dialectic phonetic variation, which makes the use of kanzi reading sound less practical as a possible means of coding. For these reasons, the use of phonetics for Chinese input seems to have been deemed less effective, and although sound is used in some systems as supplementary information, the majority of earlier Chinese input work has involved variations of full-display systems, followed by systems based on the graphic structure of kanzis. The latter, on the other hand, is less popular in Japan. In what follows we shall mention only those systems that are designed for Japanese (except for one Chinese example, in the section "Some Examples Optimized for Hand and Finger Motions"). A survey of Chinese systems can be found in, for example, Jan and Yamada (Note 8), Tajima (1981), and Yamada (1978).

Because the size of the character set makes its full display difficult to use, the most popular experimental approach in China uses the combination of several hundred character radicals as codes. Such an approach is also used in Japan as a supplementary system for the inputting of characters beyond the basic set. An NEC Company system uses 336 radicals plus eight displayed synthesis patterns in addition to 1,712 kanzis, so that kanzis other than these 1,712 can be synthesized (Hasegawa, 1975). Giiti Misaka uses a similar synthesis approach in his full-display Mishima Syntizer input system.

Another graphic approach is to use the characteristic features of kanzis at their top and bottom, or at three or four corners, on which to base the kanzi code design. This approach also appears to be popular in China, but there have been only a few serious attempts in Japan along this line. The Wides 80 system mentioned in Table 13.2 is one such product available in Japan. However, it uses 100 keys, and touch typing is not possible on it. This system is based on the "three-corner" codes originally devised by Hu Li-ren and others (Hu et al., 1978), and a kanzi is identified by three sequential strokes on the 100 keys. This code may be typed on 10-key keyboard by using six strokes per character, and a similar machine is available for Chinese. However, 10 keys are too few for the formation of good touch-typing patterns to be learned by "finger memory," although they may be learned by the "mind." This is analogous to the case of the several thousand Chinese telegraph codes, which are nothing but four-place decimal digits sequentially assigned from the top of the character list, that Chinese telegraph operators learn to use in daily telegraph dispatch and reception. For the purpose of handling nonbasic kanzis in Japan, the four-decimal digit JIS C-6626 (1978) codes are often used on 10 keys in Japan.

An experimental kanzi code that is based on the graphic structure of kanzis has been implemented at Hiroshima University on the standard keyboard (Isomichi & Shintani, Note 9), using two to three strokes per kanzi. It is reported that after about a month of training, typists have attained an input speed of 17-18 characters per minute.

One of the difficulties of such graphic coding even for laymen's use appears to be that, as is well known in psychology, people tend to grasp graphic structures in their totality rather than as the sum of components, even in cases where the components are in adjacent positions and not physically in contact. This tendency is even stronger if components are physically touching. Unfortunately, most of the time the components of a kanzi are at least touching, and if we use simpler components such as brush strokes, most of them even overlap. This makes on-the-fly extraction of codes based on those components difficult for the lay user dependent on such code extraction. This is why the experimental Chinese photocomposer Sinotype, devised at the Massachusetts Institute of Technology by S. H. Caldwell (1956) and utilizing basic brush-stroke coding, was able to achieve only the speed of longhand, that is, about 20 kanzis a minute.

Sound-Based Codes May Not Be Optimal

In order to recall some basics of learning theory (Osgood, 1953), take two learning tasks $T_1 : S_1 \rightarrow R_1$ and $T_2 : S_2 \rightarrow R_2$, where S_i is a set of stimuli and R_i is the set of corresponding responses. If after an experience with task T_1 a subject is given task T_2, then the performance of the subject on T_2 is expected to be influenced by T_1 in some manner. Depending on whether or not the experience on T_1 helps the performance on T_2, such an influence is called a *positive transfer* (PT) or a *negative* one (NT). Now the subject is again put back on T_1, and the experience on T_2 has some influence on the subject's performance on T_1 when compared with his initial performance on T_1. Again, depending on whether or not such an influence is favorable, it is called a *retroactive facilitation* (RF) or *inhibition* (RI).

Three well-known paradigms of such experiments, together with experimental laws governing them, follow. (In these paradigms, "$\sim$" denotes similarity and "$\uparrow$" and "$\downarrow$" denote an increase and a decrease, respectively.)

1. $T_1 : S_1 \rightarrow R_1 ; T_2 : S_2 \rightarrow R_1$ (i.e., $R_2 = R_1$)
   (i) $(S_1 \sim S_2)\uparrow \Rightarrow PT\uparrow$ and $RF\uparrow$ (e.g., Hamilton)
2. $T_1 : S_1 \rightarrow R_1 ; T_2 : S_1 \rightarrow R_2$ (i.e., $S_2 = S_1$)
   (ii) $(R_1 \sim R_2)\uparrow \Rightarrow NT\downarrow$ and $RI\downarrow$ (e.g., Osgood)
3. $T_1 : S_1 \rightarrow R_1 ; T_2 : S_2 \rightarrow R_2$ (general case)
   (iii) $(S_1 \sim S_2)\uparrow \Rightarrow NT\uparrow$ and $RI\uparrow$ (e.g., Gibson)
   (iv) Skaags-Robinson phenomenon, to be discussed.

Figure 13.13 is an extension of the schematic surface for transfer and retroaction by Osgood (1949). Axes SS′ and RR′ are for the types of stimuli and responses, respectively, and the markings I, S, N, O, and A along these axes denote "identical," "similar," "neutral," "opposite," and "antagonistic," respectively. The vertical axis indicates the degree of transfer and retroaction, with the upward direction corresponding to positive transfer and retroactive facilitation. Each of four laws (i)-(iv) mentioned above is indicated by a thick curve on the surface. (The surface beyond the RR′ line toward S′ is what we conjecture, and no validation for it is offered here.)

Take the case of two-stroke kanzi code typing. A straightforward reasoning goes as follows: we see kanzis (S_1) and read them (R_1) day in and day out, which constitutes task $T_1 : S_1 \rightarrow R_1$. Now we read kanzis ($S_1$) and type them in their coded forms (R_2). This is task $T_2 : S_1 \rightarrow R_2$. If the codes are different from the original sounds of kanzis, then R_2 is different from R_1. As the codes deviate more and more from the natural sounds we will be traversing curve (ii), by Osgood. From the shape of this curve, we see that the more the codes deviate from the natural sounds along the curve from (a) to (b), (c), and (d), the more negative the transfer effect becomes. A conclusion is that the codes are better if they are closer to the natural sounds of kanzis. However, this is in conflict with what we think our experience with our own codes mentioned in the preceding section tells us—that is, the codes for kanzis that are similar to their natural sounds appear to give a more negative transfer effect than do neutral codes. We must resolve this apparent paradox.

The only possible locus on the transfer surface that would explain the paradoxical experience is the one that traverses a line that is some-

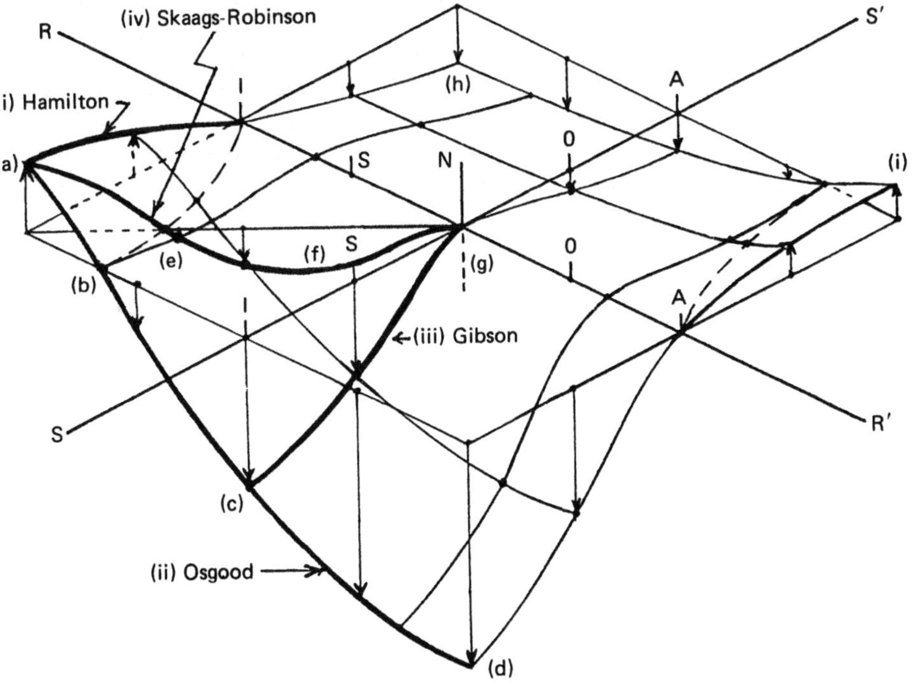

Fig. 13.13. Transfer and retroaction surface.

thing like the one from point (a) to (g) via (e) and (f). If this is the case, then the process may be explained as follows (Yamada, 1977). The set of kanzis having the same sound but different meanings corresponds to point (a) if the same sound is typed for all of them. As the codes gradually change from one kanzi to another, the response performance tends to follow (a) to (c) as long as codes are kept similar in sound. As codes deviate more and more from natural sounds, however, we begin to perceive the kanzis of the set as more and more dissimilar stimuli because now they trigger distinct sound images in our mind. After all, they have different shapes and different meanings to begin with. In other words, the difference among the kanzis is emphasized more than before, and the element of curve (iii) (i.e., Gibson) sets in. As a compound locus, the process traverses curve (iv), which is known as the Skaags-Robinson phenomenon (Robinson, 1927).

It should be noted that when we attempt to use codes that are variations of kanzi sounds, they end up constituting somewhere between 30% and 60% of the codes in various systems so far experimented with by various groups. Also, as we practice typing at point (g) while we continue to use language in a natural manner every day, the neutral nature of point (g) should cause the relative height of point (a) with respect to point (g) to become smaller, since point (g) should rise with practice. As a consequence, the coding scheme based on the *variations* of natural sounds would fall somewhere between (e) and (f) and would be inferior to the *neutral* coding at point (g).

We must emphasize here that the foregoing explanation is only a hypothesis we are proposing based on limited experience, and it should be tested by a well-controlled experiment. For example, it is possible that replacement errors among similar-sounding codes occur because they receive less attention during practice than neutral codes, since their sounds provide a memory crutch; hence they fade more easily over time. How is such a possibility explainable on the surface in Figure 13.13? (Another possible explanation for this phenomenon will be discussed later in the section on cerebral hemisphere lateralization.)

The recall of well-practiced codes is a function of long-term memory. However, as far as short-term memory is concerned, it is known that when alphabet letters are presented visually, recall of similar-sounding letters is poorer than that of dissimilar-sounding ones (Conrad, 1964). We do not know how such a property projects itself onto long-term memory and contributes to the explanation of our observations on kanzi code memory.

Another fact that may or may not have relevance to the phenomenon under discussion is that when a computer programming language is designed to emulate natural language so that it can be used with minimal training, there have been some reports that programming errors are often due to confusion with natural language. However, since such reports are not based on controlled experiments, their claims seem to lack objectivity, although plausible.

Association Codes and Interference With Pattern Typing

We have seen some ways in which kanzi codes are designed based on the reading of kanzis, mnemonics for or associations with their meanings, and descriptions of the graphic structures of kanzis. When we are faced with the task of learning 2,000 or more two-stroke kanzi codes, it is natural to feel that the task is a formidable one. Therefore, it is also quite natural to try to design the codes so that the difficulty of code learning will be minimized.

Kawakami's Rainputto code can be called a masterpiece of the art of code design. Although designed to minimize the amount of hand motion and maximize ease of hand movement (as we shall see later in "Evaluation of Codes Based on Hand and Finger Motions"), his code is still highly mnemonic and associative. Kawakami's code is proprietary; it is available only to system users and has not been made public. According to Tatuoka (1970), however, out of the codes of some 1,850 basic kanzis, approximately 44.5% are based on the reading sound, 16.5% on association with common phrases, 13.2% on component structures, 5.5% on the corresponding English words, and 20.3% on others, including fairly farfetched associations.

In order to be able to use such associative codes for so high a percentage of basic kanzis, while maintaining good characteristics with respect to hand and finger motions, Kawakami uses a custom-tailored letter arrangement on the keyboard, so that both alphabet and katakanas are strategically distributed.

The Kantec system is an offshoot of Rainputto. Unlike the latter, however, it uses the JIS standard kana keyboard (but uses two-stroke association coding, like Rainputto), thereby sacrificing good hand and finger motions. Even so, users claim that good speed is attainable, although no details have been reported. A similar associative method, called KIS, is used by the Kudan Computer Service Company (Sakamoto & Hagiwara, 1978) and others.

In order to make associative codes more uniform and easier to recall, some have advocated or used more than three strokes per character. Thus (a) Kizawa (1969) proposed the coding of kanzis by the combination of four kana strokes representing the *on-kun* sound pair for each kanzi, for example, *sa-n=ya-ma*, *ko-"=i-tu*, and *si-yo=na-sa* for *mountain*, *five*, and *sympathy*, respectively, where "=" marks the boundaries between the *on* and *kun* sounds and "-" marks the boundaries between kanas; neither symbol is part of the codes. The distinction among kanzis, hiraganas, and katakanas is made by appropriate mode shifts.

(b) The KITEN system of the Nippon Information Science Company also uses the kana typewriter and three-stroke combination codes comprising the Japanese reading of the kanzis and the initial letter of their English equivalents, for example, *ka-wa=ri*, *ka-wa=re*, and *ka-wa=su* for *river*, *leather*, and *skin*, respectively. (c) The majority of common nouns in Japanese are written in two kanzis. Taking advantage of this fact, Hotaka (1969) proposed to use as the code of a kanzi the reading of a common noun containing that kanzi, and in order to indicate which of the two kanzis in the common noun was being coded, he sandwiched the part for the coded kanzi between two periods if it was for the front kanzi or he prefixed it by a period if it was for the tail kanzi. For example, *relationship* is *ka-n=ke-i* in Japanese, consisting of the kanzis *kan* and *kei*. In order to code the *kan*, *.ka-n.ke-i* is used, while *ka-n.ke-i* is used to code *kei*.

Since three or more strokes per kanzi take more time to type than two strokes, and since two-stroke codes turn out to be no more difficult to memorize than three or more stroke associations, the ideas just presented have not been used for actual production work, to the best of my knowledge.

Also, it appears as if it saves some strokes to type kanzis in two-stroke codes and kanas in one stroke, using boundary markers in between, instead of using two strokes for the kanas as well. It turns out that the number of "strokes" per character, including non-kanzis, is almost two (i.e., 1.99 in IBM's experimental Apollo system) by the time we count spaces, shifts, and character mode changes (Clauer, Emmons, Evey, Hirsch, & Yamada, Note 10; Hirsch, Note 11). Besides, in such a system the typing error rate (including immediately corrected ones) is extremely high (an incredible .17 per stroke, measured in a controlled study (Hirsch, Note 11) because of the complex finger manipulations required. In addition, it appears more difficult to maintain and use two streams of queues—one for character codes and another for the class designations of character codes—simultaneously in the mind at a high speed. This is not only implied by the foregoing data, but also alluded to in the in-depth interview of the experimental trainees who participated in the IBM study. This phenomenon appears to be an interesting problem to study by a well-designed psychological experiment. Apparently similar phenomena were experienced by Seibel (Note 12) and Koppitz (Note 13) at the IBM Research Center when they experimented with the possibility of using abbreviations for frequent words in English text, using (multiple) shift keys to indicate abbreviations (in addition to capital letters). At any rate, there are no practical coded systems based on this mode-switch separation of character classes that are used by well-trained professional typists.

Because the majority of kanzi code input methods that have been used or proposed so far are associative mnemonic systems, such coding schemes are often called the *association method*, whether uniform-length codes or variable-length codes. The association approach may be a good compromise to offset the initial aversion to taking up the seemingly impossible task of learning two-stroke kanzi code typing. (It may also be good for those who do not intend to become expert typists, nor to type that often.) For an expert's tool, however, it is counterproductive because the associative factor most likely will stand in the way of the acquisition of superior skills.

This phenomenon may be closely analogous to a fact about the acquisition technique for Morse code. When the heightened military activities of the 1930s caused a shortage of Morse code operators, the Japanese armed forces devised a technique for their quick training, called the word association (*gôtyôgo*) method. Taking advantage of the fact that Japanese syllables are clearly separable into short and long ones, the system's originators associated a Japanese word with each of the Morse codes for kanas so that the pattern of short and long syllables of the word is the same as the pattern of dots and dashes of the Morse kana code, as in the following example.

Kana	Morse code	Associated word	Meaning
i	·—	*itô*	(Mr.) Itô
ro	·—·—	*rozyôhokô*	stroll on a street
ha	—···	*hâmonika*	harmonica
ni	—·—·	*nyûhizôka*	increase in expenditure

Initial experience with this word association method showed that signal operators could learn Morse codes quickly, and the training method was adopted by the armed services. After a few years' experience, however, it became clear that (a) although the initial pickup of codes is quick, the speed gain of signal reception thereafter is slower, and (b) that it is easier with this method to lose the continuity of reception in the middle of a sentence. Thus the Navy abandoned the method after 4 years or so, and the Army followed suit a few years later. In the meantime, the reasons for the drawbacks were investigated (Kuroki, 1943).

It is now clear why the word association method failed. First, in order to decode Morse codes, the operator must associate words to letters, then isolate the initial letters of words to find the letters sent. This means that there is an extra level of association tasks involved in the process, which would most likely require extra mental processing time. Second, the pattern matching involved in the word association process brings into consciousness the meanings of those words, which are unrelated to the meaning of the messages sent. As a consequence, the meaning of the received message becomes clear only after a concatenation of the isolated letters recovered from the association words. However, the operator's linguistic facility is mostly focused on recovering the meaning of the association words, and it tends to lose track of the meaning of the message itself. Hence, once the process goes out of phase because of the decoding delay, the operator easily loses that portion of the incoming message because its semantic context is not available to assist in removing uncertainty and filling in the gaps.

In summary, it is safe to state that for the training of professional and highly skilled Morse code operators, semantic association acts in the long run as a hindrance rather than a help. Therefore, for the training of such operators in Japan as well as in the United States, we now employ the method of direct decoding from sound to letters, starting out the reception training with sentences in a basic subset of letters, transmitted at a reasonably fast speed so that trainees are not able to resort to their own associative crutches. The speed is then gradually increased, and when it is sufficiently high, further training is continued with an additional subset of letters, and so on. We call this approach the sound imagery (*onzô*) method, or sound sensory (*onkan*) method. It is known to enable operators not only to attain an ultimately higher saturation speed sooner (even if the initial start-up slope is less steep) but also to take messages in terms of words, phrases, and sentences directly from sound, rather than in terms of letters. This ability allows the operator to lag behind the transmission for a good part of a sentence, which is not possible with the word association method. This method also makes it possible to increase reception speed because it is sufficient to be able to follow the transmission at the average speed, even if instantaneous speed at times exceeds the average. We are using a similar philosophy in the design of our method for training touch typists, as we shall see later (in "Educational Aspects").

We note here, however, that although these two approaches make use of brain functions in different ways, the language region of the left cortex of the cerebrum is still involved in both. In the case of copy typing work, even the regions of the cortex used may be different in part, depending on the types of kanzi coding, as we shall discuss later.

(We learned recently that in the Defence Force of Japan communication is now by voice or by teletypewriter, and that the association method of Morse code training has been brought back so that the code can be used in emergencies when other means are not available.)

Kana-to-Kanzi Conversion and Interactive Typing

We have seen coded kanzi input schemes in various forms. The reason we need such coding schemes in the existence of high incidences of homophone kanzi appearances, as we saw in Figure 13.5. Nevertheless, if all kanzis are coded exactly as they are pronounced, and if all homophone problems are solved by syntactic and/or semantic analyses, then kana-to-kanzi conversion might be the best solution for the input problem, at least from the standpoint of minimal effort on the part of the typist. Therefore, much effort has been expended on such research by a large number of groups for at least the past 15 years (Kurihara & Kurosaki, 1967; Mori & Kawata, 1969; Inanaga, Note 14; Sakai, Sugita, & Fujita, Note 15), and a description of this endeavor alone would require a whole chapter. At any rate, the first commercial word processor with a kana-to-kanzi conversion method, Toshiba JW-10, was placed on the market in 1978, and there are now about a dozen word processors with kana-to-kanzi conversion methods.

Unfortunately, there are too many obstacles for these systems to be ideal input devices. First, the homophone problem is a severe one. In terms of phrases or words instead of isolated kanzis, the problem of homophones is certainly smaller than what we see in Figure 13.5. Still, out of 58,431 headwords in one of the most popular pocket-size to desk-top Japanese dictionaries (Kindaiti, 1972), a whopping 36.4% has homophone words (i.e., with the same sound, but different characters and different meanings; Motizuki, 1980). I do not know the corresponding value for the English language, but it should be at least one (and possibly two) order(s) of magnitude lower. Of course the occurrence of such homophone problems would be lower in running text, but it is still a serious problem.

For example, the following are admittedly some extreme cases. However, that it is not difficult to come up with such examples indicates the annoying nature of the problem. (Note that normally we do not separate words by spaces when we write.)

(a) Kisya no kisya ga kisya de kisya sita.
(The reporter of your company returned to his office by train.)
(b) Niwa niwa niwa no niwatori ari.
(And there are two chickens in the yard.)
(c) Sikararete, huhei iiii ii ko ni natta.
(After being scolded, he became obedient grudgingly.)
(d) Ninki dewa oozi oooo oo o ooooto suru.
(As for popularity, the prince tends to overshadow the king often.)

The second problem we have is that Japanese is an agglutinate language, a member of the Altaic family consisting of the Turkic languages, the Mongol language, and Manchu and Tungus, in which the grammatical components (particles, suffixes, and the like) are affixed to the end of words one after another rather inseparably. In addition, since we use kanzis for nouns and for roots of verbs, adjectives, adverbs, and so on, word segmentation is not much needed nor used in order to facilitate reading.

In fact, the word segmentation rules usually followed by the kana writing advocates require less frequent segmentations than those followed by alphabetic writing advocates. As a consequence, we are not at all experienced in writing separated words when we phonetically spell out a sentence. Without such word separations, however, syntactic and semantic analysis of sentences by a computer is extremely difficult at present.

Third, since we may use kanzis as well as kanas to write various parts of a sentence rather arbitrarily, depending on our taste, in order to have a sentence spelled out to our full satisfaction, we must specify what parts of a sentence be written in kanzis.

In order to overcome such difficulties associated with kana-to-kanzi conversion methods, various approaches are employed by various groups. In order to assist syntactic analysis, the first approach is to make word segmentation as flexible as possible so that any reasonable segmentations will be tolerated. The second approach is to ask that the designation of kanzi (and kana) parts be indicated by the use of appropriate character class indicators (i.e., mode switch inputs).

Each of these two approaches has relative advantages and disadvantages. Word segmentation is less familiar to most of us at the outset because we do not use it in daily writing. However, it can be readily learned as we practice. The agglutinate nature of the language might make it a little harder to learn than in English, but the accommodation for the flexible rules of segmentation would compensate for the perturbation. Hence, the typing of spaces is not different from that of English as far as we can tell. On the other hand, the unit of segmentation tends to be longer than the separation length of kanzi strings and kana strings, and the system has to be more powerful in order to determine the kanzi parts in sentences. Also, some users want more kanzis and fewer kanas than others, and the system does not know exactly where to use kanzis (nor, for that matter, do other people).

The kanzi designation approach is easier to implement as a system because the latter is told exactly where kanzis are to be used. It also provides more information for syntactic and semantic analysis. On the other hand, although easier to use at the outset (especially for copy typing, because kanzi parts in manuscripts are unmistakably seen, whereas word segmentations are not), it soon becomes harder to use for fast typing. This is because it turns out that the explicit designation for kanzi and kana parts apparently requires a separate stream of attention from that of the text stream itself, somewhat analogous to the case of the association method for Morse code learning mentioned in the preceding section. And it becomes even harder when we have to compose a sentence of our own at the keyboard at a much higher speed than in longhand, because in this case the three elements of composition, keyboard manipulation, and kanzi designation have to be handled simultaneously.

Quite often the kanzi part is only a subpart of a word, and we have to break up a word to specify the end of a kanzi stream. Such an operation is a difficult task at high speed, considering that it should be performed in addition to the keeping of semantic contents in flow. However, the general experience accumulated on this psychological matter is still limited, and the difference in difficulty between the two is yet to be quantitatively determined by well-designed experiments. Since there are no expert typists in Japan in the Western sense with a very high production speed, it appears that the kanzi designation mode is preferred to word group segmentation at present by the majority of would-be users. Word processor salespersons (who usually cannot type) also encourage the former, even though the word group segmentation mode will eventually be easier and faster to use as typists acquire experience.

Within the kanzi designation method, some variations are still possible. Some early experimental systems designated each kanzi as such, by using simple boundary markers. As we saw in Figure 13.5, however, the homophone problem makes such a simple scheme impractical. For example, from a few small dictionaries we can find 58 different kanzis for the *kô* sound, 47 for the *syô*, 44 for *si*, 42 for *kan*, 35 for *tô*, 34 for *ki*, and so on; and even with context an automatic narrowing down to the right choices of kanzis in a sentence is often nearly impossible. Even if we use the kanzi word designation or the kanzi stream designation method, the number of possible choices on average is still high. For example, a few dictionaries yield 53 words for *kôsyô*, 46 for *kôkô*, 42 for *kôsi*, 38 each for *sikô* and *syôsi*, 37 for *syôkô*, and so on. Fortunately, unlike isolated kanzis, the frequency of usage declines rather quickly after the first few in each case, and the narrowing down of the possible choices from contextual information is more effective.

Toshiba's JW-10 uses a fair amount of contextual and syntactic analysis in its word group segmentation mode. On the other hand, it bases the kanzi word choices on the usage frequencies of words in its kanzi stream designation mode, and both are reasonably successful. In contrast, Fujitsu's Oasys 100 uses kanzi stream designation with "the last-used kanzi preferred" algorithm, which gives a high accuracy rate after a few pages of text typing in a given subject area.

In either case, the accuracy rate is still in the range of 85-95%, and the remaining instances require manual intervention and correction, which are usually affected by successively displaying possible choices on the CRT screen by tapping a key until the right one shows up. In order to lessen the amount of work in such procedures, a few other approaches have been devised. For example, the IDIOM experimental system developed by the Nippon Telegraph and Telephone Corporation uses up to four different kana-kanzi and kanzi-kana boundary marker keys, sandwiching between them words usually consisting of two kanzis; these boundary marker keys are so designed that they indicate the gross block structures of adjacent kanzis (Sugiyama, Takano, Kimura, Shiratori, Obashi, & Ishii, Note 16). By such a technique, they estimate that the accuracy rate would approach 96-98% of the total text.

Hitachi's experimental interactive system mentioned in Table 13.2 is so designed that it is a one-kanzi-at-a-time kana-to-kanzi conversion with the provision that, in order to resolve homophone problems, the computer asks for additional information in the form of additional reading sounds (either *on* or *kun*), the structure of the kanzi, or others, with the anticipation that experienced typists on it would provide such information before it is asked for. That is, the system starts out as an interactive kana-to-kanzi conversion processor with additional designations, but in the mind of typists it gradually transforms into a unilateral kanzi code processor as experience accumulates (Fukinuki, Fukushima, & Shimasaki, Note 17). In this respect it is an improvement over several early kanzi-by-kanzi homophone display-select systems by Oki (Saito, Nagai, Yamada, & Osako, 1969), the Electrotechnical Laboratory (Watanabe, 1972), Alps (the "cylindrical table"), or others, where all homophonic kanzis are displayed at once, and the typist selects the correct one by an appropriate designation such as keying or pointing. Hitachi's experience generally indicated that after a while typists cease to look at the display before selecting an appropriate key to identify the desired character.

In summary, the current research effort on the interactive typing, of which kana-to-kanzi conversion is the favorite choice, has two main directions. One is toward eliminating the need for kanzi designation or word group segmentation in order to allow contiguous phonetic typing. The other is toward improving the conversion accuracy rate. These two are mutually conflicting requirements and the fulfillment of both would require ever more extensive syntactic and semantic analysis of sentences. It will be some time before such perfection is realized. If and when such a goal is attained, these interactive systems will be a unilateral typing system.

Possible Hemispheric Lateralization of Cerebral Functions in Typing

Starting with the research by Roger W. Sperry and his group on the split brain of animals at the California Institute of Technology in the early 1950s (Myers & Sperry, 1953), the lateralization of functions between the left and right hemispheres of the cerebrum has been extensively studied, and a fair number of facts about it have been accumulated (Bogen, 1969; Bogen & Bogen, 1969; Bogen et al., 1972; Bradshaw & Nettleton, 1981; Gazzaniga & LeDoux, 1978). (A good exposition is seen in Blakeslee, 1980, which includes an extensive list of references, although some of the material may be overly assertive.)

The most distinguished function of the left hemisphere is its linguistic facility. The functions of the right hemisphere are not as distinctly definable as those of the left (Bradshaw & Nettleton, 1981). One of the functions that the right hemisphere is known to perform is the "manipulo-spatial mechanism," by which a spatial context is mapped onto the perceptual and motor activities of the hands (LeDoux, Wilson, & Gazzaniga, 1977). What we are aware of, and able to express verbally, involve mostly the activity of the left hemisphere. The activity of the right hemisphere hardly surfaces to the level of consciousness, hence is not verbally expressible. For this reason right hemisphere activities are sometimes likened to Freud's concept of the id. Some argue that the left-right differences in hemispheres "may be more attributable to localized differences in cerebral organization than to the overall cognitive style of the hemispheres" (LeDoux et al., 1977). In fact, extensive studies in recent years have shown that the left-right dichotomous functions are describable by the use of various pairs, such as verbal-performance, temporal-spatial, analytic-holistic, serial-parallel, focal-diffuse, similarity-difference, and propositional-appositional, depending on the nature of the tasks to be performed (Bradshaw & Nettleton, 1981).

Moreover, many studies show that, even in performing the same task, hemispheric specialization is determined by the manner in which a given stimulus parameter is processed rather than by the physical nature of the stimulus itself. For example, aphasic patients with left-hemisphere damage are known to be impaired to a much greater extent in their timing of speech than in their ability to approximate normal patterns of fundamental frequency, whereas the speech of patients with right-hemisphere damage seems to exhibit prosodic abnormalities that involve fundamental frequency more than the temporal control of speech (Cooper, 1981). And as Bradshaw and Nettleton summarized, many studies have shown that musicians and nonmusicians process the recognition of melodies by different hemispheres. For example, Bever and Chiarello (1974) first observed and Gordon (1975) later confirmed by the analysis of his earlier data (Gordon, 1970) that in effect experienced musicians depend on the left hemisphere for the recognition of melodies, whereas musically naive subjects depend on the right hemisphere. Since then, this phenomenon has been demonstrated by other researchers using diverse techniques, including dichotic listening tests and electroencephalography. Some argue that it is not the difference in musical experience but individual musical aptitude that would make such a difference in hemisphericity.

There are some indications that can be interpreted as showing that an experienced (English-language) copy typist may type more under the control of the right hemisphere than the left, whereas a novice typist may be much more dependent on the left hemisphere. If we are right in such a speculation, an experienced copy typist may be typing through a cortical reflex from the visual information of the manuscript to the execution of appropriate sequences of finger motions. This certainly involves the reflexive mapping from the letter sequence to the spatial information of the corresponding letter keys on the keyboard, and then to the perception of the locations of these keys in space, and then to the desired sequential motions of the fingers in that space, all of which are believed to be the function of the manipulospatial and subconscious right hemisphere. On the other hand, although a novice typist has to rely on the right hemisphere for the spatial sequencing of fingers over the keyboard, the execution is less reflexive, perhaps involving more left-hemisphere activities; and the more logical and conscious the typing by the novice is, the more left-hemisphere participation may be required. Hence, the difference in the degrees of relative involvement of the left and right hemispheres between an expert and a novice may be that the novice has to involve the left hemisphere more, whereas the expert is able to free it more by increasing the dependency on the right-hemisphere cortical reflexes. The first observable fact that is congenial to this conjecture is that an experienced typist is often capable of carrying out a matter of fact conversation while copy typing a text of normal complexity on a familiar subject, whereas it is our observation that a novice appears to have to stop typing in order to participate in such a conversation. This may be somewhat analogous to the fact that we can carry on a substantive conversation while walking along a familiar route, whereas a baby who can barely walk often falls as soon as it is spoken to.

Before we come to our second observation, we need to recall the phenomena of visual lateralization and lateral eye and head turning, both of which arise from the functional lateralization of the cerebral hemispheres. First, the anatomical structure of the eye is such that the nerves from the left half of the retina (upon which the image of the right visual field, RF, impinges) of *both* eyes are connected to the left cerebral hemisphere (LH), and the right half of the retina for the left visual field (LF) to the right cerebral hemisphere (RH). Hence, as Mishkin and Forgays (1952) found, when English words are tachistoscopically exposed to either the RF or LF for a short time, more words are correctly recalled from the RF, which is congenial to the fact that the LH is the language hemisphere.

In order to understand this phenomenon, we need to know something about information transmission in our nervous system. (c.f. Efron, 1963.) In 1912, A. T. Proffenberger studied the reaction time to a stimulus, which depends on the transmission speed of the nervous signal. He sent a stimulus to the right cerebral hemisphere, demanded a motor response from the left hemisphere, and measured the required reaction time, and vice versa. He found that the reaction time was about 6 msec longer for this type of case than it was for an ipsilateral response. He attributed this difference to the travel time of electrical impulses across the corpus callosum.

A study by H. Wallach, E. R. Neuman, and M. R. Rosenzweig in 1954 on the stereophonic localization of binaural clicks showed that the subjective midline localizztion is about 20 μsec to the left, and a similar study by H.-L. Teuber and S. L. Diamond in 1956 gave that to be about 170 μsec. Both the left shift of the midline and the smallness of the amount when compared with what Proffenberger gave are explicable, since each ear is known to have bilateral cortical representation, and yet the auditory cortex contralateral to the stimulated ear gives rise to larger and earlier evoked electroencephalographic (EEG) potentials than that of ipsilateral cortex.

About the same time, F. Bremer in 1958 also showed by an electrophysiological study that the time for electrical excitation to cross from one hemisphere to the opposite hemisphere is in the range of 10 msec.

The study reported by I. J. Hirsch and C. E. Sherrick, Jr. in 1961 on the ability to perceive the correct temporal order (sequence) of two light stimuli to the right and left visual fields (RF and LF) may be interpreted to show that subjective spontaneity occurs when the LF flash is 4 msec sooner than the RF flash (or the RH is stimulated 4 msec before the LH).

In 1962 A. M. Halliday and R. Mingay were interested in the time difference of transmission of electrical excitation to the brain from toes and from the index fingers, and found it to be about 20 msec. (O. Klemm in 1925 carried out a similar experiment between forehead and foot and determined the signal transmission of nerves to be about 25-30 msec.) Their evoked EEG potential data were later interpreted also to have shown left-right asymmetry.

Efron (1963) summarized most of these studies, repeated the experiments of Hirsch and Sherrick and of Halliday and Mingay, showed 2-6 msec longer delays to the RH stimuli, and also conjectured, perhaps for the first time, that the temporal order of sequenced stimuli is determined by the LH without compensation for the transmission delay of RH stimulus information across the corpus callosum, which is about 2-6 msec, depending on the intensity of the stimuli.

Filbey and Gazzaniga (1969) showed that the average "yes-no" verbal reaction time to tell whether a dot is or is not present in a tachistoscopically flashed image is shorter when the dot is in the RF (386 msec) than when the dot is in the LF (419 msec) or is absent (420 msec), by about 35 msec. When subjects' responses are made by pushing a lever with the *right* hand toward the direction of the dot in the visual field, however, the average reaction time was about 420 msec for both the LF and RF, against 380 msec for no dots. This shows that the signal arising from the visual information received by the RH reaches the LH motor cortex, which controls the motion of the right hand, much faster than the transmission of the visual information to the LH language area, which must go through the corpus callosum.

All these facts let us infer that, if written texts are linguistically processed by the LH, then it should be at advantage to send the visual stimuli directly to the LH.

The next well-known phenomenon we note here is that when the LH is more actively used (e.g., by a verbal task), eyes (and even the head) generally tend to turn to the right, even when the active use of the eyes is not involved (Gur & Gur, 1977; Kinsbourne, 1972, 1973). The turn to the oposite direction is generally less conspicuous when the subject is engaged in manipulospatial tasks. This phenomenon is reciprocal in that when the eyes are turned to the right, the LH is more activated, and vice versa (Gross, Franco, & Lewin, 1978; Hines & Martindale, 1974).

Turning now to our second observation, we note that when experienced copy typists are at work, the great majority of them place their manuscripts to the left of their typewriter. This has been so since almost immediately after typewriters became commercially available in the last century. We have asked the reason of a few people who are knowledgeable about typing both in Japan and in the United States, but have not received a really convincing answer so far.

Some possible reasons are suggested: (a) In the days of hunt-and-peck typing, some held the manuscript in their left hand and typed with their right hand, and the habit has been carried down; (b) some early typewriters had the carriage return lever at the right end of the platen (which is also unjustifiable as a reason now except as the result of inertia, since most typewriters have it at the left today, which could block the left view; or have none at all); (c) four rows of keys are arranged with a slight skew toward the left at the top, which tends to cause the slight twist of the upper torso toward the left when both hands are placed over the keyboard in touch-typing position; and finally (d) it is a carryover of the habit of hand copying, which forces dextral (i.e., right-handed) people to place the manuscript to be copied on the left. None of these reasons appears sufficient to influence professional tpists to such a degree for so long a time. It is still possible, however, that all of them combined could have produced the habit.

At any rate, in recent years some schools of typing instructors have appeared who recommend right-side placement of the manuscript. Indeed, if copy typing involves the fully committed activity of the LH (i.e., the language hemisphere), then it should be advantageous to place the manuscript at the right (i.e., in the RF), in order to send the visual image to the LH, as we have just seen. In fact, in the early stage of training, a large number of typists appear to feel more comfortable with text material at the right.

Nevertheless, on the strength of the tradition of left-side manuscript placement, it is our conjecture, based on the neuropsychological facts stated above, that an accomplished copy typist relies less on the left (language) hemisphere than on the right (manipulospatial) hemisphere (Yamada, 1982). When we consider that manuscripts are written in a language, it may seem paradoxical to prefer to handle typing through the nonlanguage right hemisphere. However, it is not the contents of the visual stimuli themselves but the type of the cognitive activities that determines the side to which the eyes and the head should be turned (Kinsbourne, 1973), and we think the paradox is no real paradox.

A relevant experimental result was shown by Levy and Trevarthen (1977) for split-brain patients. When "se" is visually injected into the RHR and "on" to the LH, by flashing the chimeric word "seon" on a tachistoscope, the choice among given *palindromes* is "sees" rather than "noon," indicating the dominance of the RH. On the other hand, a chimeric word such as "baoe" is associated with a given *picture* of a "shoe" rather than a "ball," indicating the dominance of the LH. That is, a word is processed by the RH when only word pattern matching is required, whereas a word is processed by the LH when semantic decoding is required.

If we reflect that when proofreading we hardly follow the semantic contents of the text, such right-hemisphere dependency for typing also appears less unreasonable. As we stated earlier, experienced musicians and musically naive subjects depend on different hemispheres for the same task of recognizing musical melodies. Even if the difference originates in musical aptitude, the fact remains that experienced musicians become experienced because of their natural aptitude, and it is not out of line to expect that similar circumstances may govern the hemisphericity of accomplished professional typists. Franco and Sperry (1977) have shown that when commissurotomy subjects were tested for their ability to match by touch objects that are out of sight with geometric shapes that are fully visible, the left hand (i.e., right hemisphere) not only performed consistently better than the right hand, but relative performance also improved as the structural constraints of the objects diminished from Euclidean to affine to projective to topological space. This could be explained, as Puccetti (1981) does, by assuming that the right hemisphere, through the processing of the visual stimuli, obtains the information on "what kind of shaped object to feel for," which will perhaps be utilized by the motor cortex to move the left hand. The haptic feedback from the right somatosensory cortex then is probably examined to see whether or not the prediction about the object is indeed correct.

As we stated in an earlier section, typewriting from letter sequence is an incompatible stimulus-response paradigm. It may not be unreasonable to suppose that such a paradigm is more akin to topological space tasks than to Euclidean space tasks. At the same time, well-practiced touch typing may be a different task from most of those that are employed in experiments to test brain hemisphericity in that it is likely to be a task of a reflexive nature rather than a sequentially performed task with full consciousness of each step. Only experimental investigation would be able to reveal its hemisphericity.

Nevertheless, we may offer here a possible explanation for the different degrees of compatibility among various choice versus reaction paradigms in Figure 13.10. As we may see, incompatible paradigms are those which require the transfer of information between different cerebral hemispheres, while compatible and semicompatible ones do not, although semicompatible paradigms require more complex processing than compatible ones. We will return to this subject again in the next section.

In light of the foregoing discussion, we can reexamine the transfer and retroaction surface of Figure 13.13. We mentioned an empirical observation that the associative codes for kanzis are sometimes more heavily forgotten or cause more replacement-type errors than do neutral codes. This means that their transfer effects should be expected to show up at somewhere like points (f) and (g), respectively, on the Skaags-Robinson curve in the figure, and an explanation is needed to account for the effective shift of the stimuli as perceived from I to S to N, even though typists are dealing with the same kanzis as visual input stimuli as before. We speculate that this psychologically perceived change in stimuli may occur because the cerebral area for their processing the stimuli shifts at least in part from the left hemisphere to the right, as we discussed in this section. If this were the case, we would expect the neutral codes to be more accommodating for the shift to right-hemisphere processing because they are not as involved with linguistic processing as the association codes. This is consistent with our observation, although we expect that an experimental proof for such a hypothesis will be very difficult to obtain. Strictly speaking, the Skaags-Robinson curve on which points (f) and (g) sit may deviate sideways from the diagonal line from the I-I corner [i.e., point (a)'s projection] to the N-N center [i.e., point (g)].

We note in passing that the transmission time difference of 20 msec of nervous excitation between the times for the toe and index finger to the cerebrum mentioned earlier is about one-fourth of the resolution time of consecutive actions of fingers in a good typist. In the history of typing equipment and devices, use of the feet is suggested time and time again, and still is, without much success. For example, the carriage return of the very first commercial typewriter of E. Remington and Sons in 1874 was effected by a foot pedal, which was changed to a push-down hand lever on the right side of the typewriter only several months after its introduction. Those were the days of hunt-and-peck sight typing using only the index fingers. In these present days of touch typing, the phase difference of one-fourth cycle in hand-foot coordination (together with other factors) would make smooth operation difficult even with good training.

Toward the Best Method of Copy Typing for Professionals

Starting out with hunt-and-peck typing on a conventional one-to-one full-display keyboard, we have examined various typing methods used for Japanese writing, together with their ergonomic aspects, psychophysiological implications, and underlying psychological phenomena such as choice-reaction time, phonetic confusions, interference of associative memory, and even the possibility of cerebral hemispheric lateralization, all of which appear to affect touch typing more than sight typing.

For those who would not make a profession of typing, touch typing may or may not be the best choice because it definitely requires a certain amount of initial training. At the same time, even those who do not intend to become professional typists may get the most out of touch typing, for if they intend to do a reasonable amount of typing regularly, they will not be novices after a while, and the speed and ease of touch typing would definitely make it a preferred method. At any rate, we now turn our attention to the matter of designing the best system for a professional typist.

First, we note that kana-to-kanzi conversion systems at the moment have too low an accuracy rate, even at the best current level of 95%. In the present commercial input service, it is generally agreed that the break-even error rate for profit at the first galley proof point is about .4%, and the 5-15% "error" rate seen in the first choice conversion with contemporary kana-to-kanzi conversion systems is simply intolerable. (A reasonably profitable level is said to be .2%, and .1% is excellent.) With word processors the 95% accuracy rate for first-choice homophones does not mean that the error rate is 5% because the typist would eventually find the right choice by going through the alternatives on the CRT screen. However, the time required to do so makes the actual production rate much lower. It is reported that in an office environment, close to 20% of kanzi words used in typing are not repeated within a reasonable span of typing (i.e., they would constitute the first-time appearance words in a given task). That means that the "last appearance preferred" algorithm may not work well for these words, since 36.4% of dictionary headwords have homophones.

For lack of better commercially available systems, the kana-to-kanzi conversion system is the most popular approach in Japanese word processors at present. (For example, it is claimed that the Fujitsu Company, Ltd. alone has sold, or has on order, 5,500 word processors of the Oasys family of this type, or about 30% of the cumulative word processor business in Japan as of early summer 1982, and there are about a dozen other systems of the type on the market.) However, users for whom the speed performance of their systems is of critical importance, such as stenographic reporters, have to revise their kana-to-kanzi conversion dictionaries heavily on their own, by assigning codes to many frequently used words so that the manual selection of the correct one is not necessary for multiple choices of homophones, for the preferred choices in kana versus kanzi possibilities, and so forth. The amount of such personal encoding added by them individually is known to be from 2,000 to 4,500 items. That is, even though manufacturers tend to pressure such users not to disclose the fact, the most skilled users of present-day kana-to-kanzi conversion systems have indeed changed the nature of the systems to highly coded systems of their own.

At any rate, typing with a contemporary kana-to-kanzi conversion system would not be by a good cortical reflex because the typist always has to be consciously concerned about catching possible wrong selections of homophones by the system; and when a wrong selection is caught, a conscious selection of the right word has to be made, presumably by relying on the left linguistic area of the cerebral cortex. Although the decisions and selections involved in each instance are minor, the constant succession of such conscious decisions is fatiguing. This is why in Table 13.2 we have classified interactive typing as a form of pseudo-touch typing and not as true touch typing.

In the future, the accuracy rate of kana-to-kanzi conversion will certainly improve with the use of better algorithms and more powerful processors. However, the attainment of a 100% accuracy rate is quite unlikely, since not even people would be able to do such a flawless conversion because the vocabulary of written Japanese differs substantially from that of spoken Japanese at present, and we have to rely heavily on visual information of kanzis above and beyond phonetic information in order to understand written text. But when a sufficiently high accuracy rate is achieved, such systems should become efficient, easy-to-use tools for those who want to compose right at the keyboard, and possibly for those who want to do audio typing directly from dictation or from a recording. (For audio typing, see, e.g., Kinsey, 1964.)

On the other hand, for use by professional copy typists, even if the accuracy rate reaches 100%, there still remains some doubt that the kana-to-kanzi conversion method would be the best tool. The conjecture we made in the preceding section may be correct, that a well-trained copy typist normally relies more on the direct cortical reflex of the manipulospatial right cerebral hemisphere in response to visual stimuli from a manuscript, and the linguistic left cerebral hemisphere is largely bypassed. In this case, if a typist could be taught to work this way without excessive training, then two-stroke coded kanzi typing should be a better way of typing because it involves one less step than kana-to-kanzi conversion (the involvement of the manipulospatial hemisphere cannot be eliminated in any way). Also, if we accept the theory of evolution, the use of the "instinctive" and subsconsious right hemisphere should be easier than that of the logical left because the former has been phylogenetically in use for on the order of 100 million years, whereas the latter has been in existence for only a few million years at best.

For example, it is experimentally known (Tucker et al., 1977) that, when people are under stress condition, an increased frequency of eye movements toward the left direction take place, suggesting that greater right than left cerebral hemisphere activation is involved. This fact is consistent with the conjecture that the right hemisphere is more robust and can be relied upon without high strung attention.

This, of course, is our second conjecture after the first one about right-hemisphere dependency in expert copy typing. Both have to be experimentally tested. As for the first, we are in the process of preparing for an experiment to test it by measurement of the electroencephalograms (EEGs) of our trainees on Japanese touch typing (see "Educational Aspects"). It has been claimed that EEG asymmetry is detected to reflect the lateral specialization of cerebral hemispheres in verbal tasks and in spatial tasks (e.g., Doyle, Ornstein, & Galin, 1974; Galin & Ornstein, 1972; Galin & Ellis, 1975; Galin, Johnstone, & Herron, 1978). We have been advised that such an experimental verification is a very difficult task and that there is even some doubt about the validity of the interpretation of EEG variations as demonstrating such specialization, but it is the only method we have access to at the moment among the use of others such as magnetoencephalography (e.g., Cohen, 1968), regional cortical blood flow (e.g., Lassen, Ingbar, & Skinhøj, 1978), or positron-emission tomography (e.g., Ter-Pogossian, Raichle, & Sobel, 1980). Since English is a foreign language to us, and since Japanese typists of English are not on a par with their U.S. counterparts in their proficiency, it is not our plan at the moment to test the conjecture on English typing in Japan. However, we are very much interested in eventually finding out whether there is an intrinsic difference in the way the cerebral hemispheres are used for the touch typing of English, which is a straightforward one-to-one mapping from stimulus letters to response keying, and for that of coded kanzis, which involves mapping from characters to code keying.

At any rate, if our conjecture of hemisphere lateralization in expert copy typing is correct, then it is possible that the kana-to-kanzi conversion is not an ideal tool for professional copy typing, even with a 100% conversion accuracy rate. Manuscripts are written with kanzis, and the typist has to convert them into phonetic form first, which must involve the linguistic left hemisphere because the correct reading for each kanzi must be selected from multiple choice. Only then does the execution of phonetic keying become possible. The processor would then convert the input back into the original kanzi, which is a roundabout way of inputting, even from a purely processing point of view.

We note here in passing the following two facts about contemporary kana-to-kanzi conversion systems. One is that more homophone replacement errors are expected from them, and these errors are more difficult to catch than replacement errors arising from the mistouching of keys, because the reading of wrong words makes sense phonetically. We have noticed an increase in such homophone errors in documents prepared by means of kana-to-kanzi conversion systems. The second is that reliance on the CRT display is greater with kana-to-kanzi conversion systems because operators always have to be on the lookout for homophone resolutions. As a consequence, eyestrain and visual fatigue are more intense, which is already a problem in the West with word processors with CRT displays, even without such homophone problems (Hara, 1982; NIOSH, Note 18).

For these reasons, we have turned to the study of a coded kanzi input system as a device for professional copy typists in the Western sense. At first we valued the mnemonic aspects of kanzi codes such as the sound of kanzi reading or the graphic structure of kanzis in order to assist typists in remembering codes, as we discussed earlier (in "Coding of Kanzis Based on Linguistic and Graphic Structures"). However, the experience of others, such as Kawakami's with Rainputto, Yamura Shinkô's with their SC series systems, and Itô's with his Daikei systems (all discussed in "Some Two-stroke Touch-Typing Systems"), convinced us that code learning itself is not as difficult as our first impression suggested. Besides, we gradually became aware that such crutches tend to interfere with better performance in the long run, as we discussed earlier.

One point we may raise now is that if typists are more dependent on the cortical reflex of the manipulospatial right cerebral hemisphere and less on the linguistic left hemisphere, then they will type blindly from the manuscript, without correcting minor errors it may contain, or even making their own errors because of the ambiguous handwriting of the author. Indeed this is quite common, and in the past fault has been found with such "reflex" typing, as exemplified by the complaint "They type anything." Marton and Sandqvist (1972) have shown that typists can positively utilize their left hemisphere during typing and learn the contents of what they are typing without decreasing typing speed or increasing the error rate.

Such alert typing would have been desirable in the past when an error often necessitated retyping the entire page on which the error occurred, or even the subsequent pages. However, with today's word processors, corrections and alterations of typed text can be made very easily afterward. If our conjecture is right, then alert typing with simultaneous semantic understanding demands divided attention to typing as well as to linguistic processing using both cerebral hemispheres. This would be quite exacting and, consequently, fatiguing. Therefore, it seems advisable to do these functions in two separate steps, reflex typing first and then proofreading and editing, by the same typist, possibly with much less mental tension. After all, it is our common experience that, when we are proofreading our own manuscript after typing, we often overlook missed phrases or sentences while reading for spelling, and fail to catch misspellings while reading for content.

For such reasons, we began to pay much less attention to the phonetic, semantic, or logical regularities in kanzi codes, and more to the best approach to encourage fast reflex typing. In the process, we became convinced that the ultimate typing speed by well-trained copy typists is determined by ease of finger and hand motions in typing, not by mental "reasoning," especially after we studied the history of touch typing in Western society (Yamada, 1980).

In the following sections, we shall discuss our approaches to the design of ergonomically optimal kanzi input systems, first by way of examining some past attempts by others, then by discussing our own.

Code Array Representation for Two-Stroke Codes

Yamura Shinkô's two-stroke character codes are designed (Ogawa, 1981) from the full display of a kanzi set such as the one on kantele keyboards, one of which was shown in Figure 13.8. Assume that all characters on all main keys constitute a 32 × 72 matrix, containing 2,304 elements, and divide them into four quadrants of equal size, each quadrant containing 576 characters. Now, each is further divided into 4 × 6 = 24 blocks of equal size, each block containing 4 × 6 = 24 characters. Figure 13.14a shows such a division of the character table into quadrants and blocks. Quadrant A is named left-left (L-L), and quadrants B, C, and D are, respectively, right-right (R-R), left-right (L-R), and right-left (R-L).

Figure 13.14b (Ogawa, Note 19) shows a sample array of characters in quadrant L-R. This table serves as the code table for Yamura Shinkô's two-stroke character codes for what are thought to be the most frequently used 576 characters (excepting katakanas, which are accommodated by shifting from hiraganas). In order to read a code from this table, we first note that the ISO standard keyboard has 4 × 6 printing keys for each hand. The 4 × 6 blocks in Figure 13.14b are viewed as corresponding to those keys for the left hand, and the 4 × 6 characters in each block are viewed as corresponding to the keys for the right hand. (This is the meaning of the L-R in the quadrant name.) The four blocks surrounded by the double-line square and the four characters in each of these blocks surrounded by a rectangle correspond to the home keys for the left and right hand, respectively. For example, in order to enter the Arabic numeral 8 on the keyboard, the operator first depresses the left index finger (because the corresponding block contains 8), then depresses the bottom row key, which is right below the right index finger (because that key corresponds to where 8 is situated within that block). Similarly, in order to select the quotation mark, the typist first

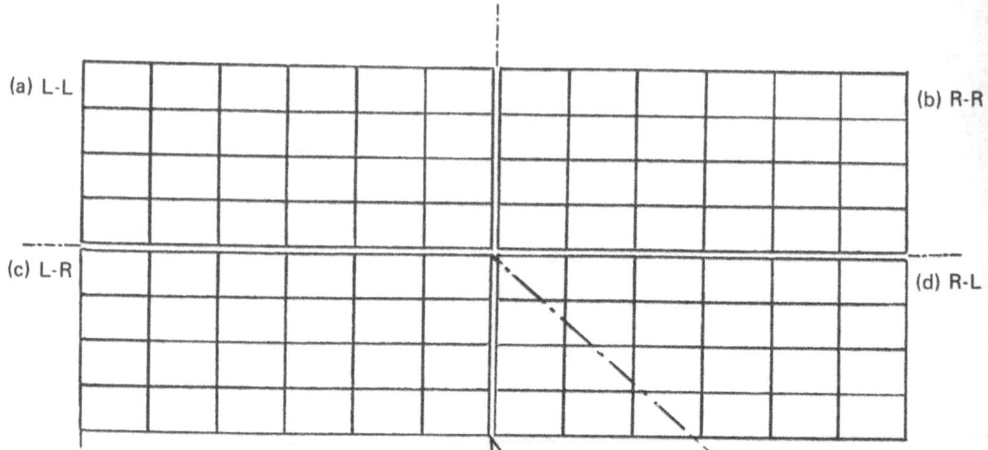

(a) Division of Character Table

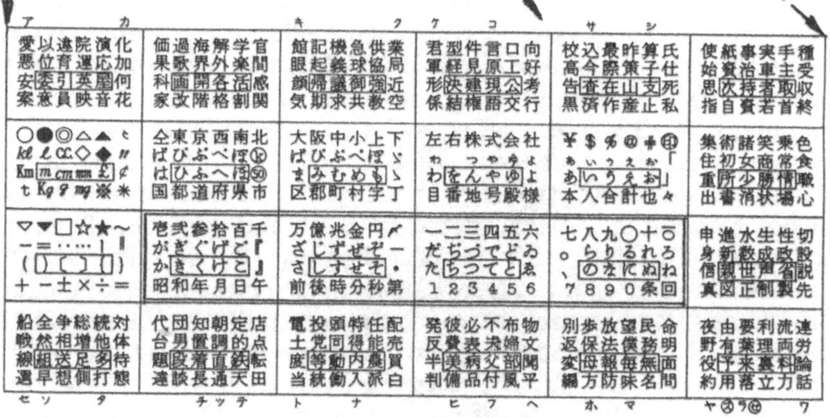

(b) Code Array for L-R Hand Sequences

Fig. 13.14. Code array for two-stroke codes.

depresses the upper row key, which is right above the left index finger, then the top row key, which is directly above the right index finger.

Codes generated in such a fashion are called *array correspondence codes* by Yamura Shinkô; however, we shall call them *array codes*. Originally this form of code presentation was devised to provide a system to be used by retrained Wabun typists, who are already familiar with the character array of kantele keyboards, because the translation from the array to two-stroke codes is immediate. On most kantele keyboards, the most frequently used characters are collected in one section of the keyboard. As a consequence, if we put that section into the L-R (or, symmetrically, R-L) quadrant, then alternate hand motion, which is not only faster (Fox & Stansfield, 1964) but also known to be desirable for good typing, will be facilitated. For example, Figure 13.15a shows the degree of alternation of hand usage when two-stroke codes are finely tuned for the purpose (Clauer et al., Note 10), where hyphens and crossed O's represent use of the left- and the right-hand fingers, respectively, when some editorials from Japanese newspapers and the like are typed. When tested with texts of about 165,600 characters (or 331,200 strokes), the expected value E of the left-right or right-left run length from an arbitrary point in the text was about 6.2 intervals, which is very good when compared with that of 1.03 for English typing on the qwerty keyboard (Hiraga, Ono, & Yamada, 1980b). The latter value is not much better than the theoretical E of 1.00 for random sequences, a computer simulation of which is seen in Figure 13.15b.

In the 720-character sample of typing sequence of Figure 13.15a, 658 characters (91.4%), represented by "⊗ –" (right-left), are from the most frequently used 576 characters; 55 characters (7.6%), represented

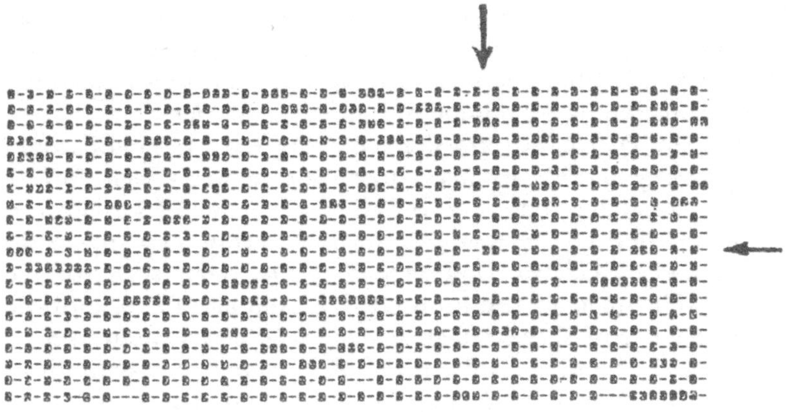

(a) Tuned sequence (E=6.2)

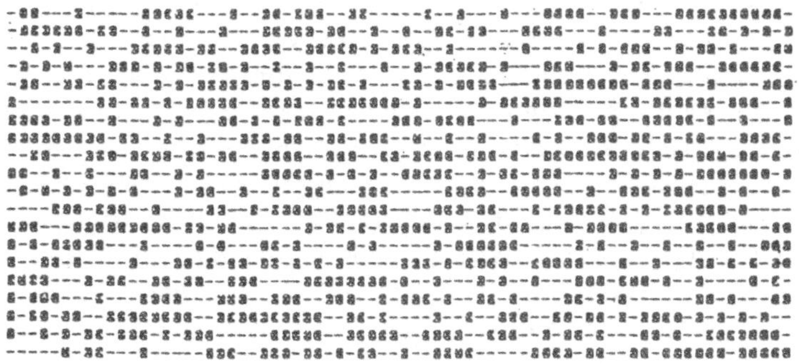

(b) Random sequence (E=1.00)

Fig. 13.15. Sequencing of hand usage (adapted from Clauer et al., Note 10).

by "⊠ ⊠" (right-right), are from the next most frequent 576 characters [i.e., the cumulative 713 characters (99.0%) are from the most frequent 1,152 characters]; 6 characters (0.8%), represented by "– –" (left-left), are from the third most frequent 576 characters [i.e., the cumulative 719 characters (99.9%) are from the most frequent 1,728 characters]; and there is only one character (0.1%), represented by "– ⊠" (left-right) from the fourth most frequent 576 characters (which is the 25th from the left on line 11, at the converging point of the two arrows in Figure 13.15a). The foregoing values fall between curves (A) and (B) in Figure 13.4, closer to the upper (B).

As we can compute from Figure 13.4, the most frequent 574 characters cover about 93.5% of the newspaper text, 98% of the text of a technical journal, and over 99% of the text of technical reports generated by a research team. Hence, the arrangement of other characters over the other three quadrants of Figure 13.14a would have little effect on the expected run length of the L-R, R-L hand sequences, so they can be arranged to facilitate recall of codes by typists. For that matter, the characters in Figure 13.14b are already arranged to facilitate recall. The eight center blocks contain the most frequently used 192 characters, and the other 382 characters are arranged around these blocks according to their *on* sounds, as is done in some dictionaries.

Yamura Shinkô's codes are derived from kantele keyboards, where characters are generally arranged according to some logic—mostly frequency of usage, but phonetic ordering or character structure can be used. This method of displaying codes in an array may appear reasonable, as claimed by Ogawa. However, if we first select a two-stroke code set that is well tuned to the economy of hand and finger motions, and if we work back from these two-stroke codes to an array correspondence, we might easily wind up with a random character distribution, with most of the L-R quadrant taken up by the high-frequency characters, the most frequently used characters showing up in the eight center blocks.

Under such conditions, it appears wise to have a code book arranged in ordinary *dictionary form* for quick reference by typists in addition to the array correspondence table. However, we reasoned that if our conjecture about the dependence of well-trained typists on right cerebral function is correct, then the array correspondence table would be a desirable approach for code reference, because when we use the code dictionary, the two-stroke code (i.e., a length 2 sequence of key names) for a character is first looked up and is then sent to the right hemisphere (RH) for manipulospatial processing. The first step in such a sequence of processing would be the function of the linguistic left hemisphere (LH), even after good training. The step becomes an automatic recall from long-term memory, and (as we discussed in conjunction with the undesirability of association codes) it remains an unnecessary extra processing step.

On the other hand, use of the array correspondence table of two-stroke codes appears to be a direct evocation of manipulospatial RH functions from a character to the depression of corresponding keys, possibly dependent much less on the LH. We suggested in an earlier section ("Touch Typing Viewed as a Choice Versus Reaction Time Paradigm") that fluent typing, from visual information to manipulo-spatial execution of key selections, is likely to be a cortical reflex of incompatible stimulus-response reactions, and such reflex skills should be developed so as to bypass as many unnecessary intermediate steps as possible. Since typing is ultimately carried out by the "finger memory," the names of keys used in the code dictionary are certainly nonessential intermediaries, even if they are known to help the memory of novice typists in the very early stages of their training.

We have just begun training four novice female typists, fresh from college, on our Superwriter II system, whose two-stroke code system, called *T-code* (T is short for Tôdai, the University of Tokyo), is optimized to require a minimal amount of hand and finger motion. (See the sections "Some Examples Optimized for Hand and Finger Motions" and "Educational Aspects"). We are using both the code dictionary and the code array for typists' quick reference, together with a computer-assisted teaching system that is now under development. It is still too early to call it definite, but contrary to our anticipation that the trainees would prefer to use the code dictionary rather than the code array, they report that the code array is easier to use than the code dictionary, at least at this stage. According to their subjective reporting, use of the code array leads naturally to finger movements, whereas the evocation of key names associated with use of the code dictionary obtrudes on, and interferes with, the reading of the text material. We intend to pursue this aspect further.

Another unexpected psychological phenomenon has been reported by our trainees. When we designed our T-code array, we used the "outside-in" approach, as in Ogawa (Note 19): The location of the key depressed first is read off as the location of the corresponding block, then the location of the key depressed next as the location of the character within the block. We thought this is the natural ordering because we have to locate a block before the letter in it. However, one of the trainees after an initial experience found this order confusing, and rewrote the code array into an "inside-out" format (in that the block location corresponds to the second key location and the character location in it to the first key location); she now claims that the "inside-out" array is easier for her to use. This opinion was subsequently supported by other trainees and the inside-out table is now our standard.

I do not know whether this phenomenon is a well-known psychological fact. If recognized by many, it may mean that our psychological space has a different topology from external space, and the inside-outside relation may have some directional symmetry. One possible explanation here is that, in the search for a particular character, our attention is focused on the immediate neighborhood of the character at the time of its discovery, hence the closer neighborhood (i.e., the "inside" information) is naturally associated with the first stroke, after which our attention shifts to the gross location, which corresponds to the second stroke.

Evaluation of Codes Based on Hand and Finger Motions

It seems to be an established fact by now that the ultimate typing speed of a well-trained English copy typist is determined by the speed limitation of the hands and fingers, not by the mental rendering of the visual input from the manuscript to the queue of commands for finger and hand motions. This had already been noticed around 1890 at the time of the invention of touch typing, and various proposals and attempts have been made since to arrive at optimized letter arrangements on the keyboard to facilitate fast and easy typing (Yamada, 1980). One notable example is the Dvorak Simplified Keyboard (DSK) arrangement patented in 1936, which may or may not be made the alternative American National Standards Institute (ANSI) standard, next to the present qwerty standard. There may be still some doubts about the very methodology for the effectiveness evaluation of various arrangements, yet it is generally recognized that the DSK is a better arrangement than the qwerty.

As mentioned in Chapter 1, the factors that August Dvorak took into consideration in order to facilitate smoother and faster hand and finger motions are (a) loading of hands, (b) loading of fingers, (c) loading among the rows of the keyboard, (d) emphasis on the alternate use of both hands, (e) avoidance of awkward motion sequences of fingers when the same hand has to be used in succession, and so on. The secondary effects of such considerations are (a) a decrease in the total travel distance by the fingers and hands, (b) the far larger percentage of words are typed on the home row alone, (c) a 50% reduction in mistyping, (d) typists' subjective report of greatly reduced fatigue, and so on.

Dvorak seems to have given more significance to roll-in keying (i.e., the successive inward use of fingers from the little to the index) than to roll-out keying. However, the effect of such a principle is not very clear to me. If flipping the hands in the roll-in direction is shown to be even somewhat easier and faster than in the roll-out direction, which seems to be the case, then an isolated same-hand roll-in keying among alternate-hand keying should in principle have a slight advantage over roll-out keying, which should be tested.

Critical examination of, or the attempted improvements over, Dvorak's work in the literature is often improperly approached. That is, people sometimes forget to take into consideration the fact that typing by an experienced typist is pattern typing, not the sequential adjoining of isolated key-to-key stroking, as we saw in an earlier section ("Touch Typing Viewed as a Choice Versus Reaction Time Paradigm"). Therefore, key-to-key stroking time is naturally expected to vary not only according to the ease or difficulty of keying in isolation and to the degree of familiarity on account of the frequency of occurrences, but also according to the nature of the contextual environment and the degree of influence it has on the specific keying under consideration.

Kinkead's critique (1975) of DSK is an example involving such an omission. Based on the analysis of key-to-key stroking times of qwerty keyboard typists, he argues that DSK typing improves typing speed over the qwerty only as much as 2.3%, which is much less than generally claimed. However, his analysis does not take into consideration the effect of the change of the frequency distribution of key-to-key strokes (not of letter-to-letter strokes, which remains the same). On the other hand, Evey's work (1980) on the construction of a typing model makes use of the frequency of occurrences of each key-to-key transition and arrives at a neat and compact model. His model also shows that the DSK should improve speed only less than 5%. Since a good typist's typing tends to be rhythmic, we suspected there would be a "leveling" effect from the context, and so the time for a key-to-key transition would be pulled to the average value of the transition times of the adjacent key-to-key transitions. Our analysis of the performance of one native Japanese typist for English indeed shows this leveling effect, although not conclusively because of the sample size of one (Hiraga, Ono, & Yamada, 1980a). However, if this effect is indeed genuine, it would account, at least in part, for the discrepancy between the often claimed advantage of DSK and the results shown by these two analyses.

The modeling attempt by Konishi, Kurematsu, and Tashiro (Note 20) appears to be quite inappropriate because, in the process of collecting key-to-key time data, they used not only the qwerty arrangement but also quasi-English text, which is a random sequence of alphabet, comma, period, semicolon, virgule (i.e., slash, /), and space, where only the frequencies of occurrences of those characters and space are made to resemble those of English text (except for the space, which is appropriately injected so that no pseudoword is longer than eight characters); otherwise the character ordering is by chance. The use of such a pseudo-English text does not take advantage of the skill of pattern typing at all. Indeed, their evaluation by simulation based on the key-to-key time data thus obtained indicated that the DSK is even less efficient than the qwerty.

Curiously enough, however, the rank ordering of keys in terms of ease of typing based on their data turns out to be a reasonable one, as seen in Table 13.7, where the effect of the difference between the two hands is omitted (Takashima, Mitsui, & Ohiwa, Note 21). This fact

Table 13.7. Ease of Key Usage

	Left Hand					Right Hand				
Row	L	R	M	I		I		M	R	L
Upper	10	8	3	5	7	7	5	3	8	10
Home	9	6	1	2	4	4	2	1	6	9
Bottom	15	14	10	12	13	13	12	10	14	15

Note. The column headings L, R, M, and I stand for little, ring, middle, and index fingers, respectively.

shows that the performance evaluation of letter arrangements on the keyboard critically depends on other factors than the mere rank ordering of the ease of key usage, obtainable from the typing performance of incoherent pseudo-English letter-to-letter transitions on the qwerty keyboard.

The second point we note here is that some authors try to improve keyboard arrangement to improve speed based on the key-to-key time data obtained for each transition in isolation, that is, the data on the finger dexterities measured for each transition separately. Such measurements were originally made in the 1920s by, for example, J. E. Coover and E. Riemer, mainly for the determination of finger dexterity (cf. Dvorak et al., 1936). R. F. Nickells, Jr. (1973) made a dexterity matrix for 30 × 30 key transitions, based on the extrapolation of the Coover and the Riemer data, and computed the relative speed performance of approximately half a million different keyboard arrangements. His computation showed that the DSK is only 6.2% faster than the qwerty. Here again, the effects of frequencies, pattern typing, and leveling are not accounted for, so such a result is expected. The relative performance of individual fingers in isolation is definitely a useful concept in the evaluation of keyboard arrangements and kanzi codes, even for Japanese touch typing (Hiraga et al., 1980a; Murayama, 1982). Beyond that, however, not much attention has been paid so far to the effect of pattern typing and the leveling effect. It is our belief that reliable performance data on a specific keyboard is obtainable only by analysis of the performance of typists who are actually trained on it, not by any simulation, at least at the present level of the art; and this goes for kanzi code typing as well.

As we already mentioned in the section on kanzi coding, the second approach to kanzi code design, after the linguistic or graphic association approach, is the facilitation, at least in part, of smooth hand and finger movement. Kawakami, a follower of Dvorak from the early days of his research, paid great attention, when designing his Rainputto system, to the smoothness of finger and hand motions in Dvorak's sense, although he designed his kanzi codes to be as mnemonic as possible (as discussed in "Association Codes and Interference with Pattern Typing").

For example, Figure 13.16 shows the loading, or usage frequency distribution, of keyboard rows for the Rainputto system, together with the ones for the DSK and qwerty keyboards for English, and the JIS kana keyboard for kana-to-kanzi conversion, our T-code and Takashima's code for Japanese, and our COS code for Chinese, the latter three to be discussed in the next section. As can be seen from these distributions, all systems except the qwerty for English and kana for Japanese are aimed at maximal loading of the home row. The DSK for English is best in this respect, but Rainputto is very good in spite of its other good features.

The loading of fingers in typing tasks should be distributed according to finger dexterity. There seems to be no complete agreement yet on the dexterity of fingers. Speed of manipulation, accommodation of different fingering patterns, and strength for key depression are mutually correlated, but not completely. For example, the little finger is anatomically better equipped than the ring finger for intricate fingering motions, but the latter may be faster for simpler typing, and may also be able to exert more force. In the days of manual typewriters, designers gave more responsibility to the ring finger than the little one because of the depression force needed for keying. With today's electric and even electronic typewriters, some designers give the little finger a better share of the load for its dexterity. But speed, dexterity, and the capacity for prolonged use can be improved by practice and training, and we cannot say what sort of loading distribution is preferable, other than that the overall distribution should be fairly evenly balanced among fingers and between the two hands, and that the index fingers should be given relatively more loading than others. If we pursue only optimal typing speed, then we generally end up with excessive loading of the fastest (index) fingers by assigning the most frequently used letters to the keys they depress, as do Nickells' algorithms (1973).

Figure 13.17 shows the finger loading distributions of the qwerty and DSK keyboards for English, the kana keyboard for kana-to-kanzi conversion, and the Rainputto for two-stroke codes. These distributions are naturally dependent on the nature of the text typed, but there the general patterns are fairly invariant. In the first three, it is assumed that the space bar is depressed by the right thumb. The percentages given for fingers are exclusive of the thumb. The amount of usage for the thumb on the kana keyboard varies for different kana-to-kanzi conversion systems, because of the different word grouping schemes used in different systems. Rainputto does not use the space bar for normal Japanese characters. These four distributions and some given in the next section clearly show that the qwerty and JIS kana keyboards are outdated (Mayuzumi, 1962; Parkinson, 1972).

The expected E value of the interval run length for alternate-hand use was discussed earlier (in "Code Array Representation for Two-Stroke

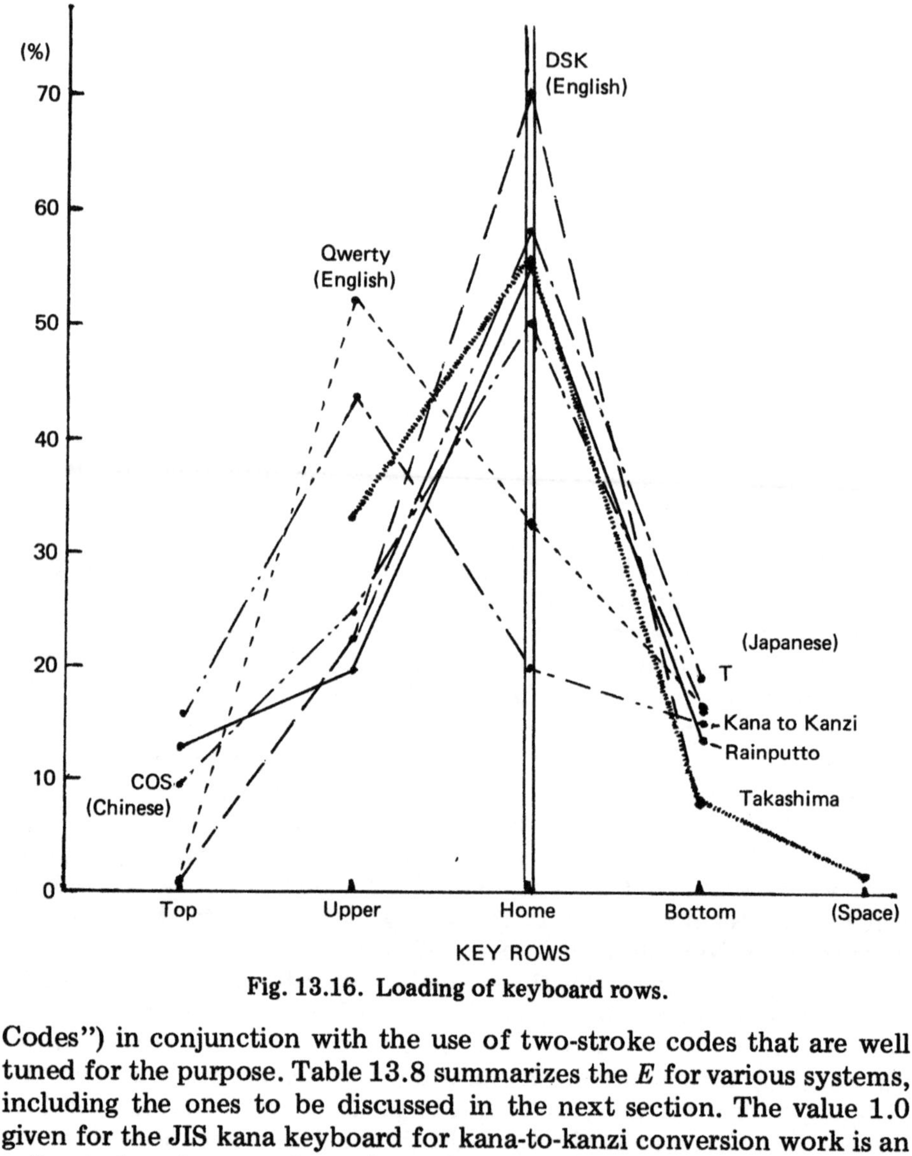

Fig. 13.16. Loading of keyboard rows.

Codes") in conjunction with the use of two-stroke codes that are well tuned for the purpose. Table 13.8 summarizes the E for various systems, including the ones to be discussed in the next section. The value 1.0 given for the JIS kana keyboard for kana-to-kanzi conversion work is an estimate based on a system whose characteristics in this respect are quite similar to those of the JIS. Rainputto's kanzi code table is not publicly available. Therefore, we have computed the value for it by using the fact that kana typing is always alternating-hand keying and by assuming that the codes for kanzis are random two-stroke codes. We also used the very high kanzi-to-kana ratio of .56-.44 determined from technical and scientific literature because it would give a more conservative computation result. Probably this estimate of 4.7 is a lower bound for Rainputto. Table 13.8 shows that the qwerty and kana keyboards give almost a chance performance.

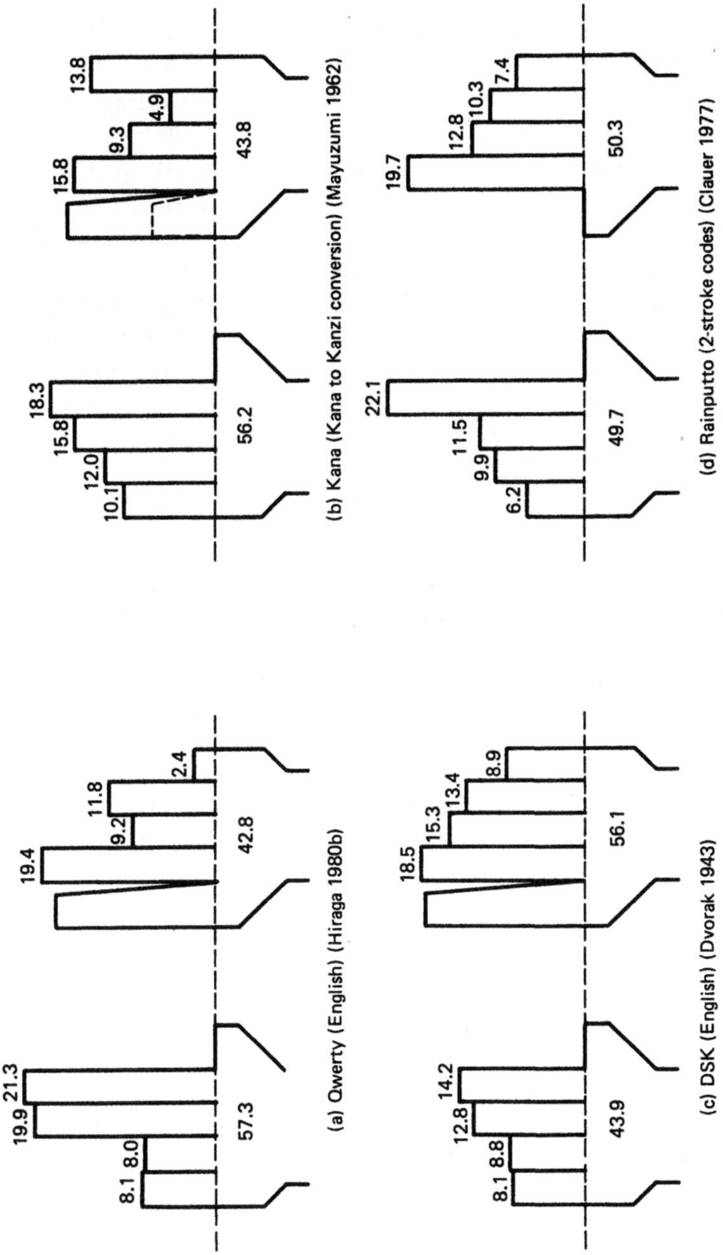

Fig. 13.17. Finger loading distributions (thumb loading not included in computation).

Table 13.8. Expected Length of Alternate-Hand Sequencing From Arbitrary Point in Text

Language	System	Expected Value of Interval Length	Comments
——	(Random sequence)	1.00	Theoretical
English	Qwerty	1.03	Shift ignored and space skipped
	DSK	1.75	(Hiraga, 1981)
Japanese	Kana	(1.0)	Estimated (cf. Clauer et al., Note 10)
	Tuned two-stroke	6.2	Clauer et al. (Note 10)
	Rainputto	(4.1)	Estimated (Clauer et al., Note 10)
	T-code	6.85[a]	Hiraga (1981)
Chinese	COS	4.4	Cf. Jan and Yamada, (Note 8)

[a] Under a restricted condition; see "Some Examples Optimized for Hand and Finger Motions."

There are different ways to represent the degree of alternating use of the hands. When we tune the system for the largest expectation of the run length of the alternating-hand intervals, if we choose LR pairs for the most frequent kanzis, the next desirable pairs to be used for the next most frequent kanzis are either RR pairs or LL pairs because an LR-RR-LR sequence of pairs or LR-LL-LR generates only two of the length 0 alternating intervals (RR or LL), whereas LR-RL-LR generates (in addition to RR or LL) a length 1 alternating interval (RL), which contributes to the shortening of the average length of the alternating intervals. With such a choice, the distribution of the length of alternating-hand sequences is a distribution around a positive value of about 3 intervals having a longer tail to the right, *and* a spike at 0 for RR and LL, which brings down the average length of the alternating interval runs to 12.4, or E=6.2.

We have used E as a measure of alternation. Another way to represent the extent of alternation is to use the average length of the alternating runs only, which would be 24.8, together with the percentage coverage of the total text by the alternating intervals.

Sometimes the latter percentage alone is used to indicate degree of alternation. However, care must be taken to distinguish this value from the percentage of individual characters of the text covered by the alternating intervals, LR or RL, which is sometimes used (Murayama, 1982). The latter quantity ignores the intervals between two two-stroke codes of characters, which constitute 50% of the total intervals. Furthermore, the philosophy behind the choice of such a measure is to account for the typing of each character separately, thus ignoring the forming of pattern typing for contiguous characters that make up a word. As a measure of the ease of typing by a well-trained typist, we consider such a choice to be less than satisfactory.

The tuning of codes to alternating-hand sequencing clearly has the side effect that every time the sequencing deviates from the alternation, the alternation is brought back as soon as possible, quite often after two intervals of alternation length 0, namely RRR or LLL. (Since the right hand is faster, RR codes are preferable after LR codes, but the difference is perhaps negligible.) Other things being equal, such a condition should be desirable. However, we do not know whether attainment of maximal alternating run length is worth the sacrifice of good distributions of keyboard-row loading and finger loading.

Next, when a consecutive same-hand typing sequence arises, it is desirable to hold down the amount of awkward finger usage sequencing, namely, finger motions involving the same or adjacent fingers over distinct key rows, such as the ones in Table 13.9. There is no complete agreement as to which sequences are more difficult to type than others. However, it is generally held that those at a higher position and more to the left in the table are more difficult than those toward the bottom and more to the right. Hence, double hurdle keying with the same finger is the hardest to execute. Even among keyings in the same class, those that involve less dexterous fingers should be harder. Taps by the same finger on the same key, although slower, are not particularly awkward sequences. In the cases of the index and little fingers, hitting of row-wise adjacent keys is difficult and classed as side reaches.

The percentage of awkward key-to-key digram strokes on various systems are summarized in Table 13.10. Since these figures vary according to the nature of the text and other factors, they should be viewed only as indications. Figures for Rainputto are based on a simulation, assuming as before the random two-stroke codes for kanzis and using texts that contain 56% kanzis. Hence, they are definitely upper bounds, and the actual figures should be lower than these. Nevertheless, the figures are much higher than in the case of the DSK for English. The reason for this is that the Rainputto must use the top-row keys in order to provide two-stroke codes to cover the basic 2,300 kanzis, thus increasing the percentages of various hurdles.

Table 13.9. Classes of Awkward Sequences

	Fingers		
Row distances	same	adjacent	remote
3	Double hurdles	Double hurdles	Double hurdles
2	Hurdles	Hurdles	Hurdles
1	Reaches	Reaches	—
0	Side reaches	—	—

Table 13.10. Percentage of Awkward Sequences

	Language			
	English		Japanese	
Sequence	Qwerty	DSK	Kana	Rainputto[a]
Same finger				
Double hurdles and hurdles	2.0	0.1	3.8	4.5
Reaches	2.6	1.3	2.4	3.1
Adjacent fingers				
Double hurdles and hurdles	5.6	0.1	9.2	5.9
Reaches	14.9	2.2	8.2	1.7
Remote fingers				
Double hurdles and hurdles	3.1	0.3	?	2.2
Total	28.2	3.9	> 23.6	< 17.4
Source	Dvorak et al. (1936)		Mayuzumi (1962)	Clauer et al. (Note 10)

[a]Upper bound based on a simulation using random codes for kanzis, and a text with 56% kanzis.

One may wonder about the effectiveness of a code optimization effort based on hand and finger motions, just as in the case of the English keyboard where persistent skepticism has been voiced about the superiority of the DSK to the qwerty. We are not yet in the position to give a definitive answer, because we have just begun training the first group of typists as our optimized Japanese touch-typing system (to be described in the next section). However, we can volunteer the following episode.

The earlier Daikei (written in kanzis) system by A. Itô (mentioned in "Some Two-Stroke Touch-Typing Systems") used a two-stroke coding system based on two kanas per character. The first kana of a code represented the initial sound of the kanzi to be coded, but the second kana was assigned more or less arbitrarily, on a "first come, first served" basis, and no particular optimization effort of any kind was made. Itô, who trained about 200 typists on his code, was in the business of Japanese input processing. His system required frequent shifting as well as the use of a third and sometimes even a fourth stroke to impose two diacritical marks, which kana writing requires.

As a consequence, his typists' hands flew all over the keyboard during typing, and he was rather pleased with the impression of speed and action that such typing gives. After we pointed out to him the futility of such "flying butterfly" hand motions, as he called them, he optimized the core codes for the several hundred basic characters in a Dvorak-like manner; he calls this optimization the Daikei (now in katakanas) system, and he took a considerable business risk and retrained his typists in his new codes. Now he estimates that the throughput speed of his typists is up by approximately 30%.

Some Examples Optimized for Hand and Finger Motions

Although we made errors and detours in the process, we have arrived at a tentative conclusion through the train of reasoning described in the preceding sections. Perhaps the best method of typing Japanese text by well-trained copy typists is to use a kanzi code system on a regular typewriter keyboard that is optimized for the easiest hand and finger motions. In this section, we shall describe four systems recently designed more or less along this line: (1) the TX620 experimental system by Ricoh; (2) Takashima's system; (3) our T-code system; and (4) our COS system for Chinese text.

Ricoh's TX620 is a relatively new development among the two-stroke code systems striving for smooth hand and finger motions. It also uses a new approach for coding the kanas, which constitute 60-70% of normal text nowadays, and this coding has a noticeable influence on the smoothness of hand and finger motions.

The earlier described Rainputto uses alphabetic representations for kana characters, and the typing of sentences in kana alone is executed in 100% alternating-hand motions over the keys only in the vicinity of home positions, an advantageous organization. However, alphabetic writing for Japanese is not a common practice, and it is generally expected to encounter strong psychological resistance from users, although this has not been the case thus far. On the other hand, the code array representation of kanas by the Yamura Shinkô system is also judged as potentially unattractive to the prospective user, because of the very nature of the superficially unappealing representation scheme of the codes. Therefore, Ricoh introduced what they call the *category key method*, using a kana keyboard of their own design (Yagi & Yamada, Note 22, pp. 43-48). It has gone through its own vicissitudes, and one type that incorporates features of the conventional kana keyboard has been adopted as the joint Ricoh-Hitachi code for their respective commercially marketed word processors.

The principal feature of the category key method is the use of one of the two strokes to indicate the category of character to be typed, namely, hiraganas, katakanas, or kanzis, further divided into subcategories that are "natural" to the Japanese people. Figure 13.18 shows one of Ricoh's category keyboards, which gives the best alternate-hand sequencing for kanas, and is also perhaps the best one to illustrate the category key principle. Hiraganas and katakanas each compromise 46

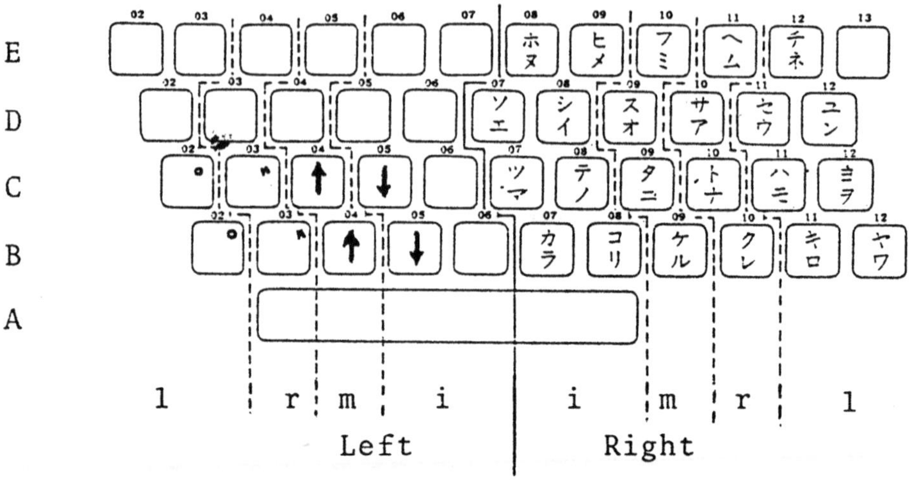

Fig. 13.18. A category key keyboard by Ricoh (adapted from Yamauchi, Note 23).

base characters and four additional smaller variants, *ya*, *yu*, *yo*, and *tu*. There are also two diacritical marks, *dakuten* (") and *handakuten* (°). Dakuten is applicable to 15 of the base kanas and handakuten to 5. In order to accommodate all of these (in either hiraganas or katakanas), a minimum of 46 + 4 + 2 = 52 distinct keyings are required. In addition, for good writing we need the smaller kanas *a*, *i*, *u*, *e*, *o*, and *wa*. If we are to type older materials, two more (*wi* and *we*) are needed. These make a total of 60 for each kana class. Thus, in order to accommodate even the minimum 52 indicated, the JIS keyboard uses the upper case for 10 kanas. In addition, frequent use of diacritical dakuten by the right little finger makes the finger loading distribution of the keyboard rather uneven, as is seen in Figure 13.17b. In Ricoh's keyboard in Figure 13.18, which has one more printing key (B-12) than the JIS keyboard, the 46 base kanas are all represented on the right-hand keys (Yamuchi, Note 23, pp. 13-23).

In order to select the upper or lower case, the upward-pointing arrows or downward-pointing arrows on the left-hand side are used as the second keystroke, where home-row arrows are assigned to the more frequent hiraganas and the bottom-row ones to the less frequent katakanas. The kanas on the right-hand keys are so distributed that each one that takes diacritical marks is uppercase on its key (except the rarely used katakana *u*, which is treated separately). The 10 small-letter variations do not take diacritical handakuten, and they are again uniquely designated by an additional key on the left-hand side (except the infrequent small *wa*, which needs sep rate handling). All other two-stroke combinations may be used for kanzis and other characters.

Thus in this system, the nine keys on the left-hand serve to identify the category of each associated character set. The advantage of this approach is that it eliminates the use of shifting or mode switching in identifying some kana characters of kana classes, while preserving the alternating-hand sequencing for kana text. The less advantageous feature compared with Rainputto is that it uses 23 right-hand keys (and 9 left) for kanas (Rainputto uses 16 on the right and 10 on the left for kana input), making the key-row loading distribution less ideal. As for the expected value of alternating-hand sequence lengths, it should be approximately the same as that of Rainputto, which was estimated to be 4.1 (see Table 13.8).

We have no further data on this system. Ricoh's other systems have these category keys distributed between both hands, which would shorten the alternating-hand sequencing, but may improve key-row loading and finger loading distributions. The key-row loading for their TX620 with such a category key method turns out to be almost identical to that of the COS Chinese system shown in Figure 13.16 (Yamauchi, Note 23, pp. 13-23). The TX620's finger loading distribution is shown in Figure 13.19a.

Takashima (1982) has developed a variable stroke length (though mostly of two strokes) coding system for Japanese, in which he uses a basically alphabetic approach for kanas. However, he uses a different approach for the handling of diacritical marks. The diacritical dakuten (") is used in Japanese to change voiceless consonants to voiced (*k* to *g*, *s* to *z*, and *t* to *d*) with one exception (*h* to *b*; historically, however, *h* was the voiceless bilabial fricative *ph*, hence not originally a complete exception). The handakuten (°) is used to change *h* to *p* (i.e., originally *ph* to voiceless bilabial explosive *p*). In order to preserve the "naturalness" of the use of diacritical marks ingrained in the Japanese mind, Takashima introduced the use of diacritical mark coding and eliminated the need for *b*, *d*, *g*, *p*, and *z* from his system. He also separated consonants to the left and vowels to the right. Hence, his system may be thought of as a hybrid of the Rainputto alphabet system and the Ricoh category key system. As for the letter arrangement on keys, he uses the little fingers much less, in favor of index fingers.

The expected value of the lengths of alternating-hand sequencing from an arbitrary point in the text is estimated to be about the same as with Rainputto or with the Ricoh category key system tuned for this goal. On the other hand, as Figure 13.16 shows, Takashima has achieved a very good key-row loading distribution, although the data were collected under certain restrictions on the text subject areas. The space bar is involved for the coding of punctuation marks.

We wished to investigate (a) the limit of ultimately smooth fingering, (b) how difficult it is to learn completely neutral (i.e., associationless) kanzi codes, and (c) the acquisition of skill in the direct mapping from kanzis to keystroking via the array representation of kanzi codes (without recourse to the dictionary-form representation of kanzi codes) as we discussed earlier. We have implemented the kanzi T-code and the KED (short for Kanzi Text Editor) on the Superwriter II system.

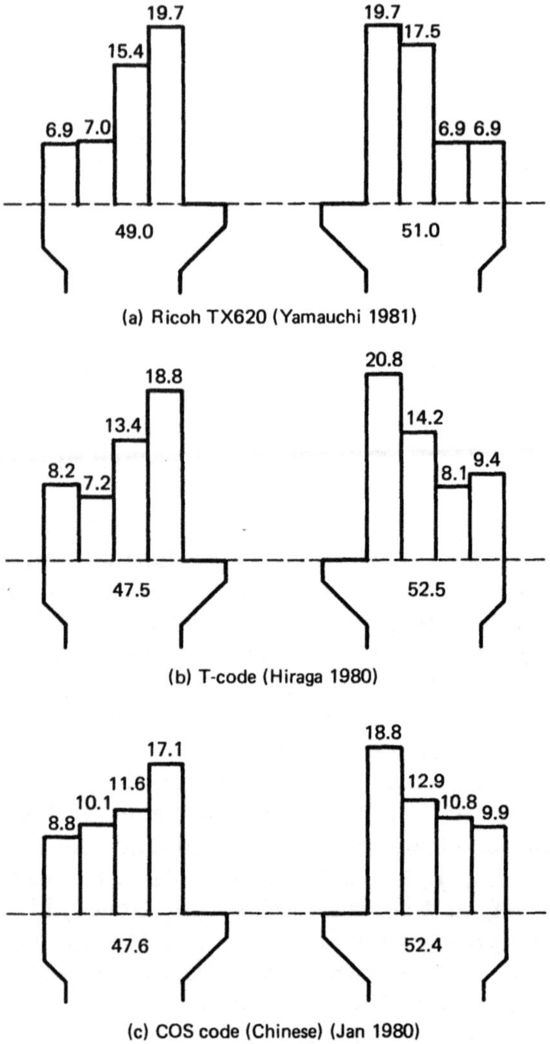

Fig. 13.19. Finger loading distributions.

For such a system, we use for coding only 40 keys from our standard 48 keys. In order to select the kanzi set to be coded, we took the rank ordering of a kanzi usage frequency given by the National Language Laboratory (1956) for newspapers and made some adjustment to suit our own needs.

The design objective of our experimental T-code is to make the smoothest hand and finger motions for word pattern typing, expected to become a cortical reflex after several months' training by a suitable method. Therefore we purposely avoided accommodating memorization by association devices for at least the codes of the basic 1,200 characters and concentrated on optimization of hand and finger motions in

Dvorak's sense. However, we made some minor modifications to his approach in order to incorporate the effect of electronic keyboards, such as the slightly increased loading of the little fingers in comparison with that of the ring fingers. This means that in coding we make no distinctions whatsoever among kanas, kanzis, and other characters.

To be more specific, the T-code has the following specifications (Hiraga, 1981).

(a) Only 40 out of 48 printing keys are used.
(b) The shift key and space bar are not involved in character codes.
(c) Out of 40 × 40 = 1,600 possible two-stroke pairs, some of those that involve the top-row keys are not used. In particular, the same-hand pairs involving the top-row keys are almost all unused. This gave us about 1,200 usable pairs, which should cover more than 95% of kanzis, or more than 98% of the total characters, in ordinary text. The coverage is almost 100% if the code set is tuned to the task of a specific group or individual (see Figure 13.4).
(d) There seem to be no scientific data indicating which is the better hand for starting alternate-hand stroking. We chose to start with the right (and stop with the left); that is, the most frequently used characters are coded in RL pairs, then in RR pairs, LL pairs, and finally LR pairs, which makes the expected length of the alternating-hand sequences largest, as we noted in the preceding section.
(e) The actual assignment of codes to characters is made to optimize various parameters in Dvorak's sense, as described in the preceding section.

The resultant codes are shown in Figure 13.20 in the inside-out array representation described earlier (in "Code Array Representation of Two-Stroke Codes"). The key-row loading by the basic 1,200 character T-code is shown in Figure 13.16, and the finger loading in Figure 13.19b. The expected length of alternating-hand sequencing from an arbitrary point in the text was found to be 6.85 when only 900 basic characters are considered (see Table 13.8). This is better than the 6.2 for the best tuned system because of the 900-character restriction, and in reality the figure would be lower. (The handling of more than 900 characters will be described shortly.)

The percentage of hurdles and reaches for same-hand sequencing against the total, again in 900 basic codes, are as in Table 13.11 (cf. Table 13.10). Since the codes for the 900 basic characters do not use the top key row, and since the codes are tuned to alternating-hand sequencing, the low percentage of awkward sequences for the T-code in this evaluation is understandable. As soon as we start using 2,304 two-stroke pairs, however, the figures should go up to levels that are somewhere between those of the DSK and the Rainputto.

Our T-code trainees reported that two-stroke kanzi codes of either the RR category or the LL category are easier to learn (by hands) than

(LL)					(RL)				
··········	··········	··········	··········	··········	··········	··········	··········	··········	··········
··········	··········	··········	··········	··········	請境系締象	邸賀岸貢漁	含喜幹丘糖	布苦圧恵固	姿絶密秘押
··········	··········	··········	··········	··········	盛革突温捕	益援周域荒	康徒景処ぜ	邦舞雑漢紡	衆節杉肉除
··········	··········	··········	··········	··········	依繊借須訳	織父枚乱香	譲へ模降走	激干彦均又	測血散笑弁
ヲ········	ゥ········	ヴ········	ヂ········	ヅ········	酸昼炭稲湯	貿捜異隣旧	攻焼闘奈夕	盤帯易速拡	汽換延雪互
果告策首農	坪買森由死	武残両在！	風階能論増	細古利ぺゃ	歩回務島開	キせ区百木	や出タ手保	コ山者発立	ナ金マ和女
報紙館夜位	音王放々応	案劇情引職	横興託側林	崎白ぐ官球	給員ど代レ	分よル千ア	７か（トれ	きっ日国二	上く８え年
婚夏彼妻善	財針裏居差	従泉厚顔量	適類御宇推	母奥郵酒伸	相家的対歴	付ブばュ作	内工ハテ見	九名川機チ	サ建バ第入
ぱ········	ぴ········	ぷ········	ぺ········	ぽ········	桜瀬鳥催障	典博筋忠乳	採羅希仏察	君純副盟標	犯余堀肩療
収際太園船	若雄査ふ賞	指氏丸続ェ	ぎ格次習火	思術広門間	中スもお定	わラ東生ろ	う４）十リ	あこ６学月	本さら高シ
種岡結進真	宅浜待取科	料土活ね参	受予切育池	英ボ加室少	３と〇てる	ーした一が	い、の５１	。◆０・２	ではになを
ヒ江別考権	及久蔵早造	投義算半県	込沢軍青清	転空性使級	ッ人三京ち	ロク万方フ	んまンつ四	けイす電地	業時「長み
··········	··········	··········	··········	··········	呼幅歓功盗	紀破郡抗幡	房績識属衣	去疑ち綿離	秒債核影麻
徳渡守登退	械刊訪融雨	帝始祭極熱	読鈴畳督況	族丁未才返	店持町所ほ	全じ自譲明	バ部六経動	後間場ニ産	問ム七住北
件友卒初阪	宮伊求技写	局頭配黒院	向府富直倉	割ぶ番望元	行ド円小ジ	通カ社野同	だり－め大	新」９子五	事田会前そ
ヨ馬証含％	判規感値ギ	済吉ゆ器昭	説週号薬派	休省央福征	海道ず西げ	当理メウグ	不合面政オ	委化ビ目市	気売下都株

Fig. 13.20. Inside-out code array for T-codes.

(LR)					(RR)				
....	....	....	....	....	....	....	....	....	....
湖礼著移郷	端飾因塩群	刷寿順危砂	麗扱片札乞	弘席票訴遺	....	....	....	....	....
借欧努底亜	紅偽豪維脱	舗錠喫粉暴	輸倒操柄魚	則存倍牛飯	....	....	....	....	....
禁硝樹句礎	絹被源願臨	批慶渉竜併	就駐揮丹鮮	綱潟創背皮	....	....	....	....	....
簡態儀宗植	承章候途複	快否街箪里	包納頼逃仙	唱募憲勉罪	....	....	....	....	....
害貸整軽評	撃折追隊角	浴秀糸春幸	積程断低減	故鉱挺児数	佐法数郎談	接備最急験	記朝知ワ送	モ資士費ィ	無石屋解募
服声任検豊	変審改昇芸	限研労統役	菱企精ざ印	令違装然確	美題非洋実	宿制集安画	セ運ツ特谷	神び打勤ャ	優公品語演
爆仲茶率比	陽構旅施曜	ァ導認健尾	殺負何履般	券悪秋非便	奏短岩巨敗	遠ォ将ぞ塚	署振練念働	閣授版効視	示即難普辺
珠遅甲致幕	陣鶴鹿貨絡	眼繁誌招季	執紹夢卸阿	岳刑弱翼窓	....	....	....	....	....
病終起路越	常張薬防得	寺質づ港条	停領容玉右	河置供試席	む南原駅物	ケ式戦関男	話座線ダ橋	べ民ソ点週	期ゾ歳強係
勢必講愛管	輸形助◆流	基好味宝争	足草築観言	婦段術額渋	要設水藤有	連鉄教力べ	デ現エ他度	車成天世文	主映書可へ
素兵専親寮	毛永申袋良	等伐鋼落命	板客師税飛	伝庭課着坂	ホ共ブ平楽	私ゴ来信午	村力製校こ	ノ完重約各	近外米ョ光
欲巣茂述則	迫災恋脳老	留列沖豆看	替沼？辞梅	還更占箱矢	....	....	....	....	....
帰庁昨城ゲ	監寄裁達芝	竹注介具失	ゅ修究答養	志抜航油深	洗羽個医静	響星討史環	司迎華許補	復並湘ユ冷	担陸巻競護
億録赤想消	色貸販編仕	左態花栄ザ	ぬ展弊型晴	根様独止堂	支協用表正	先多商八交	調松ポ決ミ	組選党歌体	銀以ヌ営治
図挙険ゼ波	之末ぼ街免	州払乗庫状	例満津準遊	字材過諸単	ヤ心界意今	再ネ～口台	団計夫食総	戸ひょ価与	身ビ勝反ズ

Fig. 13.20. (*continued*)

Table 13.11. Hurdles and Reaches

Language	System	All Hurdles	Reaches	Sum
Japanese	T-code	1.8	4.9	6.7
	Rainputto	12.6	4.8	< 17.4
	Kana	> 13.0	10.6	> 23.6
English	DSK	0.5	3.5	3.9
	Qwerty	10.7	17.5	28.2
Chinese	COS	0.39	1.57	1.96

the ones in the RL category. They think the reason is that the former two involve only one hand for each kanzi whereas the latter involves both hands. Their remark reminds us of the recent argument advanced by Lilian G. Malt of England (a personal communication in Yamada, 1980) that the speed superiority of alternate-hand keying over lateral keying (i.e., one-hand keying) should not be overly stressed. She also suggests that other factors, such as the high rate of letter confusions among vowels, are just as important, and proposes a letter arrangement for keyboards that is different from Dvorak's in its principle and somewhat reminiscent of W. W. Nelson's philosophy (1921). Since the motor cortex of the cerebrum for one hand is on the opposite hemisphere from that of the other's, pattern formation for one-hand coding may be easier than that for two-hand coding. In the case of the T-code, however, if we assign the most frequently used characters to, say, the RR category alone, then over 80% of the loading will be on the right hand (cf. Figure 13.4). If the RR and the LL categories are interspersed in use, then left-right rhythm will be seriously affected because the transition between the RR and the LL codes is not expected to be so regular. Hence we are sticking to the present T-code, although it is interesting to test the second alternative mentioned to see the trade-off between the percentage increase of one-hand keying and the increased irregularity in left-right rhythm.

There is another feature we have implemented in our Superwriter II system in conjunction with the T-code. The basic character set of the T-code is about 1,200, as shown in Figure 13.20. These are completely neutral codes. However, 48 keys can accommodate another 1,100 two-stroke codes, and these are implemented for the typists who normally type full time every day. As has been mentioned, these 1,100 characters would constitute the maximum of 2%, but normally a small fraction of 1%, of the total text. Hence, dexterity with these will not greatly influence overall typing speed, and they are arranged in systematic ways, based either on the sound or on the graphic structure of the kanzis, in order to assist the typists' recall.

For the less frequent users of the system, even looking up the codes for these 1,100 characters may be psychologically discouraging. Therefore we have provided another means, to be described next, of dealing with these 1,100 characters *and* a few hundred less frequently used subsets of the basic 1,200 characters, as well as those that are beyond the first 2,300 two-stroke coded characters (Hiraga et al., 1980a; Ono, Hiraga, & Yamada, 1981). Thus, the last 1,500 or so of the 2,300 two-stroke coded characters also have second codes for intuitive "structural" typing.

As we mentioned earlier in "Japanese Writing System," the majority of kanzis consist of easily identifiable components. We have taken the 2,965 kanzis of the JIS-C6226 first-level character set and let people try to break each into "component" characters, where the component characters may be characters, structures resembling certain characters, characters containing distinct and easily identifiable common parts, or characters that contain some components as subparts in a conspicuous manner. Figure 13.21 shows some examples of "outside" characters that are not in the core set of 1,200, together with examples of intuitively selected component characters from the core set. The W and P stand for the whole and a part, respectively of the component characters; the plus and minus signs stand respectively for addition and the subtraction relations among the components. The decompositions attempted by different people were quick and converged to a very few alternative selections. Examples of other alternatives are also shown in the figure for the first three kanzis. The outside characters are entered by first prefixing by the black diamond (see Figure 13.20), indicating that a component pair follows, and then keying the pair of two-stroke codes for the component characters (six strokes altogether for a character).

The Superwriter II system is so implemented that (a) most of the reasonable component pairs we can intuitively come up with are accepted so long as there are no conflicts with such pairs for other characters, and (b) the ordering of the component characters may be arbitrarily chosen.

We note here that such an intuitive decomposition appears to be a function of the right cerebral hemisphere and thus more appealing to people than highly logically or mathematically structured codes for which more of the left hemisphere is called on to extract the codes from the characters. (People love to cut corners.) Having the intuitive decomposition coding to fall back on in case of a memory slip should contribute to the psychological security of typists. (People love to have leeway.) However, the effectiveness of these provisions is yet to be proven.

The last system we mention here briefly is our Chinese Coding System, or COS (Jan & Yamada, 1980). The Chinese writing system has at least as many problems as the Japanese for fast typewriting, because it requires at least 3,500 kanzis, and normally 6,000, which (as we discussed earlier in "Coding of Kanzis Based on Linguistic and Graphic Structures") seems to make impractical the use of a strictly neutral code such as our T-code. But we are still interested in the possibility of true touch typing for Chinese. Hence we had to resort to certain mnemonic devices in our attempt. We were particularly interested in the degrading

	Outside Char.	Components	Other Components
(1) W+W	銅	金 同	鉄 同 (P+W)
(2) P+W	迷	道 米	米 通 (P+W)
(3) P+P	酢	配 作	酒 昨 (P+P)
(4) P–W	亜	悪 心	—

Fig. 13.21. T-Codes for outside characters (W means whole component character; P, part of the component character; +, addition of components; -, subtraction of components).

effect on the optimality of codes, in terms of hand and finger motions, of such mnemonic considerations in the process of designing the COS system to make it a humanly acceptable touch-typing system.

First we note that even in the traditional Chinese writing used in Taiwan today, we have found that a base set of 4,580 characters is sufficient for 99.6% of normal texts, and the most frequent 1,000 for 88.7%. These percentages should be higher in the more simplified writing used on the Chinese mainland today.

Hence, in designing the COS we coded the most frequently used 1,000 characters in neutral two-stroke codes, as in the case of the Japanese T-code, in order to optimize for hand and finger motions as before. Using only 40 keys, we coded the first 400 characters in RL key pairs, the next 300 in RR key pairs, and the third 300 in LL key pairs. In order to decrease the percentage of hurdles and double hurdles, the remaining 100 RR key pairs and 100 LL key pairs were not used for coding.

These assignments leave us with the 400 LR key pairs to cover at least the remaining 3,580 basic characters and more from the outside characters. Since these 3,580 characters occur in only 10.9% of the text, we feel that they have to be coded with some built-in memory-assisting structures. In order to do so, we first extracted 388 "homonymics," defined as Chinese syllables without tonal differences, expressed in the National Phonetic Symbols (NPSs), and 154 "radicals," or structural components of kanzis, of our own choice. Next, each of these two sets was separately given code assignments from the possible 400 LR key pairs, again by using the easiest ones to type. (Note that the use of the NPSs here is not an essential factor, and the alphabetic *pinyin* system is just as good.)

These steps will give us up to 388 × 154 = 59,752 possible four-stroke codes, the first two strokes representing the homonymics and the last two the radicals. We attempted to assign to each of the 3,580 kanzis a four-stroke code based on its pronunciation and most conspicuous radical. Although almost 17 times as many four-stroke codes are available as the number of kanzis to be coded by them, about 480 kanzis inevitably caused the same sound and the same radical collisions. These 480 have to be coded *ad hoc* and memorized, along with the neutral codes of the 1,000 basic kanzis. Unlike the basic 1,000 kanzis, these constitute about .5% of all kanzis in ordinary running texts, and because of their such infrequent use, there may be some recall problems associated with such *ad hoc* codes. Hence the viability of such codes should be tested by actually training the typists. In the worst case, the codes might have to be looked up when such kanzis are encountered.

At any rate, if such a coding system is indeed humanly learnable, then this COS code has rather nice properties in spite of the large character set of 4,580. Its row distribution, shown in Figure 13.16, is as good as that of the well-designed Japanese systems; its finger loading distribution, shown in Figure 13.19c is well balanced; its expected length of alternating-hand sequencing is about 4.4, which is as good as that of the Rainputto system (cf. Table 13.8); and finally, the amount of awkward sequencing is incredibly low at 1.96%, as can be seen in Table 13.11, or about half as much as the DSK gives for English. In fact, the number of difficult sequences, including taps, trills, and rocks (i.e., same-hand sequencing between nonadjacent fingers in the same key row) is 8.12%, which is still less than the 10.45% for the DSK. This good performance is achieved by (a) limiting the number of keys used to only 40, and (b) resorting to four-stroke codes early in order to avoid reaches and hurdles. Yet the average number of strokes per kanzi in regular texts is about 2.2, which makes the COS the most economical Chinese input system, as far as we know, in terms of the number of strokes per character. The COS system is now being implemented by Jan Jinn-ke for testing at the National Chung-Hsing University in Taichung, Taiwan. The details of the COS codes are described in Jan and Yamada (1980; Note 8). Some surveys of Chinese input methods in general can be found in Yamada (1978), Jan and Yamada (Note 8), and Tajima (1981).

In connection with the descriptions given in this section, two remarks can be made in passing. One concerns the question of the better hand with which to start typing an alternating-hand sequence. Most people are right handed, and, perhaps relatedly, in the majority of the countries in the world marching starts with the left foot, so there should also be a preferred first hand for alternating-hand typing. It may be the right hand. In 1959 Giiti Misaka (Note 24) of the Technical Officers School of the Japan Maritime Defence Force conducted an experiment on a group of about 80 novice typists at the school and found that the majority indeed preferred the "end with the left" pattern, exclusive of space, period, and comma. But we do not know whether such a preference would remain after typists are well trained.

Many arrangements of the alphabet on the keyboard have been proposed or used for the alphabetic writing of Japanese, and in most of them the vowels are placed on the left. Since Japanese syllables are open, this means that most often the typing pattern "start with the right" and "end with the left." We looked very hard for the justification of the design, which originated many decades ago, and finally found that it arose with the earlier double shift portable typewriters. They were used by the hunt-and-peck method with two fingers and had two shift keys, both on the left side. Since the uppercase letters at the beginning of sentences are mostly consonants, it seemed natural to place vowels on the left and consonants on the right.

Our second remark concerns the evaluation of the loading distribution on key rows. Such distributions have been one of the measures used to evaluate the optimality of the letter arrangement on the keyboard in the past, as we have used it ourselves in Figure 13.16. In normal typing motions, our hands move up and down away from the home position in order to type the off-home-row keys, not the full distances of the key row separations but a part of them. When two successive same-hand keyings take place on the same off-home row, the hand does not return to the home row in between, but lingers around the off-home-row position. In order to account for such partial and delayed hand excursions, we have constructed a simple mathematical model of typing motions and run a computer simulation test. The following is an outline and the result of the simulation (Hiraga, Note 25).

(a) The positions in which a hand can stay are listed in Table 13.12. That is, positions 2, 4, and 6 are between two key rows, and from these positions the keys in both adjacent rows can be depressed.

Table 13.12. Hand Positions Used for Simulation

Position	Corresponding key rows	Typable keys
1	Top (i.e., Rank E)	Top
2		Top and upper
3	Upper (i.e., Rank D)	Upper
4		Upper and home
5	Home (i.e., Rank C)	Home
6		Home and bottom
7	Bottom (i.e., Rank B)	Bottom

Note. By ISO, rows are called Rank A = space bar row, Rank B = bottom row, Rank C = home row, etc.

We call these *middle positions*, as opposed to 1, 3, 5, and 7, which we call *key positions*.

(b) The transition rules for the hands are as follows.
   i. When a hand is in a row position where a key to be depressed is located, no hand motion takes place.
   ii. When a hand is in a middle position and a key to be depressed is in an adjacent key position, the hand moves to the key position.
   iii. In other cases, the hand moves to the nearer middle position that is adjacent to the key position of the key to be depressed.
   iv. When a hand is idle (i.e., the other hand is keying), it stays in the last position to which it moved.

(c) In order to represent the amount of work associated with each move, a work load parameter is associated with each of the subtask categories, which are (i) choice of finger, (ii) distance of hand movement, (iii) finger stretch (i.e., reaching out to an adjacent key position from a middle position), (iv) same-hand keying, (v) same-finger keying, (vi) use of the space bar, and (vii) use of outside characters in the case of T-code. These parameters were varied over certain ranges in the simulation, and those that would give a good correlation (about .35) with the key-to-key transition time were finally chosen. (Detailed discussion is omitted here.)

The amount of work load for typing thus defined has been computed for the key and middle positions for different keyboards and different texts, and is summarized in Table 13.13. The text *Alice* is *Alice in Wonderland*, "Comp." is *Information Processing* by Marilyn Bohl (Chicago: Science Research Associates, 1971), and *Manual* is the *T-Code Manual for H-8700 Computer* (in Japanese); "With number" means that characters other than the basic 1,200 T-codes are entered by their hexadecimal codes, and "without number" means that the hexidecimal codes are ignored. The results show that the home row is indeed the home row for the English DSK and Japanese T-code, whereas with qwerty the hand moves around over the upper and home rows, centered between the two. Note that assumption (b), iv in our model penalizes the qwerty keyboard less than other models often considered do, in which idle hands are returned to the home row. This was recommended in typing by Dvorak, but does not seem to be practiced by qwerty users, and we can see why from the work load distribution.

Educational Aspects

We have just begun training four experimental typists on our Superwriter II system with the T-code described in the preceding section. The trainees are female college graduates whose ages range between 21 and 24; two of them practice 2 hours a day 5 days a week; one 4 hours a

Table 13.13. Work Load Distributions

				Position						
				1	2	3	4	5	6	7
Language	System	Text	Hand	Top		Upper		Home		Bottom
English	Qwerty	*Alice*	Left			29	35	30	6	
			Right			13	33	23	24	6
			Both			21	34	27	15	3
		Comp.	Left		1	26	33	28	11	1
			Right		1	18	32	17	26	6
			Both		1	22	33	22	19	3
		Average				21	34	25	17	1
	DSK	*Alice*	Left			2	13	83	2	
			Right			9	24	54	12	1
			Both			5	19	69	7	
		Comp.	Left		1	1	12	85	1	
			Right		1	12	27	49	10	1
			Both		1	6	20	67	6	
		Average				6	20	68	6	
Japanese	T-code	*Manual* with number	Left	6	3	6	22	42	16	5
			Right		3	6	20	54	14	3
			Both	3	3	6	21	48	15	4
		Manual without number	Left			5	21	51	18	5
			Right			5	18	59	15	3
			Both			5	20	55	16	4

day 2 days a week; and the last 4 hours a day 1 day a week. The reason for this variation in practice hours is partly that hours are chosen to accommodate the trainees, but mainly that we wanted to determine the effect of different scheduling on their progress. Experimental subjects who had no prior experience with keyboard operation, whether for English or for kana typing, were purposely chosen.

Earlier studies have been made to ascertain the effect of various training schedules on the speed of skill acquisition. Valentia (1968) found no significant changes due to different scheduling, whereas Baddeley and Longman (1978) found that learning efficiency decreases in the order of 1 hour once a day, 1 hour twice a day, 2 hours once a day and 2 hours twice a day, when speed is compared for the same number of practice hours.

We showed earlier ("Some Two-Stroke Touch-Typing Systems") the skill acquisition speed for two-stroke code typing with the systems by Yamura Shinkô, Rainputto, and Ricoh. We mentioned that the progress curves in Figure 13.11 are for a practice schedule of about 2 hours a day. However, this was not completely true for Ricoh's TX620. For certain reasons, Ricoh had to speed up the training schedule toward the end. Ricoh's learning curve in Figure 13.11 bends upward at the right. This appears to mean that when the number of practice hours is increased from 2 hours a day to several hours a day, learning becomes more efficient. That is, with respect to Figure 13.22, we do not know the nature of the envelope surface of the learning curves when the number of practice hours per day is changed from zero to several. It is likely that the shape of the surface depends on the personality and age of the students, and determination of the general property of such a surface may be nearly impossible. We chose 2 hours a day 5 days a week as the standard training schedule, but we would also like to see the data for some other combinations.

We are developing a computer program, called CATT (computer-aided typewriting trainer), that also has a built-in computer-assisted self-instruction facility (Hiraga, Ono, & Yamada, Note 26; Ono, Hiraga, & Yamada, Note 27). The lessons are designed so that each introduces a set of new characters. The trainees practice sentences, displayed on the CRT, that contain only those characters that have been introduced up to the current lesson. Trainees move on to the next set of lessons after their typing speed for the present set becomes sufficiently high, following the principle we learned from the Morse code training method as described in "Association Codes and Interference with Pattern Typing."

In order to facilitate the direct development of the right hemisphere cortical reflex for touch typing, we let the trainees use the inside-out array representation of two-stroke character code (rather than the normal dictionary-type code table), which, as was described in "Code Array Representation of Two-Stroke Codes," directly shows the two-stroke codes for kanzis in a "geographical" fashion, without any reference to the characters engraved on the keytops.

Before we began the training program, we were afraid that such an array representation of codes might meet with resistance from the trainees because people are accustomed to seeing such codes as a lexically ordered list, as in a dictionary. However, it soon became evident that our fear was unwarranted. Trainees learned to use the code array in Figure 13.20 to find codes directly without ever making reference to the letters inscribed on the corresponding keytops. They even protested against the use of the list representation when we tried to use it as part of the explanations for the lessons, for the lack of space on the CRT display screen. They volunteered the opinion that use of such a list brings in an extra association of keytop letter codes, which makes typing more difficult to execute, confirming what we predicted before we began the training program. (Of course, we first teach which finger covers which keys, as usual.)

The number of typing schools that provide training in two-stroke code typing is quite limited because the Riport Wordpal by Ricoh and Hitachi are the only word processors commercially available so far with

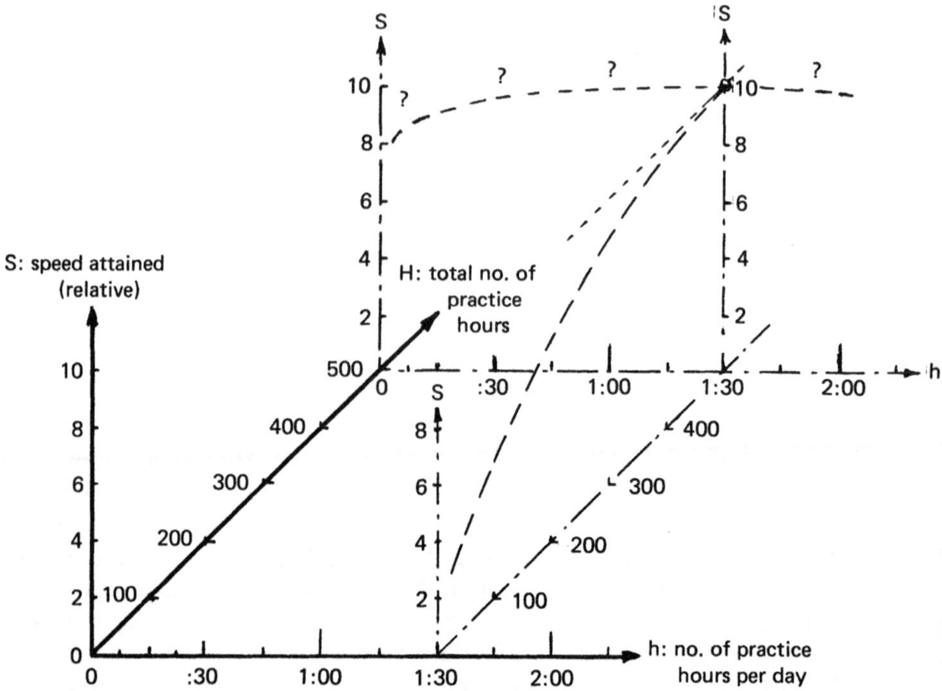

Fig. 13.22. Influence of number of practice hours per day on skill acquisition.

the two-stroke code, and they insist that training in the chain of steps from kanzi to two-stroke code recall and to code keying is necessary (Oda, Note 28). Our experience so far indicates that we need not depend on such mnemonic devices for code memorization "by brain," because the direct spatial memory of codes "by fingers" is just as easily established, and possibly better in the long run because of its "directness," as we noted earlier.

Since trainees learn kanzi codes piecemeal because of their large number, and since we avoid the prior memorization of code mnemonics in isolation from keying training, the learning curves for our T-code training appear different from the usual learning curves for English or for two-stroke kanzi codes with prior code memorization. We saw the latter curves in Figure 13.11, but ours should look like the curve of Figure 13.23a, where the speed should drop every time a set of new characters and words in them are introduced. If the training period for each new character-word set size is held constant, however, the envelope of the speed should gradually move up toward the saturation speed. Instead, our trainees train themselves on a set of lessons until their speed reaches a certain level and then move on to the next set. Figure 13.23b shows the initial portion of the learning history of one subject in such a training mode, up to 72 hours of session time. Each S stands for the average key-to-key stroke time for each hour of session time.

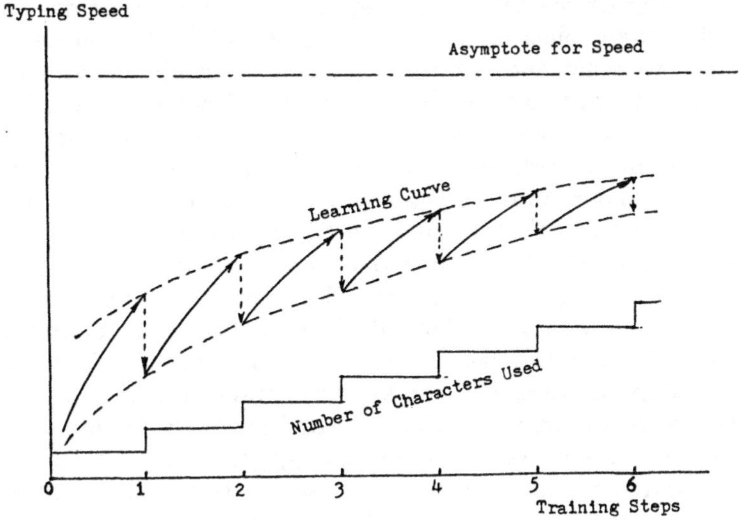

(a) Schematic Learning Curve

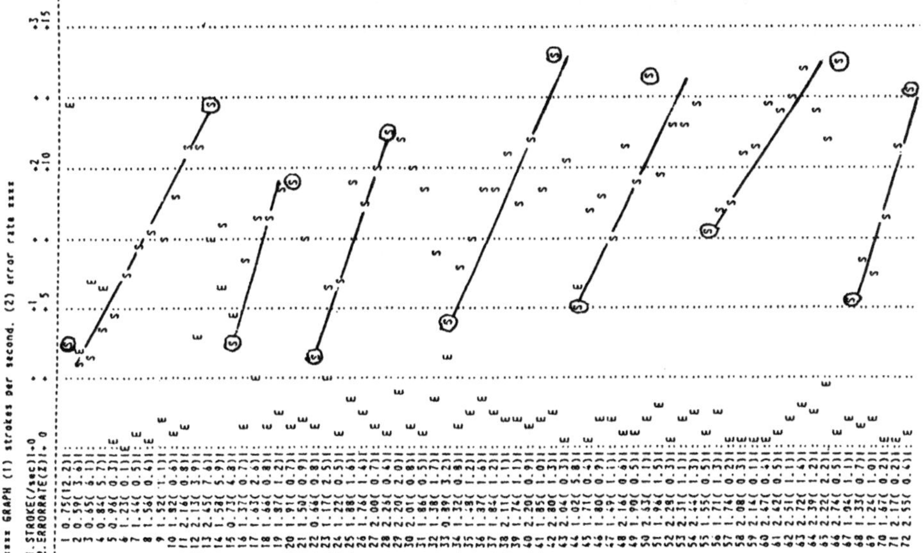

(b) Initial Section of Actual Learning Curve

Fig. 13.23. Learning curves for T-code training.

The accompanying E stands for the error rate computed in the same manner. Data are taken for each line of practice text, and if the average key-to-key time for a line is over 5 sec, then the data for the whole line are discarded in order to keep the graph data meaningful. Similarly, the cutoff point for the error rate is 50% for each line. Since two key-strokes make up a character, if stroking once gets out of phase for some reason, the rest of the line is registered as all errors. Such desynchronization often takes place in our current system because our keyboard is rather slow to react and often is not able to keep up with very fast keying. It does not allow roll-over keying either (i.e., if a keying is effected before the previously stroked key is released, then the new keying is not registered). Since we have not had very fast touch typists in the past in Japan, most of the keyboards manufactured in Japan suffer from these two shortcomings. In the future we will provide audio feedback to indicate the two-stroke segmentation of keying so that operators can immediately detect any desynchronization.

Figure 13.24 shows the effect of the cutoff parameters on the learning curve. This time, the data used are only of those text lines that have less than 700 msec average key-to-key time and less than a 1% error rate. For purposes of comparison, the lines of Figure 13.23b are also shown here as broken lines. As expected, the upper bound speeds for both parameter values remain the same, but the start-up points are vastly different because at the beginning of learning a set of new codes, trainees frequently have to look up or try to recall the codes, often spending more than 700 msec per code. Toward the right end of the graph, however, the percentage of new characters in the total is less and the difference begins to shrink somewhat. The error rate is also about one half

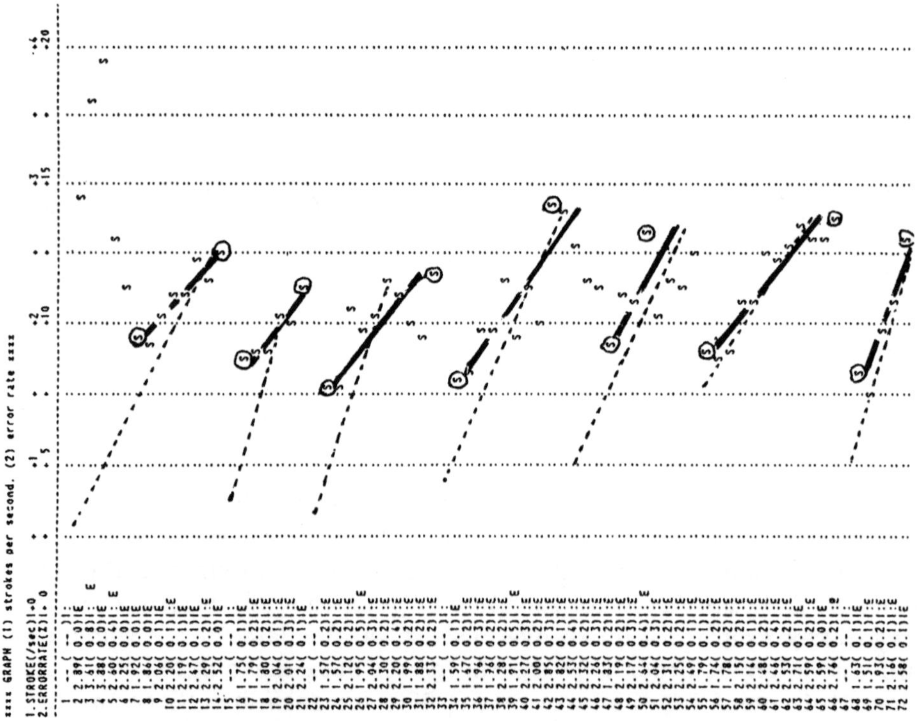

Fig. 13.24. Effect of cutoff parameters on learning curves.

or less when compared with those of other input methods (Takagi, Note 29).

The internal record-keeping data of the CATT show that the time spent actually keying is almost exactly 60% of the total log-on session time when computed at the elapsed session time of 125 hours. This result shows that the CATT is a fairly well-designed, easy-to-use teaching system.

According to the two subjects who trained for 2 hours a day 5 days a week, they felt like practicing more than 2 hours a day for their first month, then a plateau of sorts was reached in the succeeding month, during which they felt that 2 hours a day was too much. However, they soon recovered from this slump, and after 3 months the acquisition rate for new character codes accelerated. They now want to practice more than 2 hours a day. At present, we are carefully weighing an accelerated training schedule. It is possible that the optimal learning schedule is not a fixed practice time per day throughout the training period, but a varied one based on the level of acquired skill, although we do not yet know how it should be designed.

In order to trace the possible shift in the hemispheric dependency of typing from the left to the right, we have adopted the measurement of the ratio r of the power from the right-hemisphere alpha wave, p_r, to that from the left, p_ℓ; that is,

$$r = p_r/p_\ell,$$

which was used by Galin and others (Galin & Ellis, 1975). When this r is larger, it indicates that the left hemisphere is more active than the right. For those who are uninitiated, Figure 13.25 shows the power spectra of brain waves taken from the P_3-T_3 (a parietal-temporal lobe) location of electrodes for the left hemisphere and the P_4-T_4 location for the right hemisphere specified in the International Standard (Tokizane, Fujimori, Shimazono, & Sano, 1980), under the two task conditions described below. Alpha waves have power ranging around 10 Hz, and the power of beta waves, which indicates active hemisphere use, is greater than 15 Hz. The conspicuous power below 5 Hz is due to the movement of muscles of the neck, shoulder, and so on, called artifacts, and is not relevant here. The reversal of the alpha-wave power for the left and right hemisphere is clearly seen between the two different kinds of tasks.

Figure 13.26a shows the distribution of the r ratio for an experimental subject. The verbal task used here (as well as in the preceding illustration) consisted of the reading for 3 minutes of a short newspaper column, a kind of daily essay, consisting of about 800 characters (or the equivalent of about 320-400 English words) and writing the contents from memory for 5 minutes. The spatial task consisted of arranging painted blocks according to a designated pattern, which is similar to one of the performance tests of the Wechsler Adult Intelligence Score

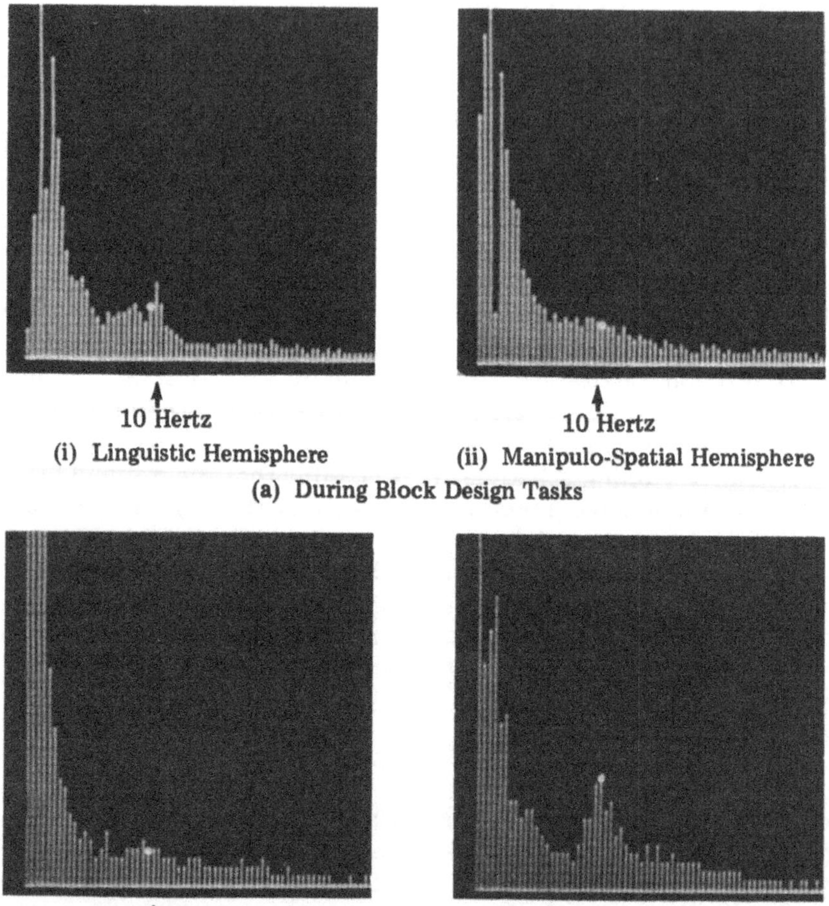

10 Hertz (i) Linguistic Hemisphere

10 Hertz (ii) Manipulo-Spatial Hemisphere

(a) During Block Design Tasks

10 Hertz (i) Linguistic Hemisphere

10 Hertz (ii) Manipulo-Spatial Hemisphere

(b) During Verbal Tasks

Fig. 13.25. Brain-wave power spectra.

(WAIS) test (Wechsler, 1941). The alpha-wave ratio during the touch typing of Japanese text falls between these two tasks, as shown. The range of r shown here is the extent that r shifts around when we compute r by using alpha waves in the ranges 9.5-10.5, 9.0-11.0, 8.5-11.5, and 8.0-12.0 Hz. We are interested in following up whether or not the ratio moves more toward the spatial task range as a subject's touch typing becomes more proficient.

This subject has learned the kanzi code by the code array representation from the very beginning. In contrast, the subject of Figure 13.26b is one of the implementers of the system who learned the kanzi code from a dictionary-type code table. Although it may be just a coincidence, his alpha-wave ratio during typing is almost that of verbal tasks.

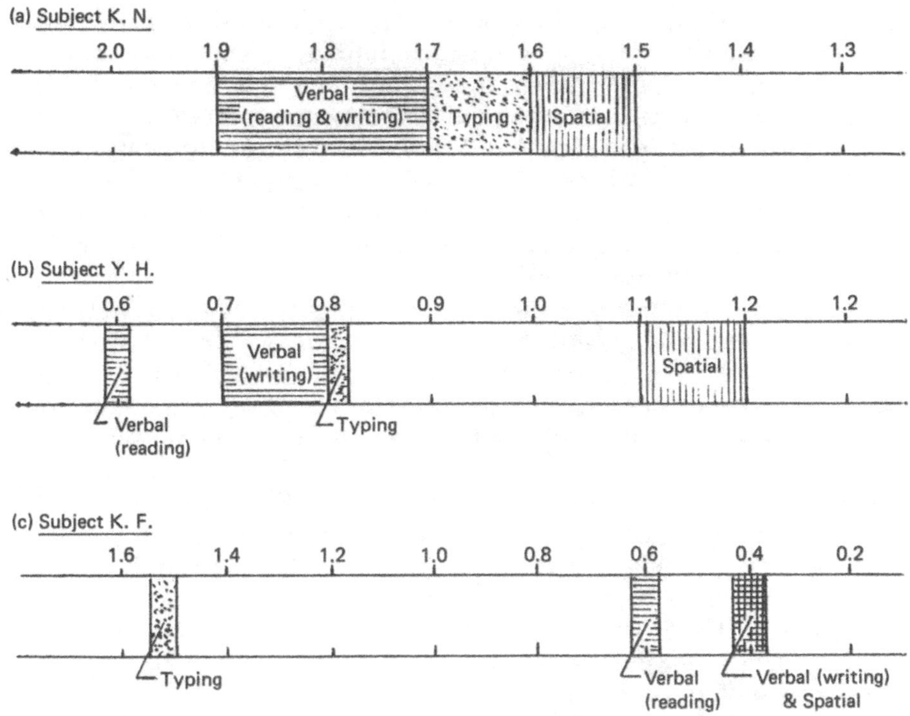

Fig. 13.26. Alpha-wave power ratio.

Note also that he has left-right reversal of hemisphericity, which happens in about 7-8% of the population. The absolute value of the ratio does not carry any significance in this figure, for it varies from one individual to another, or as a result of the shift of the attachment points of measurement electrodes on the scalp, or how they are attached. Figure 13.26c, on another experimental subject, also indicates the degree of individual variability. In this subject, the intensity of beta waves during typing is unusually high for some reason; the alpha waves seem to be drowned by the overall strength, and the r ratio tends to be unstable. In other subjects, replication of the measurements holds considerably better.

It is generally agreed that brain waves reflect the activities of the hemispheres and that the existence of strong beta waves indicates the active use of an alert hemisphere, whereas the existence of strong alpha waves indicates the idling of an awake hemisphere. At the same time, we are also aware that the interpretation of brain waves is a complicated affair. For example, in a man whose corpus callosum is cut, it has been observed (Gazzaniga & Hillyard, 1973) that when a visual discrimination task is presented by projecting, say, in the left visual field (LF; i.e., in the right hemisphere, RH, which also controls the left hand) so that the left hand is made to respond or not to respond at a given tonal signal sounded after the visual input 1 or 0, both hemispheres develop the expectancy brain wave only for stimulus 1, known as contingent negative variation (CNV), even though only the right hemisphere knows what the triggering stimulus was. This happens symmetrically for right visual field stimuli and right-hand responses. Hence, physiological brain wave activity does not necessarily reflect the psychological activity of each hemisphere. At any rate, we intend to accumulate data to study the relationship between typing activities and brain-wave variations.

It is well known that skill acquisition speed and ultimate typing speed depend on the training procedure (Malt, 1967, Showel, 1974). This is generally true with the acquisition of any motor skill (King, 1964). Hence, we are interested in finding out what is the best way to teach two-stroke kanzi code typing. With the array representation of codes to appeal to the right hemisphere, we hope we are on the right track. However, this does not mean that we would not allow the trainees to use mnemonic devices at all. In case they forget certain codes and are not able to recall "by fingers," they may use the code dictionary in terms of keytop engravings. But they will be discouraged from using it at least until they first learn codes by fingers by using the array representation. If they do so, then their associative devices will be called upon only in emergencies, and we are confident that such secondary association will not slow down the normal typing operation. This is unlike other learning approaches to use associations from the beginning, with which the elimination of the interference from intermediary association devices does not appear so easy. At any rate, the way things are unfolding, the use of the code dictionary may not be needed even for the recall of forgotten codes or for the codes of new kanzis. Our experimental subjects prefer to use the array representation of codes to the code dictionary even for such purposes, and we are developing a code book of about 100 pages, each page of which contains an array representation of codes for a few dozens of kanzis from the lexically ordered list. This will take more pages than the code dictionary, but the array representation directly appeals to the typists' spatial sense, they claim.

Concluding Remarks

We began our research on Japanese text processing with the belief that solution of the input problem would lead to wider acceptance in Japanese offices of typewriters and/or word processors operated by professionally trained typists as in Western society, making our offices much more productive and yet the work less strenuous. Since technology now enables us not only to produce what we need, but for the first time to do so at a very reasonable cost, the input method should be approached from the standpoint of human engineering. That is, in the design work, the welfare and benefits of the human being should take precedence over anything else.

At the early stage of our investigation, we felt that various attempts carried out heretofore to meet the input requirements seemed to have slighted human nature. Perhaps this happened not because we ignored human beings but because we do not really understand what human nature is. Early on in our investigation, we became convinced that the two-stroke code kanzi typing system is the best approach for a fast, minimally fatiguing touch-typing method for well-trained copy typists, and at one point we asked several manufacturers to build such a system for our use. However, assessing that there was no prospect of wide acceptance, they were quite reluctant to comply with our request and develop such a system in preference to the one-to-one display type or the kana-to-kanzi conversion type.

So we proceeded on our own and implemented our first Superwriter system for our experimental purposes (Tanaka & Yamada, Note 7). After a series of trials, setbacks, and ensuing soul searching, we gradually arrived at the conclusions we have described in this chapter. Our current Superwriter II was designed with the philosophy that the two-stroke kanzi code need not possess any memory-assisting device such as mnemonics or associations as its primary feature. As a consequence, it is designed to provide the utmost smoothness of hand and finger motions in typewriting, basically an extension of Dvorak's philosophy.

It is generally held, however, that the two-stroke input method is difficult to use, and its acceptance so far has been very slow. In such a belief there is often a confusion between the notion of difficulty in two-stroke touch typing and the necessity of training for the acquisition of touch-typing skill. As we have expounded in the preceding sections, two-stroke touch typing of Japanese text is perhaps the easiest to use after training, because its use causes less stress and fatigue when compared with other approaches, in spite of its speed advantage.

As for the necessity of prior training for skill acquisition, it is not only necessary but also desirable for optimal performance with a minimum of stress, as with any other human task involving motor skills. The necessity of pretraining is a drawback in a society like Japan, where female college graduates are employed for an average of 30 months before they retire and go into family life. Since they join their employers without prior training today, the employers must train them before they can be effectively deployed, and employers consider this to be a waste of time and money. Obviously there is a kind of chicken and egg causality between the shortage of skilled typists and the lack of willingness to make their use effective.

There is some glimpse of hope in recent developments. One is that female clerks are found to stay on their jobs longer when they are given more responsibilities beyond "gopher" (i.e., "go for") chores only, which were expected from secretaries in the United States before World War I ("Jobs: Slow Gains at Work," 1972). The other is that many responsible companies in Japan have begun to institute the rehiring of former female employees after family demands such as child care have relaxed (Sugimoto, 1981). Both of these developments would make the acquisition of special skills worth the effort.

Even without such social changes, the in-house training of touch typists should still be a worthwhile undertaking. Figure 13.27 is a schematic presentation of learning curves for typing skills with various input methods, plotted according to the claims made by the advocate for each method. The total amount of work done while an employee is on a job for 30 months is the area below the curve for each method. Note that these curves are for production (i.e., daily work) conditions, not for speed contests, which would be almost twice as fast.

We must caution here that, although the saturation speed of kana-to-kanzi conversion is shown to be about 100 characters a minute, this level appears too high. Curiously enough, no learning curves have been published so far by the manufacturers of kana-to-kanzi conversion systems, and the only graph available is by the Yokokawa Electric Works, Ltd. (Takagi, Note 29). According to this graph, the saturation level appears to be not much beyond 40 characters a minute. Therefore, the claimed speed of 100 characters a minute is either the straight kana-typing speed without including homophone selection time, or a quota-

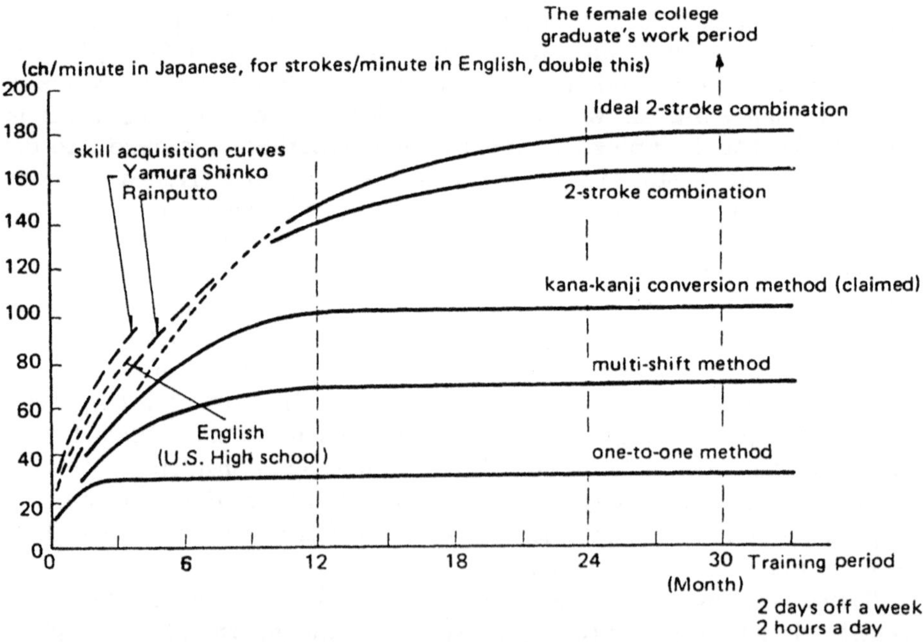

Fig. 13.27. Schematic learning curves of typing speed for various input methods under production conditions.

tion from systems that are heavily modified by the addition of kanzi coding (as discussed in "Toward the Best Method of Copy Typing for Professionals") in order to avoid homophone collisions as much as possible. It may be possible, however, to increase the speed of the kana-to-kanzi conversion system by providing a set of highly specialized dictionaries, one each for a narrowly defined subject area, thus decreasing the homophone collision rate. Even then it may not be an optimal device for professional copy typists, as was discussed in the same section.

Although the two-stroke kanzi code approach is the most efficient and least stressful method of copy typing for Japanese text from a purely technical point of view, it does not necessarily imply a quick and wide acceptance. Such advantages are not obvious to the uneducated. Besides, intense sales campaigns based on abundant funding and mobilizing of celebrities tends to have much more influence on the public than factual data, as was shown during the acceptance of the not-so-ideal qwerty keyboard over others for English at the turn of the century. We foresee the danger of that happening for Japanese word processors.

There are other factors that influence the preference of a certain item over others, as has been well expounded by Hisaaki Yasuda (1981). One of the major factors is the matter of who would use it. As was mentioned earlier (in "Typewriting in Japanese Society"), it is often said that the notion of establishing professional typists as a separate job category is not in good harmony with the Japanese management system because the latter functions in terms of group actions rather than individual leadership. However, notwithstanding cultural differences, Gregory Clark (1981) argues that the similarity between North American and/or Northern Europe and Japan with respect to the foundations of economic activities is the greatest among all the cultures in the world. He argues this in terms of a spectrum of social values ranging from emotional and practical (EP) valuations to moralistic and rationalistic (MR) valuations and concludes that although the two are on opposite sides of the optimal point for highest productivity (Japan on the EP side), both are very close to the optimal point. His argument sounds convincing to us, and we believe that there is no intrinsic obstacle in Japanese society to accepting the emergence of the typist-secretary as a separate occupation once its production value is recognized, even though it may entail some modifications in certain office practices. We side with Jon Woronoff (1981) in holding that the specialization of job functions in the office is the only possible way to attain the much needed improvement in productivity in Japanese offices. Those who are interested in finding out how good documentation contributes to the speed and excellence of research activities may find H. Itokawa's account (1981) of his own rocket research revealing.

In this connection, we believe that the necessity of initial training to develop skill in the use of two-stroke code touch typing is not a problem once its value is recognized. As Chiaki Nishiyama (1978) points out, Japanese companies have, since World War II, invested in employee training much more than the Ministry of Labor statistics suggest, at least for male employees, and the "human capital" thus developed has been the real strength of Japanese industry. He argues that the real problem confronting Japanese companies at present is the need to realize this fact and to optimize their investments in the formation of human capital. Assuming that the problem will be addressed, it should be a matter of time before the value of well-trained typists and/or secretaries will be recognized and an appropriate status will be granted to them.

Finally, we have limited our discussion in this chapter to the question of typing by professionally trained people. However, in the era of office automation and personal computers and/or word processors, the question of personal typing is as important as that of typing by typists and secretaries. For such applications, it is perhaps desirable to provide dual capabilities to word processors; kana-to-kanzi (or alphabet-to-kanzi) conversion for use by novices and two-stroke kanzi code for intensive users. When compared with the complexity of kana-to-kanzi conversion system software, the two-stroke code requires a symbol table for only on the order of 2,000-4,000 two-byte entries.

We believe that the investment of a few hundred hours at a young age in the acquisition of two-stroke code typing skill is well worthwhile when we consider that it will yield the power of typing several times faster than handwriting for the rest of one's lifetime. It has been demonstrated (Hirsch, Note 11; Takagi, Note 29) that such a skill would come back readily even after a long period of disuse, just as in the case of bicycle riding, swimming, skating, and the like. The two-stroke code typing does not interfere with the composition of sentences at the keyboard. Typing becomes as natural as the writing of kanzis, even though their structures have little to do with their pronounciation or meaning.

Before closing, we mention in passing that the present JIS kana keyboard, which is used by most kana-to-kanzi conversion systems, is not ergonomically optimized in Dvorak's sense (Kurata & Shigeta, 1961; Mayuzumi, 1962; Murata, 1967), and it becomes increasingly clear, as typists become more experienced, that it is an awkward keyboard to type on. Therefore, some efforts have been made to come up with a better kana arrangement on the keyboard. It will be interesting to see whether we adopt such a new kana keyboard as our next standard before the United States adopts the new rational standard keyboard, which has been in the making for some years (Yamada, 1980).

The kana arrangement on the JIS keyboard is mostly the result of a historical accident, and there is no apparent regularity in it. As a consequence, on the pretext that it is not an easy one for a novice to use, some have introduced letter arrangements based strictly on the "50-syllable" table of Japanese. A converter attachment for the standard keyboard was even produced some time ago (Nara System Laboratory,

Note 30). A strictly alphabetically arranged keyboard has already been experimentally shown in the West to be inferior to the qwerty, even for those who are complete novices after several hours of experience at the keyboard (Hirsch, 1970; Krankenhagen & Frädrich, 1972; Michaels, 1971; Norman & Fisher, Note 31). Judging from an analysis based on usage frequencies of kanas, the 50-syllable table arrangement is expected to be worse than the present JIS arrangement with respect to hand and finger motions. In addition, it was inferred in the study of alphabetic arrangement that the very fact of the arrangement's being an ordered one would compel users to rely on mental sequential scanning to find the intended key, which naturally slows down the operation when compared with a direct reach for keys in remembered locations. The situation should be no different for the kana keyboard.

These facts suggest that we often argue the naturalness and optimality of the means for man-machine interface without really knowing what the nature of a human being is. It is fortunate that industry is enthusiastically interested in developing new and useful products. At the same time, we feel that we should be equally attentive to basic research on an understanding of our real nature so that we will be able to tailor our equipment for optimal best fit.

Acknowledgments

I am grateful to Professor William E. Cooper for providing the opportunity to write this chapter, for his patience and understanding when personal reasons delayed the manuscript, for his numerous suggestions for improvement, and for his editing my foreign English. I am pleased with the work of the copy editor, who beautifully polished up my manuscript.

I acknowledge with gratitude the many valuable comments of Dr. Charlotte R. Lin of Schlumberger-Doll Research, Ridgefield, Connecticut, after carefully reading the manuscript.

In the preparation of this chapter, I benefited greatly from the contributions of my colleagues Yuzuru Hiraga, Jan Jinn-ke, Yoshihiko Ono, Jirô Tanaka, Hiroshi Watanabe, Kaori Furusawa, and Keiko Namba, among others, who have worked on the Superwriter project. I am also indebted to Professor Masao Saitô, Dr. Kenji Ikeda, and Mr. Ryôsuke Hosaka of the Institute of Medical Electronics of the University of Tokyo for the brain-wave measurements. Last, but not least, I am thankful to Keiko Amikura, who typed the drafts and final version of the manuscript.

Reference Notes

1. Watanabe, S. *Technical terms and character set used in "Information Processing" journal* (Workshop Paper). Tokyo: Special Interest Committee on Japanese Text Input Methods, Information Processing Society of Japan, September 1980. (In Japanese.)

2. Yamada, H. *A study of the character "ikiru" (to live)*. Privately printed by Husakazu Yamada, 1963. (In Japanese.)
3. Watanabe, S., & Ohgishi, H. *On the manipulation characteristics of kanzi input devices* (Workshop Paper EC77-25). Tokyo: Special Interest Group on Electronic Computer, Institute of Electronics and Communication Engineers of Japan, September 1977. (In Japanese.)
4. Miyamoto, K., Futamura, Y., Kanai, K., Ôshima, Y., & Inose, F. Prototype of a kanzi input device with switchable character tables (Conference Paper 1526). National convention of the Institute of Electronics and Communication Engineers of Japan, p. 6.146, 1979. (In Japanese.)
5. Tirrell, J. A., & Klemmer, E. T. *The effects of coding on keying rate* (IBM Research Rep. RC-775). Yorktown Heights, N.Y.: IBM Research Center, 1962.
6. Kojima, F. *The measurement of fatigue during input work by a touch typing system for Japanese* (Tech. Memorandum 790238). Tokyo: Ricoh Co. Technology Center, 1979. (In Japanese.)
7. Tanaka, J., & Yamada, H. *A study of touch typing input method for Japanese text* (Tech. Rep. 78-01). Tokyo: University of Tokyo, Faculty of Science, Department of Information Science, 1978. (In Japanese.)
8. Jan, J.-k., & Yamada, H. *A coding system of Chinese characters for touch typing* (Tech. Rep. 80-09). Tokyo: University of Tokyo, Faculty of Science, Deppartment of Information Science, 1980.
9. Isomichi, Y., & Shintani, J. *A kanzi input method through indexing by character patterns* (Workshop Paper 5-3). Tokyo: Special Interest Group on Japanese Text Input Methods, Information Processing Society of Japan, May 1982. (In Japanese.)
10. Clauer, C. K., Emmons, W. H., Evey, R. J., Hirsch, R. S., & Yamada, H. *A comparison of Apollo and Kawakami systems* (IBM Human Factors Center Memorandum). San Jose, Calif., 1977.
11. Hirsch, R. S. *Human factors*. Paper presented at the IBM Technology Fair, Tokyo, June 1982.
12. Seibel, R. *A feasibility demonstration of the rapid-type data entry station* (IBM Research Rep. RC-845). Yorktown Heights, N.Y.: IBM Research Center, 1962.
13. Koppitz, W. J. *Typing performance on a keyboard augmented by an overlay of multiple letter codes* (IBM Research Rep. RC-3934). Yorktown Heights, N.Y.: IBM Research Center, 1971.
14. Inanaga, H. *Transformation of phonetic sentences into ideographic sentences in Japanese*. Preprints for seminar on Input/Output Systems for Japanese and Chinese Characters, January 1971, 264-275.
15. Sakai, T., Sugita, S., & Fujita, H. *Some experiments on kanzi I/O system*. Preprints for seminar on Input/Output Systems for Japanese and Chinese Characters, January 1971, 232-253.
16. Sugiyama, S., Takano, M., Kimura, H., Shiratori, Y., Obashi, F., & Ishii, S. *A study of Japanese input system based on characteristic classification (IDIOM*)* (Workshop Paper EC79-13). Tokyo: Special Interest Group on Electronic Computer, Institute of Electronics and Communication Engineers of Japan, 1979. (In Japanese.)
17. Fukinuki, T., Fukushima, K., & Shimasaki, Y. *A kana keyboard kanzi input device with feedback corresponding to the ambiguity of character types* (Work-

shop Paper EC72-5). Tokyo: Special Interest Group on Electronic Computer, Institute of Electronics and Communication Engineers of Japan, May 1972. (In Japanese.)

18. NIOSH (National Institute for Occupational Safety and Health). *Potential health hazard of video display terminals*. Washington, D.C.: U.S. Department of Health and Human Services, 1981.
19. Ogawa, S. *Japanese text input method by array correspondence system* (Workshop Paper 4-2). Tokyo: Special Interest Group on Japanese Text Input Methods, Information Processing Society of Japan, March 1982. (In Japanese.)
20. Konishi, K., Kurematsu, A., & Tashiro, H. A study of letter arrangement on the English keyboard by keying characteristics of typists (Conference Paper 559). National convention of the Information Systems Division, Institute of Electronics and Communication Engineers of Japan, p. 2.216, 1981. (In Japanese.)
21. Takashima, T., Mitsui, O., & Ohiwa, H. *An input method of Japanese text by touch typing and its training method* (Workshop Paper 4-3). Tokyo: Special Interest Group on Japanese Text Input Methods, Information Processing Society of Japan, 1982. (In Japanese.)
22. Yagi, Y., & Yamada, Y. *Japanese text word processor Ricoh TX620* (Ricoh Tech. Rep. 2), 1979. (In Japanese.)
23. Yamauchi, S. Direct input system of Japanese text through kana-keyboard (Ricoh Tech. Rep. 2), 1981. (In Japanese).
24. Misaka, G. The relation between keying termination hands and fatigue. Personal communication, 1959. (In Japanese.)
25. Hiraga, Y. *A model of typewriting behavior based on the delayed excursion of hands*. Unpublished memorandum, 1982.
26. Hiraga, Y., Ono, Y., & Yamada, H. *Implementation of computer aided typewriting trainer for Japanese*. Paper presented at the national convention of the Information Processing Society of Japan, Hukuoka, October 1982. (In Japanese.)
27. Ono, Y., Hiraga, Y., & Yamada, H. On the text of computer aided typewriting trainer for Japanese. Paper presented at the national convention of the Information Processing Society of Japan, Hukuoka, October 1982. (In Japanese.)
28. Oda, M. *Two-stroke code input and training* (Workshop Paper 6-3). Tokyo: Special Interest Group on Japanese Text Input Methods, Information Processing Society of Japan, July 1982. (In Japanese.)
29. Takagi, T. *Input skill acquisition on kantele keyboard for Japanese word processor* (Workshop Paper 6-1). Tokyo: Special Interest Group on Japanese Text Input Methods, Information Processing Society of Japan, July 1982. (In Japanese.)
30. Nara System Laboratory *Sokutyper*. Brochure by K.K.-S.D.S., ca. 1970.
31. Norman, D. A., & Fisher, D. *Why alphabetic keyboards are not easy to use: Keyboard layout doesn't much matter* (Rep. 8106). La Jolla, Calif.: University of California at San Diego, Center for Human Information Processing, 1981.

References

Akiba, N. An experiment on the design of typewriter and performance, I & II. *Journal of Science of Labour*, 1961, *37*, 380-386; 435-441. (In Japanese.)

Baddeley, A. D., & Longman, D. J. A. The influence of length and frequency of training session on the rate of learning to type. *Ergonomics*, 1978, *21*, 628-635.

Blakeslee, T. *The right brain*. Garden City, N.Y.: Doubleday, 1980.

Bever, T. G., & Chiarello, R. J. Cerebral dominance in musicians and nonmusicians. *Science*, 1974, *185*, 137-139.

Bogen, J. E. The other side of the brain, I: Dysgraphia and dyscopia following cerebral commissurotomy; II: An appositional mind. *Bulletin of the Los Angeles Neurological Society*, 1969, *34*, 73-105; 135-162.

Bogen, J. E., & Bogen, G. M. The other side of the brain, III: The corpus callosum and creativity. *Bulletin of the Los Angeles Neurological Society*, 1969, *34*, 191-220.

Bogen, J. E., Dezure, R., Tenhouten, W. D., & Marsh, J. F. The other side of the brain, IV: The A/P ratio. *Bulletin of the Los Angeles Neurological Society*, 1972, *37*, 49-61.

Bradshaw, J. L., & Nettleton, N. C. The nature of hemispheric specialization in man. *Behavioral and Brain Sciences*, 1981, *4*, 51-91.

Bremer, F. Physiology of the corpus callosum. *Proceedings of the Association for Research in Nervous and Mental Disease*, 1956, *36*, 424-448.

Brown, C. R. Human factors problems in design and evaluation of key-entry devices for the Japanese language. In A. Chapanis (Ed.), *Ethnic Variables in Human Factors Engineering*. Baltimore: Johns Hopkins University Press, 1975.

Caldwell, S. H. The Sinotype—A machine for composition of Chinese from a keyboard. *Journal of the Franklin Institute*, 1959, *267*, 471-502.

Clark, G. Foundations of Japanese management. *Nippon Keizai Shimbun*, December 23, 1981, p. 14. (In Japanese.)

Cohen, D. Magnetoencephalography: Evidence of magnetic fields produced by alpha-rhythm currents. *Science*, 1968, *161*, 784-786.

Conrad, R. Acoustic confusion in immediate memory. *British Journal of Psychology*, 1964, *55*, 75-84.

Cooper, W. E. The analytic/holistic distinction applied to the speech of patients with hemispheric brain damage. In Bradshaw & Nettleton (1981), pp. 68-69.

Downing, H. Word processors and the oppression of women. In T. Forester (Ed.), *The microelectronics revolution: The complete guide of the new technology and its impact on society*. Oxford: Basil Blackwell, 1980.

Doyle, J. C., Ornstein, R., & Galin, D. Lateral specialization of cognitive mode, II: EEG frequency analysis. *Psychophysiology*, 1974, *11*, 567-578.

Dvorak, A. There is a better typewriter keyboard. *National Business Education Quarterly*, 1943, *12*, 51-58; 66.

Dvorak, A., Merrick, N. L., Dealey, W. L., & Ford, G. C. *Typewriting behavior*. New York: American Book Company, 1936.

Efron, R. The effect of stimulus intensity of the perception on simultaneity in right- and left-handed subjects. *Brain*, 1963, *86*, 285-294.

Evey, R. J. How typists type. *Proceedings of the International Computer Conference (Chinese Data Processing and Text Editing: The Next Frontier)*, 1980, *1*, 3.1-3.21.

Filbey, R. A., & Gazzaniga, M. S. Splitting the normal brain with reaction time. *Psychonomic Science*, 1969, *17*, 335-336.

Fox, J. G., & Stansfield, R. G. Digram keying times for typists. *Ergonomics*, 1964, *7*, 317-320.

Franco, L., & Sperry, R. W. Hemispheric lateralization for cognitive processing of geometry. *Neuropsychologia*, 1977, *15*, 107-114.

Galin, D., & Ellis, R. Asymmetry in evoked potentials as an index of lateralized cognitive processes: Relation to EEG alpha asymmetry. *Neuropsychologia*, 1975, *13*, 45-50.

Galin, D., Johnstone, J., & Herron, J. Effects of task difficulty on EEG measures of cerebral engagement. *Neuropsychologia*, 1978, *16*, 461-472.

Galin, D., & Ornstein, R. Lateral specialization of cognitive models: An EEG study. *Psychophysiology*, 1972, *9*, 412-418.

Galli, E. J. The Stenowriter—a system for the lexical processing of stenotypy. *Institute of Radio Engineers, Transactions on Electronic Computers,* 1962, *11*, 187-199.

Gazzaniga, M. S., & Hillyard, S. A. Attention mechanisms following brain bisection. In S. Kornblum (Ed.), *Attention and performance IV*. New York: Academic Press, 1973.

Gazzaniga, M. S., & LeDoux, J. E. *The integrated mind*. New York: Plenum Press, 1978.

Gelb, I. J. *A study of writing* (2nd ed.). Chicago: University of Chicago Press, 1963.

Gordon, H. W. Hemispheric asymmetries in the perception of musical chords. *Cortex*, 1970, *6*, 387-398.

Gordon, H. W. Hemispheric asymmetry and musical performance. *Science*, 1975, *189*, 68-69.

Gross, Y., Franco, R., & Lewin, I. Effects of voluntary eye movements on hemispheric activity and choice of cognitive mode. *Neuropsychologia*, 1978, *16*, 653-657.

Gur, R. E., & Gur, R. C. Correlates of conjugate lateral eye movements in man. In S. Harnad et al. (Eds.), *Lateralization in the nervous system*. New York: Academic Press, 1977.

Hara, J. *The sociology of computerized world*. Tokyo: Asahi Shimbun-Sha, 1982. (In Japanese.)

Hasegawa, J. Kanzi input and output system by method of unit pattern construction. *Information Processing,* 1975, *16*, 808-817. (In Japanese.)

Hines, D., & Martindale, C. Induced lateral eye movements and creative and intellectual performance. *Perceptual and Motor Skills*, 1974, *39*, 153-154.

Hiraga, Y., Ono, Y., & Yamada, H. An assignment of key-codes for a Japanese character keyboard. *Proceedings of the 8th International Conference on Computational Linguistics*, 1980, 249-256. (a)

Hiraga, Y., Ono, Y., & Yamada, H. An analysis of the standard English keyboard. *Proceedings of the 8th International Conference on Computational Linguistics,* 1980, 242-248. (b)

Hiraga, Y. *A human factors basis for evaluating keyboard efficiency*. Unpublished master's thesis, Department of Information Science, Faculty of Science, University of Tokyo, 1981.

Hirsch, R. S. Effects of standard versus alphabetical keyboard formats on typing performance. *Journal of Applied Psychology*, 1970, *54*, 484-490.

Hori, K. Kanzi information processing and a kanzi input device. *Administration and ADP*, 1973, *9*, 11-17. (In Japanese.)

Hotaka, R. A method of kanzi input—idiomatic phrase system. *Information Processing*, 1969, *10*, 354. (In Japanese.)

Hu, L.-r., Chang, Y.-w., & Huang, J. K.-t. The digitized Chinese dictionary—three-corner coding method. *Ming Chuan College Journal*, 1978, Taipei. (In Chinese.)

English version revised and prepared by C. A. Hoffman, *Proceedings of the International Conference of the Chinese Language Computer Society*, 1979, *2*, 213-250.

Ikeda, K., Hirohata, K., & Kiyono, T. A handy Japanese text-processing system utilizing a personal kanzi/kana tablet. *Proceedings of the 3rd USA-Japan Computer Conference*, 1978, 117-121.

Itô, A. Input method of Japanese text for computers and its code table. Japanese Patent Application S49-69234, 1974. (In Japanese.)

Itokawa, H. Japanese style conference and human relations. In *Amazing Technique of Utilizing Time*. PHP Business Library A-001, 1981. (In Japanese.)

Jan, J.-k., & Yamada, H. A coding system of Chinese characters for touch typing—a summary version. *Proceedings of the International Computer Conference (Chinese Data Processing and Text Editing: The Next Frontier)*, 1980, *1*, 1.1-1.21.

Jobs: Slow gains at work. *Time*, March 10, 1972, pp. 66-71.

Kawakami, A. Typewriter keyboard for Japanese text input. Japanese Patent Application S50-35453, 1975; Patent 830046. (In Japanese.)

Kawakami, A., & Kawakami, T. Human factors in Rainputto keyboard for kanzi input. *Proceedings of the 1st USA-Japan Computer Conference*, 1972, pp. 292-295.

Kawakami, A., & Kawakami, T. Kanzi input by touch typing. *Information Processing*, 1974, *15*, 863-867. (In Japanese.)

Kindaiti, K. *Sin-Meikai Japanese dictionary*. Tokyo: Sanseidô, 1972. (In Japanese.)

King, D. *Training with the organization: A study of company policy and procedures for the systematic training of operators and supervisors*. London: Tavistock, 1964.

Kinkead, R. Typing speed, keying rates, and optimal keyboard layouts. *Proceedings of the Human Factors Society 19th Annual Meeting*, 1975, 159-161.

Kinsbourne, M. Eye and hand turning indicates cerebral lateralization. *Science*, 1972, *176*, 539-540.

Kinsbourne, M. The control of attention by interaction between the cerebral hemispheres. In S. Kornblum (Ed.), *Attention and performance IV*. New York: Academic Press, 1973.

Kinsey, T. L. *Audio-typing and electric typewriters*. New York: Pergamon Press, 1964.

Kizawa, M. An attempt to design a mnemonic code for kanzis. *Information Processing*, 1969, *10*, 351-353. (In Japanese.)

Krankenhagen, J. H., & Frädrich, J. The influence of keyboard-layout on input-velocity and error-rate in dialling alphanumeric sequences of symbols. *Proceedings of the International Symposium on Human Factors in Telecommunications*, 1972, Session IX.

Kurata, M., & Shigeta, S. Human factors in design of keyboard. *Industrial Medicine*, 1961, *3*, 471-480. (In Japanese.)

Kurihara, T., & Kurosaki, Y. On the transformation process of phonetic sentences in Japanese. *Technology Reports of the Kyûshû University*, 1967, *39*, 659-664. (In Japanese.)

Kurishima, O. A new kanzi input/output device. *Data Communication*, 1976, *8*(5), 56-61. (In Japanese.)

Kuroki, S. On a new teaching method in [Morse code] communication skill acquisition. *Journal of the Acoustical Society*, 1943, *S18*(5), 19-22. (In Japanese.)
Lassen, N. A., Ingbar, D. H., & Skinhøj, E. Brain function and blood flow. *Scientific American*, 1978, *239*(4), 50-59.
LeDoux, J. E., Wilson, D. H., & Gazzaniga, M. S. Manipulo-spatial aspects of cerebral lateralization: Clues to the origin of lateralization. *Neuropsychologia*, 1977, *15*, 743-750.
Levy, J., & Trevarthen, C. Perceptual, semantic and phonetic aspects of elementary language processing in split-brain patients. *Brain*, 1977, *100*, 105-118.
Malt, L. G. Training methods for keyboard operators. In *Advances in Computer Typesetting (Proceedings of the International Computer Typesetting Conference*, July 1966, University of Sussex), 1967, 20-23.
Marton, F. K., & Sandqvist, G. Learning while typing. *Quarterly Journal of Experimental Psychology*, 1972, *24*, 287-290.
Matsui, N. Characteristics of character search operations. *Employment and Profession*, 1982, *39*, 34-41. (In Japanese.)
Mayuzumi, H. On typewriter keyboards. *Zitumu to Yôzi*, 1962, *1*(3), 2-16. (In Japanese.)
McWhirter, N., & McWhirter, R. (Eds.) Fastest typing. *Guinness Book of World Records*. New York: Sterling, 1977.
Michaels, S. E. QWERTY versus alphabetic keyboards as a function of typing skills. *Human Factors*, 1971, *13*, 419-426.
Miller, J. A. American shorthand machines and their inventors. *National Shorthand Reporter*, 1942, *16*(6-8), -; 289-293; 321-325.
Mishkin, M., & Forgays, D. G. Word recognition as a function of retinal focus. *Journal of Experimental Psychology*, 1952, *43*, 43-48.
Mori, K., & Hirahara, H. An evaluation method of kanzi look-up system (Conference Paper 74). National convention of the Institute of Electronics and Communication Engineers of Japan, 1969, p. 74. (In Japanese.)
Mori, K., & Kawata, T. Kana-to-kanzi conversion. *Information Processing*, 1979, *20*, 911-916. (In Japanese.)
Morikawa, E. Survival conditions for small scale, light printing industry. *New Printing Monthly*, 1982, *24*(6), 22-27. (In Japanese.)
Motizuki, Y. Homophones in Japanese and in Chinese. *Yuwen Xiandaihua*, 1980, *1*, 216-217. (In Chinese.)
Murata, T. Letter arrangements of typewriters: Roman and kana typewriters. *Gengo Seikatu*, 1967, *187*, 52-61. (In Japanese.)
Murayama, N. Two-stroke method for Japanese text input. *Information Processing*, 1982, *23*, 552-558. (In Japanese.)
Myers, R. E., & Sperry, R. W. Interocular transfer of a visual form discrimination habit in cats after section of the optic chiasm and corpus callosum. *Anatomical Record*, 1953, *115*, 351-352.
National Language Laboratory. *Kanzis in contemporary newspapers*. Tokyo: Syûei Publishing Co., 1976. (In Japanese.)
Nelson, W. W. Typewriter reforms—the combinational keyboard. *Science Progress*, 1921, *16*, 307-318.
Nickells, R. F., Jr. *The design of an optimal typewriter-like keyboard*. Unpublished master's thesis, Lehigh University, 1973.

Nishiyama, C. Human capital and Japanese economy, I & II. *Nippon Keizai Shimbun*, February 12 & 13, 1978. (In Japanese.)
Nora, S., & Minc. A. *L'Informatisation de la Société* (a report to the French President), 1978. (In French); (Japanese translation of Vol. 1 by K. Kosi, Sangyô Nôritu Daigaku, 1980.)
Ogawa, S. A device for the generation of character codes. Japanese Patent Application S56-10190, 1981. (In Japanese.)
Ogawa, S., Hori, H., & Kokubun, M. Model SC 4000 kanzi keyboard papertape puncher. *Newspaper Printing*, 1972, *62*, 65-68. (In Japanese.)
Ono, Y., Hiraga, Y., & Yamada, H. A method of handling kanzis outside the basic set in two-stroke input method for Japanese text. *Proceedings of the National Convention of the Information Processing Society of Japan*, 1981, 963-964. (In Japanese.)
Osgood, C. E. The similarity paradox in human learning: A resolution. *Psychological Review*, 1949, *56*, 132-143.
Osgood, C. E. *Method and theory in experimental psychology*. New York: Oxford University Press, 1953.
Palantype Organization, Ltd. *The Palantype method of stenotyping* (3rd ed.), England, 1963.
Parkinson, R. The Dvorak simplified keyboard: Forty years of frustration. *Computer and Automation*, 1972, *21*(11), 18-25.
Pesch, M. The French shorthand machine. *The National Shorthand Reporter*, 1955, *16*(5), 153-155.
Posner, M. I. Components of skilled performance. *Science*, 1966, *152*, 1712-1718.
Puccetti, R. The alleged manipulospatiality explanation of right hemisphere visuospatial superiority. In Bradshaw & Nettleton (1981), pp. 75-76.
Reform in typewriting. *The American Weekly*, December 2, 1945.
Ricoh Company *Ricoh TX620* [Brochure 7905 K-7905(1).] Tokyo: Business Data Show, 1979. (In Japanese.)
Robinson, E. S. The similarity factor in retroaction. *American Journal of Psychology*, 1927, *39*, 297-312.
Rutzick, M., & Swerdloff, S. The occupational structure of U.S. employment. *Monthly Labor Review*, 1962, *85*, 1209-1213.
Saitô, K., Nagai, E., Yamada, K., & Ôsako, A. Kanzi character input to machine. *Information Processing*, 1969, *10*, 294-298. (In Japanese.)
Sakamoto, S., & Hagiwara, T. A kanzi input system without the need of specific input hardware. *Business Management*, 1978, *17*, 43-47. (In Japanese.)
Sakashita, Y., Watanabe, O., & Ôkawa, K. A study of the character sets necessary for Japanese text input devices according to business categories and personal job functions. *Proceedings of the Symposium on Input Systems for Japanese Text, Information Processing Society of Japan*, 1981, 121-124. (In Japanese.)
Schoonard, J. W., & Boies, S. J. Short-type: A behavioral analysis of typing and text entry. *Human Factors*, 1975, *17*, 203-214.
Shiratori, Y., Obashi, F., Yamashina, M., & Kimura, H. A Japanese kana-to-kanzi translation method by characteristic marks of kanzi characters. *Transactions of the Institute of Electronics and Communication Engineers of Japan*, 1981, *J64-D*, 773-779. (In Japanese.)
Showel, M. A comparison of alternative media for teaching beginning typists. *Journal of Educational Research*, 1974, *67*, 279-285.
Simonson, E., & Brozék, J. Flicker fusion frequency: Background and application. *Physiological Review*, 1952, *32*, 349-378.

Sugimoto, T. The rehiring policy of retired former female employees. *Sankei Shimbun*, November 4, 1981, p. 10. (In Japanese.)

Tajima, K. Problems of Chinese language information processing. *The Asia Quarterly*, 1981, *13*(2/3), 39-52. (In Japanese.)

Takahashi, N. The current state and future trend of Japanese text input systems. *Information Processing*, 1981, *23*, 518-528. (In Japanese.)

Takashima, T. *A study of human factors in keyboard manipulations.* Unpublished master's thesis, Toyohashi University of Engineering Science, 1982. (In Japanese.)

Tatuoka, H. Rainputto system—without computer, yet speedy. *Stenography News*, 1970, *100*, 7-10. (In Japanese.)

Ter-Pogossian, M. M., Raichle, E., & Sobel, B. E. Positron-emission tomography. *Scientific American*, 1980, *243*(4), 140-155.

Thurstone, L. L. The learning curve equation. *Psychological Monographs*, 1919, *26* (Whole No. 114).

Tokizane, T., Fujimori, B., Shimazono, Y., & Sano, K. *New introduction to brain waves.* Tokyo: Nanzandô, 1980. (In Japanese.)

Tucker, D. M., Roth, R. S., Arneson, B. A., & Buckingham, V. Right hemisphere activation during stress. *Neuropsychologia*, 1977, *15*, 697-700.

U.S. Bureau of the Census. *The U.S. fact book: The American almanac for 1977.* New York: Grosset & Dunlap, 1976.

Valentia, A. A. *The effects of three laboratory arrangements associated with one type of large group instructional arrangements in the learning of typewriting.* Unpublished doctoral dissertation, Stanford University, 1968.

Watanabe, S. Input and display device for kanzis. *Electronics*, 1972, *17*, 72-78. (In Japanese.)

Wechsler, D. *The measurement of adult intelligence* (2nd ed.). Baltimore: Williams & Wilkins, 1941.

Wieger, L. *Chinese Characters: Their origin, etymology, history, classification and signification* (4th ed.; L. Davront, trans.). Catholic Mission Press, 1927.

Woronoff, J. *Japan's wasted workers.* Tokyo: Lotus Press, 1981.

Yamada, H. Unending interest in languages and characters. *Nikkei Shimbun*, July 29, 1977. (In Japanese.)

Yamada, H. An ergonomic comparison of input methods for Japanese text. *Proceedings of the Information Processing Society of Japan Symposium*, July 1978, 1-32. (In Japanese.)

Yamada, H. A historical study of typewriters and typing methods: From the position of planning Japanese parallels. *Journal of Information Processing*, 1980, *2*, 175-202.

Yamada, H. The history of typewriters and the input of Japanese text. *Information Processing*, 1982, *23*, 559-564. (In Japanese.)

Yamada, H., & Tanaka, J. A human factors study of input keyboard for Japanese text. *Proceedings of the International Computer Symposium*, Taipei, 1977, 47-64.

Yasuda, H. *Introduction to office automation.* Tokyo: Kôdansha, 1981.

Yoshitake, H. Relationship between frequency and composition of subjective symptoms of fatigue. *Journal of Science of Labour*, 1970, *46*, 584-592. (In Japanese.)

Yoshitake, H. Correlation between subjective symptoms of fatigue and critical fusion frequency (CFF) of flicker. *Journal of Science of Labour*, 1972, *48*, 69-76. (In Japanese.)

Author Index

Subject Index

GPSR Compliance

The European Union's (EU) General Product Safety Regulation (GPSR) is a set of rules that requires consumer products to be safe and our obligations to ensure this.

If you have any concerns about our products, you can contact us on ProductSafety@springernature.com

In case Publisher is established outside the EU, the EU authorized representative is:

Springer Nature Customer Service Center GmbH
Europaplatz 3
69115 Heidelberg, Germany

Batch number: 10844669

Printed by Printforce, the Netherlands